D0711695

Zanzibar
Pemba • Mafia

the Bradt Travel Guide

WITHDRAWN

Chris McIntyre
Susie McIntyre

edition
9

www.bradtguides.com

Bradt Travel Guides Ltd, UK
The Globe Pequot Press Inc, USA

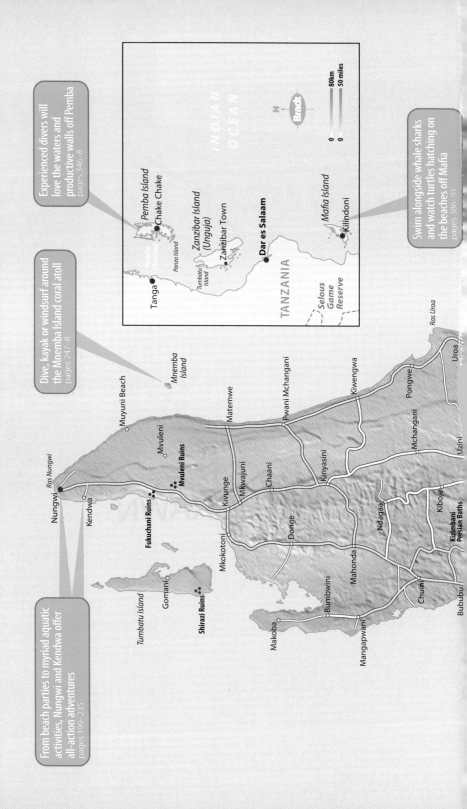

Experienced divers will love the waters and productive walls off Pemba pages 346–8

Dive, kayak or windsurf around the Mnemba Island coral atoll pages 247–8

From beach parties to myriad aquatic activities, Nungwi and Kendwa offer all-action adventures pages 199–235

Swim alongside whale sharks and watch turtles hatching on the beaches off Mafia pages 386–91

INDIAN OCEAN

Pemba Island
Chake Chake

Tanga

Panza Island

Tumbatu Island

Zanzibar Island (Unguja)
Zanzibar Town

Dar es Salaam

TANZANIA

Selous Game Reserve

Mafia Island
Kilindoni

N

Bradt

0   80km
0   50 miles

Ras Uroa

Uroa

Uzini

Mchangani

Pongwe

Kiwengwa

Ras Nungwi

Nungwi

Kendwa

Mnemba Island

Muyuni Beach

Mvuleni

Mvuleni Ruins

Fukuchani Ruins

Mkokotoni

Tumbatu Island

Gomani

Shirazi Ruins

Matemwe

Pwani Mchangani

Mkwajuni

Chaani

Kinyasini

Kivunge

Donge

Ndagaa

Mahonda

Kiboje

Kizimbani
Persian Baths

Chuini

Bumbwini

Mangapwani

Makoba

Bububu

INDIAN OCEAN

Go kitesurfing in the warm, shallow waters around Paje
pages 294–6

Encounter the colobus monkey colony in Jozani-Chwaka Bay National Park
pages 324–8

Make coconut paste and learn about village life on the Jambiani Cultural Tour
page 312

Explore uninhabited islands and sandbanks in the Menai Bay Conservation Area
pages 332–3

Gain an insight into rural life in Zanzibar on a spice tour
pages 116–17

Walk in the footsteps of Princess Sayyida Salme at Mtoni Palace
pages 185–7

Wander the labyrinthine alleyways and atmospheric market of Stone Town
pages 159–75

Embark on a snorkelling tour to the protected reef around Chumbe Island
pages 333–6

ZANZIBAR TOWN

Ras Michamvi
Michamvi Kae
Michamvi Pingwe
Michamvi
Dongwe
Bwejuu
Paje
Chwaka Bay
Chwaka
Ufufuma
Umbuji
Bambi
Dunga
Jendele
Jozani Forest
Zanzibar Butterfly Centre
Pete
Zala Park
Kitogani
Jambiani
Muyuni
Makunduchi New Town
Makunduchi
Kufile
Kizimkazi Mkunguni
Kizimkazi Dimbani
Bi Khole Ruins
Unguja Ukuu
Unguja Ukuu Ruins
Uzi Island
Menai Bay
Kisakasaka
Tunguu
Fuoni
Dunga Ruins
Heritage Conservation Park
Welezo
Mtoni
Kidichi
Kizimbani
Persian Baths
Mbweni
Chukwani
Chumbe Island
Zanzibar Channel
Kwazi Bay
Fumba

Bradt

0   10km
0   6 miles

KEY

■	Capital city
●	Main town
○	Village
✈	Airport
∴	Ancient site
	Main road (tarred)
	Main road
	Other road

Zanzibar Don't miss...

Zanzibar Town
The island's largest
settlement features
whitewashed houses,
bazaars, mosques and
museums, as well as
an old Arab fort
(pictured here)
(SC/AWL) pages 119–75

Diving and snorkelling
The seas around the Zanzibar
archipelago offer coral reefs,
sandbanks and plentiful
marine wildlife (SS) pages 95–8

Beaches
Fine-sand beaches
such as this one on
the east coast are
a major draw
for visitors
(CM) page 269

Wildlife
Kirk's red colobus
(*Procolbus kirkii*) is
native to Zanzibar
and can be seen
in the Jozani
Forest Reserve
(yu/S) pages 48–59
& 327

Culture
Locally produced
Tingatinga
paintings can
be found for
sale throughout
Zanzibar (NK/S)
pages 40–3

Zanzibar in colour

left   Tall houses line the labyrinthine alleyways of Stone Town (NF/S) pages 159–75

below left   Zanzibar Town's Market Hall is the place to track down everything from fruit and fish to spices and sewing machines (NF/S) page 161

below right   The atmospheric nightly street-food market at Forodhani Gardens is popular with diners and voyeurs alike (PS/S) page 146

bottom   The Anglican cathedral was built on the site of a former slave market in Zanzibar Town (t/S) pages 167–9

top   The newly landscaped Forodhani Gardens have become the pulsing heart of Stone Town, with three cafés, a bandstand and even a dhow-shaped adventure playground (AG/EA) page 165

bottom   The Old Dispensary was originally built in the late 19th century as the private home of an Indian merchant, one of the wealthiest individuals on Zanzibar at the time (C/S) page 162

above Part of the Songo Songo archipelago just off the coast of mainland Tanzania, Fanjove is a private island teeming with wildlife and pristine beaches (EC/EA) pages 400–1

left Zanzibar's quintessential private island, Mnemba, certainly offers unparalleled barefoot luxury, but *mkeke* beach huts on powder sand can be found for all budgets (CM) pages 247–8

below The pristine sandbars, excellent diving and snorkelling opportunities and high-quality lodges make Mafia Island an exclusive but low-key Indian Ocean retreat (KJ/S) pages 369–401

AUTHORS

Chris McIntyre went to Africa in 1987, after reading physics at The Queen's College, Oxford. He taught with VSO in Zimbabwe for almost three years and travelled extensively, before co-authoring the UK's first guide to Namibia and Botswana for Bradt Travel Guides. He now has three Bradt guides to his name: *Namibia*, *Botswana* and *Zambia*, and co-authors three others: *Tanzania, Northern Tanzania* and this guide, *Zanzibar*.

Chris is also the managing director of Expert Africa, a leading tour operator to Africa. When not travelling and researching, he works with his specialist team to organise tailor-made trips and honeymoons to southern and eastern Africa – including these Tanzanian islands.

He is a Fellow of the Royal Geographical Society, and occasionally writes and photographs for UK magazines and newspapers. Based in leafy southeast England, he enjoys country life with his wife, Susie McIntyre, and two, well-travelled children. Chris can be contacted by email on **e** chris.mcintyre@expertafrica.com.

Susie McIntyre had an adventurous childhood in Zambia and Saudi Arabia, and has spent the last two decades promoting responsible global travel, both as a PR and marketing consultant, specialising in travel and tourism, and as an author and journalist. She is passionate about southern Africa: its people, wildlife and diversity. From Indian Ocean diving to cutting-edge conservation, community development to family travel and off-grid adventures, Susie is dedicated to thorough, on-the-ground research and works tirelessly to ensure the complexities of these archipelagos are accurately represented. Well known and respected on these islands, Susie is both candid and enthusiastic about their charm.

When not traipsing around tropical isles, Susie lives in the English countryside with her husband and co-author, Chris McIntyre, and their adventurous young children. Together they all spend a significant amount of time travelling and researching in Africa to get their fix of the continent and ensure they are totally abreast with developments.

Call the author

Chris McIntyre runs award-winning specialist tour operator: Expert Africa. See *www.expertafrica.com* for the latest information on Zanzibar and the rest of Tanzania, then call Chris and his team to help you plan your own African adventure.

No bias, no hard sell: for real insight, call an Expert
UK: +44 203 405 6666
USA/Canada (toll-free): 1-800-242-2434
Australia (toll-free): 1-800-995-397

EXPERT AFRICA

NAMIBIA · SOUTH AFRICA · BOTSWANA · ZAMBIA · MALAWI · ZIMBABWE · RWANDA · TANZANIA · KENYA · MOZAMBIQUE · SEYCHELLES

info@expertafrica.com
www.expertafrica.com

Philip Briggs provided the original base information for the *Southern Tanzania Safaris* chapter and additional facts and figures. He is the co-author of the Bradt safari guides to Northern Tanzania and Tanzania. He also wrote their guides to Uganda, Ethiopia, Malawi, Mozambique, Rwanda, Somaliland, Ghana and Suriname, as well as their East African Wildlife guide, and Highlights guides to Kenya, South Africa and Ethiopia. He also contributes regular travel and wildlife features to *Travel Africa, Africa Geographic* and *Wild Travel* magazines.

Sarah Chanter wrote the original *History* section and many of the historical items for early editions of this book. She has a keen interest in the history and culture of Zanzibar, has worked as a teacher in Kenya and has travelled extensively throughout East and southern Africa.

Said el-Gheithy lives and works in both Zanzibar and London. As director of the Centre for African Language Learning (London) and the Princess Salme Institute (Zanzibar/London), he kindly provided information for the *Language* and *History* sections in early editions of this book.

David Else is a professional travel writer. He first reached Zanzibar in 1985, sailing by dhow from Dar es Salaam. Over the next two decades (and using more comfortable transport) he visited Zanzibar regularly and wrote the first five editions of this guidebook. David now lives in the north of England – a long way indeed from a tropical coastline.

Jeff Fleisher is an archaeological researcher in the Department of Anthropology at the University of Virginia, and provided valuable information for the historical and cultural sections of this book.

Tricia and Bob Hayne researched and provided the base for the section on Pemba. Formerly editorial director of Bradt Travel Guides, Tricia is now a freelance travel writer, and a member of the British Guild of Travel Writers. She and Bob have also helped to update Chris's guides to Namibia, Botswana and Zambia, as well as Bradt's guide to St Helena.

Dudley Iles is a keen ornithologist and conservationist, and provided information on the wildlife of Zanzibar. From 1993 to 1995 he worked for the Commission for Lands and Environment in Zanzibar, helping to set up environmental clubs and train conservation officers.

Christine Osborne wrote the original text on which this book's *Mafia Archipelago* chapter was based. Born in Australia, she has travelled widely through Africa and the Indian Ocean islands as a writer and photographer. Christine now runs the multi-faith and travel image libraries www.worldreligions.co.uk and www.copix. co.uk. She is a member of the British Guild of Travel Writers.

Gemma Pitcher is a travel writer who has lived and worked on Zanzibar, and travelled widely throughout eastern and southern Africa. She provided content for the early editions of this book; some of the text originally appeared in *Zanzibar Style*, which was written by Gemma, and is reproduced with permission.

Dr Matthew Richmond is a marine science and fisheries expert who has lived and worked on Zanzibar and around the western Indian Ocean since 1989. Matt is involved in numerous marine education and biodiversity projects in the region, is the author of *A Guide to the Seashores of Eastern Africa and the Western Indian Ocean Islands*, and provided the text on marine wildlife for this book.

Richard Trillo is Kenya Programme Manager at tour operator Expert Africa and is a specialist in African travel. He holds an MA in East African Ethnography, Swahili Literature and African Linguistics from London's School of Oriental and African Studies. For many years he was Director of Communications at travel publisher Rough Guides and he is the author of Rough Guides to *Kenya, West Africa* and *Madagascar*, and co-author of Rough Guides to *First-Time Africa, The Gambia* and *World Music*.

AUTHORS' STORY

Holidays in Africa have long concentrated on game-rich safaris on the mainland. Visitors since Livingstone have travelled from across the globe for great wildlife spectacles set in vast tracts of wilderness, sometimes accompanied by strange and fascinating traditional cultures. Many find themselves bitten by the Africa bug, returning as frequently as possible, but it is only recently that Africa's islands have been viewed as final destinations in their own right.

For us, the transition from bush to beach followed a similar pattern. We have both lived in southern Africa: Chris teaching in rural Zimbabwe and pioneering Bradt's travel guides to Namibia, Botswana and Zambia; Susie spending a happy childhood in Zambia's northern reaches. Our early experiences were concentrated in the heart of Africa; any travel focused heavily on the national parks and wildlife wonders of neighbouring countries.

Years later and still hooked on the continent, Chris used his experience to establish Expert Africa, a UK-based tour operator. Slowly, an opportunity became clear to offer exotic beach hideaways as a relaxing end to more traditional safaris. Keen to understand the options, we explored all the archipelagos from southern Mozambique to Tanzania's Pemba. Our first trip took us to Zanzibar and its idyllic neighbour, Mafia – we were enchanted! So when the opportunity arose to take on the Bradt guide to these islands, we leapt at the chance to research in more depth, and get a deeper understanding of these islands.

Now, as we sign off our fourth edition of this guide, we're pleased to have been able to completely overhaul some sections and extensively update many others. We remain humbled by the individuals we've encountered, amazed at the marine life in the turquoise seas, and also concerned by some of the less responsible developments that we've seen. We hope that this guide may help ethical travellers to contribute towards a better future for these striking islands and point them towards the area's extra special experiences.

PUBLISHER'S FOREWORD   *Hilary Bradt*

My association with Zanzibar goes back to 1976 when the newly 'Africanised' and socialist government of the island was hostile to foreign visitors. I have since returned many times as a lecturer on board expedition ships and have relished the changes I have seen. The beaches are still superb, and while Stone Town still has the intimacy and total otherness that I loved, the buildings have been renovated and tourists now receive a warm welcome. On my last visit I escaped my group and wandered the narrow streets away from the tourist centre, stopping to watch a small child play with a toy car made from wire and bottle tops. His father, seeing my interest, came forward with a broad grin and asked me to photograph the two of them. That brief encounter epitomised all that I love about Zanzibar.

Chris McIntyre's talent at knowing what Bradt readers are looking for has made him one of our most praised writers on Africa. Once again, he and Susie McIntyre have extensively revised one of our flagship titles, bringing their inside knowledge to an ever-widening audience of travellers to Zanzibar.

Ninth edition published July 2017   First published 1993

Bradt Travel Guides Ltd
IDC House, The Vale, Chalfont St Peter, Bucks SL9 9RZ, England
www.bradtguides.com
Print edition published in the USA by The Globe Pequot Press Inc,
PO Box 480, Guilford, Connecticut 06437-0480

Text copyright © 2017 Chris and Susie McIntyre
Maps copyright © 2017 Bradt Travel Guides Ltd; includes map data © OpenStreetMap contributors
Illustrations copyright © Carole Vincer and Annabel Milne
Photographs copyright © 2017 Individual photographers (see below)
Project Manager: Laura Pidgley
Cover image research: Pepi Bluck, Perfect Picture

ISBN: 978 1 78477 052 5 (print)
e-ISBN: 978 1 78477 506 3 (e-pub)
e-ISBN: 978 1 78477 407 3 (mobi)

British Library Cataloguing in Publication Data
A catalogue record for this book is available from the British Library

Photographs Alamy: Danita Delimont (DD/A); Ariadne Van Zandbergen, www.africaimagelibrary.com (AVZ); AWL: Danita Delimont (DD/AWL) Steve Outram (SO/AWL); Chris McIntyre (CM); Dreamstime: Sohadiszno (S/D); Expert Africa: Angela Griffin (AG/EA), Elizabeth Chapman (EC/EA); FLPA: Pete Oxford (PO/FLPA); Shutterstock: Andaman (A/S), Adwo (AD/S), Attila JANDI (AT/S), Bartosz Budrewicz (BB/S), Claudiovidri (C/S), Kjersti Joergensen (KJ/S), MattiaATH (M/S), Nick Fox (NF/S), Nicole Kwiatkowski (NK/S), Pearl.diver (P/S), Pajac Slovensky (PS/S), sivanadar (s/S), Stesh (ST/S), tr3gin (t/s), T_H (th/S), yu-jas (yu/S); SuperStock (SS); Susie McIntyre (SM)

Front cover Sailing dhow (AVZ)
Back cover Whale shark (PO/FLPA); Spice vendor at Darajani Market (DD/AWL)
Title page Cyclist on a local beach (ST/S); Cocount crab (AVZ); Anglican cathedral in Stone Town (P/S)

Maps David McCutcheon FBCart.S

Typeset by www.dataworks.co.in
Production managed by Jellyfish Print Solutions; printed in India
Digital conversion by www.dataworks.co.in

Acknowledgements

Susie and Chris McIntyre have extensively updated and rewritten the guide for this ninth edition. However, thanks are due to the many people who have helped with advice, information and contributions throughout the book's many years of life. Some are already listed as major contributors and others are named in the text. Of the rest, special thanks go to James Denny and Lyndsey Marris, Tanzania specialists at Expert Africa, for their good humour and company on hectic research trips for this edition. Also to Peter Bennett, who helped research and gather information for four early editions of this book. Further help has come from many others, including Javed Jafferji, John da Silva, Balkishna Gorolay, who greatly benefited our *History* section, and Fiona Clark and Jim Boggs, for input on wildlife and culture. For wildlife contributions, particular thanks to Rob Wild, Dr Nadia Corp, Lorna Slade and Dr Per Berggren. Thanks also to Toufiq Juma Toufiq, Ali Addurahim and Ali Khamis Mohammed for local insights; and to Adria LaViolette for historical, archaeological and anthropological input. Hildegard Kiel and Yusuf Mahmoud helped with the *Music and dance* section, whilst Haji Hafidh and Robert Pasiani of Eco+Culture gave great insight into community tourism initiatives and practical help with local transport details. For passionate and infectious enthusiasm in all things historic, cultural and local, thanks to Anjam Hassan: a pillar of Stone Town's guiding scene.

For this ninth edition we're very grateful also to all those who have so willingly offered information, insight and a place to rest our heads: Salma and Salim Abdullah, Nassor Ali, Julia Bishop, Peter Byrne, Maura Cavallo, Christian Chilcott, Nicola Colangelo, Joel Crossland, Trish Dhanak, Julia Gimadyeva, Elies Hagedoorn, Anjam Hassan, Sara Hemed, Tammy Holter, Alois Inninger, Javed Jafferji, Massimo Lancellotti, Linda Le Dirach, Kassim Mande, Elly M'langa, Dr Aviti J Mmochi, Hashir Mohammed, Mohammed Naushad Mohammed, Mustafa Mukame, Ali Mwinyi, Alok Nandan, Stefanie Schoetz, Abdul Simai, Helen Simmans, Lukáš Šinogl, The Zanzibar Collection and Edwin van Zwam.

On a personal note, thanks to our children, James and Charlotte, for their patience during days of writing, and to their wonderful grandma, Margaret Shand, for outstanding and inspirational childcare during research trips.

Contents

TANZANIA

FOLLOW BRADT

For the latest news, special offers and competitions, subscribe to the Bradt newsletter via the website www.bradtguides.com and follow Bradt on:

f BradtTravelGuides
🐦 @BradtGuides
📷 @bradtguides
📌 bradtguides

Introduction

Zanzibar is a magical, evocative African name, like Timbuktu, Casablanca or Kilimanjaro. For many travellers, the name alone is reason enough to come. Yet although expectations run high, awareness of the reality on Zanzibar and its neighbouring islands is often rather hazy.

Having travelled and lived in Africa for many years, we had many friends who had sailed from mainland Tanzania to Zanzibar decades ago, and returned eulogising about the intoxicating aroma of spices, the amazing beaches, and just how cheap it was – but somehow neither of us made it there at the time.

When we eventually visited at the start of the new millennium, Zanzibar was beginning to evolve. Stylish lodges were flourishing alongside backpackers' beach hideaways, and flights around the islands were becoming easier. On that first trip we also discovered Mafia – a smaller and quieter archipelago to the south, with fewer visitors and spectacular diving.

It's now coming up for 15 years and many trips since our first Spice Islands encounters, and a tremendous amount of change has taken place: good, bad and unexpected. It remains impossible not to be enchanted as you approach from the air, looking down on sparkling turquoise waters, darkened only by patch reefs, and punctuated by the billowing triangular white sails of passing dhows. We still smile as we step off the plane, to be enveloped by the exotic blend of warmth, humidity and aromatic spices.

For many, the islands offer a quintessential Indian Ocean experience: palm-lined stretches of powder-white coral sand line the coast for miles, while below the waves, reef fish flit amongst colourful coral gardens, overshadowed only by the occasional pelagic looming out of the blue. From the nesting turtles on Juani to the whalesharks seen annually off Mafia, there is always something unexpected awaiting the diver and snorkeller. On land, too, these islands can enthral. Kirk's red colobus monkeys can be seen in the forest, Arabian architecture provides an exotic urban backdrop, and village life remains steeped in tradition. Yet, despite the stunning raw material and depth of culture, aspects of Zanzibar have the potential to disappoint.

Development along huge swathes of Zanzibar's coastline, by both foreign and local investors, has been astonishingly fast, and much of it is lamentable. In general, there appears to be scant regard for environmental impact and a disturbing lack of real community development. The islands are also handicapped by a largely autonomous government which, at best, has combined inefficiency at regulating development with ineffectiveness at providing even the most basic of public services. At worst, and in stark contrast to the more positive situation in Tanzania, it seems to conform to the most negative stereotypes of African governance.

Despite these issues, we have found much to hearten us on recent research trips, mostly due to a sprinkling of dedicated, forward-thinking individuals who are determined not to give up on the islands and their people, and to a core of truly good islanders within the islands communities. Some really special, ethically run hotels and lodges have been established, even if they need to be carefully sought out in advance of visiting, and there are a few brilliant marine conservation projects blossoming in Mafia's waters, where close encounters with turtles and whalesharks are simply awesome. There are doggedly determined individuals pushing forward with creative projects to recycle, to train, to educate and to empower, all of which are making small, positive inroads.

For those who want to escape to intimate lodges with great diving and snorkelling, the lodges on Mafia are firm personal favourites and less visited simply because the island is less well known. Trailblazing models of responsible tourism, like Zanizbar's Chumbe Island and Mafia's Chole Mjini, continue to force the pace.

Away from hotels and lodges, opportunities for visitors to enrich their holidays whilst also making a positive impact on the people, range from original and high-quality souvenir shopping, which also happens to be fair trade (pages 149–52), to local village restaurants with impressively high standards of cuisine, and the eclectic island tours run by both Zanzibar Different and Eco+Culture, who are dedicated to funding community development. We love these primarily because they're all very good indeed – but also because these initiatives are responsible in their approach. If you take time to look beyond the gaze of most visitors, and vote with your feet to support them, you might find your trip taken to a whole new level.

While researching this latest edition, we had the absolute privilege of a day pounding Stone Town's streets with Anjam Hassan. A lifelong resident of these winding alleyways, he's now a loquacious guide, bringing to life their hidden histories and tales. He is a Muslim, a husband and father, a fountain of knowledge and insight, but most of all, a thoroughly charming, entertaining gentleman literally bursting to share his city and culture. As he revealed generations of insight into herbal medicines, unravelled the many myths surrounding patterns on carved Zanzibari doors, imparted detailed family recipes over brimming market stalls, shared our horror of religious extremists and revelled in the healing power of turmeric, time literally ran away with us. Without a plane to catch, I would cheerfully have carried on in his company. He was candid and charismatic, interested in opinion and open to discussion, and overwhelmingly warm and giving. We learnt immense amounts and had such fun.

It can be hard on these islands for visitors and community members to engage with each other in a meaningful way; the options are somewhat limited for genuine and accessible interaction with local Zanzibaris. But time with Anjam, or the equally charismatic Kassim Mande in Jambiani, are fascinating and offer tremendous insights and understanding of local thinking and sensitivities. With all this comes a breakdown of some of the negative barriers which have arisen over the years from a lack of knowledge and respect. If you make time to walk with one of these guys (details found on pages 118 or 312), you may just discover, like us, that it turns out to be one of your favourite days on Zanzibar.

Our message is clear: don't discount the less well-known areas of Zanzibar, Pemba Island or the Mafia Archipelago. And for some of the best experiences, get off the beaten track, ideally with knowledgeable residents. Your choices will make a difference not only to your stay, but also to the communities that you encounter.

These islands already receive more than 150,000 visitors each year; fewer than one in every 50 will have a copy of this guide. We hope it helps you to get there, to choose the right places to stay, and to make the most of your time on the islands. But more than that, we hope that it will open your eyes to some of the more offbeat and responsible travel opportunities on the islands, and give you the confidence to venture off on your own, away from the lodges that we've so carefully described, to explore and to meet people like Anjam and Kassim – for their sake, as well as for the good of your holiday.

HOW TO USE THIS GUIDE

AUTHORS' FAVOURITES Finding genuinely characterful accommodation or that unmissable off-the-beaten-track café can be difficult, so the authors have chosen a few of their favourite places throughout the country to point you in the right direction. These 'authors' favourites' are marked with a ✳.

MAPS
Keys and symbols Maps include alphabetical keys covering the locations of those places to stay, eat or drink that are featured in the book. Note that regional maps may not show all hotels and restaurants in the area: other establishments may be located in towns shown on the map.

Grids and grid references Several maps use gridlines to allow easy location of sites. Map grid references are listed in square brackets after the name of the place or sight of interest in the text, with page number followed by grid number, eg: [103 C3].

FEEDBACK REQUEST AND UPDATES WEBSITE

At Bradt Travel Guides we're aware that guidebooks start to go out of date on the day they're published – and that you, our readers, are out there in the field doing research of your own. You'll find out before us when a fine new family-run hotel opens or a favourite restaurant changes hands and goes downhill. So why not write and tell us about your experiences? Contact us on ☎ 01753 893444 or ℮ info@bradtguides.com. We will forward emails to the authors who may post updates on the Bradt website at www.bradtupdates.com/zanzibar. Alternatively you can add a review of the book to www.bradtguides.com or Amazon.

Part One

GENERAL INFORMATION

ZANZIBAR AT A GLANCE

Islands Zanzibar Island (Unguja), Pemba Island, and surrounding islands

Location About 40km off the coast of East Africa, in the Indian Ocean, about 6°S of Equator

Size Zanzibar 1,660km², Pemba 985km²

Climate Wet season mid March to end May; short rains November; rest of year generally dry. Average temperature 26–28°C

Status Separate state within United Republic of Tanzania, governed by Revolutionary Council and House of Representatives

Population 1,303,569 (2012 census)

Life expectancy 58 (men); 62 (women)

Main town Zanzibar Town, population 223,033 (2012)

Economy Fishing, agriculture, tourism

Languages Swahili (official), also Arabic

Religion Islam

Currency Tanzanian shilling (TSh)

Exchange rate £1 = TSh2,779, US$1 = TSh2,226, €1 = TSh2,371 (April 2017)

International telephone code +255

Time GMT +3

Electrical voltage 230v 50Hz; round or square three-pin 'British-style' plugs

Weights and measures Metric

Flag The new flag, inaugurated in 2005, consists of three horizontal stripes in blue, black and green, and features an inset of the United Republic of Tanzania flag.

National anthem 'Mungu ibariki Afrika' (God Bless Africa)

Public holidays 1 January, 12 January, 7 April, 26 April, 1 May, 7 July, 8 August, 14 October, 9 December, 25 December, 26 December (see also pages 94–5)

1

History, Politics and Economy

HISTORY

Sarah Chanter, with additional contributions by Jeff Fleisher
The monsoons that blow across the Indian Ocean have allowed contact between Persia, Arabia, India and the coast of East Africa (including the islands of Zanzibar) for over 2,000 years. The first European arrivals were Portuguese 'navigators' looking for a trade route to India. They reached Zanzibar at the end of the 15th century and established a trading station here and at other points on the east African coast.

At the end of the 17th century the Portuguese were ousted by the Omani Arabs. During this period, Zanzibar became a major slaving centre. In 1840, the Omani sultan Said moved his court from Muscat to Zanzibar, and the island became an Arab state and an important centre of trade and politics in the region. Many European explorers, including Livingstone and Stanley, began their expeditions into the interior of Africa from Zanzibar during the second half of the 19th century.

Zanzibar was a British protectorate from 1890 until 1963, when the state gained independence. In 1964, the sultan and the government were overthrown in a revolution. In the same year, Zanzibar and the newly independent country of Tanganyika combined to form the United Republic of Tanzania.

FIRST INHABITANTS AND EARLY VISITORS The first human beings, *Homo erectus*, evolved in the East African Rift Valley, within 1,000 miles of Zanzibar, about 1.5 million years ago. They migrated throughout Africa and later Asia and beyond, becoming hunter-gatherers. Near rivers and coasts these people developed fishing techniques, and it is possible that Zanzibar's first human inhabitants were fishermen who crossed from the African mainland in dugout canoes sometime during the 1st millennium BC.

At around the same time, or even earlier, the east African coast (including the islands of Zanzibar) may have received visitors from many parts of the ancient world, such as Mesopotamia (present-day Iraq) and Egypt. The Egyptian pharaohs sent expeditions to the land they called Punt (present day Somalia) in around 3000BC and again in 1492BC; these possibly continued southwards down the east African coast. This theory is supported by carvings on temple walls at Luxor showing sailing boats with slaves unloading gold, ivory tusks, leopard skins and trees of frankincense.

Other visitors may have included Phoenicians, a seafaring people from the eastern shores of the Mediterranean. Around 600BC, a Phoenician fleet sailed south along the coast, past Zanzibar, and is believed to have circumnavigated Africa before returning to the Mediterranean three years later.

By the 1st century AD, Greek and Roman ships were sailing from the Red Sea down the east African coast, searching for valuable trade goods such as tortoiseshell,

3

ebony and ivory. Around AD60, a Greek merchant from Alexandria wrote a guide for ships in the Indian Ocean called *The Periplus of the Erythaean Sea*. This is the first recorded eyewitness account of the east African coast, and describes 'the Island of Menouthesias' (most likely the present-day island of Unguja, also called Zanzibar Island) as 'flat and wooded' with 'many rivers' and 'small sewn boats used for fishing'. Another Alexandrine Greek, Claudius Ptolemaeus (usually called Ptolemy), also mentioned Menouthesias in his book *Geographike*, written about AD150.

At about the same time, it is thought that Arab and Persian trading ships from the Persian Gulf were also sailing down the coast of East Africa. They sailed south on the northeast monsoon between November and February, carrying beads and cloth, and even Chinese porcelain that had come via India. Then, between March and September, after the winds changed direction, they returned north on the southwest monsoon, carrying the same tortoiseshell, ebony and ivory that had attracted the Greeks and Romans, plus mangrove poles for timber and other goods. The Arabs and Persians traded with the local inhabitants but they remained visitors and, at this stage, did not settle.

During the 3rd and 4th centuries AD, other groups of migrating peoples started to arrive on the east coast of Africa. These people were Bantu (the name comes from the term used to define their group of languages); they originated from the area around present-day Cameroon in the centre of the continent, then spread throughout eastern and southern Africa. On the east African coast, they established settlements, which slowly grew into towns, and eventually became the major trading cities such as Kilwa, Lamu and Mombasa on the mainland, and Unguja Ukuu on the island of Unguja (Zanzibar Island). These coastal settlers traded with the Arabs, exporting ivory, rhino horn, tortoiseshell and palm oil, and importing metal tools and weapons, wine and wheat.

The Arab traders called the east African coast Zinj el Barr, meaning 'land of the black people', from where the modern name Zanzibar is derived. 'Zinj' comes from *zang*, the Persian word for 'black', and *barr* is the Arabic word for 'land'. The Arabs may also have derived the word from *Zayn za'l barr*, meaning 'fair is this land'. Zanzibar remained the name of the whole coast, including the islands of Unguja and Pemba (which together make up the present-day state of Zanzibar), until the late 15th century.

EARLY ARAB SETTLERS The 7th century AD saw the rise of Islam in Arabia. At the same time, wars in this area, and subsequent unrest in Persia, caused a small number of people from these regions to escape to the east African coast, where they settled permanently, bringing the new Islamic religion with them.

There are several accounts of emigrations from Arabia to East Africa – the history of this period is largely based on stories handed down by word of mouth through generations, which are difficult to separate from myth and legend. One story tells of two Arab chiefs from Oman who arrived in East Africa with their families around the end of the 7th century, and settled on the island of Pate, near Lamu. Another story tells of an emigration from Shiraz, in Persia, some time between the 8th and 10th centuries, when the Sultan of Shiraz and his six sons migrated with their followers in seven boats. One of the sons stopped at Pemba, while others settled in Mombasa and Kilwa. The 9th-century Arab tale of Sinbad the Sailor, one of the stories in *The Arabian Nights*, was most probably inspired by accounts of journeys by Arab sailors to East Africa and southeast Asia.

THE RISE OF THE SWAHILI During the second half of the 1st millennium, the coastal Bantu people developed a language and culture (in fact, a whole civilisation) which became known as Swahili. This name came from the Arabic word *sahil*, meaning 'coast'. Their language, Kiswahili, although Bantu in origin, contained many Arabic words. It also included some Persian words, mainly nautical terms. There was some intermarriage, and the Swahili adopted many Arab customs and traditions, including the Islamic religion. On Unguja (Zanzibar Island), Shirazi settlers are believed to have married into the family of the island's Swahili king. Several centuries later, the Mwinyi Mkuu (the great lord), the traditional ruler of Unguja, continued to claim descent from a Shirazi prince.

By the 7th century, the Swahili people were trading regularly with Arab and Persian merchants. In the same way, Swahili dhows (traditional ships based on an Arab design) also became involved in the trade and sailed regularly to and from the Persian Gulf, carrying gold, ivory, rhino horn, leopard skins, tortoiseshell, and ambergris from whales. African slaves were also carried to the Persian Gulf, probably to work in the marshlands of Mesopotamia.

Over the following centuries the trade between Africa and Arabia increased, as did trading links between East Africa and Asia. Ivory was exported to India, and later China, while Indian cloth and Chinese porcelain and silk were imported to Arabia and Zanzibar. At around this time, Indonesian sailors from Java and Sumatra are thought to have reached East Africa and Madagascar, possibly introducing coconuts and bananas.

From this period (7th to 10th centuries) archaeologists have discovered a very distinctive kind of local pottery, known as Tana Tradition, which looks the same at sites along the whole East African coast, from northern Kenya to southern Tanzania, and out to the Comoros Islands. The similarity of this pottery over such a large area shows how closely linked the people of the coast were, and also shows – for the first time – a sense of commonality and shared experience. Imported ceramics, called Sassian Islamic, from the Persian Gulf, have also been discovered.

Archaeological, linguistic and historical research conducted since the early 1980s has also led to a shift in the way that the early history of the coast is interpreted, rejecting some of the ideas put forward by scholars working during the 1950s, 1960s and 1970s. In essence, this research suggests that at its core – its foundation – Swahili culture and history are African phenomena. Until recently, archaeologists had proposed that the large towns of the east African coast (such as Kilwa, Lamu, Mombasa and Unguja Ukuu) had been built by Persian or Arab settlers, and the local Bantu people had then intermarried and 'Africanised' the Arabs, thus resulting in the Swahili people. But, through extensive excavations at many of these towns, it is now known that they were founded by people from the interior of Africa and, instead of simply starting as grand towns, were actually built up slowly over time by these same people.

Unquestionably, the links to the Indian Ocean trade were some of the most important for these towns, but there is little evidence of large-scale migrations from Arabia or Persia to the coast of East Africa until the middle of the 2nd millennium.

ZANZIBAR ENTERS THE 2ND MILLENNIUM
On Unguja, one of the earliest remaining examples of permanent settlement from Persia is a mosque at Kizimkazi, on the southern part of the island. It contains an inscription dated AH500 (Anno Hegirae), which corresponds to the Christian year AD1107, making this the oldest-known Islamic building on the east African coast. From the end of the 12th century, Omani immigrants also settled in Pemba. At around the same time, the settlement that was to become Zanzibar Town also began to grow.

As the trade between Africa, Arabia and the rest of the Indian Ocean continued to expand, Zanzibar became an increasingly powerful and important commercial centre. Major imports included cotton cloth, porcelain and copper from Dabhol, a port on the west coast of India, and exports included iron from Sofala (in present-day Mozambique). By the 13th century, Zanzibar was minting its own coins, and stone buildings were starting to replace more basic mud dwellings. In 1295, the Venetian traveller Marco Polo wrote of Zanzibar: 'The people have a king … elephants in plenty … and whales in large numbers', although he never visited the island. Other writers of the time noted that the kings and queens of Zanzibar and Pemba dressed in fine silks and cottons, wore gold jewellery, and lived in stone houses decorated with Persian carpets and Chinese porcelain.

Many Chinese imports had come to Zanzibar via India, but in the early 15th century the ports on the coast of East Africa were trading directly with China. Gold, ivory and rhino horn were transported to the East, as well as a small number of slaves. In 1414, a dhow from the city of Malindi (in present-day Kenya) carried a giraffe to China as a present for the emperor. The trade came to an abrupt end in 1443 when the new Ming emperor banned Chinese merchants from going abroad, but the demand for ivory remained, supplied by Arab dhows via markets in India.

By the mid 15th century, the islands of Zanzibar, along with Mombasa, Malindi, Lamu and Kilwa, formed a chain of thriving Swahili Islamic city states, each with its own sultan, spread along the east African coast. These cities had close trading links with Arabia, Persia, India and southeast Asia. Commerce between Africa and the Indian Ocean had become very profitable, and it seems that the sultans of Zanzibar and the other city states were more than happy for their territories to remain as gateways or conduits for it. At the end of the 15th century, though, the situation was severely disrupted by the arrival of the Portuguese on the coast of East Africa.

PORTUGUESE RULE By the mid 15th century, Prince Henry 'the Navigator' of Portugal was encouraging voyages of exploration around the African coast. He hoped to find a sea route to the East, as well as the Christian kingdom of the legendary Prester John (or 'Priest-king') of Abyssinia. With the rise of the Ottoman Empire in 1453, all goods from the East, including the increasingly valuable spices, now reached Portugal via potentially hostile Muslim countries.

In 1487, Prince Henry's successor, King John II, dispatched two expeditions to the East led by Bartholomew Dias and Pedro da Covilhan: one by sea around the southern tip of Africa, the other overland through Egypt. In 1497, another Portuguese navigator, Vasco da Gama, encouraged by the reports of Dias and da Covilhan, rounded the Cape of Good Hope and sailed northwards up the coast of East Africa, on the way to India. He passed Zanzibar and landed at Mombasa, where he received a hostile reception from the sultan. But he got a warm welcome in Malindi, an old enemy of Mombasa. Da Gama built a pillar of friendship on the shore at Malindi and employed an Omani navigator called Ahmed bin Majid to guide him across the Indian Ocean. On his return from India in 1499 he moored for a day off Unguja.

More Portuguese ships followed in the wake of da Covilhan and da Gama. They needed safe provisioning and repair bases for their voyages to and from the Far East, and so garrisons were established in the harbours of Unguja, Pemba and Mombasa.

Any early friendship was soon forgotten when the Portuguese took control of Unguja in 1503. A ship commanded by Rui Lourenço Ravasco moored off the southern end of the island while Portuguese sailors captured over 20 Swahili dhows and shot about 35 islanders. The Mwinyi Mkuu (ruler of Zanzibar) was forced to become a subject of Portugal, and agreed to allow Portuguese ships free access to Zanzibar. Additionally, he was required to pay an annual tribute to the Portuguese crown.

Portuguese domination of the region continued. In 1505, they took control of Mombasa, and in 1506, Pemba. Between 1507 and 1511, the Portuguese also occupied territories in the Arabian Gulf, including Muscat and the island of Hormuz.

By 1510, Unguja's tribute had fallen short and the people of Pemba had also become hostile to the Portuguese. Under Duarte de Lemos, the Portuguese looted and set fire to settlements on Unguja, then plundered the town of Pujini in Pemba. They soon regained both islands, and by 1525, the whole east African coast, from Lamu to Sofala, was under Portuguese control. Gold, ivory, ebony and slaves from the interior were carried to Portuguese colonies in India or back to Portugal. Iron ore and garnets from Sofala, and coconut fibre and gum-copal (a tree resin) from the islands were also exported. Cloth, beads, porcelain and metal tools were imported to the East African coast from Oman and Portugal.

Around 1560 the Portuguese built a church and small trading settlement on a western peninsula of Unguja. This was to become Zanzibar Town. But although the Portuguese occupied Unguja, and forced the local people to trade under their supervision, the islanders continued to pay allegiance to the Mwinyi Mkuu, their own king.

Portugal was not the only European power with interests in the Indian Ocean. In November 1591, the *Edward Bonaventura*, captained by Sir James Lancaster, became the first English ship to call at Zanzibar. It was supplied with fresh food and water by the Mwinyi Mkuu. Soon, more European ships were calling at Zanzibar on their way to and from the Indian subcontinent and islands of the East Indies.

John Henderson, a Scottish sailor from one English ship, was reportedly held captive on Zanzibar in 1625. He later escaped, but not until he had fallen in love with a Zanzibari princess who escaped with him back to Scotland. Today, their portraits are in the collection of the Scottish National Portrait Gallery in Edinburgh.

With the advent of English ships in the Indian Ocean, the Portuguese needed to strengthen their position on the coast. In 1594, they built a fort at Chake Chake in Pemba and, from 1593 to 1595, Fort Jesus in Mombasa was constructed. Settlers arrived from Portugal, and a Portuguese garrison was established in Fort Jesus, brutally suppressing the local population. Mombasa became known as *Mvita*, 'the place of war', and the Portuguese governor as *Afriti*, 'the devil'.

Despite these fortifications, however, the Portuguese position in East Africa began to weaken. In Arabia, Hormuz was regained by the Persians in 1622 and, in January 1650, Muscat was regained by the Omani Arabs. Following this victory, the Sultan of Oman's navy sailed to Zanzibar to help the Mwinyi Mkuu, Queen Mwana Mwema. The Omanis raided the Portuguese settlement on Unguja, killing many people and imprisoning about 400 in the church. They also attacked and burnt the Portuguese settlement on Pemba. By 1668, virtually the entire coastal area was in Omani hands. The only garrisons still held by the Portuguese were at Fort Jesus in Mombasa, and on the western peninsula of Unguja.

In 1682, the Portuguese persuaded the Queen of Pemba, who was living in Goa, to return, but this attempt to install a friendly ruler in Pemba was frustrated when her own subjects drove her out. The last Portuguese inhabitants were expelled in 1695.

By this time, Queen Mwana Mwema of Unguja had been succeeded by her son, Yusuf. After his death, towards the end of the 17th century, the island was divided between his two children, Bakari and Fatuma. King Bakari ruled the southern part of the island, with Kizimkazi as his capital, while his sister, Queen Fatuma, ruled the northern part. Fatuma supported the Portuguese, so her capital was built near the garrison on the western peninsula which later became the site of Zanzibar Town.

1

When the Omani fleet arrived at Mombasa and laid siege to Fort Jesus in March 1696, Queen Fatuma sent three dhows full of food to help the Portuguese defenders. The dhows were captured and burnt by the Omanis, who then attacked Zanzibar itself, forcing Queen Fatuma and her followers to flee into the interior of the island. The siege of Mombasa lasted until December 1698, when the Omani forces took Fort Jesus and installed an Omani governor. Once again, the Omanis attacked Zanzibar. They drove out the last of the Portuguese settlers, captured Queen Fatuma and took her to Oman, where she spent the next 12 years in exile before returning to resume her rule. While she was away, her son Hassan took the title Mwinyi Mkuu, but paid allegiance to Oman.

Thus the Portuguese were finally ousted from the whole east African coast, and the Omanis were firmly in control of the entire region as far south as present-day Mozambique (which remained in Portuguese hands until 1972).

OMANI RULE
Early sultans and the rise of the slave trade
From 1698, the Sultan of Oman ruled the islands of Zanzibar from Muscat, his capital, through appointed governors and occasional armed raids to put down minor rebellions. To consolidate his grip on the islands, a fort was built in Zanzibar Town, on the site of the Portuguese church, and by 1710 about 50 Omani soldiers were garrisoned there.

By this time, Oman had become a major trading nation. One of its major exports was dates, and the expansion of date plantations created a demand for cheap slave labour. The rules of Islam forbade the enslavement of Muslims, so Africans were imported in large numbers, many of them transported through Zanzibar. It is estimated that there were about 5,000 African slaves in Oman at the beginning of the 18th century, with about 500 new slaves arriving each year. Although most slaves were used on the plantations, others were employed as domestic workers or concubines, and some were re-exported to Persia or India.

In 1744, in Oman, the ruling Yaa'rubi dynasty (which had been in power since 1624) came to an end after a long civil war. It was succeeded by the new Busaidi dynasty led by Ahmed bin Said al Busaidi, an Omani merchant and ship owner. Ahmed was made Sultan of Oman and the east African coast; one of his first moves was to install a new governor in Zanzibar.

At this time, the governors of the east African city states paid allegiance to Oman, but in practice they enjoyed a great deal of autonomy. Zanzibar, Pemba, Lamu and

---

THE PORTUGUESE LEGACY

Zanzibar was occupied by the Portuguese in the 16th and 17th centuries. They introduced many new foods, brought from their colonies in other parts of the world, and the Swahili words used for these today are borrowed directly from the Portuguese language: cassava or manioc is *muhogo* in Swahili (from the Portuguese *mandioca*) and the cashew nut is *mbibo*, from *bibo*, both plants originally grown in Brazil. Avocado is *mpea* and guava is *mpera*, both from the Portuguese word *pera*. The Portuguese also introduced the use of dung (Swahili: *mboleo*, Portuguese: *boleo*) for cultivation, and the iron nail (Swahili: *parafujo*, Portuguese: *parafuso*) for boatbuilding.

Source: A History of East Africa by Oliver Roland and Matthew Gervase, Oxford University Press, 1963

Kilwa were all ruled by members of the Busaidi family, but Mombasa was controlled by a rival Omani family, the Mazrui. In 1746, the Mazruis declared Mombasa independent of Oman, and overthrew the Busaidi force on Pemba. In 1753, they tried to capture Zanzibar, but the governor here remained loyal to Oman and repelled the attack.

During this period, the Mwinyi Mkuu, King Hassan, had died and been succeeded by his son, named Sultan, who in turn was succeeded by his son Ahmed, and then by his grandson Hassan II.

Zanzibar was now a major commercial centre and had also become very important strategically. From the middle of the 18th century, there was a flourishing trade in slaves from Zanzibar and Kilwa to the Mascarenes (present-day Mauritius and Réunion): around 3,000 slaves a year by the 1770s. In the same period Dutch ships came to Zanzibar in search of slaves to work on plantations in the East Indies.

Until this time African slave traders had brought captured slaves to the coast, but by the end of the 18th century, the demand for slaves had increased to such an extent that Arab and Swahili traders from the coast and islands were penetrating the African interior. By the 1770s, caravan traders had already travelled inland as far as Lake Nyasa, present-day Lake Malawi (for more details, see box pages 168–9).

Sultan bin Ahmed and British involvement
In Oman a new sultan, Sultan bin Ahmed, came to power in 1792. He needed a strong ally to help him combat the Mazrui of Mombasa and also to keep the Persians out of Oman. He found this ally in Britain, by this time a powerful maritime nation with an empire expanding all over the world. In the late 18th century, Britain was at war with France and knew that the French emperor, Napoleon Bonaparte, was planning to march through Persia and capture Muscat on his way to invade India. In 1798, Britain and Oman agreed to a Treaty of Commerce and Navigation. Sultan bin Ahmed pledged himself to British interests in India, and his territories became out of bounds to the French. He allowed the British East India Company to establish a trading station in the Persian Gulf, and a British consul was posted to Muscat.

As well as defeating Bonaparte, the British had another motive for the treaty with Oman: they wanted to put pressure on the sultan to end slavery, which had been declared illegal in England in 1772. At this time, the trade from Africa to Oman was still buoyant.

At the same time, Zanzibar's position as an important trade centre was bolstered further when the supply of ivory from Mozambique to India collapsed because of excessive Portuguese export duties. The traders simply shipped their ivory through Zanzibar instead.

Sultan Said and the birth of the spice trade
In 1804, Sultan bin Ahmed of Oman was killed in battle, and his sons Salim and Said (aged 15 and 13) jointly inherited his kingdom with their cousin Bedr acting as regent. Two years later the young Said killed Bedr, who he believed was plotting to kill him; in 1806, he was proclaimed Sultan of Oman and the east African coast.

Said ruled his kingdom from Muscat and did not visit his African territories for several years. He maintained good relations with Britain because, like his father, he hoped for British help against the Persians and the Mazruis. During this period, wars and drought had drained Oman's economy, and many Omani merchants migrated to Zanzibar to participate in coastal trading and the caravans to the interior.

Meanwhile, in Europe, a campaign led by William Wilberforce resulted in the abolition of the slave trade within the British Empire in 1807. The USA passed a law against slave trading in 1808; the French and Germans did the same a few years later.

In East Africa, however, about 8,000 slaves were brought from the mainland to Zanzibar every year, many of them carrying ivory. The resultant surplus of slaves was addressed in 1812, when a Muscat-born Arab called Saleh bin Haramil al Abray introduced clove trees into Zanzibar from the island of Bourbon (now Réunion). The slaves were diverted to work on clove plantations and demand increased once again.

As the demand for slaves and ivory continued to expand, Arab traders from the coast pushed further inland. In 1820, they established a trading centre at Kazeh (near present-day Tabora, in Tanzania), over 800km (500 miles) from the coast. From Kazeh, trade routes branched north to the shores of present-day Lake Victoria, northwest to Buganda (now Uganda), and southwest to the southern end of Lake Tanganyika (see map, page 13).

Early British anti-slaving attempts To combat this expansion in slavery, the British consul in Muscat continued to put pressure on Sultan Said to end the slave trade. In September 1822, Said signed an anti-slavery treaty with the British captain Fairfax Moresby which prohibited slave transport south and east of the 'Moresby line', drawn from Cape Delgado, the southern limit of the sultan's domain in Africa, to Diu Head on the coast of India (see map, opposite).

This treaty meant that the transport of slaves from Zanzibar to the Mascarenes and India was banned, but still permitted between Zanzibar and Oman. The sultan was also banned from selling slaves to Christians, which included the French for their Indian Ocean islands. British warships gained the right to confiscate any dhows found carrying slaves in forbidden waters. Ironically, British prohibition of the slave trade to the Mascarenes only led to an increased development of the slave trade in Zanzibar itself. Sultan Said lost the revenue he would have received as duty on all slaves sold, so to make up the shortfall, he encouraged the development of more clove plantations.

Meanwhile, Sultan Said continued his attempt to oust the Mazrui Sultan of Mombasa. In 1823, the sultan asked for British protection against Oman. Captain William Owen of HMS *Leven* saw that he could use this local dispute to Britain's advantage: he sailed to Muscat and informed Sultan Said that he intended to grant the Mazrui request for British protection unless Said agreed to end the slave trade. Said refused to do this, so Owen declared Mombasa a British protectorate, along with the coastline from Malindi to Pangani, on condition that the Mazrui sultan agreed to abolish the slave trade. The sultan agreed, but within a few years, the Mazrui reverted to slave trading, and the British protectorate was lifted in July 1826.

Sultan Said in Zanzibar In 1827, Sultan Said sailed from Muscat to Zanzibar to inspect his far-flung territory. Here he met one Edmund Roberts, an American merchant from Portsmouth, New Hampshire, who suggested a commercial treaty between Said and America. Soon Zanzibar was supplying large amounts of ivory to America and western Europe. African ivory was soft and easy to carve into combs, piano keys and billiard balls. Asian ivory, in contrast, was hard and brittle. So great was the American demand for ivory in the 1830s that a town called Ivoryton was established in Connecticut, with a factory making piano keys and billiard balls out of ivory imported from Zanzibar. The Americans also purchased animal hides and gum-copal, a tree resin used in the manufacture of varnish. In return, cotton cloth (called 'Amerikani'), guns and gunpowder were imported into Zanzibar for distribution along the coast and to Arabia.

Sultan Said realised that trade with Europe and America would increase Zanzibar's wealth and strength, and thereby consolidate his own position, so at the end of the 1820s, he decided to develop Zanzibar's clove industry further. His first move was to

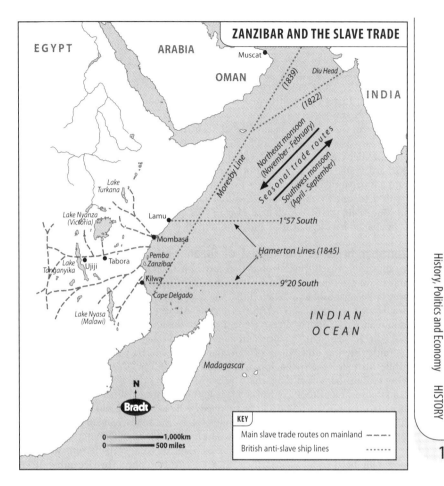

ZANZIBAR AND THE SLAVE TRADE

EGYPT

ARABIA

Muscat

OMAN

(1839)

Diu Head

(1822)

INDIA

Lake Turkana

Lake Nyanza (Victoria)

Lamu

Mombasa

Pemba

Zanzibar

Tabora

Ujiji

Lake Tanganyika

Kilwa

Cape Delgado

Lake Nyasa (Malawi)

Moresby Line

Northeast monsoon (November - February)

Seasonal trade routes

Southwest monsoon (April - September)

1°57 South

Hamerton Lines (1845)

9°20 South

INDIAN OCEAN

Madagascar

N

Bradt

0 — 1,000km

0 — 500 miles

KEY

Main slave trade routes on mainland — — —

British anti-slave ship lines ·······

confiscate the plantations of Saleh bin Haramil al Abray, who had introduced cloves to the island in 1812. Said's reason for this stemmed from Saleh's position as the leader of a political faction competing for power, and Saleh had also continued to send slaves to the Mascarenes after the Moresby Treaty had made this illegal.

Vast plantations were established on Zanzibar and Pemba, and the islands' prosperity soon grew dramatically. Said decreed that three clove trees must be planted for every coconut palm, and that any landowner failing to do so would have his property confiscated. He became the owner of 45 plantations scattered over the islands, with about 50 slaves working as labourers on the smaller plots and up to 500 on the larger ones. Cloves fetched a high price abroad, and by the end of Said's reign, Zanzibar was one of the world's leading clove producers.

Said valued Zanzibar's large harbour, abundant freshwater supply and fertile soil. He also recognised the strategic importance of a Busaidi power base on the east African coast, and decided to spend several months on the island each year. A large house was built for him at Mtoni, on the west coast of the island about 5km north of Zanzibar Town.

Over the next few years, Said came under increased pressure from the British to abolish slavery. This call was strengthened in 1833, when the Emancipation

Act abolished slavery throughout the British Empire and all slaves in British territories were freed. Recognising the need for strong allies, in the same year Said formalised the trade agreement suggested earlier by Edmund Roberts and signed a Treaty of Amity and Commerce with the United States of America. This gave the Americans freedom to set up trading posts at Zanzibar and on the mainland. In return, Said hoped for armed assistance against the Mazrui and for British anti-slavery pressure to ease. In 1837, Said finally managed to oust the Mazrui from Mombasa and install his own garrison of soldiers in Fort Jesus. His presence along the coast of East Africa was finally complete.

Links between Zanzibar and America became increasingly cordial, and a consul, Richard Waters, was appointed in March 1837. Said presented him with a horse and a boat, and Waters was often the sultan's guest at Mtoni Palace. In November 1839, Said sent his trading ship *El-Sultani* to America. The ship arrived in New York in May 1840, the first Arab boat ever to visit an American port, and returned to Zanzibar with a cargo of arms and ammunition, china, beads and 'Amerikani' cloth.

Zanzibar becomes the capital of Oman In December 1840, Sultan Said established his capital in Zanzibar, transferring it 3,000 miles from Muscat. He made this move at a time when Zanzibar's prosperity was increasing rapidly, and Oman's was in decline. Said also believed that the dual power base of Zanzibar and Oman would help safeguard his territories on the African mainland and maintain his dominance over Indian Ocean trade. Many of Oman's most influential merchants were already based in Zanzibar, and more followed him in the move from Muscat.

Said's title was now Sultan of Zanzibar and Oman. He ruled Zanzibar directly while his eldest surviving son, Thuwaini, remained in Muscat as Governor of Oman. Zanzibar's own king, the Mwinyi Mkuu, presided over local matters but Said's government took control of trade and international affairs. Zanzibar Town began to expand: when Said had first arrived in the 1820s, the buildings were mostly huts of mud thatched with coconut fronds, but by the 1850s many impressive stone buildings had been constructed by the new immigrants from Oman.

Said was also followed to Zanzibar by Captain Atkins Hamerton, who had originally been installed in Muscat to act as British consul. In December 1841, he became the first British consul in Zanzibar. France also established diplomatic relations with Zanzibar: a French consulate was opened in 1844.

Meanwhile, despite the restrictions imposed by the Moresby Treaty, the slave trade continued to expand. In 1841, Arab traders had established a trading colony at Ujiji on Lake Tanganyika, almost 1,600km (1,000 miles) from the coast, and in 1843, the first Arab caravans had reached Buganda (now Uganda) on the shores of present-day Lake Victoria. By the end of the 1840s, Arab traders had gone even further, reaching the Upper Congo (now eastern Democratic Republic of Congo), the Central Highland area around Mount Kenya, the Rift Valley lakes of Baringo and Turkana, and southern Ethiopia. About 13,000 slaves a year were arriving in Zanzibar from the mainland (see map, page 11).

Britain's opposition to the slave trade Sultan Said became increasingly concerned that British attempts to abolish the slave trade would weaken his power in the region. In 1842, he sent his envoy Ali bin Nasur to London on the ship *El-Sultani* to plead his case. Said's gifts for Queen Victoria included emeralds, cashmere shawls, pearl necklaces and ten Arab horses.

In reply, the British government told the Zanzibari ruler that it wished to abolish the slave trade to Arabia, Oman, Persia and the Red Sea. To soften the blow Queen

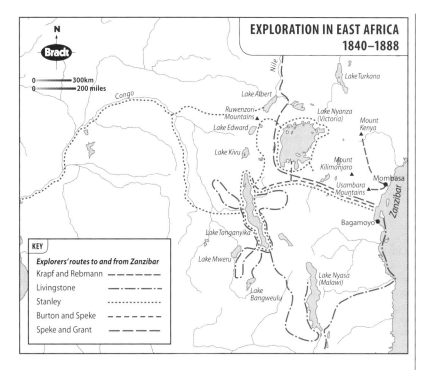

Victoria gave Said a state coach and a silver-gilt tea service. The state coach arrived in pieces and had to be assembled. It was still unused a year later, as Zanzibar had no roads, and the tea service was considered too ornate to use and was taken to the British consulate for safe keeping.

Britain continued putting restrictions on the slave trade. In October 1845, Said was virtually forced by Captain Hamerton to sign another anti-slavery treaty, which allowed slave transport only between lines of latitude 1° 57' S and 9° 20' S (between Lamu and Kilwa, the northern and southern limits of Said's dominions on the coast). This meant slaves could still be imported into Zanzibar but could no longer be exported to Oman.

Ships from the British navy were employed to help enforce the treaty by capturing any dhows carrying slaves. When a dhow was captured, it was set on fire and the slaves were taken to Aden, India, or a free slave community on the mainland coast, such as English Point in Mombasa. However, with only four ships to patrol a huge area of sea, the British navy found it hard to enforce the treaty, so the slave dhows continued to sail. Ships from France, Germany, Spain, Portugal and America also continued to carry slaves, as there were still huge profits to be made. On the mainland, slave traders continued to push further into the interior.

Early European explorers   In the 1840s, European missionaries and explorers began to venture into the east African interior. In Britain, an Association for Promoting the Discovery of the Interior Parts of Africa had been formed as early as 1788, and had since merged with the Royal Geographical Society (RGS). In the following years it would play a leading role in the search for the source of the River Nile.

Zanzibar became the usual starting point for journeys into the interior. Here, the European missionaries and explorers paid their respects to Sultan Said, who 'owned' most of the land they would pass through. They equipped their expeditions with supplies and porters before sailing to Bagamoyo on the mainland. Many explorers followed the established slaving routes into the interior, often employing slave traders to act as guides.

In 1844, the English Church Missionary Society, unable to find any British recruits, sent the German Johann Krapf to East Africa in an early attempt to convert the local people to Christianity. He was joined by his missionary colleague, Johann Rebmann, who arrived in Zanzibar two years later. They travelled widely across the areas now known as southern Kenya and northern Tanzania. In May 1848, Rebmann became the first European to see Kilimanjaro, and in December 1849, Krapf was the first European to see Mount Kenya.

Meanwhile on Zanzibar the slave trade continued. By the 1850s, about 14,000 to 15,000 slaves a year were being imported into Zanzibar from the mainland, providing Sultan Said with a large income from duties. Zanzibar traders pushed even deeper into the interior, reaching what is now northern Zambia. In 1852, a caravan reached Benguela (in present-day Angola) having completely traversed the continent from east to west, while the following year another group reached Linyanti, in the present-day Caprivi Strip of Namibia.

Through the slave caravans Said had become the nominal ruler of a vast commercial empire stretching along the coast from Mozambique to the Somali ports, and inland to the Great Lakes of Nyasa (Malawi), Tanganyika, Nyanza

THE ESCAPE TO MARSEILLES

In October 1859, Barghash was plotting to overthrow his brother, Majid, who was Sultan of Zanzibar. At the time Barghash was living in a house in Zanzibar Town, close to the palace of Beit el Sahel, with his sister Meyye and 11-year-old brother Abdil Aziz. Two more sisters, Salme and Khole, and two of his nieces, the princesses Shembua and Farashuu, all supported Barghash and wanted Majid overthrown.

Majid, aware that his brother was plotting against him, arranged to have their houses watched and ordered Barghash's house to be blockaded. Several hundred soldiers were posted outside the front of the house with strict orders to shoot any suspicious person and cut off all communications. But Barghash had plenty of provisions, and his fellow conspirators smuggled water to him through the back of the house.

Meanwhile, at the fortified plantation of Marseilles (so named by another brother, Khaled, who had a predilection for all things French), in the centre of the island, the conspirators stored arms, ammunition and food supplies in preparation for a siege. Princess Salme played an important part in the preparations because she could write, and prepared secret messages to be carried between the other conspirators. She later referred to herself as 'secretary to the alliance of rebels'.

At midnight on 8 October 1859, Salme and Khole went to Barghash's house with a large escort including Shembua and Farashuu. Bluffing their way past the soldiers on duty (Arab women did not normally speak to strange men), they were allowed to pay the prisoner a short visit. They brought women's robes and veils and Barghash wrapped himself in a voluminous black robe, which left only his eyes free. The tallest women walked alongside him to make his height less conspicuous, and the guards on the door made way respectfully for the royal party when they left the building.

(Victoria) and Turkana. By the end of his reign, Zanzibar's empire covered about 2.5 million km² (1 million square miles), or 10% of the African continent, including the whole of present-day Tanzania, plus sizeable parts of Malawi, Zambia, the DRC, Uganda and Kenya. The Arabs had a saying: 'When the flute plays in Zanzibar, they dance on the lakes.' But it was an empire in name only, and Said never attempted to conquer or develop the area.

The end of Said's reign Sultan Said made periodic visits to Muscat, leaving his son Khaled as Governor of Zanzibar in his absence. Khaled had a predilection for French goods and called his principal country estate Marseilles, after the French Mediterranean port. When Khaled died of tuberculosis in November 1854, an order came from Said in Muscat appointing another son, the 20-year-old Majid, as governor.

In September 1856, Said sailed for Zanzibar again in his boat *Kitorie*. He travelled with his family, including his son Barghash, now 19 years old. Said ordered some loose planks of wood to be loaded onto the ship, saying that if anyone should die on board, the body must not be buried at sea according to Muslim custom, but embalmed and taken to Zanzibar in a coffin. Said seemed to know it was he who was about to die: he began to suffer severe pains from an old wound in his thigh followed by an attack of dysentery. On 19 October 1856, he died on board the ship. He was 65 years old.

Once outside the town, Barghash threw off his disguise and headed for Marseilles with his supporters, while his sisters returned to Zanzibar Town. Majid soon heard news of Barghash's escape, and mustered 5,000 soldiers, while the British consul, Sir Christopher Rigby, provided nine soldiers and a gun from the British warship HMS *Assaye*.

Majid marched to Marseilles and started to bombard the house, but Barghash's supporters emerged from their fortifications, and fought off Majid's troops until sunset. Several hundred lives were lost. Majid retreated for the night but, as he and his army slept, Barghash and his supporters slipped back into town. On the morning of 16 October, Majid re-advanced on Marseilles and smashed open the gates, only to find it abandoned.

By this time, Barghash had returned to his house. Realising that his plans were thwarted, he remained concealed, refusing even to go to the window. Rigby arranged for HMS *Assaye* to be anchored just offshore, and a detachment of marines landed and marched to the front of Barghash's house, calling on Barghash to surrender. When there was no answer, the marines started to fire their guns at the front of the house. Khole, calling from her house across the street, persuaded her brother to surrender. Contemporary reports describe how cries of *Aman!* (Peace!) were heard from inside the house and how, after the firing had stopped, Rigby rapped on the door with his walking stick and demanded immediate surrender. When Barghash emerged, Rigby arrested him and put him on board the *Assaye*. He was taken to India, where he lived in exile for two years. Abdil Aziz insisted on accompanying his elder brother and stayed in India after Barghash's return in 1861.

Princess Salme was rejected by her family and, in 1866, met a German trader called Heinrich Ruete. They became lovers and moved to Germany, where Salme changed her name to Emily and later wrote a book about her life at the court of Zanzibar (see box, pages 188–9).

Barghash put his father's body in a coffin and took command of the fleet. He knew his elder brother Majid would succeed his father as the new Sultan of Zanzibar, but he also realised that Majid would be unaware of their father's death. On the night of his arrival at Zanzibar, Barghash came ashore secretly and tried to take control of the palace at Mtoni and the fort in Zanzibar Town, but he was unable to muster enough supporters and his attempt was thwarted.

On 28 October 1856, Majid bin Said was proclaimed Sultan of Zanzibar. A ship was sent to Oman with the news, but Said's eldest son Thuwaini refused to acknowledge Majid as sultan, believing that he was the legitimate successor. Majid agreed to pay Thuwaini 40,000 Maria Theresa dollars annually as compensation, but after a year the payment ceased.

Later European explorers By this time, the reports of early explorers like Rebmann and Krapf encouraged the Royal Geographical Society to send an expedition to East Africa to search for the source of the White Nile. The leaders were Lieutenant (later Sir) Richard Francis Burton and Lieutenant John Hanning Speke.

In December 1856, on the last day of mourning for Sultan Said, Burton and Speke arrived in Zanzibar. They sailed for Bagamoyo and followed the slave route towards Lake Tanganyika, which they hoped was the source of the Nile. When they arrived, in January 1858, local Arab traders told them that a river at the northern end of the lake flowed into the lake (not out of it). Burton and Speke were unable to reach the point where the river met the lake.

Bitterly disappointed, they began to return eastwards to Zanzibar. Burton became ill and was forced to stop, so Speke struck out northwards on his own and became the first European to see the great *nyanza* (meaning 'lake') which he named Lake Victoria. He was certain it was the source of the White Nile, although he was unable to prove it at the time. Speke and Burton returned to Zanzibar in March 1859, and then travelled separately to London.

To verify his theory, Speke returned to Zanzibar in 1860 with the Scottish explorer James Grant. Together they travelled inland to Lake Victoria, and this time found a great river emptying Lake Victoria at a waterfall, which they named the Ripon Falls after an earlier president of the Royal Geographical Society. Although they were still unable to prove without doubt that this river was the Nile, it was the closest any explorer had come to settling the great geographical question of the age.

The division of Oman and Zanzibar Meanwhile, back on Zanzibar, a power struggle was developing between the Omani rulers. Sultan Thuwaini of Oman planned to overthrow Sultan Majid of Zanzibar, as his promised tribute had not been paid. In February 1859, Thuwaini sailed southwards but was intercepted by a British cruiser at the eastern tip of Arabia. The British government wanted to keep control of the sea route to India, and did not want a civil war to develop in this area. Captain Hamerton, the British consul, had died, but Thuwaini was persuaded to submit his claims to the arbitration of Lord Canning, the Governor General of India. Thuwaini agreed and returned to Muscat.

But Majid was in danger from another member of the family. His brother Barghash was still plotting to overthrow him and proclaim himself Sultan of Zanzibar. Majid learnt of the plot but Barghash escaped to the Marseilles plantation. He was finally captured and exiled to India for two years (see box, pages 14–15).

In April 1861, Lord Canning declared that Oman and Zanzibar should be completely separate. The annual tribute from Zanzibar to Oman was reinstated, and in March 1862, Britain and France signed an Anglo–French declaration which recognised Majid as Sultan of Zanzibar and his territories as an independent sovereignty.

Although the Mwinyi Mkuu still lived in the palace at Dunga, his power was now negligible. Hassan II was succeeded by Mohammed, who died in 1865, aged 80. He was succeeded by his son, Ahmed, who died of smallpox in March 1873, leaving no male heir. The line of the Mwinyi Mkuu of Zanzibar had come to an end, and its passing was hardly noticed.

In 1866, in Oman, Thuwaini was murdered in his sleep by his son Salim, who succeeded him. Majid discontinued the payment of the tribute on the grounds that Salim was a usurper, and Oman withdrew into isolation. This isolation lasted for over 100 years until the accession of Sultan Qaboos bin Said in 1970.

DAVID LIVINGSTONE AND 'STINKIBAR' In 1866, the Scottish missionary and explorer David Livingstone arrived in Zanzibar. He had already travelled across much of central and southern Africa, and written at great length about the horrors of the slave trade. He wanted to introduce what he regarded as essential elements of civilisation – commerce and Christianity – to Africa as a way of defeating the slave trade. He had also been asked by the Royal Geographical Society to clarify the pattern of the watersheds in the area of Lake Nyasa and Lake Tanganyika and their relation to the source of the White Nile (still an unsolved problem for the geographers of the day).

By this period, Zanzibar's increasing trade and growing population had created its own problems and Livingstone did not enjoy his stay:

> No-one can truly enjoy good health here. The stench from … two square miles of exposed sea-beach, which is the general depository of the filth of the town, is quite horrible. At night, it is so gross and crass, one might cut a slice and manure the garden with it. It might be called 'Stinkibar' rather than Zanzibar.

During the same period, other European visitors arriving by ship claimed they could smell Zanzibar before they could see it. In the town itself, the freshwater springs were not particularly fresh. Dr James Christie, an English physician who arrived in Zanzibar in 1869, reported that the springs consisted of the 'diluted drainage of dunghills and graveyards'. Not surprisingly, this led to frequent bouts of dysentery and epidemics of smallpox and cholera. Malaria and bilharzia were also problems. Cholera epidemics had occurred in 1821 and 1836, and smallpox in 1858. Later cholera epidemics in 1858 and from 1869 to 1870 killed one-sixth of the population of Zanzibar Town, and 35,000 people throughout the island.

At this time, slavery had still not been abolished on Zanzibar. In the early 1860s, an average 15,000 slaves a year were being imported into Zanzibar from mainland Africa, and by 1866 this had grown to 20,000 a year. The slave population had reached its peak and clove production entered a phase of overproduction and stagnation, so prices dropped.

As a result of the declining profitability of clove production, there was a greater interest in the production of coconut and sesame seed oils, mainly for export to France. There was also a revival of sugar production, and rubber plantations were established along the coast.

LIVINGSTONE, STANLEY AND THE RELIEF EXPEDITIONS David Livingstone had left Zanzibar in March 1866. Lack of news in the outside world led to speculation on his whereabouts, and in January 1871, the American journalist Henry Morton

Stanley arrived in Zanzibar, having been commissioned by the *New York Herald* to search for the 'lost explorer'. In November the same year, Stanley arrived at Ujiji, where he found Livingstone and greeted him with the now immortal phrase, 'Doctor Livingstone, I presume?' (for details on the explorations of Livingstone, see boxes, page 170 and below).

HENRY MORTON STANLEY

The man known to the world as Henry Morton Stanley was born John Rowland on 29 January 1841 in Denbigh in Wales. He spent nine years in a workhouse and two years as a farmhand before joining a ship from Liverpool to New Orleans, which he reached in 1858. In New Orleans he was adopted by his employer, a cotton merchant, from whom he took his new name, Henry Stanley. 'Morton' was added later.

By 1869, Stanley was a correspondent for the *New York Herald*. The manager of the newspaper, James Gordon Bennett, dispatched him to Africa with orders to cover the inauguration of the Suez Canal, and then find Livingstone if he was alive, or bring back his bones if he was dead.

Stanley arrived in Zanzibar on 6 January 1871. He borrowed a top hat from the American consul, John Francis Webb, and went to visit Sultan Barghash, who gave him letters of recommendation to show his agents in the interior. Stanley set off from Zanzibar in March that year, just two days before the start of the rainy season. His provisions included American cloth, beads of glass, coral and china for trading, plus two silver goblets and a bottle of champagne for the day he met Livingstone.

Stanley finally met Livingstone at Ujiji, on the eastern shore of Lake Tanganyika, on 10 November 1871. According to Stanley's own description of the meeting, Stanley took off his hat, held out his hand, and said, 'Doctor Livingstone, I presume?' When Livingstone answered, 'Yes,' Stanley continued with, 'I thank God that I have been permitted to see you,' to which Livingstone gravely replied, 'I feel thankful that I am here to welcome you.'

After these traditional English niceties, and the seemingly mundane phrase that was to dog Stanley for the rest of his life, Stanley and Livingstone travelled in the area together for some time, but Livingstone was still determined to discover the source of the Nile and pressed on southwards alone. Stanley returned to Zanzibar on 7 May 1872, before travelling to London.

Two years later, Stanley gave up journalism to return to Africa as an explorer. He reached Zanzibar again in September 1874, and left for the mainland in November the same year. On this expedition he rounded the southern shore of Lake Victoria, went through Buganda (now Uganda), and followed the Congo River (through present-day DRC) to the Atlantic Ocean, which he reached on 12 August 1877, thus crossing Africa in 999 days.

From 1879 to 1884, Stanley returned to the Congo for King Léopold II of Belgium. He established and governed the Congo Free State (which was to become Zaire, now renamed the Democratic Republic of Congo), and the town of Stanleyville (now Kisangani) was named after him.

After another expedition from 1887 to 1889, Stanley returned to Britain a celebrity. He was married in Westminster Abbey in 1890, elected to Parliament as a Liberal Unionist for North Lambeth in 1895, and knighted in 1899. He died in London on 10 May 1904.

After Stanley had found Livingstone and returned alone to Zanzibar, Livingstone stayed at Kazeh until August 1872, then set off southwards on another expedition to find the source of the Nile, which he thought would take no more than a few months (he had already been in the interior for six years at this stage).

Meanwhile the RGS in London was unaware of Stanley's 'find', so in February 1872, the Livingstone Search and Relief Expedition, led by Lieutenant Llewellyn Dawson, was dispatched to Zanzibar in the steamship *Abydos*. Two months later, the expedition arrived in Zanzibar, where their ship was caught in the freak hurricane of 14 April. Every ship and dhow in the harbour was driven ashore except the *Abydos*. The town was wrecked, many people were killed, and over two-thirds of the coconut and clove trees on the island were uprooted.

A few weeks after the hurricane, in May 1872, Stanley arrived at Bagamoyo, where he met Dawson and told him that Livingstone was safe and would be arriving after a few more months. Dawson cancelled the Search and Relief Expedition and returned to London. But by the end of 1872 Livingstone had still not arrived back at Zanzibar as expected, so in February 1873 a second Relief Expedition, led by Lieutenant Verney Lovett Cameron, set out from Zanzibar to find him.

Unknown to Cameron and the rest of the world, Livingstone had grown ill, with a recurrence of dysentery. On 2 May 1873, he died in the village of Chitambo, near Lake Bangweulu (in present-day Zambia), 800km (500 miles) south of Ujiji, and even further from the actual source of the Nile. Two of his companions carried his body back towards Zanzibar. In August 1873, they reached Kazeh, where they met Cameron.

Cameron decided to march on to Ujiji, which he reached in February 1874, and where he found Livingstone's papers. From Ujiji, Cameron continued westwards, eventually reaching the Atlantic coast in November 1875, thereby becoming the first European to travel across this part of Africa from east to west.

SULTAN BARGHASH AND JOHN KIRK By this time, on Zanzibar, Sultan Majid had died, aged 36. His only child was a daughter so his brother Barghash (who had twice already tried to seize the throne and had returned to Zanzibar from exile in India in 1861) finally succeeded to the throne, and was proclaimed sultan on 7 October 1870. In the same year, Dr John Kirk (who had originally come to Zanzibar as a medical officer on Livingstone's expedition) was made acting British consul.

After the hurricane of April 1872, Sultan Barghash had announced plans to grow new plantations, and the slave trade picked up once again. By late 1872, around 16,000 slaves had been imported into Zanzibar. The hurricane hit only the southern tip of Pemba, leaving most of the clove trees on that island untouched. By the 1880s, the island was producing about 80% of the total clove harvest from Zanzibar and Pemba.

At the same time, the anti-slavery movement continued to grow, fuelled in America by the publication of *Uncle Tom's Cabin*. In January 1873, Sir Bartle Frere, a special envoy from Queen Victoria, arrived in Zanzibar to negotiate a treaty which he hoped would finally put an end to the Arab slave trade. Sultan Barghash was naturally reluctant to end slavery and Frere sailed for England at the beginning of March 1873 without a treaty. Almost immediately the British navy began a blockade of every slave port on the mainland. The number of slaves passing through the Customs House in Zanzibar Town between January and March dropped to 21, compared with 4,000 in the same period the previous year.

In June 1873, Sir John Kirk informed Sultan Barghash that a total blockade of Zanzibar Island was imminent. Reluctantly Barghash signed the Anglo–Zanzibari treaty which provided for the complete abolition of the slave trade in Barghash's territories, the closing of all slave markets and the protection of all liberated slaves. Transport of slaves was forbidden, and slaves could no longer be exported from mainland Africa to Zanzibar and Pemba, except for domestic purposes.

The large slave market in Zanzibar Town was closed immediately. The site was bought by missionaries of the Universities' Mission to Central Africa (UMCA), and work started on the cathedral which can still be seen in Zanzibar Town today (pages 167–9).

One of the main effects of the treaty, now that slavery was illegal, was to push up the price of slaves and the trade continued in a clandestine manner. Through the 1870s smugglers were estimated to be exporting between 10,000 and 12,000 slaves a year.

In 1875, Kirk brought Sultan Barghash an official invitation to visit Britain to ratify the Anglo–Zanzibari treaty. In June the same year, Barghash and Kirk arrived in London where Barghash received the Freedom of the City at the Guildhall and attended a state banquet at Mansion House. While Barghash was in London, his sister Salme had come from Germany (see box, pages 188–9) hoping to be reconciled with her brother, but Barghash refused to meet her. After four weeks of intensive sightseeing and entertainment, Barghash and his party returned to Zanzibar via Paris and Marseilles, arriving home in September.

For the British, Zanzibar was no longer a distant, obscure island, and links between the two countries became even more firmly established. In 1869, the Suez Canal had opened, making the sea voyage between Britain and the coast of East Africa much shorter and simpler. In 1872, the British India Steamship Navigation Company started a monthly mail service between Zanzibar and Aden, Yemen. It brought the first scheduled passenger and cargo service to Zanzibar, which allowed merchandise to be exported quickly. Communication was again improved in 1879, when the Eastern Telegraph Company completed their cable from Zanzibar to Europe via Aden, and a telegraphic link with Europe was established.

Inspired by his visit to Europe, Barghash decided to make many changes on Zanzibar. Advised by John Kirk (now firmly installed as the power behind the throne), he appointed Lieutenant William Lloyd Mathews (see box, page 196) to reorganise his army and enforce his sovereignty over the interior.

During his exile in India, Barghash had seen the opulent wealth of the Indian palaces and he tried to emulate them on Zanzibar. Many luxurious palaces were built, including Chukwani, to the south of Zanzibar Town, and Maruhubi Palace, to the north, for his harem. Another palace in the town became known as the Beit al Ajaib, or House of Wonders, as it was the first building on Zanzibar to have electric lighting. In all of his palaces, Barghash upgraded the dinner services from silver to gold. Divan coverings of goat and camel hair were replaced by silks and taffetas, and French carpets covered the floors.

Barghash introduced Zanzibar's first clean water system to replace supplies from local wells and rainwater: aqueducts and conduits brought pure water from a spring at Bububu into Zanzibar Town, a distance of some 6km. Other developments introduced by Barghash included a police force, an ice-making factory, electric street lighting, and telephones to connect his city and country palaces. Barghash also built and improved the roads on the island, and every year he provided one of his private steamships for Muslims wishing to make the pilgrimage to Mecca.

THE SCRAMBLE FOR AFRICA In 1884, Dr Karl Peters, founder of the Society for German Colonisation, arrived in Zanzibar, then sailed for the mainland where he made 'treaties of eternal friendship' with the local African chiefs in return for large areas of land. By the time he reached Kilimanjaro he had annexed more than 6,000km² (2,500 square miles) of land, which were still nominally under the control of Sultan Barghash.

Britain was concerned at the presence of a rival European power on its patch, but was distracted by events elsewhere. In January 1885, Khartoum, the capital of Anglo–Egyptian Sudan, fell to the forces of the Mahdi. The British general Gordon was killed and the British governor of Equatoria Province, south of Khartoum, was cut off (ironically, the governor was actually a German called Eduard Schnitzer, although he had adopted the name Emin Pasha and was working for the British).

Otto von Bismarck, the German chancellor, saw the Mahdi's victory as a sign of Britain's weakness and believed that Germany could consolidate its claims in East Africa without British opposition. In February the same year the General Act of Berlin, signed by Kaiser Wilhelm of Germany, officially proclaimed a German protectorate over the territories annexed by Karl Peters. Sultan Barghash was only formally told about his loss of land in April of the same year. He hoped for support from the British, but Britain did not want to make an enemy of Germany, and so declined.

In June 1885, the Germans claimed another protectorate over Witu and the mouth of the Tana River, near Lamu, and in August the same year, five ships of the German navy, commanded by Carl Paschen, arrived in Zanzibar harbour. Paschen demanded that Sultan Barghash recognise the German protectorates. Kirk, on the recommendations of the British government, persuaded Barghash to submit.

A few days after the arrival of the German fleet, another German ship entered the harbour, carrying Barghash's sister Salme (who had eloped to Germany in 1866). She was with her son Said-Rudolph, now 16 years old, and two other children. On Kirk's advice, Barghash tolerated Salme's presence. Barghash sent his formal recognition of the German protectorate to Carl Paschen and two months later, the British government arranged for a joint commission between Britain, Germany and France to establish their own boundaries in the mainland territories that were still officially under the control of the Sultan of Zanzibar.

After lengthy discussions the first Anglo–German agreement was signed in late 1886. Barghash's lands were reduced to Zanzibar, Pemba, Mafia, Lamu and a ten-mile (16km) wide coastal strip stretching around 1,200km (about 750 miles) from the Tana River, near Lamu, to the Rovuma River, near Cape Delgado. The rest of the mainland, east of Lake Victoria and Lake Tanganyika, was divided between Britain and Germany. Britain took the northern portion, between the Tana and Umba rivers, which became British East Africa, later Kenya. Germany took the southern portion, between the Umba and Rovuma rivers. This became German East Africa, later Tanganyika (see map, page 13).

Given no option, Barghash agreed to this treaty in December 1886 and the French government signed it a few days later. In June 1887, Barghash leased the northern section of his coastal strip (between the Tana and Umba rivers) to the British East African Association (BEAA), which had been formed by William Mackinnon in May the same year. Meanwhile the Germans and Portuguese met in Barghash's absence to discuss their own border, and Portugal gained more of Barghash's land in the south.

In February 1888, Barghash sailed to Muscat, to recuperate from tuberculosis and elephantiasis at the healing Bushire Springs on the Persian coast. He returned to Zanzibar on 26 March, but died five hours after his arrival, aged 51.

On 29 March 1888, Barghash's brother Khalifa bin Said was proclaimed sultan. In April the same year, the British East African Association became the Imperial British East Africa Company (IBEA), with its capital at Mombasa, which was beginning to take Zanzibar's place as the commercial centre for Africa.

A BRITISH PROTECTORATE In September 1889, Khalifa signed an agreement with the British government agreeing to abolish slavery in his territories. Anybody who entered the sultan's realms, and any children born, would be free. Britain and Germany were awarded a permanent right to search for slaves in Zanzibar's waters. As a sign of Britain's appreciation, Khalifa was knighted, but less than a month later he died, aged 36.

Khalifa's brother, Ali bin Said, was the fourth and last of Said's sons to become Sultan of Zanzibar. On 1 August 1890, Ali signed an anti-slavery treaty forbidding the purchase and sale of slaves. With the end of the slave trade, the only viable export from the interior was ivory, by now a rapidly waning asset.

Meanwhile in the interior, Karl Peters entered Uganda in February 1890 and claimed the territory for Germany, just ahead of Sir Frederick Jackson from England. The British politician Lord Robert Salisbury realised that control of the Upper Nile could lead indirectly to the control of the Suez Canal and thus the trade route to India. Germany was persuaded to renounce any claims over Uganda in return for British support of the Kaiser against the major European powers of the day, France and Russia.

By the second Anglo–German agreement (the Treaty of Zanzibar) of 1 July 1890, Germany agreed to recognise a British protectorate over the Sultanate of Zanzibar, and to abandon any claim to Witu and the country inland as far as the Upper Nile. Germany also abandoned any claim to the west of Lake Nyasa but, in return, gained sovereignty over the coast of German East Africa, later to become Tanganyika. The British–German border was continued westwards across Lake Victoria to the boundary of the Belgian territory of Congo, thus securing Uganda for Britain. The British coastal strip (which still belonged to the Sultan of Zanzibar) was removed from the control of the British East Africa Company and administered by the British East Africa Protectorate, later to become Kenya and Uganda.

In exchange for the thousands of square miles of east African territory, including the islands of Zanzibar (Unguja and Pemba) which it gave up to British control, Germany gained Heligoland, a strategically important small island off the German coast which lay near the mouth of the Kiel Canal.

In 1891, a constitutional government was established in Zanzibar, with General Sir Lloyd Mathews as first minister. But although Zanzibar enjoyed the status of a British protectorate, the island's importance as a commercial centre was declining further in favour of Mombasa.

The British now controlled Zanzibar, so when Sultan Ali died in March 1893, without making a will, they proclaimed Hamad, son of Thuwaini (the former sultan of Oman), as sultan.

During Hamad's reign, in November 1895, Zanzibar issued its first stamps (from about 1875 the island had been using Indian stamps with 'Zanzibar' overprinted). Then a newspaper, the *Gazette for Zanzibar and East Africa*, was produced. It was followed by others in English, Arabic, Swahili and Urdu.

THE LAST YEARS OF THE 19TH CENTURY When Sultan Hamad died in August 1896, the British recommended his cousin Hamoud as sultan. But Barghash's son, Khaled, who had already tried to seize power from Hamad, made a second attempt at snatching the throne. He was briefly successful this time but was ousted by the British, after 'the shortest war in history' (see box, page 24).

On 27 August 1896, Hamoud was conducted into the Customs House and proclaimed Sultan of Zanzibar amidst the salute of the ships. The new sultan supported the British government, and on 5 April 1897 he signed a treaty to abolish the legal status of slavery in Zanzibar and Pemba. Shortly after this Queen Victoria awarded him the Grand Cross of the Most Distinguished Order of St Michael and St George. Hamoud sent his son Ali to school at Harrow in England, where he represented his father at the coronation of King Edward VII.

Sultan Hamoud died on 18 July 1902 and the British proclaimed the 18-year-old Ali as the new sultan. From his school days he spoke English fluently, and continued to travel in Europe during his reign. In May 1911, Ali attended the coronation of King George V in England. While in Europe, his health deteriorated and he abdicated in December 1911. He spent the last seven years of his life in Europe, and died in Paris in December 1918. Khalifa bin Harub, a cousin of Ali, became Sultan Khalifa II on 16 December 1911.

ZANZIBAR ENTERS THE 20TH CENTURY Sultan Khalifa bin Harub proved to be a moderate but influential ruler, and proceeded to guide Zanzibar through the first half of the turbulent 20th century with skill and diplomacy.

Soon after Khalifa gained power, changes were made to the British way of overseeing their interests in Zanzibar. In July 1913, responsibility for Zanzibar was transferred from the Foreign Office to the Colonial Office. The post of British consul became British Resident, subject to the control of the Governor of the British East Africa Protectorate. At the same time a Protectorate Council was established. This was an advisory body with the sultan as president and the British Resident as vice president.

During World War I, the German and British armies, with conscripted African soldiers, were involved in several campaigns on the mainland. The war did not affect Zanzibar directly except for one incident when the British ship *Pegasus* was bombarded and sunk by the German ship *Königsberg* in Zanzibar Town harbour (graves marking the bodies of sailors killed in this incident can still be seen on Grave Island).

Towards the end of the war, in 1917, the British army drove the Germans out of their territory and marched into Dar es Salaam. Khaled, who had tried to seize the throne of Zanzibar during 'the shortest war' in 1896, was still there and was captured. He was exiled to the Seychelles, then allowed to return to Mombasa in 1925, where he lived quietly until 1927.

After the war, the German East African territory was administered by Britain under a League of Nations mandate and called Tanganyika. Later, in 1920, the British East Africa Protectorate became known as the Kenya Colony.

In 1925, the British Resident on Zanzibar was made directly responsible to the Colonial Office in London, and a new Legislative Council was established. The ten-mile (16km) wide strip of land along the coast of Kenya, including Mombasa, which had been leased to Kenya in 1895, was still technically 'owned' by the Sultan of Zanzibar and the new Kenyan government continued to pay the lease of £11,000 per year.

During World War II, Zanzibar was not involved in any military action. The war's main effect was to interrupt the supply of rice, a staple food for the Asian and African people, that had until then been imported from Burma.

REVOLUTION AND THE ROAD TO INDEPENDENCE After World War II, Britain gradually allowed the local people of Zanzibar to become involved in the islands' government. Several local political parties were formed and Zanzibar's first elections were held in July 1957. The Afro-Shirazi Union (which later became the Afro-Shirazi Party, or ASP) defeated the Zanzibar Nationalist Party (ZNP). Broadly speaking, the ASP was dominated by Africans, the ZNP by Arabs.

Sultan Hamad died on 25 August 1896 while the British consul, Arthur Hardinge, was on leave in England. The acting British consul, Basil Cave, recommended that Hamoud (Hamad's cousin) be appointed sultan, but when Cave and Sir Lloyd Mathews reached the palace of Beit el Sahel in Zanzibar Town, they found the doors barred. Khaled, the son of Barghash (and another cousin of Hamoud), had arrived before them with about 60 armed men, entered the palace by climbing through a broken window, and been quickly joined by more than 2,000 supporters.

Khaled proclaimed himself sultan, and raised the red flag of Zanzibar on the palace roof. But Basil Cave refused to recognise his claim: British ships in the harbour landed guards of marines, which were posted at the British consulate (where many British women sought refuge), the Customs House, and elsewhere around the town. Many foreigners gathered on the roof of the English Club, where they had a clear view of the harbour and the palace.

On the morning of 26 August, the three British ships were reinforced by the timely arrival of two others, and the following day, at dawn, the British fleet under Rear Admiral Harry Holdsworth Rawson delivered an ultimatum: Khaled was to surrender, disarm, evacuate the palace and be at the Customs House by 09.00, or the British ships would open fire. At 08.00 Khaled sent an envoy to Cave, asking for a chance to discuss peace, but his request was refused.

The palace clock struck three (09.00 British time) and at 09.02 the bombardment started. In half an hour, Beit el Sahel and the adjoining palace of Beit el Hukm were badly damaged. The lighthouse outside the palace was in flames and the nearby House of Wonders was also hit a few times. Many of Khaled's supporters had fled, leaving 500 dead and wounded lying about the palace grounds.

At 09.40 Khaled surrendered. He lowered the flag, the firing ceased and the war was over. This dispute over the succession is listed in the *Guinness Book of Records* as the shortest war in history.

Khaled escaped through the narrow streets and fled to the German consulate, where he was given asylum. As the steps of the consulate led onto the beach, Khaled was able to board the German warship *Seeadler* without risking arrest and was taken to Dar es Salaam, where he lived in exile. He died in Mombasa in 1927, aged 53.

In October 1960, Sultan Khalifa died, after ruling for 49 years, and was succeeded by his only son, Abdullah. In November the same year, Zanzibar was granted a new constitution which allowed for the elections of the members of the Legislative Council. Elections took place in January 1961, producing no clear result, and again in June 1961, but these were marred by serious interracial rioting. Nevertheless, the ZNP, along with the aligned Zanzibar and Pemba People's Party, won 13 of the seats on the council, while the ASP won ten.

Britain realised that internal self-government for Zanzibar was inevitable, and this was finally granted in June 1963. In July that year, Sultan Abdullah died following a reign filled with personal pain and involving the amputation of both legs. Abdullah was succeeded by his eldest son, Jamshid.

On 10 December 1963, Zanzibar became an independent sultanate, and the coastal strip was finally ceded to Kenya, which became independent two days later. Zanzibar was made a full member of the British Commonwealth and on 16 December became a member of the United Nations. But the new sultanate was short-lived: on 12 January 1964, the Zanzibari government was overthrown in a violent revolution.

The leader of Zanzibar's revolution was a Ugandan called John Okello who had been living in Pemba. The local African population supported Okello with great enthusiasm, and went on a rampage through the islands, during which more than 17,000 Arabs and Indians were killed in one night. As a result, the leader of the Afro-Shirazi Party, Sheik Abied Amani Karume, was installed as president of the newly proclaimed People's Republic of Zanzibar, which included the islands of Unguja and Pemba.

Karume and other prominent ASP members formed the Revolutionary Government of Zanzibar (Serikali ya Mapinduzi ya Zanzibar, or SMZ). Most of Zanzibar's Asian and Indian people left the islands; their property was confiscated and their land nationalised. On the mainland, Sultan Jamshid was given temporary asylum in Dar es Salaam, then went to Britain where he lived in exile.

Meanwhile, Tanganyika had also become independent in December 1961, with Julius Nyerere elected as president the following year. Nyerere had known and supported Karume since the mid 1950s, but the Zanzibar Revolution created problems in Tanganyika, inspiring an attempted coup in Dar es Salaam only a few days later. (To suppress this coup Nyerere received help from Britain in the form of a battalion of commandos.)

Once Nyerere had regained control, he approached Karume to discuss a political union, and on 24 April 1964 the two countries joined to form the United Republic of Tanganyika and Zanzibar. In October the same year the country was renamed Tanzania (from 'Tan' in Tanganyika and 'Zan' in Zanzibar). Nyerere became the president of the new state while Karume became vice president. The SMZ was to control all local affairs on the islands of Unguja and Pemba, while foreign affairs would be handled by the Tanzanian government.

During the negotiations, John Okello had gone to the mainland to meet Nyerere. On his return to Zanzibar in March 1964 he was sent back to Dar es Salaam. He made no further public appearances.

Despite the so-called union, Karume kept Zanzibar separate from the rest of Tanzania in many respects. The clove plantations on Unguja and Pemba were developed and the earnings from exports continued to increase, but this revenue was not shared with mainland Tanzania.

By the end of the revolution almost all of the European and Asian residents had left Zanzibar. To fill the vacuum caused by the departure of these skilled people, Karume recruited technical and military assistance from Cuba, China and the then Eastern bloc countries of East Germany, Bulgaria and the Soviet Union. Engineers from East Germany designed and built new blocks of flats in Zanzibar Town, and in 'new towns' elsewhere on the islands of Unguja and Pemba. In 1970, Karume's government was accused of human rights violations against political opponents.

On 7 April 1972, Karume was assassinated while playing cards in the ASP headquarters in Zanzibar Town. Aboud Jumbe Mwinyi, who had been a member of the ASP since before independence, became the new leader of the Revolutionary Government. Mwinyi was less hardline than Karume and introduced several reforms. He was also more sympathetic towards Nyerere and mainland Tanzania. In February 1977, the ASP united with Nyerere's party, the Tanzania African National Union (TANU), to form the Chama Cha Mapinduzi (Party of the Revolution).

After this unification, both leaders began to relax some of their policies on nationalised industries and state financial control. Relations with some Western nations, including Britain, slowly improved. In July 1979, as a sign that Tanzania was regaining some international respect, Queen Elizabeth II visited Zanzibar. Then, in 1980, the first presidential elections took place, and Aboud Jumbe Mwinyi was officially elected as President of Zanzibar.

POLITICS AND RECENT HISTORY

Zanzibar is a semi-autonomous state within the United Republic of Tanzania. It is governed by its own Revolutionary Council and 50-strong House of Representatives, whose members are elected or appointed for five-year terms. The President of Zanzibar is also the Vice President of Tanzania.

Zanzibar has seen many changes on the political front since the early 1990s. Along with the rest of Tanzania, Zanzibar ceased to be a one-party state in 1992. For the first time in almost 20 years, Chama Cha Mapinduzi (CCM) was faced with several new opposition groups, which quickly coalesced into parties. The Civic United Front (CUF), led by Seif Sherif Hamad from Pemba, became the major opposition party for Zanzibar. Elections were planned for October 1995, as all parties agreed that a gradual transition to a multi-party political system would be beneficial. Salmin Amour remained as Zanzibar's president and CCM leader, while on the mainland the CCM chose a new president, Benjamin Mkapa, in July 1995. This followed the resignation of Julius Nyerere, the 'father of the nation', who had ruled since independence, although he remained an important figure behind the scenes.

Elections were duly held in Zanzibar on 22 October 1995, a week before the mainland vote. It was a simple two-horse race between Salmin Amour and Seif Sherif Hamad for President of Zanzibar, and between CCM and CUF candidates in the islands' parliament. There was a very high turnout (over 95% of registered voters) and voting passed peacefully, but the counting took three days for just over 300,000 votes.

Although the ruling party's control of the government structure gave it an in-built advantage, it soon transpired that the CUF was polling strongly. Complaints by the CCM that the election process was flawed were withdrawn when it transpired that Amour had won with 50.2% of the vote, but then the CUF picked up the claim of unfair procedures. International observers agreed that there was evidence of serious irregularities, but the nominally independent Zanzibar Electoral Commission refused to hold a recount or to compare their figures with some of those recorded by the UN. On the mainland, a divided opposition and an even more shambolic election, not to mention the possibility of vote-rigging, meant that the CCM and President Mkapa stayed in power. The CUF brought a high-profile legal case against the CCM on the grounds that the results and the whole election process were not representative of the wishes of the people, but this was bogged down in the courts and finally dismissed in 1998.

In the lead-up to elections in late 2000, Amour rocked the boat by announcing he would stand for a third (and unconstitutional) term as president. The instant response among the people of Zanzibar was a sharp swing in support for the CUF. An equally quick response from CCM high command meant Amour was relieved of his post, and Amani Karume, son of President Karume who had been assassinated in the 1970s, was ushered in as Zanzibar's new CCM leader and presidential candidate.

At a grass-roots level, there was still considerable support for the CUF, but the strong following this party enjoyed on Pemba meant that ostensibly political differences stood in danger of degenerating into inter-island (or 'tribal') conflicts. This sense of grievance also translated into separatist aspirations; since the end of the 1990s, the desire of many Zanzibaris to be independent of mainland Tanzania has been stronger than it had been for many years. The urge for separation is also partly due to the death in 1999 of Julius Nyerere.

When elections were held in October 2000, President Mkapa and the CCM romped home with huge and increased majorities. The people of mainland Tanzania seemed happy (in fact, many seemed indifferent) about the result, and international observers agreed that voting had been free and fair. On Zanzibar, however, it was a different story. In the period leading up to the election, fist-fights erupted on several occasions between CUF and CCM supporters, local party offices were attacked or burned, and CUF demonstrations were broken up by the police and army. On election day, things were so bad in 16 constituencies that the whole process was cancelled, and a re-run vote arranged for 5 November. CUF demonstrations turned into violent protests, especially in Zanzibar Town, to be met with police tear gas, rubber bullets and even live ammunition. In disgust, the CUF pulled out of the election process, leaving the November re-runs to be easily won by CCM candidates. In response, the CUF announced its continued boycott of procedures in the House of Representatives.

In one of his first moves as newly elected president of Zanzibar, Amani Karume called for peace and reconciliation between the two sides, which he backed up by releasing from prison the group of CUF leaders who'd been held on charges of treason since 1998. Hopes for peace were dashed shortly afterwards when a series of bombs exploded in Zanzibar. The trouble simmered on, with more CUF street protests in January 2001. This time the police used even stronger tactics to break things up: in a single day, between 20 and 70 demonstrators were shot, one policeman was killed, and many more were injured. The events were reported in media around the world, the USA and the donor nations of Europe expressed concern, and aid money which had been frozen following the discrepancies of the 1995 election remained firmly out of reach.

In March 2001, at the direct behest of President Mkapa, leaders from the CCM and the CUF tentatively started to discuss their differences, and in October that year, after a long series of negotiations, the two sides signed an accord to end their dispute over the election results. By 2002, the islands had returned to their traditional calm and peaceful atmosphere, and Zanzibar was fully open for business once again.

In the elections of October 2005, the CCM and the CUF were once again vying for power, with rallies held across the island throughout the summer of 2005. Although there seemed to be little in the way of party manifestos, and despite claims by the CUF of vote-rigging and other irregularities, this time the election passed off comparatively peacefully. With a 90% turnout of the electorate, the CCM retained control, with the CUF polling 46% of the total votes, and Amani Karume retaining the presidency. Tensions remained between the parties and their supporters, with the CUF claiming in both 2000 and 2005 that election victory had been stolen from them and the Zanzibar Electoral Commission citing many irregularities in the voting. Sporadic negotiations to agree on power-sharing terms and secure a peaceful resolution took an immediate back seat. However, in April 2008 a major setback stalled the process completely: the CCM called for a referendum to approve a contentious power-sharing agreement resulting in the CUF abandoning the negotiations altogether. The political future seemed murky with the poor rural population suffering from the lack of real commitment to bettering their future.

However, on 1 November 2010, change did come. Zanzibar formally formed a government of national unity, known as the Revolutionary Government of Zanzibar, following a referendum proposal for rival political parties to share power. Overwhelmingly approving a constitutional change in July 2010, Zanzibari leaders paved the way for a possible power-sharing government.

Headed by President Ali Mohamed Shein, of the ruling CCM, and Seif Sharif Hamad, of the CUF as vice president, the two main parties involved in the coalition government pledged to work together and divided up ministerial posts accordingly. Whilst the majority of old-school politicians effectively remained in power, there was a tangible sense of hope and positivity about this move amongst the population. Great hopes were held that less infighting and diminished political violence may lead to some practical good governance and improvements for the average Zanzibari.

Sadly, yet more political upheaval hit in October 2015, when John 'The Bulldozer' Magufuli of the long-ruling CCM party triumphed in the Tanzanian presidential race on a strong anti-corruption message, taking over from incumbent Jakaya Kikwete who could not run for a third term. In the election on Zanzibar, however, things were very different.

Following a campaign filled with threats and infused with propoganda, including CCM claims that the sultan might return from British exile in the event of an opposition victory, the opposition Civic United Front (CUF) claimed an early victory (52%). This result, however, was immediately annulled by the Electoral Commission, citing 'irregularities'. Uproar, cries of foul play and condemnation from Western diplomats and the international community followed, and the opposition CUF called on voters to boycott to election re-run. Come March 2016, that's exactly what happened and in the latest election, it came as no surprise that the incumbent President Ali Mohamed Shein won with more than 90% of the votes. This conclusively ended the government of national unity negotiated in 2010.

As the island's opposition has not mounted its threatened campaign of civil disobedience following the result, world attention has drifted away from the islands. However, the impact of these elections will have long-term and far-reaching consequences for Zanzibaris, and Tanzania as a whole. The USA has already suspended US$472 million of Millennium Challenge aid to the country over the second election, calling it 'neither inclusive nor representative'.

With bubbling political tensions, a disenfranchised population, poor general governance and historic outbursts of violence, it is hard to see a positive political future for the islanders as things stand. We must hope that Zanzibar and Tanzania can find a fair and forward-looking solution to avoid future unrest.

ECONOMY

For the people of Zanzibar, fishing and farming are the main economic activities. From the beginning of the 19th century to the mid 1970s Zanzibar exported a large proportion of the world's supply of cloves, and the islands' economy was based largely on this commodity. Some diversification has occurred since then as the world market price for cloves fell dramatically in the 1980s, but they remain a major export, along with coconut products and other spices. In recent years, seaweed has also become an important export commodity. The potential for tourism to be a major earner of foreign currency has been recognised and has been developing apace for the last fifteen years.

In 2006, Tanzania, and by association Zanzibar, was one of the 32 countries worldwide designated for HIPC (Heavily Indebted Poor Countries) debt relief.

Their debt wiped, with the African Development Bank cancelling a balance in excess of US$640 million, the economy gained new buoyancy. According to accountancy powerhouse PricewaterhouseCoopers, approximately 20% of government revenue was spent in paying external debt prior to HIPC; whilst afterwards less than 8% of revenue will be spent on debt service leading up to 2010.

Under the HIPC, resources saved from debt service are allocated to key anti-poverty programmes, including education, health and infrastructure. With fewer draining economic pressures, the people of Zanzibar should, in theory, have seen significant benefits; these are not very evident though, and poor general governance remains a barrier to necessary improvements across all sectors.

SEAWEED FARMING In 1989, seaweed farming was introduced on the east coast of Zanzibar and has since become a vital source of income for coastal villagers and a valuable addition to the island's traditional exports (see boxes, pages 278–9 and 331). The seaweed is planted and tended on beach areas between the high- and low-water marks. It is harvested and dried, collected in Zanzibar Town, and then exported to several countries in Europe and Asia for use as a food thickener or stabiliser.

Despite the success with seaweed, exports are limited, and Zanzibar imports many basic foodstuffs, including rice (from Pakistan, Thailand, Vietnam, Indonesia, India, China and the USA), maize (from mainland Tanzania), cooking oil (from Kenya, Tanzania, Singapore and Dubai), sugar (from Brazil), plus wheat and flour (from France, Germany and the USA). Other imports include mineral water (from the Gulf States) and beer (from Denmark).

TOURISM Whilst tourism remains relatively marginal to life in Pemba and Mafia, it has grown rapidly on Zanzibar Island over the last 30 years. Investment here has been significant and some of the wealth has stayed on the islands, but as well as providing opportunities, this has created many new problems.

Jobs in the tourism sector have developed skills in many islanders, and there is a class of local entrepreneurs who wouldn't have existed without tourism. Popular festivals have been introduced, several traditional handicraft techniques have been revived, and some villagers, especially women, have had the chance to earn income and better their lifestyle as a direct result of growing tourism.

The benefits are easy to find, but the tourism boom has not been universally good. Pragmatic observers agree that it's not tourism that is the problem per se; it's the sensitivity and sustainability of the individual tourism developments. It's all about how responsible the tourism enterprises and visitors are with the resources and culture of the islands. This issue of 'responsible tourism' is moving up the agenda, as evidenced by the rise of consciously responsible lodges like Chumbe Island (pages 335–6) and Chole Mjini (pages 384–5). However, there's a long way to go before all of the hotels and lodges match the high standards set by these.

Officially, the government recognises this problem, and back in 1992 introduced a National Environmental Policy for Zanzibar. This stressed that the quality of life of the Zanzibaris should not be harmed by the destruction of their environment, and that cultural and biological diversity should be preserved. In the words of President Salmin Amour, 'unchecked development could soon become unsustainable for our people and our small islands'. Sadly, in spite of the policies and well-intentioned sentiment, the speed and scale of the current growth in tourism developments continue unabated, and the local population is increasingly questioning its benefits.

However, there are signs that some of the more ethical elements of the tour operator community are starting to take these issues seriously. In 2008, the independent UK-based charity Tourism Concern (*www.tourismconcern.org.uk*) conducted a review of tourism on Zanzibar on behalf of the UK members of its Ethical Tour Operators Group (ETOG). This involved analysing and inspecting some of the hotels most

HISTORY OF ZANZIBARI AGRICULTURE

The earliest peoples on Zanzibar are thought to have been hunter-gatherers who made little impact on the natural vegetation. However, the first Bantu settlers, who probably arrived sometime in the 3rd or 4th century AD, started to clear patches of natural forest to plant crops such as millet and sorghum.

At some stage, plants such as bananas, coconut palms and yams were introduced, possibly by peoples from Madagascar who in turn had originally migrated from the islands of Indonesia. As these crops became more popular, more indigenous forest was cleared.

In the 16th century, Portuguese traders established bases along the east African coast, including those on Zanzibar and Pemba, and introduced plants such as cassava and maize from their colonies in South America. More forest was felled as local people cleared the land required to grow these crops.

After the Omani Arabs gained control of the islands in the early 18th century, and the trade in ivory and slaves expanded, Zanzibar became an important import and export centre. Cassava was used for feeding the vast numbers of slaves who passed through the island's infamous market. Another major export at this time was copra (produced from coconuts) which meant more land was cleared for coconut palm plantations.

At the turn of the 19th century, cloves were introduced from other islands in the Indian Ocean, and they soon became a major export crop. Other spices, such as vanilla and cardamom, were also grown and yet more forest was cleared for plantations.

Throughout the 19th century, the powerful nations of Europe put pressure on the sultans of Zanzibar to restrict the trade in slaves. As this was reduced, the trade in cloves and other spices became even more important. During the colonial period, plantations continued to be developed and the natural forest continued to be reduced. A Forestry Department was established to exploit the forests' timber supplies, but apparently it was not until the 1950s that it came to the attention of the Forestry Department that there was very little indigenous forest left on the island of Zanzibar. The largest remaining area, Jozani Forest, to the southeast of Zanzibar Town, was purchased from an Arab landowner by the department and the felling of trees was restricted. In 1960, Jozani was declared a protected nature reserve and in 2004 it became the heart of Zanzibar's first national park: Jozani-Chwaka Bay (pages 324–8).

popularly featured and spending time with island-based industry bodies, local and international NGOs, tourists, community groups and local residents. ETOG started this project to establish the most critical issues affecting tourism businesses and communities, and to highlight examples of best practice. Armed with this information, ETOG's members aim to find a practical way to raise ethical standards.

This is a positive step by a few overseas tour operators, but to have a substantial impact on Zanzibar's tourism issues requires the Zanzibari government to engage fully in the issue, and to work for long-term sustainability.

Sadly, there is little sign of this happening in any real form. The government is doing little in the way of fairly regulating the pace of development, or trying to upgrade the island's basic water supplies, communications, rubbish collections or other island infrastructure. Despite this, as visitors, we should do our best to act responsibly towards Zanzibar's environment and cultures, and to travel as responsibly as possible.

Visitor numbers and the tourism economy The Zanzibar Commission for Tourism was founded in 1987 to promote Zanzibar as a tourist destination, and in 1992, the Zanzibar Investment Promotion Agency was created to encourage overseas investment, particularly in tourism projects. Buoyed by their presence, the first half of the 1990s saw a dramatic rise in the development of tourism, but the last few years have seen a truly staggering increase.

In 1995, over 56,000 visitors were arriving in Zanzibar each year; earnings derived from the tourism sector are said to have contributed an estimated US$1,971 million to the economy (see the Tanzanian government website, www.tanzania.go.tz/zanzibar, although we are unsure how these stats were derived, as this means that each visitor effectively contributes over US$35,000!).

By the end of 2005, numbers had exceeded 100,000 visitors per year for the first time, and by 2008 official tourism figures were sitting at 140,000 arrivals, with real figures estimating visitor numbers to be closer to 160,000. Zanzibar Association of Tourism Investors (ZATI) shows arrivals hit a record high in 2011, peaking at 220,000.

There are often some discrepancies in tourism arrival figures on account of official figures only including travellers arriving directly from abroad and not tourists coming in from Dar es Salaam or from safaris on the Tanzanian mainland. In descending order, the majority of visitors come from Italy, the UK, Germany, the Netherlands and the USA, all lured by images of pristine beaches, swaying palms and exotic island life. Tourist arrivals to Pemba and the Mafia Archipelago remain insignificant by comparison.

In 2012, the government announced a target of half a million tourists to Zanzibar annually by 2013 and, in a similar vein, the Zanzibar Commission for Tourism projected figures estimating close to 450,000 annual visitors by 2020. While far below the figures recorded by larger countries like Kenya and similarly styled tropical islands, these ever-increasing visitor numbers clearly show that Zanzibar's tourism industry has changed gear since the early 1980s. In fact, by 2013 visitor numbers had only reached around 270,000, and the half a million target shifted to 2020. Whilst government-backed think-tanks optimistically project this quadrupling of the total tourist expenditure to US$2.6 billion, if the projected growth is achieved, it is hard to see how the islands will cope, socially, logistically or environmentally, with such a significant rise in numbers.

Tourism currently represents about 25–27% of Zanzibar's gross domestic product (GDP) and over 80% of foreign direct investment (FDI), in contrast to cloves, which account for around 45% of GDP. Whilst export earnings from this traditional commodity fall (see box, pages 50–1), the income from tourism is rising to plug the gap. Some observers still expect tourism to be Zanzibar's largest generator of foreign income by 2020.

National tourism policies The Zanzibari government's current policies and development plans consistently emphasise tourism that benefits the local population, protects and conserves the natural environment and maximises local employment and locally produced goods and services. All very admirable aims, but in reality, few of these guiding principles seem to be translated into laws to regulate development.

Large developments, often European all-inclusive resorts, seem to be being built on every available plot of land on the north and east coasts, container-loads of goods are continually imported from China, and in most hotels significant numbers of employees are from mainland Tanzania and overseas. It is hard not to reach the conclusion that the government is doing its people a gross disservice by only paying lip service to these issues.

1

In spite of this, there are some stalwart hoteliers and tour operators doing the utmost to be socially and environmentally aware; throughout this book we have highlighted their achievements and ambitions, so that travellers can vote with their feet.

Issue awareness With huge question marks hanging over the sustainability of the current level of tourism to Zanzibar, and the islands' leaders exhibiting only myopia on many of the issues, alarm bells are ringing for responsible travellers. Being aware of what the issues are is a crucial step towards travelling responsibly, and some of the main issues include the following.

Fresh water depletion Fresh water is very precious on low-lying islands like these, and there is mounting evidence of groundwater depletion: water levels in wells used by villagers for generations have dropped and, in a few areas, wells that were once fresh are now becoming brackish.

Zanzibar Town draws its water from a freshwater aquifer flowing under the centre of the island; a pipe network pumps water to the main coastal communities outside the capital. The demand from hotels is rising, sometimes leaving the volume of piped fresh water for the villagers as both inadequate and unreliable. Some communities have sunk wells to directly access the groundwater, as have some hotels (whilst others ferry their water in by truck), but the pressure on this critical resource is growing. One survey claimed that, on average, tourists use 180 litres of water per day (this of course includes all use – washing, laundry, hotel cleaning, etc) compared with the average local Zanzibari's consumption of less than 40 litres.

Nungwi and Kendwa are at the end of the pipe network, and here the problem is most acute. Villagers are increasingly experiencing serious problems getting access to fresh water. With the island's mushrooming hotels drawing more water from the pipe, in addition to all of the communities along its route north, there is rarely much water left by the time it gets to Nungwi. This has led to conflict between the villagers and the hotels and, with further development under way and no real solution in place, things are set to get increasingly difficult. For recent observations, Tourism Concern's WET report (*www.tourismconcern.org.uk*) looks at these specific community water problems, though with less emphasis on the role of good governance than many believe central to the issue.

Rubbish Rubbish is a major problem on Zanzibar Island. There is minimal municipal waste collection, and that which does exist focuses almost exclusively on Zanzibar Town. At the end of 2006, the statement from the governmental Environment Department declared that 'out of about 200 tonnes of solid waste produced daily in Stone Town, the Zanzibar Municipal Council workers are only able to collect about 60 tonnes'. This situation is visibly worsening every year with the daily solid waste now estimated at 300 tonnes, and yet the collection rate remaining static. With little state investment or significant effort to manage the problem, this is only set to get worse. Currently, the waste-collection efficiency is only 45–50%, and open dumping, without proper treatment, is the prevalent method for final disposal. Researchers consistently point to the environmental pollution and potential human health risks, yet limited budget, poor equipment, the absence of decent policy or urban planning and social habits make change driven by the municipality almost impossible.

There is currently only a single stinking (and totally inadequate) landfill site for the whole of Zanzibar Island to use. The result is that much rubbish is dumped around the island, or at sea, by both local residents and irresponsible hotels and tourists. It's often noted that, as much of the island is made of coral rock, digging more landfill sites may not be easy, but despite this there are a number of active rock quarries around the island.

Several of the better hotels now have efficient waste-management plans, and separate glass for a recycling NGO, while some pay for an official collection and hope the waste is not dumped before it reaches the landfill site. Some investment comes from overseas governments and, in Jambiani and Kendwa, small NGOs and concerned residents are trying hard to address the problem on a local level. There is one reliable private waste collection company on the island, ZanRec; however, with large-scale developments mushrooming, a formal government strategy and serious financial backing are critical to curb the waste problem.

Social vices Most local people on Zanzibar regard tourism as a broadly positive industry in terms of its potential to earn money. However, increasingly there is resentment felt about the behaviour of tourists. You only need to watch bikini-clad women walking through a village, or see beer bottles piled high at a beach barbeque, to realise how inconsiderate some visitors are to local values.

Unsurprisingly, as with many traditional, reserved communities faced with a dramatic influx of international tourists, cultural erosion can also be observed on Zanzibar. As a predominantly (95%) Muslim country, alcohol and drugs have had little place in society in the past. Now, with the Western influence of tourists and growing wealth from ad hoc guiding, souvenir selling and prostitution, exposure and addiction to both is starting to become a problem among young local men, especially in Stone Town and Nungwi. This often evolves to cause problems like opportunist theft for money, and it increases village tensions with traditional elders appalled at the behaviour of the youths.

Similarly, prostitution is another fairly recent island issue, within both the tourist and local communities. Female sex workers are now travelling from the mainland in search of tourist dollars, local men are offering their services to foreign girls in beach bars, and local women are selling their bodies to other villagers flush with new-found wealth.

Many hotels and NGOs are acutely aware of these tensions and are working hard, directly or through local charities, to address social and environmental issues in their area. Many more in the tourism sector appear oblivious to the issues.

Overfishing There is growing concern about overfishing, particularly for crab, lobster, squid and octopus, to supply restaurants catering for tourists. Fishermen on all coasts are reporting difficulties in finding fish big enough to sell and, in spite of legal restrictions, fishing on the coral reef is increasing as a direct result. A secondary consequence of the voracious tourist appetite for fresh seafood has been to inflate the price of fish and shellfish beyond the means of many local villagers. Demand in some areas is making the ingredients for traditional meals, such as octopus, too expensive for purchase by the fishing communities from where they come.

Construction materials For years, beach sand, coral rock and native trees have been used for construction, leading to accelerated coastal erosion. As just one example, mangrove poles are a particularly good construction material; they are very strong, often straight and highly resistant to termites (see box, page 264). However, these have seldom been sustainably harvested. This has depleted Zanzibar's original mangrove forests, which are vital to the marine ecosystems as a nursery for many small fish as well as a buffer for the coast against the ocean.

2

People and Culture

PEOPLE

POPULATION AND SETTLEMENT The population of Zanzibar was 1,303,569 in the 2012 census, with an annual growth rate of 2.8%. Having remained fairly steady for some years, the general feeling of Zanzibari residents that recent years had seen a more significant increase was borne out in the most recent census. The current increase rate represents a 32% increase over the ten-year period since the 2002 census, one high even by African standards. At the current rate, the population of Zanzibar is set to double in the next 24 years, with a frightening lack of infrastructure, resources or community development to adequately support this.

Of the total residents, around two-thirds of the people (896,721) live on Zanzibar Island (Unguja), with the greatest proportion settled in the densely populated west. Zanzibar's largest settlement is Zanzibar Town (sometimes called Zanzibar City), on Zanzibar Island, with 593,678 inhabitants.

Currently 46% of the population live in these urban areas, but outside these towns, most people live in small, traditional villages and are engaged in farming, fishing or tourism-related industries.

On Pemba (population 406,808) the overall settlement pattern is similar. The largest town is Chake Chake, with a growing district population of 97,249; other smaller towns are Wete and Mkoani. Mafia's total population was 46,850 in 2012, with its capital Kilindoni being the largest settlement.

There is considerable disparity in the standard of living between the inhabitants of Mafia, Pemba and Zanzibar and between urban and rural populations, which are split roughly equally. The average annual income of just US$250 hides the fact that about half the population lives below the poverty line on less than US$1 per day. The census revealed that 19% of Zanzibaris have no access to any toilet facilities (42% have a pit latrine), and only 11% have a regular refuse collection, with a shocking 63% simply dumping their waste in open bush. More positively, the use of electricity as the main source of lighting was higher in Zanzibar (43%) than the mainland, with the number of households using electric lights more than doubling over the decade.

The most commonly owned asset is now a mobile phone, with 80% of island households claiming ownership; fewer own a house (75%), a hand hoe (54%), a bicycle (44%) or even a cooker (23%).

Despite a reasonable standard of primary health care and education, the mortality rate for children under five is 67 in 1,000, and it is estimated that malnutrition affects one in three of the islands' people; life expectancy at birth is 65.2 – with women faring slightly better than men, and those is urban communities having a lower life expectancy (59 years) than their rural counterparts.

While the incidence of HIV/AIDS is considerably less in Zanzibar than in Tanzania as a whole (0.6% of the population, against the national average of around 8%), it is a growing problem. The Zanzibar AIDS Commission reports that women show HIV prevalence rates that are higher than their male counterparts (0.7% and 0.5% respectively), and that understanding of infection protection is still poor in many communities. Projections from observations of two population surveys suggest 7,200 Zanzibaris are living with HIV, and this number is disturbingly three times higher in young females than in their male counterparts. In late 2006, the government unanimously adopted its first National HIV/AIDS Policy with plans for a door-to-door awareness campaign, HIV prevention education in school curricula and the promotion of condom use (the screening of visitors for HIV on arrival was omitted). This has been a positive step, but sadly trends such as increasing drug and alcohol use, the rise in prostitution, and mounting numbers of mainland Tanzanians seeking work on the island, are likely to increase the infection rate in the long term.

ORIGINS It is thought that Zanzibar's original inhabitants came from the African mainland around 3,000 to 4,000 years ago, although this is not certain and no descendants of these early people remain, having been completely absorbed by later arrivals.

Over the last 2,000 years, the records have become a little clearer. Historians know that Bantu-speaking people migrated from central Africa and settled across east and southern Africa during the 1st millennium AD (for more details, see page 3). Those who settled on the east African coast and offshore islands, including Zanzibar, came into contact with Arab traders who had sailed southwards from the Red Sea region. The Bantu adopted some customs of the Arabs and gradually established a language and culture which became known as Swahili.

From the 10th century, small groups of immigrants from Shiraz (Persia) also settled at various places along the east African coast, and especially in Zanzibar, and mingled with the local people. Over the following centuries, small groups of Arab and Persian peoples continued to settle here and intermarry with the Swahili and Shirazi. The largest influx occurred in the 18th and 19th centuries, when Omani Arabs settled on Zanzibar as rulers and landowners, forming an elite group. At about the same time, Indian settlers formed a merchant class.

Today, most of the people in Zanzibar are Shirazi or Swahili, although clear distinctions are not always possible. They fall into three groups: the Wahadimu (mainly in the southern and central parts of Zanzibar Island), the Watumbatu (on Tumbatu Island and in the northern part of Zanzibar Island) and the Wapemba (on Pemba Island), although again distinctions are hard to draw, and in fact, often not made by the people of Zanzibar themselves. The islands' long history of receiving (if not always welcoming) immigrants from Africa and Arabia has created a more relaxed attitude to matters of tribe or clan than is found in some parts of Africa.

Zanzibar is also home to groups of people of African origin who are descendants of freed slaves, dating from the 18th and 19th centuries. In more recent times, a large number of Africans have immigrated from mainland Tanzania. Additionally, some Arabs who were expelled after the 1964 Revolution have returned to Zanzibar.

Other people on Zanzibar include small populations from Goa, India and Pakistan, mainly involved in trade or tourism, and a growing number of European expatriates and volunteers, many working in the tour industry, with others employed as teachers, doctors and engineers.

LANGUAGE *with thanks to Said el-Gheithy*

The indigenous language spoken throughout Zanzibar is Swahili (called Kiswahili locally). This language is also spoken as a first language by Swahili people along the east African coast, particularly in Kenya and mainland Tanzania, and as a second or third language by many other people throughout East Africa (including Kenya, Tanzania and Uganda, and in parts of several other countries such as Rwanda, Mozambique and Congo), making Swahili the common tongue of the region. Although there are many forms and dialects found in different areas, visitors with a basic grasp of Swahili will be understood anywhere.

Swahili is an African language and includes many words and phrases of Arabic origin, plus words from other languages such as Persian, English and Portuguese. Over the centuries Swahili has developed into a rich language, lending itself especially to poetry. Zanzibar is regarded as the home of Swahili – it is spoken in its purest form here and in pockets on the coast of Tanzania and Kenya. In fact, in these areas, tradition dictates that ordinary conversation should approximate the elegance of poetry. Generally, as you travel further inland on the east African mainland, the Swahili becomes increasingly simplified.

For visitors, English, and several other European languages, such as French and Italian, are spoken in Zanzibar Town and most tourist areas. However, if you get off the beaten track, a few words of Swahili will be useful to ask directions, to greet people or even to begin a simple conversation. Even in the tourist areas, using a few Swahili words (for example, to ask the price of a souvenir or order a meal in a restaurant) can add to the enjoyment of your visit. Arabic is also spoken. For basic words and phrases, see pages 420–2.

RELIGION Most of the people in Zanzibar are Muslims (followers of the Islamic faith) and all towns and villages on Zanzibar Island and Pemba have mosques. Visitors to Zanzibar Town cannot fail to hear the evocative sound of the muezzins calling people to prayer from the minarets, especially for the evening session at sunset. And visitors cannot fail to notice the effects of the holy month of Ramadan, when most people fast during the day, and the pace of life slows down considerably (see also page 94). There are also small populations of Christians and Hindus.

Islam Islam was founded by the Prophet Muhammad, who was born around AD570 in Arabia. He received messages from God during solitary vigils on Mount Hira, outside his home town of Mecca. When driven out of Mecca by his enemies, he migrated to Medina. Here, at the age of about 53, he started to convert the world to Islam, and his message spread rapidly through the Arab world and beyond.

Muhammad died in AD632, but fired by evangelist zeal, Arab Muslims had conquered all of northern Africa by the early 8th century, and introduced the new religion there. By AD1100, Islam had spread from Arabia and the Horn of Africa along the east African coast, through the current countries of Kenya and Tanzania, all the way down to Sofala (in present-day Mozambique). Today, Islam is the dominant religion of these coastal areas, which include the islands of Zanzibar.

The five main tenets of Islam are prayer (five times a day), testimony of the faith, fasting (the period of Ramadan), almsgiving, and the pilgrimage to Mecca (the hajj). The Muslim calendar dates from the Hejira, the flight of Muhammad from Mecca to Medina, which corresponds to 16 July AD622 in the Christian calendar. The Muslim year consists of 12 lunar months of 29 or 30 days each, making 354 days. Eleven times in every cycle of 30 years a day is added to the year. This means that Muslim festivals fall 11 or 12 days earlier every year, according to the Western calendar.

Other religions There are small populations of Christians and Hindus living on the islands. The two most notable churches are the Anglican Cathedral Church of Christ and the Catholic Church of St Joseph in Zanzibar Town; Hindu temples are also present to serve the local community.

Alongside the established world faiths, traditional African beliefs are still held by most local people, and there is often considerable crossover between aspects of Islam and local custom (for more details, see box, page 40).

CULTURE

ARTS AND CRAFTS

Music and dance As you wander around Zanzibar Town, you will hear calls to prayer from the many mosques as well as the sounds of American rap music and Jamaican reggae. Around the next corner, however, you are also likely to hear film music from India or the latest chart-toppers from Egypt and the Gulf States. Thankfully the islands have not entirely lost their own cultural traditions, and equally popular in Zanzibar are local musical forms, in particular the style known as *taarab*.

Taarab Zanzibar has been at the crossroads of trade routes for thousands of years as peoples of Africa, India, Iran, China and other parts of Asia and the Arab world have all played their parts in influencing the music, architecture, food and culture of the region. In its origins, *taarab* was court music, played in the palace of Sultan Barghash. The sounds of Arabic musical traditions and those from India, Indonesia and other countries of the 'Dhow region' (the Indian Ocean basin) are clearly distinguishable even today, mingling to form a unique flavour and providing the frame for the Swahili poetry which makes up the heart of taarab music.

Currently, two major taarab groups exist in Zanzibar: Nadi Ikhwan Safaa and Mila na Utamaduni (also called Culture Musical Club, or just Culture). Of the two, Culture are the more professional and have become quite well known internationally, not only through CD releases such as *Spices of Zanzibar* or the more recent *Bashraf* albums, but also because they have successfully toured Belgium, France, Germany, Switzerland, the United Arab Emirates, Réunion and many other countries. Nadi Ikhwan Safaa, affectionately known by local people as Malindi Music Club, are Zanzibar's oldest group, who trace their roots back to 1905. The group plays a style of taarab in which the distant Middle Eastern origins are still very much to the fore.

Different theories abound about the real origins of taarab in Zanzibar. Legend has it that in the 1870s Sultan Barghash sent a Zanzibari to Cairo to learn to play the *qanun*, a kind of zither, common to the Arab-speaking world. Among the first singers to record taarab music in the Swahili language was the legendary Siti binti Saad, who was taken to India by a film director. Siti stopped performing in the 1940s, but her records – solo and in duet with Sheikh Mbaruk – continued to be issued on 78rpm throughout the 1950s and are still much in demand. Besides the qanun, other instruments that came to feature in the taarab groups (or orchestras) include the oud, violins, *ney*, accordion, cello and a variety of percussion. Thus, much of the traditional taarab music sounds like a more Africanised version of some of the great Egyptian popular classical orchestras that played alongside singers like Oum Kulthoum, who is still played on Radio Zanzibar to this day.

The best way to experience taarab is at a local concert, but visitors to Zanzibar are also welcome at the orchestras' rehearsals in Malindi or at Vuga Clubhouse in the evening. What Andy Morgan (*Roots* magazine) says in an article on Zanzibari music definitely holds true: 'There's hardly anything in the whole of Africa as uplifting as the swelling sounds of a full taarab orchestra in full sail.'

Kidumbak The suburb of Ng'ambo – the 'other side' of Zanzibar Town, where the lower-class living areas spread out and where poorer families and more recent arrivals to the city live – is the home of *kidumbak*. This music style, which is less refined and more upbeat than taarab, could be located musically somewhere between Stone Town big-orchestra taarab and the rural *ngoma* music. It is most often performed at weddings and other celebrations and is closely related to taarab. In fact, contemporary kidumbak often makes use of the latest taarab hit songs and is sometimes called *kitaarab*, which means 'a diminutive type of taarab' or 'derived from taarab'. Historical evidence suggests that Swahili taarab was originally performed in a very similar way to kidumbak and only later changed to resemble court orchestra music.

The kidumbak ensemble consists of a single melodic instrument, customarily a violin (played in frantic fiddle-style), a *sanduku*, or tea-chest-bass, two small clay drums (*ki-dumbak*), which form the rhythmic core of every such ensemble, and other rhythm instruments, such as *cherewa*, a kind of maracas manufactured from coconut shells filled with seeds, or *mkwasa*, short wooden sticks played like claves. In contrast to taarab, kidumbak is much more rhythmic and the lyrics more drastic than the poetic settings of the taarab songs, often criticising other people's social behaviour. At wedding performances, the singer has to be able to string together a well-timed medley of ngoma songs, and she or he must have the ability to compose lyrics on the spot. At a Zanzibari wedding, one kidumbak set usually lasts for an hour; as one song joins the next, the intensity heats up, with the main attraction being the interplay between the music and song of the players and the dancing and chorus response of the wedding guests.

Beni This brass band music originated around the end the 19th century as a mockery of colonial-style military bands. It was soon incorporated into the competitive song-and-dance exchanges so popular on the Swahili coast and spread

BI KIDUDE

A description of the music of Zanzibar would not be complete without mentioning the late Bi Kidude, one of the island's most famous singers. She performed with Siti binti Saad, toured the world and sold thousands of cassettes before her death in 2013. When she performed, she claimed to feel like a 14 year old, and for once, to see was to believe. Her voice was raw and unfiltered, and her singing and drumming with a large drum strapped to her hips was an exhibition of sheer energy. With the agility of a teenager and the sly wisdom of a thoroughly experienced performer, her stage presence was absolute and intense. She became most famous for her performance of *unyago ngoma*, which is played at all-female initiation rituals for brides to prepare them for their wedding night, featuring explicit lyrics as well as movements.

from there all over East Africa. *Beni* (from the English 'band') is a popular wedding entertainment with a strong focus on rhythm and dance and audience participation.

Beni borrows choruses from the latest taarab hits and arranges them in extended medleys with the female wedding audience joining in for the chorus and as dancers. It is funny music, vivacious, raucous and lively. If you can imagine a deranged military marching band playing as loud as possible on half-broken trumpets, trombones, drums – only vaguely in tune with each other, but having a great time – then you will get the idea!

In Zanzibar, beni is performed both as a street parade and, stationary, for a wedding dance. The band Beni ya Kingi usually kicks off the opening parade for the Festival of the Dhow Countries (page 44), which winds its way slowly with a great crowd through the narrow streets of Stone Town before reaching Forodhani Gardens at the waterfront, where it then turns into a wild and lively party.

Ngoma *Ngoma*, literally translated, means 'drum' and is a term used to encompass all local African traditional forms of dancing, drumming and singing. There are literally hundreds of different ngoma styles throughout Tanzania, variations often being so slight that untrained eyes and ears can hardly notice the difference. A number of these originate from Zanzibar and Pemba and all are spectacular to watch. The often-elaborate native costumes emphasise the unity of the dancers' steps and the rhythm section, which usually consists of several handmade drums and percussion instruments (such as oil tins beaten with a stick). *Ngoma ya kibati* from Pemba, for example, consists of a very rapid declamatory style of singing which is an improvised dialogue to drum accompaniment with singers/dancers coming in for a chorus every so often. Even if you can't follow a single word of the firework-like exchange between the two main singers, *kibati* is hilarious; if you understand all of the references and hints implied, it is of course even more so. Another example is *msewe*, supporting the rhythm section, and named after the material which is strapped to the ankles of the male dancers.

Each ngoma style has its own special costume. In *kyaso*, men dance dressed in shirts and *kikois* (special woven cloth from the east African coast) with a long, narrow stick in their hand, all movements beautifully co-ordinated. In *ndege*, women in colourful dresses all hold bright umbrellas, moving forwards with slightly rotating steps and movements of the hips. In *bomu*, the women dress up like men and in other funny costumes and dance around in a circle.

The variations are endless and performances are never dull. According to Abdalla R Mdoe, choreographer for Imani Ngoma Troupe, a privately initiated performance ensemble that specialises in all kinds of ngoma, three different types can be differentiated: ceremonial ngomas, which are performed at weddings, circumcision and other festivities; ritual ngomas (eg: *kisomali* to cure a sick person, or *pungwa* to avert evil); and religious ngomas, which in Zanzibar are closely related to the Muslim festivities of Zikri, Duffu, Maulidi and Hom.

Modern taarab Undoubtedly a pop-phenomenon (and therefore ephemeral) is a modern style of taarab, called *rusha roho*, which translates literally as 'to make the spirit fly' and has some untranslatable meaning approximating to 'upsetting someone' or 'making the other one jealous'. Modern taarab is also the first style of taarab designed to be accompanied by dance, and features direct lyrics, bypassing the unwritten laws of lyrical subtlety of the older groups. Much of modern taarab music is composed and played on keyboards, increasing portability; hence the group is much smaller in number than 'real taarab' orchestras and therefore more readily available to tour and play shows throughout the region. This fact has led to its enormous popularity in Zanzibar, boosted by the prolific output of cassette recordings, which, though not up to European studio quality standards, still outsell tapes by any other artist local or international.

Visual arts

Tingatinga *paintings* Among the visual arts, by far the best-known contemporary Zanzibari style is *Tingatinga* (or *tinga-tinga*). Paintings in this distinctive style can be found for sale at souvenir stalls and shops all over Zanzibar, as well as at tourist centres on the Tanzanian mainland and in Kenya. The subjects of Tingatinga paintings are usually African animals, especially

THE SHETANI OF ZANZIBAR   *Gemma Pitcher*

Throughout the centuries Zanzibar Island (Unguja) and, to a greater extent, Pemba Island have been famous as centres of traditional religion and witchcraft, alongside their better-known role as centres of the spice and slave trades. Today the cult of the *shetani* (meaning a spirit or spirits, the word is singular or plural) is still going strong in Zanzibar and Pemba – a dark undercurrent unseen and unknown by the majority of visitors.

According to local traditional beliefs, shetani are creatures from another world, living on earth alongside animals and humans, but invisible most of the time and generally ill-intentioned. Many of the ebony carvings on sale in Zanzibar's curio shops depict the various forms a shetani can take – for example, a hunched and hideously twisted old woman, a man–dog hybrid, or a young girl with the legs of a donkey.

There is no real way, say the locals, of protecting yourself from the possibility of being haunted or attacked by a shetani. The best thing is simply to keep out of their way and try to make sure they keep out of yours – for instance by hanging a piece of paper, inscribed with special Arabic verses, from the ceiling of the house. Almost every home or shop in Zanzibar has one of these brown, mottled scraps attached to a roof beam by a piece of cotton.

Should the worst happen in spite of these precautions and a shetani decide to take up residence in your home – or even, in the worst-case scenario, your body – the only thing to do is to visit a *mganga* (sorcerer). To be a mganga is a trade that generally runs in families, with secrets and charms passed on from father to son or mother to daughter. *Waganga* (the plural of mganga) meet periodically in large numbers to discuss their business (patients must pay handsomely for their services) and initiate new recruits. A committee of elderly, experienced practitioners will vet a younger, untested mganga before declaring him or her fit to practise.

Each mganga is in contact with ten or so shetani, who can be instructed to drive out other shetani from someone who is possessed, or to work their power in favour of the customer. The waganga are also herbalists, preparing healing medicines where spirit possession is not indicated, or combining both physical and occult treatment in severe cases.

But there are some shetani, goes the current thinking, which even a mganga cannot control. The latest and most famous of these was (or is) Popo Bawa – a phenomenon of far greater significance than just a run-of-the-mill shetani, which gripped Zanzibar's population in a wave of mass hysteria in 1995.

Popo Bawa (the name comes from the Swahili words for 'bat' and 'wing') began on the island of Pemba, where he terrorised the local population to such an extent elephants, leopards, hippos, crocodiles and gazelles, as well as guineafowl, hornbills and other birds. The main characteristics of the style include images which are both simplified and fantastical, bold colours, solid outlines and the frequent use of dots and small circles in the design.

The style was founded by Edward Saidi Tingatinga, who was born in southern Tanzania in 1937 and came to Dar es Salaam looking for work in the 1950s. After doing various jobs, in the early 1960s Tingatinga became unemployed and looked around for a way to earn money. At that time, carvers and sculptors, notably Makonde people, were producing some indigenous work, but most local painters favoured pictures based on European representational styles or Congolese styles from central Africa (in fact, in the 1950s and 1960s many painters from Congo and

that they called upon their most powerful sorcerers to drive him across the sea to Zanzibar. There the reign of terror of the 'shetani-above-all-shetani' continues.

The experiences of those who claimed to be visited by the demon were terrifying. They awoke in the middle of the night to find themselves paralysed and with the feeling of being suffocated. They then saw a squat, winged figure, around 1m tall, or slightly smaller, and with a single eye in the middle of his forehead, approaching the bed. Helpless, they were powerless to move or cry out as the demon raped them, men and women alike. Only when Popo Bawa had departed were they able to raise the alarm.

During the height of the Popo Bawa hysteria, people took to the rooftops and village squares, following a rumour that safety could only be had by those who slept outside, in a group. Despite precautions like these, tales of the demon's progress around the island spread, until the government was forced to broadcast announcements on the radio pleading for calm. Despite this, a helpless, mentally handicapped young man was beaten to death by a mob that had become convinced he was the demon. This seemed to be the climax of the whole affair – after that, the hysteria abated somewhat and Popo Bawa retreated. He is widely expected to return, however, and when local people talk of him, it's with a nervous laugh.

American psychologists came to Zanzibar to study the events and write papers, and stated that the case of Popo Bawa is simply a Zanzibari version of a phenomenon known as a 'waking dream'. One of the characteristics of such a dream is a feeling of being weighted down or even paralysed. Other characteristics include extreme vividness of the dream and bizarre or terrifying content. It is this same phenomenon that is used by sceptics in the USA to explain the stories of those who claim to have been abducted by aliens.

Nevertheless, to the people of Zanzibar, Popo Bawa was very real and proof that shetani exist. Of course, they are not all as horrific as Popo Bawa; the lesser shetani come in all shapes, sizes and colours – beautiful Arabic women, hideous Ethiopian hags, or tall, handsome white men. Shetani can be forced to work for humans, but it's a risky business. Some successful businessmen are said to keep a whole room of shetani in their houses to promote material success and make mischief on their adversaries. But the price of such supernatural intervention is high – a goat, a chicken or a cow must be sacrificed regularly and its blood sprinkled in the four corners of the room. If this sacrifice is not faithfully and regularly made, the shetani will take a terrible substitute – it will demand instead one of its master's male children …

To get a flavour of the unique experience of Zanzibari music, recommended recordings are listed below. For an unforgettable live experience, your best option is the Festival of the Dhow Countries around the beginning of July each year (page 44). You can also stop by the Dhow Countries Music Academy, Zanzibar's first music school, which opened in the Old Customs House on the waterfront of Stone Town in 2002. The school provides music lessons as well as instruments at minimal cost to anyone interested in studying music from the Dhow region or acquiring mastery of an instrument. Particular emphasis is on teaching traditional Zanzibari music styles, with most of the teachers coming from Zanzibar. It is a great place to meet local musicians and get further information on Zanzibari music and cultural events.

Bashraf: Taarab Instrumentals from Zanzibar (Dizim Records, 2000)
Beni ya Kingi – Brass Band Music of Zanzibar (Dizim Records, 2003)
Kidumbak Kalcha: Ng'ambo – The Other Side of Zanzibar (Dizim Records, 1997)
Mtendeni Maulid Ensemble – The Moon Has Risen; Zanzibara 6 (Buda, 2012)
Sauti za Busara – Zanzibar Festival Classics (Fourth World Records, 2008)
Shime! – Culture Musical Club (World Village, 2009)
Spices of Zanzibar – Culture Musical Club (Network Medien GmbH, 2004)
The Music of Zanzibar, vols 1–4 (Globestyle Recordings, 1988)
Waridi: Scents of Zanzibar – Culture Musical Club (Virgin France, 2004)
Zanzibar: Music for Celebration (Topic Records, 2000)
A Hundred Years of Taarab in Zanzibar – Zanzibara 1 (Buda, 2006)
The Diva of Zanzibari – Bi Kidude; Zanzibara 4 (Buda, 2006)

Zaire, now the DRC, came to Kenya and Tanzania to sell their work to tourists and well-off residents). Legend has it that Saidi Tingatinga decided he could do what the Congolese artists did – paint pictures and sell them for money.

With no training, he produced pictures that were initially simple and straightforward. Subjects were the animals and people he remembered from his home in southern Tanzania. He used just four or five different colours (actually house paint – and the only colours available) and painted on wooden boards. But despite this humble beginning, Tingatinga quickly sold his early paintings, mainly to local European residents who admired the original, 'naïve' style.

Within a few months, Tingatinga's paintings were in high demand. He couldn't keep up with the orders which flooded in, so he employed several fellow painters to help him produce more. There was no concept of copyright, and Tingatinga encouraged his colleagues to base their works on his style. As their success grew, soon the artists were able to afford to use bright enamel paints (the type used for touching up paintwork on cars and bicycles) and painted on canvas so tourists could take home pictures more easily. By the end of the 1960s, Tingatinga painting had become recognised as truly original contemporary African art.

In 1972, Saidi Tingatinga died, but the artists he'd encouraged formed a group named in his honour, and continued to produce and sell works in his style. Today, demand from tourists is still high, and vast numbers of Tingatinga artists produce paintings on cloth, wooden boards and other objects such as trays, plates and model wooden cars. There's even an aeroplane at Zanzibar Airport with its tail decorated in Tingatinga style.

With so many Tingatinga paintings available in Zanzibar and around East Africa, the quality of the work varies considerably; many pictures for sale in the streets have been bashed out quickly with little care or attention to detail. But if you search hard among the dross, or visit a shop where the trader has an interest in stocking better-quality stuff, you can often find real works of art (and still at reasonable prices) which do justice to the memory of Saidi Tingatinga – the founder of a fascinating, entertaining and quintessentially African style.

TRADITIONAL GAMES Stroll casually around any village or town on the islands of Zanzibar, and eventually you'll be sure to come across two hunched, intent figures seated on a *baraza* bench (see box, page 160) – their grunts of satisfaction or derision accompanied by the click of counters on wood. Sometimes a crowd of spectators will have gathered, pointing and shouting garbled instructions. Look closer and you'll make out the object of all this excitement: a flat wooden board, 32 little round holes and a lot of brown polished seeds. This is *bao* – Zanzibar's favourite pastime.

Games of bao – the name simply means 'wood' in Swahili – can go on for hours or even days at a time. Experienced players develop little flourishes, scattering the counters (known as *kete* – usually seeds, or pebbles or shells) expertly into holes or slapping handfuls down triumphantly at the end of a turn. Bao is played, under various different names and with many rule variations, across Africa, western India and the Caribbean. Swahili people are proud of their version, known as 'king' bao, and claim it as the original and purest form of the game. Tournaments are held periodically in Zanzibar and on the coast of the mainland – as in chess, one grandmaster eventually emerges.

The object of the game is simple: to secure as many of your opponent's counters as possible. Bao masters (usually old men) are said to be able to think strategically five to seven moves ahead, a level comparable to professional chess players. Children learn bao as soon as they can count, scratching little holes in the ground in lieu of a board and using chips of wood or stones as counters.

The African love of carving has produced a proliferation of bao boards of many different sizes, shapes and forms. The board can be represented as resting on the back of a mythical beast, grows human heads from either end, or is smoothed into the shape of a fish. Bao boards make excellent souvenirs and are sold in almost every curio shop, often along with a badly photocopied set of printed instructions that are guaranteed to bamboozle even a maths professor. It's far better to find a friendly local to teach you – the game is actually surprisingly simple to pick up.

Keram is the second most popular game in Zanzibar, and probably first arrived here from India. It's a fast-paced, raucous game played on a piece of wood carefully shaped into a small, square snooker table with cloth pockets at each corner. The game is similar to pool, with nine black disks, nine white disks, one red 'queen' disk and one larger white striker. Players flick the striker from their side of the board in an effort to get their own-colour disks into the pockets. Boards are kept smooth and speedy by liberal applications of talcum powder.

Bao and keram, like their Western equivalents chess and pool, have very different characters. While bao is traditionally a daytime game, played in shady village squares by elderly, dignified men, keram is popularly played at night in bars, often in the midst of a noisy and tipsy crowd of Jack the Lads.

FESTIVALS
Sauti za Busara Music Festival (February) The 'Sounds of Wisdom' annual festival, occasionally called the Zanzibar Music Festival, is a fabulous fiesta

celebrating the best of African music. Held every February in key venues across Zanzibar, with the biggest stars performing in Stone Town's Old Fort amphitheatre and Forodhani Gardens, it is a great opportunity to see live performances from a range of regional artists. For three days, the beats of jazz, taarab, pop and a host of other ethnic genres fill the evening air (17.00–01.00), as hundreds of artists and thousands of revellers descend on the capital. It's a joyous, fun-filled time to be in town … just be sure to book accommodation well in advance!

A three-day festival pass will cost around US$120 for international visitors (online booking available); all children under 12 years are admitted free of charge (\ *024 223 2423;* m *0773 822294;* e *busara@busara.or.tz; www.busaramusic.org;* ￼ *sautizabusara*).

Festival of the Dhow Countries – Film Festival (July) Without a doubt, the highlight of Zanzibar's artistic and cultural calendar is the Festival of the Dhow Countries – a 16-day event usually held in early July every year, and touted as East Africa's premier cultural event and among the most significant cultural events in all of Africa. The 'dhow countries' are those of Africa and the Indian Ocean basin, and so include east and southern Africa, northern East Africa, west and central Africa, the Horn of Africa, Arabia, Iraq, Iran, the subcontinent of India, Madagascar and the Indian Ocean islands, plus what the organisers call 'their global diaspora'.

The festival has grown from strength to strength since its humble beginnings at the Zanzibar International Film Festival (ZIFF) back in 1998, and now includes theatre, performances of traditional and contemporary music and dance, plus exhibitions of paintings, sculptures, craftwork and photography. However, the central part of this event is still the film festival, with its large, interesting and eclectic mix of films from the dhow countries and further afield. Several film-makers are also present, there are prestigious awards for new films (short and long features and documentaries) and the festival also includes workshops, talks and discussions, as well as an energetic series of entertainments called the Children's Panorama.

On the more serious side, film- and media-related workshops have included Women Film-makers, Making Current Affairs Programmes for African Audiences, Constructing African History in the Cinema, and Creative Journalism.

The main venue for the festival is the open-air theatre at the Arab Fort, with films and performances on the main stage of the amphitheatre and live music in the adjoining Mambo Club, while other events are held at the Palace Museum, the House of Wonders and the Old Dispensary (Stone Town Cultural Centre). The Old Customs House, which became the home of the Dhow Countries Music Academy in 2002, is the venue for musical masterclasses. There's also a series of free shows in Forodhani Gardens, just outside the fort.

Many events are free and admission charges are kept to a minimum (around US$0.50 for Tanzanian residents, US$5 for non-residents) to encourage local participation. The festival's directors have always aimed to deliver an event which is accessible to the local population; pricing them out would fail their objective. There's also an ambitious (but highly successful) programme of 'Village Events', which transports a selection of everything the festival offers in Zanzibar Town (film, music, theatre, women's workshops, children's shows, etc) out to the rural areas of Unguja and Pemba islands. The Festival of the Dhow Countries' organisers are keen to promote July as 'culture month' on Zanzibar, and this is undoubtedly an excellent time to visit the islands, although of course it's likely to be busy at this time. You can get more information from ZIFF,

Philip Briggs

The word 'dhow', commonly applied by Europeans to any traditional seafaring vessel used off the coast of East Africa, is generally assumed to be Arabic in origin. There is, however, no historical evidence to back up this notion, nor does it appear to be an established Swahili name for any specific type of boat. Caroline Sassoon, writing in *Tanganyika Notes & Records* in 1970, suggests that the word 'dhow' is a corruption of *não*, used by the first Portuguese navigators in the Indian Ocean to refer to any small local seafaring vessel, or of the Swahili *kidau*, a specific type of small boat.

The largest traditional sailing vessel in wide use off the coast of East Africa is the *jahazi*, which measures up to 20m long, whose large billowing sails are a characteristic sight off Zanzibar and other traditional ports. With a capacity of about 100 passengers, the jahazi is used mainly for transporting cargo and passengers over relatively long distances or in open water, for instance between Dar es Salaam and Zanzibar. Minor modifications in the Portuguese and Omani eras notwithstanding, the design of the modern jahazi is pretty much identical to that of similar seafaring vessels used in medieval times and before. The name jahazi is generally applied to boats with cutaway bows and square sterns built on Zanzibar and nearby parts of the mainland. Similar boats built in Lamu and nearby ports in Kenya are called *jalbut* (possibly derived from the English 'jolly boat' or Indian *gallevat*) and have a vertical bow and wineglass-shaped stern. Smaller but essentially similar in design, the *mashua* measures up to 10m long, has a capacity of about 25 passengers, and is mostly used for fishing close to the shore or as local transport.

The most rudimentary and smallest type of boat used on the Swahili coast is the *mtumbwi*, which is basically a dugout canoe made by hollowing out the trunk of a large tree – the mango tree is favoured today – and used for fishing in mangrove creeks and other still-water environments. The mtumbwi is certainly the oldest type of boat used in East Africa, and its simple design probably replicates that of the very first boats crafted by humans. A more elaborate and distinctive variation on the mtumbwi is the *ngalawa*, a 5–6m-long dugout supported by a narrow outrigger on each side, making it sufficiently stable to be propelled by a sail. The ngalawa is generally used for fishing close to shore as well as for transporting passengers across protected channels such as the one between Mafia and Chole islands in the Mafia Archipelago.

The largest traditional boats of the Indian Ocean, the ocean-going dhows that were once used to transport cargo between East Africa, Asia and Arabia, have become increasingly scarce in recent decades due to the advent of foreign ships and other, faster modes of intercontinental transport. Several distinct types of ocean-going dhow are recognised, ranging from the 60-tonne *sambuk* from Persia to 250-tonne boats originating from India. Oddly, one of the larger of these vessels, the Indian *dengiya*, is thought to be the root of the English word 'dinghy'. Although a few large dhows still ply the old maritime trade routes of the Indian Ocean, they are now powered almost exclusively with motors rather than by sails.

There's an excellent small exhibition on boats in the Pemba Museum in Chake Chake, and in the House of Wonders in Zanzibar Town. Don't miss the fascinating examples of traditional 'stitched dhows', with their timbers 'sewn' tightly together.

People and Culture CULTURE

2

the festival organisers, who are based at the Old Fort in Zanzibar Stone Town (m *0777 411499;* e *ziff@ziff.or.tz; www.ziff.or.tz*).

Mwaka Kogwa – Shirazi New Year (July)
In a very different vein, the festival of Mwaka Kogwa is held every year in several villages around Zanzibar, but most famously and most flamboyantly at the village of Makunduchi, in the south of Zanzibar Island. The traditional festival originated in Persia and celebrates the arrival of the New Year according to the Shirazi calendar. This one-day festival normally occurs during July, but check the dates locally as changes are possible (for more details, see box, page 314).

3

Natural Environment

PHYSICAL ENVIRONMENT

This place, for the goodness of the harbour and watering and plentiful refreshing with fish, and for sending sorts of fruits of the country, as cows … and oxen and hens, is carefully to be sought for by such of all ships as shall hereafter pass that way.

James Lancaster, captain of the Edward Bonaventure,
first English ship to visit Zanzibar (1592)

LOCATION AND SIZE Zanzibar consists of two large islands, plus several smaller ones, about 40km off the coast of East Africa, in the Indian Ocean, about 6°S of the Equator. The two large islands are Unguja (usually called Zanzibar Island) and Pemba. Zanzibar Island is about 85km long and between 20km and 30km wide, with an area of 1,660km². The smaller Pemba Island, at around 985km², is some 67km long and between 15km and 20km wide.

The islands are generally flat and low lying, surrounded by coasts of rocky inlets or sandy beaches, with lagoons and mangrove swamps, and coral reefs beyond the shoreline. The western and central parts of Zanzibar Island have some low hills, where the highest point is about 120m above sea level. Pemba Island has a central ridge, cut by several small valleys, and appears more hilly than Zanzibar Island, although the highest point on Pemba is only 95m above sea level.

CLIMATE

February 19th. We anchored off Zanzibar at dawn. A day of fierce heat. The island is said to enjoy a cool season. I have never struck it. An hour's stroll ashore sufficed to revive old memories, then I retired to the ship for a cold bath and an afternoon under the electric fans.

Evelyn Waugh, Tourist in Africa *(1959)*

The climate of Zanzibar is dominated by the movements of the Indian Ocean monsoons, and characterised by wet and dry seasons. The northeast monsoon winds (known locally as the *kaskazi*) blow from November/December to February/March, and the southwest monsoon winds (the *kusi*) blow from June to September/October. The main rains (the *masika*) fall from mid March to the end of May, and there is a short rainy season (the *vuli*) in November.

Throughout the year, humidity is generally quite high (less so in the rainy season), although this can be relieved by winds and sea breezes. Temperatures do not vary greatly throughout the year, with daytime averages around 26°C (80°F) on Zanzibar Island from June to October, and around 28°C from December to February, although in this latter period the humidity is often higher, so

47

temperatures feel hotter. Pemba tends to be cooler and gets slightly more rain than Zanzibar Island.

WILDLIFE

Unlike on the African mainland, there are no large wild animals on Zanzibar. Forest areas are inhabited by monkeys and small antelopes, while civets and various species of mongoose are found all over the islands. Birdlife is varied and interesting, with over 200 species being recorded, although bird populations are not as high as in other parts of the east African region. The marine wildlife, in the coral reefs that surround the islands, is particularly rich.

FLORA The islands of Pemba and Zanzibar were originally forested, but human habitation has resulted in widespread clearing, although a few isolated pockets of indigenous forest remain. Formed about 27 million years ago and seven million years ago respectively, both islands were originally coral reefs which became exposed as sea levels dropped, so the main rock type is a coralline limestone, known locally as 'coral rag'.

On the eastern side of Zanzibar Island, and in parts of the northern and southern areas, the landscape is very flat where coralline rock is exposed or covered by a thin layer of a calcareous sandstone soil, which supports low scrubby bush, known as coral rag thicket, quite dense in some areas. The western and central parts of the island are slightly more undulating, with a deeper soil cover: red, iron-rich and more fertile. Additionally, the western sides receive more rain than the eastern sides of the islands. Thus the western parts of Zanzibar Island were once covered in forest, similar in most respects to the low coastal forest which existed on the east African mainland, but today very little of Zanzibar's indigenous natural forest remains, as it has mostly been cleared and used for agriculture. Local people grow crops on a subsistence basis, and this area is also where most of Zanzibar Island's commercial farms and spice and fruit plantations have been established.

The only significant areas of natural forest remaining in Zanzibar are at Jozani, a forest reserve on the south-central part of Zanzibar Island, and at Ngezi, a forest reserve in the north of Pemba Island, although smaller patches do exist elsewhere. The water table around Jozani is particularly high (during the rainy season the water can be over 1m above the ground) and the trees are mainly moisture-loving species.

Trees and deforestation Despite the establishment of forest reserves such as Jozani and Ngezi, Zanzibar's forests continue to be cut down at an unsustainable rate. A lack of definitive boundaries, ignorance and need prevailing. Timber is used for construction, boatbuilding and furniture-making, and as fuel, both for domestic purposes and to burn coral to produce lime for building works. This last use has grown particularly quickly as the number of hotels in Zanzibar has increased.

The island's **mangrove swamps** are critically important: they are nurseries for a number of coastal fish, shrimp and crab species, they assist in shore protection, and play an important role in reducing the effects of pollution. Sadly, the mangrove wood from coastal areas is also being cut down at an alarming rate. Forestry Department figures show that in 1992, about ten million poles were cut in Chwaka Bay Forest, compared with 2.5 million in 1990. This wood is used for fuel

COCONUTS

Coconuts are the second most important crop on Zanzibar after cloves. They grow on a certain species of palm tree which are generally planted where clove trees cannot survive, although as diversification is encouraged, it is not uncommon today to see coconut palms and clove trees on the same plantation.

Coconuts are picked throughout the year, and large quantities are consumed locally as food, with the milk used for cooking. The pickers skilfully climb up the palm trunks using only a short loop of rope, then drop the nuts to the ground. The outer husks of the coconuts are removed by striking them on a sharp stick or metal bar fixed in the ground.

Coconut products – mainly the 'kernel' (the white edible parts) – are also exported. The process involves splitting the coconuts in two and leaving them to dry so that the white fleshy kernels can be easily removed from the shells. The kernels are then dried for a few more days in the sun or in a special kiln. Gangs of workers separating the husks and kernels, and small coconut kilns, can be seen in the plantation areas outside Zanzibar Town.

When the kernels are properly dried, the resulting substance is called 'copra', which is widely used in the food industry as a flavouring, or for decoration. Copra is also processed into an oil that is used in some foods and in the production of soap, candles and hair oils. In the days before aerosol foam, copra was particularly good for making shaving soap as it helped produce a good lather.

The coconut husks are not wasted: they are buried under sand on the beach for several months, which helps to soften the fibres and make them separate from the rest of the husk. They are periodically dug up and beaten on rocks to help this process, and then buried again for another few months. The fibre is called 'coir', and is used for mats and rope-making. In the areas outside the towns you will often see local women working with coir in this way.

and furniture, and in the construction and repair of buildings, but unfortunately the cutting of poles in the mangrove swamps leads to beach erosion and the destruction of habitats for fish and other marine life.

To replace some of the disappearing forest, through the 1990s, the Zanzibar Forestry Department planted acacia, casuarina and eucalyptus trees in Zanzibar and Pemba, as well as orange, coffee and cinnamon plants in Pemba. Another scheme, called the Zanzibar Cash Crop Farming System Project (ZCCFSP), discouraged farmers from cutting clove trees for firewood. All logging, and even the removal of dead wood, has officially been stopped in the Jozani and Ngezi reserves, although how carefully this new rule will be policed remains to be seen.

A relatively new project outside Zanzibar Town is engaged in the use of timber from coconut palm trees, which are found all over Zanzibar and Pemba islands. Traditionally, palm has not been used as a timber because it is very hard to cut or plane. However, modern high-quality joinery tools mean coconut wood can now be turned into beautiful furniture and fittings such as doors and window frames. The aim of the project is to use the local palm trees after they have come to the end of their natural fruit-producing life. By using this local source of timber, it is hoped that other trees will not be cut down or imported to Zanzibar from the mainland. Several of the hotels and tour companies around Zanzibar are now using coconut-wood items.

Cloves are the buds of a tree which, when dried, produce a unique flavour and aroma that is beloved of chefs the world over. The name comes from the French word *clou* meaning 'nail', which the buds resemble.

Cloves were introduced to Zanzibar at the end of the 18th century from the French colonies of the Seychelles, Ile de France (now Mauritius) and Réunion, where they had earlier been introduced from the Moluccas in Indonesia by French sailors. Sultan Said (sultan between 1804 and 1856) recognised their value and encouraged the setting up of plantations on Zanzibar and Pemba. When the plantations were established, it was found that growing conditions on Pemba Island were superior to those on Zanzibar, and the bulk of the clove crop actually came from there.

At the height of the clove trade, in the second half of the 19th century and the early 20th century, the islands of Zanzibar produced more than 90% of the world's supply of cloves, and the power and wealth of Zanzibar were based largely on this trade. Today, about 75% of the islands' total produce comes from Pemba.

Clove trees (*Eugenia aromatica* or *Eugenia caryophyllata*) grow to a height of around 10–15m and can produce crops for over 50 years. In the first eight years of growth, the buds are left to turn into colourful pink flowers. When a tree reaches maturity, however, the buds are painstakingly picked by hand before they open, when they are still white, then separated from their stems. Buds and stems are dried in the sun on palm-leaf mats or on a special stone platform called a *sakufu*, during which time they turn brown. During the harvest season, between July and January, with a break during the November rainy season, the scent of cloves is carried on the breeze right across Pemba in particular, where you can often see sacks of cloves being loaded at Mkoani for shipping to Zanzibar Island. Here, they are offloaded at the port, or on the beach near the Tembo Hotel, and carried by truck to the nearby distillery.

Other trees occurring on Zanzibar include mango (*mwembe*), which is used for its fruit and as timber for boatbuilding, kapok (*capoc*), and *Bombax rhodographalon*, which is used in light construction, and also produces a substance similar to cotton, traditionally used to make stuffing for mattresses and pillows. Other fruit-producing trees, grown in plantations or singly around local villages include guava, breadfruit, orange and pomegranate.

Spice trees and food plants The main crops grown in Zanzibar are coconuts and cloves. Bananas, citrus fruits and other spices are also grown commercially. As well as the famous clove trees, other spice plants found on Zanzibar and Pemba include black pepper, cinnamon, cardamom, jasmine, chilli and henna, whose small leaves are dried, ground and mixed with lemon to give the paste familiar to Eastern beauticians. The main crops grown by local people for their own consumption include maize, cassava, yams, bananas and pumpkins (see box, page 30).

MAMMALS As described above, much of Zanzibar's indigenous forested area has been cleared, so natural habitats for all wild animals are severely restricted. Probably the best places to see indigenous mammals are the Jozani Forest Reserve on Zanzibar Island and the Ngezi Forest Reserve on Pemba.

In this section, scientific names of species are given according to information provided by the Jozani Forest Reserve and Ngezi Forest Reserve. Other authorities

All cloves in Zanzibar have to be sold to the government, which buys at fixed rates, then sells on at market rates to the users and producers. So important is the crop that, on Pemba, vehicles have to stop as they pass police checkpoints to give the opportunity for vehicles to be checked for smuggled cloves. Sometimes, however, the government rates paid to the clove growers are so low that a harvest is not economically viable, and the cloves are left on the trees. As a result, some plantations have been completely abandoned in recent years, creating anger and resentment among the local farmers.

Most of the cloves that are harvested are processed into oil at the distillery on Zanzibar Island. This oil is used mainly as a flavouring device in foods such as cakes, pickles, cooked meats and ready-made mixes. It is also used in some antiseptic solutions, such as mouthwashes, and in mild painkillers for toothache. Its other major use is in cosmetics, where it gives a sweet-spicy note to many different kinds of perfumes.

The best-quality dried buds are kept separate and used whole in cooking, pickling or the making of spiced wines and liqueurs. These buds are also distilled into a high-grade oil for use in particularly fine perfumes. In the cosmetics industry, the oil from good Zanzibar clove buds is reckoned to be the best in the world.

Today, Zanzibar is still a major exporter of cloves and clove products, representing about 75% of foreign-exchange earnings – although these are highly dependent on the fluctuating world market price. Agriculture's contribution to Zanzibar's gross domestic product (GDP) currently stands at around 32%, a figure which has been static in recent years, and shows little evidence of increasing significantly anytime soon.

disagree on some classifications and nomenclature, especially regarding subspecies, but this is unlikely to be important for most visitors.

The Jozani Forest Reserve is well known for its population of **red colobus monkeys**. This animal is found elsewhere in Africa, but those on Zanzibar form a distinct species, called Zanzibar red colobus or Kirk's red colobus (*Procolobus kirkii*), endemic to the island and one of the rarest primates in Africa.

Although hard to see in the forest canopy, one group of red colobus in Jozani is partly habituated to human presence, so you are quite likely to spot some if you visit. These monkeys are mainly reddish-brown in colour, with a darker back and 'cap', and a paler forehead-patch, but their most striking and unusual feature is the male's white crest on the forehead. On closer inspection, particularly of facial areas, you will notice that each monkey has slightly different coat patterns and colourings.

In Jozani and some other patches of forest, you are likely to see the **blue monkey**, also called Sykes' monkey, the mitis monkey or the Zanzibar white-throated guenon (*Cercopithecus mitis albogularis*), which on Zanzibar is bluish-grey, or even a greenish-grey, with a distinct white throat-patch. Although the two types of monkey compete for some food items, they are often seen foraging peacefully in mixed groups. The Swahili word for monkey is *kima*. On Zanzibar, the blue monkey is more commonly given this name.

Blue monkey

When distinguishing between the two, the blue monkey is called *kima mweusi*, and the red colobus *kima punju* – 'poison monkey' (probably because the colobus has a stronger smell than other monkeys, and is reputed to have an evil influence on trees where it feeds).

A local subspecies of **vervet monkey** (*Cercopithecus aethiops nesiotes*) occurs on Pemba, but it is thought not to be on Zanzibar Island. This monkey is smaller than the red colobus and the blue monkey, generally greyish with a dark, rusty-brown back and black feet.

Other mammals found on Zanzibar, mainly in forested areas, include the **bush pig** (*Potamochoerus porcus*), although its numbers are reported to be greatly reduced; **Zanzibar tree hyrax** (*Dendrohyrax arboreus neumanni*), a rodent-like animal the size of a rabbit (this subspecies is endemic), with hoofed feet and rounded ears, and a loud piercing scream when threatened; **Ader's duiker** (*Cephalophus adersi*), a species of small antelope found only on Zanzibar and, until recently, the Kenyan coast; and **Zanzibar suni** (*Nesotragus moschatu moschatus*), another endemic subspecies of antelope which is even smaller than the duiker. The endemic **Pemba blue duiker** (*Cephalophus monticola pembae*) occurs at Ngezi Forest. All of these animals are nocturnal or extremely shy and are unlikely to be seen.

Ader's duiker

Leopard (*Panthera pardus adersi*), or *chui* in Swahili, have been recorded in Jozani, and elsewhere in Zanzibar. Again, this is an endemic subspecies, smaller than the mainland version and with finer markings, and also very unlikely to be sighted. Recent studies have concluded that this animal is now extinct on Zanzibar (see box opposite).

The small-eared **greater galago** or **bushbaby** (*Otolemur garnettii*) and the Zanzibar **lesser galago** (*Galagoides zanzibaricus*) both occur on Zanzibar, the latter listed as vulnerable by the IUCN. The **small-eared galago** (*komba* in Swahili) is about the size of a rabbit, generally brown, with very distinctive large ears and eyes, and a large bushy tail. The **Zanzibar galago** (*komba ndogo*) also has large eyes and ears, but it is smaller (about half the size of the greater galago) and grey in colour. Both animals are nocturnal, especially active at dawn and dusk, and have distinctive cries – sometimes like a child crying (hence their name), other times loud and shrill, and positively spine-chilling. They are known to be inquisitive and will forage around huts and villages at night. They are attracted to bowls of locally brewed palm wine, and often get captured when intoxicated and incapable of escape. A local saying, *mlevi kama komba*, means 'as drunk as a bushbaby'!

Also found in Zanzibar is the **African civet** (*Viverra civetta schwarzi*; *orngawa* in Swahili); it looks like a very large domestic cat with a stocky body, thick tail, and black, white and grey markings which form rough stripes. The **Javan civet** (*Viverricula indica rasse*) occurs on Pemba and Zanzibar, probably introduced by southeast Asian traders.

Smaller mammals include the **Zanzibar slender mongoose** (*Herpestes sanguineus rufescens*), most often seen running across roads with its tail vertical, and the **bushy-tailed mongoose** (*Bdeogale crassicauda tenuis*) – rarely seen anywhere. The **marsh mongoose** (*Atilax paludinosus rubescens*) occurs only on Pemba and may be seen at Ngezi Forest. The banded mongoose is a non-indigenous species, introduced to Zanzibar Island.

Populations of rats, mice and shrews (plus 14 species of bat) occur on both Zanzibar and Pemba islands. Those worthy of note include the **Zanzibar four-toed**

LEOPARDS IN ZANZIBAR

Leopard

The Zanzibar leopard (*Panthera pardus adersi*), is a local subspecies. Two different types have been recorded: the *kisutu*, which is similar to the mainland leopard, but with a more compact spot pattern and lighter background; and the *konge*, which is larger than the kisutu with dark fur and faint spot pattern.

Leopard tend to be shy and mainly active at night. Perhaps because of their elusive, nocturnal habits, they have traditionally been considered unlucky by local people, and are often associated with witchcraft, so have been actively hunted. They are also hunted because they are seen as vermin by farmers, and for their skins which can be sold to dealers. The leopard has been further pushed to the edge of extinction by an ever-growing loss of suitable habitat, as forest areas are cleared, and by a loss of prey, as Zanzibar's small antelopes are also hunted unsustainably.

By the 1980s, the leopard was believed to be extinct in Zanzibar, but in 1994, an American researcher called Scott Marshall found evidence of three leopards on Zanzibar, including prints, droppings and a suspected den near Chwaka. In his report, Marshall suggested that these leopards were trapped and 'domesticated' at a young age, to be used in ceremonies by local witchdoctors or traditional healers. He also suggested that there may be several more leopards similarly kept in captivity at other villages in Zanzibar, although this assumption was based on local anecdotal evidence, rather than on positive sightings.

However, in 1998, the South African wildlife experts Chris and Tilde Stuart published a report describing their exhaustive methods to locate any signs of leopard on Zanzibar Island, and concluded that none existed in a wild state. They also looked into the possibility of a few 'kept' leopards remaining in existence but found no hard evidence. They further concluded that even if a small number of 'kept' leopards were being held in secret, there was no hope at all for long-term survival of this species on Zanzibar.

Natural Environment   WILDLIFE

3

elephant shrew (*Petrodromus tetradactylus zanzibaricus*) with distinctive long slender legs and a trunk-like snout for eating insects, and the **Pemba flying fox** (*Pteropus voeltzkowi*), a large fruit bat with distinctive rufous colouring and fox-like face, found only on Pemba Island (page 354).

REPTILES, AMPHIBIANS AND INVERTEBRATES Of all the reptiles on Zanzibar, undoubtedly the easiest to spot is the **giant tortoise** (*Geochelone gigantea*) that inhabit Prison Island, a few kilometres offshore from Zanzibar Town. They were introduced here from the island of Aldabra, in the Seychelles archipelago, in the 18th century.

If you visit Jozani, you'll probably see some of the forest's population of tiny black and gold **frogs**. In the rainy season, when the ground floods, you'll see their tadpoles too. **Chameleons** can also be seen in Jozani and other parts of the island. Like the mongoose they are often seen crossing roads, but often very slowly, and very precariously. Other reptiles include **snakes** (rarely seen) and **geckos** (frequently seen on the inside walls of buildings – particularly the budget hotels in Zanzibar Town – although this is no cause for worry as they're small, timid and harmless).

The long black **millipedes** which you'll see on paths, especially after rains, are also harmless, and will curl up in a ball if you disturb them. Smaller still, though much more dangerous, is the **mosquito**. These are relatively common on Zanzibar, so see page 84 before you arrive.

One of the best places to see some of Zanzibar's reptiles (among other animals) is at the Zanzibar Land Animals Park (ZALA) a few kilometres west of Jozani Forest on the road to Kizimkazi (pages 328–9).

BIRDS *Dudley Iles*

Zanzibar is not noted as a major birdwatching area, but over 200 species of bird have been recorded on the archipelago. The avifauna of Zanzibar includes the resident birds, plus visiting migrants and seabirds. For any keen birdwatcher travelling on the east African mainland, polishing off the holiday with at least a few days in Zanzibar can make the trip-list even more impressive – the islands boast several species and races which are unique. Even for the more casual birdwatcher, Zanzibar provides some fine opportunities. Knowing the name of the bird that flew over the beach, or sings from a bush in your hotel garden, will make your time in Zanzibar even more rewarding and enjoyable.

Overview Like the majority of offshore islands, Zanzibar and Pemba have a smaller avifauna than the mainland of East Africa. Zanzibar can claim about 220 species, and Pemba slightly fewer. Of these, about 35 have been added since 1994, an indication of increasing tourist interest and observations. On Zanzibar, visitors are able to make a larger contribution to natural history records than on the mainland, since there have been fewer observers until recently.

Although Zanzibar and Pemba are similar in size, geography and position, they provide an interesting avifauna comparison. Zanzibar has woodpeckers, shrikes, cuckoo-shrikes and bulbuls, while Pemba has none of these. But Pemba has its own species of green pigeon, scops owl, white-eye and sunbird found nowhere else in the world.

As well as the resident birds, migrants from Eurasia, the Middle East and southern Africa pass through or remain to winter on the islands. Those from the north arrive in September/October and leave again in February/March. For European visitors it is a delight to see a familiar spotted flycatcher in the hotel garden, or hear the sound of a curlew calling from the shore at low tide.

Habitats The main bird habitats on Zanzibar, and some of the species found there, are described below. If the name of a bird is singular (eg: golden weaver), it refers to one species. If the name is plural (eg: bee-eaters, kingfishers), it refers to several species of the same or similar genus.

Parks and gardens Perhaps surprisingly, some of the best places to see birds are the parks and public gardens of Zanzibar Town, or the gardens of the many hotels situated along the coasts of Zanzibar and Pemba. The seed- and fruit-bearing trees, and the insects they attract, in turn attract many mannikins, warblers, coucals, sunbirds and swifts.

A bird you cannot miss in towns and around the big hotels on the coast is the Indian house crow (see box, page 55).

Dudley Iles and Helen de Jode

The Indian house crow (*Corvus splendens*) was introduced to Zanzibar in 1891. The bird is a scavenger and 50 crows were sent by the Indian government to help clear domestic waste building up in Stone Town at the time. Although the Indian house crow did consume some of this rubbish, it is by nature an aggressive bird and it began to attack many of the island's small birds and their eggs. As early as 1917 it was realised that the crows had become a pest, and they were subject to various control efforts including trapping, shooting and poisoning, but to little effect. By the 1940s, the Indian house crow had spread throughout Zanzibar Island, and by the 1970s its population had increased to such an extent in Zanzibar Town that many small bird species were rarely seen.

The crow population continued to grow, and by 1990 their impact on the indigenous bird population was considerable, with the town becoming virtually devoid of all other species. In addition, the Indian house crow was affecting agricultural and livestock production: feeding on germinating maize, sorghum and soft fruits, eating young chicks and ducklings and attacking calves and sometimes even cattle.

Between 1990 and 1995, the Finnish International Development Agency funded a control programme organised by wildlife expert Tony Archer and a team from the Zanzibar Commission for Lands and Environment. They used firstly a Malaysian-designed crow trap, and later a poison which was developed in the USA to control starlings as agricultural pests. The trapping and poisoning strategies were combined with a bounty on the collection of Indian house crow eggs and chicks during the breeding season. According to a report issued by Tony Archer, almost 45,000 crows were killed between 1993 and 1995. An estimated 95% of the crow population was killed in Stone Town and 75% across the island as a whole, allowing the small bird populations to return.

Unfortunately, since 1995, as funding dried up, there has been little continued effort to control the numbers of crows in Zanzibar. Increasing amounts of rubbish generated by a growing human population in Zanzibar Town, and a growth in tourism in coastal areas, are partly to blame for the rise in the number of crows. Current levels are having a serious impact on the indigenous bird population and are becoming an environmental health hazard.

In Dar es Salaam, where a similar crow problem exists, the Wildlife Conservation Society of Tanzania (WCST) has succeeded in killing over 43,000 crows using crow traps paid for by hotel owners and with some limited funding from the Canadian Fund for Local Initiatives.

In Zanzibar, several hotels and individuals around Zanzibar have now established their own crow traps, but many more are needed if the island is to be rid of the Indian house crow.

Natural Environment WILDLIFE

3

Farmland The more fertile areas of Zanzibar, mostly the centre and west of Zanzibar and much of Pemba, are occupied by the majority of the rural population. Over the centuries natural coastal scrub and forest have been cleared and turned over to agriculture, either for small-scale subsistence farming or for commercial plantations growing fruit and spices. The plentiful supplies of seeds, fruits and insects here attract many birds, including the beautiful long-tailed paradise flycatcher and parties of golden weaver (the only widespread weaver in Zanzibar). You may also see green wood-hoopoe, crested guineafowl (although these are now rare) and the diminutive emerald-spotted wood dove.

The telegraph wires along the roads provide vantage points for lilac-breasted roller and occasionally for the rufous-coloured broad-billed roller, and in winter for the blue-cheeked bee-eater.

Lesser-striped swallow hunt for flying insects over the countryside, and visit pools to collect mud for nest building. In areas where there are coconut palms you will see palm swift.

Freshwater ponds and grasslands Some farming areas consist of grassland, grazed by cattle, and often flooded after rain. Some of these wet areas are used to grow rice. Here you will see black-winged bishop, a small bright red weaver, plus herons and egrets, especially cattle egret, and maybe even a goshawk or harrier.

Where undisturbed, ponds and marshes support breeding jacana (or lilytrotter) and black crake, and possibly Allen's gallinule. You may also see small parties of pygmy goose, white-faced whistling duck and occasionally the rare white-backed duck. In winter months, purple heron and yellow wagtails (from Eurasia) feed in the rushes along pond edges.

Other birds seen in these areas include little grebe, red-billed teal and moorhen.

Bush Many areas of Zanzibar, especially the north and east, are not fertile and have not been cleared. They are covered in low scrubby vegetation called coral rag bush. It grows on well-drained rock which was once a coral reef, but was exposed when sea levels dropped many millions of years ago. The poor vegetation here does not attract great numbers of birds, but a few exciting species can be seen, especially in the early morning or late evening, including the pale-eyed sombre bulbul, eastern bearded scrub robin, crowned hornbill and collared sunbird. You might also see birds of prey such as African goshawk or black kite, plus rollers and shrikes. With luck a Gabon nightjar may rise suddenly from near your feet.

Forests and woodland Only a small percentage of Zanzibar's indigenous forest remains, following centuries of clearing for farms and plantations. The main areas are Jozani Forest on Zanzibar and Ngezi Forest and Kiyuu Forest on Pemba, characterised by tall trees with buttressed roots and a convergent canopy, interspersed with ferns and smaller bushes. Masingini Forest, near Bububu north of Zanzibar Town, can also be rewarding. The forest birds of Zanzibar are shy and hard to spot, but your chances are better in the early morning, when you might see Fischer's turaco, wood owl, crested guineafowl or tambourine dove, plus swifts, hornbills, woodpeckers and weavers.

In patches of woodland, on the edge of areas which have been cleared for farming, you may see more weavers, plus coucals, sunbirds, flycatchers and bulbuls.

Mangroves Mangroves occur on small offshore islands or around estuaries, in or near areas which are covered by water at high tide. Individual mangroves can grow to 5m in height, and close together, which creates a forest-like atmosphere (the mangrove vegetation of Zanzibar is discussed on page 59). This habitat is rich in marine life, which is exploited by humans as well as resident and migrant shore birds including herons and kingfishers. Other species you are likely to see include mouse-coloured sunbird and blue-cheeked bee-eater.

Seashore and sandbars Naturally, as a group of islands, Zanzibar is surrounded by seashores, made up of beaches, low cliffs, creeks and tidal coral-mud flats. On the beaches you will find various wading birds, including plovers, whimbrels and sandpipers; many of these will be familiar to European naturalists, as Zanzibar becomes an increasingly important wintering ground for these northern species.

Also look out for the greater sand plover (which comes from central Asia) and the striking crab plover, which breeds along the Somali coast. Another notable shore bird is the dimorphic heron, which feeds along the tide line: about 49% of these birds are mouse grey, and another 49% are pure white, while the rest show intermediate plumages. Perhaps the most striking seashore bird is the African fish eagle, which may be seen in some areas.

On the numerous sandbars off the west coast of Zanzibar you can see more waders, plus flocks of terns, gulls and cormorants. The sooty gull often seen here is a visitor from the Red Sea.

Open sea Some birds spend most of their time at sea, in (or above) deeper water, and rarely come to the shore. You will see these only if you are out on a boat, possibly diving or fishing, or crossing to Zanzibar Town on a ship from Pemba or Dar es Salaam. Oceanic birds are rare, but you may occasionally see frigatebirds or a roseate tern, or a masked booby from the breeding colony on Latham Island, south of Zanzibar.

Birdwatching areas
There are many places where you can watch birds on Zanzibar, and we list just a few recommended areas here.

People's Gardens This small park in Zanzibar Town (pages 172–3) has flowers and flowering trees and attracts a good range of birds. Here you might see scarlet-breasted sunbird, the Indian race of house sparrow, bronze mannikin, black-and-white mannikin, and the neat but skulking green-backed camaroptera, a complex name for Zanzibar's only widespread resident warbler. Overhead, parties of little swift hawk for insects.

Mbweni Ruins Hotel garden On the outskirts of Zanzibar Town (pages 178–9), this good hotel has a beautiful garden, and is an excellent birdwatching area. You don't have to be a guest to come here for lunch and a walk around their nature trail. At least 50 species have been recorded here by the hotel management, who are very knowledgeable on local wildlife and can advise on good birdwatching places on Zanzibar. The hotel's dining veranda overlooks a beach where many shore birds, including oystercatchers, whimbrels, sooty gull and lesser crested tern, await the retreat of the tide. Nearby is an area of mangrove. In the hotel gardens you'll see bronze mannikin, mangrove kingfisher, little swift and scarlet-chested sunbird, plus Eurasian golden oriole and blue-cheeked bee-eater in winter. During the heat of the day, the hotel pond is beloved by black-breasted glossy starling, dark-capped bulbul (more widely known as common, black-eyed or yellow-vented bulbul), golden weaver and as many as 50 Java sparrows (introduced around 1857 but now resident).

Bwawani Marsh Situated near the port on the edge of Zanzibar Town, this is the largest reed swamp on Zanzibar, although it was formed by accident when the Bwawani Hotel was built. Some 20% of Zanzibar's birds have been recorded here including a few, like the hottentot teal and purple gallinule, which have not been recorded elsewhere on the island.

Other species to look out for are lesser swamp warbler, Allen's gallinule, jacana, wood sandpiper, night heron, purple heron and the African race of the little bittern. The best viewing spots are on the Bububu road and on the smaller road leading to the hotel. Unfortunately, the swamp has become a dumping ground for local rubbish. Beware!

Jozani Forest A good area for keen birders, particularly if you visit early or late in the day, is Jozani Forest Reserve (pages 324–8), although the birds here typically hide themselves in the undergrowth or high canopies. The area south of Jozani Forest itself, on the other side of the main road, where the semi-habituated monkeys are found, is also good for birding (for more details, see page 328). Birds occurring here include the olive sunbird, the little greenbul (a racial endemic), dark-backed weaver, paradise flycatcher, east coast batis (a neat black-and-white flycatcher), crowned hornbill and cardinal woodpecker. Local specials include the east coast akalat and Fischer's turaco. At dawn or dusk you may also see African wood owl.

In the nearby mangrove forest, where a walkway has been constructed, you can see mangrove kingfisher, mouse-coloured sunbird and maybe tropical boubou.

Chwaka Bay This is the largest and most complex area of mud and sand on Zanzibar. It is an important area for local fishing, seaweed production, and for wintering shore birds, most notably the crab plover. Much of the east coast, from Chwaka to Nungwe, can offer good birdwatching along the shore – and even beyond the reef at low tide. Birds occurring here include waders, terns and gulls, plus herons such as the green-backed heron and dimorphic heron.

Matemwe This is a small village about halfway between Chwaka and Nungwi – with typical east coast conditions. There is a wide beach here, backed by palm groves and coral rag bush, and each habitat attracts typical species. The Matemwe Lodge's gardens (pages 241–2) are typical of many carefully planted and well-watered lodge gardens; they attract sombre greenbul, collared sunbird and paradise flycatcher, among others.

Chumbe Island This small island lies off the west coast, within easy reach of Zanzibar Town. About 63 bird species have been recorded here since 1992, but these are mostly sea and shore birds. The resident land birds are limited to about six common species, including African reed warbler, and most notably the small colony of mouse-coloured sunbird.

Perhaps Chumbe's main avian interest lies in the vagrants which occasionally appear, such as a wood warbler (only the third recorded sighting in all Tanzania) and, in 1999, a peregrine falcon. In 1994, around 750 pairs of roseate tern bred on two islets off Chumbe, but, although some 500 young were reared, the birds have not returned. House crows, fish eagles, rats (now eliminated) and bad weather were the probable reasons for their staying away (for more details on visiting the island, see pages 333–6).

Misali and Panza islands Misali Island lies close to Pemba Island while Panza Island lies off Zanzibar. Each has coastal forest and typical shore habitats. Like all small islands they are limited in bird species but are attractive for migrants. Misali is noted for a small population of Fischer's turaco, while on Panza brown-necked parrot occur. Panza also has large colonies of fruit bat and white-winged bat which attract bat hawks.

Ngezi Forest On Pemba Island, Ngezi Forest (pages 366–7) is a good birding destination. Birds recorded here include palm-nut vulture, African goshawk, and four endemics: Pemba scops owl, Pemba white-eye, Pemba green pigeon and Pemba violet-breasted sunbird. Ngezi is also home to a good population of fruit bats.

THE SEAS AND SHORES OF ZANZIBAR   *Matt Richmond PhD*

For anyone visiting the islands of Zanzibar, Mafia Island or the coast of mainland Tanzania, the diversity of marine life in the surrounding shallow waters may not be immediately obvious. However, the main marine habitats (mangroves, coral reefs and seagrass beds) are part of an extremely diverse, productive and vitally important marine ecosystem. Other marine habitats include the beaches and cliffs fringing the shore, and the vast areas of open water. The species of plants and animals which make up these habitats around Zanzibar and off mainland Tanzania are mostly the same as those found elsewhere in the western Indian Ocean (eg: Mozambique, Madagascar, Mauritius and the Seychelles), though slightly different from those in similar habitats as far away as southeast Asia, Australia and the South Pacific islands. Some species of fish and other creatures do, however, span this entire Indo-Pacific region.

MARINE HABITATS

Beaches and cliffs Around the main islands of Zanzibar (ie: Unguja and Pemba), many shores are fringed by either coconut-lined coral-sand beaches, where ghost crabs scamper, or rocky limestone cliffs. Remains of ancient reefs once below the sea (over 100,000 million years ago), then exposed as sea levels, dropped, now undercut and battered by high-tide waves. The cliffs provide a home to the brilliant red-yellow grapsid rock crabs and the bizarre eight-plated chiton snail, plus numerous other small snails, rock oysters and rock-skipper fish.

Mangroves In sheltered bays and inlets, where wave action is reduced, mangrove stands and forests are commonplace. Mangrove trees are specially adapted to survive in the sea, and all ten species found in the western Indian Ocean occur in Zanzibar. At high tide mangroves attract numerous species of fish, crabs and shrimps which depend on the forests as nursery grounds for their young. At low tide, red-clawed fiddler crabs carry out their formal challenges when not sifting the mud for food, while mud-skippers flip from pool to pool or from branch to branch when the tide is in. One of the best places to experience these fascinating marine forests is the mangrove boardwalk at Jozani Forest (page 326) – especially when the tide is in. You can also snorkel around a mangrove forest on Misali Island, off Pemba, or in many other inlets around the main islands.

Seagrass beds and lagoons The intertidal areas or zones lie between the high- and low-tide marks. Where beaches slope sharply, this is a narrow strip. Where old coral beds slope imperceptibly and are almost flat, this area may extend 2km or more. Intertidal zones provide a habitat for thousands of molluscs, crabs, sea cucumbers, seaweeds and several species of seagrasses, which are themselves food for fish at high tide.

Seagrass (Cymodocea rotundata)

Seagrass (Thalassodendron ciliastumm)

Along the east coast of Zanzibar (and the east coasts of the other islands and the mainland) shallow lagoons occur, extending to the reef crest. The lagoons support assorted coral, seagrass and seaweed communities and often great selections of starfish and beautiful nudibranch (sea hares and their relatives).

Blue starfish

Coral reefs

Corals are not plants, but animals belonging to the *Coelenterata* group (which also includes sea anemones and jellyfish). Corals exist in clean, clear, shallow, warm water, and so are found only in tropical regions. A coral begins life as a soft, many-tentacled 'polyp' around 1mm in size, and then produces a hard calcium carbonate skeleton around itself for protection. These types of coral are called **hard corals.** A coral colony develops from a single polyp by a process called 'budding' (where a new polyp grows out of an existing one). When polyps die, their hard skeletons remain, and the colony expands as new polyps form on the skeletons of old dead polyps. In this way colonies grow, and the growth rate varies from about 1cm to 5cm per year depending on species, depth and water conditions. Groups of colonies together make up the coral reefs found fringing the islands. Different types of hard coral form their colonies in different shapes; the commonly known varieties include staghorn coral, plate coral, mushroom coral, table corals and brain corals – all abundant in shallow water.

Crown-of-thorns starfish feeding on brain coral

Coral also uses a form of sexual reproduction where sperm and eggs are mixed (either internally with a coral embryo or larvae later being released, or by 'spawning' where eggs and sperm are released by polyps to mix in the water). In both ways the corals can colonise new areas.

Within the polyps exist microscopic algae-type organisms called *zooxanthellae*, which trap the sunlight needed to power the chemical reactions that produce the coral's hard calcium skeleton. It is the *zooxanthellae* which give the coral its colour – usually pink or pale brown in a variety of shades – as the coral polyps themselves are virtually transparent. Thus when coral is picked, and taken out of the water, the corals and the *zooxanthellae* die and lose colour, leaving only the pale 'bleached' chalky-white skeletons. During daylight hours, the coral colonies use sunlight in much the same way as plants do, but at night-time on a reef, most hard coral species are busy, with polyps extending their tentacles to catch planktonic foods.

Staghorn coral

Soft corals, on the other hand, do not have a hard external skeleton and do not form reefs. They are far more colourful than hard corals, although they also require light to build the tiny crystal fibres embedded in their soft pink, lilac or cream-coloured tissues. The daytime feeding of the eight-tentacled polyps, a feature of this group, is clearly visible on soft corals which can, in places, dominate underwater scenes.

On the east coasts of Zanzibar and Pemba, typical fringing reefs are marked by a continuous line of surf resulting from Indian Ocean swells. At low tide the reef crest dries out revealing pink algal-rock and boulders – the coral itself usually only becoming prolific on the seaward slope below 5m. On Zanzibar, the coral-covered reef slopes dip down to about 20m, after which a fairly bare sandy seabed continues down a further 4km to the ocean bottom. On the more sheltered west coasts of the Zanzibar Channel, smaller, isolated patch reefs with sandbars, and island reefs (around Chapwani, Changuu, Bawe and Chumbi islands), provide coral gardens in the relatively shallow waters. In contrast, parts of the reef around Pemba Island drop down over 50m or more offering spectacular vertical coral walls. Some of the most dramatic dive sites along the Tanzanian coast are found on the steep slopes of Pemba Island.

On any of these coral reefs you will immediately note the amazing variety of colourful fish of all sizes and shapes, incredible in their patterns and forms: butterflyfish, parrotfish, surgeonfish, damselfish, emperors, goatfish, pufferfish, angelfish, triggerfish, groupers and grunts to name a few. Most of these typical coral reef fish are territorial and reside over small areas of reef, rarely leaving their patch and aggressively protecting it from others of their own species. Some, like the butterflyfish, pair up for life and occupy a patch the size of a tennis court; others, such as the blue-lined yellow snappers, roam around the reefs in schools of a few hundred.

Emperor fish

Grouper

Because of the rich diversity of life forms, coral reefs have been compared to tropical rainforests. With Zanzibar's waters containing more than 700 fish species associated with coral reefs, over 100 species of hard corals, 150-odd species of seaweed and 300-plus species of seashells, to mention just a few of the more obvious sea creatures, the comparison is certainly a valid one. Then there are sponges, anemones, brittlestars, sea cucumbers, sea-squirts, feather-stars and crustaceans, all forming a seemingly chaotic, mind-boggling complexity which has fascinated scientists since Darwin's time.

The loss of the microscopic *zooxanthellae* from the coral, resulting in bleaching, was a major feature of the reefs around Zanzibar and elsewhere in the tropics in 1998, as the region experienced increased seawater temperatures (up to 32°C) associated with a severe, and much-publicised, shift in global climate conditions called El Niño. Although coral bleaching had occurred in the past, this event was on a scale not witnessed before. Much coral (both hard and soft) bleached and failed to regain its *zooxanthellae*. Within about five months vast areas of previously rich and diverse coral communities died. In many reef areas since then, new, small colonies have begun to emerge from settlement of coral larvae, and the coral component of these reefs is beginning to return to that prior to 1998. In other areas, total recovery to pre-1998 conditions may take decades or centuries. For reasons that are still unclear, much more coral around Pemba eventually died, whereas on Zanzibar corals recovered after bleaching.

Open waters The open waters, though mostly empty at first glance, can be very busy at times. They are home to vast schools of small, plankton-feeding, pelagic fish species such as sardines, silver-sides and Indian mackerel, continuously on the move and relentlessly pursued by larger pelagic fish, like skipjack, yellowfin tuna, kingfish, sailfish and marlin. Out at sea, in the Pemba Channel or off the east coast, flocks of hundreds of white terns identify tuna feeding frenzies as they dart into the shoals of small pelagic fish forced up to the surface by the tuna below.

Sailfish

Also feeding out at sea for most of their lives are turtles, coming into shallow waters when looking for a mate. Green and hawksbill turtles are the most common (for more details, see pages 65–7).

Both the friendly bottlenose dolphin and the less bold humpback dolphin can be seen in small groups, or pods, quite close to the shore (see box, page 322). Around Zanzibar there appear to be a few pods of 10–15 members, each with its own territory. One area where they are commonly seen is off Kizimkazi in southwest Zanzibar (viewing is easily arranged with a local boat), or around Mnemba Island in the northeast, or, with a bit of luck, even off Zanzibar Town. Watching dolphins is especially enjoyable if you're also sipping a cool beer on the Africa House Hotel terrace at sunset. At Kizimkazi and Mnemba it's also sometimes possible to see groups of spinner dolphins, providing an unforgettable memory.

Less common are whales, though humpback whales have been spotted several times around October/November in the Zanzibar Channel and off Nungwi in the north, leading their recently born young back to the summer feeding grounds in Antarctica.

Yellow fish tuna

Tides and weather Tides, the daily rise and fall of sea level, are a noticeable feature along the east coast of Africa. They are dictated mostly by the moon (and to a lesser extent the sun) and there are two main types. The smaller tides, known as neap tides, occur during the half-moon phases and result in a tidal range (the difference between high and low water) of only 1.5m. From this period onwards the tidal range increases until a full or new moon (ie: every two weeks), when spring tides occur. These result in the largest tidal range, of about 4m between high tide and low tide. Spring tide low water always occurs at around 10.00–11.00, for about three days, twice every lunar cycle (at full moon and new moon). Through the rest of the lunar cycle, the time of each tide changes from one day to the next by an average of 50 minutes (about 30 minutes during spring). So if high tide is at 15.00 on one day it will be about 15.50 on the following day.

During spring low tides the low-water mark can be a couple of kilometres out, and these days are ideal for walking out on the intertidal flats and reef crest to explore the kaleidoscope of life. Take care to avoid trampling on living coral and on sea urchins or blue-spotted stingrays. Good footwear (trainers, plastic sandals or neoprene booties) is strongly recommended. Even the tiniest cut or graze can flare up into a nasty tropical ulcer which will keep you out of the sea for days recovering. Also be aware of the speed with which the tide comes in and don't be caught out on the reef crest of the east coast with the incoming tide around your waist – you'll have an exhausting swim back to the beach if you do. And remember, tidal currents are strongest during spring tides so be careful not to swim too far out, or into tidal channels.

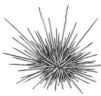

Needle spine urchin

Prevailing weather also greatly influences sea conditions and travellers should be aware of the main seasons (these are described in more detail on page 69).

LOCAL PEOPLE AND MARINE LIFE It won't take you long to realise that a great number of Zanzibaris are dependent on the surrounding seas and shallows for their variety of foods. Various fishing methods are used to catch this vital source of protein which contributes over 70% of the needs of the local population.

On dark new-moon nights in the Zanzibar Channel, sardine boats with lights attract and net vast shoals; on the same nights gill-netting boats, with 15cm-mesh nets, are after the large pelagic species (tuna, kingfish and billfish) in the southern Pemba Channel, operating mostly from Nungwi. Conventional hook-and-line fishing and passive fish-trapping using baited basket-traps (*madema*) are still practised all around the islands.

During the low spring tides thousands of women and children collect octopus, shells, sea cucumbers and moray eels from the intertidal flats, whilst other women tend to their seaweed (*mwani*) farm patches in the lagoons on the east coast. The lines of sticks protruding out of the water at low tide can't be missed (for more details see box, pages 278–9).

Kingfish

Mangroves are also harvested: the wood has been used for building poles for centuries because of its resistance to rotting and insect infestation. However, the rapid increase in demand over the last few years, with overcutting in places, has led to deterioration of the forests and the marine life which relies on them. Recently, the felling of planted *Casuarina* (Australian pine, though not actually a true pine) has produced, so far, acceptable insect-resistant poles, easing some of the pressure on the mangroves.

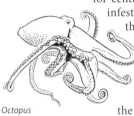
Octopus

CONSERVATION Owing to the rapid increase in human population (at present doubling every 20 years), the availability of new fishing materials, the development of a number of destructive fishing methods and the inability of the government to enforce fisheries regulations, the delicate balance of life in the shallow seas (and therefore this vital source of food) is beginning to be destroyed. Spear-fishing is on the increase and because of its effectiveness can quickly strip the reefs of the larger fish, and even of small species such as butterflyfish. Not only does it reduce fish numbers and make them wary of snorkellers, such as around the shallow reefs close to Zanzibar Town or in the lagoon on the east, but by removing these vital predators the balance within the ecosystem is being lost. Netting around reefs, and the type of fishing known locally as *kigumi*, where corals are broken deliberately to force fish out into the surrounding net, are also practised and extremely damaging. Dynamite-fishing is also very destructive, but mostly restricted to the mainland coast. Also restricted to the mainland and Mafia coasts, fortunately for Zanzibar, is the collecting of shallow live coral (mainly of the genus *Porites*) for baking on open kilns into lime. On Zanzibar at least, quarried coral rock is used instead.

Careless anchoring of boats on coral reefs can also, over a short time, cause considerable localised damage. In 1994, a project funded by the Dutch embassy of Dar es Salaam through the Institute of Marine Sciences established, in conjunction with the tourist boat operators who use the reefs, 15 permanent moorings for the islands and reefs close to Zanzibar Town, thus reducing tourism-related damage. Although these have since deteriorated and are no longer functional, the project did serve to increase the awareness of the importance and needs of living coral reefs, and in general boat operators around Zanzibar Town are careful when dropping anchor, attempting to set it in sand or rubble. Perhaps in the future the shallow coral gardens around Bawe Island and the sandbanks off Stone Town will come under some form of management to conserve their productivity and attractiveness

3

to visitors. The main threat to these shallow coral reefs, some of which have superb hard coral communities, remain the *kigumi* fishermen.

The local demand for marine curios (shells, dead coral and turtle products) has increased with the growing number of tourists, further adding to the overexploitation of the marine resources. The collection of large, colourful, attractive mollusc shells like the giant triton (*Charonia tritonis*) and the bull-mouth helmet shell (*Cypraecassis rufa*) have secondary effects which are not that obvious. These feed on the crown-of-thorns starfish (*Acanthaster planci*) and sea urchins respectively. Absence of the molluscs again upsets the balance, and populations of these echinoderms can increase alarmingly, furthering the destruction of the coral reefs. Collection of live hard corals is, of course, extremely damaging to the reef ecosystem. A colony the size of a football can take over 20 years to grow and the implications of mass removal for sale to tourists or export need no further explanation. Don't buy the stuff!

Giant triton shell

Bull-mouth helmet shell

Some steps are being taken to try and address the problems. With the involvement of donor organisations and conservation bodies such as the Worldwide Fund for Nature, private enterprise, the Institute of Marine Sciences, and the Zanzibar authorities (Department of Fisheries, Commission of Environment and Department of Tourism), plans to create marine protected areas have made some progress. On Pemba the only marine protected area is Misali Island Conservation Area, which involves local fishermen in conservation and charges fees to visiting divers and snorkellers. On Zanzibar, a few miles south of Zanzibar Town, Chumbe Island Coral Park (CHICOP), a private investment, includes a protected forest and coral reef on its western shores. Chumbe can be visited for a day, or you can stay overnight, and funds generated contribute to raising awareness of marine issues through the educational centre used by local school pupils. Further south, the Menai Bay Conservation Area brings fisheries and mangrove issues to local community groups supported by the government in an attempt to manage the resources for the long term. The only other marine protected area is a zone 200m wide around Mnemba Island, an exclusive private island resort off the northeast coast. However, the spectacular turquoise waters around Mnemba Island extend beyond this boundary and the 20km of fringing reefs are accessible to divers and snorkellers from several beach hotels operating from the north and east coasts of Zanzibar.

Tourism development, now a rapidly growing industry, also has a role to play in marine conservation. By acknowledging that the marine resources on which it depends are finite and also vital to the neighbouring coastal villages, and by attempting to come up with methods which assist all of the users, tourism can contribute to a healthy future for all concerned. Survival of both may be in the balance.

So, when bobbing around over a coral garden, or simply sitting on the seabed, 10m down, watching the coral reef world around you, or wading through the dark mud in a mangrove forest, think about it … and enjoy it. There's a whole lot going on: between individuals, between species, between habitats and between the ecosystem and the people who use it. This section has touched upon some of the more salient issues and examples of life in the seas and on the shores of Zanzibar. Many more exist to be discovered and pondered; while doing so, the following are a few points to remember:

- Don't touch living coral. There's no need to and it is more sensitive than it looks. Be careful when reef walking and snorkelling or diving. Be aware of what your flippers are doing and avoid landing on coral when entering into the water. Maintain good buoyancy control at all times.
- Help prevent anchor damage. Insist on the use of permanent moorings, if available, or anchor only in sand.
- Don't buy shells, turtle products or corals.
- Spread the word. Explain what you now know about the local marine ecosystems to other visitors and locals.

SEA TURTLES *Original text by Fiona Clark, updated by Lorna Slade, ecologist, Zanzibar Sea Turtle Survival Project*

Five types of sea turtle occur in the western Indian Ocean: the **green turtle** (*Chelonia mydas*), the **hawksbill turtle** (*Eretmochelys imbricata*), the **loggerhead turtle** (*Caretta caretta*), the **Olive Ridley turtle** (*Lepidochelys olivacea*) and the **leatherback turtle** (*Dermochhelys coriacea*). All are endangered species. The most commonly found turtle in Zanzibar is the green turtle, followed by the hawksbill. Both nest in Zanzibar. Leatherback and loggerhead are sometimes seen, but don't nest. There have been no records of the Olive Ridley since 1975.

Zanzibar is not a major turtle nesting site, but appears to be a feeding ground for sea turtles from other areas; nesting is more prolific on Pemba. Conservationists have recovered tags from captured turtles showing that green turtles come to Zanzibar from Aldabra Island, in the Seychelles, and from Europa and Tromelin islands. Loggerheads that nest in KwaZulu-Natal (South Africa) also feed in Tanzania – one loggerhead was captured in Tanzania just 66 days after being tagged in South Africa.

The current turtle scene The IOSEA (Indian Ocean and South-East Asian) Marine Turtle policy is an intergovernmental agreement that aims to protect, conserve, replenish and recover marine turtles through partnership organisations. According to its country report on Tanzania, there remain a number of challenges to sea turtles, including artisanal/subsistence fishing using gill nets, illegal harvesting, mangrove depletion, coastal (especially tourism) development, human and light disturbance, pollution, coral destruction, limited knowledge of genetics and population dynamics, and other inherent threatening factors. All of this occurs in spite of a number of protection and conservation initiatives being spearheaded by the government in collaboration with local communities, NGOs, the National Turtle Committee and development partners.

Zanzibar's turtle conservation work has so far centred on working with communities to raise general awareness about surveillance, nesting activities, monitoring, beach cleaning and potential ecotourism benefits. This community education and involvement is critical but it must be matched with workable solutions to help the traditional fishing industry better adapt to the necessary conservation goals.

The number of turtles caught in the nets of bottom trawlers has declined steadily from the mid 1990s, though it remains at approximately 70–80 turtles annually at present (many of these survive capture only to be later slaughtered for their shells). In addition, almost 600 turtles annually become trapped in the long, curtain-like gill nets used in traditional fishing methods (85% of fish in Tanzanian waters are caught in this way). Illegal and unregulated turtle fishing also continues with dynamite-fishing, the use of spear guns and lethal entanglement in monofilament fishing lines. The future is not entirely bleak though. A dedicated government committee has been formed to address all of these problems and there are a number of techniques and devices which can yet be employed to protect the turtles. We must only hope that adequate financial and human resources will back up the new policies and protect these graceful sea creatures.

On Mafia, the marine conservation NGO, SeaSense, is doing some marvellously successful turtle conservation and ecotourism work. Hatchings are utterly delightful to watch and community support for the project is genuine, profitable and sustainable. It's a magical trip to see the baby turtles and well worth supporting (see box, page 399).

The bad news The sea turtle population is decreasing in Zanzibar. This is bad because turtles are part of a food web which includes seagrasses, sponges, jellyfish and tiger sharks, and also because living turtles are attractive to tourists and (like dolphins) can sometimes be a way for local people to earn money.

The number of nesting sites has been reduced dramatically, and turtles are hunted and trapped by more efficient means than previously. Local fishermen tell how, 20 or 30 years ago, some beaches would contain 100 or more turtle nests every year. But these days the same beaches contain only two or three nests. Places where nests can still be found include Mnemba Island, the beaches north of Matemwe Bungalows, and around Kizimkazi. Pemba is home to the most important nesting beaches; turtles nest on Misali Island, at Ras Kiuyu and on the beaches near Ngezi Forest – especially Vumawimbi. Unfortunately, except for the island sites, few of these nests are successful: many eggs are taken by people, while others are lost to the sea when erosion has formed steps on some beaches forcing turtles to nest in places that are vulnerable to the high tide.

The burgeoning tourist industry also has its costs. In the last ten years, many hotels have been built on turtle-nesting beaches. Buildings often extend right to the beach, vegetation is cleared and the beach lit up at night, disturbing any turtles coming up to nest and disorientating any hatchlings. For example, Nungwi on the north coast and Kiwengwa Beach on the east coast of Zanzibar are now wall-to-wall hotel with no space or peace for turtles.

Turtle-hunting in Zanzibar only became illegal in October 1993. Although penalties are quite severe (a large fine, or two years in prison, or both) enforcement of the new law is unlikely. The Fisheries Department is under-resourced and has many other problems to deal with (such as dynamite-fishing).

Turtles are usually captured with gill nets, which are set on the seabed, while others are caught with spear guns. They are brought ashore and have their flippers and shell removed, often while still alive. The number of turtles caught increased dramatically in the 1960s when gill nets, snorkelling gear and spear guns were introduced. Some local fishermen claim that their increased catch proves the population is increasing too, but the same fishermen also agree that nesting turtles have all but disappeared. Uroa on the east coast of Zanzibar is a renowned area for turtle-hunting and the beach sometimes looks like a turtle graveyard.

In March 1996, there were two incidents of poisoning in Pemba through the consumption of turtle meat, resulting in the deaths of 37 people. Hawksbill turtles, in particular, are known on occasion to harbour toxins thought to originate from toxic algae in the food chain. These toxins do not harm the turtle, but have disastrous effects on any humans eating the meat. These unfortunate incidents helped reduce turtle slaughter, but apparently only for a short while.

The good news Since 1992, there have been several small-scale turtle-protection projects run with volunteer help through the government of Zanzibar's Department of the Environment. These include the following:

- A Swahili-language education package for schools and other youth groups, emphasising the plight of sea turtles and their need to be protected. A poster carrying the same message has also been produced both in English, aimed at visitors, and in Swahili, aimed at locals.
- A nest protection scheme, run by Matemwe Bungalows, a hotel on the east coast. Local villagers are paid a small fee if they report an intact nest, and a further bonus for each successful hatching. To avoid the problems of beach erosion, some nests are moved to safer sites.
- A survey and protection scheme carried out by the management of the exclusive lodge on the private Mnemba Island. This is an ideal site for turtles, with safe beaches (no local fishermen are allowed to land) and deep-water access.
- A nest protection and monitoring scheme on the protected Misali Island, off Pemba, now a marine conservation area, patrolled by local rangers and still one of the best turtle-nesting areas in Zanzibar.
- Community education and involvement in nest-recording and monitoring in both Pemba and Zanzibar, including the successful production of an educational drama and video, has played a key role in reducing threats to turtles. Through active inclusion of local community members in conservation activities, the role of turtle security has become a source of employment and social status, reinforcing the benefits of protecting the creatures.
- There are plans afoot to try and introduce the use of turtle excluder devices (TED) in the country's fisheries legislation. In essence, the TED is a metal grid of bars that attaches to trawling nets and allows larger animals, like turtles and sharks, to escape whilst still keeping prawns, shrimp and the like inside. With a hatch opening at either the top or the bottom, the heavy weight of the sea turtles, sharks and larger fish causes the hatch to open on impact, providing them with an escape route. The success of the TED has varied around the world, but it is a start at further regulating fishing methods, and may help a few more adult turtles to escape in the future.
- In areas where turtle mortality is critically high through animal and egg poaching, cash rewards for conservation have been used. This is clearly not financially sustainable and has had mixed results in the archipelago. On Zanzibar Island, incentive-driven conservation has proven to be counter-productive in obtaining committed public participation; however, on Mafia, modest incentives have been highly effective in involving local communities and in protecting nests. This is a short-term solution though and it is generally agreed that generating revenue to fund turtle conservation through turtle tourism and park entry fees is a far more positive and sustainable method. Mnarani Aquarium below is one successful example.
- Mnarani Aquarium (pages 225–7) in Nungwi is a local conservation initiative to protect turtles and educate villagers and tourists. Managed by a group of local fishermen, in a large tidal-fed rock pool, the water has been stocked with several species of fish and around ten green and hawksbill turtles. The Department of the Environment has allowed this group (only) to keep a maximum of eight turtles for educational purposes and any excess brought in by fishermen are periodically tagged and released. Although generally keeping turtles in captivity is not to be encouraged, in this case the local community benefit, and the educational value to locals (school children are allowed in free) and tourists are judged to be worth it. The aquarium does not keep mature female turtles.
- Both green and hawksbill turtles are now being tagged for monitoring on Pemba and Mafia islands, with the latter project also undertaking genetic studies.

Turtle-shell products Zanzibar used to be a major centre for turtle-shell, usually called 'tortoiseshell', and at the height of the trade (the early 20th century) some 3,300kg were exported every year from the islands and nearby mainland coast. Demand dropped, but has recently been revived by the growth of tourism. Less than half the tourists who bought turtle-shell items knew what it was, or that turtles were endangered. However, local conservationists and aware tourists complained to such a degree that many shops now refuse to stock turtle-shell products. Tourists are asked by conservation organisations to boycott any shops that continue to sell turtle products, although these are rarely seen nowadays.

Local police and customs officials are now also aware that turtle-shell products are illegal. Tourists buying whole shells from hawkers should be aware that conservationists and hoteliers will report them to the police for possession of turtle shells, and if caught they will be reprimanded and the shell confiscated.

Local perspectives Lest we get too self-righteous about all of this, we should perhaps remember that Zanzibar is a poor country and that a large sea turtle is worth about a month's wages for an office worker, and considerably more than that to a fisherman or farmer. Turtle meat is also held traditionally to have healing properties. Stopping the local people from catching turtles will inevitably make some of them poorer, yet if the turtle-hunting continues, there will soon be none left anyway. But many Zanzibaris can't afford the luxury of thinking ahead. Life is hand to mouth and the 'if I don't catch it someone else will' attitude is of course understandable.

Having said that, there does need to be a halt to turtle killing as populations are in danger of extinction. In addition to finding alternative food and income sources for local communities, it is also essential that continued education, improved law enforcement and government protection for important nesting beaches are maintained, to ensure that the turtle has a place in Zanzibar's future.

4

Planning and Preparation

Truly prepossessing was our first view … of Zanzibar. Earth, sea and sky all seemed wrapped in a soft and sensuous repose … The sea of purest sapphire… lay basking … under a blaze of sunshine.

Richard Burton, British explorer (1856)

WHEN TO VISIT

The best time to visit these islands is during the dry seasons – December to February and June to October (see page 47 for more details) – but generally speaking, from December to February any wind comes from the northeast, so beaches on the southern and western parts of the islands are more sheltered. Conversely, from June to October it tends to come from the southwest, so northern and eastern coasts are best. Ultimately, however, these islands are at the mercy of the ocean and their weather patterns can be unpredictable at any time of year. Even during the 'dry' seasons, afternoon showers are not unknown, although they tend to be short and pleasantly cooling (for more details, see box below).

It is also possible to visit during the rainy season, when there are fewer visitors and you're more likely to get good bargains from lodges and hotels (the ones that remain open) and trips. The rain can be heavy, but is not usually constant; the sunsets can be particularly magnificent; and pineapples are in season! Travel can be trickier, with roads damaged and buses delayed, but you'll get there eventually.

At holiday times, such as Christmas and Easter, the islands are popular with expats from Dar es Salaam and Nairobi as well as overseas visitors. Expect full flights and higher hotel rates. Conversely, during the Islamic fasting period of Ramadan (page 36), many restaurants and shops are closed during the day, and life runs at a generally slower pace.

If you're going scuba diving or game fishing, see box, page 98. If local festivals appeal, then see pages 43–6. Sports fans may like to tie in their visit with the Zanzibar International Marathon, held every year in early November.

CLIMATE CHART

	Jan	Feb	Mar	Apr	May	Jun	Jul	Aug	Sep	Oct	Nov	Dec
Temp (°C): av min	25	25	24	23	22	20	19	19	19	21	22	24
av max	31	31	31	30	29	29	28	28	28	29	30	31
Hours of sun/day	8	8	7	5	6	8	7	8	8	8	8	8
Rainfall (mm)	80	70	140	390	250	60	45	40	50	90	220	160
Av days of rain	7	6	12	19	14	4	5	6	6	7	14	12

We feel the real highlights of these islands are often away from the resorts and obvious places, and in the unscheduled interactions with the local people that you meet and the unspoilt areas you stumble across whilst exploring (read the book's introduction for more). That said, we recognise that a little initial direction can help to make the best of a trip, so here are a few pointers.

WHERE TO STAY The choice of accommodation is endless – but a few places really stand out. Top of the list, and most people's budgets, is **Mnemba Island** (pages 247–8) on Zanzibar. It's very expensive, but it's also exceedingly good, and remains the best by far in the archipelago. We approached it fully expecting to comment that it was overpriced, but the reality is that it is in a different league from the other places in this guide. It's very polished, yet also very simple; the ultimate in barefoot luxury. The arrival of **Kilindi** (page 229) in Kendwa, opened up a fabulous island alternative at a significantly reduced (relative) cost; its understated elegance, impressive space and super service quite possibly make this Zanzibar island's premium property for escapists. Whilst more recently, Paje's premium pick **White Sand Luxury Villas** (page 287) is designer safari chic on the beach, **Tulia** in Pongwe (page 258) is going for all-out lux and fine dining, albeit minus the beach, and money-no-object groups can kick back on the simply stupendous private island of **Thanda** (page 386), off Mafia's west coast.

For small, high-quality beach lodges with more reasonable price tags, our top tips would be the four spacious villas at **Matemwe Retreat** (pages 239–40); its more relaxed sister property, **Matemwe Lodge** (pages 241–2); the fabulous new hotel sharing its beach, **Green & Blue** (page 240); stylish **Sunshine Marine Lodge** (page 242) at Muyuni beach; couples-only **Zawadi** (page 274) beside the Blue Lagoon; and kick-back cool **Upendo Beach Retreat** (page 275) and **Matlai Boutique Hotel** (page 272), both in Michamvi Pingwi. For consistently high levels of service, individually styled accommodation and access to stunning beaches and watersports, try **Ras Nungwi Beach Hotel** (pages 211–12) in Nungwi; **Shooting Star** (page 255) in Pwani Mchangani; social **Sunshine Hotel** (page 243) in Matemwe; bijoux **Anna of Zanzibar** (page 271); chic **Indigo Beach** (page 281) in Bwejuu; and **Fumba Beach Lodge** (page 332) in the quiet southwest of Zanzibar.

Whilst looking at these, compare them with the three main lodges on Mafia Island: **Pole Pole** (pages 381–2), **Kinasi** (page 382) and **Chole Mjini** (pages 384–5). Mafia doesn't offer the extensive beaches of Zanzibar, but it's much quieter and in many ways gives a great deal of exclusivity for your money, with the added bonus of some superb diving and snorkelling. It's a great favourite of ours, and very undervalued.

For small, secluded beach retreats that cost even less, have a look at **Warere Beach Hotel** (page 214) on Nungwi's northeast coast; friendly **Nur** (page 303) in Jambiani; and **Pongwe Beach Lodge** (page 259).

Budget travellers might want to check out **Sunset Bungalows** (pages 231–2) in Kendwa, which offers good-value bungalows on the beach; the delightful **Bellevue Bungalows** (page 283) on the Michamvi Peninsula, which has neat rooms, good food and a thoroughly chilled vibe; **Karamba** (pages 316–17) in Kizimkazi; and cheerful **Zanzistar** (page 304) and **Blue Oyster** in Jambiani (page 302). Also try **Santa Maria Coral Park** (page 260), a small and simple place in a coconut grove beside a sweeping bay; quiet **Kimte Beach Inn** (page 303), on a quiet stretch of Jambiani beach; and **Demani** (pages 307–8), off the beach but with a fabulous pool and immaculate budget rooms and dorm – proof that you can still find magical places to match tight budgets. For self-catering, **La Papaye Verte** (page 305) and **Mango Beachhouse** (page 306), both in Jambiani, are good options.

If you're looking specifically at the busy Nungwi area, then at the top end, **Z Hotel** (page 201) claims to be a 'boutique on the beach', and has raised the hospitality bar in the area. The mid-range **Flame Tree Cottages** (page 206) offers a more laidback, great-value place to stay a few minutes' walk from the buzzing heart of town; and a little further away, **Mnarani Beach Cottages** (pages 212–13) is very friendly and reasonably priced, with one of Zanzibar Island's best views.

If you're taking a family, lack mobility, or are simply seeking the extensive facilities of a larger resort, then good-value **Breezes** (pages 274–5) is first class; **Karafuu Resort** (pages 273–4) in Michamvi and **La Gemma Dell'Est** (pages 229–30) in Kendwa are both worth considering. We feel all of these are a step above most of the island's other big resort offerings. They are well managed and the facilities and beach locations are excellent.

For something completely different, those interested in ecology or conservation shouldn't miss a few days at **Chumbe Island** (pages 335–6) for a terrific all-round experience!

The best hotels in Stone Town change quite fast, as new ones start up and often raise the bar, but currently theatrical **Emerson Spice** (page 130), central **Jafferji House & Spa** (page 126) and **Zanzibar Palace** (page 132), and treasure-filled **Kholle House** (pages 130–1) are our pick of the finest upmarket, boutique guesthouses. The **Park Hyatt Zanzibar** (pages 126–7) has brought international city hotel style to the Stone Town waterfront and is the undisputed best large hotel in town. The **Zanzibar Serena Inn** (page 128) remains reliably efficient with a distinctly African air, whilst for something less expensive, but still with a pool, **Dhow Palace** (page 133) is a good choice. Slightly cheaper in price, but brimming with character, central **Maru Maru** (page 142), intimate **Kisiwa House** (page 128) and **Zanzibar Coffee House** (page 133) are excellent. For backpackers and the budget-conscious, funky **Rumaisa Hotel** (page 134), ethical **Zenji Hotel** (page 136) and the renovated **St Monica's Hostel** (page 138) should be top of the list.

If you are keen to stay by the beach just outside Zanzibar Town, **Maruhubi Beach Villas** (page 181) has some good sea-view rooms. Equally, if exclusive use is more your thing, there are now some excellent options: **Che Che Vule** (page 240) and **Upendo Beach Retreat** (page 275), are just a couple of highlights.

WHERE TO EAT AND DRINK If you enjoy good food, then Zanzibar can be a great place to visit – though choose your lodges and restaurants carefully or you may be disappointed in the lack of culinary variety and quality. You can expect to eat well in most of the top lodges, but only a few stand out. In Stone Town, the roofop **Spice Tea House** at Emerson Spice (page 139) is hard to beat for its five-course degustation menu and atmospheric panorama, whilst its marketplace courtyard barbeque is magical menu after dark. **Qambani** (page 273), **White Sand Luxury Villas** (page 287), **Tulia** (page 258), **Kilindi** (page 229), **Ras Nungwi Beach Hotel** (pages 211–12) and **Green & Blue** (page 240) offer excellent seaside dining in top-end settings, whilst **Pongwe Beach Hotel** (page 259), **Sunshine Hotel** (page 243) and **Seconda Stella a Destra** (page 309) all pride themselves on delivering fine food with an affordable price tag. They share this with the vastly cheaper, superb village cuisine served in **Okala Restaurant's** (page 310) implausibly simple makuti banda, tasty dishes at **Bellevue Bungalows** (page 283), and super sharing platters and fresh cocktails in the beach chic surroundings of **Upendo Bar & Restaurant** (page 276). For some of the island's finest coffee and cake,

4

hang out with the kitesurfers at **Mr Kahawa** (page 293) on Paje beach. A tasty meal with a worthy cause, students at the Jambiani Tourism Training Institute offer dinner every Friday night at **Alibi's Well** (page 308) as part of their course.

For up-to-date advice on Stone Town's best independent restaurants, we'd always suggest that you ask locally; things change quickly and some of our recommendations in the main listings are likely to be out of date sooner than they're printed. However, a clutch of newcomers have been added to our list of all-time favourites, to make for a much more varied and exciting culinary collection in the city. Our current top recommendations by day are: the **Stone Town Café** (page 145) for filling breakfasts, cheerful **Lazuli** (page 145) for smoothies, and **Zanzibar Coffee House** (page 145) for coffee pick-me-ups. Appetisers and sundowners on **Tatu's** (page 144) top floor (or a nightcap from its extensive whisky collection if you visit later) are fun before dinner at newcomer **6 Degrees South** (page 141), **Abyssinian Maritim** (page 139) for authentic Ethiopian or **La Taverna** (page 142) for a friendly, family-run Italian. **Rendezvous Les Spices** (pages 143) is perfect for delicious, fresh Indian dishes. Sundowner cocktails on the **Park Hyatt** (page 126–7) terrace are a treat; romantics will love **The Secret Garden** (pages 140–1) and all Stone Town diners should book a rooftop dinner at the **Hurumzi Tea House** (page 139) at Emerson on Hurumzi.

WHAT TO SEE AND DO   Whilst lazing on the beach can be very relaxing, if this is the limit of your activities then you will miss out on a lot. At least accept the offer of a local beach masseuse if there is one; they can be surprisingly good.

A highlight of many trips to Zanzibar and Mafia is the **diving**, which is good at many places around these islands. The best spots would certainly include the reef around Mnemba Island (page 248), those in Mafia's marine park (pages 386–91), and for advanced divers, the challenging waters around Pemba (pages 346–8). The less aquatic might prefer to go **snorkelling**, and if so they should add Chumbe Island to this short list of reefs, with its world-class, pristine coral; no scuba diving is allowed there. Chumbe is also worth visiting for its guided **forest and intertidal walks** (pages 333–6), especially for nocturnal sightings of huge coconut crabs.

A sunset dhow cruise can be magical and romantic, but better still is a **dhow trip to a remote sandbar**: lie on a deserted beach, snorkel on the reef, eat fresh seafood and look out to nothing but tropical ocean. The upmarket lodges on Mafia (pages 379–86) all arrange these trips from Chole Bay, whilst on Zanzibar Island, Fumba Beach Lodge (page 332), Unguja Lodge (page 317) and ethical operator Eco+Culture (page 114) all run similar trips in the Menai Bay Conservation Area.

If you're in the Nungwi area, then do wander along to see the turtles at the **Mnarani Natural Aquarium** (page 225). It's a great conservation project and a rare chance to see hatchling turtles at very close quarters. For the ultimate turtle-hatching experience though, plan your trip between June and September and head to Juani Island, off Mafia, for a magical day trip to see the natural nests and mad-dash to the ocean of these tiny turtles.

More generally, any trip to Zanzibar Island should include a **spice tour**: ask around to make sure you will have a knowledgeable guide. The trip idea may seem clichéd, but plucking everyday spices from what seems like a tangled bit of unruly forest can be fascinating. For something slightly different, combine the spices with some Zanzibari history on the acclaimed **Princess Salme Tour** (see box, page 186). Starting at Mtoni Palace, the day trip takes in the palace ruins, a traditional coffee ceremony, the Kidichi plantations and a delicious Swahili lunch, and even helps fund the palace conservation initiatives.

For animal lovers, visit the colobus monkey colony in **Jozani-Chwaka Bay National Park** (pages 326–7), and maybe even drop into the **Zanzibar Butterfly Centre** (page 328) next door. Meanwhile, those in search of a much more original, albeit less predictable, experience should consider visiting the community beside **Ufufuma Forest** (pages 264–7). Perhaps the ultimate wildlife experience is the opportunity to see and **swim with whale sharks** (see box, page 393) off Mafia's coast. Between September and March annually, there are some fabulous trips through Kitu Kiblu to learn and interact responsibly with these enormous plankton-eating fish. A spectacular encounter!

For some genuine community insight and interaction, the **Jambiani Cultural Tour** (page 312) is really very good. Tailored to the particular interests of the visitor, it offers some hands-on entertainment and enlightening insights into the lives of the rural population, and ensures a percentage of the tour is reinvested into necessary village development. Equally, the newly opened **Seaweed Center** in Paje (page 294) offers tours and valuable insight into the importance of this marine agriculture to local villagers.

No trip to Zanzibar is really complete without a night or two in **Stone Town**. Whilst here, take a walk around the narrow alleys – ideally with a great guide (see box, page 118) – venture into the bustling market on Creek Road, stroll through Forodhani Gardens, relax in Mrembo Traditional Spa, and treat yourself to a rooftop meal on a balmy evening. For more insight, most of the local tour operators (pages 114–17) can arrange guides for half- and full-day excursions.

ORGANISED TOURS AND TOURIST INFORMATION

If you're staying on a low budget (eg: US$20–30/night bungalows) or want to travel without a fixed schedule, then it'll be best to arrange your own accommodation and flights, booking things as you go or a few days in advance during high season – then you can just travel where and when the mood takes you. The advantages of such a trip hinge on the freedom that you have to make and change your arrangements, as well as from the increased choice of lower-budget options available to you. The disadvantages mainly arise from the problems you may have when places are full, and you are forced to spend time and energy finding somewhere different to stay.

However, if you're planning to book your trip in advance, and you want to stay in more comfortable places (eg: US$100+ per night), then you will probably find it easier and cheaper to arrange your trip through a specialist tour operator.

A few tour operators offer scheduled trips to Zanzibar (ie: you join a group on fixed dates and with a pre-determined itinerary). However, most will work on a tailor-made basis (ie: they design a trip for you, around your dates and what you want to do). The main advantage of such trips is that using a specialist, you have their experience and knowledge of the island, and its various options, at your command. You should discuss your preferences with them in detail, and then a good tour operator will be able to plan a trip that will suit you well – discussing all the pros and cons of the various choices, and answering all of your questions along the way. Hence you're much more likely to get a trip that will really suit you well!

A very good secondary reason is if you're visiting top-end lodges and camps, then it will almost certainly be cheaper to book your trip through a good specialist than it would be to arrange the trip for yourself. And, of course, you pay one price upfront which includes most things (flights, transfers, accommodation, etc), so you simply sit back, relax and enjoy the trip, knowing you don't need to worry about the logistics of it.

The main disadvantage of using a tour operator is the fixed itinerary: you cannot change your plans on a whim (or at least not without a cost), say to spend more or less time at a particular place.

The best way to find a trip that suits your own interest and pocket is to phone a knowledgeable tour operator direct. Ask for their brochure, study their website, and then discuss your ideas with them.

TOURIST INFORMATION

Tanzania Tourist Board ☎+255 022 211 1244; e info@tanzaniatourism.go.tz; www.tanzaniatouristboard.com

Tanzania Trade Centre (UK) ☎+44 (0)207 758 8070; e info@tanzatrade.co.uk; www.tanzatrade.247logistics.co.uk

TOUR OPERATORS Finding a good tour operator for a trip to Zanzibar and the islands isn't always easy. Endless companies can get you there, but you will get the best trip if you work with one who really knows the area and has visited all of the islands and lodges.

Don't let anyone convince you that there are only half a dozen decent beach lodges here: it's simply not true. If the operator that you're speaking to doesn't know most of the places in this book and offer a wide choice to suit you – then use one that does.

Here we must admit a personal interest in the tour-operating business. Chris McIntyre runs the specialist UK tour operator **Expert Africa** (☎ 020 8232 977; e info@expertafrica.com; www.expertafrica.com; see ads, pages i & 68). We organise trips to Tanzania and these islands for travellers from all over the world. Booking your trip with us will always cost you the same as, or less than, booking the safari camps and beach lodges directly.

We advise our travellers from personal experience, and then allow them to make up their own minds. None of the team works on commission – so unlike many companies, we'll never push you into buying anything. Similarly, we have no financial ties to anywhere in Africa, so can offer truly independent advice on the full range of the choices available. Our only aim in advising you is to arrive at a trip that suits you perfectly.

Our trips are completely flexible, and they start from about US$900/£700 per person sharing for a week, including transfers, accommodation and most meals. We believe that Expert Africa has the best-value programme of high-quality lodges and hotels on Zanzibar and the islands – and the most extensive and comprehensive website. Chris will happily send you a detailed colour brochure and start to help you plan your trip. However, for a comparison, some of the specialist African tour operators who also feature Zanzibar and the islands include the companies listed below. If you're looking for a pure diving trip, perhaps including a live-aboard, then you should consider one of the UK's specialist diving operators (page 76).

In the UK

Aardvark Safaris Aspire Business Centre, Ordnance Rd, Tidworth, Hants SP9 7QD; ☎01980 849160; e mail@aardvarksafaris.com; www. aardvarksafaris.com. Small, reliable upmarket safari specialist to Africa & Madagascar.
Abercrombie & Kent St George's Hse, Ambrose St, Cheltenham, Glos GL50 3LG;

☎01242 547760; www.abercrombiekent.co.uk. Worldwide holidays for groups & individuals to upmarket destinations with upmarket price tags.
Acacia Expeditions 23a Craven Terrace, London W2 3QH; ☎020 7706 4700; www.acacia-africa. com. Adventure holidays & overland/camping safaris throughout Africa.

Africa Travel Resource Westcott Rd, Dorking, Surrey RH4 3NB; ☎ 01306 880770; www. africatravelresource.com. Web-based tour operator highlighting its own Zanzibar favourites.

Cazenove & Loyd Argon Mews, Fulham Broadway, London SW6 1BJ; ☎ 020 7384 2332; enquiries@cazloyd.com; www.cazloyd.com. Top-end tailor-made trip specialists to Africa, the Indian Ocean islands, Latin America & the Indian subcontinent.

Expert Africa 9/10 Upper Sq, Old Isleworth, Middx TW7 7BJ; ☎ 0203 405 6666; info@ expertafrica.com; www.expertafrica.com. Specialist team including Chris McIntyre, this book's co-author, offering a wide range of unbiased tailor-made choices.

Gane & Marshall ☎ 01822 600600; e info@ ganeandmarshall.com; www.ganeandmarshall. co.uk; see ad, page 104. Worldwide operator with a Zanzibar programme.

Hartley's Safaris The Old Chapel, Chapel Lane, Hackthorn, Lincs LN2 3PN; ☎ 01673 861600; info@ hartleysgroup.com; www.hartleys-safaris.co.uk. Long-established tailor-made holiday specialists to southern & East Africa & the Indian Ocean islands.

Imagine Africa Riverbank House, 1 Putney Bridge Approach, London SW6 3JD; ☎ 020 3797 4509; www.imaginetravel.com/imagine-africa. Small, motivated tour operator with wide coverage including Africa, Asia, India, Latin America & riding holidays.

Natural High 1 Chaldicott Barns, Semley, Shaftesbury, Dorset SP7 9AW; ☎ 01747 830950; e enquiries@naturalhighsafaris.com; www. naturalhighsafaris.com. Small tailor-made trip specialists to Africa, run by old African hands, focusing on Tanzania.

Original Travel ☎ 020 7978 7333; e ask@ originaltravel.co.uk; www.originaltravel.co.uk. Upmarket holidays to Africa, the Indian Ocean islands & Latin America.

Pulse Africa ☎ 01865 591097; info@pulseafrica. com; www.pulseafrica.com. Specialist operator featuring Egypt, Gabon & southern & East Africa, including Zanzibar.

Rainbow Tours 2 Waterhouse Square, 138–140 Holborn, London EC1N 2ST; ☎ 020 7666 1250; e info@rainbowtours.co.uk; www.rainbowtours. co.uk. Established specialists to South Africa & Madagascar, plus Latin America & the rest of Africa, including Tanzania's islands.

Safari Consultants ☎ 01787 888590; www. safari-consultants.co.uk. Long-established tailor-made trip specialists to southern & East Africa, & the Indian Ocean islands, with a very good knowledge.

Scott Dunn Riverbank House, 1 Putney Bridge Approach, London SW6 3JD; ☎ 020 3411 8456; www.scottdunn.com. Tailor-made programmes to Tanzania, Zanzibar and worldwide.

Steppes Travel 51 Castle St, Cirencester, Glos GL7 1QD; ☎ 01285 601776; e enquiry@ steppestravel.co.uk; www.steppestravel.co.uk. Upmarket tailor-made specialists to Latin America, Asia, Africa & the Indian Ocean islands.

Tribes Travel The Old Dairy, Wood Farm, Ipswich Rd, Otley, Suffolk IP6 9JW; ☎ 01473 890499; www.tribes.co.uk. Small, highly responsible operator, particularly strong on cultural trips, offering holidays worldwide on fair-trade principles.

Zanzibar Travel ☎ 01242 222027; e info@ zanzibartravel.co.uk; www.zanzibartravel.co.uk. Small tailor-made tour operator focused on Kenya, Tanzania & Tanzania's islands.

In France

Wild Spirit Safari ☎ +33 1 45 74 11 14; +33 1 47 49 91 50; e infos@wild-spirit-safari.com; www. wild-spirit-safari.com. Kenya & Tanzania specialists offering add-on trips to Zanzibar, with offices in Paris & Arusha (Tanzania).

Zanzibar Voyage ☎ +33 1 53 34 92 77; e contact@zanzibar-voyage.com; www.zanzibar-voyage.com. Paris-based Zanzibar specialist with a good range of hotels & Tanzanian safari add-ons.

In North America

Africa Adventure Company ☎ 954 491 8877/1 800 882 9453; e safari@AfricanAdventure.com; www.africa-adventure.com. Reputable Florida-based African operator with a good tailor-made safari business.

African Horizons ☎ 847 905 0296/1 877 256 1074 (toll free); e safariplans@gmail.com; www.africanhorizons.com. Small Illinois-based operator offering safari & some Zanzibar trips.

Expert Africa ☎ 1 800 242 2434; e info@ expertafrica.com; www.expertafrica.com. Californian office of the African specialist run by one of this book's authors, with an emphasis on high-end safaris with decadent beach add-ons.

In Australasia

Africa Safari Company ☎+61 2 9541 4199/1800 659 279 (toll free); e enquiries@africasafarico.com.au; www. africasafarico.com.au. Sydney-based tailor-made operator with trips to the Indian Ocean.

Classic Safari Company ☎+61 2 9327 0666/1300 130218 (toll free); e info@ classicsafaricompany.com.au; www. classicsafaricompany.com.au. Established operator based in Australia (NSW) offering tailor-made & specialist group trips across Africa.

Expert Africa ☎(New Zealand) +64 4 976 7585 or (Australia) + 1 800 995 397; e info@ expertafrica.com; www.expertafrica.com. Antipodean office of the African specialist which is run by one of this book's authors, focusing on tailor-made safaris & beach retreats.

Dive specialists

Dive Tours e info@divetours.co.uk; www.divetours.co.uk

Dive Worldwide ☎01962 302087; e reservations@diveworldwide.com; www.diveworldwide.com

RED TAPE

Most foreigners entering the country need a **visa** for Tanzania or a visitor's pass, depending on their own nationality. Whether you first arrive in Dar es Salaam or Zanzibar, you will be asked how long you want to stay. Up to three months is usually not a problem, and you'll receive a stamp in your passport. Currently, most visas can be obtained on arrival in Tanzania – although the airport queues can be long and they must be paid for in hard currency cash, so it's often best to get them in advance. A visa will often take several weeks to issue, so apply well in advance of your trip. The charge for issuing a single-entry (90-day) visa ranges from US$20 to US$100, depending on your nationality. At the time of writing, it is US$40 for UK citizens and US$100 for US passport holders, but do check the latest charges with your local embassy. Visa applications by researchers and journalists will need to be cleared by the Commission for Science and Technology (COSTECH) before being granted.

If you are planning to come via Nairobi or Mombasa, you may also need a visa or visitor's pass for Kenya. You may also need a return ticket out of Tanzania or Kenya, or be required to show that you have sufficient funds to cover your stay (for other currency matters, see page 89).

Tanzanian regulations, which also cover Zanzibar, forbid the import or export of Tanzanian shillings worth more than US$100 without a permit. Similarly, if you wish to import or export more than US$10,000 in foreign currency, you should also seek advice from your local Tanzanian embassy or high commission.

There is no longer any legal requirement for a yellow-fever vaccination certificate, unless you have come from a country where yellow fever is endemic. In theory you might also be asked for a cholera-exemption certificate; in practice we've never experienced this.

If you intend to hire a car or motorbike, then it's best to bring an International Driving Permit (IDP), which is easy to obtain from your national motoring association (in Britain contact the AA or RAC), and also a few spare passport-size photos. Entry regulations do change, so double-check the above with your nearest Tanzanian embassy, high commission or tourist office before you leave.

A full list of **embassies and consulates** in Tanzania (as well as Tanzanian embassies abroad) can be found on www.embassypages.com/tanzania. Consulates are generally unable to assist with visas or with simple problems such as illness or theft of belongings, but they will try to help in more serious cases such as wrongful arrest or imprisonment. If you lose your passport, you can get an Emergency Travel Document from the Ministry of the Interior in Zanzibar. This will allow you to leave Zanzibar and either go directly back to your own country, or reach Dar where most countries have representation and you should be able to get a replacement.

GETTING TO ZANZIBAR

BY AIR There are no direct scheduled flights to any of the islands, or even to Dar es Salaam, from the UK, Europe or USA. Consequently, most visitors fly first to Dar or Nairobi (via the Middle East or another African capital), and then take a regional service across the Zanzibar channel.

Scheduled flights Britain is one of the cheapest places in Europe to buy scheduled flights to Zanzibar, Dar, Mombasa or Nairobi. Specialist African agencies can also arrange regional flights to/from Zanzibar, and whole trips, including safari-and-beach combinations. The cheapest flights from London to Zanzibar start from around £600 in the low season, and rise to around £1,000 in the high season – plus an additional amount for airport and departure taxes and fuel surcharges, which is currently about £40. The relatively high taxes and surcharges are direct reflections of both the price of aviation fuel (oil) and also the increasingly high taxes levied by many governments on air travel.

For details on getting to Pemba and Mafia, see pages 340–2 and 375–7.

The best deals are usually found by buying a long time (9–12 months) in advance; tickets for travel in the near future almost always command a premium. To buy just flights, you should talk to the 'seat-only' travel agents. To find them, look through the advertisements in the travel supplements of the Sunday newspapers. Be prepared to shop around, and to find that many of the bargain fares offered in ads are unavailable when you phone.

To mainland Africa

✈ **British Airways** www.ba.com. Daily to Dar from London via Doha.

✈ **Emirates** www.emirates.com. From most major European cities, via Dubai, to Dar daily.

✈ **Ethiopian Airlines** www.ethiopianairlines. com. Daily flights to Dar via Addis, with connections to most European & several American cities.

✈ **Fly Dubai** www.flydubai. 3 weekly direct flights from Dubai to Dar (5hrs 40mins), with connections to Eastern Europe.

✈ **Kenya Airways** www.kenya-airways.com. 5 flights daily between Nairobi & Dar (1hr 15mins), with good connections to Europe & around Africa.

✈ **KLM** www.klm.com. From Amsterdam to Dar daily (10hrs 30mins), via KIA.

✈ **Qatar Airways** www.qatarairways.com. From Doha to Dar daily (6hrs), with good connections to most major European cities.

✈ **South African Airlines** www.flysaa.com. To Dar from Johannesburg twice daily (3hrs), with connections to most major European cities & the US.

To Zanzibar There are a handful of direct flights between Zanzibar and Nairobi with Kenya Airways, which are very convenient when combining Zanzibar with a safari itinerary in Kenya. There are also direct flights between Europe and the Middle East and Zanzibar, but currently all of the direct services from Europe are charter flights run by mass-market tour operators based in Italy, France and Spain.

4

From Dar es Salaam, there are a number of scheduled flights to Zanzibar, and although airfares vary slightly you should expect to pay around US$80 one-way.

✈ **Air Tanzania** www.airtanzania.co.tz. The national carrier operates 5 flights/week from Dar (Mon, Thu, Fri, Sat, Sun), In addition to their main office in Dar, they have a base at Dar Airport & within the Tembo House Hotel (page 131).

✈ **Coastal Aviation** www.coastal.co.tz. A reliable small operator with a good reputation & strong network of scheduled flights connecting Zanzibar daily to Dar, Arusha, Tanga, Pemba, Selous Game Reserve, Ruaha National Park, Mwanza, Serengeti, Ngorongoro & Manyara.

✈ **Fly Dubai** www.flydubai.com. 4 weekly flights from Dubai to Zanzibar (*5hrs 50mins*).

✈ **Kenya Airways** www.kenya-airways.com. 3 daily flights between Nairobi & Zanzibar (*1hr 40mins*).

✈ **Mango Airlines** www.flymango.com. Low-cost carrier flying twice weekly (*Tue & Sat; 3½hrs*) from Johannesburg to Zanzibar.

✈ **Oman Air** www.omanair.com. From Muscat to Zanzibar 8 times/week (*5hrs 25mins*) with a good network of international connections.

✈ **Precision Air** www.precisionairtz.com. This company has a few daily flights between Zanzibar & Dar, Arusha & Kilimanjaro, as well as connections to several other destinations in East Africa.

✈ **Qatar Airways** www.qatarairways.com. Daily flights from Doha to Zanzibar via Kilimanjaro (*6hrs*).

✈ **Turkish Airlines** www.turkishairlines.com. 3 weekly flights from Istanbul to Zanzibar, via Kilimanjaro (*9hrs*).

✈ **ZanAir** www.zanair.com. Based on Zanzibar, with offices in Zanzibar Town & at the airport. There are several daily flights from Dar to Zanzibar, & these usually tie in with the timetables of long-haul flights to/from Europe. There are also connecting flights to Selous, Arusha & Pemba.

Charter flights

For visitors from mainland Europe, another option to consider may be holiday charter flights. Charter flights from Europe (and particularly Italy, France and Spain) fly direct to Zanzibar, although currently there are none from the UK. These are usually sold only as part of a week or two-week package visiting one of Zanzibar's larger 'resorts'. However, if the planes are not full then tour operators will sometimes sell 'flight only' deals, which are good value.

Departure taxes

There is a departure tax in US dollars (currently US$40) when flying out of a mainland Tanzanian or Zanzibar airport on an international flight. This is payable in US dollars, either in cash or, increasingly, included in the cost of pre-paid airline tickets. If you do need to pay in cash, then travellers' cheques, other currencies and even Tanzanian shillings are not accepted for this; you must have US dollars. You can change whatever you have into US dollars at an airport bureau de change, but often the exchange rates given are very poor. However you carry your money, it's always worth carrying some dollars in cash to cover costs like this. For domestic flights, the airport tax is US$9.

Before you pay anything, especially if you've come to Zanzibar on an international return flight, check that the departure tax isn't already included in your ticket price (even better, check what taxes are included when you buy your ticket). If you are flying to Dar to pick up an international flight, you need only pay the international departure tax once (probably at Dar), although you will still pay the domestic departure tax for your flight out of Zanzibar.

Zanzibar airport

Located about 7km inland from the capital, **Abeid Karume International Airport** has not traditionally offered the best island welcome. However, after much neglect, recent years have seen Zanzibar's airport finally getting some attention and investment. In the first phase of work, 2010 saw the single runway extended and renovated to allow larger aircraft to land, paving the way for increased direct flights from long-haul destinations.

Arguably, a more significant development has been the addressing of dire terminal facilities. Funded by the Chinese, construction began on an additional, modern international terminal building some years ago, and the building has essentially been complete for some considerable time now; however, it remains unopened. Therefore, if you are arriving or leaving Zanzibar on a large international flight (as is the case with most European charters), you will probably still have to queue outside under the beating African sun – long, slow, muddled queues necessitate a cool hat, some water and lots of patience. When it does eventually open, though, the terminal should certainly improve the waiting times and general experience, and may even serve to ease pressure on the crumbling existing terminal for the Dar arrivals, though sadly any actual upgrades here seem unlikely. Be prepared for the worst until then though, especially if travelling with young children.

Dar es Salaam airport Dar's domestic terminal is a 5-minute drive from the international terminal. If you already have a connection to Zanzibar booked you will be met at the international terminal and transferred in a small minibus. If you haven't arranged anything, take a taxi for a few dollars and seek out the next flight with space. If you have arranged a tailor-made trip with a good tour company, then they will usually arrange for a member of staff to guide you through the check-in process and will often help you to circumvent any long queues for charter planes.

BY SEA Zanzibar's main port is at the heart of Zanzibar Town's waterfront, towards the northern end of Mizingani Road. Several large passenger ships run daily between Dar es Salaam, Zanzibar and Pemba, and – more rarely – to other points on the mainland. As the number of flights between Dar and Zanzibar has increased, and their airfares have become more competitive, the number of passenger boat services has declined.

Ships that are used by occasional tourists are listed below. In both Dar es Salaam and Zanzibar Town, all the ship booking offices are at the main passenger port, very near the city centre. Schedules and prices are chalked up on boards outside each office and you can easily buy tickets on the spot. Reservations are not essential but if at all possible you should buy a ticket in advance (a few hours to a couple of days) to make sure. Non-Tanzanians usually have to pay in US dollars and prices are quoted in this currency; Tanzanian residents enjoy cheaper rates, and can pay in Tanzanian shillings.

Note that all non-Tanzanian passengers leaving Dar must pay a port departure tax of US$5. The departure tax office is near the ship booking offices, and tickets are carefully checked before you board. Most of the shipping companies include this charge in the ticket price, so check very carefully whether this is included to avoid unnecessarily paying again at the port tax office.

In Zanzibar, in particular, many touts and hustlers hang around the boat ticket offices, encouraging you to go to one company instead of another. This can be time-consuming, irritating and disconcerting, so as an alternative you can buy your ticket through one of the reliable tour companies listed on pages 114–17. This will often save time and hassle, and it usually does not cost you any more money (the tour company gets a commission from the shipping company). Some tour companies do charge extra for this service, however, so check before you make arrangements. At Dar es Salaam, there are fewer hustlers, but still it's best to decline assistance politely.

Travellers at the port have also reported problems from over-zealous porters. If you drive into the port by taxi, you might want to ask your taxi driver to carry your bags for an extra tip, simply to avoid hassle.

Passenger ships and ferries
The main passenger ships used by visitors between Dar and Zanzibar are:

Azam Marine & Coastal Fast Ferries
022 212 3324; e info@azammarine.com; www.azammarine.com. These are the best of the commercial passenger boats with multiple ferries travelling between Zanzibar & Dar. Azam currently has 8 vessels, including fast catamarans (*Kilimanjaro, II, III, IV*) & RIB speedboats. The fastest Dar–Zanzibar crossings are reasonably comfortable & the open-top deck allows for some lovely views on the final approach to Stone Town. Ferries depart Dar at 07.00, 09.30, 12.30 & 15.45 daily (*40mins*). There is also a twice-weekly service (*Wed & Sat; 3hrs*) from Zanzibar to Pemba, departing at 07.00. In Zanzibar Town, the booking office is on the right at the far end of the parade between the port gates & the water. *One-way fares: Dar–Zanzibar US$35/60pp (economy/Royal class); Zanzibar–Pemba US$35/45pp (economy/first class); children US$10 reduction in economy only.*

MV Flying Horse 022 212 4507 (Dar); m 0784 472497/606177 (Zanzibar); e asc@raha. com. This large catamaran, run by the African Shipping Corporation, has a capacity of more than 400 passengers. The daily daytime service from Dar

to Zanzibar departs at 12.30 (*3hrs*), & the return trip from Zanzibar departs at 21.00, but does not arrive in Dar until 06.00 the following day. The boat runs deliberately slowly, stopping at sea for a time on this overnight journey so passengers don't have to disembark in the middle of the night. The seating areas have AC & a video is usually shown. The ship also has a small bar & restaurant. It's possible to travel on the deck, which has a few seats & an awning to keep off the sun, but little else. Some travellers view this as a very pleasant way to travel, especially when leaving Zanzibar port at sunset, & for budget travellers it is a good way to save on a night's accommodation. There have been some claims of a lack of reliability on *Flying Horse* so best to check locally with a reputable your operator before booking. In Zanzibar Town, the booking office is the first on the left inside the port gates. *One-way fare: US$25pp.*

Sea Star Services 022 213 9996. This large catamaran is also among the most efficient services between Dar & Zanzibar, with one daily departure (*2hrs*). *One-way fares: first class US$35pp; second class US$45pp.*

Traditional dhows
Dhows do operate between Dar es Salaam, Zanzibar and the ports along the Swahili coast, but – following a spate of incidents in which tourists drowned – the government imposed strict safety standards on

2011 SPICE ISLANDER FERRY DISASTER

On 10 September 2011, the MV *Spice Islander I*, a passenger and cargo ferry carrying around 3,500 people and goods from Zanzibar Town to Pemba, capsized and sank off the northern coast of Zanzibar. The carrying capacity of the ferry was 690, including crew, yet officially 2,967 people were reported missing or dead, 203 bodies were recovered from the sea and 619 passengers, many injured, were rescued. The ferry was woefully overloaded, and the consequences utterly tragic. The harrowing details recounted by rescue teams, made up of dive operators and fast ferries, are horrific: dead bodies afloat, desperate and drowning people clawing at crammed dive boats, and picturesque beaches littered with body bags and the injured. An official investigation into the sinking took place, and further accidents have happened since, so whether ferry operators genuinely address the issues of poor maintenance and overloading remains to be seen. What is abundantly clear though, is the need to be highly cautious in choosing to travel by local ferry. If it looks too busy – do not board the boat!

any dhows wanting to carry tourists. They now need to have radios, lifejackets and various other fairly standard pieces of marine safety equipment – which are notably lacking from most dhows!

We advise strongly against travelling illegally on any dhow unless the captain is very clearly aware of these regulations, and working within them. Not only is it illegal, but many 'normal' working dhows are dangerously overloaded, and quite frightening and unpleasant vessels in which to cross a busy stretch of open ocean.

Departure taxes Even ship passengers cannot escape departure taxes! Tourists leaving by boat from Zanzibar are charged a US$5 'seaport departure service charge'. This also is payable in dollars only, but many of the ship companies include this tax in the ticket price. Check this carefully to avoid paying twice.

HEALTH *with Dr Felicity Nicholson*

People new to exotic travel often worry about tropical diseases, but it is accidents that are most likely to carry you off. Road accidents are very common in many parts of Zanzibar so be aware and do what you can to reduce risks: try to travel during daylight hours, always wear a seatbelt and refuse to be driven by anyone who has been drinking. Listen to local advice about any areas where crime is an issue.

When travelling around Zanzibar or East Africa, the different climatic and social conditions mean visitors are exposed to diseases not normally encountered at home. Although you will have received all the vaccinations recommended below, this does not mean you will be free of all illness during your travels: certain precautions still have to be taken. You should read a good book on travel medicine (page 427) and be aware of the causes, symptoms and treatments of the more serious diseases. But don't let these colourful descriptions put you off – with a little care and attention most of these illnesses can be avoided.

If you do need medical attention, there are several hospitals and medical centres in Zanzibar Town, and the larger and more upmarket hotels have on-call European doctors who can be called out for a fee. Pharmacies in Zanzibar Town have a basic range of medicines, but specific brands are often unavailable, so bring with you all that you will need.

PREPARATIONS Sensible preparation will go a long way to ensuring your trip goes smoothly. Particularly for first-time visitors to Africa, this includes a visit to a travel clinic to discuss matters such as vaccinations and malaria prevention. A list of recommended travel clinic websites worldwide is available at www. itsm.org, and other useful websites for prospective travellers include www. travelhealthpro.org.uk and www.netdoctor.co.uk/travel. The Bradt website now carries a health section online (*www.bradtguides.com/africahealth*) to help travellers prepare for their African trip, elaborating on most points raised below, but the following summary points are worth emphasising:

- Don't travel without comprehensive medical **travel insurance** that will fly you home in an emergency.
- Make sure all your **immunisations** are up to date. Officially, proof of vaccination against yellow fever is only needed for entry into Zanzibar if you are coming from another yellow fever endemic area, but the Zanzibari authorities have been known to request proof of vaccination for visitors coming from Tanzania – which effectively incorporates most visitors. The decision to vaccinate or not is a complex one as the actual risk of yellow fever in Tanzania, including Zanzibar, is considered to be very low indeed. Having the vaccine, assuming that there were no contraindications, would only be warranted if you were spending time in another country where there is active disease. If the vaccine is not suitable for you and you are not at risk of disease then most health-care professionals would issue an exemption certificate instead. It's also reckless to travel in the tropics without being up to date on tetanus, polio and diphtheria (now given as an all-in-one vaccine, Revaxis) and hepatitis A. Immunisation against, typhoid, hepatitis B and rabies may also be recommended.
- The biggest health threat is **malaria**. There is no vaccine against this mosquito-borne disease, but a variety of preventative drugs is available, including mefloquine, atovaquone/proguanil (Malarone) and the antibiotic doxycycline. The most suitable choice of drug varies depending on the individual and the country they are visiting, so visit your GP or a travel clinic for medical advice. If you will be spending a long time in Africa, and expect to visit remote areas, be aware that no preventative drug is 100% effective, so carry a cure too. It is also worth noting that no homeopathic prophylactic for malaria exists, nor can any traveller acquire effective resistance to malaria. Those who don't make use of preventative drugs risk their life in a manner that is both foolish and unnecessary.
- Though advised for everyone, a **pre-exposure rabies vaccination**, involving three doses taken over a minimum of 21 days, is particularly important if you intend to have contact with animals, or are likely to be 24 hours away from medical help.
- Anybody travelling away from major centres should carry a **personal first-aid kit**. Contents might include a good drying antiseptic (eg: iodine or potassium permanganate), plasters, suncream, insect repellent, aspirin or paracetamol, antifungal cream (eg: Canesten), ciprofloxacin or norfloxacin (for severe diarrhoea), antibiotic eye drops, tweezers, a digital thermometer and a needle-and-syringe kit with accompanying letter from health-care professional.
- Bring any **drugs or devices relating to known medical conditions** with you. That applies both to those who are on medication prior to departure, and those who are, for instance, allergic to bee stings, or are prone to attacks of asthma.
- Prolonged immobility on long-haul flights can result in **deep-vein thrombosis** (DVT), which can be dangerous if the clot travels to the lungs to cause pulmonary embolus (see box, page 85).

COMMON MEDICAL PROBLEMS

Malaria Since no malaria prophylactic is 100% effective, it makes sense to take all reasonable precautions against being bitten by the nocturnal *Anopheles* mosquitoes that transmit the disease (see box, page 84). Malaria usually manifests within two weeks of transmission, (though it can be as short as seven days) but it can take months, which means that short-stay visitors are most likely to experience symptoms after they return home. These typically include a rapid rise in temperature (over 38°C), and any combination of a headache, flu-like aches and pains, a general sense of disorientation, and possibly even nausea and diarrhoea. The earlier malaria is detected, the better it usually responds to treatment. So if you display possible symptoms, *get to a doctor or clinic immediately*. A simple test, available at even the most rural clinic in Africa, is usually adequate to determine whether you have malaria. And while experts differ on the question of self-diagnosis and self-treatment, the reality is that if you think you have malaria and are not within easy reach of a doctor, it would be wisest to start treatment.

Travellers' diarrhoea At least half of those travelling to the tropics/developing world will experience a bout of travellers' diarrhoea during their trip; the newer you are to exotic travel, the more likely you will be to suffer. By taking precautions against travellers' diarrhoea you will also avoid typhoid, paratyphoid, cholera, hepatitis, dysentery, worms, etc. Travellers' diarrhoea and the other faecal-oral diseases come from getting other peoples' faeces in your mouth. This most often happens from cooks not washing their hands after a trip to the toilet, but even if the restaurant cook does not understand basic hygiene you will be safe if your food has been properly cooked and arrives piping hot. The most important prevention strategy is to wash your hands before eating anything. The maxim to remind you what you can safely eat is:

PEEL IT, BOIL IT, COOK IT OR FORGET IT.

This means that fruit you have washed and peeled yourself, and hot foods, should be safe but raw foods, cold cooked foods, salads, fruit salads which have been prepared by others, ice cream and ice are all risky, as are foods kept lukewarm in restaurant or hotel buffets. Self-service or buffet meals are safest to eat when the food is hot and freshly cooked – for example, a late buffet lunch eaten in the mid-afternoon will have been sitting around a long while.

Rabies This deadly disease can be carried by any mammal and is usually transmitted to humans via a bite or deep scratch. Beware village dogs and habituated monkeys, but assume that *any* mammal that bites or scratches you (or even licks your skin) might be rabid. First, scrub the wound with soap under a running tap, or while pouring water from a jug, then pour on a strong iodine or alcohol solution, which will guard against infections and might reduce the risk of the rabies virus entering the body. Whether or not you underwent pre-exposure vaccination, it is vital to obtain post-exposure prophylaxis as soon as possible after the incident. However, if you have had the vaccine before exposure treatment is very much easier. It removes the need for a human blood product (Rabies Immunoglobulin (RIG)) which is not pleasant to have, expensive and often hard to find. Death from rabies is probably one of the worst ways to go, and once you show symptoms it is too late to do anything – the mortality rate is 100%.

The *Anopheles* mosquitoes that spread malaria are active at dusk and after dark. Most bites can thus be avoided by covering up at night. This means donning a long-sleeved shirt, trousers and socks from around 30 minutes before dusk until you retire to bed, and applying a DEET-based insect repellent (around 50% DEET) to any exposed flesh. It is best to sleep under a net, or in an air-conditioned room, though burning a mosquito coil and/or sleeping under a fan will also reduce (though not entirely eliminate) bites. Travel clinics usually sell a good range of nets and repellents, as well as Permethrin treatment kits, which will render even the tattiest net a lot more protective, and helps prevent mosquitoes from biting through a net when you roll against it. These measures will also do much to reduce exposure to other nocturnal biters. Bear in mind, too, that most flying insects are attracted to light: leaving a lamp standing near a tent opening or a light on in a poorly screened hotel room will greatly increase the insect presence in your sleeping quarters.

It is also advisable to think about avoiding bites when walking in the countryside by day, especially in wetland habitats, which often teem with diurnal mosquitoes. Wear a long loose shirt and trousers, preferably 100% cotton, as well as proper walking or hiking shoes with heavy socks (the ankle is particularly vulnerable to bites), and apply a DEET-based insect repellent to any exposed skin.

Bilharzia Also known as schistosomiasis, bilharzia is an unpleasant parasitic disease transmitted by freshwater snails most often associated with reedy shores where there is lots of water weed. It cannot be caught in hotel swimming pools, but should be assumed to be present in any freshwater river, pond, lake or similar habitat, probably even those advertised as 'bilharzia free'. The riskiest shores will be within 200m of villages or other places where infected people use water, wash clothes, etc. Ideally, however, you should avoid swimming in any fresh water other than an artificial pool. If you do swim, you'll reduce the risk by applying DEET insect repellent first, staying in the water for under ten minutes, and drying off vigorously with a towel. Bilharzia is often asymptomatic in its early stages, but some people experience an intense immune reaction, including fever, cough, abdominal pain and an itching rash, around four to six weeks after infection. Later symptoms vary but often include a general feeling of tiredness and lethargy. Bilharzia is difficult to diagnose, but it can be tested for at specialist travel clinics, ideally at least six weeks after likely exposure. Fortunately, it is easy to treat at present.

HIV/AIDS Rates of HIV/AIDS infection are high in most parts of Africa, and other sexually transmitted diseases are rife. Condoms (or femidoms) greatly reduce the risk of transmission.

Tick bites Ticks in Africa are not the rampant disease transmitters that they are in the Americas, but they may spread tickbite fever along with a few dangerous rarities. They should ideally be removed complete as soon as possible to reduce the chance of infection. The best way to do this is to grasp the tick with your finger nails as close to your body as possible, and pull it away steadily and firmly at right angles to your skin (do not jerk or twist it). If possible douse the wound with alcohol (any spirit will do) or iodine. If you are travelling with small children, remember to check their heads, and particularly behind the ears, for ticks. Spreading redness around the bite and/or fever and/or aching joints after a tick bite imply that you have an infection that requires antibiotic treatment, so seek advice.

Skin infections Any mosquito bite or small nick is an opportunity for a skin infection in warm humid climates, so clean and cover the slightest wound in a good drying antiseptic such as dilute iodine, potassium permanganate or crystal (or gentian) violet. Prickly heat, most likely to be contracted at the humid coast, is a fine pimply rash that can be alleviated by cool showers, dabbing (not rubbing) dry and talc, and sleeping naked under a fan or in an air-conditioned room. Fungal

LONG-HAUL FLIGHTS, CLOTS AND DVT   *Dr Felicity Nicholson*

Any prolonged immobility, including travel by land or air, can result in deep-vein thrombosis (DVT) with the risk of embolus to the lungs. Certain factors can increase the risk and these include:

- History of DVT or pulmonary embolism
- Recent surgery to pelvic region or legs
- Cancer
- Stroke
- Heart disease
- Inherited tendency to clot (thrombophilia)
- Obesity
- Pregnancy
- Hormone therapy
- Older age
- Being over 6 foot or under 5 foot

A deep-vein thrombosis causes painful swelling and redness of the calf or sometimes the thigh. It is only dangerous if a clot travels to the lungs (pulmonary embolus). Symptoms of a pulmonary embolus (PE) – which commonly start three to ten days after a long flight – include chest pain, shortness of breath, and sometimes coughing up small amounts of blood. Anyone who thinks that they might have a DVT needs to see a doctor immediately.

PREVENTION OF DVT
- Wear loose comfortable clothing
- Do anti-DVT exercises and move around when possible
- Drink plenty of fluids during the flight
- Avoid taking sleeping pills unless you are able to lie flat
- Avoid excessive tea, coffee and alcohol
- Consider wearing flight socks or support stockings (*www.leghealthwarehouse.com*)

If you think you are at increased risk of a clot, ask your doctor if it is safe to travel.

Planning and Preparation   HEALTH

4

infections also get a hold easily in hot moist climates, so wear 100% cotton socks and underwear and shower frequently.

Sunstroke and dehydration Heatstroke, heat exhaustion and sunburn are often problems for travellers to Zanzibar, despite being easy to prevent. To avoid them, you need to remember that your body is under stress and make allowances for it. First, take things gently; you are on holiday, after all. Next, keep your fluid and salt levels high: lots of water and soft drinks, but go easy on the caffeine and alcohol. Third, dress to keep cool with loose-fitting, thin garments – preferably of cotton, linen or silk. Finally, beware of the sun. Hats and long-sleeved shirts are essential. If you must expose your skin to the sun, then use sunblocks and high-factor sunscreens (the sun is so strong that you will still get a tan). Be especially careful of exposure in the middle of the day and of sun reflected off water, and wear a T-shirt and lots of waterproof suncream (at least SPF25) when swimming. The glare and the dust can be hard on the eyes, too, so bring UV-protection sunglasses and, perhaps, a soothing eyebath.

UNUSUAL MEDICAL PROBLEMS
Snake and other bites Snakes are very secretive and bites are a genuine rarity, but certain spiders and scorpions can also deliver nasty bites. In all cases, the risk is minimised by wearing closed shoes and trousers when walking in the bush, and watching where you put your hands and feet, especially in rocky areas or when gathering firewood. Only a small fraction of snakebites deliver enough venom to be life-threatening, but it is important to keep the victim calm and inactive, and to seek urgent medical attention.

Insect-borne diseases Although malaria is the insect-borne disease that attracts the most attention in Africa, and rightly so, there are others, most too uncommon to be a significant concern to short-stay travellers. These include dengue fever and other arboviruses (spread by diurnal mosquitoes), sleeping sickness (tsetse flies), and river blindness (blackflies). Bearing this in mind, however, it is clearly sensible, and makes for a more pleasant trip, to avoid insect bites as far as possible (see box on page 84). Two nasty (though ultimately relatively harmless) flesh-eating insects associated with tropical Africa are *tumbu* or *putsi* flies, which lay eggs, often on drying laundry, that hatch and bury themselves under the skin when they come into contact with humans, and jiggers, which latch on to bare feet and set up home, usually at the side of a toenail, where they cause a painful boil-like swelling. Drying laundry indoors and wearing shoes are the best way to deter this pair of flesh-eaters. Symptoms and treatment of all these afflictions are described in greater detail on Bradt's website (*www.bradtguides.com/africahealth*).

CRIME AND SAFETY

As in most countries, crime in these islands is gradually on the increase. Similarly, problems tend to occur with greater frequency in the cities and tourist heartlands than in the rural areas. Perhaps inevitably, the juxtaposition of relatively wealthy tourists and a high density of relatively poor local people causes envy and leads to the occasional crime.

THEFT Zanzibar Town is notorious for opportunist pickpockets, and occasionally tourists do have bags and cameras snatched while walking around the narrow streets of Stone Town (for more specific details on places to be careful, see box, page 127). There have also been robberies on some of the beaches around Zanzibar Town; it is better not to go there alone, especially at night. The authors have yet to hear of any crime problems on Mafia Island – but this is a small, rural island with a low population density.

You can reduce the chances of having anything stolen by not displaying your wealth. Don't bring valuable jewellery to these islands; leave it at home. Keep your valuables secure, out of sight and preferably back in the safe at your hotel. Keep most of your money there too, and do not peel off notes from a huge wad for every small purchase. Wandering around the town with a camera casually slung over your shoulder or a state-of-the-art MP3 player is insensitive and simply asking for trouble. A simple, dull-looking bag is much safer than something smart or fashionable.

Theft from hotel rooms is unusual, though not unheard of. Most hotels have safes, where valuables can be stored, although reports of stuff disappearing from the safes of more basic budget hotels are not unknown (for more details, see box, page 127).

In contrast to the comments above, there have in past years been some very serious incidents indeed. On a few occasions, an organised, armed gang has attacked and robbed a remote beach lodge or resort. These incidents are thankfully rare – but they can happen. In response, some of the more upmarket resorts now have armed security teams or armed policemen patrolling at night. Whilst these cannot guarantee the safety of visitors, it does give some reassurance that such serious crime is being tackled by the Zanzibari police.

TERRORISM Islamic terrorist groups are present in East Africa, and to a varying degree, pose a threat across the entire region. In Zanzibar specifically, in 2013, there were two explosions in Zanzibar Town: one near Mercury's and another at the Anglican cathedral. There was also a bomb attack near a mosque in Stone Town in June 2014, which killed one person and injured several others.

With the rise of global terrorism, some travellers have looked nervously towards East Africa, citing Islamic influences, porous borders, long coastlines and a relative availability of arms as reasons to be wary of terrorism there.

The truth is that there are large Islamic communities on the islands, especially on Pemba and Zanzibar. These communities are largely very peaceful, though they probably have their extremist elements, very much like the extremists who live in communities in the UK, Europe and the USA. So whilst Zanzibar (and, to a lesser extent, Pemba) has many factors that may cause initial concern, at the time of writing the British Foreign and Commonwealth Office do not cite the risk from terrorism as higher than in Western Europe or the USA.

WHAT TO TAKE

CLOTHING You are unlikely to experience great extremes of temperature on Zanzibar, although days can be very warm and some nights chilly. Clothing should be light and loose-fitting for daytime, and you may need something slightly more substantial for evenings. Even in the dry seasons, a rain jacket is a good idea (though you may not need it). Umbrellas (should you need them) are available locally. You'll need a good pair of shoes for sightseeing, and a pair of sandals for relaxing. A hat to keep off sun and rain completes the outfit.

Plastic beach shoes, rafting sandals or something similar to avoid the spiky sea urchins are useful for walking out into the sea across old coral beds. Remember, though, never to tread on live coral. In a few seconds you can break off chunks that will take several decades to re-grow.

Dress codes are very relaxed, even in the smartest hotels and restaurants, so you won't need black tie or a ball gown. However, it's important to be sensitive towards local customs. When wandering around towns and villages you should be aware of local Muslim sensibilities: dress modestly and do not expose too much bare flesh. Remember that a woman walking around a Zanzibar town with bare shoulders and a short skirt, or a man without a shirt, is as unacceptable as someone parading naked on your local high street.

Of course, tourists don't need to don robes, veils and turbans, but around town it is important for women to have knees and shoulders covered. This is recommended for men, too. Therefore, for men and women, long trousers are better than shorts, although baggy surf-shorts or culottes are acceptable, and long-sleeved shirts and blouses are better than vests and skimpy T-shirts. For the beach, normal swimming gear is fine, although going into local fishing villages in briefs or bikinis shows a complete lack of sensitivity.

EQUIPMENT If you're planning to base yourself in one place during your stay, or if your transfers are pre-arranged, then carrying your stuff in a suitcase or kitbag is absolutely fine. However, if you're likely to have to carry your own luggage, particularly if you're travelling around and visiting the islands as part of a longer trip, then it is usually easier to carry all your clothing and equipment in a rucksack.

Most rucksacks have internal frames, whilst some turn neatly into travel bags, with a zipped flap to enclose the straps and waist-belt. Both are fine, although if the straps can be zipped away then they are less likely to be damaged on bus roof-racks or airport carousels.

If you're staying in the cheaper hotels, sheets are not always very clean, so a light sheet sleeping bag is useful. It's unlikely you'll need a full sleeping bag; if you do hit the islands in a cold snap, most smaller hotels provide blankets. The better hotels and lodges have good facilities including towels and clean bed linen.

To avoid getting malaria, it is important to protect yourself from mosquitoes. Most hotels provide nets over the beds, but in the smaller cheaper hotels these are often in bad condition and riddled with holes. Either take your own **mosquito net** (visit a good camping shop before you travel), or take a needle and cotton to make running repairs. For added protection, bring a roll-on **insect repellent** and use mosquito coils (available locally) in your room at night. Remember: it takes only one mosquito to give you malaria.

Free-camping, outside an organised campsite, is illegal on the islands and there are no official campsites, so it is not worth bringing a tent. Fortunately, basic beach hotels and hostels can be very cheap.

All but the cheapest hotels provide towels. Personal items to bring include **toiletries, lipsalve, sun protection cream** and **sunglasses**. Soap, toothpaste and some medicines can be bought locally if you run out. Suncream is available in some hotel shops, but it's expensive, so it's advisable to bring all you need. Equally, condoms can be extremely difficult to buy on the islands, so bring your own supply if you are likely to need them. You'll almost certainly bring a **camera**; make sure you bring spare batteries and memory cards.

A **first-aid and medical kit** is recommended (page 82), but what you need depends on your type of holiday, the amount of travel, and how far you plan to get off the beaten track. Whatever, you should include the basics.

If you're staying in the smaller, cheaper hotels, the following items will be useful: a **torch**, as power cuts are frequent and some places only have power for a few hours at night; a **pocket multi-tool** for making minor repairs or preparing fresh fruit; a **water bottle and purification tables** if you're heading to more remote areas; and a **universal sink plug**, as these are more often than not missing in basic hotels.

Finally, if you're keen on snorkelling, it is worth taking your own **mask, snorkel and fins**. Hiring these is usually easy and cheap, but hired kit from all but the best operators can fit poorly, spoiling the whole experience.

MONEY AND BANKING

CURRENCY Tanzania's unit of currency, used throughout these islands, is the Tanzania shilling (TSh). However, as non-Tanzanians have to pay for some items, such as flights, ferry tickets and hotels, in foreign currency, the US dollar has effectively become an unofficial second currency. The prices of many other items, such as tours or rental cars, are also often quoted in US dollars, although these may be paid in TSh at the current rate. All of the watersports and dive operators currently quote prices in US dollars, though this trend has been known to switch to euros as they strengthen.

Prices in TSh, and exchange rates against hard currencies, are likely to vary considerably in the future, but prices in US dollars tend to remain more constant. As much as is possible, we have tried to quote in US dollars in this book to allow for sensible cross-comparisons. At the time of going to press, the rate of exchange was as follows: £1 = TSh 2,779; US$1 = TSh 2,226; €1 = TSh 2,371. For visitors to the islands, the most convenient currency to use is US dollars. Ideally, it should be carried in cash, in a mix of high and low denominations; this is handy as it can be used almost anywhere

CHANGING MONEY On the islands, the easiest place to change money is Zanzibar Town, where there are banks and many bureaux de change. It is also possible to change money in Chake Chake on Pemba. Around Zanzibar Island, money can also

KANGAS AND KIKOIS

A *kanga*, the traditional coloured wrap worn by local women, makes an ideal souvenir. You can wear it, use it as a beach mat on the coast or a sheet to cover bare mattresses if you're in cheap hotels, and then hang it on your wall, throw it over your sofa or turn it into cushion covers when you get home. A kanga normally comes as a large rectangle which the women then cut into two pieces, each about a metre square. One half is worn as a wrapover skirt and the other is worn as a headscarf (a knot is usually tied in one corner and used for keeping money). Prices for a kanga, from the market or a local cloth shop, start at about US$5.

On Zanzibar and elsewhere on the coast, men traditionally wear a *kikoi*, a wraparound 'kilt' of woven cotton, usually striped and thicker than a kanga. Once again, a kikoi also has many practical travel uses before you take it home to use as a seat cover. Prices start at US$8.

If you want to combine African and Western clothing, you could even have a local tailor make up a shirt or pair of baggy shorts from a kikoi. For more ideas see the excellent little book *101 Uses for a Kanga*, by David Bygott, available in Zanzibar's bookshops.

be changed at most large and medium-sized hotels – although often the rates are poor. Several tour companies are also licensed to change money. For those travelling via Dar es Salaam Airport, there are a couple of convenient bureaux de change just outside the international terminal; the domestic terminal has no change facility.

Both banks and bureaux de change offer tourists free-floating market rates; there is no black market in currency in Tanzania. Generally, the private bureaux offer better rates for cash, particularly for large denomination bills, and also tend to have a faster service than banks. Both accept most foreign currencies, but staff are most familiar with US dollars and euros, and these get relatively better rates than other currencies.

Try not to change more than you will need into Tanzanian shillings (TSh); it can be difficult to get a good rate when changing this back. When calculating the amount of money you need to change into TSh, remember that under Tanzanian law, visitors from overseas must pay for many items, such as the larger hotels, car hire and air tickets, in foreign currency (usually US dollars). Most other large purchases, like boat trips and costly souvenirs, can also be paid for with US dollars.

CREDIT CARDS You can use your credit card (or debit card) at most larger souvenir shops, travel agents, and better hotels and lodges (even just to settle the bill for 'extras'); however, you may be charged as much as a 10–15% handling fee. This will seem unreasonable, until you talk to owners of businesses about their difficulties in dealing with the banks in Zanzibar, then you'll understand!

There are a scattering of ATMs in Stone Town, and we'd be surprised if these don't gradually multiply with time. Generally situated at banks or larger hotels, with the machines themselves in a secure ante-room, they all have a permanent security guard on the door and tend to operate a one in/one out policy to card holders.

In theory, drawing cash may also be possible through larger hotels or tour companies, but again, expect high commissions (more information on using credit cards is given on page 93).

COSTS AND BUDGETING The cost of a visit to the islands depends very much on your standard of travel. Zanzibar Town has the most choice and, in many ways, the lowest prices for the quality that you get.

At the bottom end, the very cheapest hotels cost between US$10 and US$30 per person per night and will be extremely basic. If you have meals in local eating-houses and small restaurants (snacks US$3; curry US$6; grilled seafood US$4–12; pizza US$6–8), supplemented by lunches of fruit and bread from the market, plus tea or soft drinks (US$1–3) or the occasional alcoholic sundowner (US$3–6), then your food and drink budget will be around US$15–20 a day. Hotels in the expansive middle range cost between about US$75–150 for a double, and meals in smarter restaurants cost the equivalent of around US$15 per person. Towards the top of the range, good-quality hotels are US$150–300 for a double, with meals in the best establishments from around US$25 per person.

Outside Zanzibar Town, most places are beach lodges. The cheapest of these, supplying little more than a (sometimes clean) room, will again be around US$20–30 per person per night. Pay between about US$40–75 per person per night and you can find clean and pleasant places by the dozen. US$75–150 per person per night buys you somewhere smart – usually places that need booking in advance; whilst you can pay up to US$1,250 per person sharing for the exclusive delights of Mnemba – but then this is one of Africa's top lodges.

You also need to take into account the costs of getting around. Buses are very cheap, costing the equivalent of only a few dollars to cross the island.

For independent travel, you can hire bicycles for around US$5 per day, motor-scooters for US$25 or cars from around US$40.

Organised tours of the spice plantations, Jozani Forest or boat trips out to the smaller islands start from about US$25 per person for a small group. If you want a vehicle or boat to yourself, this can go up to about US$75 for a day's outing. Snorkelling trips are around US$30 whilst a single dive to local reefs starts at US$35; both activities command a supplement if conducted on the reefs off Mnemba Island, which ranges from US$15–60. PADI Open Water dive certification courses range from US$450–700; centres are now obliged to sell the teaching material (around US$50) for these courses, but this is not always included in the price. Game-fishing trips are notoriously costly with a half-day coming in at around US$500. Entry to most of the historical sites and ruins on the island is free, as is lying on the beach!

ACCOMMODATION

For visitors to Zanzibar, the accommodation and food available are amongst the most important aspects of a visit. This section describes briefly what you can expect, but these things do change with time and you should be ready for this.

Aside from style, throughout the guide, the accommodation listings have been subdivided into six price brackets to help you choose something best suited to your budget. The price code is based on the nightly cost of a standard double room.

Hotels offering full-board (FB) or all-inclusive (AI) stays have details of their rates at the time of going to print, to help with budget planning.

HOTELS AND GUESTHOUSES

Zanzibar Town At the upper end of the range, Zanzibar Town had only one large, international-standard hotel for decades: the Serena Inn, part of a chain of other properties in Tanzania and Kenya. Double rooms cost around US$265. In 2013, Hilton opened in this bracket and even more recently, the Park Hyatt Zanzibar raised the bar yet higher. There is little else in Stone Town of the same quality and size, although several grand old buildings have been renovated and opened as quite lovely, smaller boutique hotels. They combine good quality with local flavour and often some style, although they lack some of the extensive facilities of the Serena. Prices range from US$125–300 for a double room.

Zanzibar Town has a wide choice of mid-range hotels, costing between US$50 and US$120 for a double, where rooms are en suite, clean and comfortable, perhaps with air conditioning at the upper end of the scale.

At the lower end of the price range there are many small hotels and guesthouses which offer a basic room for US$10–20 per person. Rooms may not be spotless, and facilities are likely to be shared, but these are generally popular with budget travellers and it's worth looking around for the better places. All hotels in Zanzibar include breakfast in the room price, unless otherwise stated.

Zanzibar Island Around Zanzibar Island, away from Zanzibar Town, nearly all of the hotels and guesthouses are built on, or very near, idyllic tropical beaches, complete with palm trees, white sand and warm blue waters. Some travellers come here for a couple of days, just to relax; others linger for weeks. Places to stay range from large hotels and resorts with many facilities to small but comfortable lodges and bungalows to very basic local-style guesthouses. More recently, this range includes private villa rentals.

HOTEL PRICE CODES

Rates for a standard double room are:

Exclusive	♕	US$300+
Luxury	$$$$$	US$200–300
Upmarket	$$$$	US$100–200
Mid range	$$$	US$50–100
Budget	$$	US$25–50
Shoestring	$	< US$25

At the top end are a dozen or so fairly stylish, **smaller beach lodges** which cater to individual visitors, usually on pre-arranged trips. Typically they'll have between about ten and 30 rooms. Staying here you can expect good food, very comfortable accommodation and a fairly exclusive atmosphere. Expect to pay around US$75–250 per person per night for somewhere smart – or considerably more in the case of Mnemba.

Next there are a number of **large beach resorts**, with upwards of 50 rooms each. These are generally used by pre-booked package tourists who fly in and spend most or all of their time on Zanzibar within the resort. Some focus so clearly on packages bought overseas (typically in Italy) that their rates are in euros, and they will not even accept 'walk-in' guests.

At the **lower end of the market**, US$10–60 will give you a night at one of a diverse range of places. These have little in common except that they normally deal largely with walk-in guests. At the better places, reservations are recommended during the busy season. There's a huge choice, ranging from places that are aspiring to be the next exclusive beach lodge, down to basic bungalows beside a beach where even if you did succeed in reserving a room (if they had a phone, and if it was working), it would be a very unusual thing to do.

As the number of tourists visiting Zanzibar continues to grow, the number of places on Zanzibar's coast – and the range of places – increases also. Expect to find more new places when you arrive, and expect a few old places to have disappeared or been renamed.

Pemba and Mafia Visitor numbers to Pemba and Mafia are absolutely minuscule compared with Zanzibar; these islands therefore offer far less choice. Mafia's clutch of small beach lodges represents particularly good value if you value a fairly high degree of exclusivity without wanting anything that is too luxurious or expensive. Pemba has only a few real beach lodges, all very different.

SELF-CATERING Cooking for yourself is not common at all. A few budget hotels and guesthouses might allow you to use the kitchen, but this would be very unusual. For places that do allow self-catering, this is always noted in our listings. Perhaps the obvious candidates are Flame Tree Cottages in Nungwi, Che Che Vule in Matemwe or Le Papaye Verte and Mango's Guesthouse in Jambiani.

In a relatively recent trend, there are several private villas for rent, based all across the island. Whilst these in theory would allow for self-catering, they invariably come fully staffed with a chef prepared to shop and cater to your party's needs.

CAMPING Informal camping on Zanzibar is illegal and, as yet, there are no official campsites on the islands. Camping is permitted in the grounds of some budget hotels on the coast, but this is far from usual as the hotels are so cheap anyway. There are some lovely bell tents set up at Big Blu on Mafia that offer a great under-canvas experience with good facilities, and a rock-bottom price.

PAYMENTS AND RESERVATIONS Officially, all non-Tanzanian visitors must pay hotel bills in foreign currency, usually US dollars, so all prices are quoted in this currency. Residents and citizens are sometimes charged lower rates (typically 50–80% of the visitor rate), and can usually pay in Tanzanian shillings (TSh). In many places foreigners can also pay in TSh – at the current rate of exchange so it makes no difference to the price – but US dollars are usually easier to carry and deal with. Smaller hotels often accept only cash. Larger and smarter hotels (typically over the 'US$50 per night' bracket) will usually accept credit cards, and sometimes accept US dollar travellers' cheques – although many will add a surcharge of 5–15% for the privilege. To avoid surprises, always check a hotel's policy on payments before reserving a room.

Hotels and lodges which remain open during the low season (March to early June) often have substantially lower prices then. Conversely, many places will charge additional premiums (over and above their normal high-season rates) for accommodation over Christmas and the New Year. At any time of year, rates may be negotiable if you're in a small group (six people or more), or plan to stay for a long time (more than about five or six nights); this is especially true of the smaller, lower-budget lodges and hotels.

If you intend to stay in budget hotels and lodges, then it is usually possible simply to arrive and get a room on the spot; there's normally lots of choice. However, the smartest hotels and lodges on these islands are generally the busiest, and for them, advance reservations are always wise, if not essential. Unless you book at least three to four months in advance, it can be difficult to secure consecutive nights at any of the island's top 20 or so beach lodges between July and October.

EATING AND DRINKING

RESTAURANTS In **Zanzibar Town** there are several good restaurants catering specifically for visitors, specialising in local dishes, seafood or curries; meals usually cost between US$7 and US$20 per person. There are also smarter restaurants, where prices are a little higher.

Zanzibar Town also has restaurants where meals and snacks are less elaborate and prices are around US$5–7. There are also some small eating-houses catering mainly for local people where you can eat for around US$2–3. They usually only have one or two types of food available, such as stew and rice, but they also serve chapattis, samosas and other snacks.

Outside Zanzibar Town, in the smaller towns and villages on Zanzibar, Pemba and Mafia, there are relatively few places to eat. Local people tend to eat in their

---

THE FRUIT SEASONS

Between December and March is the main mango season on Zanzibar, and the markets are full of these tasty green-to-yellow fruits. From March to mid June it's the wet season (*masika*), when pineapples are plentiful, and July to September is when oranges are in abundance.

own houses and there are not enough tourists around yet to create a substantial market for cafés and restaurants. On the coast, hotels and guesthouses usually have restaurants attached, where food and service generally reflect the overall standard of the accommodation. A few small restaurants have opened by the most popular beaches, catering for the growing influx of visitors.

You have to try hard to really splash out on food in Zanzibar, but throughout this book listed restaurants are accompanied with a price code to give an indication of expense.

CAFÉS AND BARS In Zanzibar Town, many places serve drinks as well as food, although at busy times you may be required to buy a meal rather than have a drink on its own. You can buy international and Tanzanian brands of fizzy drink, plus local and imported beers. Prices vary greatly according to where you drink: a bottle of Coke from a shop or small backstreet café costs US$1, but may cost four times this in a smarter café or restaurant. A bottle of local beer (including Safari, Tusker or Kilimanjaro) costs US$1.50 in a local bar, and at least double this in smarter places.

At larger hotels and restaurants in Zanzibar Town or on the coast you can also buy imported beers, wines (mostly from South Africa) and spirits.·

SELF-CATERING If you plan to provide for yourself in Zanzibar Town, there are several shops selling locally produced bread and cakes, plus a reasonable choice of food in tins and packets imported from Kenya and beyond. Zanzibar Town has a market that's good for fruit and vegetables, plus fresh meat and fish if you have a means of cooking it. Other towns have small markets where you can buy meat, fish, fruit and vegetables, and shops with a limited but adequate supply of tinned food.

PUBLIC HOLIDAYS

The islands share most public holidays with the rest of Tanzania. Offices and businesses are usually closed on these days, although some tour companies remain open. Public holidays with fixed dates include:

1 January	New Year
12 January	Mapinduzi 'Revolution' Day
7 April	Sheikh Abeid Amani Karume Day
26 April	Union Day: Zanzibar and Tanganyika
1 May	Workers' Day
7 July	*Saba Saba* (Seven Seven)
8 August	Peasants' and Farmers' Day
14 October	Nyerere Day

9 December	Independence Day
25 December	Christmas Day
26 December	Boxing Day

Christmas Day, Boxing Day, New Year's Day and Easter are public holidays, and celebrations are low key on this largely Muslim island.

The Muslim feasts of Idd il Fitri – the end of Ramadan – and Idd il Maulidi (also called Maulidi ya Mfunguo Sita) – Muhammad's birthday – are celebrated by many people and are effectively public holidays. Dates of these holidays depend on the lunar calendar, and fall 11 or 12 days earlier every year. Approximate dates for Ramadan for the next few years are as follows: 16 May–14 June 2018; 6 May–4 June 2019.

On Revolution Day (12 January), don't be surprised if you hear live gunfire from the army barracks or even heavy anti-aircraft artillery fire (also live!) from warships moored off Zanzibar Town, particularly at night (when the tracer makes a nice arc through the sky). It's just the military celebrating – not another revolution!

WATERSPORTS

These islands have some superb destinations for diving, fishing and watersports enthusiasts, and even if you're only a casual snorkeller or angler, there's plenty to attract you. Some diving and fishing companies are based in Zanzibar Town, but most operate from the coastal hotels around the islands (for details on the best seasons for diving and fishing, see box, page 98).

DIVING Diving is an important element of an increasing number of people's trips, so here are some general comments on the various areas for diving around the islands. See individual sections for more details.

Dive sites The seas around these islands offer some of the best diving conditions in the Indian Ocean. As well as coral reefs, the marine life is a major attraction. All around the islands you'll find coral and colourful reef fish, while encounters with larger fish such as groupers, barracudas, sharks, rays and mantas, plus turtles, dolphins and even whales, are possible at the better dive sites.

Zanzibar Island **Off the west coast**, and within easy reach of Zanzibar Town, are numerous small islands, sandbanks and reefs where divers can experience good corals with slopes and drop-offs. There are also some good sites for experienced divers, including a couple of wrecks (there are no wrecks on the east coast).

Off the north coast and northern part of the east coast are many more reefs. There's also Mnemba Island (sometimes more fancifully termed Mnemba Atoll), a tiny island standing on the edge of a much larger circular coral reef upon which you'll find some of the finest dive sites on this stretch of the east African coast. It is popular though, so you'll find many dive boats floating above different sites on this reef; all come from around Nungwi and Zanzibar's northeast coast. Tumbatu Island also has some good reefs, used by one or two of the operations in Kendwa and Nungwi.

One long barrier reef runs along virtually the whole of the **east coast**. Although this is seldom quite as colourful as the Mnemba reef, it does offer good variation between its different sites, and many are good. You are much more likely to be on your own here, especially towards the south, than anywhere around the northern tip of Zanzibar.

Southwest Zanzibar has long been ignored with few divers being able to dive here, but the relatively new dive centres at Fumba Beach Lodge (page 332) and Unguja Lodge (page 317) are changing this. On the evidence so far, the diving here is a match for anywhere around Zanzibar, with the possible exception of some of the best Mnemba reefs. However, with usually no other divers or boats around, the whole experience here is arguably much better.

Pemba Island Pemba, and the numerous smaller islands nearby, has some spectacular diving spots. A number of Pemba's wall and drift dives are notable for variable and strong currents, and so are really more suitable for very experienced divers – hence the island is a favourite amongst live-aboard operations.

Mafia Island By contrast, Mafia has a real mix. Inside Chole Bay is generally sheltered and shallow; an ideal place for novice divers to learn with some lovely, gentle diving. Outside the bay is more dramatic fare, capable of surprising even experienced divers with big ocean fish and breathtaking sights, including a particularly spectacular ocean-facing coral wall. The corals here probably aren't generally as lush as Mnemba's – but larger fish are much more common.

Dive companies The main diving seasons are outlined in the box on page 98, but it's worth noting that at any time of year, the east coast areas are exposed to the Indian Ocean swell, while the west coast tends to be more sheltered.

The diving operators on the island are detailed within the individual chapters of this book, under the relevant area section. Prices for dives vary slightly between them, but of the main, and arguably best, centres, there is little difference between them. Pricing is invariably in US dollars, with good reductions available for multi-dive packages.

Diving is a dangerous sport and some of the better operators will insist on divers doing a formal refresher course if they have not been underwater within the previous six months. Treat this as a valuable reintroduction, and a testament that the dive centre takes safety seriously; it's a sensible precaution.

Nearly all the dive centres on the islands are based at hotels and beach lodges, and can be contacted either directly or through the hotel/lodge. With the exception of Mnemba, you rarely need to be staying at a hotel to use the dive centre facilities, although some places give a discount to guests. The individual dive operations are listed in the relevant areas in which they operate, but there are a few centres on Zanzibar Island (as well as on Pemba and Mafia) that are worthy of mention for appearing to us (we're divers, although we're not specialist dive-centre inspectors) to offer especially high-quality trips, and for displaying a responsible attitude towards safety and their community.

On Zanzibar Island, listed clockwise by location from Zanzibar Town, our pick from the sub-aqua scene are: the largest of the dive chains, **One Ocean** with centres in Stone Town and several on the east coast; **Scuba Do Diving** in the heart of Kendwa Beach; long-established **East Africa Diving & Watersport Centre** on Nungwi's West Beach; **Zanzibar Watersports** at Ras Nungwi Beach Hotel and Paradise Bungalows in Nungwi and Kendwa Rocks; **Mnemba Island Lodge Dive Centre** (for guest use only); **Rising Sun Dive Centre** at Breezes and Royal Zanzibar; and **Fumba Beach Lodge Dive Centre** in the island's southwest.

Courses Most – but not all – of Zanzibar's dive operators are affiliated with PADI, and offer at least the introductory courses. Of these, the most popular is Discover Scuba which, for around US$90 per person, incorporates a theory session, usually

PADI International recognises that there can be issues with some unlicensed dive centres and instructors passing themselves off as registered centres, particularly in remote locations. Their advice to all divers is 'don't take anything at face value – certificates, flags and branding can be forged and obtained outside official channels'. In a bid to combat these unscrupulous operations and individuals, PADI has set up a searchable database of licensed members and resorts so that divers can access reliable, up-to-date information (*www.padi.com/about-padi/consumer-alerts*). It is equally possible to search by location for instructors and companies that are under investigation or have been suspended. It may be wise to check both before donning any sub-aqua kit.

With all dive centres, PADI registered or not, divers are well advised to talk with the staff (and management where possible) to ascertain their commitment to providing a quality service. Are they eager to listen? Do they understand the kind of dive experience sought? Are they willing, perhaps even eager, to prove their credentials? Are they willing to demonstrate the quality of their equipment before requiring a commitment to hire or dive with it? Can they demonstrate that the air in the cylinders is from a reputable source, and is recently certified as clean (air quality should be sampled and checked quarterly)? Is there a sense of pride among the staff that they are working for a trustworthy and reputable company?

There are many operations on Zanzibar, Pemba and Mafia offering safe, enjoyable diving, with well-maintained modern equipment, clean air and a keen eye for customer service, but asking questions and getting a feel for an operation is critical before taking the decision to venture underwater.

based in a pool, followed by a boat dive to around 40ft (12m). The course may be completed in half a day, but is sometimes spread out over a day with a break for lunch.

The first of PADI's certification courses is the Open Water, which includes tuition in both diving theory and practical skills, and four open-water dives. Prices for this start at around US$470, rising to over US$700. Rates for the Advanced course, which incorporates five dives, are slightly lower than those for the Open Water, which is a prerequisite. As a rule, all of these 'entry' courses include equipment; for more advanced courses, equipment hire may incur an additional charge.

The equivalent Open Water referral (where the classroom element has been completed in advance) comes in at nearer US$370. PADI (*www.padi.com*) has recently introduced **PADI eLearning**, a new way in which prospective divers can take the Open Water course. Applicants nominate a dive operator, then complete all the paperwork online while still at home. They then print out the results, and take them down to their chosen operator, who will conduct the practical part of the course, and pose an 18-question review. While costs are the same as for taking the course in the more traditional way, the benefits are significant in terms of convenience at home, as well as time saved when on holiday. Several dive centres have signed up to this scheme and highly encourage clients to make use of the system.

Nitrox diving is gaining popularity for the extended bottom time it can give at shallow depths. By adjusting the mix of air in a tank to 32/68 oxygen/nitrogen (the norm is 21/79), divers can dive to a maximum of 30m (100ft) but can stay at that depth for up to 30 minutes on a first dive. On 50/50 oxygen/nitrogen, divers are limited to 9–12m (30–40 ft) but bottom time is increased by up to 50%.

Planning and Preparation   WATERSPORTS

4

If you are coming to Zanzibar specifically for scuba diving, there are some points you need to know. Diving is possible at any time of year, and divers visit different parts of the archipelago according to conditions. Having said that, most people avoid the main rainy season from March/April to May, even though during this period there can be some very good days. The weather is especially changeable at this time, and in less than an hour can switch from beautifully calm and sunny conditions to a full-blown tropical rainstorm, reducing visibility on the surface to a few hundred metres and churning up the water.

Generally speaking, from June/July to October, when the winds come from the south, the northern coasts of Zanzibar Island and Pemba Island are better, although during August some days can offer perfect conditions, while on other days the sea may be rough. September to December is usually the calmest time, and from November to February/March, the southern coasts are preferred, as the winds come from the north. Pemba enjoys some of its best visibility of the year in February.

At any time of year the western sides are more sheltered, while the eastern sides (the ocean side) are more prone to swells and rough days. As in many other parts of the world, the weather and sea conditions on Zanzibar are unpredictable and there's always a chance of a bad day during the 'good' times, and perfect conditions at the heart of the 'bad' times.

If you're seriously into game fishing, the best time is from August to March, although conditions are also reasonable from July to September. August to November boasts excellent sport fishing for yellowfin tuna, sailfish and marlin. Marlin are even more prevalent between November and March during the billfish season, when striped marlin are positively prolific (schools of up to ten recorded) and blue and black marlin are common.

Nitrox certification is offered by only a handful of companies on Zanzibar. It takes two days for an initial course, and costs around US$300.

SNORKELLING Most of the dive centres mentioned above will also cater for snorkellers, by hiring out snorkels and fins. You'll have to take a boat from virtually all the lodges and hotels throughout the islands in order to reach decent reefs for snorkelling. Some places will offer excursions of an hour, at other places snorkelling is a half-day trip and you'll share the boat with divers.

Zanzibar Off the west coast, Chumbe Island stands out as having some of the best-preserved and most easily accessible coral in the region; it really is in pristine condition, outshining any of the coral gardens known elsewhere near the islands.

Off the northeast coast, the house reef close to the shore on the western side of Mnemba Island is used by many lodges from Nungwi and the northeast coast. Residents of Mnemba have the relaxing luxury of being able to walk into the water rather than sail for several hours to get there, but they share the same reef. Further south, on the **southeast coast**, snorkelling is along the main barrier reef.

The **southwest** has been explored relatively little compared with most of Zanzibar's other areas, although it's perhaps worth noting that the teams from Safari Blue and Eco+Culture (page 333) offer snorkelling on the tiny islands south of Fumba.

Pemba and Mafia The place most often used for snorkelling off **Pemba** is known as Misali Island. After a speedboat ride here from Fundu Lagoon, you can snorkel from the beach (often while the boat takes divers elsewhere to dive). Live-aboards obviously have more scope, although they tend to concentrate on the diving rather than snorkelling. From the lodges on **Mafia**, snorkelling is usually an hour or two's gentle dhow ride away. The reefs around the mouth of Chole Bay are interesting and quite tidal; the sandbanks exposed by the ocean around low tide are idyllic – magical empty places to laze around, beachcomb and snorkel from the beach.

FISHING The waters around Zanzibar and Pemba islands offer some of the best fishing in the world, especially the Pemba Channel, between Zanzibar and Pemba islands, or around Mafia Island, south of Zanzibar. Big-game fish include barracuda, kingfish, sailfish, billfish, wahoo, dorado and blue marlin.

Fishing companies There are several fishing companies based on Zanzibar: some are experienced and reputable, others seem less so. When making bookings or enquiries you should ask about the equipment they use: what type is it? How suitable is it for big-game fishing? How old is it? How often is it serviced? Ask about safety equipment too: are the boats fitted with radios? Do they carry spare outboard motors, life jackets and so on? You may also feel it important to assess their 'catch and release' ethos; with numbers of big-game fish dwindling, 'catch and release' really should be the norm.

A few of the dive centres listed above can also organise fishing trips on request, but serious game-fishermen may be best starting their enquiries with Zanzibar Watersports, Fishing Zanzibar and Game Fish Tours, all in Nungwi (pages 220–2) or Blue Reef Sports & Fishing Lodge in Jambiani (page 302).

SHOPPING

If you're looking for souvenirs, collectables or gifts to take home, then the islands have a lot to offer. Most of the shops and stalls are in Zanzibar Town (pages 149–55), but you can also buy things at many of the lodges and hotels elsewhere. The villages do not tend to have much in the way of curios visibly displayed as in other African countries, though some beaches now have Maasai market stalls.

Zanzibar Town market is particularly good for the aromatic spices that make Zanzibar so famous. Wander around the Old Town to find endless shops and stalls selling wooden carvings; paintings in the Tingatinga style (pages 40–3); jewellery in stone, gold and silver; models or mobiles made from coconut shells; and a plethora of other souvenirs. Carved boxes inlaid with shells, or decorated with hammered brass, are very popular.

Several curio shops sell antiques and original hand-crafted pieces; very many more sell genuine junk. Some antiques have been brought to the islands by Arab or Indian traders in the last couple of centuries; virtually all are now reproductions. The Zanzibar clocks, originally used by Zanzibari merchants, are unique. Carpets, rugs and mats, made in the Persian or Arab style, are easy to carry home. Traditional Zanzibar furniture, such as tables, beds and wardrobes decorated with stained glass and mirrors, can be found but these are less easy to get back!

Some shops still sell shells and coral, taken from the reefs and beaches around the islands. They wouldn't do this if thoughtless visitors didn't buy them. This trade encourages people to catch and collect live molluscs, and to break off live coral. Reefs take decades to grow, and if you buy these items, then you are helping to degrade, and eventually destroy, the islands' fascinating marine life.

4

You may also see turtle shells, or items made from turtle-shell such as bracelets or earrings. Again, turtles are an endangered species in Zanzibar and you should not buy these things (for more details, see pages 65–8). Similarly, in this part of the world, anything made from ivory is likely to have come from a poached elephant: avoid it. All of the above marine objects are illegal to export, so beware if you do try to take anything through the airport.

For the very best in quality and ethics, visit some of the 'Made in Zanzibar' suppliers (pages 149–52).

MEDIA AND COMMUNICATIONS

MEDIA Unlike mainland Tanzania's vibrant and diverse media scene, Zanzibar's independent press comes under a different set of regulations and has had a long, rough ride. In November 2003, *Dira*, the island's first post-revolution, independent newspaper, was forced to cease publication after the Zanzibar government alleged that it had violated registration procedures and professional ethics. The popular private paper had been previously almost bankrupted by a huge libel fine of TSh660 million (about US$500,000) following the publication of 'false and harmful' reports about the Zanzibar president's family: namely two articles that accused his children of using their father's influence to buy up state-owned companies.

Following this, a period ensued where, in spite of international pressure to allow free expression, the media scene was wholly government-run; private broadcasters and newspaper publishers were banned. Then, at the end of 2005, 13 new private publications were granted licences, including four newspapers (*Zanzibar Wiki Hii* (Zanzibar This Week), *Marhaba, ZIFF* and *Fahari*), followed by an additional seven in the last few years. However, it must be noted that their content is far from independent and impartial, and state-run daily *Zanzibar Leo* (Zanzibar Today) dominates. State-operated TV Zanzibar and its radio counterpart, Voice of Tanzania-Zanzibar, still dominate, and continue to act as a channel for government opinion, with little, if any, room for political criticism of those in power. The current media environment may be private but it is far from wholly independent, with strict laws effectively leading to some censorship.

However, international media rights organisation Reporters Sans Frontières (*rsf.org*), who campaign for global press freedom and the right to be informed, have acknowledged some improvements on the island. Press laws remain strict, with rigorous local government monitoring, but censorship and harassment have declined, and access to the mainland media has increased for the local population.

Many Zanzibaris now receive local and mainland broadcast channels, and satellite television is increasingly widespread. The BBC World Service is also available on FM in both Zanzibar (94.1) and Pemba (93.5).

Whilst is was hoped that press freedom on the islands will increase by allowing a private press to operate and the creation of a revised Freedom of Information Act, there is still a very long way to go, and the impact of curtailing free press expression on the mainland cannot be ignored. In November 2016, President Magufuli quietly enshrined into law the controversial Media Services Act, which supersedes the 1976 Newspaper Act, and displayed vagrant disregard for the voice of the Media Council of Tanzania, whose recommendations were largely ignored, along with large swathes of the general population.

The new act saw the abolition of independent self-regulation of the media and the creation of a government-controlled Media Council to oversee all publishers, from major news outlets to social network users. It now has the right to ban newspapers and prohibit non-accredited journalists from publishing, as well as enforcing tough criminal penalties, both fines and lengthy prison sentences, for journalists charged with offences such as defamation, sedition and publishing false statements. Journalists have already been threatened and prosecuted in the last year for their reporting of presedential and public affairs, with many now feeling unable to speak freely for fear of the consequences. It began with a few radio stations being closed down and a dozen individuals being prosecuted over their posts on social media, but there can be little doubt that it will impact the wider media scene.

Tanzania has sadly fallen 34 places in the press freedom index since 2010 and is now ranked 75th out of 180 countries. We watch and hope for future improvement.

POST Most towns and large villages on these islands have post offices, or at the least a postal collection, but it's best to send all your mail from Zanzibar Town. The main poste restante service for Zanzibar is also in Zanzibar Town (page 155). The post service is reliable, with letters taking about a week to ten days to reach destinations in Europe and North America (Australia takes a bit longer).

ZANZIBAR TELECOMMUNICATIONS

Changes to telephone codes are a frequent occurrence in Tanzania, Zanzibar and the other archipelago islands. Every effort has been made to ensure this book is accurate; however, further numeric variations are inevitable in the future. The key dialling codes and most significant recent changes are detailed here.

CALLS TO ZANZIBAR The area code for all of Zanzibar (Zanzibar Island and Pemba Island) is 024, if you are calling from elsewhere in Tanzania, Kenya or Uganda. For calls from other countries, individual numbers must be prefixed with the international code for Tanzania +255, then 24 for Zanzibar (minus the first 0).

CALLS WITHIN ZANZIBAR Calling within Zanzibar, you simply dial the number you want, without the 024 area code. For emergency calls dial 112, and for directory enquiries dial 118.

CALLS FROM ZANZIBAR Phoning out of Zanzibar to mainland Tanzania, Kenya or Uganda, you will need the city or area code, followed by the individual number. For all other countries, it is necessary to dial the international access code (000), plus the country code (eg: 1 for USA, 44 for Britain, 27 for South Africa), followed by the city or area code (minus the first 0), then the individual number.

Area codes on the Tanzanian mainland that have changed include:

Area	Code	Area	Code
Dar es Salaam	022	Mtwara	023
Tanga	027	Dodoma	026
Arusha	027	Tabora	026
Kilimanjaro	027	Mwanza	028

Letters to destinations inside Tanzania cost about US$0.20, while postcards to countries outside Africa are about US$0.50 (slightly more for letters).

TELEPHONE The best place on the islands for calling from a landline is the public call office, next to the old post office in Zanzibar Town. There are several private phone bureaux around here also. International calls to Europe or the USA cost between US$2.50 and US$5 per minute, depending on where you go. Note that most places charge per full minute; go over by one second and you might as well speak for the next 59 (more details are given on page 156). Elsewhere on the islands the better hotels and lodges will usually allow guests to make international calls, although rates are high.

There are now a handful of mobile phone (cell phone) networks and increasingly good signal coverage in the islands. These work around most larger towns and main arteries, and increasingly in more isolated spots, too. You'll get a signal in most parts of Zanzibar Island, in the busier areas of Pemba Island and Mafia and even in the lodges on Mafia Island, and the exclusive Mnemba Island.

If you're bringing a mobile phone from home, those with GSM capability should work here; check with your own service provider before you depart. For longer stays, consider picking up a Tanzanian SIM card to cut costs; it's very easy and highly cost-efficient. Details of how best to do this are given on page 156.

INTERNET These days, Wi-Fi is available in most mid-range and high-end accommodation and restaurants, with even a number of the budget operators boasting the service. It's rarely fast or consistently reliable, but it should be more than possible to send the odd message home, post a picture or check the news; just don't try streaming a movie! For details of internet cafés, see pages 156–7.

BUSINESS HOURS

Most shops and travel company offices in Zanzibar Town are open every day, although some close on Fridays, the Muslim holy day, or on Sundays, the official day off. Normal business hours are from between 08.00 and 09.00 until noon, then from 13.00 or 14.00 until 17.00 or 18.00. Some private shops and tour agencies take a longer break at midday and stay open later in the evening. In the low season, some souvenir shops stay closed, while others open mornings only. Government offices and banks are closed on Saturdays and Sundays; post offices are closed Saturday afternoons and Sundays. Opening hours on Pemba and Mafia are similar, but less predictable.

BECOMING INVOLVED

CULTURAL ETIQUETTE
- Dress and act sensitively: locals consider revealing clothing or public displays of affection offensive. Keep swimwear for the beach, and in towns or villages keep your upper legs and shoulders covered. Sporting bare chests or bikini tops as you stroll around the market is the height of rudeness and arrogance.
- Support locally owned, small-scale shops and businesses. This is the best way for your money to benefit the grass-roots economy.
- Buy locally made crafts, but avoid wildlife products, such as ivory, skins, coral, shells from turtles or any other kind of marine animal, and even wooden carvings, unless the material comes from a sustainable renewable source.
- Always ask permission before photographing local people. And accept refusals.
- Non-Muslims should not enter mosques without permission.

- During the holy month of Ramadan, local people fast, and you can show understanding for this tradition by not eating or drinking in public places (eating in tourist restaurants is fine).

GETTING INVOLVED Shopping in some of the fair-trade shops listed in the *Made in Zanzibar* section, pages 149–52, booking through an ethical tour operator and donating money to lodge-sponsored community projects are all ways in which visitors to Zanzibar are able to actively contribute to the social and environmental development of the island and its poorest communities. For those who would like to take that a step further, we have listed a few local NGOs (Non-Governmental Organisations) on the island which seem to be doing excellent charity and development work, and very much need sustained support.

During our research, we visited and contacted a number of possible NGOs, but we know from experience that they're not always good at responding to enquiries – perhaps partly due to the pressures that they're under, and partly due to the limitations of their communications. A few stood out for not only doing some great work, but also for having a clear mission, good leadership and relatively easy communication channels. We have listed them here for travellers keen to 'give something back' in a real sense when they visit or return from a trip to Zanzibar.

Hands Across Borders Society (HABS)

+1 250 721 9009; e habszanzibar@yahoo. ca; www.handsacrossborderssociety.org. HABS was established in 1999 in British Columbia to provide complementary health & education services to communities in need within the developing world, including from its excellent base in Jambiani on Zanzibar Island. In addition to providing complementary health-care services & education to the villagers at its Chiropractic Wellness Centre, HABS is also involved in assisting & funding a number of other village projects & amenities, with the most recent being the construction of the Jambiani Tourism Institute where local people are now trained to help them secure employment in the burgeoning hotel scene. Health-care practitioners are welcome to volunteer here for placements of 1 month & over, financial contributions are gratefully received to fund everything from electricity to supplies, & unlike many charities, the Jambiani base is happy to receive material donations from walk-in visitors. The most useful supplies to donate are orthopaedic supports, straps, bandages & antibiotic creams.

Health Improvement Project: Zanzibar (HIPZ)

01453 767561; e admin@hipz.org. uk; www.hipz.org.uk. Registered as a charity in 2006, HIPZ is an ambitious & successful health-care development scheme, being spearheaded by 2 British consultant surgeons. It aims to establish a unique public/private partnership with the Zanzibar government to improve health care in Zanzibar through fundraising & professional support. Their original & flagship project, is to renovate, equip & run the district hospital in Makunduchi (southern Zanzibar), where many of the 60,000 locals currently have little or no access to health care. Such is their current success that HIPZ have recently taken on another hospital, a triage centre & a dental clinic in Kivunge. Makunduchi Hospital is 1 of only 2 district hospitals on Zanzibar, but its facilities have been neglected for years. HIPZ aim to build a new hospital, train local staff, provide medical & IT equipment, offer high standards of clinical care, & expand medical services to include everything from A&E to maternity & dental care. A significant recent success is the newly constructed maternity unit, which is now delivering comprehensive obstetric care free of charge, as well as operating an ambulance retrieval service to bring labouring women from remote communities to deliver safely in the unit. Hot on its heels, the children's ward is the next target for improvement. The hope is that the hospital will become a model for the introduction of similar facilities across the island, & that a sustainable, locally managed facility can vastly improve access to high-quality community health care.

SOS Children's Village Zanzibar

Terrington Hse, 13–15 Hills Rd, Cambridge CB2 1NL, UK; 01223 365589; e hello@sos-uk.org.uk;

4

For additional online content, articles, photos and more on Zanzibar, why not visit www.bradtguides.com/zanzibar.

www.soschildrensvillages.org.uk. The Zanzibar SOS Children's Village was built in 1988, in a residential district near the airport. 11 family houses are now home to 110 orphaned & abandoned children, providing them with a safe place to live, a 'mother', love & care. The construction of a nursery school, primary & secondary school, health-care centre, sports fields & mosque, has led the village to become a real neighbourhood centre, serving the local community as well as the orphans. Away from the village, 3 youth houses are home to older children & young people taking their first steps towards independence. The orphanage is doing excellent work but it relies on the continued charity of many people: for financial donations to fund school books, desks, a generator, construction & renovation; gifts from footballs to pens; & child sponsorship. If you are interested in helping, they have a clear website which can accept donations & arrange child sponsorship. They're trying to provide as normal an environment as possible for their children & this understandably precludes impromptu visits from curious visitors, although existing sponsors are warmly welcomed.

Part Two

THE GUIDE

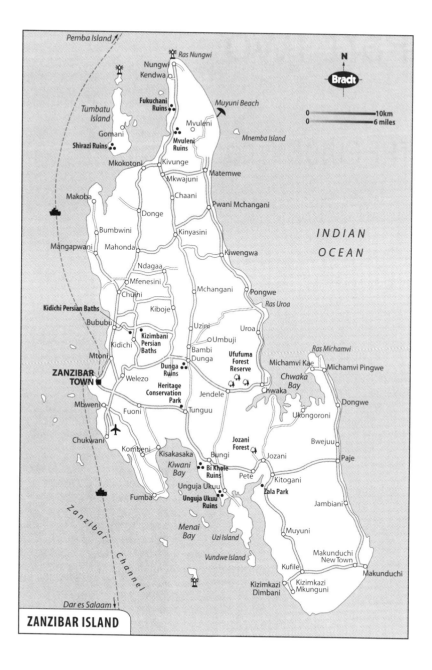

ZANZIBAR ISLAND

5

Zanzibar Island Essentials

GETTING AROUND

You can travel around Zanzibar Island in several different ways: by hire car, motorbike, scooter, bicycle, tourist minibus, *dalla dalla*, bus, taxi, organised tour, walking, hitchhiking, or a combination of all of these. Outside Zanzibar Town, the main roads are predominantly tar these days, whilst minor routes are dirt or graded gravel. All are highly variable in quality, from smooth, newly resurfaced tar to appallingly rutted gravel, where travel can be slow and uncomfortable. Happily, there are increasingly fewer of the latter. As in the rest of southern and East Africa, traffic drives on the left in Zanzibar; however, the greatest risk on the road is the other drivers: be very aware.

HIRED VEHICLES

Car hire   Car hire is possible on Zanzibar Island, although whether it's wise for most visitors is a real question. There are no international car-hire companies on the island, so vehicle quality is highly variable. Driving standards are not good and roads can be in poor condition, so accidents are frequent. We do not generally recommend that visitors hire cars here, but if you choose to do so exercise great caution and never drive at night: it can be exceedingly dangerous.

If you do want a car, it's probably best arranged through one of the tour companies (pages 114–17). A few have their own vehicles, while others will make arrangements on your behalf. Rates vary but are generally between US$50 and US$60 per day for a small car (eg: a Suzuki 'jeep') and around US$100 per day for a larger car (eg: a Toyota Land Cruiser). There are also a few local car rental companies springing up, offering slightly more competitive rates: Zanzibar Car Hire (*www.zanzibarcarhire.com*), Zanzibar Express Car Hire (*www.zanzibarexpresscarhire.com*) and Kibabu Cars (*www.kibabucars.com/car-hire*) all offer SUVs for around US$35–45 per day. However, quality is more variable than price, and standards on Zanzibar are often low; check your car *very* carefully for defects and even go for a short test drive before accepting it. The price usually includes unlimited distance, but you pay for the fuel. Be aware that there is likely to be virtually none in the tank on collection!

Insurance is normally included in the rental, although some companies are vague about this. It's always important to check your exact legal position should you be unfortunate enough to have an accident involving another car or person. Get this in writing, which may be harder than you realise. A deposit, proof of identity and your driving licence are usually required, and you will need a local driving permit, which must be arranged in advance (at least 24 hours prior to car collection). The police road blocks around the island will fine you without this paperwork, so do not leave without it (see below). It is not a bad idea to also carry a valid International Driving Permit (IDP).

Driving licences Unlike mainland Tanzania, you need an International Driving Permit (IDP) or a 'local driving permit' to drive either cars or motorcycles legally on Zanzibar. Enforcing this, the traffic police on Zanzibar routinely stop any tourist they see behind a wheel. There are several checkpoints on the roads between Zanzibar Town and the north and east coasts. If you do not have either an IDP or a local driving permit then you'll have to repeatedly pay small bribes or a heftier official fine.

An IDP is easy to obtain from your national motoring association – eg: in Britain contact the AA (*www.theaa.com*), or the RAC (*www.rac.co.uk*), provided that you have a standard driving licence at home. If applying by post, the process takes time, so order one well in advance of your trip. In the UK, it is also possible to apply for an IDP in person at major post offices.

The alternative is a local driving permit, which can be issued for you in Zanzibar. The rental company can usually organise this for you with minimal fuss for about US$10, and we would recommend that you do this for smooth passage at police encounters.

Beware of eager tour companies who are keen to rent you a car and say that IDPs are not essential. Also watch out for a scam where local papaasi rent you a motorbike claiming that an IDP is not needed, before informing the police, who then find and fine you.

Petrol and diesel Petrol is now widely available in Zanzibar Town and across the island, notably *en route* to Nungwi, and at Kinyasini, Chwaka, and at Kitogani, near the junction where the road turns off to Paje. New petrol stations are springing up along the roads with surprising regularity.

Petrol costs are increasing on the island, as in the rest of the world, with prices currently about US$1 per litre for petrol and just a little more for diesel. Occasional fuel shortages in outlying parts of the island are rare these days but it is generally worth filling up as and when you see a petrol station, and certainly prior to leaving Zanzibar Town. In an emergency, however, it is normally possible to locate 'black market' fuel at about 20% above the standard pump price.

Maps The most up-to-date area maps you will find are likely to be within this book. We spend a great deal of time plotting all of the listings and roads using GPS co-ordinates and tracks that we generate whilst researching. Many of the larger, more colourful maps available are sadly out of date as development on Zanzibar far outstrips the time between reprints. However, for those keen to get hold of some larger island maps than we are able to include here, there are a few possibilities.

A straightforward tourist map of Zanzibar Town and Zanzibar Island is available from the Zanzibar Tourist Corporation offices, and from some bookshops and hotels in the town. It costs around US$2. Far better than this is the attractive, hand-drawn map of *Zanzibar Stone Town and Zanzibar Island* produced by local artist Giovanni Tombazzi, which is widely available for around US$8, and highlights landmarks and a little of their historical background. This is part of a wider series of maps, including many of the national parks and mountains of mainland Tanzania. They are all many years old now, and hotels change frequently, but for general sense of the place and attractions they are still the best available.

The *Gallery Map of Zanzibar* is available in the Gallery Bookshop (page 154). The map of Zanzibar Island is not as easy to read or detailed as Giovanni's map, but the map of Stone Town is clear and useful.

A map called *Pemba: The Clove Island* is available in some book and gift shops, and is well researched, again at a scale of 1:100,000. There are two versions, however: one from 1992 and a better one from 1995. The date is on the back cover.

Most commercially produced maps of Tanzania also include Zanzibar. One of the best is the *Tanzania Travellers Map* published by Macmillan, which shows the mainland at a scale of 1:2,000,000 and has more detailed maps of Zanzibar Island (1:500,000) and Pemba Island (1:830,000) on the back, although even these contain a few errors.

Good-quality maps of Zanzibar and Pemba islands (produced by the British Directorate of Overseas Surveys at scales of 1:50,000 and 1:10,000) are available in Zanzibar Town from the Map Office in the Commission of Lands and Planning, part of the Ministry of Environment, near the People's Bank of Zanzibar and the fort. Maps cost about US$2.

Motorbike and scooter hire
It is possible to hire motorbikes (almost all are Honda 125cc or 250cc trail bikes or similar) or scooters (mostly Vespas and Piaggios) from many of the tour companies (pages 114–17). Prices vary, but are generally around US$25–30 per day for a scooter, US$35–40 per day for a motorbike.

For a cheaper deal, try Nasor Aly Mussa's Scooter Service, usually shortened to Fundi Nasor, a small garage just off New Mkunazini Road in Zanzibar Town, near the Anglican cathedral. As with cars, you should take your scooter for a test drive to make sure everything works before agreeing to hire.

Some tourists to Zanzibar hire scooters, imagining them to be similar to Greek island-style mopeds. However, scooters have larger engines and are harder to handle than mopeds, and there have been a number of accidents and injuries. You should not hire a scooter if you have never ridden one before; the dirt tracks and pot-holed roads of Zanzibar are not ideal places to start learning.

If you're keen, however, do check beforehand that your travel insurance policy covers you for using this type of transport, as not all do.

Bicycle hire
For getting around Zanzibar Town, or going further afield around the island, fit and adventurous visitors will find bicycles ideal. Most bikes are heavy steel Chinese-built roadsters, so you shouldn't plan on covering too many miles (it's generally too hot to cycle fast anyway). You can also hire mountain bikes, but most of these are pretty basic all-steel models, and only slightly lighter than the Chinese roadsters. They do have gears, however, which makes them easier to ride.

Bikes can be hired through several of the tour companies listed (pages 114–17) and daily rates start at US$10 for the Chinese roadsters, and US$15 for mountain bikes. Take your bike for a short test ride before hiring to make sure everything works. Unless you plan extensive off-road forays, make sure your tyres are pumped up fairly hard, especially on the mountain bikes, where semi-flat fat tyres can make for hard going. Your bike should come with a puncture outfit and pump, but if it doesn't these can be bought from the bicycle *fundi* (mechanic) in the market in Zanzibar Town.

Roads can be rough, but are generally flat, and traffic is very light once you get away from Zanzibar Town. If you get tired, you can put your bike on top of a bus or dalla dalla and come home the easy way.

Keen cyclists might like to contact Mreh Tours (page 115) – the only company as far as we know to offer specific cycle tours of Zanzibar.

Taxis The saloon-car taxis available around Zanzibar Town can be hired to take you further afield, but some drivers do not like to go off the tar roads as the rocky dirt lanes are liable to damage the undersides of their beloved vehicles (the minibuses have higher clearance, or at least the bus drivers seem not to worry).

A short ride through town will cost just over US$3, a trip further afield to Mbweni Ruins or Mtoni Marine Centre around US$7–10 (one-way), and an airport transfer to/from Zanzibar Town US$10–15. A taxi to Jozani Forest is US$20–25 one-way, or around US$30–35 return, possibly more if you plan to spend all day in the forest. To Nungwi or Bwejuu is around US$40–50 one-way. If you're going this far, then it's probably best to arrange for a proper minibus and guide to take you.

Tourist minibuses On Zanzibar Island, most travellers will get between Zanzibar Town and one of the beaches using a minibus. These can be arranged by the *papaasi* (see box, pages 122–3) who lurk at budget hotels looking for custom. A ride in one of these vehicles can cost as little as US$5, although often the papaasi will have their own favourite beach places, which pay them a commission for each visitor who stays; make sure you are very clear about your destination, the timings and the cost before getting on board.

If haggling with the papaasi is not for you, most local travel agents can arrange a reliable private minibus from Zanzibar Town to any beach lodge for about US$50 per vehicle. For most people this is the preferred way of getting around. Alternatively, if you know which lodge you want to go to, call them and ask them to arrange a minibus for you; they will often do this through a reliable travel agent with whom they work and at a reasonable rate.

If you have pre-arranged your trip, then you'll probably be met at the airport by a driver with a vehicle who will transfer you to your chosen lodge. Sometimes it's easy, especially for short trips, to incorporate a visit to a spice farm on the way, as part of these transfers.

PUBLIC TRANSPORT
Buses It is possible to reach many parts of Zanzibar Island by public bus, although few visitors use their services – most use tourist minibuses or dalla dallas. All buses leave from Darajani Bus Station on Creek Road in Zanzibar Town. Fares are very cheap: for example, it costs only a few dollars to travel half the length of the island between Zanzibar Town and Bwejuu. Note, however, that prices can rise suddenly if there is a fuel shortage.

On a few routes, especially the longer ones, there are only a few buses each day. They often wait until they are full to depart, usually leaving Zanzibar Town around noon to take people back to their villages after visiting the market. They reach their destinations in the evening, and 'sleep' there before returning to Zanzibar Town very early in the morning (between 02.00 and 04.00) in time for the start of that day's market. Some of the longer journeys can be very slow. For example, Zanzibar Town to Nungwi takes 3–5 hours, and Zanzibar Town to Makunduchi 4–6 hours.

Buses do not always go to their final destination. For example, bus No 1 (the route for Nungwi) may only go as far as Mkokotoni. Therefore, always check that the bus is going to the destination you think it should be.

Route number	To	Number per day	First	Last
NORTH				
1	Mkokotoni (occasionally continuing to Nungwi)	15	05.30	20.00
2	Bumbwini & Makoba, via Mangapwani	3	05.30	18.00
14	Nungwi, via Mahonda, Kinyasini & Chaani	7	07.00	18.00
NORTHEAST				
6	Chwaka (some continue to Uroa & Pongwe)	5	07.00	16.00
13	Uroa	5	08.00	16.00
15	Kiwengwa	5	08.00	18.00
16	Matemwe	6	07.00	18.00
SOUTHEAST				
9	Paje, sometimes to Bwejuu & Jambiani	7	06.00	17.00
10	Makunduchi, via Tunguu, Pete & Munyuni	4	07.00	16.00
SOUTHWEST				
7	Fumba, via Kombeni	4	06.00	16.00
8	Unguja Ukuu	4	06.00	16.00
CENTRAL				
3	Kidichi & Kizimbani, via Welezo	7	06.00	18.00
4	Mchangani, via Dunga, Bambi & Uzini	5	06.00	17.00
5	Ndagaa, via Kiboje	4	06.00	16.00
11	Fuoni, via Tungu & Binguni	10	07.00	18.00
12	Dunga, then north to Bambi	5	07.00	17.00

Some of the bus routes listed above are also covered by public minibuses or dalla dallas, which fill the gaps in the bus service 'timetables'. These are usually slightly more expensive than the buses, but also tend to be quicker.

Public minibuses and dalla dallas For independent travellers, local minibuses and small converted trucks called dalla dallas cover many routes around Zanzibar Island. Minibuses and dalla dallas are faster than buses, and are gradually replacing them on the roads. Fares are cheap: typically about US$0.50 around Zanzibar Town and a few dollars to cross the island.

Buses and dalla dallas from outlying villages heading for Zanzibar Town tend to leave very early in the morning but, apart from that, there are no truly fixed timetables: most vehicles simply leave when they're full. At any bus or dalla dalla station, don't expect an information board: you will need to ask around to find the transport you need. Be aware that the last buses to some coastal villages will leave Zanzibar Town by mid afternoon.

Dalla dalla journeys are invariably an experience, with time to interact with local people, but comfort is limited. Seating is on hard timber benches along the sides of the vehicle, and it's quite likely that parcels and packages of all shapes and sizes will be packed in around you.

Zanzibar Island Essentials   GETTING AROUND

5

In spite of their erratic appearance, dalla dallas do have standardised route numbers and destinations. There are three main terminals in Zanzibar Town: Darajani Bus Station on Creek Road (opposite the market), Mwembe Ladu and Mwana Kwerekwe. The latter two stations are a few kilometres from town and are best accessed by a short hop on a dalla dalla from Darajani.

The most useful dalla dalla routes and times are listed in the box below; the name in brackets is the destination as written on the front of the vehicle.

DALLA DALLA ROUTES AND FREQUENCY

Dalla dalla number	Departs	To	Number per day	First	Last
AROUND ZANZIBAR TOWN					
502/534	Darajani	Bububu, via Marahubi & Mtoni	Lots	06.00	21.00
505	Darajani	Airport (U/Ndege)	Lots	06.00	21.00
510	Darajani	Mwana Kwerekwe (m/Kwerekwe)	Lots	06.00	21.00
511	Darajani	Kidichi Spice (K/Spice), via Kidichi Persian baths	Lots	06.00	21.00
NORTH					
101	Creek Rd	Mkokotoni	15	05.30	21.00
102	Darajani	Bumbwini, via Mangapwani	5	10.00	16.00
116	Creek Rd	Nungwi	25	05.30	21.00
121	Darajani	Donge & Mahonda	5	10.00	18.00
NORTHEAST					
117	Creek Rd	Kiwengwa, some continue to Pwani Mchangani	9	06.00	19.00
118	Creek Rd	Matemwe	10	06.00	19.00
206	Darajani or Mwembe Ladu	Chwaka, via Dunga Palace	10	06.00	18.00
209	Mwembe Ladu	Pongwe	3	07.00	16.00
214	Mwembe Ladu	Uroa, via Dunga Palace	7	06.00	18.00
SOUTHEAST					
309	Darajani or Mwana Kwerekwe	Jambiani, via Jozani	5	07.30	16.00
310	Darajani	Makunduchi, via Jozani	10	06.30	21.00
324/603/340	Darajani	Bwejuu, via Jozani, Paje & Kae Michamvi	Lots	09.00	14.00
SOUTHWEST					
308	Mwembe Ladu or Mwana Kwerekwe	Unguja Ukuu	4	08.00	15.00
336	Darajani or Mwana Kwerekwe	Kibondeni	Lots	06.00	20.00
326/507	Darajani or Mwana Kwerekwe	Kizimkazi, via Jozani & Zala Park	5	07.00	16.00

Hitchhiking Hitching around Zanzibar Island is possible, but traffic can be light so you will need patience. However, a combination of public transport, walking and hitching is sometimes the only way to travel for budget travellers – and simply a matter of taking the first vehicle which will give you a lift. You should usually expect to pay a few dollars for a lift.

ORGANISED TOURS

In Zanzibar Town, it seems that every other shop or office is a tour company, and it's always easy to find someone to arrange and organise tours within Zanzibar. The problem is finding a good tour company. This section is designed to help you locate something suitable for your needs and budget.

The most popular tours organised from Zanzibar Town are boat excursions to Prison Island and the trips around the plantations called 'spice tours' (see box, pages 116–17). Most companies also arrange tours to Jozani-Chwaka Bay National Park to see the colobus monkeys (see box, page 327), to Kizimkazi to see the dolphins (pages 321–4), and visits to old palaces and other ruins in the Zanzibar Town area (pages 184–7) or elsewhere on the island. You can also usually arrange transport to the beaches on the north or east coasts and other parts of Zanzibar with a tour company.

Many companies can also make hotel and ship reservations, flight bookings, car-hire arrangements, and so on. Check the arrangement before organising this: some make no charge for the service (instead getting commission from the transport company or hotel), whilst others charge a small fee. Watch out for those charging a hefty fee for the service, which can sometimes be no more than a couple of phone calls on your behalf.

Tour prices are usually quoted in US dollars (although they can be paid for in TSh or other currencies), and tend to vary considerably between the different companies. A lot depends on the quality you're looking for. At one end of the scale, budget outfits offer cheap and cheerful tours, where you'll be sharing a basic minibus or dalla dalla with several other tourists, the quality or knowledge of your guide may be poor, and their social and environmental ethics highly questionable. At the other end of the scale, you can arrange a private tour for just a couple of people, in a good-quality vehicle, often with air conditioning, and a knowledgeable, responsible guide. Good companies can provide guides who speak English, French, German, Italian and often other languages.

This is not to knock the cheaper outfits: many tourists go on budget tours and have an excellent time. In the same way, some of the so-called upmarket companies may rest on their laurels a bit and not be up to scratch. It is therefore worth comparing a few tour companies before finally arranging your tour, and when comparing prices it is also very important to compare exactly what you get for your money. Your best source of recommendations (good or bad) is always other tourists and travellers, so talk to some of them if you can before signing up for anything. All the companies listed here have been recommended by the authors or readers of previous editions of this book.

To get an idea of prices, companies running tours that you share with (four-eight) other people offer the following rates: City Tour (*US$20*); Prison Island Tour (*US$30*); Dolphin Tour (*US$40*); Spice Tour (*US$28*); Jozani Forest Tour (*US$35*). All these rates are per person, but for the tour only, and do not include extras like entrance fees (ie: for the Palace Museum this is US$2, for Prison Island US$4, for Jozani Forest US$4).

If you want a private tour, with a mid-range or top-quality tour company, the rates are more likely to be around US$15–30 more expensive per person, for a minimum of two passengers, and usually include all entrance fees, although you should check this when booking or comparing prices.

While in Zanzibar you can also use tour companies to set you up with tours to Pemba, the Tanzanian mainland, Kenya and even further afield. In recent years there's been significant growth in the number of companies offering fly-in safaris to the national parks of Selous and Ruaha in southern Tanzania. Logistically it's easier to get there than to the northern parks of Serengeti and Ngorongoro, although many companies offer this option, too.

All tour companies have to be licensed by the government of Zanzibar and, if you have a reason to be dissatisfied, you can complain to the Ministry of Tourism who may take action against the company on your behalf. In reality, there's little control but it's still best to use only registered companies. If you decide to use unofficial operators, take care.

Most of the companies listed here can arrange tours on the spot (or with a day's notice), but you can also make prior arrangements by phoning or emailing in advance.

TOUR COMPANIES Tour companies based in Zanzibar Town include the following (listed alphabetically):

✳ **Eco+Culture Tours** [125 F3] ✆024 223 3731; m 0755 873066/0777 410873; e ecoculturetours@gmail.com; www.ecoculture-zanzibar.org. This tour company (situated on Hurumzi St) is different to its competitors. For example, instead of the ubiquitous 'standard' spice tour, it takes guests to plantations & gardens guided by a local herbalist, & as well as a visit to Jozani Forest, walks in the community forest at Ufufuma are arranged. Well-guided, insightful village tours are another great option – a genuine opportunity to meet local people in the company of respected local guides. Trips are sometimes slightly more expensive than those arranged by some other tour companies but they are refreshingly different, ethically minded & well guided. A percentage of all tour revenue is returned into funding solid community projects, telling of the organisation's origins as an NGO. Robert & Haji in the Zanzibar office are gentle & very friendly, & we highly recommend them as an island operator. See also page 333.
Fernandes Tours & Safaris [125 F7] ✆024 223 0666; m 0777 413352/474344; e fts@zanlink.com; www.fernandestoursznz. com. This small, friendly & well-connected company on Vuga Rd used to work mainly with incoming tour groups from Britain, South Africa & elsewhere, but is now branching out to

provide good-quality tailor-made trips around Zanzibar for groups & individuals in the mid-range price bracket. You can arrange things on the spot, or in advance.
Fisherman Tours & Travel [125 E7] ✆024 223 8791/2; m 0777 440044/441144/412677; e reservations@ fishermantours.com; www.fishermantours.com. This well-established & experienced company on Vuga Rd has skilled & efficient staff, & caters for overseas tour groups, as well as individuals & small parties. Offering a complete guide & escort service, they have their own fleet of vehicles, & most drivers are equipped with mobile phones. Other services include the organisation of wildlife safaris on mainland Tanzania, as well as the usual tours around Zanzibar, plus car hire, hotel bookings, ground transfers & so on. In the past, Fisherman Tours received quality awards from business organisations in Europe & America, & do (fairly) consistently deliver a good service. The office is near Air Tanzania & they have full credit-card facilities.
Gallery Tours & Safaris m 0777 853824/0774 305165; e info@gallerytours.net; www. gallerytours.net. Celebrating its 10th birthday in 2016, Gallery Tours & Safaris is owned by local businessman Javed Jafferji, owner of Gallery Bookshop, Jafferji House & author of

several coffee-table books on the Swahili coast. Positioned as a high-end tour operation, it aims to raise the standard of guiding, vehicles & customer service found amongst the ground handlers. Catering for both groups & individuals, the team here is geared up to deal with everything from standard spice tours to weddings. Smart branding & attention to detail make this one of the best operations around. In conjunction with Zanzibar Serena Inn, Gallery Tours also owns the company Original Dhow Safaris. Its fleet of 3 traditional dhows departs every sundown from the Serena Hotel for a luxury sundowner trip, complete with a well-stocked bar & tasty canapés. This trip must be booked at least 1 full day in advance & is highly recommended as a pre-dinner holiday treat. All Gallery tours can be booked at any of the owner's Stone Town businesses, or in advance by email.

Island Express Safaris & Tours `024 223 4375/64; m 0774 111222/111888; e info@islandexpress.co.tz; www.islandexpress.co.tz. This smart, efficient operation has offices in central Stone Town on Kajificheni St, as well as beside the airport. Offering a more personal service than most other tour operators on the island, tours & transfers with Island Express are never for groups, but are only ever arranged on a private basis. This does make them slightly more expensive, though not prohibitively so, & of course gives complete flexibility on your trip. Staff are friendly & professional with fluent English, Spanish, French & German guides available. A recommended operation.

Mreh Tours `024 223 3476; e mrehtours@zanzinet.com. This company offers all the usual tours, & is especially keen on bicycle hire & tours by bike. One itinerary is a 9-day cycling trip around the island (no doddle even on Zanzibar's flat roads, as the bikes are the traditional steel Chinese models, not tip-top lightweight jobs), though shorter, more manageable variations are possible. Costs are around US$50 a day including bike, food, drink & backup vehicle. Basically, if you have the slightest interest in cycling, call in at their office on Baghani St & discuss the options with Saleh Mreh Salum, the energetic & friendly owner.

Sama Tours [125 E4] m 0777 430385/431665; e samatours@zitec.org; www.samatours.com; see ad, page 176. As well as spice tours, boat trips & all the usual services, the helpful team based

on Gizenga St (behind the House of Wonders) arranges cultural tours, giving visitors an opportunity to meet local people: recommended by clients as a great opportunity for photos. Guides speak English, French, German & Italian. They also offer 'special' spice tours, organised by one of the knowledgeable, multi-lingual owners, Salim Abdullah. Sama Tours caters for both groups (anything from cruise ships to overland trucks) & individuals seeking tailor-made tours, airport & port collection, hotels, excursions, transfers, car hire, & so on. They are friendly & recommended. Prices depend on the length of the tour, the services required & the number in the group.

Sun N Fun Safaris `024 2237381/7665; m 0774 662342; e zanzibarsun@hotmail.com. In the same building on the waterfront as Sea View Indian Restaurant, & with the same enthusiastic management, this company can set you up with absolutely anything, usually at a very reasonable price. It runs tours of Zanzibar Town & the island, provides transfer services to the airport or east coast, & can help with general tourist information on the island & beyond. It can also assist with visas, car & bike hire, boat trips, flight tickets & bus tickets in Zanzibar & on the mainland. The office sells postcards, stamps (it has a mailbox), maps & souvenirs of the 'I love Zanzibar' variety. Students carrying an ISIC card are eligible for a 5% discount on all their services.

Suna Tours `024 223 7344. Suna is run by the formidable Naila Majid Jiddawi, a former Zanzibari MP & bastion of Zanzibar tourism promotion. The company represents some mid-range hotels on the east coast & can assist with reservations for any other hotel on the coast, as well as arranging transport, good-quality spice tours & trips to the islands. The company office is in a small white building at the end of Forodhani Gardens, near the Old Fort, & the staff here are very happy to provide general tourist information, even if you don't take one of their tours.

Tropical Tours & Safaris [124 C5] `024 2236794; m 0777 413454; e info@tropicaltoursandsafari.com; ☐ TropicalToursZanzibar. From a small but highly efficient office on Kenyatta Rd, this straightforward & friendly budget company has been recommended by several travellers, & offers the usual range of tours plus car hire, & ferry & air ticket reservations. More recently it's started handling everything from mainland safaris to beach weddings.

ZanTours [120 C2] ☎024 223 3116; e contact@zantours.com; www.zantours.com. The largest operator on Zanzibar, it has a large office in the Malindi area, efficient staff, a fleet of clean vehicles & an impressive range of tours, transfers, excursions & safaris. They cater for groups of any size (from several hundred to just a few) including individuals wanting tailor-made services. You can walk in & they'll set something up on the spot, although most of their clients arrange things in advance by email. ZanTours is closely allied to ZanAir (page 78) & some tours utilise their fleet of planes. One of their most popular tours is a short fly-in excursion from Zanzibar direct to the Selous National Park in southern Tanzania.

✳ **Zanzibar Different** ☎024 223 0004; m 0777 430177; e info@zanzibardifferent. com; www.zanzibardifferent.com. Owned by the delightful Stefanie Schoetz of Mrembo Traditional Spa (see box, page 166) & creator of the Princess Salme Tour (page 186), this small, deliberately different (as its name suggests) company is a great addition to the ever-expanding selection of island operators. Small & personal, they have put a new spin on some classic Zanzibari tours, as well as adding original offerings in music, cookery & the arts, & they are very flexible with all tours being specially adapted for children if necessary. Superb city walking tours, tailored to your interests as you go, with engaging, knowledgeable guides, are highly recommended. Ethical & responsible in their outlook, a percentage of profits goes to the Mtoni Palace Conservation Project. This is a little operation, but well worth seeking out at Mrembo Traditional Spa on Cathedral St.

Zenith Tours ☎024 2232320; m 0777 413084/0774 413084; e info@zenithtours.com; www.zenithtours.com. This very professional & efficient organisation, situated behind the Old Fort, offers transfers, accommodation &

SPICES AND SPICE TOURS
Gemma Pitcher

Sooner or later every visitor to Zanzibar Island (Unguja) will be offered a 'spice tour' – a trip to the farmlands just outside Stone Town to see aromatic plants and herbs growing wild or cultivated in kitchen gardens. Even if you decline a tour, the array of spices on offer in the souvenir shops or heaped in baskets in the local markets will tell you that spice is central to Zanzibar's history and economy.

The history of spices in Zanzibar begins early in the 16th century, when the 'spice race' between the major European powers to control the lucrative trading routes to the Far East was at its height. Portuguese traders gained a toehold on Zanzibar as part of their plan to rule the coast of East Africa and imported various plants, including spices, from their colonies in South America and India. Some land was cleared for plantations, but the Portuguese never really developed their presence on Zanzibar beyond a military one.

It was left to the Omani Arabs, who ruled Zanzibar from the early 19th century, to develop Zanzibar economically as a spice-producing entity. Sultan Seyyid Said, the first Omani sultan to govern Zanzibar, quickly realised the potential of his new dominion, with its hot climate and regular rainfall, as a location for spice farming. With the demise of the slave trade in the late 19th century, spices became Zanzibar's main source of income.

When the era of the sultans ended and the long arm of the British Empire reached Zanzibar, the island's new colonial administrators encouraged the farming of spices and other useful plants, bringing European scientists to establish experimental agricultural stations and government farms such as those at Kizimbani and Kindichi. Today these areas still contain spice plantations controlled by the modern Tanzanian government.

excursions in the mid-range price bracket, including safaris to the mainland. They are also linked to World Unite, a German-based international volunteering organisation, with details of internships & volunteer opportunities across a range of sectors (nursery schools to medical & environmental placements) in Tanzania & Zanzibar.

INDEPENDENT GUIDES If you prefer not to use a tour company, it is possible to arrange a tour of the spice plantations, a boat trip to the islands or transport to the east coast with an independent guide. Many double as taxi drivers; in fact many are taxi drivers first, and guides second. One driver, a **Mr Mitu**, has been doing these tours for many years and has been recommended by many visitors, although sometimes he subcontracts work to other drivers. These days he's so popular that instead of Mr Mitu in his taxi you might find yourself joining a large group touring the island in a fleet of minibuses. He's even got his own office (✆ *024 223 4636;* m *0777 418098*) – a tiny room tucked away behind the old Ciné Afrique with the walls covered in photos, from where his tours leave every morning at 09.30, returning about 15.00. They cost around US$15 per person and are highly recommended by those who have been.

There are several other taxi drivers who also organise their own spice tours. Most will undercut the tour companies (about US$35 for the car seems average), although you may not get the same degree of information that you would get with a specialist guide.

You are almost certain to meet some of the local independent 'guides' who are in fact just hustlers (see box, pages 122–3) who tout for business outside hotels and

But spices in Zanzibar today are by no means simply the preserve of governments keen to produce cash-rich export products or a useful tourist attraction. For the ordinary people of Zanzibar, spices and useful plants are a vital part of everyday life and a rich element in the island's strong and vibrant culture. The spices grown in village kitchen-gardens give their flavour to the distinctive cuisine of Zanzibar, provide innumerable cures for everyday ailments, and yield the dyes and cosmetic products needed to celebrate weddings and festivals.

A spice tour is probably the best way of seeing the countryside around Stone Town and meeting rural communities. Guides take you on a walking tour of the villages and plantations at Kizimbani or Kindichi, picking bunches of leaves, fruit and twigs from bushes and inviting you to smell or taste them to guess what they are. Pretty much all the ingredients of the average kitchen spice rack are represented – cinnamon, turmeric, ginger, garlic, chillies, black pepper, nutmeg and vanilla among many others. Local children follow you all the way round, making baskets of palm leaves and filling them with flowers to give to you. At lunchtime, you'll stop in a local house for a meal of pilau rice and curry, followed by sweet Arabic coffee and perhaps a slice of lemongrass cake. Many spice tours include a visit to the Persian baths built by Sultan Said for his harem, and stop at Fuji or Mangapwani beaches just outside Stone Town for a swim on the way back.

All in all, even if horticulture isn't one of your interests, a spice tour is still an excellent way of gaining an insight into one of the most important aspects of rural life in Zanzibar.

For more information on the spices you'll encounter on your tour, see the box on pages 192–3.

CULTURAL GUIDES IN STONE TOWN

Although the narrow streets of Zanzibar are like a labyrinth, Stone Town is not very large and getting seriously lost is unlikely. (If you don't know where you are, just keep walking and you'll soon come out onto Creek Road or one of the streets alongside the sea.) In fact, for many visitors getting lost in the maze of narrow streets and alleys is all part of the fun. However, if your time is limited, you prefer not to become disorientated, or you want to find some specific sites of interest, it's possible to hire a knowledgeable guide from most local tour companies.

If you don't want a formal tour, but would still like to be accompanied by a local, you could engage the services of the *papaasi* (see box, pages 122–3), although generally they will be more interested in taking you to souvenir shops (where they might earn a commission from your purchases) than museums. It might be wiser to ask your hotel or a reputable tour company to put you in touch with someone who will happily walk with you through the streets, and show you the way if you get lost. We have heard from readers who employed a local schoolboy, who was also very happy to practise his English, and this seems an excellent idea. About US$5 (in Tanzanian shillings) for a day's work would be a suitable fee.

A few local individuals worth contacting, who are both reliable and knowledgeable, are the delightfully engaging and loquacious **Anjam** (m *0777 430117 (via Zanzibar Different);* e *anjam_znz@yahoo.com*); cultural radio presenter **Farid Himidy** (m *0777 484734*), who gives fascinating and amusing, cultural and historical tours for around US$15 per person, and who can also tailor his tours for children; **Said El-Gheithy** (m *0779 093066;* e *selgpsm@gmail.com*) who speaks beautiful English and has special interests in anthropology and traditional medicine; and the recently trained guides from the dedicated guide-training and youth capacity-building NGO **KAWA Training Center** on Kiponda Street (m *0777 957995; kawatrainingcenter.com* ⊕ *09.00–17.00 Mon–Fri*). You can either make contact in advance and agree a rendezvous, or simply make some calls on arrival. Tours typically last a couple of hours and usually start from an iconic landmark, such as outside the Old Fort.

restaurants, or along the streets of Stone Town. For spice tours, papaasi prices are often cheaper than those offered by regular companies, but the tours are usually shorter, the vehicles out of condition, and without a proper guide, which usually makes the whole thing pointless unless you are a fairly skilled botanist.

For short boat trips, it doesn't usually make much difference if you go with the papaasi or a regular company, although if you deal with the papaasi be aware that safety equipment is likely to be inadequate, if available at all, and if things go wrong, it is very difficult to complain or get your money back.

6

Zanzibar Town

> The streets are, as they should be under such a sky, deep and winding alleys, hardly twenty feet broad, and travellers compare them to the threads of a tangled skein.
>
> *Richard Burton, British explorer (1857)*

Zanzibar Town, sometimes called Zanzibar City, is situated about halfway along the west coast of Zanzibar Island. Many visitors are surprised by its scale and sprawl; the 2012 recorded population of 223,033 – making it by far the largest settlement in the archipelago. When combined with the census districts immediately surrounding the capital, the population figure rises to a staggering 593,678, and gives a greater sense of the urban sprawl focused on this part of the island. So, whilst the city centre district (Mjini) has grown by only a little over 17,000 people in the last decade, the regional concentration of growth has been more dramatic: a consequence of the combined impact of natural population growth and immigration. That said, Zanzibar Town has always been a bustling, significant city and during the colonial period, before the development of towns such as Dar es Salaam, Nairobi and Mombasa, Zanzibar Town was the largest settlement in the whole of East Africa.

Zanzibar Town is divided into two sections by Creek Road, though the creek itself has now been reclaimed. On the west side is the 'heart' of Zanzibar Town: the evocative old quarter, usually called Stone Town. This is the more interesting section for visitors: many of the buildings were constructed during the 19th century (although some date from before this time), when Zanzibar was a major trading centre and at the height of its power. The trade created wealth which in turn led to the construction of palaces, mosques and many fine houses. Discovering the architectural gems hidden along the tortuous maze of narrow streets and alleyways that wind through Stone Town is part of the island's magic for many visitors. Aside from the souvenir Tingatinga paintings, neatly folded kanga fabrics and beaded jewellery, it's a scene virtually unchanged since the mid 19th century (see Burton's description above).

On the east side of Creek Road is Michenzani, or the 'New City', though this part of town used to be called Ng'ambo (literally 'the other side') and is still often referred to by its unofficial name. It's a sprawling area of mainly single-storey houses, local shops and offices, covering a significantly wider area than Stone Town. This used to be where the poorer African and Swahili people lived, while wealthier Arabs, Indians and Europeans lived in Stone Town, and to a large extent this rich–poor division still exists today. Some attempt has been made to 'modernise' this area: at the centre of Michenzani are some dreary, uninviting blocks of flats (apartment buildings) that were built in the late 1960s by East German engineers as part of an international aid scheme. Few visitors go to this eastern part of Zanzibar Town, as there is little in the way of 'sights', though a visit here certainly helps to broaden your understanding:

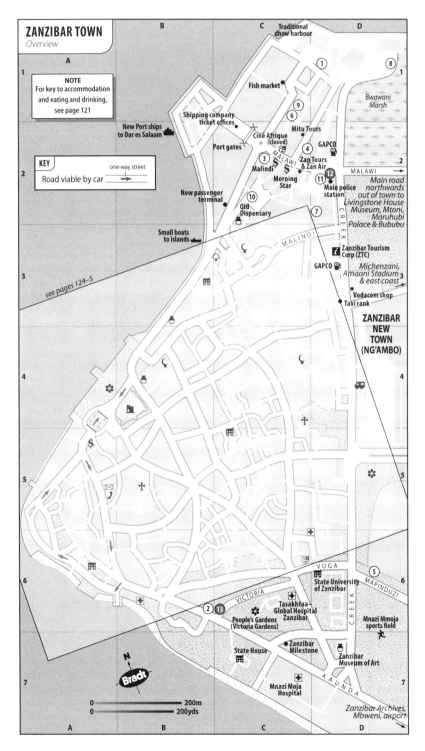

ZANZIBAR TOWN
Overview

NOTE
For key to accommodation
and eating and drinking,
see page 121

KEY
Road viable by car — — — one-way street

Traditional
dhow harbour

Fish market

New Port ships
to Dar es Salaam

Shipping company
ticket offices

Cine Afrique
(closed)
Port gates

Mitu Tours

GAPCO

Zan Tours
& Zan Air

Malindi

Morning
Star

Main police
station

New passenger
terminal

Old
Dispensary

Small boats
to islands

see pages 124–5

Bwawani
Marsh

Main road
northwards
out of town to
Livingstone House
Museum, Mtoni,
Maruhubi
Palace & Bububu

Zanzibar Tourism
Corp (ZTC)

GAPCO

Michenzani,
Amaani Stadium
& east coast

Vodacom shop
Taxi rank

ZANZIBAR
NEW
TOWN
(NG'AMBO)

VUGA

State University
of Zanzibar

MAPINDUZI

Mnazi Mmoja
sports field

VICTORIA

Tasakhtaa–
Global Hospital
Zanzibar

People's Gardens
(Victoria Gardens)

Zanzibar
Milestone

Zanzibar
Museum of Art

State House

KAUNDA

Mnazi Moja
Hospital

Zanzibar Archives,
Mbweni, airport

N

Bradt

0   200m
0   200yds

you'll realise that beside Stone Town is a city where thousands of real people live and work in far less exotic, but no less authentic, surroundings.

The best way to explore Stone Town is on foot, but the maze of lanes and alleys can be very disorientating. To help you get your bearings, it is useful to think of Stone Town as a triangle, bounded on two sides by sea, and along the third by Creek Road. If you get lost, it is always possible to aim in one direction until you reach the outer edge of the town where you should find a landmark.

Although many of the thoroughfares in Stone Town are too narrow for cars, when walking you should watch out for bikes and scooters being ridden at breakneck speed! It's also useful to realise that paths wide enough for cars are usually called roads while narrower ones are generally referred to as streets. Hence, you can drive along New Mkunazini Road or Kenyatta Road, but to visit a place on Kiponda Street or Mkunazini Street you have to walk. When looking for hotels or places of interest, you should also note that most areas of Stone Town are named after the main street in that area: the area being referred to as Kiponda Street or Malindi Street, instead of simply Kiponda or Malindi. This can be confusing, as you may not be on the street of that name. But don't worry: at least you're near!

GETTING AROUND

Most visitors and locals get around the town on foot, and in Stone Town this is the best and often the only way, but there are other means of transport available. Note that if there is a petrol shortage, as periodically happens, taxi fares automatically go up and petrol prices can increase exponentially.

TAXI Private taxis for hire wait at taxi ranks around town; they do not usually cruise for business, although if you see a taxi in the street it is always possible to flag it down. The main taxi ranks are near the Gapco petrol station on Creek Road [120 D3], outside the ZanAir office just east of the Port Gates [120 C2], beside the House of Wonders [124 D3], in front of the Serena Inn in Kelele Square [124 A5], and at the northern end of Kenyatta Road [124 C4].

There are no meters. Wherever you go, you should agree the fare with the driver before starting your journey. A short ride through town costs US$3–4; all the way across town costs around US$5–6. A longer ride, from town out to Mtoni Marine Centre or Mbweni Ruins Hotel, will be about US$8–10. From town to the airport is around US$10–15, and it should be the same the other way, but from the airport into town taxi drivers may quote fares of US$20 or higher.

DALLA DALLA Converted small lorries with two rows of wooden seats at the back called dalla dallas (or dallas for short) carry passengers on local runs around town and to outlying suburbs. There are several routes, all starting at the Darajani Bus Station on Creek Road. The most useful routes for visitors are detailed in the box on page 112. Fares rise from pennies up to a maximum of US$1.50–2 for trans-island journeys. Safety and driving standards are fairly questionable, and comfort levels nil, but they are very cheap and certainly give a feel for local life.

BICYCLE A bike is very handy for getting around Zanzibar Town and the surrounding area, and bikes can be hired from several of the tour companies listed on pages 114–17. They are either sturdy steel Chinese-made models, or more modern-looking (though almost as heavy) mountain bikes. Prices for Chinese bikes are about US$10 per day; mountain bikes are US$15 per day. A deposit of around US$50 may be required.

CAR AND MOTORBIKE A car or motorbike is not really necessary or practical for getting around Zanzibar Town as distances are short, road signage is minimal, other drivers are erratic, and parking is often difficult. There are no international car-hire companies on the island; however, both can be hired from various tour companies listed on pages 114–17. Prices vary, but are generally around US$25–30 per day for a scooter, US$35–40 per day for a motorbike, between US$50 and US$60 per day for a small car (eg: Suzuki 'jeep') and around US$100 per day for a larger 4x4 (eg: a Toyota Land Cruiser). Check your vehicle carefully before driving off, make sure you have reliable contact numbers in the event of vehicle problems, and ensure you have a signed Zanzibar Island driving permit and your usual licence before heading anywhere. Zanzibar Town driving is not for the faint-hearted!

GUIDES AND THE *PAPAASI*

Nearly all tourists who come to Zanzibar Town use the services of a guide at some stage during their visit. If your trip was arranged from outside Zanzibar, it will sometimes include the services of a guide. Even if you organise something simple through a tour company in Zanzibar, like a visit to the spice plantations, the price usually includes a guide to show you around. Guides from reputable companies have to be registered with the Tourism Commission, and will carry identity cards, which they receive on completion of a short instruction course.

There are also many other 'guides' in Zanzibar who are not registered, most of whom are not really guides at all, but touts and hustlers who make their money showing tourists to hotels and souvenir shops, arranging transport or getting groups together to share boat rides. These touts are known locally as beach-boys or *papaasi* – literally meaning 'ticks', ie: parasites or irritating bloodsuckers.

When a ship comes into Zanzibar from Dar es Salaam, there is usually a group of papaasi on the dockside. Some can be quite aggressive, but a few are not too unpleasant and will help you find a place to stay (which may be useful, as the labyrinth of alleys in Stone Town is disorientating at first). Tell them exactly what you want in terms of standard and price. In theory, it should not cost you any more money and could save you a lot of walking but in practice it does not always work so well. The papaasi will usually expect a commission from the hotel for bringing them a guest. Some hotels pay more commission than others, and some do not pay at all, so the papaasi will only take you to the places where they get a decent cut. Hence their hotel recommendations are usually far from impartial.

We have heard from several travellers who arrived on Zanzibar, aiming to stay in a certain hotel, only to be told by the welcome party of papaasi that it was 'full', 'closed' or even 'burnt down'. If you're in any doubt, it is best to be polite but firm

The following selection of places to stay in and around Zanzibar Town is not exhaustive, as new places continually open and existing ones change name, location and ownership; however, it is as comprehensive as we can possibly make it, and it does aim to highlight the best accommodation in each price bracket.

If you are coming from the airport (or elsewhere on the island) by taxi, and don't have a reservation, be firm about which hotel you want to go to, otherwise the driver will most likely take you to wherever offers him the best commission, not necessarily the best quality or value (see warning on pages 122–3). Do also remember that many hotels in the older part of Zanzibar Town cannot be reached by vehicle because of the narrow maze of lanes, and you may have to walk a few hundred metres through the streets to reach it. If the driver shows you the way, and this is advisable if you haven't been before, then he'll probably help with your luggage, in which case it's usual to give a fair tip for this extra service.

Much of the accommodation is in, or very near, Stone Town, which is the best area for atmosphere and ease of getting around. Several places do not have exact street addresses, and many lanes and house numbers, even if they exist, are unmarked. For ease, we have tried hard to mark the lanes, landmarks and all listed properties on the Zanzibar Stone Town maps (pages 120 and 124–5).

Unless stated otherwise, hotels listed below offer air conditioning and en-suite bathrooms as standard. For details of price categories, see page 92. The Bwawani Hotel and House of Spices are best avoided.

(or simply ignore them completely), and find your own hotel. Even better, make a phone call or send an email to reserve a room in advance; some hotels even give discounts for advance bookings. They should also be able to arrange for someone to meet and escort you to their establishment.

After arranging your hotel, most papaasi will want to be your 'guide', offering to show you around the sights or souvenir shops of Stone Town, find companions for dive trips or boat excursions, or arrange transport to the east coast. Use these services if you need them but be prepared to pay. Always be aware that the owners of the souvenir shops, boats and dive centres will usually pay commission to the papaasi, a charge that will, of course, be effectively passed on to you.

Some papaasi are outright crooks, and involved in robberies and other crimes like drug dealing. Others are conmen, and some travellers have been stung arranging budget hire cars where a papaasi has taken a deposit then simply disappeared. Changing money is another potentially expensive operation, where initially tempting good rates precede sleight-of-hand tricks or simply snatch-and-run theft. Budget travellers have also reported having drugs planted on them by papaasi they befriended, who then reported them to the police; any fines (official or unofficial) paid out included a kickback to the informant.

If you deal only with reputable tour companies (whether low or high budget) you'll have none of these problems. Although trustworthy guides have identity cards, some papaasi have managed to get some too (they could be fakes, or simply stolen – it's hard to tell). This of course is confusing for tourists. There is a need for legitimate guides on Zanzibar, who can help tourists without hassling them, and it is hoped that the government will apply itself to this matter in the near future. For a list of reputable guides and operators, see pages 114–17.

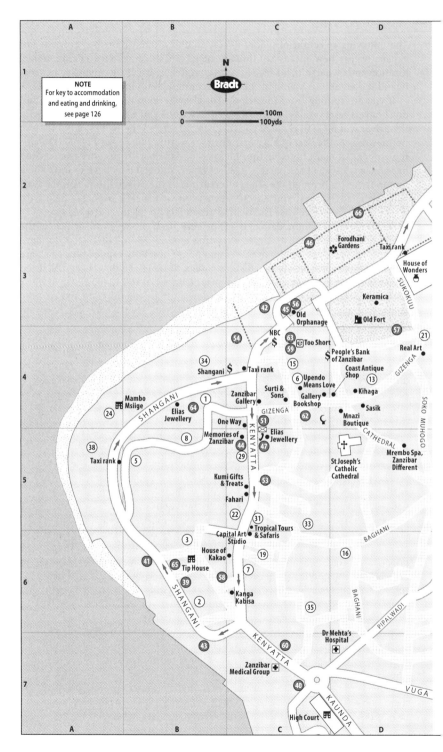

NOTE
For key to accommodation
and eating and drinking,
see page 126

N

Bradt

0 ——————100m
0 ——————100yds

66

46   Forodhani
      Gardens   Taxi rank

                            House of
                            Wonders

                 Keramica

42 45 56
        Old
        Orphanage   Old Fort

NBC   63 Too Short   57   21
54   59   People's Bank
                       of Zanzibar   Real Art

34   15   Coast Antique
Shangani Taxi rank   6 Upendo   Shop
                             Means Love   13
Mambo   Surti &
Msiige   Zanzibar Sons   Gallery   Kihaga
         Gallery   Bookshop
24   64   Sasik
        Elias   1   62   Mnazi
        Jewellery   Boutique
                One Way
        8   Memories of   Elias
             Zanzibar   44   Jewellery
38   29 47
Taxi rank 5   St Joseph's   Mrembo Spa,
                                    Catholic   Zanzibar
        Kumi Gifts   53   Cathedral   Different
        & Treats
        Fahari
             22
                  31 Tropical Tours 33
        3   Capital Art & Safaris
                  Studio
        41 65   House of   19   16
            Tip House Kakao
        39   58   7
        2   Kanga
                  Kabisa   35
        43   Dr Mehta's
                   60   Hospital
             Zanzibar
             Medical Group
                   40
                                  VUGA
                        High Court

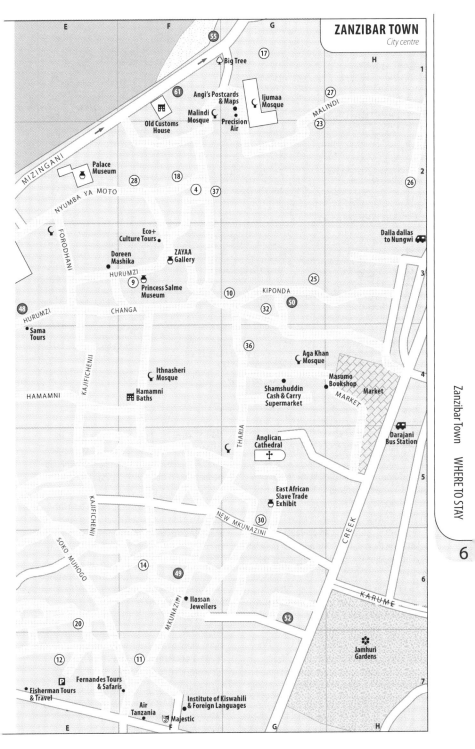

Big Tree

Angi's Postcards & Maps

Ijumaa Mosque

Malindi Mosque

Precision Air

Old Customs House

MALINDI

Palace Museum

MIZINGANI

NYUMBA YA MOTO

FORODHANI

Eco+ Culture Tours

Doreen Mashika

ZAYAA Gallery

HURUMZI

Princess Salme Museum

CHANGA

KIPONDA

HURUMZI

Sama Tours

Dalla dallas to Nungwi

KAJIFICHENII

Ithnasheri Mosque

HAMAMNI

Hamamni Baths

Aga Khan Mosque

Masumo Bookshop

Market

MARKET

Shamshuddin Cash & Carry Supermarket

THARIA

Anglican Cathedral

Darajani Bus Station

East African Slave Trade Exhibit

NEW MKUNAZINI

KAJIFICHENII

SOKO MUHOGO

CREEK

KARUME

Ilassan Jewellers

MKUNAZINI

Fernandes Tours & Safaris

Fisherman Tours & Travel

Air Tanzania

Majestic

Institute of Kiswahili & Foreign Languages

Jamhuri Gardens

125

Where to stay

1	Abuso Inn	B4	15	Karibu Inn	C4
2	Africa House	B6	16	Keki House	D6
3	Al Johari	B6	17	Kholle House	G1
4	Asmini Palace	F2	18	Kiponda	F2
5	Beyt al Salaam	B5	19	Kisiwa House	C6
6	Coco de Mer	C4		Lemongrass	(see 47)
7	Dhow Palace	C6	20	Manch Lodge	E6
8	DoubleTree by Hilton	B5	21	Maru Maru	D4
9	Emerson on Hurumzi	F3	22	Mazsons	C5
10	Emerson Spice	G3	23	Narrow Street	G2
11	Flamingo Guest House	F7	24	Park Hyatt Zanzibar	A4
12	Haven Lodge	E7	25	Pearl Guesthouse	G3
13	Jafferji House & Spa	D4	26	The Rosal	H2
14	Jambo Guesthouse	F6	27	Safari Lodge	H1

28	The Seyyida	F2
29	Shangani	C5
30	St Monica's Hostel	G5
31	Stone Town Café & Bed & Breakfast	C5
32	The Swahili House	G3
33	Tausi Palace	C5
34	Tembo House	B4
35	Zanzibar	C6
36	Zanzibar Coffee House	G4
37	Zanzibar Palace	F2
38	Zanzibar Serena Inn	A5

Where to eat and drink

39	6 Degrees South Grill & Wine Bar	B6	51	La Taperia	C4
40	Abyssinian Maritim	C7	52	La Taverna	G6
41	Amore Mio	B6	53	Lazuli	C5
42	Archipelago	C3	54	Livingstone Beach	C4
43	Baboo Café	B7		Lulu Restaurant & Lounge	(see 28)
	Baharia	(see 38)		Maru Maru	(see 21)
	Beyt al Chai	(see 5)	55	Mercury's	F1
44	The Book Café	C5		Mistress of Spices	(see 13)
45	Buni Café	C3	56	Monsoon	C3
46	Café Foro	C3	57	Old Fort	D4
47	Café Miwa	C5	58	Pagoda Chinese	B6
48	Clove	E3	59	Radha Vegetarian	C4
49	Green Garden	F6	60	Rendezvous Les Spices	C7
50	House of Spices	G3	61	Sea View Indian	F1
	Hurumzi Movie Café	(see 9)		The Secret Garden	(see 10)
	Hurumzi Tea House	(see 9)			

62	Sforno Pizza & Sweet	C4
63	The Silk Route	C4
	The Spice Tea House	(see 10)
	Stone Town Café	(see 31)
	The Swahili House	(see 32)
	Taarab	(see 8)
64	TAMU Gelateria Italiana	B4
65	Tatu	B6
	Zanzibar Coffee House Café	(see 36)
66	Zenji Forodhani Garden Café	D2

EXCLUSIVE

✱ 🏠 **Jafferji House & Spa** [124 D4] (8 suites & 2 rooms) 📱 0774 078442/1; e info@ jafferjihouse.net; www.jafferjihouse.net. In early 2012, Javed Jafferji opened up his childhood home as an elaborately crafted boutique hotel. Resident publisher, shopkeeper & tour operator, Javed is well known in Zanzibar for his photographs, & a selection of them can be found adorning the walls. Recently renovated with a loving approach, this certainly has the wow factor: an artistic blend of old & new, fine antiques, sumptuous fabrics & eclectic tribal objets d'art create an extravagant & theatrical spectacle. Zanzibari doors, old wall clocks & gramophones are reminiscent of days gone by, while rich colours, AC & flatscreen TVs give a thoroughly modern edge. The suites & rooms all have baths, & are overflowing with exquisite furniture & traditional fabrics. Bedrooms are named after important figures in Zanzibar's history, such as the Princess Salme suite with its large ornately carved bed, stained-glass windows,

old-fashioned telephone & terracotta walls. The Jafferji suite, on the top floor, is most impressive of all, with an enormous copper bath, a varnished wooden floor & traditional Zanzibari shuttered wooden frontage, plus, of course, fabulous views & Stone Town's only outdoor shower! Up on the rooftop is a tiny but gorgeous outpost of Amani Spa, with Zanzibari therapists offering massages in an open-sided treatment room with a standalone bath & shower & the best spa views in town. Downstairs, the Mistress of Spices restaurant (page 140) offers freshly prepared international food from an à la carte menu & there's also a useful internet point & TV room. Despite all the opulence, the hotel still feels warm & welcoming, like a home, albeit a very stylish one. B&B. ♨

✱ 🏠 **Park Hyatt Zanzibar** [124 A4] (67 rooms) 📞 024 550 1234; e zanzibar.park@ hyatt.com; www.zanzibar.park.hyatt.com. For location, grandeur & elegance, the imposing Park Hyatt Zanzibar is hard to beat. Opened in March 2015, in arguably Stone Town's

Theft from hotel rooms is very unusual, but we'd always recommend that you pack your things in a locked bag when you leave your room for any length of time, and that you store any valuables in the hotel's safe, preferably within a sealed, lockable bag or pouch, to prevent tampering. This is not really an issue at hotels in the middle and upper price ranges because many offer individual safety-deposit boxes, either at reception or in the rooms, and several budget hotels in Zanzibar Town now run an organised system with a book for guests to write in exactly what they leave.

Historically, the more serious robberies (sometimes with violence) have occurred on some of the beaches in and around Zanzibar Town. You should not walk here alone, particularly after dark, and sadly there are parts of town where drugged and drunken youths wander the streets looking for kicks (just as they do in many other parts of the world). Another time to be wary is the hour or two just after sunset during the period of Ramadan, when everybody is inside breaking their fast, and the streets are deserted.

most prestigious location, it has brought a luxury brand & international levels of hotel sophistication to the city. Sandwiched between leafy Kelele Sq & the Indian Ocean, & just mins on foot from the quintessential labyrinthine alleyways & city hustle, this hotel offers calm & pampering to its high-end, image-conscious guests.

The hotel itself spans 2 buildings: the UNESCO-listed Mambo Msiige mansion (page 175) & the brand new Zamani Residence, a contemporary take on Swahili architecture, with strong Middle Eastern influences. From the first striking sight of the arched reception courtyard, guests glimpse the hotel's style: Modernist minimalism meets historic Swahili. Stark, whitewashed interiors & formidably high ceilings sit alongside soaring Omani arches, cool courtyards, wide marbled corridors & intricate timber latticework. Rooms are extremely comfortable, light & contemporary, with timber 4-poster beds, intelligent lighting, fabulous rain shower, a free-standing bath, & all the best in toiletries, mod cons & refreshments. It's the wide balconies & idyllic Indian Ocean views that really catch the imagination though: the chance to peep through sweet almond trees to watch dhow flotillas is worth the ocean-front upgrade cost. The public areas are equally grand in scale: the glazed Terrace Bar with its giant metal lampshades, blue backlit bar & iced magnums of Roederer Cristal; the breezy waterfront veranda beautified with clipped bougainvillea; & the

airy Dining Room, dressed in turquoise & white herringbone marble, complete with slow spinning fans & a gentle efficiency. Menus ooze freshness & flavour, with culinary options ranging from crispy falafel (US$10) to nasi goreng (US$15) & pan-fried king prawns (US$25); children are well catered for, & memorable barefoot dinners on the beach (US$150 for 2) can be arranged.

The atmosphere is fairly formal & the service is slick & understated throughout, with a distinct air of wealth permeating both the building & its guests. Perusing the bling on display at the in-house jewellers & rejuvenating in the Anatara Spa are appealing options; whilst less extravagant visitors can still enjoy that Hollywood feel from a dip in the stunning glass-sided swimming pool, a complimentary beach class with the resident yogi, and a chance to dress up for dinner. There's even a gallery tucked into the back of the ground-floor lobby area, exhibiting a good collection of watercolour sketches by the late Zanzibari artist, John Baptist Da Silva. Insulation from the frenetic city beyond its heavy carved doors make this a hotel for those wanting to visit Stone Town but with the option to escape its hot, hectic reality. For some, the hotel is joyful relief, but for others it lacks the bustle of a stay in the city. For most, however, it is hard not to take great pleasure in its relaxed & beautiful seafront terrace, even if only for stylish sundowners. For now, the Park Hyatt is Stone Town's ultimate hotel haven. B&B. ♛

⌂ **Zanzibar Serena Inn** [124 A5] (51 rooms)
☎ 024 223 1015/3051/3587; e zanzibar@serena.
co.tz; www.serenahotels.com. Part of this efficient
East African chain, the Serena is both efficient &
decidedly African. This large, impressive hotel sits
between the sea & Kelele Sq on a green & pleasant
corner of Shangani. Converted from 2 historic
buildings & restored at great expense, the Serena
was originally the External Communications
('Extelcoms') headquarters, built in the early 20th
century by the British colonial administration. The
neighbouring house is much older & was known
originally as the Chinese Doctor's Residence, where
explorer David Livingstone stayed before one of his
journeys to the African mainland. It later became
the private home of the British consul.
Empty & in a bad state of repair prior to
restoration, their 1997 conversion into today's
hotel was handled sensitively, with a design
reflecting Zanzibar's Indian, Arabic & colonial
heritage. Walls are decorated with historic
prints & contemporary paintings, but perhaps
the most interesting relics are the pieces of old
telecommunications equipment unearthed from
the basement & now on display in some of the
top corridors. Beyond its historic appeal, the staff
here are consistently excellent, in part due to the
hotel's very good training scheme, & will go out
of their way to engage & assist. The bedrooms are
a little dated, but well furnished in mahogany,
with gleaming polished floors & crisp white linen.
Every room – from standard to state – boasts
all the in-room & public facilities expected of an
international-class hotel, including an inviting
seafront swimming pool, 2 excellent restaurants, a
coffee shop, Wi-Fi, satellite TV & reasonably priced,
in-house massage treatments. If you happen not
to be on holiday here, there's a business centre
& conference facilities. Generous discounts are
available in the low season & sometimes also
during quiet midweek periods, & it's worth noting
that here, like many of the top-end hotels, cheaper
rates are often available if you book through an
overseas tour operator. B&B. ⏝

LUXURY

⌂ **DoubleTree by Hilton** [124 B5] (58 rooms
& 4 suites) ☎ 024 223 4062; e ZNZST_Res@hilton.
com; www.doubletree.hilton.com. This branch
of DoubleTree became only the 2nd international
hotel chain to make its mark on the city, following

the Serena. Located in the centre of town, this is
a modern hotel with traditional touches. Rooms
& suites are relatively small but comfortable &
clean with a good range of facilities & helpful
guest services. The rooftop Taarab Restaurant
& Bar (🕐 06.30–22.00 Mon–Fri; 07.00–22.00
Sat–Sun $$$$) serves drinks, snacks & both buffet
& à la carte meals. Business travellers benefit from
a large separate conference centre on Kelele Sq
with 24hr business centre, 8 conference rooms &
outdoor café. B&B. **$$$$$**

⌂ **Kisiwa House** [124 C6] (11 rooms) ☎ 024
223 5654; e info@kisiwahouse.com; www.
kisiwahouse.com. Neighbouring Dhow Palace,
Kisiwa House opened in 2009 as an elegant
& welcoming hotel. Rooms are divided into 3
categories – Burdani, Malkia & Sulaima – all
decorated in pure white with splashes of sea blue.
Burdani are the only suites without sitting rooms,
while Suliama rooms are simply huge (perfect for
families) & have standalone baths. All rooms are
kitted out with fans, safes, TV, AC, fridges, kangas
& silk-edged mosquito nets. Spacious bathrooms
contain both baths & showers, plus 2 sinks &
various sweet-smelling lotions & potions. With a
cheery, light-filled reception, filled with potted
plants & vases of anthuriums, & a double-height
courtyard lounge for chilling, this place displays
calm, class & imagination throughout. For dining,
Darini, the sunny rooftop restaurant & bar, has
both an indoor & outdoor section with the hint
of a sea view. Easy listening music accompanies
meals of local-style seafood with an international
twist: seafood broth with lemongrass (US$7.50),
vermicelli salad with sweet chilli prawns
(US$7.50); or risotto with calamari, octopus & fish
(US$20). Kisiwa also has a seaside sister property
in Paje. B&B. **$$$$$**

⌂ **Maru Maru** [124 D4] (50 rooms) ☎ 024 223
8516/7/8; e reservations@marumaruzanzibar.
com; www.marumaruzanzibar.com. In Jan 2012,
after a 6-year renovation, Maru Maru opened in a
prime spot just behind the Old Fort & the House
of Wonders. On the site of an old Hindu temple,
it's a gleaming, modern hotel ('*maru maru*' means
'marble tile' in Kiswahili), created from the merger
of 3 adjoining buildings, the last of which was
added in 2016 to allow for the creation of a rooftop
swimming pool, spa, gym & 6 new rooms. The hotel
is spotless, well finished & bright throughout, with
a host of polite, well-trained staff. The modern

rooms are all identical bar bed size (twin, queen or king); Wi-Fi, safe, fridge, in-room tea & coffee facilities & a flatscreen TV are all standard. Furniture is crafted locally; linen is crisp & white with trademark turquoise cushions & throws. The rooms are all en suite, 6 with traditional hammam baths & the remainder with showers. There's a choice of 2 dining areas: The Bakery, serving freshly baked bread, pastries & cakes in the fountain courtyard, & the Terrace Restaurant up on the roof. The latter offers a great view across town, the cathedral spires & out towards the water, making this a popular choice for laughter & cocktails at sunset, followed by spicy Indian suppers made from locally sourced produce ($$$–$$$$). On a more practical note, Maru Maru is one of very few hotels in Stone Town to have a lift, & for the very few who self-drive, there's parking. B&B. $$$$–🐘

🏠 **Africa House Hotel** [124 B6] (15 rooms) m 0773 884606; m 0777 212621; e gm@africahousehotel.co.tz; www.africahousehotel.co.tz. This sea-facing hotel was once among the most popular places to stay in Zanzibar Town, but sadly it would be unlikely to make the cut these days. Situated along the Shangani waterfront, Africa House served as the English Club from 1888 until the end of the colonial era, but is perhaps best known for its expansive balcony bar, which, remains a good sundowner venue offering a winning combination of fruity cocktails & frothy coffees, a cracking ocean view & tasty bar food. Under new Indian management since mid 2015, there have been some renovations to the interiors, but somehow the atmosphere is lacking warmth & style. The rooms are clean & functional with a mix of traditional décor & modern facilities (AC & TV), albeit the tasselled cushions, heavy velvet curtains & tiled floors seem incongruous together. With some great new accommodation options in the city, the unattractive frontage, variable service & steep bar prices perhaps make this a less attractive an option than it once was, but it's remains a good low-season deal. $$$$–$$$$$

🏠 **Beyt al Salaam** [124 B5] (11 rooms) 024 223 2592; e reservations@beytalsalaam.com; www.beytalsalaam.com. Standing across Kelele Sq from the Serena, behind thick walls & antique shuttered windows, Beyt al Salaam was previously the fêted boutique hotel, Beyt al Chai. Sadly, ownership change & a desire to squeeze more rooms into this once lovely little hotel have robbed

it of its former charm & glory. The lounge & bar have been sacrificed to allow for a doubling of bedrooms, resulting in no public areas & a darkening of corridors as windows disappeared behind doors. Arranged over 3 floors, its bedrooms are simple & clean with high ceilings, some authentic Zanzibari furniture & pretty views over the square. The downstairs restaurant serves b/fasts, light lunches & tasty dinners to guests & city visitors (page 140). It's hard not to conclude that whilst passable, the heart has left this place. B&B. $$$$–$$$$$

🏠 **Emerson on Hurumzi** [125 F3] (22 rooms) 024 223 2784; e reception@emerSononhurumzi.com; www.emerSononhurumzi.com. Reincarnated many times, this hotel grande dame is a Stone Town institution. The hotel itself sprawls across 3 venerable buildings dating from 1840–70, one of which was originally the home of Tharia Topan, a prominent Ismaili Indian merchant who also built the Old Dispensary (page 162) & Zanzibar Coffee House (page 133). The original merchant house was gutted & completely restored, opening in 1999 to reveal a thoroughly original & innovative transformation. Nowhere before in the city had Swahili style looked so theatrical or sexy – the concept was game-changing. Vibrant to the point of kitsch & decorated with antique Zanzibari furniture & carpets, its distinctly bohemian atmosphere brought glamour & romance to the back streets. Each of the 22 rooms is different in character, including the open-sided Pavilion Room, the vast Crystal Room with its intricately carved balcony & the airy South Room – reached by a small bridge. Very deliberately, none have a TV or fridge. Some have AC, others rely on natural cooling – shutters, shades, deep balconies & a sea breeze. Sadly, this hotel is looking a little tired these days – for all its initial trendsetting, there are now other places offering a more sophisticated version of Swahili boutique chic. However, having been imaginatively reinvented in the past, anything is possible. Next door, **240 Hurumzi** has a further 6 rooms, which all have shared kitchens & are aimed at long-term visitors, but are sometimes booked on a per-night basis. These newer rooms are all on the top 2 floors of the building & are brimming with antiques & Zanzibari furniture. For those not self-catering, b/fast is taken in the hotel's Hurumzi Tea House restaurant, the 2nd-highest building in Zanzibar Town, with some of the finest skyline views to boot (page 139). B&B. $$$$–$$$$$

6

✷ 🏠 **Emerson Spice** [125 G3] (11 rooms)
\024 223 2776; e reservations@emersonspice.
com; www.emersonspice.com. Opened in 2012, this
exotic & historic hotel is the brainchild of the late
Emerson Skeens, with strikingly theatrical rooms,
each dedicated to a leading lady & each with a
colourful twist on traditional Swahili design. Ceilings
are immense, vibrant colours adorn the walls, &
potted plants, stained-glass windows & intricately
carved wooden doors add to the atmosphere.
Rooms are kitted out with fans & AC, fridges & bright
mosquito nets, & eclectic curtain fabrics & dark
wooden furniture. Some rooms even have hand-
painted murals on the wall, such as the Ancient
Eqyptian scene in the Aida room, & all come with a
dramatic tale attached to their interior design. Open-
plan bathrooms feature Arabic baths & twin sinks,
bordered with decorative painted ceramic tiles.
The attention to detail continues throughout the
communal areas of the property where the interior
courtyard & its twinkling blue pool are reminiscent
of a Moroccan *riad*. There's now also a cool, palm-
filled walled garden & the enchantingly atmospheric
Secret Garden restaurant (pages 140–1). Culinary
creativity is worth noting on the rooftop here, too
(page 139). B/fast can be served in the entrance
hall, on the rooftop or on your own balcony. With
its exciting design, beautiful rooms, bijoux oasis &
impressive food, Emerson Spice is unquestionably
one of the best choices for an atmospheric stay in
Stone Town. B&B. **$$$$–$$$$$**

UPMARKET

🏠 **The Swahili House** [125 G3] (20 rooms)
m 0777 510209; e info@theswahilihouse.
com; www.theswahilihouse.com. A serious
regeneration project in 2008, took this
dilapidated, 19th-century Indian merchant's
home & converted it into Swahili House. Towering
behind a café courtyard filled with potted palms,
it is a traditional hotel built around a central
roofed atrium, with an authentic Zanzibari feel &
good management courtesy of Moivaro Lodges
(the East African operators also behind Fumba
Beach Lodge, page 332). It's not fancy, but rather
a cool, calm & efficient establishment with a
genuine Stone Town vibe & central location. The
rooms are decked out in locally produced furniture
& antiques, with polished stone floors, narrow
wooden balconies (some rooms) & a touch of
modernity in the form of AC. There are 3 room

types of increasing size – Deluxe, Suites & Sultan
Suites – spread over 4 floors, with those nearest
the top offering excellent views of Stone Town's
alleyways. As of 2015, there is also a blissfully
efficient lift from reception all the way to the roof
– welcome relief for hot, weary travellers! Alight
at the rooftop restaurant to one of the largest
hotel rooftops, where you can lounge on batik-
covered baraza benches, sip a cool drink & look
out over ramshackle rooftops towards the sea;
there's even a jacuzzi up there! B&B. **$$$$–**👑
🏠 **Al Johari** [124 B6] (15 rooms) \024 223
6779; e info@al-johari.com; www.al-johari.com.
Flanked by 2 golden lions, the heavily carved door of
Al Johari brought a touch of boutique bling to Stone
Town's hotel scene when it opened. The Mauritian
owners carefully refurbished the 2 old buildings,
which now combine to make up the hotel, & tried
hard to strike a balance between traditional Zanzibari
influences & modern amenities. Meaning 'jewel' in
Swahili, the vision certainly had a good degree of
opulence: a multi-storey cascading waterfall at its
heart, fine wines & an array of antiques. The shine
may have faded a little with time, though. Whilst
rooms remain tastefully furnished with crisp linen
on Zanzibari beds, marble floors, massage showers
(plus jacuzzis in suites), glass sinks & organic herbal
products, there are little signs of minor maintenance
issues: the odd broken lock, noisy AC or leaky shower.
There is, however, a lovely rooftop bar where guests
enjoy flavoured shisha pipes in a décor reminiscent
of a bygone era. Adjoining the bar, in a glass AC area,
is the formal restaurant, Fusion. Al Johari is most
easily found by following the Shangani Rd towards 6
Degrees South, then taking the signed alleyway away
from the sea. B&B. **$$$$**
🏠 **Kholle House** [125 G1] (10 rooms)
m 0772 161033; e info@khollehouse.com; www.
khollehouse.com. Kholle House opened its carved
wooden doors in Feb 2011 & has become a hit with
those seeking a traditionally inspired boutique
bolthole. Named after Princess Kholle, who once
used the rooms here to display her most treasured
possessions of artwork & ceramics, the house makes
the most of its fascinating past by including many
original historic features. It's beautiful & much
thought has gone into the high-quality furnishings.
Rooms are split into 3 categories (Classic Rooms,
Deluxe Rooms & Prestige Suites), varying in size
(some quite bijoux) but all boasting beautiful
beds, nets & AC, as well as a selection of bathroom

products infused with local spices. Some of the Prestige Suites have French décor & furniture, which is a little more contemporary, whilst others have Indian influences. B/fast is, unusually, à la carte & is served in the downstairs b/fast room, overlooking the garden. Outside, various loungers & cushions are scattered amid palms, frangipani trees & a small but lush lawn. There's also a thoroughly inviting pool, complete with an alluring tinkling of water, which is a precious rarity in the heart of Stone Town & a very welcome relief after a hot day. Kholle House can be something of a mission to locate at first – something to note if arriving by taxi or asking directions is the Kiswahili pronunciation of this hotel name sounds more like 'holy house'. B&B. **$$$$**

⌂ **Tausi Palace Hotel** [124 C5] (40 rooms) m 0773 539944; e; www.tausipalacehotel.com. Situated in Baghani St, just off Kenyatta Rd, Tausi Palace (formerly Chavda Hotel) is now part of the same hotel group as Africa House (page 129), Zanzibar House (page 243), & African Sun, Sand & Sea in Bwejuu (pages 282–3). Under gentle, female management, it reopened in July 2015 after some renovation & shows signs of being well kept & ordered. The generally spacious bedrooms have dark wood, antique-style Indian furniture, Persian carpets on tiled floors, white walls & lacquered timber ceilings. Zanzibari beds, minibar, safe, TV, phone, AC, mosquito nets & large bathrooms are standard. There are some excellent sized family rooms with 2 adjoining en-suite bathrooms upstairs. Matching linens & sunlight casting rainbows through the coloured glass door arches add a cheerful edge to the rooms, & a calm atmosphere pervades (aim for a lighter room in the new block). Upstairs is a restaurant & very pleasant rooftop bar, offering one of the best skyline views of St Joseph's Cathedral spires, Shangani mosque & the city beyond. The rooftop terrace is shaded by a high, timber-framed roof & there is also an umbrella-filled courtyard bar on the ground floor, a passable gym & 2 conference centres. Free collections from the port or airport for pre-booked guests. B&B. **$$$$**

⌂ **Tembo House Hotel** [124 B4] (40 rooms & 8 apts) ☎024 223 3005/2069; e reservations@ tembohotel.com; www.tembohotel.com. This hotel has a great location on Shangani Rd, just west of Forodhani Gardens, leading right down to the sea. Easily identified by its grey elephant sculpture at the entrance ('tembo' means 'elephant' in Kiswahili), Tembo has long been a popular

option. Part of the hotel was the 1834 American consulate, & there are 2 more recent wings, both overlooking the ocean & quite Indian in décor. The bedrooms are all off chequerboard-tiled corridors, lined with Arabesque arches & plants in colourful ceramic pots. All have a mosaic Turkish bath, heavily carved furniture, mosquito nets, fridge & TV. Most have a sea view or overlook the large courtyard swimming pool (⌚ 08.00–19.00), whilst some look out over the attractive gardens of the Park Hyatt. It's possible to pay a US$10 'good view supplement' on booking, otherwise you may want to check out available rooms on arrival. The 2 large corner rooms are fabulous for a trpl or couple wanting space, as they have huge private terraces with good sea views. The public spaces are good & varied: a lounge on the upper floor of the old building boasts a huge stained-glass window that fills the room with coloured light, & the beachfront Bahari restaurant has neat tables on decking under clipped sweet almond trees (non-residents welcome). Whilst the hotel is on the beach & deckchairs are laid out, it's not really a beach hotel, but rather a city hotel with a seafront location. There is a reasonable amount of passing local trade on the shoreline, so expect some hassle to buy cashews & sunglasses if you choose to sit out. Equally, the water is relatively polluted this close to the harbour & city so swimming is not advisable. It's also worth noting that, as with its sister property, the Dhow Palace (page 133), the Muslim owners do not serve any alcohol.

Due to a high demand for interconnecting family rooms, Tembo has created 4 apartments across the road & 4 in nearby Mercury House. Tembo Apartments, all named after exotic spices, offer spacious rooms, each with a sitting area, TV, en suite & a small balcony overlooking the Shangani Rd. There are no kitchen facilities, & realistically most short-stay visitors are probably better off in the main hotel. Around the corner, with its entrance in the middle of Zanzibar Gallery shopfront, Mercury House Apartments are squarely aimed at the self-catering market, & offer a private kitchenette & basic crockery. If you're seriously thinking of self-catering, choose Malaika for the largest facilities, although these rooms can also be booked on a B&B basis (b/fast at Tembo Hotel). Guests at both apartments are free to use all main hotel facilities. B&B. **$$$$**

⌂ **The Seyyida** [125 F2] (17 rooms) ☎024 223 8352; m 0779 377 850; e info@theseyyida-zanzibar.com; www.theseyyida-zanzibar.com. The Seyyida, meaning 'lady of the manor' in Swahili, opened as a very welcome addition to the mid-market scene. It offers a cool & quiet haven from the heat & bustle of Stone Town, with spacious rooms set around a verdant linear courtyard, varying in size & views. All are equipped with various mod cons including a flatscreen satellite TV, minibar fridge, internet connection & very effective AC. The tasteful décor is a mixture of modern & Zanzibari, with attractive wooden furniture & billowing gold curtains. At the top of the building, Lulu is a cheerful rooftop bar & restaurant (page 139) whose sweeping sea & harbour views make this a popular sundowner spot, even if you're not staying the night. There's also a massage treatment area & a sofa-filled lounge, which occasionally hosts jazz & taarab nights. B&B. **$$$$**

☐ **Zanzibar Grand Palace Hotel** [120 C2] (34 rooms) ☎024 223 5368/9; m 0773 303703; e bookings@zanzibargrandpalace.com; www.zanzibargrandpalace.com. Just opposite the port gates, on Turky's Sq, stands this rather unremarkable hotel. The rooms & 2 suites have drab décor but are well finished & clean; the suites have the added bonus of a spacious lounge. Alcohol-free minibars & safes are the norm, while cable TV, free Wi-Fi & room service suggest that this hotel is aimed firmly at the business market. This is backed up by the presence of the Busara Convention Centre, one of Stone Town's largest conference rooms, seating 150. The hotel is one of few in town to have a lift, which whisks guests up to Top Roof Restaurant, where chefs rustle up a selection of largely seafood dishes made with organic ingredients (*main course US$6*) but sadly with an unappealing view of container ships & the ugly dock. Downstairs & out on the square the Dock Café doles out strong espressos & quick snacks to weary businessmen. B&B. **$$$$**

☐ **Zanzibar Hotel** [124 C6] (11 rooms) m 0778 717800; e frontdesk@zanzibarhotel.co.tz; www.zanzibarhotel.co.tz. Under the same ownership as Africa House (page 129) & with a large garden plot, this grand hotel should be buzzing. But more often than not its fading public spaces, dilapidated garden & spacious rooms are empty & its staff hard to find. There is some promise – the high-ceilinged rooms are furnished with antiques, including a wonderfully ornate carved wooden clock in the foyer, island artwork & crisp, colourful linens giving it an old-

fashioned feel. Mosquito nets, TV & tea-/coffee-making facilities are standard throughout. The Royal Deluxe rooms have king-sized beds whilst the Twin Deluxe have queen sized; the latter can be found in rooms with lovely views over the fountain courtyard. There's a compact b/fast room in the main foyer, while in the garden stands the independently run Lemon Spa. Hopefully, investment & good management in the future can turn this hotel into the success story it should be. B&B. **$$$$**

☐ **Zanzibar Palace Hotel** [125 F2] (9 rooms) ☎024 223 2230; e info@zanzibarpalacehotel.com; www.zanzibarpalacehotel.com. Since opening in Jul 2006, Zanzibar Palace Hotel quickly gained a reputation as one of the best boutique hotels in Stone Town, & with delightful European owner-managers, it remains a friendly, gentle & reliable place. The hotel's interiors have a distinctly Zanzibari feel: steep staircases, a central atrium, handcrafted wooden furniture, antique Arab *objets d'art*, rich fabrics & atmospheric glass lanterns. Yet for all the historic furnishings, modern creature comforts abound: AC throughout the public areas & bedrooms, Wi-Fi, in-room cable TV & a DVD library & in-room player. Each bedroom is individually named & has its own particular décor, but all are beautifully finished to a high standard with ornate chairs & sumptuous fabrics, & boasting impressive bathrooms (the luxury rooms have a shower & no bath, whereas the deluxe & suites have both). The 3rd-floor suites – Sherali, Dunia & Arabica – are particularly luxurious & would make wonderfully romantic honeymoon hideaways; Dunia has possibly the highest bed in Zanzibar & comes complete with a step! Juicy mango wedges or sugared French toast may lure you to b/fast (both continental & cooked) in the ground-floor dining room (room service is available), where à la carte meals are also served: try gazpacho Andaluz (*US$5*), carpaccio of springbok (*US$6*), pan-seared kingfish with bacon (*US$15*) or pancakes with ice cream (*US$4.50*). Occasionally, there's a Swahili buffet night laid on, which is well worth sampling. Helpful staff are on hand for travel tips, the small bar serves cold drinks throughout the day & board games are available for when you tire of city explorations or the heat. Alternatively, you could head for the tranquil new spa next door. With state-of-the-art equipment & a continuation of the opulent interiors of the main hotel, this is a great place to spoil yourself. B&B. **$$$$**

MID RANGE

⌂ Asmini Palace [125 F2] (12 rooms)
m 0774 276464/5; e info@asminipalace.com;
www.asminipalace.com. Located on Forodhani Rd in
the Kiponda area, Asmini is a striking white building,
constructed with traditional architecture in mind: an
arched entrance, central courtyard & carved timber
doors, shutters & balconies from every bedroom.
The staff are delightful & its rooms are clean &
uncluttered, with king-size Zanzibari beds, crisp
embroidered linen & a small seating area. Mosquito
nets, cable TV & fridge are provided in every room.
There is a sunny rooftop restaurant for lunch &
dinner & a large b/fast area on the ground floor filled
with fresh flowers, while free Wi-Fi is available in
public areas, & there's a lift. A good-value option in
this price range. B&B. **$$$–$$$$**

⌂ Zanzibar Coffee House [125 G4] (8 rooms)
☏024 223 9319; m 0773 061532; e coffeehouse@
zanlink.com; www.riftvalley-zanzibar.com. Housed
in an 1885 Arabic home, originally built by Sir Tharia
Topan, *wazir* (high-ranking advisor) to Sultan Said
Barghash & described by Stanley in *Through the Dark
Continent* as 'one of the richest merchants in town',
Zanzibar Coffee House is by contrast an understated,
unpretentious haven. Tucked in the maze of streets
behind the Creek Rd market, & with pedestrian access
only, its individually styled bedrooms, each named
after a type of coffee, sit above the excellent café
of the same name (page 145). Well proportioned
& modestly furnished, the rooms are simple &
atmospheric, with traditional Zanzibari 4-poster beds,
antique dressers & glass lamps. Most are en suite,
whilst a few share bathrooms; there are few modern
trappings except AC, & no telephones, TVs or gadgets.
A stay here is made all the more pleasurable for its
simplicity. Coffee aromas permeate the building, the
gracious staff provide a very friendly service & the
stunning tower-top terrace offers one of Stone Town's
most appealing aerial hangouts. B&B. **$$$–$$$$**

⌂ Abuso Inn [124 B4] (24 rooms) ☏024 223
5886; m 0777 425565; e abusoinn@gmail.com.
Set back from the Shangani Rd, almost opposite
the Tembo, this convenient family-run hotel is
much better than first impressions imply. The
building was a renovation project of the close-
knit Abubakar family, & its spick & span rooms
are pretty good: polished timber floors, comfy
king-size & twin Zanzibari beds, fresh linen, good-
quality furniture & even some sea views. Fans, AC,
mosquito nets, hot water & attractive traditional

furnishings are standard. Guests can relax with a
cold drink (no alcohol is served) in the sofa-filled
TV & lounge area, while b/fast is served on the
rooftop restaurant. The spacious rooms & central
location continue to make this one of the best
deals in this range. B&B. **$$$**

⌂ Coco de Mer Hotel [124 C4] (13 rooms)
m 0774 001302; e cocodemerznz@gmail.com;
www.cocodemerhotel.wordpress.com. This
straightforward place has rooms set around an
airy courtyard, decorated with potted plants – all
are different so it's well worth looking at a few on
arrival as standards & size vary. Rooms downstairs
are a bit dark, but those upstairs are generally
brighter. All have ceiling fans & hot-water showers
of questionable cleanliness; 3 have a small TV.
The restaurant does basic food around main meal
times (order in advance) & there's an adjacent
ground-floor bar which serves a variety of snacks
& sandwiches. US$10/car transfers are available
from the port/airport but be sure that you have a
confirmed reservation at the hotel in Shangani as
there have been rumours of people being taken to
a less salubrious annex. B&B. **$$$**

⌂ Dhow Palace Hotel [124 C6] (31 rooms)
☏024 223 3012/0304; e reservations@dhowpalace-
hotel.com; www.dhowpalace-hotel.com. In the
Shangani area, just off Kenyatta Rd, this is an
excellent & frequently recommended hotel. It's a
renovated old house built in 1559 around
2 cool central courtyards, complete with a tinkling
fountain & swimming pool respectively. From
the blue mosaic pool & its adjacent juice bar, the
distinctive harlequin stained-glass windows of
the newer rooms & their balconies rise upwards.
By contrast, the original rooms all access a private
section of shared balcony & boast more space, &
a less kitsch interior. All of the rooms are nicely
furnished with Zanzibari beds, mosquito nets,
genuine antiques, a refreshing amount of space &
bathrooms complete with Persian baths. All
mod cons are provided, including fridge, cable TV &
Wi-Fi. The whole place is spotlessly clean, the staff
are friendly & the atmosphere is very tranquil. B/fast
& other meals are served in the à la carte restaurant
downstairs, while upstairs is a lovely sundowner
lounge & snooker table, overlooking the city's
rooftops. It lacks only a seafront location, although if
it had this the rates would be significantly higher, so
instead you get real comfort & a heat-busting pool
at an excellent price. B&B. **$$$**

6

⌂ **Hotel Marine** [120 C2] (24 rooms) ☎024 236069; **m** 0777 411102; **e** hotelmarinestar3@ hotmail.com. This stand-alone hotel is in a large house opposite the port gates & overlooking the Mizingani Road roundabout. Inside, a grand staircase winds around an inner courtyard to rooms on 3 upper floors. The rooms are of fair quality but run-down & dusty, & guests appear something of an inconvenience to the staff. B&B. **$$$**

⌂ **Keki House** [124 D6] (11 rooms) **m** 0774 664646 **e** kekihouse@outlook.com. Undergoing several name changes) & owners in recent years, Keki House is currently under Egyptian management & sadly feeling the strain of constant change. The century-old building is now in need of some maintenance & aesthetic upgrades, but it does offer an array of clean budget rooms, many sizeable, but fairly spartan. Each is furnished with 1 or 2 Zanzibari beds, most have functional en-suite bathrooms, & the higher Superior rooms have a view over a small green square. There's an enormous 'Penthouse' – which, bar its top-floor location, forsakes all other luxurious connotations its name implies! Downstairs there's a covered courtyard adorned with mediocre local art & a lime green massage treatment room: the Coconut Spa (local Maisha spice scrub US$70/hr; Swedish massage US$40/hr). Meals are served at the adjoining apricot-coloured restaurant: Zanzibar Cousin's. Raised above street level, diners sit at 6 tables beside shuttered ceiling-to-floor windows, listening to Arab music & sampling the Indian influenced menu: chicken pilau (*US$4.50*), spiced stewed okra (*US$2.50*), vegetarian samosa with sweet chili (*US$1.50*). B&B. **$$$**

⌂ **Mazsons Hotel** [124 C5] (36 rooms) ☎024 223 3062/3694; **e** mazsons@zanlink.com/ reservationmazsonshotel@zanlink.com; www. mazsonshotel.com. This hotel on Kenyatta Rd has an interesting history: old records show it was built in the mid 19th century by Said bin Dhanin, who is thought to have settled here about the time that Sultan Said moved his court to Zanzibar from Muscat. Ownership changed hands several times, & during the early part of the 20th century the building was a Greek-run hotel before becoming a private dwelling once again. After the 1964 Revolution, the house, along with many others, fell into disrepair. Today, it is a hotel & once again beginning to look a little tired. The reception area is large & dated in décor, &. the slightly soulless

bedrooms have white tiled floors with beige linen & walls hung with tacky plastic 'flowing' waterfalls. Large TVs, safes, small fridges & functional bathrooms feature in all. There's an overpowering smell of insect repellent, but at least the mosquitoes should stay away. Some rooms have access to the shared balcony at the front of the hotel, overlooking the square & Kenyatta Rd. Its reasonable restaurant, Yungi Yungi, serves à la carte international food, which is popular with locals, & there's a business centre & 3 conference rooms. B&B. **$$$**

⌂ **Rumaisa Hotel** [120 D1] (7 rooms) **m** 0777 410695; **e** inforumaisa@yahoo.com; www.rumaisahotel.blogspot.co.uk. This funky little place opened in 2011 & trendy travellers & 'flashpackers' have been recommending it ever since. Located in the Funguni area, it's quite a walk from the centre but allows for lower prices than there would otherwise be for the standard of room. All rooms are well finished & furnished in different vivid colours in Zanzibar style with TV, hot water, Wi-Fi, fans, fridge, & a solar emergency light. They are simple but very pretty, with cheerful touches from stained glass to tropical fish shower curtains & Indian furniture giving a homely feel to ensure guests feel like they're staying over with a friend. Staff are very helpful & friendly, & there's a lovely clean smell pervading the air. The blustery rooftop bar is filled with music in the evenings, when the owner's father plays the guitar & drums for guests. At the front, a communal balcony has a sea view with Prison Island in the distance. Remarkably, there is also a 52-seat cinema within the hotel, showing an array of family, Bollywood & Hollywood action movies for around US$3! B&B. **$$$**

⌂ **Shangani Hotel** [124 C5] (28 rooms) ☎024 223 6363/3688; **m** 0777 411703; **e** shanganihotel@ hotmail.com. On Kenyatta Rd, opposite the old post office, this hotel is an adequate mid-range choice. Enter reception by passing through the bureau de change, in the knowledge that the rooms are better than this 1st impression may give. They are little more than functional, but they are all clean with distinctive flowery bedspreads. AC, fan, fridge & satellite TV are standard, though the ambient noise level is definitely less towards the back of the hotel. B/fast & other meals are taken in the rooftop restaurant & a consistently reliable internet café is attached. B&B. **$$$**

⌂ **Stone Town Café & Bed & Breakfast** [124 C5] (8 rooms) **m** 0778 373737; **e** baraka@

zanlink.com; www.stonetowncafe.com. Above the bustling Stone Town Café (page 145) on Kenyatta Rd, this family-owned & run B&B offers delightful modern rooms with dbl polished wooden Zanzibari beds, AC, fans & fridges. Each room has a small seating area with a TV & en-suite shower with hot water as standard. Cool floors & warm colours make this a cosy place to spend a night or 2, while high-quality accessories & sturdy furniture raise the standard above the average Stone Town guesthouse. B/fast is included at the popular Stone Town Café downstairs, where guests can order what they want from the menu up to a value of US$7, with anything over this costing extra. Advice & assistance are readily given by owner Judi & her team, & if you plan to stay here, do consider visiting Pack for a Purpose (*www.packforapurpose.org*) before you travel; the owners here also fund & operate a super school for disadvantaged Zanzibari children. A top choice in this budget. B&B. **$$$**

BUDGET

☗ **The Rosal Stone Town Hotel** [125 H2] (13 rooms) m 0752 850400/0765 939393. In the Kokoni area, between Malindi St & Creek Rd (follow the alleyway at the People's Bank of Zanzibar), the Rosal is a big old house with distinctive red baraza benches outside, & rooms spread around the internal courtyard; some are large & airy with old wooden shutters leading onto a small balcony, while others are smaller. All rooms have en-suite showers, AC, a mini fridge & some also have satellite TV. Rose & Alnashir are friendly owners & their rooftop restaurant has good views across Stone Town. Quiet & good value. B&B. **$$$**

☗ **Safari Lodge** [125 H1] (28 rooms) ☎ 024 223 6523; m 0784 606177; e info@safarilodgetz. com. Constructed from 2 adjoining houses, this is a well-signed, 3-storey building with impressive carved timber balconies spanning the width of its upper floors. One half is older than the other, & the hotel's spacious rooms vary in standard depending on which side you're in. The newer rooms are impressively bright & immaculately clean, with the 3 good-value suites being bang up to date, with soft white & brown furnishings. Inside, each has a large Zanzibari bed or 2, AC & fan, & cable TV. It has a convenient location for exploring the Old Town, & a decent rooftop restaurant for skyline b/fasts. B&B. *Dbl* **$$$**; *dorm* **$**

☗ **Kiponda Hotel** [125 F2] (15 rooms) ☎ 024 223 3052; m 0777 431665; e info@kiponda.com; www. kiponda.com. On Nyumba ya Moto St in the Kiponda area, not far from the main seafront, this is a small, quiet hotel in a building that used to house part of a sultan's harem. It has been renovated in local style & still has an original carved wooden entrance door. The Zanzibari management team, headed up by the very helpful Salma, give the place a relaxed & friendly atmosphere, & although it's a touch more expensive than other budget hotels, it is also a lot quieter & better value. The older rooms are looking somewhat forlorn, but the newer ones are cleaner & much more colourful with simple furnishings & efficient fans; there is even a deep sink for washing laundry. Some rooms have AC, & 2 have their own bathroom located outside the room. Good b/fasts are available in the airy restaurant, & this area mutates into a casual coffee bar from 11.00 to 18.00, serving cold drinks, including beer, making it a nice place to hang out in the heat of the day. The hotel has good connections with Sama Tours (page 115) & can help with flights & ferry reservations. Discounts are available for long stays & for groups, with extra reductions in low season. B&B. **$$–$$$**

☗ **Princess Salme Inn** [120 C1] (10 rooms) ☎ 024 223 6588; m 0777 435303; e info@ princesssalmeinn.com; www.princesssalmeinn. com. To the northern side of the port, in a building with distinctive turquoise shutters, the Princess Salme Inn is set back a little from the Mizingani Rd, beside Bandari Lodge & Warere Town House. In keeping with the name, a framed photo of Princess Salme (see box, pages 188–9) greets guests in reception, where they are offered a warm welcome, bijou bedrooms & an airy rooftop complete with self-catering facilities (fridge, cooker & crockery). There are pastel-shaded walls, white bedding & fluffy towels, mosquito nets over the beds & windows, & efficient fans. The majority of the rooms share 2 central bathrooms, whilst the en-suite dbl, complete with Zanzibari bed, is best used by people who know each other well as the only divider to the bathroom is a plastic shower curtain adorned with leaping dolphins. The rule here is simple: the more you pay, the more facilities you get. B&B. **$$–$$$**

☗ **Warere Town House** [120 C1] (12 rooms) m 0782 234564; e info@warere.com; www.warere. com. Situated in an unexpectedly leafy corner (albeit not in the smartest part of town), neighbouring the

Princess Salme Inn, this pleasant 3-storey lodge has been popular for many years with travellers on a tight budget. With super friendly staff, it's located in an early 20th-century homestead, & offers a simple, comfortable haunt, with rooms offering traditional Zanzibari furnishings, kanga curtains & sparkling bathrooms with hammam baths. 4 rooms boast breezy flower-filled balconies, albeit overlooking the unattractive back of Bandari Lodge, & all guests can access the bright rooftop terrace, where b/fast is served with a sea view. Warere has a good sister property (page 214) by the beach on the quieter side of Nungwi, & negotiating a price on combination trips may be possible. B&B. **$$–$$$**

🏠 **Zenji Hotel** [120 D2] (9 rooms) m 0774 276468/0776 705592; e info@zenjihotel.com; www.zenjihotel.com. Opposite the now defunct Ciné Afrique, this Dutch–Zanzibari hotel is a haven of calm with the hustle & bustle of Malawi Rd literally on its doorstep. In fact, it is only the noisy location that lets down this quirky little place, which is a real find among the shabbier options near the port. The rooms have been given poetic & exotic-sounding names such as Spirit of Nature & Room of Wonder, each of which is priced differently depending on facilities. All have AC, fans & hot water, but 2 share a bathroom, only some have balconies & 1 has a private toilet in the corridor, rather than in the room. Kitted out in locally handcrafted furniture, with colour-trim mosquito nets, pastel shades on the walls & tie-dye sheets, the rooms are full of charm & light. A tasty buffet b/fast served up on the roof includes homemade bread & cake, while caffeine fiends will be happy to note that cappuccinos & espressos from the Zenji Café (page 145), made with coffee from the Zanzibar Coffee House (page 145) are included in the room price. Wi-Fi is free, & the hotel has laptops that guests can borrow. While maintaining high standards, Zenji is also conscious of giving back to the community. All staff here are local & many are uneducated. The hotel gives them free English lessons twice a week, & this must be working, as they are some of the friendliest staff in any Stone Town hotel. There's a small curio shop in reception where quality local crafts are sold, & the hotel has a strong involvement in women's aid projects. B&B. **$$–$$$**

🏠 **Funguni Palace Hotel** [120 D1] (13 rooms) 📞 024 223 3525; m 0777 411842; e info@ fungunipalace.com; www.fungunipalace.com. New in 2011, the rooms are clean & comfy if a little soulless, with chunky polished wooden beds, yellow walls & gold-trim mosquito nets. Fans, AC, phones & TV are found in all rooms, while some have balconies. Giant sofas are crammed in to the reception room where vases of flowers brighten the place up a bit, while up on the roof is the unremarkable b/fast room. B&B. **$$**

🏠 **Garden Lodge** [120 C6] (18 rooms) 📞 024 223 3298; e gardenlodge@zanlink.com. This simple but friendly place is situated in a house on the busy Kaunda Rd, near Victoria Gardens & the main hospital. The vehicle entrance is surrounded by a small garden terrace of tropical flowers & palms, whilst the building is clad in cerise bougainvillea, making this feel like a pretty lush retreat for Zanzibar Town. Catering primarily to students, tour groups & backpackers, the bright yet shabby rooms here all have dbl twin beds, with good-quality furniture & linen, fans, mosquito nets & reliable hot water. Upstairs rooms are brighter & airier; try to get one at the back to avoid traffic noise disturbance. There are small balconies at the front of the hotel laid out with deckchairs & a cool 1st-floor lounge with crimson Zanzibari chairs. There is a vivid orange rooftop terrace for b/fast & a few good restaurants within easy walking distance. Good choice for the price. B&B. **$$**

🏠 **Haven Lodge** [125 E7] (9 rooms) 📞 024 223 5677; m 0777 437132; e thehaven@yahoo. com. This is a friendly & good-value place, in the southern part of Stone Town between Soko Mohogo St & Vuga Rd. Makame, the manager, aims to offer simple bedrooms & separate bathrooms, hot water, a big b/fast & as much tea & coffee as you like, & broadly he succeeds. There's a good deal of space for the price, cheerful embroidered bedspreads, fans, a generator in case of power cuts, an organised safe-deposit system, luggage storage, a kitchen for self-catering (free) & cheap transfers to the coast, boat trips & tours; they even have bikes for hire. If you do stay, look out for the distinctive reception desk covered in coins & be sure to visit nearby Nyambuni Restaurant for great Swahili fare. B&B. **$$**

🏠 **Jambo Guesthouse** [125 F6] (9 rooms) 📞 024 223 3779; m 0777 496571; e info@jamboguest. com; www.zanzibar.net/hotels/jambo_guest_ house. In a quiet & peaceful quarter of the Mkunazini area, 5mins from the Anglican cathedral & opposite the pleasant outdoor Green Garden Restaurant (page 142), this straightforward little hotel has a range of room sizes, all of which share bathrooms. Most of the simple, yellow rooms are on the wood-panelled 1st floor, & all have coconut-wood beds, neatly edged mosquito nets & ceiling fans, while decoration comes in the form of plastic sunflowers. The rooms are looking a little scuffed but they do have AC & this helps with the heat & humidity. Bathrooms are small & unremarkable but the water is always hot. B/fast is served beside reception & is usually accompanied by Sky News. It's a good-value budget place, offering thoughtful little extras such as a free luggage store & tea & coffee, all of which have made it justifiably popular with backpackers for many years. With advance bookings, it's also possible to arrange a free pick-up from the port or airport. B&B. **$$**

🏠 **Karibu Inn** [124 C4] (25 rooms) 📞024 223 3058; m 0777 417392; e karibuinnhotel@yahoo. com. On a narrow street, parallel with Kenyatta Rd, in the Shangani part of town, this hostel-like place caters mainly for young travellers, budget tour groups or people on overland truck expeditions. There is a laissez-faire vibe here, a consistent crowd of braided backpackers hanging around the reception & a very basic lounge. Rooms are dispersed around a warren of levels & corridors; they are clean but basic & primarily sgl/dbl en suites. Dorms are available, each of which sleeps between 5–8 people with sgl beds, plenty of space, ceiling fans & an en-suite bathroom. The friendly management can set you up with budget tours, & also run a safe-deposit scheme. They will not tolerate stains from henna tattoos on sheets or towels & will charge for any damage. B&B. *Dbl* **$$**; *dorm* **$**

🏠 **Malindi Lodge** [120 C2] (8 rooms) 📞024 223 2359; e malindilodge2007@yahoo.com. On Malawi Rd, close to the port gates & next to Ciné Afrique, Malindi Lodge is in a convenient location if you're arriving or departing by boat. 2 rooms boast a fridge & en-suite shower, others share 2 central bathrooms. Rooms are all fairly small & some overlook the busy road below, making them a less quiet option. However, with simple Zanzibari beds, bright turquoise linen & floors to match which consistently kept spotlessly clean, this is a good choice within its price range. B/fasts are served at the banquet table on the ground floor & offer a good time to chat to the staff about directions & onward plans. B&B. **$$**

🏠 **Manch Lodge** [125 E6] (23 rooms) 📞024 223 1918; m 0778 202038; e manchtime_72@hotmail. co.uk; www.manchlodge-zanzibar.net. A stone's

throw from Haven Lodge, this budget place on Vuga Rd usually has a friendly bunch of locals hanging out on the veranda, lending to its relaxed air. The interiors here are unusual: large posters showing worldwide scenes, chintzy sofas on the balcony, & a crazy patterned floor seeming particularly curious choices. Rooms are quite cramped with heavy brown furniture, while the en suites are unventilated concrete cubes literally within the bedrooms (take a shower before bed & it won't be amorous gestures making the place steamy!). To escape the heat there's a breezy balcony on the 1st floor &, unusually for Stone Town, at least a few trees to break the view. B/fast is in the flower-filled garden & is an indulgent affair including pancakes & eggs for those staying for 4 nights or more. British visitors may smile at Heinz baked beans on the menu, while for lunch & dinner there's an array of burgers, pizzas, samosas & salads for US$5–7. It's just about acceptable for the price but phone in advance for a free pick-up from the port or from airport for US$2. B&B. **$$**

🏠 **Mnazi House** [120 D6] (10 rooms) m 0778 881213; e info@mnazihouse.com. Constructed entirely using the skills of local carpenters, painters, craftsmen & suppliers, this gleaming property is in the Kikwajuni residential area of Stone Town, allowing visitors to watch everyday life passing by right on the doorstep. Rooms are Zanzibari in style & fresh flowers make guests feel at home. The hotel is opposite a football field, so there is a possibility of watching, or even joining in, a friendly local game. Due to the location, guests are asked to be quiet after 22.00 so as not to disturb local residents. B&B. **$$**

🏠 **Pyramid Hotel** [120 D2] (11 rooms) 📞024 223 3000; m 0777 461451/0748 255525; e pyramidhotel@yahoo.com. On Kokoni St, between the Malindi & Kiponda areas, this old hotel is just behind the Ijumaa Mosque, a short walk back from the seafront. A budget travellers' favourite for many years, & deservedly so, it gets its name from the very steep & narrow staircases (almost ladders) that lead to the upper floors. The rooms have nets, AC, fan & hot water, yet vary in atmosphere: some are large & bright, others small & dark, so choose carefully. The manager Ibrahim & his staff are very friendly & the rooftop restaurant does great b/fasts. Overall, it's a good budget choice, offering a US$10/car pick-up from the airport or port, free use of a rather slow computer in reception, as well as a book-swap service. **$$**

⌂ **St Monica's Hostel** [125 G5] (16 rooms)
📞024 223 0773; e monicaszanzibar@hotmail.
com; www.zanzibarhostel.com. Beside the
Anglican cathedral, St Monica's whitewashed walls
sit behind its lush front garden. Built in the 1890s
to house teachers, nurses & nuns working at the
UMCA mission, it now offers a warm welcome
to both church guests & younger backpackers.
A recent programme of major renovations & an
enthusiastic manager have rejuvenated the hostel's
buildings & soft furnishings. There is a pleasant,
reverential atmosphere, largely emanating from
the bold architecture: cool thick walls, wide
staircases, Arabesque arches, traditional wooden
shutters & rooms with large balconies overlooking
the cathedral or pretty palm gardens. Rooms – 7
en suite, 9 with shared bathrooms – are clean &
simple with mosquito nets. There is a restaurant,
run by the parish's Mothers' Union, offering fresh
Swahili cuisine for b/fast, lunch & dinner (no
alcohol); a long-standing art shop selling vibrant
paintings & hand-printed T-shirts; & an airy lounge
area for games & gossip. A great-value, friendly
place in this price range. B&B. **$$**

SHOESTRING

⌂ **Flamingo Guest House** [125 F7] (15
rooms) 📞024 223 2850; m 0777 491252;
e reservations@flamingoguesthouseznz.
com; www.flamingoguesthouseznz.com. In a
fairly noisy area of Mkunazini St, this no-frills
place has little charm. Behind reception, an
external concrete staircase ascends to an array
of en-suite & shared-facilities rooms. The beds
are basic & all rooms have a sink (no plug) &

ceiling fan, though several smell of damp & the
shared showers & toilets can be grim. When
the washing line isn't obscuring the view, the
roof terrace has great views of the Anglican
cathedral. B&B. **$**

⌂ **Narrow Street Hotel** [125 G2]
(8 rooms) 📞024 223 2620; m 0774 281010;
e narrowstreethotel@ymail.com. In an interesting
bit of town, this old hotel is in the maze of narrow
alleys off Malindi St. The Zanzibari-style rooms are all
neat & tidy with carved furnishings, TVs, AC & pretty
pink mosquito nets. They are quite small though, so
ideally you should know your room-mate well before
checking in. The en-suite bathrooms are also bijou
but they are simple & clean & the water is always hot.
The staff are a bit sleepy, & don't be surprised to find
them all gawping at the TV in the lounge area, but
this is a fair low-budget choice in a central location.
B&B. **$**

⌂ **Pearl Guesthouse** [125 G3] (13 rooms)
📞024 223 7611. This dark & dingy place opened
in 1992 & appears to have remained in the same
state ever since. Pale yellow interiors match
the fading sheets & it needs a good clean but is
otherwise fine. Some of the rooms have an outside
bathroom, & all have a separate toilet. All rooms
have fans & 2 also have AC, which costs an extra
US$5/room. Guests also have the option of b/fast
for an extra US$2pp, or they can use the somewhat
dubious kitchen. You'll have to carry your food
upstairs to the roof to eat, where high walls &
drying laundry obscure what would be a decent
view. Pearl is cheap as chips, but you get what you
pay for. B&B. **$**

✕ WHERE TO EAT AND DRINK

The dining experience in the city has taken a dramatic turn for the better over
recent years, with some stylish evening eateries opening, a burgeoning selection
of cool cafés, and even a more organised street food area in Forodhani Gardens'.
Several hotel restaurants, such as those at **Emerson Spice**, **Park Hyatt**, **DoubleTree
by Hilton** and the **Serena Inn**, deserve a special mention for their cuisine, and are
listed below (though most of the upper- and mid-range hotels welcome residents
and visitors to their dining rooms). At the other end of the scale, there are many,
seemingly nameless, basic eating-houses that you may just stumble across as you
walk around the streets. Menus are rare in these establishments, and some of the
very small places may only have one meal available. These places are harder to keep
track of, so look for the longest queues to spot the current best bets.

The following list, arranged very loosely into categories of quality and price (for
codes, see page 94), cannot hope to be complete given the current pace of change,

but it indicates the type and range of places available. Nearly all those included are open in the evenings for dinner, and most also open for lunch; some are open all day. At busy times, reservations may be necessary in some of the smarter and better-known restaurants, and it's always worth booking any rooftop dining in advance simply because space is often extremely limited.

RESTAURANTS
Gastronomic

✘ **Abyssinian Maritim** [124 C7] m 0772 940556/0713 359054/0752 940556; ⏰ noon–16.00 & 18.00–22.00 daily. This great little Ethiopian place is easy to find on the corner opposite the High Court in Vuga, serving authentic cuisine, great coffee & shisha pipes amid a north African décor. Receiving consistently enthusiastic praise & popular with both Zanzibari expats & visitors alike, this culinary departure from Swahili curries is a very welcome addition to the restaurant scene. Worth experiencing. $$$$$

✘ **Hurumzi Tea House** [125 E3] ☎ 024 2232784; ⏰ noon–16.00 & 18.00–22.00 daily. After a blip in service & food quality, it looks like this iconic spot at Emerson on Hurumzi (page 129) may be regaining its past glory & still boasts one of Stone Town's most beautiful rooftop views. Up 4 flights of increasingly steep & narrow stairs, this colourful little cushioned spot is wholly decadent in its simplicity. Sitting cross-legged on the soft Persian carpet, sipping a cool midday mocktail & gazing out towards the sea over ramshackle roofs, make this a very easy place to like. Lunch offerings are African–Asian–Arabian fusion, filled with aromatic spices & served on low beaten metal trays. Courgette, green pea & turmeric burgers (US$5.50), fish kofta (US$6) or a refreshing trio of sorbet (US$3) tempt diners & all are washed down with freshly mixed drinks, chilled bottles of beer & wine. Evening meals (US$25pp) are equally relaxed affairs, starting with sunset drinks & cocktails at 18.00, accompanied by the sound of muezzins calling from the minarets around town. Guests then select a rich Arabic–Swahili meals from a seasonal set menu (spiced salted squid served with baobab & lime; baba ganoush & flatbread; slow-cooked goat with plum & hibiscus; butternut & saffron tagine) & enjoy performances of live traditional music. Reservations essential. $$$$$

✘ **Livingstone Beach Restaurant** [124 C4] m 0773 164939. Laidback Livingstone consists of a large, uncluttered & attractively decorated dining room leading out to a private beach where you can dine with your toes trailing in the sand & watch picturesque passing dhows at sundown. The (mostly seafood) menu is priced relatively high, with most main courses falling into the US$14–20 range, & there's shisha available. Although its location is good, service speeds can be slow & paying in foreign currency (US$) will significantly increase your bill. $$$$$

✘ **Lulu Restaurant & Lounge** [125 F2] ☎ 024 223 8352; e info@theseyyida-zanzibar.com; www.theseyyida-zanzibar.com. Up on the roof of the Seyyida Hotel (pages 131–2), Lulu is a peaceful light lunch or evening retreat serving a tempting selection of dishes such as king prawns with dry martini sauce & lyonnaise potatoes (US$20) or fruity flavoured shisha pipes (US$5). Receiving well-deserved praise for its food & friendly staff, it is most popular for late-afternoon sundowners where hotel guests & passers-by can enjoy the cocktail of the day (US$8) under the shade of giant umbrellas. There's can enviable view of the sea from its sunny terrace & it's worth a pit stop for that alone. $$$$$

✳ ✘ **The Spice Tea House** [125 G3] ☎ 024 223 2776; m 0775 046395; e reservations@ emersonspice.com; www.emersonspice.com; ⏰ 17.30–23.00, closed Thu. On the rooftop of Emerson Spice (page 130), this intimate, open-sided dining experience offers a lovely bird's-eye vista over town, a buzzing atmosphere & an impressive 5-course degustation menu. Open by night for a single sitting (cocktails from 18.00; dinner 19.00), the US$40pp set menu (excl drink) is excellent value, consistently delicious & worth booking to avoid disappointment. Accommodating only 25 diners, at individual tables under the central rooftop canopy, it's highly personal & delightfully engaging. Be sure to arrive in time for sundowners to take full advantage of the evening breeze & sunset atmosphere: hear muezzins call the faithful to prayer, look down on traders heading home & watch warm pinks fill the sky before nightfall. Cocktails (US$5) are made to order & aromatic food is cooked by a small smiling team in the corner of the terrace. Presented beautifully, the food is also

6

quite delicious, with inventive ingredients & Swahili fusion flavours. The tempting menu changes daily based on seasonally available produce & freshly landed seafood: calamari ceviche, lobster on green papaya salad, black pepper-seared tuna, Tambi prawns with grilled mango, & coconut chilli kingfish, to name but a few. Desserts such as baked bananas or plum tart round off the seafood feast, & are happily washed down by reasonably priced bottles of imported wine. (Note: The fixed menu means any food allergies should be mentioned at the time of booking). For special occasions, traditional music or dancing may also be arranged, & is a real treat for diners! $$$$$

✗ **Baharia Restaurant** [124 A5] ✆ 024 223 3051. Not as flamboyant as Hurumzi Tea House, this place at the Serena Inn (page 128) is good quality nonetheless. The food is a mix of Asian, African & European, with a popular Swahili night every Sat, which includes live music. Starters like salads or mini kebabs are US$5, while main courses include curries (*US$15*), fish in garlic & ginger (*US$12.50*), lobster (*US$25*) & a pasta station (*US$9–12*). In the Mdele Coffee Shop & patisserie, you can have snacks & light meals (*US$5*) or coffee & cakes (*US$4*). $$$$–$$$$$

✗ **Beyt al Salaam Restaurant** [124 B5] m 0773 000086; e reservations@beytalsalaam. com; www.beytalsalaam.com; ◷ 07.00–10.00, noon–15.30 & 18.00–22.00 daily. Overlooking Kelele Sq, this pleasant little restaurant at Beyt al Salaam (page 129) serves light lunches & enjoyable dinners. Diners are seated at neatly laid tables amid twinkling candles; service is friendly & polite, if sometimes a little slow. Imaginative dishes such as yellowfin tuna degustation (*US$6*), warm crab gratin (*US$7.50*), beef fillet mignon (*US$14*), tagliatelle with lobster ragu (*US$12*), coconut crème caramel (*US$5*) & a reasonable wine list are always on offer. $$$$–$$$$$

Creative cooking

✗ **Mistress of Spices** [124 D4] m 0773 740888; e info@jafferjihouse.net. Part of Jafferji House (page 126), this is a wonderfully atmospheric dining room, with silk-covered ceilings, antique mirrors & Moroccan lamps casting their delicate shadows across the tables. Several tables are tucked into intimate alcoves, with seating on low baraza benches: they look beautiful but for comfort over dinner, you may prefer one of the more conventional chairs. B/fasts, lunches &

dinners are created using high-quality, fresh local ingredients &, of course, the spices that pervade the air. Try the 'Signature Jafferji House Juicy Meaty Beefburger', which comes with avocado salsa & potato wedges (*US$10*). No alcohol is served, but there are ample spice-infused coffees & fresh juices to quench your thirst. $$$$

✗ **Monsoon Restaurant** [124 C3] m 0777 410410; e monsoon@zanzinet.com, www. monsoon-zanzibar.com. ◷ 11.30–22.30 daily. Near the fort & seafront, this is a French-run place serving a good selection of Mediterranean & spicy Zanzibari food, accompanied by live taarab or *ngoma* music on Wed, Fri & Sat nights. There are 2 parts: a bar & a massive open space covered in rugs & cushions. You leave your shoes at the door & lounge around kasbah-style. Thick walls & good ventilation mean it's always cool, & so are a number of the clients. If you want to relax even more there is also a very pleasant & shady terrace with about 10 tables facing Forodhani Gardens. Main courses cost US$7 upwards, while 3-course dinners with a glass of wine are great value at around US$16. $$$–$$$$

✗ **Sambusa Two Tables Restaurant** [120 B6] ✆ 024 223 1979; m 0777 416601. Usually just called Two Tables, this place is particularly worthy of mention because for a long time there was nothing else quite like it on Zanzibar. This is a small place it really does have only 2 tables (although 1 seats about 8 people) on the balcony of a family's private house, set back off Victoria St, between the junction of Kaunda R & Beit al Amaan, but is clearly signposted on a roadside tree. The entrance is tucked around the back of the building, in a leafy corner past dozing cats & well-tended chickens. Food is cooked by husband-&-wife team Salim & Hidaya in their own home, with help from the rest of the family. Phone or visit in the afternoon to make a reservation. A full meal of spiced rice, curries & innumerable local delicacies costs about US$10. The food is generally highly rated, but do pace yourself: if you fill up on the snacks & starters you may not do justice to the main course when it arrives! This is not a regular restaurant, but rather a window on genuine Zanzibar family life, & the reality of Stone Town living & dining may not be for everyone. BYOB. $$$$

✳ ✗ **The Secret Garden** [125 G3] ✆ 024 223 2776; e reservations@emersonspice.com; www.emersonspice.com; ◷ closed Wed. Quite unlike any other dining experience on the island, the newly opened Secret Garden is simply magical. Part of Emerson Spice (page 130), this tumbledown, former Swahili marketplace has been transformed into an utterly enchanting open-air restaurant. The flickering light of candles illuminate the crumbling windows & arches & help create the impression of a grand opera set. Yet within the semi-derelict buildings an impeccable experience awaits: efficient waiters serve chilled glasses of wine at neat triangular tables, aromatic waves of spiced Swahili dishes (US$8–15) drift from an open *braai* (BBQ), & oversized potted palms add exoticism and intimacy. Occasionally, taarab musicians play from above the restaurant; it all feels very James Bond! Wedding celebrations & exclusive parties can be arranged, but simply coming here for a casual dinner is something special in itself. Highly recommended. $$$$

✖ **Taarab Restaurant** [124 B5] ☎024 223 4062; ⏰ 07.00–22.00. On the rooftop of DoubleTree (page 128), Taarab is a smart, slick restaurant where chef Alan, his team & the friendly waiting staff deliver consistently good food in thoroughly pleasant surroundings. With tables indoors & on the wrap-around rooftop terrace, you can gaze over the castellation across the city from a stylish setting whilst indulging in fresh, healthy & imaginatively presented food: try the crab soup served in a coconut shell, utterly scrumptious piri-piri prawns, melt-in-the-mouth ceviche or a yummy rum baba. While you're here, have award-winning barman Dismas fix you up a totally tropical cocktail. For something smart, slick & special, Taarab is worth checking out. $$$$

Mid range

✳ ✖ **6 Degrees South Grill & Wine Bar** [124 B6] m 0620 644611; e info@6degreessouth. co.tz; www.6degreessouth.co.tz; ⏰ 10.00–01.00 daily. 'Quirky. Imaginative. Breezy. This culinary hotspot is all degrees of cool.' That's the claim made by 6 Degrees, & indeed many of the cocktail-sipping visitors & expats who hang out here would concur. Opened in late 2013, its expansive, open-fronted restaurant & bars overlook the Shangani Waterfront from 3 levels. The striking street-level restaurant, complete with soaring arched glass roof, pristine white-&-lime linens, high-backed chairs & square pillars, serves a selection of Zanzibari favourites – from vanilla chicken (US$9)

to catch of the day with coriander-infused rice (US$11) – & lunchtime sandwiches (US$6–8), wraps (US$6–10) & salads (US$8). Tucked behind is a swish, chillout with a 2-storey, chilled glass wine tower, plush sofas, barrel tables & a glass spiral staircase to a mezzanine extension. A further flight of stairs up is the popular cocktail bar Up North @ 6 Degrees (pages 147–8). $$$–$$$$

✖ **House of Spices** [125 G3] ☎ 024 223 1264; m 0773 573727; e info@houseofspiceszanzibar. com; www.houseofspiceszanzibar.com. Offering tempting fusions of local & Mediterranean cuisine from the top floor of an attentively renovated Zanzibari house, House of Spices is justifiably popular with both expats & tourists. Most diners sit on the lantern-lit roof terrace, where there's also a bar, & the friendly waiters can help you choose from the varied menu, which includes a range of curries & salads, as well as tapas & thin-crust pizza. Alternatively, the fresh seafood plates come with a choice of 5 tasty sauces, each made with a different aromatic spice. To accompany the meal, there's a choice of beers, a long list of spirits & a couple of wines. More recently, a calm & breezy wine & tapas bar has opened on the 2nd floor, presenting a great option for a pre-dinner drink or a light bite. On the ground floor is a small spice shop selling neatly packaged spices, & offering hot or iced tea & coffee on a lovely cushion-covered floor, & for those who can't leave, rooms are now available. $$$–$$$$

✖ **Café Miwa** [124 C5] m 0778 933144; e info@cafemiwa.com; ⏰ 10.00–22.00 daily. This small, all-day cafe offers a wide variety of food but is a little dishevelled inside. If you're on a health kick, detox with a US$3 'Refresher' juice (celery, cucumber, lime & pineapple), or there's decent coffee (US$3), milkshakes (US$3.50), smoothies (US$3–4) & even shisha pipes from 16.00 (excl Tue). Food ranges from carpaccios & salads (US$5–6) to burgers (US$7–9), plus disappointing sushi, noodles, curries & grilled meats & fish (US$11–13). Passable, but nothing special. Cash only. $$$–$$$$

✖ **Lemongrass** [124 C5] m 0778 933144; ⏰ noon–15.30 & 18.00–22.00, closed Tue. Immediately above the Old Post Office on Kenyatta Rd, this offers an array of oriental fusion food. Most diners sit on director's chairs at tables along the length of the balcony, though there is a large, more formal indoor restaurant, too. Under the same ownership as neighbouring Café Miwa in spite of different menus & branding, the food from both kitchens is available at either venue. Fare is fresh but nothing exceptional. However, for a taste of China & southeast Asia, you'll find an array of dishes: sour & spicy tom yum soup (*US$5*), nasi goreng (*US$9*), green chicken curry (*US$8*), kung po beef (*US$8*) & seafood hotpot (*US$18*). Cash only. $$$–$$$$

✘ **Maru Maru** [124 D4] ✆024 223 8516/7/8; e reservations@marumaruzanzibar.com; www. marumaruzanzibar.com; ⊕ 07.00–10.00, 12.30–15.00, 19.00–22.30 daily. Launched in 2015, the bakery (⊕ *10.00–19.00 daily*) within this hotel (page 128) sells fresh bread, petit fours, cupcakes & tempting slices. Sit at the little round tables in the courtyard while sweet staff brew coffee, sample some childhood favourites (vanilla cupcakes with a plump cherry on top), or grab a take-away loaf & head to La Taperia (page 143) for some deli goods to accompany it. Come sundown, head up to the hotel's spacious rooftop terrace. Lounge on coconut-wood chairs & loungers, pull up a bar stool for a friendly chat, fresh cocktails & distance ocean views, or sit at the neat restaurant tables, complete with colourful runners & fresh flowers. There's a snack menu available all day – East African skewers (*US$4*) or vegetarian samosas (*US$2–3*) – & a varied à la carte menu: chicken Caesar salad (*US$4.50*), a trio of mini burgers (*US$7*), pizza (*US$7*), & a good seafood section (grilled red snapper for US$10). The real highlight though is the Indian food prepared by the resident chef – every Sat evening there's a culinary South Indian Special featuring an array of authentic curry & tandoori dishes (from 19.00). $$$–$$$$

✘ **Amore Mio** [124 B6] m 0776 211071; e e_walzl2yahoo.it; f amoremio.zanzibar; ⊕ 10.00–22.00 daily. Look for the neon ice-cream cone at the bend in Shangani Rd between the Serena & Africa House Hotel. This long-standing, unfussy 'Cafeteria Italiano' has a breezy waterfront location & offers the obligatory array of pasta & pizza from an extensive menu. Pizza costs around US$7–9, hot paninis are in the US$3–4 range, & it serves good strong coffee as well as a variety of ice creams. For a late-night bite, after nearby sundowners, or a post-dinner ice-cream, it's a reliable choice. $$$

✘ **Archipelago Restaurant** [124 C3] ✆024 223 5668; m 0777 462311. Opposite the National Bank of Commerce on Kenyatta Rd, this 1st-floor restaurant has long established itself as one of the most popular lunch spots in Stone Town, thanks in large part to its bright décor & elevated balcony overlooking the beach. The other chief ingredient in its success is that the food – curries (*US$9*), fish dishes (*US$9–11*), burgers (*US$6–8*) & pizza (*US$7–11*) – is very good, reasonably priced, & the product of a sustainable fishing policy. No alcohol is served but the fresh juices more than make up for this. Archipelago has the same great Aussie–Zanzibari owners as the Stone Town Café & Café Foro (in the gardens). $$$

✘ **The Book Café** [124 C5] ✆0774 164866. In a beautifully restored building on Kenyatta Rd, this café (formerly Hot Spot Bistro) is a relaxed spot to sip coffee (of which there is an extensive range), smoothies & milkshakes surrounded by a selection of paperbacks & attractive African coffee-table books, often produced & published by the owner. It's laidback & efficient in a very central spot. $$$

✘ **Green Garden Restaurant** [125 F6] m 0773 849636; ⊕ 11.00–22.00 daily. In the southern part of town, opposite Jambo Guesthouse, this appropriately named restaurant is a delightfully chilled, open-air eatery, set on raised terraces under tall palms. Behind its timber wall, neat concrete paths meander between well-tended gardens to shady tables & a cool makuti-thatched bar/lounge, complete with fans. It's a friendly, unpretentious place to relax or write postcards home. Food ranges from tapas-style dishes to more substantial options, with refreshing snacks & wood-fired pizza. $$$

✳ ✘ **La Taverna** [125 G6] m 0776 650301; www.latavernazanzibar.com; ⊕ 11.00–23.00 Mon–Sat. A little off the main tourist trail, towards the market, this is a gem of a restaurant with a host of happy regular customers, delightful young Italian owners & consistently tasty, homemade pasta/pizza. In a brilliantly whitewashed single-storey house, food is served under broad umbrellas on the terrace: delicious handmade ravioli, myriad pasta shapes with tempting seafood & fresh vegetable sauces & crisp pizzas (far superior to most you'll experience on the island). Wine is inexpensive & free flowing, which all adds to the relaxed, casual vibe. $$$

✕ **La Taperia** [124 C4] e lataperiazanzibar@ gmail.com; ◷ 10.00–22.00 daily (deli shop ◷ 10.00–18.00). On one end of the balcony above the Shangani Post Office, La Taperia is relative newcomer, offering – as its name suggests – tasty tapas. There's a well-stocked bar, casual indoor dining area & popular tables & bar stools on the terrace. It's a buzzy place to grab a bite above the bustle, & uniquely in Stone Town, there is also a separate, glass-fronted delicatessen where you can buy imported cheese, a wide selection of cold-cut meats, olive oil, wine & fresh bread. Pick up some delicious treats or order a freshly made sandwich & head to Forodhani for a seafront picnic. Access to this upper level is from Gizenga St: a small but well-signposted first right if you come from Kenyatta Rd. Cash only. $$$

✕ **Mercury's Bar and Restaurant** [125 F1] ◌024 223 3076; m 0777 413081; e mercurys. zanzibar@gmail.com. Named after Zanzibar's most famous son (see box, page 144), this place has a fine setting on the bay, overlooking a small beach, the bobbing fishing & pleasure boats of the new port, & the historic seafront buildings of Mizingani Rd. It's a real Stone Town institution: perennially popular & always with a relaxed, island atmosphere. Wooden tables & chairs are set out on the large wooden deck under broad sunshades & a huge almond tree (growing through the roof). You can sip thirst-quenching spiced ice tea, choose from the extensive cocktail list & a menu that unashamedly cashes in on the former Queen singer's apparent dietary preferences – Freddie's Favourite Salad (*US$6.50*), anyone? Despite this corniness, the food is reliably good: soups (*US$4.50*), oriental-inspired stir-fries (*US$9*), & Zanzibari curries (*US$8.50–13*).For hungry friends, there's a Seafood Extravaganza sharing platter (lobster, squid, prawns, crab, octopus & catch of the day; US$22) & a baffling range of cocktails for US$7–9 – try the 'Monica Lewinsky' (blue curaçao, triple sec, gin, Sprite & lemon juice) 'to find out what a bubbly body can do in a blue dress'! There's live music on Sat night (◷ *20.30–23.00*), ranging from traditional *bashraf* & *kidumbak* to reggae & pop. $$$

✕ **Old Fort Restaurant** [124 D4] m 0744 278737/0741 630206; ◷ for lunch & dinner 08.00–20.00 daily. Opposite Forodhani Gardens, Zanzibar's Old Fort (page 164) has been here for

centuries, but was renovated in the early 1990s. As well as a historical landmark it's now a cultural centre, with a semicircular open-air theatre, several souvenir shops, & this shady outdoor café-restaurant, where an eclectic group of locals & sightseers mix. Sandwiches for around US$4 & local dishes such as chicken & *ugali* (maize meal) or fish curry & chapatti for around US$5 are on offer but it's unlikely to be your trip's culinary highlight. Every Tue, Thu & Sat, there's an evening of entertainment (taarab music, African dance, etc) & a BBQ – you may need to book ahead. $$$

✕ **Pagoda Chinese Restaurant** [124 B6] ◌024 223 4688; e pagoda888@hotmail.com; ◷ 11.30–14.30 & 18.30–22.30 daily. The Pagoda, just off Kenyatta Rd near the Africa House Hotel, is run by Mr Chung, who has lived on Zanzibar for many years. They proudly & justifiably claim to serve the only genuine Chinese food in Zanzibar. The restaurant offers good service, kitsch décor, generous servings & fresh food, though recent reviews are mixed. Starters range from 5 spring rolls (*US$2*) to crispy deep-fried squid (*US$4*), & main courses include sweet & sour fish, prawns piri-piri, chicken in oyster sauce & satay beef (*US$7*) plus roast duck (*US$10*). The menu also includes a few specialities, such as Chinese curried crab (*US$8*). There are a lot of vegetarian options, & meals include crisp, fresh vegetables specially flown in from Kenya. Rice & noodles are around US$2.50. $$$

✕ **Rendezvous Les Spices** [124 C7] m 0777 410707; ◷ 11.30–15.30 & 18.30–23.30 Tue–Sun. This French-owned restaurant serves some of the best Indian food on the island. Easily located on Kenyatta Rd, it's buzzing most evenings & the vibrant murals give the place tremendous colour & atmosphere. It's reasonably priced too, with starters for around US$3–4, & main courses such as crab masala, chicken tikka, lamb biriyani or various tandooris for US$7–8. Vegetarian dishes are available, & specials, such as prawn curry, are around US$8.50. Cash only. $$$

✕ **Sea View Indian Restaurant** [124 C1] ◌024 223 2132; ◷ 07.00–22.00 or later. On the seafront near the People's Palace, this is one of the oldest tourist-orientated restaurants in Zanzibar Town, founded back in the 1980s & still going strong. With tables on an upstairs balcony & a beautiful view across the bay, it's ideal for b/fasts, lunches & evening meals. During the day (until 18.00) you can enjoy spicy snacks with your drinks – a plate of spring rolls, samosas & bhajis is about US$2 – plus toasted sandwiches for US$2.50, & omelette & chips from US$4. For larger lunches or evening meals the choice is very small, but the quality consistently good. Vegetarian thalis (a mixture of dishes) cost US$7.50, & fish, chicken, squid or octopus in coconut sauce with poppadoms, plus snacks for starter, a fruit dessert & tea or coffee costs US$7. $$$

✴ ✗ **The Silk Route** [124 C4] ☎ 024 223 2624; ⓕ silkrouteznz; ◷ noon–15.30 & 18.30–22.30. Just around the corner from Forodhani Gardens, beside the tunnel, look for the distinctive turbanned doorman welcoming you to Silk Route. This long-standing Indian fusion restaurant rustles up a range of hot & fiery curries served with a dozen different freshly baked naans (*US$1–2*) & spiced rice (*US$2–3*). Fresh prawns & fish feature in many of the dishes, but beef & chicken versions are also available. Vegetarians can enjoy a wide selection of dishes from dedicated appetisers to tandoori, curry & biryani options. Tandoori *changu* (snapper marinated overnight), Goan beef vindaloo & kebabs fit for the Moguls (*all US$9*) are enough to entice most spice addicts. The restaurant is spread over 3 floors, with the most prized dining spots being on the 2-tier, top floor open-sided rooftop. Decorated in orange & grey, this fresh & breezy setting also helps overly ambitious chili eaters to cool themselves down! Prices are reasonable, starting at US$5 for a seafood curry, rising to US$10 for a beef-based dish, with 3-course lunches a steal at US$8p. The gold-&-red clad staff are friendly, & the quality consistent. Worth a visit. $$$

✗ **The Swahili House** [125 G3] ⓜ 0777 510209; ⓔ info@theswahilihouse.com; www. theswahilihouse.com. There are 2 dining options at this hotel (page 130): the casual courtyard café at its entrance, where snacks (chapatti wraps for US$8) are served all day in an open-fronted, shaded terrace; & the rooftop restaurant. It is worth the trip to the top (there is now a lift, too!) for both breeze & beautiful vista. Possibly the largest traditional rooftop in Stone Town, the large wooden bar, neatly set tables & cushioned baraza benches, invite casual dining (lunch & dinner) & lingering sundowners (Happy Hour 16.00–19.00 daily). Stop for a lite bite: tandoori chicken salad (*US$5.50*) or Mexican beef guacamole (*US$7*), or splash out on the Seafood Platter for 2, where US$24 will buy you prawns, snapper, lobster, octopus & calamari, or just take a break from sightseeing to enjoy the skyline somewhere cool. $$$

✗ **Tatu** [124 B6] ⓜ 0778 672772; ⓔ info@ tatuzanzibar.com; ⓕ tatuzanzibar; ◷ 10.00– 01.00 daily, kitchen noon–22.00 daily. Meaning '3' in Swahili, 'tatu' is a reference to the 3-storey building that's home to this bar/restaurant. The 1st floor is a social little pub area, complete with free Wi-Fi & a satellite TV enjoyed by sports fans & expats; the 2nd floor is a reasonably good restaurant open for lunch & dinner; whilst the top floor is a fine, open-sided cigar & whisky bar serving super snacks by day (try the excellent prawn tempura), sea view sundowners & serious nightcaps. Open from noon until the wee hours, there are 85+ single malts to sample here – allegedly East Africa's largest collection of the 'water of life'. $$$

FREDDIE MERCURY

The late Freddie Mercury, lead singer and front man for the rock band Queen, was born on Zanzibar on 5 September 1946. His name then was Farouk Bulsara, and his father was an accountant working for the British government in the House of Wonders. His family had emigrated to Zanzibar from India but were originally of Persian extraction. When he was nine, Farouk was sent to boarding school in India, and never returned to Zanzibar. He later went to a college in London, and in the 1970s formed Queen with three other former students. The current inhabitants of various houses around Zanzibar Town will tell visitors 'Freddie lived here', and given that the family moved house several times, the claims could all be genuine.

Cheap & cheerful

Lazuli [124 C5] **m** 0777 456277; 11.00–21.00 Mon–Sat. With a simple, unassuming exterior, Lazuli's little whitewashed room, azure shutters & jaunty coloured tablecloths give it a somewhat Mediterranean air. It's a small, cheerful café & a welcome find amid the dust & heat of a day's sightseeing. The menu boasts refreshing drinks & a selection of light meals – the spiced iced coffees are simply delicious & the main reason to come here. Food reviews have become a little hit-&-miss in recent times but ingredients are always fresh & food is homemade. That said, service is notoriously – sometimes painfully – slow: don't come in a rush; instead appreciate that everything is made to order. **$$–$$$**

Radha Vegetarian Restaurant [124 C4] 024 223 4808. Tucked away up the narrow street which runs parallel to Kenyatta Rd near the Karibu Inn, Radha is very reasonably priced, proudly serving exclusively vegetarian Indian food. With consistently delicious fare, it is deservedly popular & at busy times it's wise to book ahead. A thali consisting of dhal, rice, lentil & vegetable curries, okra, roti, poppadom & lassi costs US$5. You can also get savoury snacks such as samosas & spring rolls, cakes & sweets, fresh juices & beers. **$$**

Baboo Café [124 B7] **m** 0777 499297. Tucked under 2 shady sweet almond trees, with a concrete terrace overlooking the sea, this tiny little café is a friendly, unpretentious hangout. Engaging service, under the guidance of owner Baboo, & tasty Swahili food, courtesy of his wife Mariam, both make for happy customers. Iced coffees, freshly squeezed juices, salads (*US$3.50–5*), seafood platters (*US$7.50*) & curries (*US$4*) are all on offer. Find it on the southern end of the beach behind Africa House Hotel, where sunset views are particularly good. **$$–$$$**

Cafés of Forodhani Gardens In the revamped Forodhani Gardens, there are now 3 small waterfront cafés, the best of which are **Café Foro** [124 C3] (nearest the children's playground) & **Zenji Forodhani Garden Café** [124 D2] (*www.zenjiforodhani.com*). Each has an identical pavilion building by the sea & shaded outdoor seating. Selling a selection of cold drinks & with varying menus of fish, burgers, wraps, salads & sweet treats, they are all open for b/fast, lunch & snacks, & offer a very pleasant sense of calm & green space. **$$–$$$**

Stone Town Café [124 C5] **m** 0778 373737; **e** baraka@zanlink.com; www. stonetowncafe.com; 08.00–22.00 daily. Alongside Kenyatta Rd, below the popular B&B of the same name (pages 134–5), the scents of spiced tea & falafel waft from this buzzing Aussie–Zanzibari-run café. Marked out by an oasis of lush potted palms & umbrellas, an eclectic array of passers-by queue for unfussy, tasty dishes served by friendly staff. Busy in the morning, when hungry tourists & B&B guests pop in for the all-day b/fast, but popular all day for its cheesy pizzas (*US$6*), fresh fruit shakes & smoothies & tasty teatime treats like sticky date pudding with caramel sauce (*US$3*). The Arabic Kitchen menu offers a tasty selection of mezze treats (*US$2.50 each inc flatbread*), & bigger dishes like chicken shwarma with chips & salad (*US$4*). A thoroughly recommended stop for foot-weary sightseers. **$$**

Zanzibar Coffee House Café [125 G4] 08.00–18.00 daily. This friendly café on Mkunazini St, behind the main Creek Rd market, is an excellent place to break a morning of sightseeing with a cold drink, strong coffee or a light snack. The fresh juices are creative – watermelon, cucumber & ginger (*US$2.50*) – & crêpes are delicious sweet treats (*US$3–4.50*). Drop by for b/fast of homemade date & nut muesli (*US$3.50*) or feast on a light lunch of salad (*US$4.50–6*), bruschetta & chapati wraps (*US$5–6*) or try the house special soup with freshly baked bread (*US$4.50*). As its name suggests, the coffee here is excellent (head barista Asmah Jamah Shabani winning the 1st Tanzania Barista Championship in 2009); all of the beans are grown by the café's owners on fair-trade estates in Zanzibar & in the Southern Highlands, & there's an adjoining roasting & grinding room. The resulting serving options are varied – from creamy cappuccinos to iced delights. Good accommodation is also available (page 133). A very pleasant Stone Town experience. **$$**

Zenji Café [124 D2] **m** 0777 247243; www.zenjicafeboutique.com. Just below the friendly Zenji Hotel (page 136) is this great café, whipping up a selection of milkshakes, velvety ice creams, fruity smoothies & revitalising coffees. The Dutch–Zanzibari owners claim to bake the best brownies in Zanzibar, a claim well worth testing – they are rich, decadent & wickedly good. Community is the key here with a local project providing the raw ingredients & a small boutique on the side of the café selling gifts made by Tanzanian projects such as the Sewing Enterprise for Women (SEW), based in Arusha, who have crafted batik cushions & remarkable bags made from unopened condoms. The only drawback here is the location, right on busy Malawi Rd, but strategic planting around the terrace at least partially shields the view of the traffic, & watching the world go by is arguably something of its city charm. $$

Sforno Pizza & Sweet [124 C4] m 0772 555388. Sit on stools made from car tyres, beside oil drum tables, read the 'get active' quotes on the walls… & ultimately enjoy homemade ravioli (*US$3–5*), pizza (*US$1.50*), fresh focaccia (*US$1.50*) or yummy cakes & coffee. Owned by Roman lady Annarita, this simple spot, furnished with upcycled furniture, offers fresh, tasty bites in its tiny space amid the Gizenga St shops. End your meal with one of TAMU's Italian ice-creams (below) in tropical flavours. $–$$

TAMU Gelateria Italiana [124 B4] m 0772 459206; ⏱ 10.30–23.00 daily. This Italian-owned & run establishment is one of Stone Town's best ice-cream spots, with a happy following among residents & visitors, offering an array of traditional & exotic flavours: coco-cardamom & tamarind

alongside rich chocolate & vanilla. Open long hours to tempt both hot sightseers & those seeking something sweet after dinner. Cakes, fresh pasta & pizza, courtesy of another local Italian eatery (Sforno, above) are also on offer. $–$$

Rock bottom

Buni Café [124 C3] ⏱ 08.00–18.00 daily. With a prime central location, opposite the National Bank of Commerce, this small café serves great fresh coffee (iced for hot days) along with cakes & a selection of sandwiches & light lunches for around US$4–8. The raised terrace is an excellent spot for people-watching over a late b/fast or light lunch. $

✕ **Clove Restaurant** [125 E2] Run by a friendly group of Swahili women, this is an open-air place in a small & shady garden square alongside Hurumzi St. Their busiest time seems to be lunch, so you should ask in advance if you'd like to eat here in the evening to ensure food is still available. Local dishes such as meat & *ugali* (maize meal), rice & fish, or curry & chapatti cost around US$5. $

✕ **Hurumzi Movie Café** [125 F3] m 0659 921121; f hurumzini; ⏱ 11.00–22.00 Mon–Sat. This is a small, relaxed little café with a twist: movies. A film is shown at 17.00 &

FORODHANI NIGHT MARKET

For very cheap eats, and a wonderful taste of the local atmosphere, by far the best place to eat in the evening is at the nightly food market at Forodhani Gardens. Once a ramshackle collection of waterfront stalls, the renovation of the gardens has led to the creation of a purpose-built, hard-standing food area. The smarter surroundings, organised litter collection and arrival of chefs' hats for the traders have certainly improved the market's hygiene and image, although in many ways the experience is unchanged. The food stalls remain a social gathering place for both locals and tourists, and as the sun sets the stallholders fire up their braziers and hurricane lamps, serving fish and meat kebabs (*mishkaki*), grilled squid and octopus, samosas, chapattis and 'Zanzibar pizzas' – akin to a filled savoury pancake. Try the nutritionally challenged *chipsi mai yai*: an omelette filled with chips, sometimes served with shredded cabbage. Most food is grilled on hot coals in front of you, and served on a paper plate. Other stalls sell sugar-cane juice, ice cream and cold drinks – look for the refreshing local pineapple drink named Zed. The sweet-toothed could seek out *haluwa*, made from tamarind, oil and sugar: it's so sweet and sticky that a little goes a long way. Prices are very reasonable, and a filling plate will cost between US$2 and US$4. The food is invariably highly regarded but it is worth choosing from a stall doing brisk trade to ensure fresh ingredients.

19.00 Mon–Fri, & between 11.00 & 16.00 visitors are welcome to pick from the movie selection & put on whatever they fancy watching. Buy a drink or a snack & the accompanying film is free. Alternatively, pop by for Sat brunch (⏱ *11.00–16.00*) & tuck into a selection of pain au chocolat, pancakes, poached eggs & smoothies: 2 items & a drink is only US$4.50. The weekly film schedule is on display, & it's a cool spot to break sightseeing. Residents & volunteers get a 10% discount. **$**

✕ **Passing Show Hotel** [120 D2] ⏱ lunchtime only. Despite the name, this is not a hotel, but a Zanzibar institution nonetheless. Serving generous bowls of rice with an assortment of meats, vegetable sauce or beans (*US$2*), or larger plates of rice & meat or chicken (*US$3*), the food is good & cheap & the service quick. It caters mainly for local people, although visitors are always welcome. Lunchtimes can be very busy but turnover is reasonably quick & tables are available both inside & streetside. **$**

BARS, CLUBS AND ENTERTAINMENT

The number of bars in Zanzibar Town grows steadily each year. Some bars cater almost exclusively to tourists, others mainly to local Tanzanians who have migrated to Zanzibar from the mainland (indigenous Zanzibaris are generally Muslim so don't drink alcohol). Tanzanian, Kenyan, South African and a selection of international beers are usually available, as are soft drinks and a smattering of local and imported spirits. Wines are mostly South African, with international fine wines really only available at the top-end restaurants affiliated with hotels, like the Park, Hyatt, Serena or DoubleTree by Hilton, and a few of the smarter restaurants and cocktail bars. In addition, many of the larger hotels have separate bars, open to non-guests, and many of the restaurants and cafés mentioned in the section above also serve drinks.

Once upon a time, no visit to Zanzibar would have been complete without a visit to the Sunset Bar at the Africa House Hotel (page 129), but recently prices have risen and standards fallen, and there are far better options for sundowners with a sea view: notably the Terrace Bar at the Park Hyatt and Up North @ 6 Degrees. Mercury's, Tatu, Lulu, Baboo Café and the Forodhani Gardens' cafés all have the view and a decidedly more low-key vibe. For the ultimate sundowners though, try a dhow cruise: check out **The Original Dhow Safaris** (m *0772 007090;* e *info@dhowsafaris.net; www.dhowsafaris.net*), or **Dhow Zingatia** (m *0778 925800;* e *reservation@zingatia-zanzibar.com; www.zingatia.com*) for something a little more laid-back.

BARS AND CLUBS Don't come to Zanzibar Town to go clubbing; it's simply not the done thing. There a few bars where live music or a DJ may play a few tunes after sundown but it's very low key by international standards, and there's certainly nothing close a serious nightclub.

Ⓨ **Mercury's** [125 F1] Aside from its all-day meals (page 143), Mercury's is a good spot for sundowners & long evenings by the waterfront. Excellent range of cocktails & ever-popular shisha pipes are available, & there's live evening music to keep you entertained on Sat. If you're here for the scenery more than the booze, in May–Sep the angle of the sun means the sunsets are easier to appreciate at Mercury's than at 6 Degrees or Tatu.
Ⓨ **Sunset Bar** [124 B6] m 0773 884606; www.africahousehotel.com. Despite what is said

above, for the history & wide terrace, there is still appeal here. Cocktails are *de rigueur*, with an extensive menu to tempt you, & especially popular among locals & the more adventurous visitors are the shisha pipes. The sun usually sets around 18.30, so try to get there in good time (say an hour before) if you want the best terrace seats. You can also order snacks & meals (*US$4–10*) to enjoy on the veranda.
✳ Ⓨ **Up North @ 6 Degrees** [124 B6] www.6degreessouth.co.tz; ⏱ 17.00–01.00 daily.

6

This hip rooftop cocktail & music bar above the restaurant 6 Degrees South (page 141) is the current hot favourite for Stone Town sundowners.

Sip cocktails at the wrap-around white bar, hang out with friends, or dance the night away on Fri or Sat disco nights. Happy Hour 17.00–19.00.

LIVE MUSIC There is no one particular venue in Zanzibar Town for live music, but local artists – from traditional taarab to Afro-pop and rap – often perform at the larger hotels, bars and rooftop restaurants. To find out what's going on, ask at your hotel or look for posters around town advertising special events.

The **Dhow Countries Music Academy (DCMA)** (*www.zanzibarmusic.org*) is based in the Old Customs House on Mizingani Street [125 F1] and is dedicated to music teaching and the promotion of traditional instruments and sounds. They host weekly concerts in their building and other venues: check out the jam sessions at Livingstone (page 139) on Tuesday and Friday nights (⊕ *21.00–midnight*) or listen over a glass of wine at La Taperia (page 143) on the first and third Friday of every month (⊕ *19.30–22.00*). They also host public workshops, often free of charge, and visiting musicians are welcomed with open arms. The **Old Fort** [124 D3] and **Mtoni Ruins** (north of Zanzibar Town) are atmospheric venues for live music, hosting mostly traditional musicians and dancers, but occasionally contemporary performances, too. A couple of times each week a 'night at the fort' evening is organised, which includes at least two performances plus a barbeque dinner. There are often performances on other nights, too. The best thing to do is visit the fort during the day, and ask the staff at the desk what's happening during your stay. On a larger scale, Zanzibar Town also plays host to the annual **Sauti Za Busara festival** (see box, below), and this is certainly the time to visit, if African music appeals, though it can be very busy.

CINEMAS In the 1920s, Zanzibar boasted the first cinema in East Africa: the Majestic Cinema (not to be confused with the Majestic now on Vuga Road), designed by British resident and architect John H Sinclair. Sadly, it burned down as the result of a projector fire in 1953. Somewhat remarkably, in spite of Majestic's missing roof and broken chairs, old faithful movie-goers do continue their cinematic pilgrimage here on occasion.

Until recently, the only real options for big-screen films were the rare showings in the atmospheric **Old Fort amphitheatre** [124 D3] during the annual Zanzibar International Film Festival (ZIFF) in June/July, or the very tired **Majestic Cinema** on Vuga Road [125 F7], where kung-fu flicks and Hindi melodramas

---

SAUTI ZA BUSARA – ZANZIBAR'S ANNUAL MUSIC FESTIVAL

If you're heading to Stone Town in early February, be sure to buy tickets for Sauti Za Busara. Centred on Stone Town's atmospheric Old Fort, this four-day extravaganza celebrates the best of African music, traditional and modern. Over 200 musicians and artists take to the stage during this highly successful festival, which also includes screenings of documentaries and music videos. An electric atmosphere of African beats and friendly festival-goers from all over the world, plus a variety of souvenirs and street food, make this eclectic festival one of Africa's best. Tickets can be purchased through the festival's website, (*www.busaramusic.org*), or bought on the door, but expect to queue. Do bear in mind that city accommodation sells out fast around festival time, so book early for a guaranteed room.

predominate. However, with the opening of the little cinema attached to the **Rumaisa Hotel** (page 134) and **Hurumzi Movie Café** (pages 146–7), visitors have more reliable options to get their movie fix. Weekly film schedules for both are available on their Facebook pages and at the venues themselves.

SHOPPING

Zanzibar Town is something of an Aladdin's cave for visiting shoppers, with a vast array of shops, large and small, catering for the ever-growing tourist influx. Even die-hard deal-hunters will be hard pushed to visit them all, and there are bound to be even more by the time you visit. A selection of both favourites and perennials are listed here; aside from their positive credentials, their products are without question some of the best quality and most original around. For a long time, quality and variety were an issue for visiting shoppers, with cheap, mass-produced, imported tat almost all that was available. However, a handful of international designers have set up in Stone Town in the last few years, raising the bar not only in terms of the shopping experience, presentation, quality and originality of goods, but also in training up local Zanzibari and mainland Tanzanians in the value of creating and selling better goods. Prices for these items are understandably considerably higher, but it is very much the case that you get what you pay for.

In the larger tourist shops and boutiques listed, prices are fixed and you can pay in US dollars or by credit card (surcharges are usual), whilst in the market and at smaller locally run outlets, cash (Tanzanian shillings) is necessary and bargaining is part of the experience. There are no hard and fast rules to the latter, and sensible judgement is required, but a basic rule of thumb is to start negotiations at half the asking price and if you ultimately pay around 75% of the initial price, then it's likely both parties will walk away happy.

MADE IN ZANZIBAR – FAIR-TRADE AND HIGH QUALITY In recent years, there has been a welcome trend towards training the local community, especially women, to produce high-quality, well-designed clothing and accessories. These are then sold to delighted tourists through some of the better hotel gift shops and a growing number of stylish boutiques, whilst the individual Zanzibaris benefit from a new skill and a fair price for their efforts. In all of these places, prices are fixed; save bargaining for the markets.

Several of the brands below belong to the 'Made in Zanzibar' producers' network (*madeinzanzibar.com*), a collective aiming to cross-promote quality products from Zanzibar to support the local 'eco-nomy', and provide an identifiable brand for visitors. A little more information is available online, but do look out for the logo when shopping. Currently, the best projects, products and shopping outlets are:

Fahari [124 C5] 62 Kenyatta Rd; ☎ 0772 661065/0714 541537; e info@fahari-zanzibar. com; www.fahari-zanzibar.com. Opposite the Stone Town Café, this beautiful boutique showcases well-made, stylish products: leather bags, accessories & jewellery. Established by an experienced British accessories designer, Julie Lawrence, it's made a big impact as both a super social enterprise & NGO, & as an excellent addition to the high-end shopping scene. Fahari means 'to have a sense of pride' in Swahili, & that's exactly what's instilled in the Zanzibari women trained here. Since its inception, 54 local ladies have been trained in the fields of creative design, manufacture, marketing & sales, with 14 now working full-time, with profit share, in the shop. Other trained staff benefit from new & improved skills, experience & occasional work.

All this means purchases here genuinely support local women in building a sustainable future. In addition, a fusion of traditional Zanzibari skills (woodcarving, henna painting, kitenge design and palm weaving), locally sourced Indian Ocean products, international expertise & cutting-edge designs, ensure the products are genuinely appealing to visitors, especially those with a keen eye for originality & quality. All design & manufacture is done on Zanzibar, to exacting standards, with traditional concepts & techniques given a modern twist to ensure consistency & quality. Items are not cheap, but neither should they be; these are ethically produced, handmade & high-quality goods. A great place to treat yourself or take back some impressive souvenirs.

Kanga Kabisa [124 B6] 024 223 2100; info@kangakabisa.com; www.kangakabisa.com; 09.00–19.00 daily. Founded in 2004 by Lotta Gillving, Kanga Kabisa produces women's, men's & children's clothes, as well as a few accessories, made exclusively from vibrant locally produced cotton kanga cloth. Colourful fabrics, cool cotton & functional Nordic designs courtesy of its Swedish initiator – often with a nod to '60s & '70s fashion – are perfect attire for summer- or beachwear. With locally sourced materials & a strong desire to minimise environmental impact in island production, it is a real model for simple, ethical businesses in the region. Available for purchase in their Shangani shop (beside Africa House Hotel), as well as some hotel gift shops.

Kihaga [124 D4] mwarabually@yahoo.com. This little NGO is a relative newcomer to the ethical shopping scene, established by well-respected designer Mwarabu Ali Said Majondo, which runs a youth training scheme teaching local people to become proficient tailors. Their neat, colourful boutique displays vibrant off-the-peg chitenge & kanga cotton clothing, & also offers a great bespoke service. Choose a fabric of your liking from the vast array of colours & patterns, select a design from the catalogue of images or a piece in the shop, get measured up, & collect your custom-made outfit 3 days later. Should any alterations (*marekebisho*) need to be made, they can be turned around within a day. Prices are very reasonable (ladies' dress US$40–50, skirt US$25, men's shirt US$25–30, shorts US$30–35, children's dress US$25) & quality is

good. Quite reasonably, you will be asked to pay a deposit at the time of ordering.

Moto 0777 466304; moto@madeinzanzibar.com; www.motozanzibar.wordpress.com. Initiated in 1997 by Antje Förstle, this island-wide handicraft co-operative aims to work as a competitive small industry to better develop the rural economy, ensure the continuation of traditional crafts & further train Zanzibari artisans. Impressively, it is as environmentally responsible as it is socially aware: soil, roots & barks provide the products' striking natural dye colours & solar cookers are used exclusively in their production. The latter significantly save on valuable natural resources, whilst educating its members about alternative energies and giving them a competitive edge on final sales. The finely made array of vibrant palm basketry, wide-brimmed straw hats, household decorations & woven fabrics are striking & immediately appealing in both design & quality. They may be slightly more costly than some on the market, but the craftsmanship is significantly better & Moto currently operates in 9 Zanzibari villages, providing an umbrella for 19 co-operatives, totalling over 100 men & women, all of whom benefit from the supportive structure, work ethic, shared business opportunities & established route to market through its shop on Hurumzi St & a handful of hotel gift shops. If you are interested in the traditional skills involved in making these products, ask at the shop about hands-on tours at the community workshop in Pete (near Jozani Forest).

Dada dada@madeinzanzibar.com; www.dadazanzibar.wordpress.com. Initiated by the same environmentally & socially aware team behind Moto, Dada began in 2007 as a 'wholesome food & e-cosmetics' network. Meaning 'sister' in Swahili, it offers training & employment for women in the Matemwe area, whilst producing some delicious homemade foodie treats & spiced cosmetics. Using seasonal ingredients (often organic), locally sourced, produced on a small scale with solar equipment, & then beautifully packaged, the women here take great pride in their lovely wares. Packets of dried spices & tropical fruits, bottled Swahili cooking sauces, tropical mustards (try the sweet date mustard with cognac) & chutneys (take home some tasty baobab chutney for your next ploughman's lunch!), imaginative snacks (from chilli 'n' cashew date balls to coconut-crusted ginger), spice teas & even pasta (from traditional varieties to the likes of beetroot and wholegrain tagliatelle) certainly tempt the taste buds & make excellent souvenirs. Or for something more personal, cleansing, moisturising & exfoliating soaps are also handmade in their workshop, alongside natural mosquito repellent, solid shampoo, body oils & a dedicated men's grooming range, 'Jambo Bwana'. On a practical level, they make a chemical-free mosquito repellent from beeswax & lemongrass, which is worth a try! In addition to creating these fabulous products & Dada's own product training, the parent NGO goes far beyond this remit & is involved in everything from rainwater harvesting & the promotion of accessible alternative energy to hygiene & training in sustainability & business skills. Products can be purchased in the Moto shops, several hotel gift shops & now even in some Zanzibar Town supermarkets.

JENGA m 0777 209576; e info@jengazanzibar. com; www.jengazanzibar.com. A Dutch-backed social enterprise, JENGA works hard to help local craftsmen & women & small co-operative groups to promote & sell their handicrafts. By teaching practical sales & marketing skills, & opening craft shops in Nungwi & Michamvi to display these beautiful island products, this organisation is offering practical support & a real route to market. Their work is worth supporting not only because it is directly benefitting talented local people, but because their crafts – from clothes to jewellery to soap – are high quality & thoroughly Zanzibari.

Malkia In 2003, Danish designer Iben Djuraas established a women's co-operative in Bwejuu, making clothing for women & children. Named Malkia, the Swahili word for 'queen', Iben's project was one of the first on the island to mix chic Scandinavian fashion design with vibrant ethnic textiles. Made entirely from Swahili kanga fabrics, the wrap skirts, summer dresses and tunic tops are fun and flattering attire. Training and improving the women's sewing skills, creating simple, stylish patterns and providing a route to market, Iben sought to ensure that the Malkia women learnt valuable skills and an income to better the lives of themselves and their children. Iben no longer lives on the island, so the operations of the

project have been handed over to the women whom she trained. Now working with JENGA, they continue to produce contemporary, stylish clothing at reasonable rates from their workshop on Michamvi Peninsula. Malkia purchases can be made at several hotel shops on the island, including Matemwe Beach Village and Mtoni Marine Centre, as well as at Mrembo Spa (page 166) in Stone Town or directly from Malkia's 10 female tailors in Bwejuu.

Sasik [124 D4] e sasikaznz@hotmail.com; www.sasikzanzibar.blogspot.co.uk. Sasik, an acronym formed in part from its initiator's name (Saada Abdulla Suleiman Industry Karibuni), began in 1994 when Saada taught herself the art of appliqué & encouraged friends & family to learn, too. Seeing a potential market for the colourful products they made, she applied for & received a grant from the UK-based Tanzania Gatsby Trust to set up a local women's co-operative. Initially, the funds were used for the simple workshop at the back of their current shop on Gizenga St. Here, 12 local women were taught the fine hand-stitched technique & their distinctive Swahili–Arabic soft furnishings began to emerge. Now 45 women are employed (there are plans to triple this in time), many earning an income for the first time & actively improving their standard of living & the education of their children. The intricate appliqué cushion covers, bedspreads & wall hangings are made on the spot & you can buy off the shelf or order bespoke colour schemes & designs.

Surti & Sons [124 C4] m 0777 472742; www. surtiandsons.wordpress.com; ⊕ 09.00–14.00 & 14.30–19.00 daily. In a small unassuming shop on Gizenga St, the family craftsmen here have been handmaking leather sandals & bags for 4 decades., Their beautiful, durable footwear is made under the careful supervision of Pravin Surti, a softly spoken man with a genuine desire for customer satisfaction. Well known for quality within the community, & favoured footwear supplier of expats & more affluent Zanzibaris, the sandals here are made with good leather, finely stitched for comfort, & are available in a variety of lovely colours & styles. Leather belts & bags are also available. This family are true artisans & a purchase here is certainly an enduring souvenir.

Upendo Means Love [124 C4] www. upendomeanslove.com; ⊕ 09.00–17.00 Mon–

Sat. In a lovely little shop next to the Coco de Mer Hotel, Upendo sells gorgeous cotton children's clothing & some stylish ladies' summerwear. Initiated by Danish resident Dorthe Davidsen Langås, Upendo operates a multi-faith sewing school & workshop on site, & seeks to empower local women through education, employment & economic independence. Every year, 80 Zanzibari ladies are given vocational training to Tanzanian national diploma level, invited to seminars on business skills, & are offered interest-free loans to purchase their own sewing machines. Many go back to set up their own small businesses & 12 are employed in the Stone Town workshop to make the beautifully cut, colourful clothes, which are for sale in the shop. The easy-to-wear outfits are ideal for summer, & more importantly, all of the profits are ploughed back into sustaining & developing the project.

Zenji Boutique [120 D2] Malawi Rd; www. zenjicafeboutique.com. This little boutique within Zenji Hotel & Café (page 136) makes excellent browsing after one of the café's famously gooey chocolate brownies. A real treasure trove of eclectic Zanzibari & Tanzanian arts & crafts, lovingly displayed with impressively detailed descriptions of all of the products, their production method & ethical pedigree. The boutique sells products made by both talented individuals & several inspiring groups: women's co-operatives, the disabled & environmentally conscious. There are rice & flour sacks transformed into attractive bags, lovely dishes & cutlery produced from recycled metal, hand-dyed fabrics, glass & beaded jewellery & a host of other enticing gifts. There is a small workshop where local women create delightfully decorative & original paper beads; buy something ready-made or join a workshop to learn & create your own. Worth a stop for a wide selection of original souvenirs in a range of budgets.

TOURIST SHOPS There are many shops on Kenyatta Road and along Gizenga Street, as well as its continuations Hurumzi Street and Changa Bazaar. In addition, these streets are lined with pavement traders offering carvings, paintings and beaded trinkets. Most of the shops and stalls stock contemporary carvings as well as older, traditional statues and artefacts from mainland Tanzania and elsewhere in Africa. Tingatinga paintings on canvas or wooden trays, assorted gold, silver and stone jewellery, packets of spices, and mobiles made from coconut shells in the shapes of dolphins, dhows or tropical fish are readily available at every turn. Some of the paintings and craftwork stocked in the souvenir and craft shops is bashed out and of very poor quality, but occasionally, if you search hard enough, you'll find real works of art which have been more carefully made. It's worth spending a bit more time and money (if indeed the stallholder charges more for better quality – some don't seem to) to get something that will still look good when you get it home.

Souvenirs One of the best places to start any shopping trip is the **Zanzibar Gallery** [124 C4] (*zanzibargallery.net*), which sells a range of carvings, paintings, jewellery, materials, maps, clothes, rugs, postcards, antiques and real pieces of art from all over Africa, plus a good selection of books. You can also buy local spices, herbs, pickles and honey, and locally made oils such as pineapple bath oil or banana-scented bubble bath – all made naturally from Zanzibar fruit. It's owned by local photographer and publisher Javed Jafferji, whose own books (signed) are also for sale, including some beautiful large-format photo books, plus illustrated diaries and address books featuring photos from Zanzibar and Tanzania. The Jafferji family also runs The Book Café (page 142).

Another all-round place on Kenyatta Road is **Memories of Zanzibar** [124 C5] (*www.memories-zanzibar.com*), opposite the post office, selling everything from beaded flip-flops and silver bracelets to carpets and gourd-lamps, as well as a good selection of books about Zanzibar, and African music CDs. Further along the same road, opposite Stone Town Cafe, is **Kumi Gifts & Treats** [124 C5].

It's cool, friendly, neatly laid out and has a particularly good display of kikois (see box, page 89), as well as soft kanga toys, a selection of imported swimwear and Ipanema flip-flops, costume jewellery and beach bags. For Tanzanian designer chic, check out **Doreen Mashika's** [125 E3] fashionista fare (*www.doreenmashika. com*) – the expensive shoes and handbags are stylish and offer a taste of African design talent. For postcards you can't go wrong at **Angi's Postcards & Maps** [125 G1], on Mizingani Road, near the Big Tree; there's a truly massive selection here, all at good prices. **ZAYAA Gallery** (Zanzibar Young Artist Association) at the eastern end of Hurumzi Street [125 F3] showcases young artists and has some especially lovely women's art, inspired by henna patterns. **Real Art** (m *0784 460419*) on Gizenga Street offers a good, if more expensive, selection of Tanzanian and Zanzibari art. Paintings and sculptures are organised by style and artist, with quality works selected by the knowledgeable owner, Anita. Inside the **Old Fort** [124 D3], seek out the small art shop beside the restaurant for original watercolours, oil paintings and well-observed pen-and-ink drawings. The friendly artists are on site and many of their works are impressive. Alternatively, a few doors down, **Keramica** [124 D3] sells original, slightly more contemporary products, in the shadow of the amphitheatre.

ANTIQUES Around Zanzibar Town there are also several shops selling antiques from Arabia and India, dating from Omani and British colonial times. **Coast Antique Shop** [124 D4] on Gizenga Street has a particularly good selection of Zanzibar clocks, whilst the enthusiastic staff at **Zanzibar Curio Shop** have a great range of timber souvenirs from doors to carvings. There are several more options on the street between St Joseph's Cathedral and Soko Mohogo crossroads (opposite Mrembo Spa), with Abeid and Tamin curio shops good places to come for genuinely hand-crafted chests.

TAILORS The current best bet for reliable, well-made bespoke clothing is **Kihaga** (page 150). Alternatively, also on Gizenga Street, the tailor at **Mnazi Boutique** [124 D4] can copy any shirt, skirt or trousers you like, from material you buy in the shop or elsewhere in town. If you prefer traditional African clothing, consider a kanga or a kikoi (see box, page 89). Alternatively, **Osman**, the tailor opposite ZAYAA Gallery at the end of Hurumzi Street, is highly recommended (in spite of his tiny, fabric-strewn workplace). He'll happily assist in fabric purchase and will sew mock-ups of bespoke clothing before committing to your chosen material. On Kenyatta Road, the smarter **One Way** boutique [124 C5] also sells piles of T-shirts embroidered with giraffes and elephants or emblazoned with Kenyan and Tanzanian slogans and logos.

JEWELLERY The last few years have seen a significant increase in the number of gem stone and jewellery shops in Stone Town, with posters for beautiful tanzanite springing up on many a shopfront. It's worth looking around and choosing any expensive purchases carefully. **Hassan Jewellers** [125 F6] on Mkunazini Street (m *0773 453575*), close to the market, is reliable and reputable. The family team here are lovely, speak excellent English and stock a good range of tanzanite, for which they will be able to supply authentication certificates showing the stone's size, cut and clarity. Sourcing gems from the owner's own mine in Arusha, they are knowledgeable and efficient, and have an onsite workshop for setting. Jewellery can be custom made in three to ten days depending on the complexity and delivered anywhere on the island or to international addresses.

For something more contemporary and a little unique, **Elias Jewellery** (m *0777 414686;* f *eliasjewellers*) is certainly worth a look. It currently has two branches, one on Kenyatta Road [124 C5], above the post office (access from stairs a few metres along Gizenga Street, signed to Lemongrass and La Taperia), and another on Shangani [124 B4], opposite Tembo Hotel. A family business, stemming from the marriage of two jewellery families, you'll find tanzanite set in gold and silver, as well as some unusual pieces incorporating materials such as ebony wood and recycled rubbed. For serious sparkle, with an equally dazzling price tag, **Lithos Africa** inside the Park Hyatt may fit the bill.

Do be aware when purchasing tanzanite anywhere that it is a soft stone that scratches easily; it's better to have it set as earrings or in a necklace than as a daywear ring.

NEWSPAPER AND BOOKSHOPS Newspapers from Kenya and mainland Tanzania, some international magazines and a reasonable range of books are available from the **Masumo Bookshop** [125 G4], off Creek Road, and from some of the souvenir shops along Kenyatta Road near the Old Post Office. Coffee-table books fact and fiction can all be purchased from the well-stocked **Gallery Bookshop** [124 C4] on Gizenga Street, which is open from 09.00 daily, though shuts at lunchtime on a Sunday, or their sister shop **The Book Café** on Kenyatta Road (page 142).

The best bookshop is the **Zanzibar Gallery** on Kenyatta Road (page 152), which has a good selection of guidebooks and coffee-table books on Zanzibar and other parts of Africa, animal and bird field guides, maps, histories and a range of general novels for those seeking some beach reading material.

CAMERA SUPPLIES For photographic traditionalists, slide and print film is still available in Zanzibar Town souvenir shops (the ones along Kenyatta Road have the best stock); memory cards and camera batteries may be available in the larger hotel shops but stocks are very limited. It's well worth taking spares to avoid disappointment. For pictures from a different era, visit the **Capital Art Studio** on Kenyatta Road. The shop itself gives the impression that it has been unchanged since colonial times, with a good selection of old photographic prints from the 1950s and 1960s, and a few earlier ones, all taken by the owner's father. They also sell camera film and batteries, and offer a one-day developing service.

FOOD SHOPPING If you are self-catering or just going on a picnic for the day, Zanzibar Town has a large **market** selling a vast array of exotic fruit and vegetables, plus fresh fish and meat, though the latter is not for the faint-hearted. You can also buy fresh bread in the market from the salesmen who ride in from the bakeries in the suburbs with large baskets on the backs of their bicycles. Dotted around the town are many small shops with a supply of basics, such as bread, biscuits, some fruit and vegetables, and maybe a few tinned items. As these foods are mainly for local people, prices are low. For more choice go to the '**container stores**' (built in converted shipping containers) along Creek Road or to the shops in the street near the Ciné Afrique, where you'll find a good range of imported food in tins and packets. Most items are reasonably priced, only slightly more than if bought in Dar or Mombasa. The best supermarket with the widest stock in Stone Town is the **Shamshuddin Cash & Carry Supermarket** [125 G4], off Creek Road, near the market. If you're after something more European in flavour, **Maru Maru** (page 128) has an in-house bakery selling take-away loaves and cakes, or for a more extensive range, **La Taperia** (page 143) has a lovely little delicatessen selling cured meats, imported cheeses and other tasty morsels; they'll even make up take-away sandwiches from freshly baked bread. For a sweet indulgence, try the gourmet Tanzanian chocolates on sale at **House of Kakao** [124 C6] (*77 Kenyatta Rd, opposite Dhow Palace;* ⏰ *10.00–19.00 daily*). Made from 100% premium, fair-trade cocoa, sourced directly from Tanzanian co-operatives and packaged organically, **Chocolate Mamas** is Tanzania's first and only indigenous producer of fine chocolate. Pop in for a free tasting with friendly Cecilia and take away a tasty treat from one of their 16 flavoured bars, cocoa nibs or powders.

OTHER PRACTICALITIES

AIRLINES If you need to book or reconfirm a ticket while you are on Zanzibar, this is most easily done through one of the tour operators recommended on pages 114–17. For further details of the airlines represented on Zanzibar, see pages 77–8.

BANKS AND MONEY CHANGING Hard-currency cash can be changed into local currency at most banks as well as at a number of private bureaux de change dotted around Stone Town. These days, there isn't much to choose between the rates offered by banks and the private 'forex bureaux'; indeed some of the private bureaux offer an inferior rate to the banks, but you'll generally find the transaction takes a minute or two at a private bureau whereas changing money at banks often involves long queues and plenty of paperwork. Good private bureaux de change include the **Shangani Bureau de Change** [124 C4] (at the northern end of Kenyatta Road, near the Tembo Hotel), **Malindi Bureau de Change** [120 C2] (east of the port gates) and **Morning Star Bureau de Change** [120 C2] on Gizenga Street opposite United Travel Agents. Most large hotels will also change money, although some deal only with their own guests, and they often offer poor rates. There are also currency bureaux at the port and airport. The only place that exchanges travellers' cheques is the first-floor 'Foreign Trade Dept' at the **National Bank of Commerce** [124 C4] on Kenyatta Road. The rate here is pretty good and the commission (0.5%) is negligible. You can draw cash against Visa cards at the security-guarded ATM outside the same bank, but the only place where you can draw against MasterCard is at the excellent Barclays Bank headquarters and ATM a couple of kilometres out of town along the road towards the north coast.

Currently, getting cash on a debit or credit card is virtually impossible anywhere else; however, the first bank outside Stone Town is currently under construction in Kiwengwa on the east coast (page 256).

COMMUNICATIONS
Post Although letters can be sent from other post offices around Zanzibar Island, it's best to send all your mail from Zanzibar Town. The service is reliable, with letters taking about a week to ten days to reach destinations in Europe and North America (Australia takes a bit longer).

✉ **General Post Office (GPO)** [120 D3] ⏰ 08.00–12.30 & 14.00–16.30 Mon–Sat, 08.00–12.30 Sun. Zanzibar Town's main post office is a large building in the new part of town on the road towards the Amaani Stadium.
✉ **The Old Post Office** [124 C4] Kenyatta Rd; ⏰ 08.00–13.00 & 14.00–16.30 Mon–Thu, 08.00–noon & 14.00–17.00 Fri, 09.00–noon

Sat. This post office is much more convenient for tourists. It's possible to buy stamps here, & this is also the place to collect letters sent by poste restante (although some items may get sent to the main post office by mistake – so make sure anyone writing to you addresses the envelope: 'Old Post Office, Kenyatta Road, Shangani').

6

Telephone Zanzibar Town has a wide choice of places where you can make calls. Some are properly equipped, others are just a dusty phone in the corner of someone's shop, which is nevertheless proudly touted as an 'international communication centre'.

One of the best phone centres is **Tanzanian Telecommunications (TTCL)** international telephone office [124 C5] (⏰ *08.00–21.00 daily*), next to the Old Post Office on Kenyatta Road. Calls cost US$1 for 10 minutes inside Zanzibar, US$1 for 3 minutes elsewhere in Tanzania, and US$1–3 for other international destinations. The office is large, cool and quiet, and the staff members are very friendly and helpful. Another option for international calls is to buy a phonecard from here (they are also sold at some shops and hotels) and use this in the direct-dial phone booth outside: a US$10 card gives you ten minutes to Europe or the USA.

If the international telephone office is closed, local boys loiter by the phone booths outside with cards and will charge you per unit to use them. There will probably even be a few young entrepreneurs with mobile phones, who allow international calls at negotiable rates. It makes you wonder who is really paying the bill.

At the private phone bureaux around Zanzibar Town, international calls are about the same price as those charged by the TTCL, although a few places manage to undercut this rate, and some can be considerably more, so it's worth checking if you've got a lot of calls to make. For cheaper international calls, try one of the **internet cafés** for options such as Skype. For current phone codes, see box, page 101.

Mobile phones If you bring a mobile phone from home, it's emphatically worth the minor investment in a Tanzanian SIM card (which costs around US$2.50 and gives you a local number) and airtime cards (available in units of Tsh1,000 to 5,000).

For the best coverage on the islands at present, we recommend you purchase a Zantel SIM – visit Asko Tours and Travel [124 C4], next to the post office on Kenyatta Road, to purchase the relevant SIM card and ask them to help you set it up. Buy a reasonable amount of credit whilst in Stone Town as only tiny credit bundles are available once you leave the capital, and each one has to be loaded individually into your phone.

International text messages and calls out of Tanzania are seriously cheap: at the time of writing, a few dollars will buy you around 20 text messages to anywhere in the world, and international calls work out at around US$0.50 per minute.

By contrast, you can expect to rack up a hefty bill very quickly by using your home SIM for calls and/or messages, since in most instances these are charged at international rates out of your home country, even when you are phoning home.

Email and internet Wi-Fi is relatively easy to access in Zanzibar Town these days, and many a café, hotel and restaurant will advertise free Wi-Fi for customers. Speeds and reliability vary considerably, but connectivity is eminently possible!

If you are one of the island's rare visitors without a mobile, tablet or laptop, you'll still find a few internet cafés around town. Like the phone offices (indeed, many are also phone offices), some are large and air conditioned with several terminals, while others are in the corner of someone's shop and you connect to the outside world crammed between boxes of soap and tinned meat. The cost of internet use from a PC is a pretty standard US$1 per hour across town, and most charge per 30-minute increment, starting at a few dollars, and if you go over this by a few seconds you'll be charged for the next 30 minutes. Some of the more reliable and well-equipped internet cafés include:

Shangani Internet Café [124 C5] Kenyatta Rd; 📞024 223 2925. This is one of the best places in Zanzibar Town. It has long opening hours, fast connections, about 15 computers, a fridge full of ice cream & cold drinks, & charges US$1/hr.

Too Short Internet [124 C4] ⏲ 08.00–23.00. Opposite the National Bank of Commerce, this is centrally located with long hours, & around 8 quick machines at the standard rate of US$0.50/30mins. If you're travelling with a laptop & fancy a night in, for US$2 you can also rent DVDs here (US$10 refundable deposit).

HOSPITALS, DOCTORS AND PHARMACIES Zanzibar's main public hospital is Mnazi Mmoja General Hospital, on the south side of Stone Town. Like many hospitals in developing countries, the staff are dedicated but the wards are badly underfunded, undersupplied and in very poor condition. Equally distressing is the pile of rubbish (including drip-feeds and needles) simply dumped on the beach behind the hospital. In case of a real emergency, it's likely that you'll want to be flown to one of the private clinics in Dar es Salaam.

Private medical clinics Most tourists in need of urgent medical attention should go to one of Zanzibar's private medical clinics where the staff speak English and the service is better. There is now even quality dental care available. Of course, any treatment has to be paid for, and it will cost around US$50 for a consultation. All fees should be covered by decent travel insurance, and we would highly recommend ensuring you have this prior to travel. Most medical centres also have pharmacies selling medicines and other supplies.

Dr Mehta's Hospital [124 D7] 3353 Pipalwadi St (opposite the High Court); 📞024 223 1566, emergency m 0777 419999, ambulance m 0656 959595; e drmehtashospital@gmail.com; 📘 Drmehtashospital. For 24hr medical treatment, ultrasound, x-rays, ECGs, & competent care, it's a good choice. Dr Ameesh Mehta is fluent in 5 languages, & is the chosen doctor for most expats, wealthy Zanzibaris & visitors. Ambulance transfer available.

Tasakhtaa – Global Hospital Zanzibar [120 C6] 📞024 223 2341, emergency 📞024 223 2222; m 0779 770577; e info@tasakhtaahospital.co.tz; www.tasakhtaahospital.co.tz. Part of an Indian hospital chain, this facility opened in 2015 on Victoria St. Open 24hrs for emergencies (visiting 11.00–noon & 16.00–18.00), this has a team of GPs as well as an orthopaedic surgeon, cardiologist & gynaecologist. Ambulance transfer available.

Zanzibar Medical Group [124 C7] 📞024 223 3134. Another good-quality private clinic on Kenyatta Rd.

Other medical centres Whilst we would strongly advise visiting one of these private clinics for any significant or potentially dangerous medical issue, if your insurance covers only major medical problems, and you want to keep costs down for something minor, you could go to one of Zanzibar's other medical centres:

Afya Medical Hospital 📞024 223 1228; m 0777 411934. Off Vuga Rd at the southern end of Stone Town, Afya is large & well stocked, with friendly staff. Consultations cost around US$5, blood or urine tests are available, & there's also a pharmacy.

Fahaud Health Centre Near St Joseph's Cathedral. This very basic centre offers consultations for US$5 & malaria blood testing.

Pharmacies If you need to buy medicines, Zanzibar Town has several pharmacies; however, stocks are not always reliable, so if you know you're likely to need a specific drug during your visit, then it's best to bring a full supply with you. There are pharmacies near to Emerson on Hurumzi (page 129), and another

6

highly recommended outfit opposite the Shamshuddin Cash & Carry Supermarket [125 G4] (the pharmacist here is excellent if you are in need of medical advice). Straightforward medicines, toiletries and tampons are also available at the 'container stores' on Creek Road.

POLICE In case of emergency in Zanzibar Town, the main police station [120 C2] (✆ *112 or 024 223 0772*) is in the Malindi area, on the north side of Stone Town. This is also the central police station for the whole of the island. Robberies can be reported here (travel insurance companies usually require you to provide a copy of the basic report on the incident from the local police if you are making a claim), but you should not expect any real action to be taken as the police are not particularly well motivated and corruption is rife.

Zanzibar also has a platoon of **tourist police**, supposedly to assist and protect the island's foreign visitors, although many people question their effectiveness. They are mostly seen driving around town in fancy new patrol cars, while touts continue to hassle tourists unimpeded.

SWAHILI LESSONS If you would like to learn a few words (or even more) of the local language, Kiswahili, there are options with formal classes as well as a number of local people willing to assist. For experienced teachers and structured learning, the best place to start is the **Institute of Kiswahili and Foreign Languages** [125 F7] (✆ *024 223 0724/3337;* e *takiluki@zanlink.com; www.glcom.com/hassan/takiluki. html*). Inside the State University on Vuga Road, the institute offers individual lessons and courses. Classes are normally 08.00–noon and cost US$4 per hour, or US$80 for a week's course. Single lessons away from the institute and longer courses, which include lodgings in the house of a teacher or local family, are also available.

SWIMMING The hotel swimming pools at the Serena and Tembo hotels are no longer open to non-guests; however, Dhow Palace (page 133) will allow visitors to use their pool for US$5 per person during low season or quieter periods. If it's hot and you're desperate for some aquatic relief, **Maruhubi Beach Villas** (page 181) slightly out of town, also allows non-residents to swim in its large beachside pool for US$5 per day, or for something more entertaining, the new **Mtoni Marine Water Park** (15 minutes north of Stone Town) promises to open its doors in 2017 with water slides, wave pools and a raft of aquatic fun stuff for families.

TOURIST INFORMATION The **Zanzibar Tourist Corporation (ZTC)** is the state travel service. It has offices in Livingstone House [120 D2], on the northeast side of town on the main road towards Bububu, where you can make reservations for the exceedingly basic ZTC bungalows on the east coast. For general tourist enquiries, you're better off asking at the ZTC office on Creek Road [120 D3], where the members of staff are a bit more helpful, and there are postcards and maps for sale.

For general information, hotel staff and most tour companies are happy to help, even if you don't end up buying a tour from them. Try **Eco+Culture** [125 F3], **Sama Tours** [125 E4] or **Zanzibar Different** [124 D5], listed on pages 114–17. Also worth visiting is the information desk at the **Old Fort** (page 164), which has details of local musical, cultural and sporting events.

For less formalised (but equally useful) information, check the noticeboard at the open-air restaurant inside the fort. Local events are advertised here, alongside details of companies selling tours, spare seats on charter flights and local residents selling cars or motorbikes.

One writer has compared the old Stone Town of Zanzibar to a tropical forest where tall houses stretch to the sky instead of trees, and the sun filters through a network of overhanging balconies instead of foliage. Its labyrinth of twisting streets and alleys is a stroller's paradise, with new sights, sounds or smells to catch the imagination at every turn: massive carved doors, ancient walls, tiny tempting shops with colourful wares and bustling shoppers, old men hunched over a traditional game, kids with homemade toys, ghetto-blasters at full volume, little boys hawking cashews or postcards or fresh bread, the sound of the muezzin calling from the mosque and the scent of cloves or ginger or lemongrass – and everywhere the echoes of Zanzibar's rich and fascinating history, the sultans, shipbuilders, explorers, slave markets, merchants and exotic spice trade.

Stone Town was originally built on a peninsula that has probably been inhabited since the first people arrived on Zanzibar (although the creek that separated its eastern edge from the rest of the island has now been reclaimed). Ras Shangani, at the western tip of the peninsula, is thought to have been the site of a fishing village for many centuries, and at least one of Zanzibar's early Swahili rulers, the Mwinyi Mkuu, had a palace here.

In the 16th century, Portuguese navigators built a church and trading station on the peninsula as it had a good harbour and was easy to defend. When the Omani Arabs began to settle on the island in the 18th century, they built a fort on the site of the church, and today's Stone Town grew up around the Old Fort.

Most of the houses you see today were built in the 19th century, when Zanzibar was one of the most important trading centres in the Indian Ocean region. The coralline rock of Zanzibar Island was easy to quarry for use as a construction material, so many of the houses were built in grand style with three or four storeys. Previously most of the houses on Zanzibar had been much smaller, built of mangrove poles and palm thatch, making the fine white buildings in Stone Town even more exceptional.

Today, nearly all of these old houses are still inhabited, although many are in a very bad state of repair. The coralline rock was a good building material but it is also soft, and easily eroded if not maintained. Crumbling masonry, along with dilapidated woodwork, is sadly an all too familiar sight in Stone Town – and in some places where the surface has disintegrated it reveals the rough blocks of ancient coral beneath.

However, since the end of the 1980s and through the 1990s, several buildings in Stone Town have been renovated. The Zanzibar government, with assistance from the United Nations Centre for Human Settlements (the Habitat Fund), plans to preserve many more, eventually restoring the whole of Stone Town to something like its original magnificence. The Stone Town Conservation and Development Authority has been established to co-ordinate this work, although it is sometimes hampered by a lack of co-ordination with the local government authorities.

During the 19th century, many of Stone Town's inhabitants were wealthy Arabs and Indians. Consequently the houses were built in two main styles: the Arab style, with plain outer walls and a large front door leading to an inner courtyard; and the Indian style, with a more open façade and large balconies decorated with ornate railings and balustrades, designed to catch sea breezes and dispel the humid atmosphere.

Many of the buildings have doors with elaborately carved frames and panels, decorated with brass studs and heavy locks. The size of the door and the intricacies of its decoration were signs of the family's wealth and status. Today, the Zanzibar door has become a well-recognised symbol of the town and island's historic and cultural background, and many new buildings incorporate one into their design – either a genuine one removed from an old building, or a reproduction (see box, page 173).

Among the houses and tucked away in the narrow streets you will come across mosques, churches and other public buildings, almost hidden in the maze. Stone Town also has a few streets of shops, some of them still called bazaars. Some shops are very small, no more than a kiosk, with a few dusty food tins or a couple of jars of sweets on the shelf; others are larger, catering for locals and visitors, with a wider range of goods. There are also antique and curio shops (bargain hard here), and an increasing number of places selling a wide and inventive selection of locally produced arts and crafts, aimed specifically at the growing tourist market.

As you explore the narrow streets with all their historic links, remember that Zanzibar Town today is very much a real community, where people live and work. It is not a museum piece created for tourists. You should not enter any private house or courtyard unless expressly invited to do so, and before you peer through a window or doorway, stop and ask yourself – would you appreciate a stranger

BARAZA BENCHES
Gemma Pitcher

Baraza benches, often simply called *barazas*, have been a focal point of community life in Zanzibar for centuries. These thick benches of solid stone are built into the walls around courtyards or flank the heavy doors of distinctive Arab-style townhouses. The houses that line the long, narrow streets of Stone Town often have barazas outside – and you will also see barazas on the verandas outside traditional Swahili homes, while in the villages a palm-leaf shelter, flanked by wooden seats, fulfils the same function.

Barazas evolved as a way for Islamic men to receive visitors in their homes without compromising the privacy of their womenfolk. Coffee and sweetmeats would be served on the baraza to anyone who arrived, with only the closest friends or family members being invited into the house. The Omani sultans held public meetings, also known as barazas, outside their palaces to receive petitioners or give visiting dignitaries a public audience.

Today, barazas are still a meeting point for all sections of Zanzibari society. Every urban baraza area is lined with people lolling on the warm, smooth cement benches, gossiping, playing games of *bao* or cards, drinking sweet, thick Arabic coffee or simply idling away a long afternoon with a nap. Draughts boards are scratched in chalk on the stone surfaces, ladies sit comfortably to plait each other's hair, and for traders with no market stall of their own, a baraza provides a flat surface on which to pile their tiny pyramids of oranges, tomatoes and mangoes.

In the rainy season, when torrents of water, sometimes laced with rubbish, make walking down the streets of Stone Town uncomfortable and even hazardous, the barazas outside the houses provide a useful elevated pavement, and pedestrians jump from one to the next in an attempt to keep their feet dry.

The baraza as an architectural feature is an idea that seems to have caught on in a big way among the designers of Zanzibar's smarter hotels; almost every courtyard, nook and cranny – and even bathroom – now boasts its own baraza bench, often whitewashed to match the coral walls or inlaid with mosaic tiles.

doing the same in your home? You should also show respect for local sensibilities (page 87). Mosques are not usually open to non-Muslim visitors. Taking photos of buildings is generally acceptable, but you should never photograph people without their permission (page 102). It's much easier to feel comfortable exploring like this, and taking photos where permitted, if you're accompanied by a good cultural guide (see box, page 118).

THE MARKET [125 H4] The market is about halfway along Creek Road and a good place to visit even if you don't want to buy anything. At the end of the 19th century, the town's marketplace was inside the Old Fort. Today's market hall was built in 1904, and some very early photographs of the market displayed in the museum show that very little has changed since then.

The long market hall is surrounded by traders selling from stalls, or with their wares simply spread out on the ground. It's a very vibrant place where everything, from fish and bread to sewing machines and secondhand car spares, is bought and sold. People bring their produce here from all over the island, and others come to buy things they can't get in their own villages. You could spot dog-eared schoolbooks, anonymous tangles of metal being soldered into usefulness, rough wooden chairs, suitcases, shoes, baskets, kitchenware, clocks and watches, CDs, mobile phones and doubtless the occasional kitchen sink. Some food displays may be best avoided by the squeamish: the massive deep-sea fish heads, jaws agape; dark haunches of beef and slabs of less identifiable meat; pearly squid tentacles; grubby recycled bottles and jars containing oil, honey, pickle and goodness knows what else … and the inevitable accompanying buzz of flies. Don't miss the swathes of multi-patterned cotton fabrics, the fragrant spices and mound after mound of exotic fruit and vegetables though – and just enjoy people-watching and being part of a Zanzibar experience which hasn't yet become especially touristy. On occasional evenings, a public auction is held in the street behind the market where furniture, household goods, old bikes, and all sorts of junk are sold. It is very entertaining to watch, but make sure you don't bid for anything by mistake: keep your hands still!

LIVINGSTONE HOUSE MUSEUM [120 D2] (m *0779 093066;* e *selgpsm@gmail. com;* ⊕ *opening hours to be finalised*) On the northeast side of the town, in the Kinazini waterfront quarter, this old building now serves as the headquarters of the Zanzibar Tourist Corporation (ZTC).

It was built around 1860 for Sultan Majid (sultan from 1856 to 1870), a time when Zanzibar was used as a starting point by many of the European missionaries and pioneers who explored eastern and central Africa during the second half of the 19th century. David Livingstone, probably the most famous explorer of them all (see box, page 170), stayed in this house before sailing to the mainland to begin his last expedition in 1866. Other explorers, such as Burton, Speke, Cameron and Stanley, also stayed here while preparing for their own expeditions. The house was later used by members of the island's Indian community, and in 1947 the colonial government purchased it for use as a scientific laboratory for research into clove diseases. After independence and the Revolution it became the Zanzibar headquarters of the Tanzania Friendship Tourist Bureau, the forerunner of today's ZTC. Although not all the rooms are being used, a large, downstairs room was due to be opened as a Livingstone Museum in early 2017 by Said El-Gheithy, the local academic and guide who is the curator of the Princess Salme Museum (page 163). When open, it will offer displays of original artefacts and reproductions of items associated with Livingstone's life, as well as story boards recounting his travels.

OLD DISPENSARY [120 C2] (🕐 *09.00–18.00 daily; admission free*) Opposite the new port buildings, on Mizingani Road, this grand four-storey building has a set of particularly decorative balconies. Also called the Ithnasheri Dispensary or Hospitali Kongwe, it was designed by Indian architect Hasham Patel and built in the 1890s as a private house for prominent Ismaili Indian merchant Tharia Topan, a customs advisor to the sultans, and one of the wealthiest Zanzibaris of his era. Still unfinished when he died in 1891, it passed into the hands of Haji Nasser Nur Mohammed who founded a dispensary in the building; this fell into disrepair during the 1970s and 1980s, and was later renovated in 1997 with funding from the Aga Khan Charitable Trust. A few years later it opened as the Stone Town Cultural Centre. The building has now largely been taken over by offices, but a couple of handicraft stalls operate from the ground floor. The Aga Khan Trust for Culture is hopeful that the building will one day become the Indian Ocean Maritime Museum and we wait in anticipation for more news of this impressive building's future.

OLD CUSTOMS HOUSE [125 F1] (🕐 *09.00–18.30 daily; admission free*) On Mizingani Road overlooking the sea, this large building has a plain façade and is fairly featureless apart from the beautiful set of carved wooden doors, decorated in the Arab style with fish, lotus and anchor-chain motifs. Hamoud, grandson of Sultan Said, was proclaimed sultan here in 1896. In 1995, it was renovated with the help of UNESCO; the building comes to life best when the Dhow Countries Music Academy, which is based here, hosts taraab concerts (check for details on www.zanzibarmusic.org). You can visit at any time and follow your ears to see if rehearsals are taking place.

PALACE MUSEUM [125 E2] (🕐 *08.30–18.00 daily; admission adult/child US$3/1.50; guides available with fees to be agreed beforehand (around US$5 is fair)*) Housed in a large white building with castellated battlements situated on Mizingani Road, where the latter runs very close to the sea, this palace was built in the late 1890s for members of the sultan's family and was originally called the Sultan's Palace (it is physically connected by a little covered bridge at the top floor level to its neighbour the Beit el Sahel, page 174). From 1911, the palace was used as the Sultan of Zanzibar's official residence, but was renamed the People's Palace after the 1964 Revolution, when Sultan Jamshid was overthrown. It continued to be used as government offices until 1994 when the palace was turned into a museum dedicated to the history of the sultans of Zanzibar. Remarkably, much of their furniture and many other possessions survived the revolutionary years and can now be seen by the public.

Despite the dark and disheveled reception area, the exhibits themselves are relatively well organised and labelled. The ground floor is dedicated to the early years of the sultanate (1828–70) as well as displaying a Gatling gun (an early kind of machine gun) obtained by the sultan in the 1890s, a fine Zanzibar chest and large portraits of various sultans, most of which were restored in 1994 by an Italian conservator.

The upper floors are largely devoted to exhibits from the later, more affluent period of 1870–96, with thrones, banqueting tables (the banquet room is said to be still used on occasions) and ceremonial furniture, plus personal items such as beds (look out for the intricately carved ebony love seat and the Indian sofa with Krishna on its back) and the sultan's mobile water closet with its unusual arrangements. You can't fail to notice the incongruous examples of early 1960s Formica furniture and a 1936 bathroom complete with bidet and footbath for pre-prayer ablutions.

The state room furniture is all a bit dusty (note the huge Venetian chandelier dating from the 1930s), but there are fascinating exhibits everywhere: note the grandfather clock by Maple & Co., London, and a copy of the entire Quran printed on one large sheet of paper printed in West Germany, with each of the 30 chapters occupying a single column.

Finally, while the Sultana's Sitting Room was closed on our last visit, don't miss the room devoted to Princess Salme (see box, pages 189–90), the daughter of Sultan Said, who eloped to Hamburg with a German merchant in 1866.

Outside, overlooked by the palace balconies, the royal cemetery is still maintained by the Omani Consulate and includes the graves of sultans Said, Barghash, Majid, Khaled, Khalifa and Abdullah.

An excellent leaflet, with concise historical background and room plans, is sometimes available from the ticket desk, which also offers a small range of books.

PRINCESS SALME MUSEUM [125 F3] (m *0779 093066:* e *selgpsm@gmail.com;* ⏰ *11.00–18.00 daily; admission adults/child US$5/free, inc guided tour with the curator US$10/free*) Within the Emerson on Hurumzi hotel building (page 129), this fascinating small museum, opened by Zanzibari scholar and cultural guide Said El-Gheithy, offers a unique insight into Zanzibar in the 19th century, through the lens of Sayyida Salme. With photographs, family trees, story boards, artefacts and reproductions, the story of the youngest daughter of Sultan Said and a concubine from Circassia in the Russian Caucasus is brought vividly to life. Salme famously left Zanzibar in 1866 when she became pregnant by German merchant Heinrich Ruete. They moved to Germany and had three children before Heinrich's accidental death in 1871. It's a fascinating story, told by the princess herself in her book *Memoirs of an Arabian Princess*, (see box, pages 189–90). Salme died in Jena, Germany, in 1924.

HOUSE OF WONDERS (BEIT AL AJAIB) [124 D3] (⏰ *09.00–18.00 daily, although periodically closed for repairs; admission US$5*) This grand building dominates the waterfront area of Zanzibar Town, and is one of its best-known landmarks. A perfect rectangle, it is one of the largest buildings on the island, rising over several storeys, surrounded by tiers of pillars and balconies, and topped by a large clock tower. After more than a century of use as a palace and government offices, it opened in 2002 as the Museum of History and Culture. After part of its roof collapsed in 2016, the building was closed, and some of its exhibits moved to the Zanzibar Museum of Art (page 171). If it is open during your stay in Stone Town, it is well worth a visit – though a jumble of crafts stalls fills much of the tree-shaded parking area in front of the building, making access somewhat confusing.

Built in 1883 as a ceremonial palace for Sultan Barghash, Beit al Ajaib was designed by a marine engineer (hence the great use of steel pillars and girders in the construction), and located on the site of an older palace used by Queen Fatuma, the Mwinyi Mkuu (ruler of Zanzibar) in the 17th century. In its heyday, the interior of the palace had fine marble floors and panelled walls. It was the first building on Zanzibar to be fitted with electric lighting, and one of the first in East Africa to have an electric lift, hence its local nickname 'Beit al Ajaib', meaning 'House of Wonders'.

In 1896, the building was slightly damaged by naval bombardment during an attempted palace coup, started when Sultan Hamad died suddenly and his cousin Khaled tried to seize the throne (see box, page 24). From 1911, it was used as offices by the British colonial government and after the 1964 Revolution it was used by the ASP, the ruling political party of Zanzibar. In 1977, it became the headquarters of the Party of the Revolution (the Chama Cha Mapinduzi or CCM), Tanzania's sole political party at the time. In the early 1990s, Beit al Ajaib

6

was virtually abandoned by the government and the party and stood empty for some years, gradually falling into disrepair.

Even when its doors are open, the museum is permanently under development, with displays in various stages of completion. Those already finished cover a variety of subjects relating to Zanzibari and Swahili culture and history, including the early history of Stone Town and the Swahili trading empire of the 19th century, the maritime history of the Swahili coast, and dhow-building (one of the amazing traditional 'stitched dhows' is displayed here, its timbers literally sewn together). Further displays covering the Portuguese period and Omani and British colonial times are in progress. Among many items, you should be able to find David Livingstone's medical chest, a section of railway track from the short-lived Zanzibar Railroad, some old bicycle lamps customised to run on coconut oil, and the old lighthouse lamp.

Beyond the displays themselves, the building itself is fascinating, with the ground floor offering extraordinary views up through the central courtyard to the roof. At first-floor level the floor is tiled in marble and has four massive, carved wooden doors, which are found on the other floors as well. On the floor above the exhibition room you can go out onto the upper balcony and walk right around the outside of the building from where there are spectacular views cross Stone Town and the bay.

Outside the House of Wonders are two old bronze cannons with Portuguese inscriptions. It is thought that these were made in Portugal sometime in the early 16th century, but the Omanis probably brought them to Zanzibar, after taking them from Persian forces who had originally captured the guns from the Portuguese in 1622.

OLD FORT [124 D3] (⏱ *07.00–19.00 daily; admission free except during special events; photography permitted*) The Old Fort (also called the Arab Fort, and by its local name Ngome Kongwe) is a huge building, containing large open courtyards, and with high, dark walls topped by castellated battlements. It was built between 1698 and 1701 by the Busaidi group of Omani Arabs, who had gained control of Zanzibar in 1698, following almost two centuries of Portuguese occupation. The fort was used as a defence against the Portuguese and against a rival Omani group, the Mazrui, who occupied Mombasa at that time. The fort was constructed by the Busaidi Omani Arabs on the site of a Portuguese church that had been built between 1598 and 1612 (remnants of which can be seen in the main courtyard). In the 19th century, it was used as a prison, and criminals were executed or punished here, at a place just outside the east wall. The Swahili word *gereza*, meaning 'prison', is thought to be derived from the Portuguese word *igreja*, meaning 'church'. In the early 20th century, the fort was also used as a depot for the short railway line that ran from Zanzibar Town to Bububu. In 1949 it was rebuilt and the main courtyard used as a ladies' tennis club, but after the 1964 Revolution it fell into disuse. Today, the fort has been renovated, and is open to visitors. It is easy to walk around the top of the battlements and enter the towers on the western side, which house 'Colours of Zanzibar' in the southwest tower and the 'Collective Art Gallery' in the northwest tower, from where local art can be purchased.

In 1994, the eastern courtyard was turned into an open-air theatre. The development was imaginative yet sympathetic to the overall design and feel of the original building: seating is in an amphitheatre, and the fort's outer walls and the neighbouring House of Wonders form a natural backdrop. It's used for contemporary and traditional music, drama and dance, including most performances in the annual Sauti za Busara (see box, page 148) and the Zanzibar International Film Festival.

The entrance area also houses a tourist information desk, with details on performances in the amphitheatre and other events around town, plus a selection of books for sale and a range of tour company leaflets to browse. There are also several spice and craft shops, a pleasant café and public toilets. With so many attractions and facilities, it's easy to spend an hour or so here.

FORODHANI GARDENS [124 D3] The Forodhani Gardens (Jamituri Gardens on some maps) are between the Old Fort and the sea, overlooked by the House of Wonders. Forodhani means 'customs' and this is close to the site of the original Customs House. The gardens were first laid out in 1936 to commemorate the Silver Jubilee of Sultan Khalifa (sultan from 1911 to 1960), and were known as Jubilee Gardens until the 1964 Revolution. In the centre of the gardens stands a podium where the band of the sultan's army used to play for the public. Nearer the sea is a white concrete arabesque arch which was built in 1956 for the visit of Princess Margaret (sister of Queen Elizabeth II of Britain), although this was never officially used, as the princess arrived at the dhow harbour instead. She did visit the gardens, however, and planted a large tree, which can still be seen today.

In 2009, after years of neglect, the gardens were re-landscaped by the Aga Khan Trust for Culture and are now the pulsing heart of Stone Town every evening when the food stalls come into their own. Everyone agrees the new gardens are a vast improvement, with the street lighting, waste collection, a new sea wall of salvaged stone, and an organised food court for the evening stallholders (see box, page 146). Cafés, the bandstand, a dhow-shaped adventure playground and tropical planting amid manicured lawns make it look like the central park it is. We hope this project will prove a catalyst for ongoing urban upgrading and economic opportunity in Stone Town, as well as improving the rest of the waterfront's aesthetic appeal.

ST JOSEPH'S CATHOLIC CATHEDRAL [124 D5] This large cathedral, with prominent twin spires, is off Kenyatta Road in the Baghani part of town. Although its spires are a major landmark from a distance, the cathedral can be surprisingly hard to find in the narrow streets, and it's best to follow the small sign off Gizenga Street. The cathedral was built between 1893 and 1897 by French missionaries and local converts, who had originally founded a mission here in 1860. The plans were drawn by the same French architect who designed the cathedral in Marseilles, France. The tiles and the stained-glass windows were imported from France, and the murals on the inside walls, painted just after the cathedral was completed, also show a clear French influence. Unfortunately, some of the murals have been badly restored.

The cathedral is in regular use by the town's Catholic community, a mixture of Zanzibaris, Tanzanians from the mainland, Goans and Europeans. There are several masses each Sunday, and one or two on weekdays too. Outside mass times, the main cathedral doors may be locked, and entrance is via the back door reached through the courtyard of the adjoining convent. You will need to ask someone to gain access.

HAMAMNI BATHS [125 F4] (⏱ *09.00–17.30 daily; admission US$1.50*) Located in the Hamamni quarter, which means simply 'the place of the baths' from the Arabic *hammam* (bathhouse), opposite the Shia Mosque, this was the first public bathhouse in Zanzibar, commissioned by Sultan Barghash and built by an architect called Haji Gulam Hussein. It is one of the most elaborate on the island, and is constructed in the Persian style. Today the baths are no longer functioning, but the various rooms are still largely intact, complete with black-and-white tiled floor. The first octagonal area was for undressing and storing clothes and footwear, with a central fountain for feet-washing. There are still six visible barazas (resting niches – see box, page 160) around it, which would have provided seating and refreshments. A corridor leads to the back, past the old toilet, and to the main baths. There's a large, central atrium with a single, multi-holed rooflight, and closets off to one side for urinating and shaving pubic hair. The available baths were a Cool Water Bath, a Hot Water Bath and a Very

MREMBO TRADITIONAL SPA

[124 D5] (*Call or visit to book appointments;* \ *024 223 0004;* m *0777 430117; mrembospa.com;* ☉ *09.30–18.00 daily*)
Recently, a number of spas have sprung up around Zanzibar as the Western craze for wellness treatments has descended on the island. Many are little more than a massage table, some lemongrass oil and a friendly, untrained, local masseuse, while a few, in the larger hotels, are more sophisticated and professional and staffed by Thai therapists. All can prove a thoroughly enjoyable distraction, but the most engaging and original by far is Mrembo Traditional Spa.

In an old antique store halfway along Cathedral Street, close to St Joseph's Cathedral, Mrembo is a small, wonderfully unassuming place offering the finest traditional treatments from Zanzibar and Pemba. Their flagship treatment, *singo*, is a natural exfoliating scrub traditionally used when preparing Zanzibari girls for marriage. Prepared by hand with a pestle and mortar (*kinu*), the fresh jasmine, ylang ylang, rose petals, *mpompia* (geranium), *mrehani* (sweet basil) and *liwa* (sandalwood) combine to create the most wonderfully aromatic blend. Perfuming the skin for days after treatment and leaving it soft as silk, it's equally popular with honeymoon brides today. For men, the clove-based scrub *vidonge* is said by Pemba islanders to increase libido and stamina, and is even offered in souvenir packages. Hot sand massages, authentic henna painting and beauty treatments are available too, with all the herbal products coming fresh from the owner's garden and skillfully prepared in front of you. The treatment rooms are cool and candlelit, with simple kanga-covered massage tables and sweet-smelling incense. There is a cold-water shower for post-scrub rinsing and a very chilled taarab music room for relaxing in before and afterwards.

Although not their *raison d'être*, Mrembo is also an impressively inclusive community project. The three local therapists have disabilities: two, Ali and Zubeiri, are deaf, and Asha is blind. Trained in therapeutic massage by professional therapists from African Touch (a Canadian-funded, community-based organisation in Kenya), they have benefited enormously in confidence and social standing from their practical education and employment. Each has an able-bodied assistant at Mrembo to ease understanding, though Ali will cheerfully encourage you to try a little Kiswahili sign language, using the alphabet poster for guidance.

For a lazy afternoon of complete beauty pampering or a simple massage or manicure whilst the sun's at its peak, Mrembo Traditional Spa is a great place to while away the time with a cup of refreshing ginger tea and friendly staff. It is a true oasis of calm in the centre of Stone Town, and an experience not to be hurried.

Hot Water Bath. There's also a door at the back (ask the ladies at the front desk to unlock it), where you can climb upstairs to the roof and see what the domed ceilings looked like from the outside.

TIP HOUSE [124 B6] The house where the notorious slaver Tippu Tip once lived is close to the Africa House Hotel (turn right after 6 Degrees South if walking west on Shangani). Until the 1960s the house was a private residence, then after the Revolution it was converted into social housing. The house has not been maintained since its transformation – indeed one writer called it 'the most magnificent squat in all of Africa' – and it now stands empty and derelict-looking. While it is not open to visitors, the huge carved front door (an indicator of Tippu Tip's great wealth) can still be seen, and there is often a cluster of visitors outside.

The real name of the slave trader known as Tippu Tip (also spelt Tippoo Tib and Toppu Tob) was Hamed bin Mohammed el Marjebi. Born in the 1840s, he began to participate in the slave trade at the age of 18 and roamed East Africa through the middle of the 19th century, trading in slaves and ivory and assisting explorers such as Livingstone and Stanley with their supplies and route planning.

Contemporary records describe him as tall, bearded and strong, with dark skin, an 'intelligent face' and the 'air of a well-bred Arab'. His nickname derives from a local word meaning 'to blink', either because of a nervous twitch in his eyes, or because they resembled the characteristic blinking eyes of a bird known as tipputib.

A feared and respected figure of his time, he reportedly visited his concubines twice a day, and is said to have argued with missionaries that the prophets Abraham and Jacob, who appear in both the Bible and the Quran, were themselves slave owners. Tippu Tip became immensely wealthy and by 1895 owned 10,000 slaves and seven plantations. He died in 1905.

ANGLICAN CATHEDRAL [125 G5] (⊕ *daily, Sat evensong in Swahili 16.30–17.15, Sun holy communion in Swahili 06.30–08.00, in English 08.00–09.15, & sung in Swahili 09.30–11.30; admission US$5 inc guide & access to St Monica's Hostel & Slave Trade Exhibit*) The Cathedral Church of Christ, also called the Cathedral of the Universities' Mission to Central Africa (UMCA), is near the junction of Creek Road and Sultan Ahmed Mugheiri Road on the eastern side of Stone Town. The commonest access to the complex – consisting of the Anglican cathedral, St Monica's Hostel and the Slave Trade Exhibit – is from Sultan Ahmed Mugheiri Road, where visitors go through a security check.

The cathedral stands on the site of the slave market, used in the 18th and 19th centuries when Zanzibar was a large slave-trading centre. A group of UMCA missionaries had originally come to East Africa in 1861, following the call of the explorer David Livingstone to oppose the slave trade and spread Christianity across Africa. In 1864, they settled in Zanzibar, after a number of earlier sites proved unsuccessful. When the slave market was closed by Sultan Barghash in 1873, the missionaries took over the site and almost immediately started building the cathedral. Further adjoining land was donated to the mission by a wealthy Indian merchant called Jairam Senji. Today, nothing of the old slave market remains (but see pages 169–71).

When the first service was held in the cathedral on Christmas Day 1877, the roof was not finished; it was finally completed in 1880. Tradition has it that the cathedral's altar stands on the site of a tree to which the slaves were tied and then whipped to show their strength and hardiness. Those who cried out the least during the whipping were considered the strongest, and sold for higher prices.

6

The man who was the force and inspiration behind the building of the cathedral was Bishop Edward Steere, Bishop of Zanzibar from 1874 to 1882. (He was also the first compiler of an English–Swahili dictionary, using the Roman alphabet; until then Swahili had been written using Arabic script.) He trained local people as masons and used coral stone and cement for building materials. Sultan Barghash is reputed to have asked Bishop Steere not to build the cathedral tower higher than the House of Wonders, which was being completed at the same time. When the bishop agreed, the sultan presented the cathedral with its clock. The tower was finished in 1883.

The legacy of David Livingstone lives on in the cathedral: a window is dedicated to his memory, and the church's crucifix is made from wood from the tree that grew above the spot where his heart was buried at the village of Chitambo, in present-day Zambia.

The mosaic decorations on the altar were given to the cathedral by Miss Caroline Thackeray (a cousin of the English novelist William Makepeace Thackeray), who was a teacher at the mission here from 1877 to 1902.

Behind the altar are the bishop's throne and 12 other seats for the canons, decorated with copper panels and showing the names, in Swahili, of several biblical figures. The window behind the altar is decorated with pictures of African saints, from Egypt, Carthage and Ethiopia. Around the church are many plaques dedicated to the memory of missionaries who died here, and to the sailors and airmen who were killed in action during the East Africa Campaign of World War I. The pipe organ is said to be the only one in Africa outside of South Africa.

THE EAST AFRICAN SLAVE TRADE

From the earliest times, slaves were one of the many 'commodities' exported from Africa to Arabia, Persia, India and beyond. In the 18th century, the demand increased considerably and Arab trading caravans from Zanzibar penetrated mainland Africa in search of suitable slaves. Various contemporary accounts describe all aspects of the trade, from the initial capture of the slaves to their sale in the infamous market of Zanzibar Town.

In the interior, the Arab traders would often take advantage of local rivalries and encourage powerful African tribes to capture their enemies and sell them into slavery. In this way, men, women and children were exchanged for beads, corn and lengths of cloth.

When the Arab traders had gathered enough slaves, sometimes up to 1,000, they returned to the coast. Although the Quran forbade cruelty to slaves, this was frequently ignored on the long journey to Zanzibar: the slaves were tied together in long lines, with heavy wooden yokes at their necks or iron chains around their ankles which remained in place day and night until they reached the coast.

The trade in slaves was closely linked to the trade in ivory: the Arab traders also bought tusks from the Africans and some of the captured slaves may have had to carry these on their heads as they marched towards the coast. If a woman carrying a baby on her back became too weak to carry both child and ivory, the child would be killed or abandoned to make the ivory load easier to carry. Any slaves unable to march were also killed and left behind for the vultures and hyenas. The passage of a slave caravan was marked by a long line of decaying corpses.

After many weeks or months of marching, the slave caravans reached the coast at ports such as Kilwa and Bagamoyo. Here, the slaves were loaded onto dhows, seldom more than 30–35m long, and taken to Zanzibar. Each dhow carried

In a small garden outside the cathedral is a dauntingly expressive sculpture in concrete, Memory for the Slaves, by the Swedish sculptor Clara Sörnäs. Finished in 1998, it portrays five life-size slaves chained in an empty, waist-high pit, their concrete forms shackled with original slave chains. There is something overwhelmingly affecting about the rigid rectangular pit in which they stand, calling to mind their grim reduction in stature as human beings. It's a shocking testimony to the suffering of generations of people.

ST MONICA'S HOSTEL AND THE EAST AFRICAN SLAVE TRADE EXHIBIT [125 G5]
(⏰ 08.00–18.00 daily; admission US$5, inc guide & cathedral access) St Monica's Hostel is an impressive old stone building that encompasses hostel accommodation (page 138) and, in its basement, an evocative reminder of the dehumanising horror of the slave trade. A stone staircase leads from the entrance hallway down to what is reputed to be a dungeon where slaves were kept before being taken to market. Opened in June 2016, the East African Slave Trade Exhibit 1800–1909, to give it its full title, is perhaps the first detailed, culturally unambiguous slavery museum in Africa. Although it consists mainly of display boards, the superb illustrations, engravings, reproductions and early photographs bring the story imaginatively and movingly to life with graphic enlargements and excellent captioning. The exhibition, which takes about an hour to walk through, lays out the full economic and social history of East African slavery from its early origins to the post-slavery Empire years as freed slaves and their descendants tried to restructure their lives and establish their place in society.

between 200 and 600 slaves, all crammed below decks on bamboo shelves with barely 1m of headroom. There was barely room to sit, kneel or squat, just a crippling combination of the three. […]

By the time the slaves reached Zanzibar, they were suffering from starvation and the effects of torturously cramped conditions: it was sometimes a week after landing before they could straighten their legs. The slave traders paid customs duty on all slaves who landed, so any considered too weak to live were thrown overboard as the ship approached the port. Even so, many more slaves died in the Customs House or on the streets between the port and the market.

Before being put on sale, the slaves who did survive were cleaned so that they would fetch a better price. Men and boys had their skins oiled and were given a strip of material to put around their waist. Women and girls were draped in cloth, and sometimes even adorned with necklaces, earrings and bracelets. Generous layers of henna and kohl were smeared onto their foreheads and eyebrows.

The slaves were put on sale in the market in the late afternoon. They were arranged in lines, with the youngest and smallest at the front and the tallest at the rear, and paraded through the market by their owner, who would call out the selling prices. The owner would assure potential buyers that the slaves had no defects in speech or hearing, and that there was no disease present. Buyers would examine the arms, mouths, teeth and eyes of the slaves, and the slaves were often made to walk or run, to prove they were capable of work. Once their suitability had been established, they were sold to the highest bidder.

Source: Charles Miller, The Lunatic Express, *Macmillan, 1971*

David Livingstone is the best known of all the European explorers who travelled in 19th-century Africa, and many of his journeys began and ended in Zanzibar.

He was born on 19 March 1813 in the village of Blantyre, near Glasgow, in Scotland. In 1841, at the age of 28, he went to South Africa as a missionary doctor. There he married Mary Moffat, a missionary's daughter. On his early expeditions in southern Africa he crossed the Kalahari Desert and, in November 1855, became the first European to see Mosi oa Tunya ('the Smoke that Thunders'), which he renamed the Victoria Falls. Livingstone made his fourth major expedition from 1858 to 1864 in the area around the Lower Zambezi and Lake Nyasa (present-day Lake Malawi). He was accompanied by Dr John Kirk, another Scot, who joined the expedition as a medical officer and naturalist. After the expedition, in April 1864, Livingstone spent a week in Zanzibar before travelling back to Britain.

Livingstone returned to Zanzibar in January 1866 as he had been asked by the Royal Geographical Society to explore the country between Lake Nyasa and Lake Tanganyika, to solve the dispute over the location of the source of the Nile. He left for the mainland on 19 March 1866 and travelled around the southern end of Lake Nyasa.

After several years of exploring the region, during which time little news of his travels had reached the outside world, Livingstone met with the American journalist Henry Stanley at Ujiji on Lake Tanganyika on 10 November 1871 – the famous 'Dr Livingstone, I presume' incident (described in more detail in the box, page 18). At this meeting, Livingstone was suffering terribly from foot ulcers, fever and dysentery, and had only a few days' supply of cotton with which to buy food. But two weeks later his strength had returned sufficiently for him to set out on a small expedition with Stanley. They explored the northern shores of Lake Tanganyika, establishing that the River Ruzizi flowed into (not out of) the lake, and could not therefore be a headwater of the Nile.

Livingstone and Stanley left Ujiji on 27 December 1871 and reached Kazeh, halfway to the coast, in February the following year. Livingstone was in good health, so Stanley continued on alone and arrived in Zanzibar in May 1872.

Livingstone stayed at Kazeh until August 1872, then set out on a short expedition around the southern shores of Lake Tanganyika. He was still looking for the source of the Nile when he became ill again with dysentery. He died at the village of Chitambo, a few miles south of Lake Bangweulu (in present-day Zambia) on 2 May 1873. Two of his loyal companions, Susi and Chumah, removed his heart and buried it under a tree at the spot where he died. They dried his body in the sun for two weeks, then carried it to Zanzibar, wrapped in bark and cloth, where it was identified by a broken bone in the left arm, once crushed in the jaws of a lion. Livingstone's body rested at the British consulate before being taken to London for burial. Stanley and Kirk were among the pall bearers at his funeral in Westminster Abbey on 18 April 1874.

The tree under which Livingstone's heart was buried eventually fell down, and a stone monument now stands in its place. However, some of the wood from the tree was made into a cross, and this now hangs in the Anglican cathedral in Stone Town (page 167).

Almost any one of these display boards provides engrossing, if often appalling, accounts of human suffering and brutality, but they can reveal nuances you might not expect, often at the hands of unattributed illustrators or photographers. The demonstrative lady shown in '5.3: Freedom' fiercely telling a British naval officer about her treatment, or the face of the bearded seaman photographed giving a piggyback to a newly freed child on the preceding board, are almost unbearably moving.

Among a barrage of unexpected, if sometimes unpleasant, insights, are the story of Swema, near death and buried alive as an annoying loss, the description of physical examinations in the market place, and the fact that wealthier slaves sometimes bought their own slaves – a measure of how truly ingrained an institution slavery was.

After the British outlawed slavery and imposed their new laws by force, many freed slaves on Zanzibar returned to various forms of economic bondage for want of any alternative. Post-slavery conditions were often brutal, in different ways: '5.5: Freedom' shows a bizarre 'pairing off' of ex-slaves with women onshore, organised by the British. This seems at the very least like forced marriage, or even people-trafficking.

For a fresh take on the whole story of slavery, try visiting the exhibition backwards, in counter-chronological order. The comparatively recent era of the trade is hard to grasp: some slaves taken from Zanzibar to the Persian Gulf were seeking manumission at British consulates in Basra and Bahrain as recently as the 1930s.

Entering at a quiet time, with few other visitors and a good guide who can set the scene and recount the history while you are in the cells, is a chilling experience. The two dank cells – more like tombs – are cramped and airless, with low doorways and tiny windows. Even today it's a sombre place – but imagine it crowded with slaves, sick and exhausted after their gruelling sea voyage from the African mainland, crammed on to the narrow stone slabs and shackled with chains (see box, pages 169–70). The guides will tell you that these two, low-ceilinged slave chambers held as many as 75 women and children on the right and 50 men on the left. Whatever the veracity of the tales, it's a grim and memorable experience, intensified by the chains still embedded in the walls.

ZANZIBAR MUSEUM OF ART [120 D7] (⏰ 06.00–18.00 daily; admission US$3)

Also known as the Peace Memorial Museum, this impressive edifice stands in the Mnazi Mmoja neighbourhood, at the southern end of Stone Town near the junction of Creek and Kaunda roads. With its distinctive dome, arabesque windows and whitewashed walls, the building, often known colloquially as Beit al Amaan (the House of Peace), looks like a mosque or basilica church. It was designed by the British architect J H Sinclair, who was also responsible for the High Court, the British residency and several other public buildings around town.

For years, 'museum' was something of misnomer, as the viewable exhibits were relocated to the House of Wonders (pages 163–4). However, with the closure and planned restoration of the House of Wonders, many exhibits have been moved back here, although the displays – which are more a collection of crafts and artisanal items than the name 'museum of art' would suggest – are not interesting enough to detain you for very long. As you move around the interior in a clockwise direction, you'll encounter small, inadequately labeled sections devoted to architecture, costume and clothing, a good section on kanga sarongs, Swahili male skull caps (the cultural coding in these kofia is as complex as that in female kanga, though there is no explanation here), musical instruments, Zanzibari doors; and, inevitably, Freddie Mercury. There is a small group of paintings by Zanzibari artists, and do look out for the huge and beautiful drum belonging to the Mwinyi Mkuu (the traditional ruler of Zanzibar – see page 5).

6

The giant tortoises that once lived in the grounds now live on Prison Island (page 195). The Zanzibar Natural History Museum, located in the 'Museum Annexe' across the road, appears to be definitively closed.

ZANZIBAR ARCHIVES [120 D7] (☉ *07.30–15.30 Mon–Fri, 07.30–14.00 Sat; admission free*) For history aficionados, the Zanzibar Archives, or Nyaraka za Taifa in Swahili, contain some fascinating material. The trove includes many books and manuscripts in Arabic dating from the 17th century, when the Omani sultans took control of Zanzibar, consular and protectorate records from British colonial times, papers and documents relating to the various European expeditions that started from Zanzibar in the second half of the 19th century, and a great deal of other contemporary material such as stamps, newspapers, maps and photographs. If there is something of special interest, the staff on duty can help you search through the collections. If you just want to browse, there is an exhibition room with some items of interest on display.

The archives are situated outside central Stone Town, about 2km along Nyerere Road from the Mnazi Mmoja Hospital, in an area called Kilimani. To get there take a dalla dalla on Route U and ask to be dropped at Nyaraka za Taifa, or at the prison. It will stop at the bottom of Kinuamiguu Hill (the only hill on this road); turn left (north) off Nyerere Road, then take the first road on the right.

OTHER PLACES OF INTEREST IN ZANZIBAR TOWN Although the following sites aren't major objectives in themselves, you'll probably find yourself walking nearby as you visit some of the more important palaces and museums, and the following background information will be useful.

Mnazi Mmoja sports field [120 D6] Opposite the Museum of Art, on the other side of Creek Road, is Mnazi Mmoja sports field (Mnazi Mmoja means 'One Coconut Tree'). This area used to be a swamp at the end of the creek that separated the Stone Town peninsula (at one time itself a small island) from the rest of Zanzibar. The land was reclaimed and converted to a sports field during the colonial period, hence the English-style cricket pavilion in the corner. In the 1920s, part of the sports ground was set aside for exclusive use by members of the English Club, and contained tennis courts, a croquet lawn and the only golf course on the island. Today, Mnazi Mmoja is used mainly for informal football matches and as a jamboree and public show ground. Meanwhile, although the creek itself has been reclaimed, the sports field is still prone to flooding in the rainy season.

Nyerere Road The road leading southeast out of the town was originally built by Bishop Steere of the Universities Mission in Central Africa as a causeway across the Mnazi Mmoja swamp. Today, it is a pleasant avenue lined with giant casuarina trees.

People's Gardens [120 C6] At the southern end of Stone Town, near the main hospital, these gardens were laid out originally by Sultan Barghash for use by his harem. Sir John Kirk, the British consul to Zanzibar from 1873 to 1887, subsequently added many trees and bushes, including eucalyptus, coffee, tea and cocoa. The gardens were formally given to the people of Zanzibar by Sultan Hamoud on the occasion of Queen Victoria's Jubilee in 1897, when they were renamed Victoria Gardens. The building in the centre of the gardens was called Victoria Hall, built over the baths of the harem and used as the Chamber of the Legislative Council from 1926 to 1964. After the Revolution, the hall and gardens

Around Zanzibar and particularly in Stone Town, you'll come across massive, carved and decorated doorways, some on imposing frontages and others tucked incongruously down narrow alleys.

When a house was built in Zanzibar, the door was traditionally the first part to be erected. The greater the wealth and status of the house's owner, the larger and more elaborately carved his front door. Symbolic designs and quotations from the Quran were added to exert a benign influence: a kind of hand-crafted insurance policy. Waves of the sea climbing up the doorpost represent the livelihood of the Arab merchant to whom the house belonged, while frankincense and date palms symbolise wealth and plenty. From a darker side of history, chains carved at the side indicate that slaves were held in the house. Some designs are thought to pre-date the Quran: the stylised lotuses could relate to Egyptian fertility symbols, and the fish may possibly represent the protective Syrian goddess Atargatis or the ancient Egyptian fish god.

Many doors are studded with brass spikes and bosses, which may stem from the Indian practice of studding doors of medieval castles with sharp iron spikes to prevent their being battered in by war elephants. In AD915, an Arab traveller recorded that Zanzibar Island abounded in elephants, and around 1295, Marco Polo wrote that Zanzibar had 'elephants in plenty'. But they must have been extinct long before the Arabs built houses in Stone Town, and the studs and bosses seen today are purely decorative.

The oldest carved door in Zanzibar, which dates from 1694, is now the front door of the Zanzibar Museum of Art.

fell into disrepair, but they were renovated in 1996, with help from the German government, and Victoria Hall is now rather ignominiously the office of the Zanzibar Anti-Corruption Body.

The large house opposite the gardens, on the south side of Kaunda Road, was built in 1903 as the official British Residency. After the 1964 Revolution, when Victoria Gardens were renamed the People's Gardens, this became State House – the official residence of the president. The building next to it is the former Soviet Embassy, and now serves as the headquarters of the Zanzibar Investment Promotions Agency (ZIPA), a government body set up to attract foreign business capital to Zanzibar.

Africa House [124 B6] Near the seafront, in the southwest corner of town, this venerable, four-storey hotel (page 129) is worth visiting in its own right, even if you're not staying here. Full of character, it is bursting with paintings, old photographs and other ephemera. While the black marble staircase is a newer addition, considered by some locals to be a vulgar affectation, the glimpses of old Zanzibar on the walls are highly recommended – as are the views of contemporary Stone Town from the second-floor Trade Winds restaurant terrace.

Big Tree [125 G1] About 100m west of the Old Dispensary along Mizingani Road stands a huge Indian banyan tree (*Ficus benghalensis*) originally planted by Sultan Khalifa in 1911. Known simply as the Big Tree (or in Swahili as Mtini – 'the Place of the Tree'), it has been a major landmark for decades. It can be seen on numerous

The Palace Museum (formerly the People's Palace, and before that the Sultan's Palace) was constructed on part of the site of an even older palace called Beit el Sahel, the House of the Coast, which was originally built for Sultan Said between 1827 and 1834. Contemporary accounts describe Beit el Sahel as a two-storey whitewashed palace, with a roof of green and red tiles, separated from the beach by a high wall, with a grove of pomegranates behind. The accounts go on to describe how Sultan Said spent three days of each week at Beit el Sahel, and the rest of the time at his country palace at Mtoni (pages 185–7), about 5km north of Zanzibar Town. He often walked from the town to Mtoni even though his stables were full of Arab horses. Every morning, the best horses were brought out from the stables and hitched to the seaward side of the wall with long leads, to roam about in the soft sand at low tide.

Another palace, called Beit el Hukm (the House of Government), was built later behind Beit el Sahel. Then, in 1883, Beit al Ajaib (the House of Wonders) was built. These three palaces were connected by a series of covered passages. A lighthouse at the front was nicknamed the 'Sultan's Christmas tree' by British navy officers, on account of its many rows of lamps.

Beit el Sahel, Beit el Hukm and the lighthouse were all destroyed in the bombardment of 1896 (see box, page 24). A private house was built on the site of Beit el Hukm, which is now the offices of the Stone Town Conservation and Development Authority, easily seen between the Palace Museum and the House of Wonders, set back from the road. The building has a well-maintained garden with palm trees and shrubs. Outside the main entrance is a pair of cannons, made in Boston, Massachusetts, in 1868.

old photos and etchings of Stone Town and is still clearly visible on the seafront from ships approaching the port. Today, traditional dhow builders use the tree as a shady tree for their open-air workshops and taxi drivers congregate around the makeshift car park around its base. While its future is hopefully assured, it spent most of 2016 surrounded by undignified fencing during the construction of a new road alignment in the port area – the Mizingani Seawall and Promenade.

Old Orphanage [124 C3] Just south of the Old Fort, the road runs through a tunnel under a large building that until very recently served as the island's orphanage. Built in the late 19th century, it was used as a club for English residents until 1896, and then as an Indian school until 1950. With a prime location, there's every chance that this building is earmarked for some form of tourism development. However, the Aga Khan has also talked about making it into a Maritime Museum.

Upimaji Building Between the orphanage and the People's Bank of Zanzibar, this building is now the Commission for Lands and Environment. In the 1860s, it was the offices and home of Heinrich Ruete, the German merchant who eloped with Princess Salme (see box, pages 188–9).

Old British Consulate This fine old house was used as the British Consulate from 1841 to 1874, after which the consulate was moved to the Mambo Msiige building. The first consul was Lieutenant Colonel Atkins Hamerton, posted here

As most of Zanzibar's population is Muslim, Zanzibar Town has several mosques. The oldest is the **Malindi Mosque** [125 F1], also known as the Bamnara or Mnara Mosque, an inconspicuous place of worship near the port, with a conical minaret unique along the East African coast except in Kenya (where there are two others). The mosque is thought to be several hundred years old and has an intricately carved door frame.

Three of Zanzibar's larger mosques are in the northern part of Stone Town, all built in the 19th century: the **Ijumaa Mosque** (Sunni) [125 G1], the **Ithnasheri Mosque** (Shia, opposite the Hamamni Baths, pages 165–6) [125 F4] and the **Aga Khan Mosque** (Ismaili) [125 G4]. Compared with the large mosques of other Islamic cities, often decorated with domes and tall minarets, Zanzibar's are relatively unpretentious. However, in 1994 the Ijumaa Mosque was renovated in a modern arabesque style, and the other large mosques may follow this trend.

Non-Muslims are not normally allowed to enter any mosque in Zanzibar Town, but if you have a genuine interest a good local guide might be able to speak to the mosque's elders on your behalf and arrange an invitation. Men will find this easier than women. There are usually no restrictions on non-Muslims (men or women) visiting the area around a mosque, although photos of local people praying or simply congregating should not be taken without permission.

to represent the interests of Britain after Sultan Said moved his capital from Oman to Zanzibar.

Later consuls played host to several well-known British explorers, including Speke, Burton, Grant and Stanley, before they set out for their expeditions on the East African mainland. In 1874, the body of Livingstone was brought here before being taken back to Britain for burial at Westminster Abbey.

From 1874 to 1974 the building was used as offices by the trading company Smith Mackenzie, but it was taken over by the government in the late 1970s. It is still used as government offices today, and visitors cannot enter, but there is not much to see on the inside; most of the building's interest lies in its grand exterior.

Mambo Msiige [124 A4] Now the heritage core and minimalist reception at the Park Hyatt Zanzibar's seafront development, this grand house (whose rather obscure name means 'Look but do not imitate') formerly incorporated a variety of architectural styles. It was originally built around 1850 for a wealthy Arab, but the building was sold to the British Foreign Office in 1875 and served as the British consulate until 1913. From 1918 to 1924, it was the European hospital, after which it became government offices and then the headquarters of the Zanzibar Shipping Corporation.

Zanzibar Milestone [120 C7] Near the People's Gardens this admittedly rather insignificant octagonal pillar, built with marble taken from the palace at Chukwani, shows the distances from this exact point in Zanzibar Town to other settlements on the island. The distance to London by sea, via the Suez Canal, 8,064 miles, is also shown. Before the opening of the canal, in 1870, voyages were much longer, via the Cape of Good Hope.

176

7

Around Zanzibar Town

All the places listed in this chapter lie within 20km of Zanzibar Town, the majority being very close. Most can be reached easily as a day trip, by taxi, hired scooter, bike or a combination of foot and public transport. Equally, visits can be arranged with a tour company, with some of the palaces and bathhouses included in standard spice tours. Of the palaces, Mbweni lies south of Zanzibar Town, whilst Maruhubi and Mtoni, and the Persian Baths of Kidichi and Kizimbani, lie to the north.

SOUTH OF ZANZIBAR TOWN

The main attraction on the coast immediately south of Zanzibar is the Mbweni area, which is 3km from the town centre and hosts a number of ruined and extant buildings dating from the late 19th century. There are a few hotels dotted around these southern suburbs of Zanzibar Town, and while they are not as convenient for sightseeing, shopping or visiting restaurants as their more central counterparts, they lie close to the airport, making them useful for very early departures or late arrivals. Most also run free shuttle services for guests to and from the centre. The hotels outside town are generally quieter, and many are used by those on business trips, as some government and NGO offices are also in this area.

MBWENI AND ENVIRONS The coastal area of Mbweni is almost directly south of Zanzibar Town and is a historically and botanically important area. Receiving relatively little settlement by the 7th-century Arabs, 12th-century Persians or 16th-century Portuguese, it was the site of a wealthy Omani family retreat in September 1871 when Bishop Tozer (Bishop of Zanzibar 1863–73) purchased 12ha of land, then called Mbweni Point Shamba for the UMCA (Universities' Mission to Central Africa). The stated intention was to create a village for freed slaves and an Anglican mission. Tozer's successor, Bishop Steere (Bishop of Zanzibar 1874–82) oversaw the building of the church and other coral-rock mission buildings in what was the first large-scale missionary settlement in East Africa. The initial plot was extended over time to cover about 60ha and developed to build schools, workshops, homes and a market, as well as sugar, coconut and maize plantations. Several of the buildings are still standing today.

At Mbweni Ruins Hotel and good bookshops in town you will be able to find the informative *Zanzibar: History of the Ruins at Mbweni* by Flo Liebst, which provides great insight into what's around, as well as the UMCA missionaries of East Africa and a general history of Zanzibar.

Getting there and away To reach Mbweni, take the main road out of town towards the airport. Go uphill through the area called Kinuamiguu ('lift your legs') and then Mazizini. After a few kilometres, at a signpost to Mbweni and Chukwani,

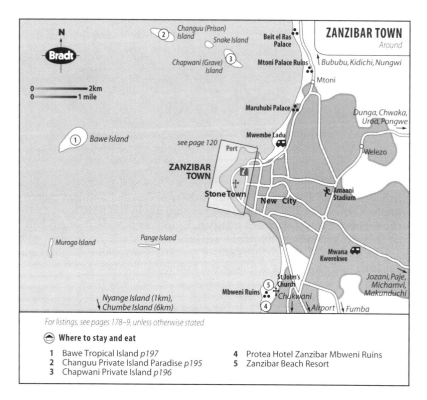

For listings, see pages 178–9, unless otherwise stated

🔶 **Where to stay and eat**

1	Bawe Tropical Island *p197*
2	Changuu Private Island Paradise *p195*
3	Chapwani Private Island *p196*
4	Protea Hotel Zanzibar Mbweni Ruins
5	Zanzibar Beach Resort

fork right, then after 500m turn right again onto a smaller road. Continue down this road towards the sea to reach Mbweni. **Dalla dalla** number 505 runs between the town and the airport, going past the main Mbweni and Chukwani junction.

🏠 Where to stay and eat *Map, above*

🔶 **Zanzibar Beach Resort** (86 rooms)
📞024 223 6033/44; m 0788 410297; www.
zanzibarbeachresort.net. About 7km from
Zanzibar Town & 3km from the airport, the hotel
is set in large, open grounds, the front section
of which overlooks the sea, & caters primarily
to East African conference groups. En-suite
rooms are in 2-storey chalets with whitewashed
walls & thatched roofs, some with a sea view
from the balcony. All have dark furniture, AC,
mini fridge, TV & safe but something of a damp
smell & ageing fixtures & fittings. The hotel's
Spice Restaurant serves local food, while the
Jahazi Restaurant cooks seafood. There's also the
Discovery Bar & disco, an assortment of sports
facilities, large pool & 100-person conference
room. B&B. **$$$$$**

🔶 **Protea Hotel Zanzibar Mbweni Ruins**
(13 rooms) 📞024 223 5478; www.marriott.com/
hotels/travel/znzmr-protea-hotel-mbweni-ruins.
In the grounds of the Mbweni Ruins, this small
hotel is often rated as one of the best of its type
in & around Zanzibar Town. The botanically
named bedrooms are bright & comfortable, each
with a large bathroom, canopy bed & practical
additions like a kettle. For the personal touch,
look carefully at the in-room artwork, the
handiwork of one of the owners, Flo Montgomery.
Every room has a small private balcony, a mere
hop, skip & jump to the pool or beach. Room
14, Ylang Ylang, has arguably the best view
over the palm oasis to the sea beyond, & the
Baobab honeymoon suite boasts its own lovely
rooftop terrace. Food at the Raintree Restaurant
(*lunch US$10–20; dinner US$10–35*) is made
to order with fresh ingredients & it's a popular
lunchtime spot for a few doting cats & visitors.
The ruins are open to visitors & sometimes the

hotel arranges atmospheric weddings or open-air dinners amongst the pillars & arches of the school chapel. Alfresco yoga classes are held here 3 nights a week. The hotel is set in extensive well-maintained grounds with a lush botanical garden (inspired by botanist John Kirk) & nature trail through its shady terraces. Nearby mangroves provide good birding, & the hotel has its own list of birds & butterflies.

The staff are keen naturalists, & can advise visitors on all aspects of local natural history. From the beachfront swimming pool to the Bustani Spa or the waterside Mangrove Bar, Mbweni Ruins is a relaxing spot & a good choice for those who want to experience Stone Town but escape the bustle. A free shuttle service runs to/from town 3 times a day; transfers to/from the port or airport cost US$20 for 4 people. B&B. **$$$$–$$$$$**

What to see and do

St John's Church (*www.zanzibaranglican.or.tz;* ⊕ *Anglican services 08.00–10.00 every Sun, Holy Communion 10.30–11.00*) At the heart of Mbweni, on a small road lined with large old 'rain trees' (should you visit in a shower, you'll find the leaves all closed), is the English-style St John's Church, complete with a tower and surrounding cemetery. Nearby is the old clergy house, which was more recently the Inn by the Sea Hotel (now closed).

St John's was opened in 1882 by UMCA missionaries and converts, and consecrated in 1904. The church has a marble altar inlaid with colourful mother-of-pearl shell and a wooden chair made for Bishop Tozer by the sailors of HMS *London*, the British naval ship famous for its slave-dhow captures. In the interesting cemetery there are also a number of very prickly cycads, naturally endemic on the east coast of Zanzibar, and thought to have been planted here by the Mbweni missionaries.

A number of descendants of freed slaves continue to live in the area and today you can visit the church and cemetery with the help of the church sexton, Peter Sudi. He is a direct descendant of John Swedi, the first African deacon of the UMCA and one of the first five slave boys to be freed and taken in by Bishop Tozer at the mission.

St Mary's School for Girls Past St John's Church towards the sea, a dirt road leads to Mbweni Ruins Hotel (page 178), whose grounds house the remains of the St Mary's School for Girls. This Victorian school was constructed by missionaries in 1871–74, under the guidance of bishops Tozer and Steere, on a property known as Mbweni Point Shamba. The school was a large square building, based around a central courtyard, incorporating the old Arab house on the property into its entrance.

The school educated orphaned girls who had been freed from captured slave-dhows and the daughters of freed slaves who lived at the mission, each with their own house and small garden. Most of the girls were trained as teachers, and were taught reading, writing, arithmetic, geography and sewing. The headmistress from 1877 until 1902 was Caroline Thackeray (a cousin of the English novelist William Thackeray). In 1877, Ms Thackeray paid for the construction of an 'Industrial Wing' in which her less academically inclined pupils were given vocational training in basketry, stitching, laundry and cooking to enable them to run a home and seek employment. In 1906, the school became a convent and in 1920 the buildings were sold by the church to a consortium including the Bank of India. Over the following years, they slowly became ruined, although the chapel, whilst lacking a roof, is still in good condition today.

Sir John Kirk's House Along the road that passes northwards in front of St John's Church is the house of Sir John Kirk, British consul-general in Zanzibar from 1873 to 1887. Kirk first came to Africa in the 1850s as the medical officer and naturalist on Livingstone's Zambezi expedition. As consul-general he was very active in the suppression of the slave trade and he is often regarded as the 'power behind the throne' during the rule of his close friend, Sultan Seyyid Barghash. Some historical records claim that this house was in fact a gift from Barghash, built as a country retreat for Kirk and his family when he was promoted from vice-consul to consul-general. It is certainly known that Kirk used the house frequently and that as a keen and experienced botanist he established a large experimental garden here, which later provided the core species of all the botanical gardens of Zanzibar and mainland Tanzania. He imported many new plant species to the islands from the Royal Botanic Gardens at Kew as well as from India, the Far East and South America, and worked on improving varieties of useful and edible crops. He established spices such as nutmeg, cardamom, cinnamon, vanilla, black pepper and ginger, as well as exotic fruit trees from avocado to lychee, palms and cycads, and even rubber vines, both endemic and imported. He also planted cinchona, the source of quinine, along with other known medicinal plants. Kirk collected trees and flowers from the mainland of Africa which formed the basis of the then standard work, *Flora of Tropical Africa*.

In 1887, Kirk left Zanzibar and sold his house to Caroline Thackeray (page 179), and each subsequent year she opened the impressive grounds to the public for an annual garden party. Although Thackeray retired as headmistress of St Mary's in 1902, she inhabited the house until her death aged 83 in 1926. She was buried in the cemetery at St John's Church and bequeathed the property to the UMCA. The house was subsequently sold to a wealthy Arab, who used it until the early 1960s. Today the property remains privately owned and is not open to the public, and although the gardens are somewhat wild and overgrown Kirk's rare and exotic species stand strong.

NORTH OF ZANZIBAR TOWN

Along the coast north of Zanzibar Town, stretching over a distance of about 5km, are several palaces dating from the 19th century. Built for the various sultans who ruled Zanzibar during this period, it was commonplace for these wealthy families to retreat from the heat, smell and disease of the city in the hotter months to less populated corners. Some of the palaces and homes are in good condition and worth a visit; others will appeal only to keen fans of historical ruins and those with exceptionally good imaginations.

For the palaces that are open, the entrance price is very low and the ticket you buy at the first place you visit will also allow you access to many other historical sites on the same day. This includes the baths at Kidichi, the caves at Mangapwani and several other sites around the island.

The main settlement in this area, the amusingly named Bububu, is approximately 10km north of the Stone Town and is known for the attractive Fuji Beach and a number of small coastal hotels which are strung along the water's edge.

GETTING THERE AND AWAY Many of this area's historical sites are included in spice tours, and all are easily accessed with a hire car or private vehicle. On public transport, the Route **2 bus** that heads north to Mangapwani village will often continue to the coast and coral cave with a little persuasion.

For Bububu and Mtoni, take **dalla dalla** Nos 502 or 534 from Zanzibar Town, a route that can also be used for the Persian Baths at Kidichi, alighting at Bububu and continuing on foot in a westerly direction for 3km. Kidichi is also the final stop on dalla dalla No 511 and public bus Route 3.

WHERE TO STAY AND EAT The hotels below all lie alongside or within a few hundred metres of the main tar road between Stone Town and Bububu/Fuji Beach, listed in the order you would pass them coming from Zanzibar Town. The **Mtoni Marine Water Park** is currently under construction on the site of the long-standing Mtoni Marine hotel. A promotional video shows banks of water slides, clips of multiple pools and myriad fountains: we await news of what is actually delivered.

Unless stated otherwise, they offer air conditioning and en-suite bathrooms as standard.

Maruhubi Beach Villas (12 rooms) m 0777 451188; e maruhubi@zanlink.com; www.sites. google.com/site/maruhubizanzibar. Situated close to the eponymous ruins some 3km north of Stone Town, this attractive, low-key resort is clearly signposted off the main road. It has a superb location on a sandy beach offering views back to the House of Wonders on the Zanzibar waterfront as well as to Mtoni Beach. Accommodation is in airy & spacious semi-detached bungalows, running in a single row perpendicular to the sea. The majority are set in beautiful tropical gardens, but rooms 1–4 are set on a coral rock pier with wonderful panoramic views up & down the coast. Interiors are lovely in their simplicity with large, coconut wood Zanzibari beds, subtle apricot walls, sparkling bathrooms & wide verandas, complete with mattress-covered sun loungers. The huge makuti Sunset Restaurant offers lunch & dinner at neat tables with turquoise director's chairs. Menu options are varied & reasonably priced – vegetarian pancake (*US$5*); calamari tempura (*US$7*); beef kebab (*US$10*) – & it serves alcohol. The pool above the beach is a big asset & non-residents can pay US$5/day to indulge. B&B. **$$$–$$$$**

THE WIVES AND CHILDREN OF SULTAN SAID

During his lifetime, Sultan Sayyid Said (Sultan of Oman and Zanzibar 1804–56) had three legitimate wives, or *harino* (singular *horme*). Under Islamic law, at any one time, he was allowed up to four harino.

In 1827, he married his cousin Azze Binte Seif bin Ahmed, daughter of Seif bin Ahmed and grandchild of Sultan Ahmed, who was considered to have equal status with her husband. She was reported to be strong-willed and to rule the royal household with a firm hand. Apparently, no act of state was carried out without her advice and approval.

In 1847, Said married his second wife, Binte Irich Mirza, nicknamed Schesade (or Scheherazade), a beautiful, extravagant princess, and the granddaughter of the Shah of Persia. She came to Zanzibar in 1849 and Said built the baths at Kidichi for her in 1850, using stonemasons and plasterers from her homeland. Schesade had no children so Said divorced her and sent her back to Persia. By the late 1850s, Schesade had become a prominent member of the Persian army, fighting against her former husband with the hellish fury of a woman scorned.

Said's third wife was Binte Seif bin Ali, of whom little is known. He also possessed a great many pan-African concubines and once these women had given birth, they were known as *sarari* (singular *surie*), immediately freed and given equal status with the legal wives.

During his lifetime, Said is credited with fathering 120 children (99 daughters and 21 sons) and when he died in 1856, he left a single widow, his first wife Azze Binte Seif, and 75 sarari. Of his children, only 36 were still alive: 18 sons and 18 daughters. Two of his sons, Thuwaini and Turki, became sultans of Oman; four more sons, Majid, Barghash, Khalifa and Ali, became sultans of Zanzibar.

🏠 **Imani Beach Villa** (9 rooms) 📞 024 225 0050; 📱 0777 061308; 📧 info@imani-zanzibar. com; www.imani-zanzibar.com. About 9km from Stone Town, Imani Beach Villa is clearly signposted off the main road at Bububu. From here, a bumpy coral-rock track meanders downhill towards the sea & Imani's beachfront plot. Tucked away in a mass of cerise bougainvillea & banana trees, it is a small & delightful home-from-home hotel. From clearing up the beach to creating some of the island's most original cocktails, managers Simon & Kristen Bennett have a hands-on attitude & strong service ethic. Under their guidance, Imani has been re-energised & revamped into a gem of a hidden hideaway. All rooms feature enormous Zanzibari beds & clean bathrooms. Centred on the villa's small, antique-filled lounge/entrance, the ocean view from the daybed, the sound of rolling waves & the constant breeze all create a distinctly exotic air. Outside, billowing orange & monochrome fabric panels conceal a cool Arab-style bar & restaurant in the tropical garden. Tasty meals (*US$20*) are served at low tables with seating on piles of cushions & Persian carpets. Check out the treehouse for sundowner drinks. A taxi to/from town is around US$10 & the hotel also has bikes which are free for guest use. B&B. **$$$**

🏠 **Bububu Beach Guesthouses** (6 rooms) 📞 024 225 0110; 📱 0777 422747; 📧 kilupyomar@ hotmail.com; 📘 BububuBeachGuesthouse. Set in Bububu village about 100m apart, these 2 guesthouses are simple but clean, friendly & very relaxed. Each can sleep up to 8 people (2 dbls; 1 quad) in adequate rooms & seem reasonably good value. There's a living room, dining room & kitchen. Although mainly geared to longer-stay visitors & family groups, the rooms can be rented individually, with self-catering or FB options available. Owner Omar Kilupi can arrange spice tours, rental cars & motorbikes, or challenge you to a game of chess as he's one of the island's master players! There's a free transfer service to/ from town twice a day or you can catch one of the frequent dalla dallas running between Bububu village & Zanzibar Town. From the dalla dalla stop on the main road in Bububu village, it's a short walk down a dirt track towards the beach to reach the hotel. B&B. **$$**

🏠 **Ngalawa Lodge** (18 rooms) 📧 ngalawa. lodge@yahoo.com. Ngalawa is marketed primarily as a business-orientated hotel, & the arresting entrance gates don't give the best first impression, though some holidaymakers might enjoy this place. It's set on a large plot of land, far back from the mangroves & beach. The airy dbl rooms are simple & clean, with coconut wood furniture, large beds covered in starched white linen & all with a TV, fan & safe; the bathrooms unusually contain both a bath & a shower. In the gardens, a pool, surrounded by shaded chairs & tables, is an attractive spot to lounge among the flowers. There is a battered tennis court (rackets & balls provided), but it's a prickly trek through long grasses to reach it. There's no official lounge but guests can relax in front of the TV in the Mbudya bar & restaurant boma, where pizzas (*US$5*), steaks (*US$9*) & pot roast (*US$8*) are made to order. A few more guests would likely improve the hotel's atmosphere significantly, though with heavy competition from other resorts on better beaches, the likelihood of success is slim. B&B. **$$$**

🏠 **Furaha Resort** (13 rooms) 📞 0773 658841/0776 200607; 📧 info@furahazanzibar. com. At the end of a very bumpy access road, past the Unique Learning School, Furaha is a cluster of small, low-key white bungalows set around an inviting swimming pool. There are tropical gardens, access to beach coves, clean rooms with reasonable facilities (AC, mini fridge, TV) & secure car parking for self-drivers. B&B. **$$$**

🏠 **Hakuna Matata Beach Lodge & Spa** (13 rooms) 📱 0756 144605; 📧 info@zanzibar- resort.com; www.hakuna-matata-beach-lodge. com. Owned by accommodating Rose & Fritz &12km north of Zanzibar Town, Hakuna Matata is built amid the ruins of Sultan Barghash's Chuini Palace (page 187), lending it a crumbling, historic charm. The 13 thatched stone cottages are divided into 3 categories, the difference being the increasing size of the room & bed. Brightly patterned blue sofas, lamps carved into elephants & wooden Maasai figures all seem a bit gaudy, but the standard of finish is high, with carved queen- or king-sized beds, hot water & sunlit terraces. Being raised up on a cliff, many cottages have a wonderful view out to sea or of the secluded bay below. Pretty, well-tended gardens have been designed to complement the ruins rather than hide them, & the 2-tier pool even has an aqueduct guarded by lion statues. Diners consistently recommended the seafood restaurant, which also serves up produce from the lodge's own gardens, & the atmospheric beach bonfire BBQ dinners. Down on the sand by day, beached dhows, sunloungers & a sheltered lagoon await. As the name suggests, there is a spa – it's particularly popular with brides-to-be beautifying before their big day. Hakuna Matata is a peaceful place with a lot of history. B&B. **$$$$$**

🏠 **Mangrove Lodge** (10 rooms) m 0777 436954; e info@mangrovelodge.com; www. mangrovelodge.com. Just north of Hakuna Matata, this is a relaxed seaside retreat on a pretty slice of mangrove beach. The Zanzibari owner, manager & former guide Haji & his Italian business partner Paolo have admirably taken a variety of measures to try to reduce the environmental impact of the lodge. There's purposely no energy-devouring AC, most cooking is done over fire & rainwater is harvested. Locally sourced materials, brought in by cart, were used to construct the buildings; local carpenters built the furniture & carved the door frames; & the furnishings were sewn by local tailors. Now, pathways through gardens & lawns link the pretty thatched bungalows, each with either a dbl or a sgl bed & a kitchenette. Inside, the simple rooms with net-draped beds are brightened by local touches: traditional ceilings & kanga-covered chairs, Zanzibari doors & hand-stitched mats. The restaurant looks out over the fishing boats bobbing in the bay &, in keeping with the eco policy, ingredients for the Italian–Swahili food are purchased locally, all leftovers are composted & no plastic bottles or bags are used. Sunbathers can choose between 2 secluded beaches: Mangroves, which surrounds a small lagoon, & Mawimbini, also home to the Mangrove bar & Haji's trinket shop. Haji arranges hygiene & language classes for his staff, & guests are welcome to join in should they wish to improve their Swahili. Mangrove plans to further improve its eco-credentials by using a photovoltaic solar-power system in the future – a stay here will help fund this ambition. B&B. **$$$–$$$$**

🏠 **Zanzi Resort** (7 villas) m 0777 111333; e office@zanziresort.com; www.zanziresort. com. This Polish-owned hotel complex 20 mins' drive north of Stone Town offers sweeping clifftop views & luxurious villas with peace & seclusion in tropical gardens spread over 6ha. Sleeping up to 4 in each, they are well appointed with king-sized beds, lounge & bathroom, a huge private garden, swimming pool with a current machine & an outdoor shower. Those with adventure-seeking

children might like to request a villa where rooms are nestled into the surrounding trees, giving the impression of sleeping in a treehouse. Villa exteriors are painted in hues of terracotta & orange with modern designs by artist Szymon Adamczyk. Next to each villa is a path leading down to a secluded beach. The resort offers a personal concierge service, 1 per villa, & on request private meals are rustled up by the imaginative chef & served in your villa, on the beach or the open-sided restaurant; budding cooks can even join chef Rafal for personal cookery classes. Alternatively, a range of massages & treatments are offered by resident Thai therapists. B&B. **$$$–$$$$**

🏠 **Sea Cliff Resort & Spa** (120 rooms) m 0767 702241; e info@seacliffzanzibar.com; www.seacliffzanzibar.com. Despite being an enormous international-standard resort offering a plethora of holiday activities, Sea Cliff just about manages to retain some Zanzibari flavour. A 20min drive from Stone Town, the high-quality rooms follow a muted colour scheme of creams & golds, with antique Zanzibari furniture & elegant lanterns. With the resort's enviable clifftop location, all but the garden rooms have private balconies with ocean views. Each room has a high-quality finish, mod cons from LCD satellite TV to iPod docking, & an outdoor seating area. Sea-view & deluxe rooms contain jacuzzis & twin basin bathrooms, whilst deluxe also boasts a balcony & patio over 2 levels. Guests have an exhaustive list of activities on offer – from darts to football – plus a modern gym containing a squash court, 2 tennis courts (rackets & balls free) & a mini climbing wall, whilst the watersports centre has a range of options including sailing, waterskiing, windsurfing, pedalos & even deep-sea fishing operated by ScubaFish (page 246); all non-motorised activities are free. The more sedate can drift off on a sunset cruise or explore the area by bicycle. The 80m kidney-shaped pool is split over 2 levels & consists of 2 infinity pools & an artificial beach, surrounded by impressive gardens with manicured bright green lawns splashed with the deep pink of bougainvillea. At the Shwari Spa, treatments include facials & scrubs & there's also a sauna & pool. There's also a very well-equipped gym where yoga classes take place, & while you're there, the kids' club (🕐 09.00–17.00) will keep the little ones entertained. Remarkably, at the far north of the property is a paddock with a number of well-groomed horses, & rides can be tailored

7

for all levels. Finally, there's a verdant 9-hole golf course, complete with seafront clubhouse & resident golf pro! Recharge from all the action at one of 2 restaurants – Mangapwani, with local & international buffets, or Kobe for light lunches by the pool – or at the 4 bars. The lounge is a popular place for a spot of afternoon tea & cake, & there's a weekly entertainment programme that includes acrobats & the 'Coconut Band'. The business market is equally catered for, with the 3 conference rooms & a separate dining area for delegates. Daily transfers (free) to/from Stone Town are offered: depart 09.00, return 13.00. HB; AI available. **$$$$$–♛**

WHAT TO SEE AND DO
Palaces
Maruhubi Palace (☉ *daily; admission US$5 for guided tour on arrival*) The Maruhubi Palace, on the seashore about 4km north of Stone Town, is named after the original landowner, but the palace itself was built in 1882 for Sultan Barghash, who ruled from 1870–88, and built five palaces in total. At one time he reputedly kept 100 women here, including his official wife and 99 concubines, while he himself resided in his main palace in Stone Town.

The Maruhubi Palace was built of blocks of quarried coral stone and wood, and was considered to be one of the most comfortable and ornate residences on the island. Large walls, thought to have been inspired by the park walls seen by Sultan Barghash on his visit to England in 1875, were built around the palace grounds. The House of Wonders in Zanzibar Town (pages 163–4), contains a photo of the palace taken at the end of the 19th century when it was still in use, and guides here often carry copies of the same photo. Perhaps the most impressive element is the overhead aqueduct that would have brought water from Mwanyanga spring further inland.

The palace was destroyed by fire in 1899 and today not much more than the pillars, the bathhouse and the original water tanks, now filled with refuse or overgrown with water lilies depending on the season, are still standing. To the north of the pillars, at the back of the beach, is a small set of arches and steps, which was part of the palace's reception area. You can still see the remains of a marble staircase set into the masonry.

The palace's pillars, which supported the upper storey, were built of red sand, white lime and coral rag. Note the remains of the massive, thick-walled, strong room at the south corner of the palace, with its secret hole in the floor, which would have been accessed by a trapdoor and covered in carpets. There's also a remaining bit of marble at the base of one of the pillars. On the north corner of the palace, on the outer wall, there's a furnace niche with smoke vents above, where firewood was used to heat hot water for the baths.

The Persian-style bathrooms, with separate chambers for the women, and a large bath for the sultan's own use, are still remarkably intact. Note the holes in the walls so that the ladies' private conversations could be overheard. The large bath for the sultan and his male guests includes substantial steam and massage areas, with hot and cool pools. It all used to be floored with black-and-white marble tiles, only one or two of which remain. Today, this part of the complex is frequently used for sacrificial offerings, usually of chickens, performed by those in pursuit of good luck. The headless bird flies around after being released, scattering blood everywhere, hence the spattered walls.

The palace was something of a beach house and at high tide the sea is barely 50m from the edge of the ruins – with the local economy inching towards the ruins with their artisanal fish-processing works on the seashore. Huge sacks of tiny fish weighing 150kg or more and selling for up to Tsh800,000 are piled under makuti shades just a stone's throw from the ruins. Much of the fish from here is exported to DRC, and you'll see the Congolese traders sizing up the goods. There's also some traditional boat-building going on under the trees: a small *ngalawa* canoe sells for around Tsh300,000–500,000.

To reach the palace, take the main road north out of Zanzibar Town towards Bububu. Pass Livingstone House on your right and, after a few kilometres, the Maruhubi Palace is signposted on your left. Dalla dallas on route B run between the town and Bububu village, past the palace entrance gate. For atmospheric photos, the palace is best seen early or late in the day.

Mtoni Palace (Beit el Mtoni) (m *0782 500011;* *mtonipalace*) About 2km north of Maruhubi, this palace was built for Sultan Seyyid Said in 1828, as he moved his court from Oman to Zanzibar. It is said that the land previously belonged to Saleh bin Haramil al Abray, the Arab trader who first imported cloves to Zanzibar (page 10). Mtoni, which means 'place by the river', is the oldest palace on Zanzibar and was the largest during Sultan Said's reign. It was home to his first and only legitimate wife, many of his secondary wives, their children and the hundreds of slaves who worked for them. With its impressive atria, living areas, baths and concubine (*suriya*) quarters, it is well worth a visit, either on its own or as part of the Princess Salme Tour (page 186). The impressive scale of the inner courtyard, bathing complex and palace gardens can still be appreciated and the visit offers a glimpse into the world of the royal family who once lived there.

While walking around the ruins is easy, and there are several small, explanatory boards, it is difficult to make out exactly how the harem quarters really worked unless you are accompanied by a good guide (we recommend those on the Princess Salme Tour). The women apparently had an aqueduct beneath the rooms, carrying waste out to sea, and supposedly there were 75 concubines here, though there doesn't appear to be space for that many women. One can only conclude that parts of the palace have vanished completely.

One of the palace's most notable residents was Princess Sayyida Salme, the youngest of Sultan Said's many daughters. Born here, she became well known as the princess who fell in love with a German merchant, Rudolph Heinrich Ruete, and eloped to Hamburg (see box, pages 188–9).

In her very readable 1888 chronicle about life on Zanzibar, *Memoirs of an Arabian Princess from Zanzibar*, Salme recalls her paradisiacal childhood home:

> *Beit il Mtoni, distant about five miles from the city of Zanzibar, lies on the sea coast, surrounded by most beautiful scenery, and quite hidden in a grove of palm and mango trees, and other gigantic specimens of tropical vegetation. The house of my birth is called 'Mtoni house', after the little river Mtoni, which rises only a few miles inland, runs through the whole palace into numerous fountains, and flows directly behind the palace walls into the splendid and animated inlet which severs the island from the African continent.*

Of the building itself, she states:

> *It had a large courtyard where gazelles, peacocks, ostriches and flamingos wandered around, a large bath-house at one end and the sultan's quarters at the other, where he lived with his principal wife, an Omani princess whose name was Azze.*

Salme records that more than 1,000 people were attached to the sultan's court in the palace. She describes how her father, the sultan, would pace up and down on a large round tower overlooking the sea, where he could see his fleet anchored off the shore. If visitors came by boat, he would greet them on the steps of his palace as there was no landing pier, while Salme and the other princesses were carried out to their boats on chairs. Sadly, she also goes on to describe her return visit to Zanzibar in 1885, after the death of Sultan Said, and the abandoned, decaying palace that she found at Mtoni. It was used as a warehouse during World War I, which did nothing to slow its decline.

In the early 1990s, the Zanzibar Directorate of Archives, Museums and Antiquities (DAMA) initiated a project aimed at conserving the ruins and surrounding gardens. Archaeological survey drawings and historical research were commissioned and undertaken, excavations of the reservoir and impressive aqueduct in front of the palace were completed, and by 2005, substantial progress had been made in clearing the gardens, replanting original species, restoring walls using original techniques and providing visitors with some insight into the palace's history and importance. There is still a tremendous amount to be done but this work is set to continue with involvement of students from the local archives and archaeology institutes.

It is a slow, careful and expensive process, but the Mtoni Palace Conservation Project is working hard to generate the necessary funds through a number of special events and tours (see box, below), though visitor donations are obviously welcomed. With more resources, it may just be possible to restore significant sections of Mtoni Palace and its gardens to their former splendour and to save any further dilapidation to the parts of the palace that are now beyond repair. For Zanzibaris, this is vital work to preserve a tangible reminder of their past, on an island where so many historical buildings have been destroyed. With gas works

THE PRINCESS SALME TOUR

(024 223 0004; m 0777 430117; e info@zanzibardifferent.com; www. zanzibardifferent.com; bookings must be made at least one day in advance)
In 2008, the dedicated team at Mtoni Palace Conservation Project initiated a lovely tour combining a number of historical palaces and traditional ceremonies, as well as an informative spice tour and delicious Swahili lunch.

Escorted by a guide from the conservation project, small groups (approx 4–6) are taken around the evocative ruins of Mtoni Palace, Princess Salme's birthplace, in a colourful, thatched cart pulled by a donkey. They're then taken to Bububu for a traditional coffee ceremony with tasty local treats (kashata (peanut brittle) and candy-like halua). After a short walk, perhaps into the grounds of Salme's cousin's home, the group visits the lush Kidichi plantation area. Here, there's a guided tour of Mzee Yussuf's spice farm before he and his wife serve a deliciously fresh, homemade meal. Expect pilau rice, coconut curry, fish masala, roasted meats, stewed beans, kachumbari salad (East African coleslaw), an array of tropical fruits and spiced tea.

Heading back down the hillside after lunch in a private dalla dalla, there are great views towards the Indian Ocean and Stone Town before the vehicle arrives at the Kidichi Persian Baths (page 191).

The tour leaves Stone Town at 08.30, returning at 14.00 and costs US$55 per person (US$5pp supplement for fewer than three people), including all entrance fees and lunch. It's an original and varied way to see these sites and enjoy traditional Zanzibari cuisine, and US$5 of the charge is donated to the valuable work of the Mtoni Palace Conservation Project.

on its north side and a big offshore land reclamation scheme to the south facing Prison Island, it's to be hoped that the fragile Mtoni Palace will not be ignored.

For those staying in Stone Town for a few nights, the twice-weekly taarab dinner concerts (⊕ 18.00–21.00 Tue & Fri; US$45) held within the ruins offer a uniquely atmospheric view on the palace. It's a really delightful evening with genuine Zanzibari cuisine and music, and quite magical under the candlelit arches.

Beit el Ras Palace (⊕ *daily during term time; admission free*) Further north along the coast, the construction of this palace was commissioned by Sultan Said as an 'overflow' house for his children and their servants when Mtoni Palace became too crowded. Building started in 1847 but was not completed by the time of Said's death in 1856. Sultan Majid (Said's successor) did not continue the project and much of the stone from the palace was used during the construction of the Zanzibar railroad (see box, page 190). The remaining ruins were abandoned and finally demolished in 1947 to make room for a school and teacher-training centre. Today, the palace is within the grounds of the Nkrumah Teacher Training College (Chuo Cha Ualimu Nkrumah) and only a giant sea-view baraza from the original palace remains – a 10m cube-like plastered hulk of a building, with high arches and a steep staircase up one side. Beit el Ras means 'the palace on the headland' and from the seating area the former residents would have had good views over this part of the coast and out towards the group of small islands off Zanzibar Town. It is reached by turning off the main road a few kilometres beyond Mtoni, though the latter is by far a more interesting stop.

Chuini Palace About 10km north of Zanzibar Town, on the coast near the village of Chuini, lie the ruins of Chuini Palace. Meaning 'place of the leopard', it was built for Sultan Barghash, added to by Sultan Ali bin Said, and destroyed by fire in 1914. The ruins are on private land and can only be visited by those dining or staying at Hakuna Matata Lodge (page 182), which is built among a section of them.

Bububu Bububu is a linear, rural village with a police station and checkpoint. The main road continues north from here towards Mahonda and Nungwi, and a new minor tar road branches off east to reach the agricultural area of Kidichi, where most visitors on spice tours arranged in Zanzibar Town are taken. If you stay on the main road for a few more kilometres, near the village of Chuini (about 10km north of Zanzibar Town) a wide dirt road forks off left, signposted to Bumbwini, and this leads to Mangapwani.

Cheetah's Rock (m 0778 875681/0757 962590; e info@cheetahsrock.org; www. cheetahsrock.org; ⊕ pre-booked visits at 14.15–18.45 Tue, Thu & Sun only; admission US$140 inc transfer from most hotels, US$120 without transport, no under-15s) Cheetah's Rock is an extensive animal rescue centre where visitors interact directly with the inmates. It's a petting zoo on a large scale, where the theory of positive reinforcement has been fine-tuned to enable visitors to get close to a number of large mammals in (relative) safety. The facility is the life's work and passion of German animal trainer, Jenny Amman, and all her 'boys' and 'girls' are treated as a rather bossy psychotherapist would treat a human patient.

The tour begins, with cold coconut juice and a detailed briefing in the reception area, at which you sign an indemnity form. The first appointment is with Chaka, a plains zebra stallion, to whom guests are introduced one by one in a kind of circus ring, with a ball game for Chaka, and Jenny very much in control. Guests then file out to meet a group of bushbabies, and feed them on (surprisingly) morsels of spaghetti. These cute primates are followed by a short visit to a lonely vervet

The daughter of Sultan Said and *a surie* (secondary wife) from Circassia, in southern Russia, Salme was born at Mtoni Palace in August 1844, and resident there for her first seven years. Describing her early childhood at Mtoni Palace, she tells of learning sewing, embroidery and lacemaking from her mother. She and her siblings had a private teacher and lessons were conducted in an open gallery containing a single large mat and a Quran on a stand. The royal children were taught the Arabic alphabet, reading and a little arithmetic. The boys were also taught to write, using homemade ink, and the well-bleached shoulder blade of a camel for a slate. But Salme was rebellious and taught herself to write in secret.

Twice a day, early in the morning and in the evening, all children over five had riding lessons. When they had made sufficient progress, the boys received Arabian horses, while the girls received white donkeys from Muscat. When the princesses rode their donkeys to the clove plantations, slaves ran by the side of each animal with a large parasol to protect the riders from the sun. The children also learnt to swim in the sea at an early age.

Salme was given her own African slaves as personal attendants. At bedtime, one slave would massage her, while another fanned gently, until the princess fell asleep, still fully dressed. Slaves fanned the princess all through the night. In the morning, her slaves massaged her gently until she awoke. Her bath was filled with fresh spring water. Slaves laid out the day's clothes, on which jasmine and orange blossoms had been strewn overnight, and which were scented with amber and musk before they were worn. Windows and doors were left open throughout the year, even in colder, wetter weather when a charcoal fire was burning. The fresh air helped to disperse the strong scents. Slaves washed the linen daily. Due to the heat, it dried in little more than half an hour, was smoothed flat (not ironed) and put away.

As a child, Salme was allowed to mix freely with boys of her own age. After she was nine years old, the only men allowed to see her were her father, close male relatives, and her slaves. She wore trousers, a shirt reaching to her ankles, and a handkerchief on her head. The shirt and trousers were always of a different pattern. On her walks, she wore *a schele*, a large shawl of black silk. When she appeared before a stranger, the law required her to be veiled; part of her face, her neck and chin had to be completely covered. Most importantly her ankles also had to be hidden.

In October 1859, Salme became involved in family intrigue between her elder brothers, Barghash and Majid. She helped Barghash escape to the Marseilles clove plantation after his attempt to overthrow Majid failed (see box, pages 14–15). Majid never punished Salme for her part in the plot but by siding with Barghash she lost the friendship of many of her other brothers and sisters. When she renewed her friendship with Majid, she isolated herself from her fellow conspirators.

monkey rescued from Stone Town lads, and then a session with a large group of ring-tailed lemurs from Madagascar in their huge aviary – again with much leaping from shoulder to shoulder – while peacocks and duiker antelopes (not dik-diks as described) step between the visitors' legs. From here, the group moves on to meet Gismo, a striped hyena, from the safe side of his bars. One of two specimens confined to neighbouring, concrete-floored cages, Gismo paces hungrily as Jenny,

By 1866, Salme was living in Zanzibar Town. Although 22 years old, she was still unmarried. Rejected by her family, she began socialising regularly with many of the foreigners on the island. She became friendly with a young German merchant from Hamburg, called Heinrich Ruete, who was living in a house next to hers. They began a covert relationship, speaking to each other from their balconies across the narrow street, and meeting secretly in the countryside.

In July 1866, Salme discovered she was pregnant. Some historians have suggested that she was forced to leave Zanzibar in a hurry, as an illegitimate pregnancy would have brought disgrace to her family and the whole Busaidi dynasty and could have resulted in her death; others have described her romantic 'elopement' with Heinrich Ruete. However, an analysis by Said el-Gheithy of the Princess Salme Institute presents events in a slightly different light:

> No doubt, her pregnancy sent shock waves through her clan and threatened the position of the European traders, reliant on the goodwill of the sultan. Yet following extensive research, and through a knowledge of her personality from at least one person who knew her, it seems Salme was a very organised and stable individual, with a strength of personality which made her adverse to irrational movements. We must not overlook or underestimate her ability to choose rationally from the options available. The concept of an 'elopement' represents her as somewhat flighty. Rather, the move to Germany should be understood as a planned emigration and her departure could be described, to use a Swahili phrase, as 'leaving without saying goodbye'.

Salme left Zanzibar on a British warship, and for several months after her departure a wave of anti-European feeling spread through Zanzibar Town. Another British warship was sent to suppress any possible reprisals against Europeans. When Salme reached Aden, she stayed with some European friends, renounced Islam and was baptised into the Anglican Church, with the name Emily. In Zanzibar, Heinrich wound up his affairs, and then travelled to join Salme in Aden. They were married immediately and travelled to Heinrich's home in Hamburg.

In the following three years Salme and Heinrich had two daughters and a son. Tragically, in August 1871, Heinrich fell while jumping from a tram, and was run over; he died three days later. No longer welcome in Zanzibar, Salme remained in Germany, making one short visit to London in 1875, and two brief returns to Zanzibar in 1885 and 1888, but her attempts at reconciliation with her family were unsuccessful. She lived in exile in Syria until 1914 and died in Germany in 1924. Among the possessions found after her death was a bag of sand from the beach at Zanzibar.

In Zanzibar Town, Princess Salme is remembered at the relatively new Princess Salme Museum (page 163), devoted to her life and writings.

inside the cage, describes the power of his jaws while offering him chicken legs by hand. One cannot help noticing her missing finger. From here, the group moves to the white lion, Aslan, and the chance to feed him chunks of beef through his chain-link fence in a carefully choreographed set of moves designed to avoid alarming the lion or exposing the guests to his very obvious teeth and claws. The tour ends with the *pièce de résistance*, a close encounter with Tyson the cheetah who obligingly

In the early 1900s, a light railway (36-inch gauge) was built and operated by an American company. Running from a point outside the Arab Fort in Zanzibar Town, it travelled along the seafront and up the coast to the village of Bububu. Constructed in 1904–05, the service was used mainly by locals but a special first-class coach was joined to the train so that passengers from the steamers could get a brief glimpse of the island. The line was closed in 1928, but railway buffs can still see the remains of bridges and embankments, as today's main road between Zanzibar Town and Bububu runs parallel to the line (and in some cases over it). Bits of the original track can be seen at Bububu.

In his 1907 book *Sketches in Mafeking and East Africa*, Lord Robert Baden-Powell quotes from a description of the Zanzibar train by an American writer called Miss Kirkland. 'Have you ever been to Bu Bu Bu? If not, do not call yourself a travelled person', she wrote. 'Bu Bu Bu is a settlement in a shady grove on the island of Zanzibar, and is the terminus of a new and important railroad – six and a half miles long.'

It has been suggested that the name Bububu comes from the sound made by the train's hooter, but maps dating from before the building of the railway show the village already had this title. It is more likely that the name was inspired by the sound of the freshwater springs that bubble to the surface just outside the village. Most of Zanzibar Town's water supply still comes from here.

poses next to each visitor in turn while they sip sparkling wine (included) and Jenny's staff take photos. Some groups go back after this to feed the striped hyena, in an enclosure outside his cage, with elaborate instructions on how to place the meat in your palm to avoid including a finger in his meal. But after a couple of glasses of bubbly this may not strike you as a wise activity.

To describe Cheetah's Rock as an unusual attraction would be a major understatement. The owners were previously based in Mallorca and secured sponsorship to leave Spain – lock, stock, barrel and white lion – by jumbo jet direct to Zanzibar, where their arrival has caused some consternation among locals and expats. The ethos here is obsessively (one might say exclusively) animal-centric – though nobody is giving a thought to the conditions endured by domestic animals on Zanzibar butchered for the carnivores, or to whether some of the charges (the hyenas for example) might not be capable of survival in the wild.

The Cheetah's Rock website states: 'Our wild animals are either rescues or have been gifted to us by legal conservation centres. There is a story behind each of them. We are happy to tell you these stories as you meet our animals on your visit. No animal has been captured in the wild. All our animals have legal papers. We use 100% violence-free animal handling methods only, based on trust, respect and reward.'

There is no question about their commitment to the welfare of their animals, and giving visitors the opportunity for close interaction. To be clear, though, the range of animals here is very limited (all of them are mentioned above, though a vast new cage complex being built in 2016 suggests new inmates may be on the way): much of the 3½ hours is occupied by the non-stop commentary of the tour leader describing how dangerous the animals are and how her methods have tamed them – for example, emphasising how the zebra stallion could kill her with a kick, or why the striped hyena might view visitors as food.

It's much less clear where they stand on rare species conservation and the safety of their visitors. Cheetah's Rock feels like an accident waiting to happen and if you decide you want to visit, you're very strongly advised not to feed the carnivores.

The Cheetah's Rock turning is about 5km north of Bububu, just before the junction to Mangapwani. From the highway, it's a 1.1km drive down a sandy road, and then another left turn with a further 1.4km sandy track to reach the complex.

Kidichi Persian Baths ($\oplus$ *daily, mainly pre-booked tours; admission free*)

The Persian Baths at Kidichi lie to the northeast of Zanzibar Town, about 4km inland from the main coast road, in the island's main clove and coconut plantation area. The baths were built in 1850 for Sultan Said, who owned land in this part of the island, and he and his second wife, Binte Irich Mirza (also called Schesade, more often written Scheherazade), would come here for hunting or to oversee the work being done on their plantations. The bathhouse was constructed so that they could refresh themselves after the journey from town. Schesade was a granddaughter of the Shah of Persia, so the baths were built in the Persian style, with decorative stucco work. An underground furnace kept the water warm. A small resthouse was also built nearby, but none of this remains.

Today, you can enter the bathhouse, and see the changing room, bathing pool and massage tables. Unfortunately, the bathhouse has not been especially well maintained over the years, and there is mould growing on much of the stucco. A colony of bats seems to have taken up residence as well. At the top of the domed ceiling is a circle of small windows: these used to be stained glass, which cast patterns of coloured light over the white walls. The conservation team from Mtoni is already looking at ways to repair and preserve the baths, and teams of specialists have been to investigate. With funding to match their care and enthusiasm, there is hope that further decay can be averted.

To reach Kidichi, continue up the main road northwards from Zanzibar Town to Bububu. At the police station, turn right onto a new tar road that leads through coconut palms and clove plantations, and past a long row of souvenir stalls selling spices and other goods. After about 4km the bathhouse, a domed white building, is seen on the right, just a few metres off the dirt road. There are several more spice–souvenir stalls here, and in the surrounding area houses where tour groups go for lunch.

Kizimbani Persian Baths ($\oplus$ *daily; admission free*) Near Kidichi and similar, if more simple, in style, these baths were also built in the Persian style for Sultan Said at about the same time. The surrounding plantations originally belonged to Saleh bin Haramil, the Arab trader who imported the first cloves to Zanzibar (they were confiscated by Sultan Said on the grounds that Saleh was a slave smuggler, see page 11). Today the experimental station here is the island's centre for agricultural research.

To reach the baths from Kidichi, continue eastwards along the tar road. After about 2km, at a crossroads, there are roads left (north) to Mfenesini and Selem, and right (south) to Mwendo and Mwera. Go straight on, along a dirt road, passing through plantations, to reach the Kizimbani Experimental Station headquarters. The baths are on the right side of the track.

Mangapwani

Mangapwani Coral Cave Mangapwani (meaning 'Arab shore') lies on the coast, about 20km north of Zanzibar Town. The Coral Cave is a deep natural cavern in the coralline rock with a narrow entrance and a pool of fresh water at its lowest point. Water was probably collected from here by early inhabitants of this part of the island, but at some point in the past vegetation grew across the entrance and the exact position of the cavern was forgotten.

Later, the area became the property of a wealthy Arab landowner called Hamed Salim el Hathy who had many slaves working on his plantations. During this time, the cavern was rediscovered by a young boy searching for a lost goat. Local people were able to use the water again, and Hamed Salim arranged for his slaves to collect the water regularly for his own use. It has been suggested by historians that the cave may have been used as a hiding place for slaves after the trade was officially abolished in 1873.

Most people come here on an organised tour, or by privately hired car or bike. Buses on Route 2 link Zanzibar Town with Mangapwani village, as do dalla dallas No 102, but services are not frequent. To reach the cavern from Zanzibar Town, take the main road through Bububu to Chuini, then fork left towards Bumbwini. After 6km, in Mangapwani village, fork left again and head westwards towards

ISLAND SPICES

A spice tour has long been one of Zanzibar's most popular excursions into the interior of the island, giving visitors a chance to experience familiar flavours from the kitchen growing naturally. A typical tour lasts about 1½ hours and is likely to include the following:

- The laurel-like **nutmeg tree** (Sw: *kungumanga*), used as an aphrodisiac, and native to Indonesia. The fleshy fruit contains the hard nutmeg nut that is wrapped in a lacy coat. This, when dried and ground, is known as mace and has a similar flavour.
- The **clove tree** (Sw: *darafuu*) is another Indonesian species, a tall, willow-like tree with delicate leaves. The flower buds are picked when pinky-green and then dried to make the familiar, stud-like cloves used in cooking.
- **Vanilla** (Sw: *vanilla*) is a Mexican vine, grown on a support tree, and takes five years to reach maturity. Every single flower has to be pollinated by hand (in the wild, it's pollinated by a single species of bee).
- **Turmeric** (Sw: *vizari*) is a fleshy-leafed plant related to the yam, which produces tubers and requires plenty of water. Women on Zanzibar make a turmeric face mask based on egg white that is good for spots and minor infected injuries. Turmeric is also drunk with milk to ward off illness. Dried, it's really only a colorant, but the fresh tuber has a pleasant taste.
- **Henna** (Sw: *henna*) is used for hair colouring and decorative skin-painting. The very small leaves of this tree are dried and crushed. Traditionally, the poisonous roots of henna were also used to induce an abortion
- Both the leaves and bark of the **cinnamon tree** (Sw: *dalasini*) are flavoursome and usable.
- **Pepper** (Sw: *pilipili*) is a creeper or vine plant. The minuscule fruits or berries start green, then turn steadily yellow and finally red. So-called white pepper is the peeled and dried red berry, while black pepper is the whole dried fruit, complete with its hard skin.
- The large cocoa pods of **cacao** grow directly from the branches of this low, large-leafed tree, but disappointingly, there's no tradition of chocolate-making on Zanzibar.

the coast (the Mangapwani Serena Beach Club is also signposted this way). About 1km from the junction, a narrow dirt road leads off to the left (there's a small signpost). Follow this to reach the cavern. A flight of stone steps leads through the entrance down into the cave itself.

Mangapwani Slave Chamber The Mangapwani Slave Chamber is a few kilometres further up the coast from the Coral Cave. Although sometimes called the Slave Cave, it is a square-shaped cell that has been cut out of the coralline rock, with a roof on top. It was originally built for storing slaves, and its construction is attributed to one Mohammed bin Nassor Al-Alwi, an important slave trader. Boats from the mainland would unload their human cargo on the nearby beach, and the slaves would be kept here before being taken to Zanzibar Town for re-sale, or to plantations on the island. It is thought that sometime after 1873, when Sultan Barghash signed the Anglo–Zanzibari treaty officially

- The small red berries of the **Arabica coffee tree** (Sw: *kahawa*) are dried, fermented and roasted to create our familiar coffee bean. Arabica can grow to 10m or more in height and the white flowers have a delightful, jasmine-like scent.
- By contrast, the **Robusta coffee plant** is a much smaller bush, whose beans have a powerful, bitterer flavour.
- **Ginger** (Sw: *tangawizi*) is a low-growing herb, whose leaves look like little bamboo shoots coming up above the subterranean tubers.
- **Ylang-ylang** (Sw: *ylangilangi*) is a flowering tree producing heavily scented blooms. Pickers have to climb the tree to pick the large, yellow flowers.
- The thin **allspice tree** is originally from the Caribbean. The unripe, dried berries are ground to produce a spice that seems to combine the flavours of several other spices, hence the name.
- **Cardamom** (Sw: *iliki*) is a small plant that produces fleshy seed capsules containing the intensely flavoured black seeds.
- **Tandori fruit** (Sw: *tandori*) is also known as the lipstick tree, as your guide's helper will probably demonstrate, and produces a brilliant red dye.

As well as the spices and food plants above, you're likely to see various banana trees (another southeast Asian import, though a very old one), of which there are 32 varieties on Zanzibar, including tiny 'ladies' fingers' and fat, sausage-like red bananas. You're also bound to see lychees, green oranges and passion fruit vines. Your guide may well point out rice fields and show you how lemongrass, sweet potatoes and pineapples grow (the latter just once a year, directly from the top of the previous year's fruit). Look out, too, for oil palms (bane of dwindling rain forests around the world) on whose commercial production so many Western food-manufacturing and chemical industries depend.

At the end of the walk you'll be treated to an extended fruit-based meal probably consisting of several kinds of oranges and bananas, watermelon, papaya, mango and custard apple. And, of course, you'll be encouraged to buy some souvenirs of your visit – plastic bags of dried spices, scented soap and other toiletries.

7

abolishing the slave trade, the cave was used as a place to hide slaves, as an illicit trade continued for many years.

To reach the Slave Chamber from Zanzibar Town, follow the directions to the Mangapwani Coral Cave. Instead of turning into the Coral Cave, continue on the dirt road for another 1km to reach the entrance to the Mangapwani Serena Beach Club. Just before you reach it, a small dirt track branches off to the right. Follow this for 1km through palm trees and bushes to reach the Slave Chamber. With care, you can reach the steps that lead down onto the chamber floor. Nearby a small path leads to a secluded beach, separated from the main Mangapwani Beach (described below) by some coral-rock outcrops.

Mangapwani Beach Mangapwani Beach lies a few kilometres west of the village. This has long been the location of the Stone Town Serena's beach outpost: **Mangapwani Serena Beach Club** (no accommodation). Set out in tiered timber terraces, hidden amidst dense tropical vegetation, there are natural enclaves set with director's chairs and tables, winding sandy paths and glimpses of the gorgeous stretch of sandy beach, framed by flame trees. You can come here for a tasty seafood lunch (⏱ *lunch 12.30–15.00 daily; US$30 for 3 courses*) or something less gargantuan like grilled catch of the day in lemon butter (*US$18*), a grilled vegetable sandwich (*US$10*), or prawn and lobster salad (*US$13*). A scattering of loungers on the sand entice sun worshippers to the exceptionally beautiful high-tide beach. It's a fabulous place to relax in the company of chirping insects, a good book and a chilled glass of wine (*US$4*), but do watch for strong currents offshore. Lovely hot showers (complete with toiletries) and towels are available for guests, and free transfers can be arranged by the Serena Inn in Zanzibar Town (see page 128; daily trips depart 10.00, return 15.00), or you can pay to travel here any time with local tour companies or taxis.

ISLANDS NEAR ZANZIBAR TOWN

Several small islands lie a few kilometres from Zanzibar Town that are good for a relaxing day's outing. Boat trips to the islands can be arranged with a tour company, with one of the *papaasi* (touts) who look for business around town and along the seafront (see box, pages 122–3) or direct with one of the boat captains. Costs range from US$15 to US$70 for the boat, or from US$5 to US$25 per person, depending on who you deal with, the number of hours you want, the quality of the boat and whether you're prepared to share with other people or want a boat to yourself. Other factors might be lunch or snorkelling gear included in the price. You can hire a boat for yourself, or reduce costs by getting your own small group together. If you're alone, it's usually easy to link up with other travellers. Boats go across to the islands every morning from the beach by the Big Tree on Mizingani Road (the seafront), from the beach near the Tembo House Hotel and the beach opposite Africa House Hotel (see pages 173, 131 and 129).

When staying on the islands overnight, check that security is provided by the hotel, and do bear in mind that these islands are isolated, without mains electricity and most of Zanzibar's boats do not have lights, making travel by sea highly treacherous after dark. There has been at least one serious 'pirate' raid on a hotel in the past, albeit some time ago now, so exercise caution after dark and consider a stay here carefully if you have small children or any existing medical conditions.

CHANGUU ISLAND Lying in the Zanzibar Channel, 6km northwest of Zanzibar Town, Changuu is a coral-rag islet, also known as Prison Island and at one time Kibandiko

Island. It was originally owned by a wealthy Arab trader who used it as a detention centre for disobedient slaves. After the abolition of slavery in 1873, the island was bought by General Lloyd Mathews, commander of the sultan's army, who built a house here (see box, page 196). In 1893, a prison (recently converted into a café, library and boutique) was built on the island but it was used instead as a quarantine station for the whole East African region. In the 1920s, passengers arriving from India had to spend between one and two weeks on Changuu before proceeding to Zanzibar Town.

Today, it is most famous for providing sanctuary to a creep of giant tortoises (*Geochelone gigantea*), descendants of four gifted from the Seychellois governor to his opposite number in Zanzibar in the 18th century. Shipped from their home on the island of Aldabra in the Seychelles, they started to breed and by 1955 there were 200 tortoises. Sadly, their numbers began to drop after independence, partly because people started to steal them to sell abroad, either as unusual pets or as food for 'exotic restaurants'. Numbering only seven by late 1996, measures were taken to protect them and in the same year 80 hatchlings were moved to Zanzibar for protection – ironically, 40 of them still disappeared. Today the tortoises are protected in a large sanctuary compound provided by the Zanzibar government with help from the World Society for the Protection of Animals. At any one time, there are usually around 15 adults, 80 juveniles and up to 100 hatchlings at the sanctuary, all individually identified and protected by microchips injected under the skin. You can go into the sanctuary to see the tortoises close up and even feed them (they delight in fresh mango peel), but please do obey the signs and do not lift or sit on the tortoises.

Changuu Island has a small beach and there's reasonable snorkelling on the nearby reef. There's a secluded beach hotel and daily tours to see the historical ruins and tortoises are organised by many of Stone Town's operators (pages 114–17), invariably making the 20-minute crossing by dhow under sail. For a cheaper option, a local boat will take four people to the island for around US$30.

Where to stay and eat *Map, page 178*

Changuu Private Island Paradise
(27 rooms) m 0773 333241/2; e info.changuu@ privateislands-zanzibar.com; www.privateislands-zanzibar.com. The team here has restored & converted many of the crumbling Arab & colonial buildings on the island, built 15 individual beachfront cottages & introduced a host of guest facilities from a pool to a floodlit tennis court in the forest. 'Deluxe' thatched cottages in the northwest of the island offer the most privacy & boast outdoor showers & baths, whilst the 'standard' rooms to the southwest are in the former 1931 Quarantine Area & have good views across to Stone Town's waterfront. The décor in all is bright & cheerful with vibrant paint & fabrics, with a good amount of space & veranda deckchairs for soaking up the sun. There is no mains electricity, & whilst there is generator power from 18.00–23.00, there is no AC & it's

worth remembering to bring a good torch for evening beach walks. In a restored 19th-century home, Mathews' Restaurant serves extensive 4-course dinners & a good, predominantly seafood, lunch menu. There's a pleasant little beach & whilst swimming & snorkelling in the sea is possible, serious caution is advised as these are busy shipping waters. On land, guests have free run of the island nature trails, whilst day visitors are confined to the ruins & Aldabra tortoise sanctuary. For all the pleasures of privacy though, Island life is not for those who plan on several excursions or for those seeking lively evenings – the 20–30min boat transfers to Zanzibar Town soon mount up (US$60 boat/return – unless you hitch with the touring day trippers). It is very isolated here, & remember it's not possible to travel to/from the island after dark as few boats out of Stone Town will have lights. HB. ⚓

CHAPWANI ISLAND This is also called Grave Island as a small section of it has been used as a Christian cemetery since 1879. Most of the graves belong to British sailors who were killed fighting against Arab slave ships, including Captain Brownrigg, who died with most of his men at the hands of the notorious slave-trafficker Hindi bin Hattam as he attempted to rescue 100 slaves on board Hattam's dhow to Pemba. A number of graves belong to crew of the World War I British ship *Pegasus*, which was bombarded and sunk by the German *Königsberg* in Zanzibar Town harbour. (This latter event is described in detail in the book *Königsberg: A German East African Raider*, listed on page 425.)

There is a small beach on the island, and a lovely patch of indigenous forest, with a population of small duikers, some massive coconut crabs and a colony of fruit bats, which every evening do a few circuits of the island then zoom off to Zanzibar Town in a dark cloud. There are about 100 species of bird in the area, including a small population of black heron in the northeast, whose presence the new lodge is trying hard to encourage.

⌂ Where to stay and eat *Map, page 178*

⌂ **Chapwani Private Island** (11 rooms) m 0777 433102; e chapwani@zitec.org; www. chapwani-resort-zanzibar-hotel.com; ⊕ mid Jun– mid Apr. The island resort hosts 10 simple rooms in small, semi-detached bungalows plus the family Sunset Villa, all open onto the sandy beach. All are en suite with Zanzibari beds, mosquito nets & a timber-decked terrace, complete with a lounger & chairs. There is generator power most of the day, but it goes off at midnight, so don't elect to stay here if AC is a must, & certainly don't forget your torch. Activities are limited, but there's a nice pool tucked in the trees or, for a more natural dip, a tidal outlet in a coral crevasse on the northeast of the island, which is a pleasant place to swim at high tide. At low tide, the exposed reef offers interesting exploration, with coral, starfish & barnacle-clad rock pools around the island, & a pleasant wooded interior (watch out for little dik-dik antelope). Food has an injection of pizzazz from the French chef & a free shuttle boat allows for a daily excursion to Zanzibar Town if shopping & sightseeing are on your agenda. The environment & the multi-lingual management make this a pleasant place to stay but like the other islands in the channel off Zanzibar Town, it lacks the feeling of real 'desert island' isolation by being so close to the main shipping routes, & yet doesn't benefit from the evening buzz of Stone Town. HB. $$$$$

SNAKE ISLAND Sometimes known by its Swahili name, Nyoka, this is a very small island between Changuu and Chapwani. Tourist boats rarely land here as there is no beach, and local legend claims it was once infested by snakes, which has long kept the local community away from its shores.

BAWE ISLAND About 6km due west of Zanzibar Town, Bawe is a beautiful little island with broad sandy beaches and a densely vegetated centre. In 1879, it was given to the Eastern Telegraph Company by Sultan Barghash to be used as the operations station for the underwater telegraphic cable linking Cape Town with Zanzibar, the Seychelles and Aden in Yemen. A second line was run from Bawe Island to the External Telecommunications building in the Shangani area of Zanzibar Town. The old 'Extelcoms' building has now been converted into the Serena Inn, but the original phone line is largely redundant.

Lovely as the beach may be, it is firmly on the busy shipping route to Zanzibar Town and isn't visited as frequently as Changuu. In theory, it's possible to combine trips here with the tortoise excursions or simply arrange an out-and-back voyage with a boat captain in Zanzibar Town, though access prices do tend to be higher than those to Changuu.

Where to stay and eat *Map, page 178*

⌂ **Bawe Tropical Island** (15 rooms) m 0773 333241/2; e info.bawe@privateislands-zanzibar. com; www.privateislands-zanzibar.com. Ochre cottages with vibrant interiors & pole-shaded terraces are a stone's throw from the sea, though a good awareness of the shipping traffic is important here. There is little more to do than sit on the beach, & access to Stone Town is possible only on short day trips, making a stay less attractive to those keen to experience Stone Town by night. FB. ☗

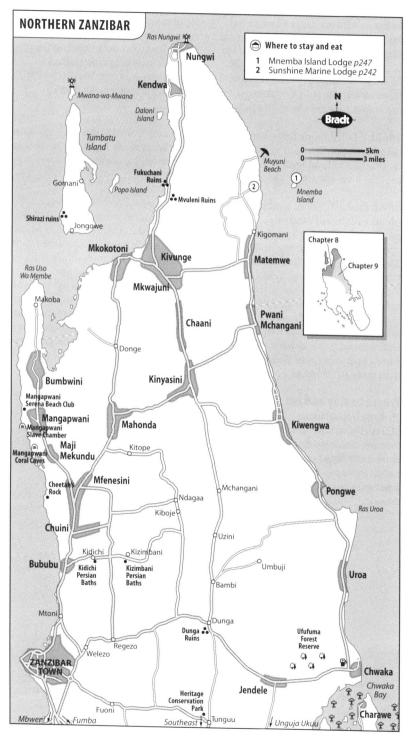

NORTHERN ZANZIBAR

Ras Nungwi

Nungwi

Kendwa

Mwana-wa-Mwana

Daloni Island

Tumbatu Island

Fukuchani Ruins

Gomani

Popo Island

Mvuleni Ruins

Muyuni Beach

Mnemba Island

Shirazi ruins

Jongowe

Kigomani

Mkokotoni

Kivunge

Matemwe

Ras Uso Wa Membe

Mkwajuni

Makoba

Chaani

Pwani Mchangani

Donge

Bumbwini

Kinyasini

Mangapwani Serena Beach Club

Mangapwani

Mahonda

Kiwengwa

Mangapwani Slave Chamber

Kitope

Maji Mekundu

Mangapwani Coral Caves

Mfenesini

Mchangani

Pongwe

Cheetah's Rock

Ndagaa

Ras Uroa

Kiboje

Chuini

Uzini

Kidichi

Kizimbani

Umbuji

Uroa

Bububu

Kidichi Persian Baths

Kizimbani Persian Baths

Bambi

Mtoni

Dunga

Ufufuma Forest Reserve

Regezo

Dunga Ruins

ZANZIBAR TOWN

Welezo

Chwaka

Chwaka Bay

Heritage Conservation Park

Jendele

Charawe

Mbweni

Fuoni

Fumba

Southeast

Tunguu

Unguja Ukuu

Where to stay and eat

1. Mnemba Island Lodge *p247*
2. Sunshine Marine Lodge *p242*

N

Bradt

0   5km
0   3 miles

Chapter 8

Chapter 9

8

Northern Zanzibar

Ageing hippies, gap-year students and bright young things escaping European city jobs are all drawn to the white sand, stage-set palm trees, turquoise sea and sparkling sunshine of northern Zanzibar. Burgeoning guesthouses and vast resort complexes; beachfront activity overload and vibrant nightlife; an ever-expanding community and immense pressure on natural resources: these are the things that now characterise northern Zanzibar above its pleasant beaches, warm sea, nautical heritage and good diving opportunities. Less than 2 hours' drive from Stone Town on the fast tar road past increasingly rural villages, this area vies for the island's budget tourism industry with Paje, but is now also home to an increasing number of large, luxurious resorts. Focused around Nungwi village on the northernmost tip, and spreading near-continuously along the golden sands of Kendwa, on the northwest coast, this bustling centre initially appears to offer every component of the perfect holiday: a wide range of accommodation, watersports galore, fresh seafood washed down with daily cocktails, and a lovely ocean vista.

Sadly, however, there are some serious social and environmental problems bubbling in this area and many visitors, as well as a good number of the foreign and local investors, appear to be blind to the spiralling situation. The alarming growth in the number and scale of developments is quite staggering. Once-small backpackers' boltholes have grown from a handful of rooms to resort hotels, mid-range places have added literally dozens of rooms to their original quota, whilst large-scale luxury or all-inclusive resorts now sit cheek-by-jowl on vast tracts of land around the north coast. Quite literally every beachfront plot from Ras Nungwi to Kendwa now has some tourist accommodation, either operational or under construction. Every single property listed in this chapter has expanded either up or out, or has been newly built since the last edition of this book, a continuation of the trend seen in the previous editions, too. It is crowded and the development not always attractive: high breeze-block walls now obstruct the once-stunning views along the northeast coast and ever-taller hotels jostle for a spot on the low coral cliffs at the seaside. It's still just about possible, however, to escape the 'Nungwi Strip' to seek out the quieter, more spectacular beaches of the northeast coast and Kendwa, but it's getting more challenging with every month that passes, and even once-quiet Kendwa has succumbed to the developers and long-standing backpacker haunts have been replaced with stylish all-inclusive resorts. That said, those places that have remained have had to raise their standards as competition has increased, and generally speaking, that's rarely a bad thing.

NUNGWI

Nungwi is traditionally the centre of Zanzibar's dhow-building industry, and over the last decade the coastline here has rocketed in popularity to become one of the island's busiest beach destinations. The ramshackle fishing village has been largely sidelined by an ever-increasing number of guesthouses, bars, shops, restaurants and bikini-clad Europeans.

In the last eight years, the number of hotel rooms in Nungwi has rocketed from 405 to over 1,000 – a staggering 259% increase! Hotels have sprung up in literally every direction, roads have been repeatedly re-routed and costs have escalated. With the exception of the World Bank-funded tar road to Stone Town, and the police post paid for by local hoteliers, there has been little thought given to the pressure on natural resources, specifically fresh water, with this vast increase in visitor numbers, and sadly the local population has suffered the brunt of the negative consequences, in very direct contrast to those who come to enjoy their 'island paradise'.

That said, the Nungwi beach scene has matured in recent years and become a little more comfortable in its own skin. The beachfront hassle has declined in favour of clusters of local curio stalls; basic shops and small businesses have been established offering everything from massage to snorkel hire; the wild nights have tempered, making way for tables set for feet-in-the-sand beach dinners, and a couple of cool cocktail spots have taken the place of pop-up makuti bars. Professionalism has spread, too, with benefits to the community through training and employment, and, of course, to the visitor's experience. The dive operations are now universally reliable and reputable; the accommodation standards are on the rise (at all budgets) and the village is benefitting from some decent efforts at hotel-funded community projects.

After a few crazy years of incessant building and change, things are finally settling down. Gardens have flourished in those dusty construction sites, and though changed irrevocably from the sleepy island backwater, it is perhaps once again reclaiming some of its exotic charm. The backpackers of old still come here looking for a cheap, fun beach break, but now so do city executives, honeymooners, retired couples and families – and all appear to be having a good time. Within the village, population numbers have spiraled with immigration (local and from the mainland) driven by the prospect of employment and tourist dollars; for the first time, Nungwi's population hit 10,000 in the 2012 census.

Ironically, given its current state, Nungwi was one of the last coastal settlements on Zanzibar to have a hotel, or any tourist facilities. As recently as the mid 1990s, proposals for large developments in the area were fiercely opposed by local people. Today, in spite of the influx of tourists, Nungwi remains a fairly traditional, conservative place with proudly independent villagers. They are not unfriendly, however, and most visitors find that a little bit of cultural respect, politeness and a few words of Swahili go a long way. It is very important to behave and dress appropriately in the village (see also page 102) so please be a considerate traveller.

GETTING THERE AND AWAY Nungwi can be reached by **bus**, **tourist minibus** or **hired vehicle**. From Zanzibar Town the main road to Nungwi goes via Mtoni, Mahonda, Kinyasini and Kivunge. There is a more scenic route directly north of Mahonda to Mkokotoni, which, once the preserve of 4x4s only, is now wonderfully accessible on the new tar road.

As you enter Nungwi, a conglomeration of signs advertising accommodation and activities marks a fork in the road and the end of the tar. Head right for Nungwi's east coast hotels and the village, or straight on for the beachfront properties of North, South and West beaches.

If you are travelling by public transport, there are daily **dalla dallas** (No 116) leaving Creek Road in Zanzibar Town for Nungwi, roughly every 30 minutes between 05.30 and 21.00. Alternatively, between 07.00 and 18.00 there are half-hourly **public buses** (Route 14) departing Darajani Terminal, Zanzibar Town. On arrival in Nungwi, the main stop is opposite a large football pitch inland of the village [202 D3], from where it's a 15-minute walk through the village to the heart of the tourist throng. The shared tourist minibuses, a more popular option, will stop in the centre of the action, beside Amaan Bungalows. Departures south leave from the same locations.

It has also been known for onward travellers to pay local fishermen at the harbour to take them by **boat** to their next destination, even as far as Matemwe on the northeast coast. Ask around to ensure reliability and safety, make sure people know where you're going, and do check that there's a decent motor and safety equipment (like life jackets and working radios or mobile phones) for longer trips.

GETTING AROUND Most places in and around Nungwi are within walking distance, but if you're staying on the slightly more upmarket east side of the peninsula, and fancy letting your hair down on the lively west side, the local **taxi** service charges US$8–10 each way. Ask your hotel to put you in touch with a responsible driver, or contact the reliable brothers at **One Stop Tours & Safaris** (m *0777 433652/461517*).

If you want to tour this part of the island, for example to visit Fukuchani and Mvuleni Ruins (page 236), then it's possible to hire **motorbikes**, **jeeps** and **bicycles**. Ask your hotel or a reputable ground operator to help you arrange this.

WHERE TO STAY Unless stated otherwise, hotels listed below offer air conditioning and en-suite bathrooms as standard.

South Beach The road into Nungwi from Zanzibar Town comes to a fork on the village outskirts. To reach places at the southern end of the west side of the peninsula, go left here, along a dusty track, towards the sea.

Just west of the village, South Beach is effectively the busiest beach. There is no reef in front of the shore here, so the water is deep enough for swimming, whatever the state of the tide. As the beach faces west, it is also a great spot for watching the sun go down. A number of the cheaper places to stay are located here, though it is also home to the imposing, contemporary Z Hotel, so its original 'budget basics' image has somewhat changed. Whatever the accommodation, this remains the liveliest part of Nungwi.

Exclusive

☀ ☖ **Z Hotel** [202 A4] (35 rooms) m 0774 266266; e info@thezhotel.com; www.thezhotel.com; ☉ Jun–mid Apr. One of the swankiest hotels in Nungwi's heartland, Z Hotel opened its heavy designer doors in 2008. It is the seaside dream of London property developers, Keith & Julian, who brought some city-boy bling previously unseen on the Nungwi beach scene. Billed as 'boutique on the beach', the rooms are divided into 6 levels of luxury with sophisticated interiors featuring billowing voile curtains, striking wallpapers, bespoke coconut-wood beds & cool travertine stone floors. In each, there are iPod docking stations & plasma TVs, & Inaya toiletries & stocked minibars complete the indulgent feel. Every room has a balcony & the sea or lush palm-filled garden can be seen from each one; for real ocean lovers the cantilevered decks in the cottages & the 3rd-floor terrace of the Z Suite are favourite lookouts. Elsewhere in the compact complex, the natural stone pool above the beach is a cool, crowded hangout, surrounded with parasols & even a few 4-poster daybeds, each with their own integrated plasma TV. There's a quiet reading lounge, complete with Moroccan lanterns, gentle music & a few computers; the small Mnazi Spa, an outpost of East Africa Diving Centre (page 220); a tiny take-away café & souvenir shop.

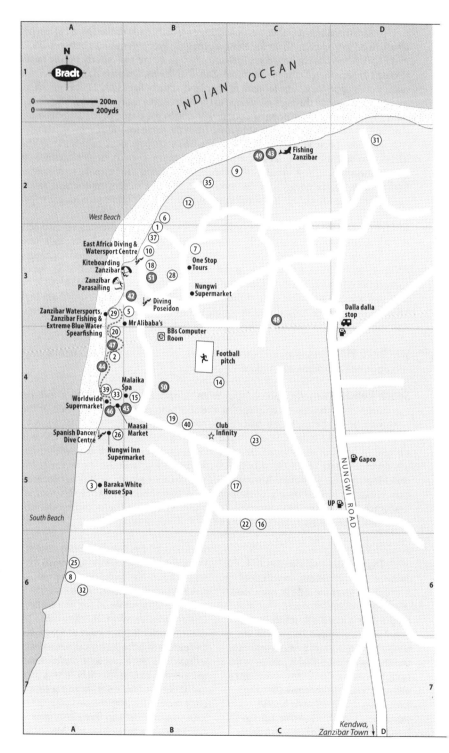

INDIAN OCEAN

N

Bradt

0 ——— 200m
0 ——— 200yds

31

49 43 🎣 Fishing
Zanzibar

9

35

West Beach

12

6

1

37

East Africa Diving &
Watersport Centre

10

Kiteboarding
Zanzibar

18

51

28

7

One Stop
● Tours

Zanzibar
Parasailing

42

Nungwi
● Supermarket

Diving
Poseidon

5

29

Zanzibar Watersports,
Zanzibar Fishing &
Extreme Blue Water
Spearfishing

20

● Mr Alibaba's

BBs Computer
Room

47

2

48

Dalla dalla
stop

44

Football
pitch

14

Malaika
Spa

39

33

50

15

Worldwide
Supermarket

46

45

NUNGWI ROAD

Spanish Dancer
Dive Centre

19

40

Club
Infinity

☆

26

23

Maasai
Market

Gapco

Nungwi Inn
Supermarket

3

● Baraka White
House Spa

17

UP

South Beach

22

16

25

8

32

Kendwa,
Zanzibar Town

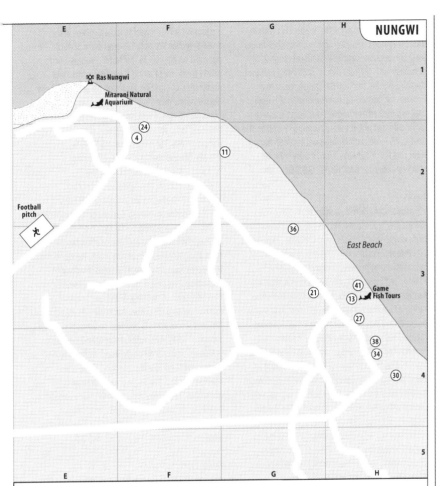

NUNGWI

Ras Nungwi

Mnarani Natural Aquarium

㉔
④

⑪

Football pitch

㊱

East Beach

㊶ Game
⑬ Fish Tours
㉑

㉗

㊳
㉞

㉚

For listings, see pages 201–17

After sundown, Cinnamon Bar (page 217) with its multi-coloured ceiling fans mixes cocktails & finger food; the popular Saruche Restaurant (page 215) gets busy with seafront diners; & Z's latest hangout, the fairy-light lit Rooftop Bar transforms into a hot spot for dressed-up honeymooners. Z is now well established as Nungwi's chic heart & whether staying here or not, it's worth coming to chill on the uber-cool, rooftop dhow sofas with a US$5 Happy Hour cocktail; it's always a fun, if busy spot. No children under 12. B&B/HB/FB. $$$$$–🍽️

Luxury

🏠 **Royal Zanzibar Beach Resort** [202 A6] (96 rooms) 📞024 224 0512; e info@royalzanzibar. com; www.royalzanzibar.com. The large, castellated accommodation blocks of this resort occupy a substantial plot between Nungwi & Kendwa. Planted with tropical gardens & above a pleasant sandy cove, Royal Zanzibar is owned by the same family as Southern Palms Beach Resort in Kenya & operates in a similar all-inclusive, entertainment-focused vein. Eating & drinking are heavily emphasised with a staggering 8 restaurants & bars, from à la carte Samaki with its oriental dining to the swim-up Upendo pool bar. For those who want to work off the calories, there's an on-site subsidiary of the east coast's Rising Sun Dive Centre, & both residents & passers-by can organise dive excursions (other watersports equipment is for guest use only). For younger guests, the kids' club is open 10.00–18.00 daily or there are 4 free-form pools, games & racket sports. HB. $$$$$

Upmarket

🏠 **Baobab Beach Bungalows** [202 A5] (105 rooms) m 0776 014164; e fo.baobab@ gmail.com. This resort remains one of the larger establishments on this stretch of coast, but is no longer marketed & filled exclusively with Italians. At the southernmost end of South Beach, Baobab boasts its own small sandy cove, but the rise in visitor numbers to the area & bead-selling Maasai make it busier than ideal. Above this enclave, the hotel has moved sand onto the coral rock to create a raised 'beach' for scores of loungers & makuti parasols. From here, the blocks of rooms stretch back inland & are all reasonably clean with a private balcony. Set back from the sea, some still maintain a view of the water & all are close to the central swimming pool. The buffet-only Baobab

Restaurant serves passable Italian cuisine & there's a sea-view bar. We noted several signs of decline in our most recent visit to this hotel – rooms a little musty from lack of airing & gardens a little less manicured. Competition is tough on Zanzibar these days & hotels here simply do not survive without good maintenance and happy customers: Baobab will have to up its game to survive. B&B/HB. *Bungalow* $$$$; *lodge/deluxe* $$$$$

🏠 **My Blue Hotel** [202 A6] (87 rooms) 📞(Italy) +39 0521 1917481; e info@ mybluehotel.com; www.mybluehotel.com. Sandwiched between Royal Zanzibar & Sunset Beach, this Italian-owned & managed all-inclusive resort attracts a young, social crowd on reasonable package holidays. The accommodation blocks have a slightly Mediterranean feel & surround the free-form swimming pools. Rooms are divided into categories based on terrace, sea view & overall size (2–4 people), & all have fairly simple interiors with dark timber furniture offsetting brilliant white walls & beamed ceilings. Flatscreen satellite TVs, Wi-Fi & minibar are standard. There is a poolside bar & an open-sided, buffet-style restaurant serving adequate food. Atop the seafront coral cliff, a large area of thatched umbrellas, & loungers sit on a manmade raised beach, with lovely sea views, & there's direct access to the beach for walks linking Kendwa & Nungwi when the tide is low. FB. $$$$

Mid range

🏠 **Langi Langi Beach Bungalows** [202 A4] (33 rooms) 📞024 224 0470; e reservations@ langilangizanzibar.com; www.langilangizanzibar. com. The name Langi Langi is a Swahili derivation of ylang ylang, the perfumed Asian tree (*Cananga odorata*) planted in the hotel's lush gardens. The hotel is divided into 2 sections by the main pedestrian footpath: the 3-storey blocks & restaurant on the seafront & the original rooms & swimming pool in the lush garden on the other. The 20 en-suite rooms are compact & clean, each with AC, fans & constant hot water. Mosquito nets are available upon request & you can even borrow a hairdryer from reception. They are a couple of mins' walk from the beach, but are of a good standard, & do sit right in the heart of Nungwi's tourist scene, with a densely tropical garden & refreshing pool. At the base of the oceanfront rooms, set on a large cantilevered deck over the water, is the reasonably good Marhaba Café where the food, especially curries, have made it popular with visitors & expats alike; bring your own alcohol if you wish or try one of the excellent cappuccinos. Alongside this, are 13 rooms including the Penthouse at the top, where tunnel-vision sea views are framed by the steep makuti thatch. These newer rooms are large, if a little spartan, & some of the furnishings are an acquired taste. If you can live with the look, there are dbl beds, French doors onto a sea-view balcony & plenty of mod cons to keep you comfortable: AC, fan, fridge & shortly safes, too. Aim for rooms higher up for the best views. The older garden rooms across the path, however, continue to be a terrific option, & probably still get our vote as the rooms of choice. In spite of being smaller, they are clean & comfortable, with AC, fan, a nice veranda & are surrounded by a totally tropical scene. The brilliant blue pool (⊕ 07.30–18.30) around which they now stand, is wonderful, too. Bordered by cerise bougainvillea, shady palms, comfortable loungers & neat makuti parasols, it's an understandably popular hangout for guests in the heat of the day or when beach hassle gets too much. Watch out, too, for the pair of rescued dik-diks & their ever-growing family! The friendly owner, Mansour Saleh Said, is clearly investing heavily in this property & is keen to see it succeed, employing only local staff. With the quality he's providing, regardless of whether the décor is to your particular taste, this remains a great option within the price bracket. B&B. $$$–$$$$

⌂ **Amaan Bungalows** [202 A4] (86 rooms) \024 550 1152; m 0775 044719; e info@ amaanbungalows.com; www.amaanbungalows. com. Heralded by rows of fluttering international flags, this sprawling, whitewashed, castellated complex is in the heart of Nungwi's accommodation cluster. A Nungwi scene stalwart, Amaan's rooms are divided into 4 broad categories: deluxe, garden, pool view & sea view. The last perch on a coral-rock cliff above the sea, within easy earshot of the sound of rolling waves, the large picture windows & cantilevered decks more than justify the upgrade cost for the sea-view category. The pool-view rooms are the most recent addition to the complex, opened in 2013, & set back from the open pool area in 2-storey blocks. Regardless of category, all rooms are clean & well cared for with en-suite tiled bathrooms, hot

& cold water, ceiling fans (AC in deluxe, pool & sea view), mosquito nets, mains electricity, UK-style 3-pin sockets & a private terrace throughout the complex. Most rooms can be made up for sgl to trpl occupancy, & 4 are interconnecting for groups & families. This is an ever-developing complex, popular with a young crowd seeking to be at the very centre of the action & older visitors on a budget. Bordering the main footpath through town, Amaan also has a practical grocery, a souvenir shop & a reliable internet café. The bureau de change inside reception will convert virtually any major currency into Tanzanian shillings & a safety deposit system is in operation. Marina Blue & Infusion (pages 216 & 215), immediately opposite on the seafront, are affiliated with Amaan & are good places to eat pizza & seafood, drink virtually anything & be merry at any hour of the day (HB & FB rates include meals at either place). Guests staying here for 3 nights are eligible for a 25% discount at Pemba Misali Sunset Beach (page 351), & the staff can assist in arranging necessary ferry transfers. B&B. $$–$$$$

⌂ **The Nungwi Inn Hotel** [202 A5] (28 rooms) m 0777 418769; e thenungwi_inn@ hotmail.com/info@nungwiinnhotel.com; www. nungwiinnhotel.com. The sea-view rooms here are right on the beach, just behind Spanish Dancer Dive Centre (page 220), whilst the other rooms are set in gardens across the dirt road. The reception is roughly between the 2, at the back of the large beachfront restaurant. Rooms are bright & airy, with starched white bedding, mosquito nets, 24hr electricity (generator for night-time power cuts only) & hot water (electricity dependent). The hotel's newest rooms are in semi-detached thatched cottages which offer slightly more space. If a true sea view is your priority, opt for rooms 1–4 or 7/8. The restaurant (page 216) is on the sand & offers nice, simple food, usually from the BBQ. Rooms can be booked directly or through the Spanish Dancer Dive Centre website (www. divinginzanzibar.com), & confirming the agreed rate is recommended. B&B. $$$

Budget
⌂ **Coccobello** [202 A6] (2 rooms) Beyond the bar (page 215), there are 2 bungalows covered in vibrant murals, painted by owner Nicole, which offer surprisingly cheerful, clean & comfortable accommodation. Painted furniture, patchwork

flooring, kanga curtains & plenty of space are all positive, & the rates are cheap to account for the lack of sea access & other facilities. Not recommended if you're after peace & quiet, but otherwise it's a very passable budget option. B&B. **$$**

⌂ **Safina Bungalows** [202 A4] (30 rooms) m 0777 415856; e info@newsafina.com; www.newsafina.com. Under the enthusiastic management of Ali Omar, Safina continues to be renovated to a good standard. In spite of the lack of sea view, it's a comfortable & spotlessly clean bedtime retreat. The staff remain as accommodating as ever & the garden continues to flourish. All rooms benefit from 24hr electricity (inc backup generator) & hot water. Dbls have duvets in addition to the standard sheets, & the basket of plastic flowers in each room shows care & effort, if not contemporary taste. B/fast is served upstairs in the half-finished building overlooking the central garden & marooned, &

increasingly weather-worn, 'Welcome Safina' dhow. If post-beach chilling on the veranda isn't enough, there is a small massage room, the Malaika Spa, where Conchesta offers spiced oil massages (*US$25–30/hr*), basic beauty therapies & henna painting. B&B. **$$**

⌂ **H&H Beach Bungalows** [202 B4] (20 rooms) ☎024 225 0630; m 0777 416937/413769; e bububu@zanzinet.com. Tucked behind Safina, Hamim & Hamida Abdallah's bungalows are a basic but great-value option. Dbl, twin & trpl rooms are set out around a small, sandy quad, where fruit & eggs are served each morning. Rooms are clean, if in need of airing, & there are small newly tiled terraces, & the bathrooms have hot water & good-quality fittings. There are ceiling fans, mosquito nets & mains electricity (no generator, so susceptible to power cuts). Hamim is a tour operator in Stone Town, so transfers & excursions can be arranged with ease. B&B. **$$**

West Beach
Northwards from Paradise Beach Bungalows, still on the west side of the peninsula, is another stretch of beach which, for the purposes of this book, we'll call West Beach. Parts of this stretch are now delineated from coast with neat rope and a post-lined coastal path.

Upmarket
⌂ **Flame Tree Cottages** [202 B2] (16 rooms) ☎024 224 0100; e etgl@zanlink.com; www. flametreecottages.com. This fabulous little place on the edge of Nungwi village is owned by a delightful Zanzibari–Scottish couple, Seif & Elizabeth, comprising a house (inc a large honeymoon/ family suite on the 1st floor) & 15 red-roofed, whitewashed bungalows spread out in extensive gardens beside the beach. Some of the rooms are interconnecting making them perfect for families, though all offer homely comfort. Inside, the rooms are immaculate with lovely linen & well-finished wardrobes made by the local carpenters, & wide, shady verandas. There's even a thoughtfully placed mini-hose for washing the sand off your feet. All the rooms have electricity, Wi-Fi, constant hot water, & a tea/coffee station. Outside, the lovely raised pool is thoroughly inviting, & the surrounding gardens & space lend a refreshing feeling of space & peace – something increasingly difficult to find in Nungwi. Lounging in one of many hammocks around the garden, listening to the windchimes & twittering birds or just reading & relaxing is lovely, & the quiet staff are happy to help with any

requests. The activities on offer are gentle & range from lemongrass oil massage (*US$12/30mins*) to snorkelling trips aboard the owner's dhow; plus there's a Zanzi Yoga pavilion on site (page 225) offering popular beachside classes with Marisa. For culinary indulgence, chef Simai's delicious dishes – fish goujons with tartare (*US$7*); beef goulash (*US$8*); steamed chilli crab claws (*US$9*) – make this one of Nungwi's nicest dining experiences, especially when enjoyed overlooking the dhows in the harbour. Flame Tree's website is as clear & organised as the place itself, & it's well worth a look for a calm retreat within easy reach of all Nungwi's livelier activities & attractions. B&B. **$$$$–** ⚊

⌂ **DoubleTree by Hilton Resort** [202 C2] (94 rooms) m 0779 000008; e znzdt_info@ hilton.com; www.doubletree3.hilton.com. Set in spacious grounds on the northernmost stretch of West Beach, this has a touch more character than you might expect from an international hotel chain. The well-kept standard rooms come with showers or baths, kettle, safe, mosquito nets &, depending on location, either a pleasant pool or a sea view. Larger suites are found in houses built closer to the beach, at the front of which there is a narrow balcony, with red concrete floors & a neat balustrade, leading to 2 separate rooms. Each has high ceilings, Zanzibari beds, good-quality furniture & the usual mod cons. There is a split-level restaurant, where Moroccan lanterns hang from the ceiling & half an old dhow is mounted on the wall. Here, themed evenings with local musicians entertain, while grilled meats & creamy desserts grace the table. Alternatively, a more informal all-day restaurant is found on the beach & serves a selection of freshly caught seafood & light snacks, or drinks can be purchased from the swim-up Dolphin Bar, & enjoyed poolside with views towards the turquoise sea. The usual array of watersports is available, along with table tennis, pool, volleyball, a gym & the Reflections wellness centre (*massage US$50/hr*). Both East Africa Dive Centre & Zanzibar Parasailing have desks onsite affording easy access to activity planning elsewhere in Nungwi. Overall, it's a family friendly & unpretentious resort at the quieter end of town. B&B/HB/FB. **$$$$**

Mid range

🛏 **Smiles Beach Hotel** [202 B2] (16 rooms) m 0773 444105; e info@smilesbeachhotel.com; www.smilesbeachhotel.com. An architectural medley has produced Smiles' appearance. Spaced in an arc around a flower-filled, semicircular garden & large, new pool, the 4 striking villas are pale yellow, with tiled pagoda roofs & elaborate exterior spiral staircases. Zanzibari-owned & one of the best-quality, quieter options in Nungwi, Smiles is a firm favourite with passing overland groups & repeat visitors. The rooms are immaculate, bright & airy & Indian in flavor, each with a sliding mosquito net, high-quality security locks, satellite TV & beach towels; some also have minibars. The spacious trpl, which could fit 6 people, is made up with 3 large Zanzibari beds. The 'Honeymoon Sweet' [sic] features a giant corner bed as its centrepiece &, like the others, offers indulgent b/fasts in bed. For those who can drag themselves the few metres to the beach, there's an open-sided restaurant-cum-smoothie bar & coffee lounge, complete with a mosaic mirrored wall & wicker lanterns swaying in the sea breeze. B&B. **$$$–$$$$**

🛏 **2 Benches** [202 B3] (4 rooms) m 0777 411314; e rosazanzibar@hotmail.com. The pizza restaurant of the same name is heralded by the eponymous red-brink benches lining the

beachfront pathway. Check in here with one of the red-clad waitresses & they'll show you to the rooms in the neighbouring building. The 2-up 2-down block offers large en-suite rooms with good sea views from their terraces, but sadly not terribly appealing interiors. The slightly musty smell bares out guest complaints of damp, but there is nonetheless a fridge, microwave, AC, fan & kettle alongside the large beds. Meals can be eaten in the restaurant: homemade pasta to order (*US$5–15*), pizza (*US$4.50–7.50*) or various grilled seafood (*US$9–15*). B&B. **$$$**

🛏 **Beach Baby Lodge** [202 B2] (9 rooms) m 0745 028606; e beachbabylodge@gmail. com. Opened in 2015, Beach Baby is the dream venture of a young South African couple, Michelle & Mike. Named after their rescue pet bushbaby, Ajuba, it's a small but efficient little lodge with neat, flat-roofed terraced rooms set around a pretty, well-tended garden. The room interiors are whitewashed concrete with rustic coconut-trunk beds, lantern fairy lights, lacy mosquito nets, simple fittings & a large open-plan en-suite bathroom. Each room is loosely themed around a sea creature with corresponding artwork & textiles. The front of the property is the contemporary, bleached coral rock restaurant & rooftop bar: sip cocktails at semi-circular tables with one of the best sea views in town, order food from the braai & hang out in this pleasant spot. Both managers here have aquatic backgrounds (one a former game-fishing charter captain, the other a dive instructor), so they're well placed to advise on marine activities, & may yet open their own dive centre. B&B. **$$$**

🛏 **Casa Umoja** [202 B2] (9 rooms) m 0777 487570/ 0777 851922; e casa.umoja@email. de; www.casaumoja.info. Set back from the busy waterfront (behind Beach Baby & 2 Benches), this is a thoroughly laidback place. Its Zanzibari–German owners have worked hard over many years to build the house & bungalows & to cultivate the lovely tropical garden. There is a gentle Rasta vibe, although the owners are not often around. There are 5 rooms in Casa Umoja itself & 4 in little bungalows tucked under the tall palms & casuarinas. Interiors are clean & spacious with simple furnishings, swept concrete floors, fans & en-suite bathrooms. Each room has a small veranda & there is a nice raised terrace, with plenty of spots under the trees to chill – swinging chairs, double hammocks & a baraza around the firepit for social evenings. B/fasts of fresh fruit & eggs are served daily; other meals can be purchased at any number of places within a few mins walking distance. There are several resident dogs roaming here for security. Cash only. B&B. **$$$**

⌂ **Ebony & Ivory** [202 B3] (4 rooms)
m 0777 128141; e lauracroci30@gmail.com. In Dec 2014, Italian Laura & her Zanzibari husband Abdi acquired 4 rooms from long-standing budget operator, Union Bungalows (see below). Freshening up the basic interiors a little & adding some red-covered coir loungers to the beach directly in front of the rooms has proved popular. All rooms have hot water (electricity allowing), ceiling fan, electricity, mosquito nets & an en-suite shower room. Wi-Fi is available but be aware that there is no backup generator here during the not-so-infrequent power cuts. Bed linen is fresh & clean, & Laura is usually on the beach to deal with any issues. There is no formal reception or central area here, & all bookings are made in advance to ensure someone is around to meet-&-greet. This is a very simple place, right on the beach, but with extremely limited facilities for the rate. At the end of 2015, the owners also opened a 4-bedroom self-catering village house with a pool for rental to families & groups. B&B. **$$$**

Budget

⌂ **Baraka Beach Bungalows** [202 B3] (16 rooms) m 0777 422910/415569; e barakabungalow@hotmail.com; www. barakabungalow.atspace.com. In the shadow of Paradise Beach Bungalows, these solid, makuti-thatched bungalows surround a small tropical garden beside West Beach. The rooms have undergone significant improvement of late, with AC, fans, electricity & hot water now standard. The interiors remain simple with tiled floors & traditional Zanzibari furniture, but they are very clean. The small terraces overlooking the palms, fuchsias & hibiscus make this a perfectly pleasant corner. There's a selection of room sizes, accommodating 2–6 people, so small groups of friends may be comfortable here, & being a mere coconut's throw from the pleasant West Beach, it's also well placed for sun worshippers. However, this proximity does also mean that the music from Cholo's (page 217) is likely to drift towards the rooms until around midnight,

though the days of really wild parties appear to be in the past. The affiliated restaurant is a tranquil, feet-in-the-sand place under brilliant blue umbrellas at the back of the beach. Open all hours & serving stir-fries, pasta, grilled seafood (all US$6.50) & frothy cappuccinos (US$4), it's a breezy hangout with classical music & a very chilled vibe. B&B. **$$–$$$**

⌂ **Jambo Brothers Bungalows** [202 B3] (9 rooms) m 0777 473901; e jambobungalows@yahoo.com. Razed to the ground by a neighbouring electrical fire in 2010, long-standing Jambo Brothers has since been rebuilt & expanded into a new building slightly further away from the beach. The split locations have led to a somewhat disjointed feel, to add to an already erratic management. There is no formal reception, just a beached ngalawa boat behind East Africa Diving Centre, where staff tend to hang out. The 7 simple beachfront bungalows are located alongside it, whilst additional rooms, in the imaginatively titled Annex Jambo Brothers, are in a whitewashed building perpendicular to the sea on an unattractive side street. The bungalows are very simple with timber beds & beach views; all have fans (5 also have AC), mosquito nets & hot-water showers, although with no back-up generator, the AC & hot water depend on the unreliable electricity supply. The Annex rooms are better, & in fact a good option if on a budget. Green concrete floors, floral purple kanga curtains, *mkeke* mats & Zanzibari beds are thoughtfully chosen, whilst the whole place is quite clean. There is an open-sided makuti restaurant, Waves, next to the Union Bungalows reception, whilst (confusingly) the similarly named Jambo Restaurant on the beach is of no affiliation. B&B. *Bungalows* **$$**; *new rooms* **$$$**

⌂ **Union Bungalows** [202 B3] (18 rooms) m 0776 583412; e unionbungalow@hotmail. com; f unionbeachbungalows. A few steps along the beach from Ebony & Ivory, Union Bungalows has a rock-top reception building, complete with a small shop & internet point. Check in here or at the large open, makuti-thatched restaurant in front of the neat little cottages. All rooms here have hot water, fans, electricity & mosquito nets; bed linen is colourful & floors are tiled. The 9 newer rooms have AC, mini fridges & even a hat stand, whilst the deluxe category are unexpectedly good: don't expect stylish but they are sparkling clean & neatly arranged. This is certainly a budget option, & a little rough around the edges, but it's all perfectly acceptable. B&B. *Dbl* **$$**; *new room* **$$$**

⌂ **Paradise Beach Bungalows** [202 A3] (20 rooms) m 0778 677691/0773 203786; e info@nungwiparadisebungalows.com/ shaabani_makame@hotmail.com; www. nungwiparadisebungalows.com. Accessed beside the high gate at Langi Langi, Paradise Beach Bungalows no longer has any bungalows. Following sustained, albeit fairly slow, redevelopment, it now offers virtually identical rooms & a dormitory in a concrete accommodation block. Whilst the building is aesthetically challenged & the landscaping sparse, the clean rooms have fans, 24hr electricity & large, tiled bathrooms. The dorm sleeps 7 in 3 bunk beds & a sgl shrouded in mosquito nets, & has its own bathroom, though the lighting & an unsightly green carpet are both poor. Equally, decent bedding has not yet reached this corner of Nungwi. That said, all rooms benefit from being positioned in front of a stepped access point to the beach – a broad sandy stretch at high tide & a small cove at low: perfect for a quick dip in the heat of the afternoon sun. The independently run restaurant, Mama Mia (⊕ *food noon–21.00; drinks 10.30–23.00*) has an extensive shaded deck overlooking the sea & West Beach. It serves an array of pizzas (*US$4.50–9.50*) fresh from its stone oven, & fresh 'n' fruity cocktails (*US$3–4*). The Zanzibar Watersports (page 224) dive & activity centre at the entrance to this little complex has certainly had a positive impact on the place & makes it a convenient location for those who are travelling on a budget but are keen on sub-aqua activities. B&B. **$$**

Nungwi village

Away from the beaches, in Nungwi village itself, there are a number of options.

Mid range

⌂ **Kipangani Villas** [202 C5] (3 villas) m 0777 971776; e info@kipanganivilla.com; f habibu.ame. About 10mins' walk from the beach & local amenities, these self-catering villas are marketed to urban escapists & international volunteers. Using very simple timber-&-thatch constructions & with distinctly ethnic-influenced interiors (mkeke matting, kanga trimmed mossie nets, rustic timber beds), this place offers the more adventurous a spacious place of their own. Villas have simple bedrooms, moulded-concrete or stone-clad bathrooms, a small open-plan kitchen (inc fridge), a shaded balcony & baraza-based lounge areas. The villas are set back from the road behind a shared garden filled with bananas, papayas, suitably tropical flowering trees, chickens & a dhow bar. Although children are welcome, the rustic nature of the buildings & garden, & relative isolation may not suit all families; equally, the proximity to the Club Infinity may become an issue. Discounted rates are available for volunteers & families. B&B. **$$$**

⌂ **Zanzibar Star Resort** [202 C3] (14 rooms) ☏024 223 0233; m 0773 663503/0713 348216; e info@zanzibarstarresort.com; www. zanzibarstarresort.com. Managed by Munaa, an astute young woman from Arusha, Zanzibar Star Resort opened the doors to its immaculate rooms in Nov 2011. Behind its perimeter wall, well-tended gardens filled with bananas, flowering shrubs & some of Nungwi's most verdant lawns lead to the Arabesque reception & 2-storey accommodation block. Rooms are arranged in a staggered diagonal to create a little terrace privacy, whilst inside they are clean & modern with pale tiled floors, dark timber furniture, smart en suites, & an array of mod cons, including a digital safe & flatscreen TV. The restaurant serves b/fast to hotel guests & lunch & dinner to all, with the likes of seafood masala (*US$7.50*), BBQ tuna (*US$6.50*) & penne bolognaise (*US$6*) gracing the menu in a typical Swahili–Italian fusion menu. There is a pleasant pool with both stone & sand underfoot options for the surrounding loungers (some of which come with an integrated shade panel!). It's certainly a pleasant little hotel, but it is impossible to escape its location issues: not only distanced from the beach along a quiet road (be careful at night if walking) but immediately neighbouring 'Club Infinity' – whose structure may be soundproofed, but the departing guests are not! B&B. **$$$**

Budget

⌂ **G Oasis** [202 B4] (10 rooms) ☏(UK) 01284 725437; m 0718 023177; e gantanas@live.com; www.goasisznz.com. On the edge of the village, a 10min walk from the beach, G Oasis was created by a British–Zanzibari family. There are 5 small, well-ordered bandas under low makuti thatch with twin beds; detached, castellated Castle Rooms; 2 2-storey houses (Twiga & Simba) offering 2-bed accommodation with en-suite bathrooms & a handy fridge; & even a 3-bedroom house for travelling families. There's a very pleasant open-sided lounge area in lilac & rhubarb tones, with a long boat-shaped table, coir chairs, lovely hammock zone & even a baby swing. There's CCTV for security, back-up generator to ensure electricity & secure parking for self-drivers. In spite of a perhaps less-than-perfect location, G Oasis has a chilled, organised air & clean, comfortable accommodation. B&B. **$$–$$$**

⌂ **Highland Bungalows** [202 C2] (9 rooms) m 0757 619761; highland-zanzibar.com. Behind a clearly marked white wall on the road towards the beach, this German-owned & run establishment has been quietly accepting visitors for several years. The circular makuti area, with its upstairs Sky Lounge, houses the bar (US$1.50 local beer), whilst behind is a gated area for accommodation: 9 spacious dbl & twin rooms, including 2 relatively new, with tiled floors, simple furnishings, en-suite bathrooms & a small private terrace with plastic chairs. There are rustic grass gardens, neat flowerbeds & some shady pomegranate, sweet almond & flame trees. B&B. **$$**

⌂ **James' Guest House** [202 B4] (9 rooms; 1 dorm) m 0772 525484/0785 091255; e bookings@jamesguesthouse.com; www. jamesguesthouse.com. James' proclaims to be 'Backpacker Paradise Nungwi'; a fact disputed by many who stay. The buildings are festooned with tattered flags from an eclectic selection of countries, & although rooms are spacious & bathrooms clean, it would be wise to avoid. Travel forums show repeated complaints about the owner's aggressive & threatening behaviour, notably towards women, as well as overbooking & increasing rates here. The author's own negative experience with the owner make these comments entirely believable; there are better options even at the bottom end of the market. B&B. **$$**

⌂ **Magharibi House** [202 C5] (4 rooms) m 0777 484165. Inside the home of Ahmed Kassim, this basic B&B accommodation is a good

10min walk from the coast. Rooms are very simple: red concrete floors, Zanzibari beds, fine blue curtains & a functional bathroom (often cold water only). It is relatively isolated from the main tourist drag so taxis are recommended for dinner & evening transfers. B&B. **$$**

⌂ **Romantic Bungalows** [202 D2] (6 rooms) m 0773 354112; e h_ellen_85@hotmail.com/ pierogentile47@msn.com. Behind its high gates are thatched terraced rooms set around a small, green, open courtyard, which is the only real view given Romantic Bungalows' location between the beachfront properties & the village. Rooms are basic, with concrete floors, simple Zanzibari furniture & dim lighting; b/fasts are served in the small open-sided dining area, with fresh fruits, eggs & toast on offer. B&B. **$$**

Shoestring

⌂ **Nungwi Guesthouse** [202 B3] (10 rooms) m 0777 494899; e nungwiguesthouse@yahoo. com. Located at the western edge of the village behind the nursery school, close to the football pitch & shops, Nungwi Guesthouse (formerly Ruma Guesthouse) is easily identified by the Bushman-esque paintings on its ochre walls. Zanzibari-owned, it offers very basic rooms with striking wraparound murals in a simple concrete building. There's a central chill-out courtyard under makuti thatch with hammocks, cushioned coir-rope sofas & a few playful kittens, & the atmosphere is decidedly relaxed. Free-spirited backpackers are most warmly welcomed. B&B. **$–$$**

⌂ **Mama Fatuma Village** [202 C5] (7 rooms; dorm & camping) m 0778 899383. Opened in 2014 & primarily catering to Swedish NGO volunteers (bus4africa.tumblr.com), this is a very basic place. Rooms are functional, with plastic flooring, Zanzibari beds & a fan in most rooms. There's also a 16-person dorm & an area for tents (although camping is illegal on Zanzibar). A kitchen is available for use, as are bikes, & many people here are volunteers so stay for longer periods. The piles of rubble, broken palm gates & location are far from inviting, but it is very cheap & the local manager, Khalid 'Eddy Murphy', has a reputation for trying to help his guests. B&B. **$**

East Beach
At the tip of the Nungwi Peninsula is the lighthouse; from here, the coast curves back sharply to the south. This eastern side of the peninsula has developed significantly more slowly than the South and West beaches, but in the

last decade tourism development has started with a vengeance and every plot from Mnarani to Ras Nungwi is now under construction or operational as a hotel. It still offers some great accommodation choices set on low cliffs of coral rock above sandy beaches, but the exclusivity is fast diminishing.

Exclusive

⌂ **Essque Zalu Zanzibar** [203 G2] (40 rooms, 9 villas) m 0778 683960; e reservations@ essquehotels.com; www.essquehotels.com. The imposing makuti construction that makes up Essque Zalu's reception area & restaurant is visible from quite a distance, while up close it's reminiscent of Sydney Opera House. The suites are set in lush landscaped gardens & have a spacious bedroom, separate lounge, 2 flatscreen TVs, a desk filled with branded notepaper, a walk-in wardrobe & an enormous bathroom. Furnished beautifully using contemporary African fabrics, art & wallpapers, the interiors are both clever & thoughtful. Amid the curious *objet d'art*, colourful textured cushions & original sculptures, they also boast a wine fridge, coffee machine & an electronic safe, which ingeniously has a plug socket inside it so you can charge your camera or laptop while it's locked away. The individual suites differ only in their view, which is of either the sea or the lush garden, although some rooms have views of both from their balcony. The resort is centred on the huge, saltwater pool, complete with a whirlpool, water jets & multi-coloured lighting. Looking out over the pool are the 2 restaurants: the casual, deli-style Market Kitchen downstairs, & the more upmarket à la carte Middle Eastern restaurant & shisha lounge upstairs. A further, laid-back lunchtime restaurant – The Jetty – is at the end of the long wooden jetty, where in spite of the wind you can take in an unrivalled view of the coastline. On the other side of the pool are the vast villas, which contain 3–4 bedrooms, a lounge, kitchen (self cater or arrange a private chef), bathroom with stand-alone bath, outdoor plunge pool & private massage room where the masseuses from the adjacent Zalu Zanzibar spa can offer a personal pampering session. The spa (page 224) itself is an oasis of calm, with treatment rooms, a steam room, super-cool gym & sauna, & a range of therapies on offer, including the quirky Maasai treatment, arranged in a series of distinctive red tartan teepees. There's no need to worry about the little ones either, as they can head off to the Petit VIP kids' club (*www.petitvip.com;* ⊕ *08.00–* *20.00*), where a range of supervised crafts, games & activities will keep them amused. Facilities abound, the rooms are top-notch & Essque Zalu is making a name as one of northern Zanzibar's premier resort options. B&B/HB/FB. $$$$$–👑

✳ ⌂ **Ras Nungwi Beach Hotel** [203 H4] (33 rooms) ☏ 024 294 0125; e info@rasnungwi. com; www.rasnungwi.com. A perennially popular choice for high-end honeymooners, this is by far one of the most reliable upmarket places to stay in Nungwi & retains a calm, low-key atmosphere. Rooms are set in compact, well-tended gardens & all have good electronic safes. Broadly speaking, the higher the room category here, the closer it is to the sea & the more it has to offer. The lodge or garden rooms sit in a row above the central area & car park & only a couple of these have distant sea views but each has a traditional Zanzibari bed with mosquito net & a veranda, & any can be made up for sgl, dbl or trpl occupancy. The rondavels of the superior deluxe chalets all enjoy sea views, but only the latter offer dressing gowns & stereos. In addition, set slightly away from the rondavels, the Ocean Suite operates as a private, separate villa & has a private plunge pool & sundeck; this is Ras Nungwi's premium accommodation. Alongside the hotel's large central bar & split-level dining room, there's an internet point (although Wi-Fi is available in all public areas), satellite TV room & a games area with a pool table, table tennis, board games & darts. The exceptional food & a great wine list are highlights of any stay here – delicious fresh, often organic, dishes served in the Ubora Restaurant are the norm. There's an extensive b/fast buffet laid out every morning, an à la carte lunch menu & 4-course table d'hôte dinner. Weekly tasty seafood BBQs with Swahili cuisine classics also feature, often accompanied by some gentle live music. In front of the main restaurant area is a small freshwater swimming pool & sundeck with paths radiating down to the beach & secluded reading areas. There's an excellent PADI dive centre (page 220), offering courses & recreational dives as well as a range of other watersports, & big-game fishing available through Zanzibar Fishing (page 222). Alternatively, play tennis, or for something more gentle, the Peponi Spa is a highly professional operation with superb treatments: try the Pinotage Deep Tissue Aromatherapy Ritual (*US$55/hr*) or a Hydrating Jade Crystal Ceremony facial (*US$65/hr*) HB/FB. **$$$$–☕**

☝ **The Zanzibari** [203 H3] (11 rooms) \024 550 0590; m; 0772 222919; e info@thezanzibari.com; www.thezanzibari.com. Utterly transformed in the last decade, The Zanzibari is a lovely spot: friendly, tropical & independent. Amid extensive climbers & flowering shrub borders, the entry-level dbl rooms are set back from the water's edge, but the interiors are cool & clean: smart 4-poster beds made up with crisp white sheets with vibrant turquoise accents, large en suites with a bath & separate shower, a handy sofa & sliding glass doors onto wide coconut-wood verandas (book the 1st floor for better views), private balcony or terrace. Mini fridges, AC & fan are standard throughout, & the rooms' only real negative is they are a reasonable distance from the sea & pool area. The 2 luxury villas, however, are right above the raised beach. Complete with their own plunge pool, they are a good option for families who want some private space alongside regular hotel facilities. Inside, there's a dbl bedroom downstairs & a lounge, complete with satellite TV, which opens onto a private terrace. Upstairs is 1 large room with open-fronted makuti thatch to keep the place cool & provide a pleasant background of swishing palms & gentle waves. It usually comprises a dbl & sgl bed, & a lounge area. There's a large pool with loungers dotted around the surrounding stone patio & a pole & bougainvillea shade for sunbathers. All other guests can enjoy the 3 cliff-top jacuzzi pools for dhow-spotting dips or book a treatment in the thatched treatment room & gaze out to sea while enjoying a massage. The restaurant menu is predominantly

seasonal & Swahili in flavour, with many ingredients grown onsite: passion fruit, banana & coconut abound. There's a new mezzanine chill-out level above the central meeting area & a friendly bar. HB/FB. **$$$$–☕**

Upmarket

☝ **Game Fish Lodge** [203 H3] (4 rooms) m 0753 451919; gamefishlodgezanzibar. wordpress.com. On the site of the old Mkadi Guesthouse, this small, laidback South African-owned lodge specialises in fishing trips (page 222), as its name suggests. It is very much a family-run operation, with Colin & Lesley providing most of the necessary services themselves – transfers & tours – & doing the catering. Guests often drink & dine together, too, lending this place a homely vibe. The original guesthouse rooms remain, though they have been renovated, & sit on a terrace beside the road looking down the steep hill towards the cliff edge & sparkling sea – a cracking view. The rooms all have pine furniture, appliqué bedspreads & a cheerful kanga-clad coir sofa; a small ceiling-mounted fan, TV, CD & DVD player are also included. Down the rocky hill, past the chicken coop, is an impressive open-sided restaurant/ bar with some particularly good map murals of Zanzibar & Pemba; chill out here in a fishing-net hammock, stroke the friendly cats or have a game of pool. Advance notice of arrival is recommended, as the gates are not always manned. HB/FB. **$$$$**

☝ **Mnarani Beach Cottages** [203 F2] (31 rooms) \024 224 0494; m 0777 415551; e mnarani@zanlink.com; www. lighthousezanzibar.com. Mnarani means 'at or near the lighthouse' in Swahili, & aptly describes this resort's situation. Close to the northernmost tip of the island, from where it is possible to see

---

WATER, WATER ALL AROUND ...

There's ocean on both sides, but Nungwi often suffers shortages of fresh water. Nearby wells are shallow and, as an increasing number of tourist developments tap into the natural water table, the local people justifiably fear their supply will run dry. For many existing guesthouses, the flow is already erratic, and at most larger hotels the water has to be trucked in for bathroom and kitchen use. For drinking, you can buy bottled water. Nevertheless, Nungwi is a place to seriously watch your water consumption – that is, go easy on the lingering showers, not the rehydration!

the sun rise & set, this is a delightful place. Neat sand paths, bordered by masses of established pink hibiscus, lead between the rooms & to the beachfront bar/restaurant area. Here, overlooking a stunning stretch of beach, the deck provides a perfect spot for sunbathing, sundowners or simply chilling on the swings. This is a very civilised place to recharge your batteries. In small, melon-coloured cottages, rooms 1–8 have perfect sea views, interrupted only by an occasional coconut palm, whilst rooms 9–12 are set in lush gardens close to the pool. The standard rooms are small but spotlessly clean, tastefully decorated & with good en-suite facilities. Coconut-wood furniture sits on broad terraces at the front of each one, whilst loungers & inviting rope hammocks hang between palms & shady casuarina trees. There is even a raised, manmade beach for relaxing during high tide. There are also 4 family cottages with large galleried interiors, lounge & useful information pack, plus some 2- & 3-bed family flats in Fisherman House, & the very rustic Mahaba Honeymoon Cottage: a woven palm structure with basic interiors. The sizeable Zanzibar House contains spacious rooms (all named after islands), each filled with good-quality furniture, fridge & large, sea view balcony complete with giant hammock (opt for the 1st & 2nd floors for the finest views). Alternatively, honeymooners on the 2nd floor can escape up the spiral stairs to the roof terrace for some of the area's best panoramic views. Dhow snorkelling trips can be arranged (*US$45/4 people inc soft drinks, snack & equipment*), or it's possible to hire watersports equipment (*3hr rental US$10/15 sgl/dbl kayak*). Kayaks are free for those on snorkelling trips. The lagoon immediately in front of the hotel is also a great place for kitesurfers. The beachfront Cinnamon Spa is a simple affair under thatch & resident Kenyan therapist offers local scrubs (*US$30*), massage (*US$30/hr*) & a popular sunburn treatment (*US$25*). For alternative relaxation, the bar has a relaxed vibe, daily cocktails & very handy tide timetables, & Mnarani's staff are some of the friendliest on the north coast. Among Mnarani's real assets is the dense vegetation that separates it from the lighthouse, for unlike any other plot on this coast, it does not feel boxed in by development. Another positive is its environmental consciousness – rainwater is collected, leftovers are composted, all materials are

local, & solar panels provide the power. On top of this, owner Nassor is active in the local community & is involved in various much-needed projects supporting Nungwi village; 90% of the staff here are directly from this village & all are extremely positive. HB/FB. **$$$$**

⌂ **Sazani Beach Hotel** [203 H4] (11 rooms) **m** 0774 271033; **e** bookings@sazanibeach.com; www.sazanibeach.com. Adjacent to Ras Nungwi Beach Hotel, Sazani Beach has been in its current form since the new millennium. There have been rumours of luxury renovations here for some time, but for now it retains its slightly offbeat & laidback character, with decidedly low-key management. Set high up on coral rock, there are 2 very simple dbl rooms in the main house, 2 large rooms suitable for dbl or trpl occupancy, which run perpendicular to the sea in a semi-detached block, standard dbls in semi-detached bungalows, & a beach banda. All are basic but neat, clean, & have 24hr electricity, mosquito nets, fans, hot water & a stunning sea view. Early-morning tea can be brought to your room, before b/fast is served on the small patio area. Homemade jams & freshly brewed coffee feature alongside traditional eggs & bacon. The restaurant area is tucked behind billowing cotton panels, or BBQs can be organised for successful game-fishing guests. Sazani has traditionally been a hangout for kitesurfers, keen to catch the shore trade winds (up to Force 6) in the clear lagoon immediately in front of the hotel, & there's a branch of Zanizbar Kitesurfing on site here. B&B. **$$$$**

⌂ **Tanzanite Beach Resort** [203 G3] (17 rooms) **m** 0777 485022; **e** info@ tanzanitebeachresort.com; www. tanzanitebeachresort.com. If you can ignore the huge, rusting satellite dish at the entrance & the immature gardens, Tanzanite has a stunning ocean outlook from its raised location. It caters mainly to German & Italian visitors & delivers a reasonably good level of accommodation. Large rooms, 2 of which are classed as seafront, are in semi-detached thatched bungalows with sparse furnishings, standard dbl beds (crazy given the size of room), small fans, mosquito nets, small bathrooms & a shaded terrace. There is a restaurant (⊕ *to non-residents 12.30–22.00*) serving a fairly limited 'fish 'n' mash' menu, a popular pool table, & a lovely kidney-shaped swimming pool, complete with token coconut palm & raised stone decking. There is no beach in front of the hotel as the coral-rock shelf extends below the property, but a faux beach festooned with hammocks has been engineered on the cliff top, with sea swimming possible at high tide & coastal walking at low. B&B. **$$$$**

Mid range

✳ 🏠 **Warere Beach Hotel** [203 H4] (15 rooms) m 0782 234564; e info@warere.com; www. warere.com/beach. Opened in 2015 by the owners of Stone Town's Warere (page 135), this is a great-value little gem. The soaring white entrance, filled with intricately carved columns, offers fabulous reaching sea views from the moment you arrive. At the top of the cliff, the central area serves as the bar, lounge & restaurant, & the breeze & view certainly invite lingering lunches & super sundowners on strategically placed swinging chairs & batik cushioned sofas. From the immaculate entrance, coral-sand pathways lead down through stepped lawns, tropical flowers & swishing grasses, past the rooms to the pool area & sea. Lovely bedrooms are divided into 3 categories, with the deluxe boasting amazing uninterrupted ocean views. Interiors are all spacious, spotless & beautifully furnished with mossie nets trimmed in navy & orange. A contemporary take on Zanzibari beds & stylish glass-block & moulded-concrete en suites are both pretty & practical. The semi-circular pool & kids' splash pool enjoy shade from sweet almond trees & mkadi palms, whilst loungers are grouped under white umbrellas; all are right on the top of the coral cliff with fabulous ocean views. Activities are limited & quiet (kayaks, bikes & yoga mats are available), but with Nungwi's centre a 5min taxi away, guests here are either happy to simply indulge in the peace on offer, or to retreat after a visit to town. B&B/HB. **$$$–$$$$**

Budget

🏠 **Baraka's Aquarium Bungalows** [203 F2] (4 rooms) m 0777 484165; e barakabungalow@ hotmail.com; barakabungalow.atspace.com Adjacent to the tidal pools at Baraka's Turtle Aquarium are 2 bungalows, each housing 2 spacious dbl rooms, each with built-in concrete beds, timber-framed mosquito nets, a table & chairs, & a curtain screening the toilet & shower. They are clean & functional, but not very inspiring. There are wide verandas, staggered to offer guests some privacy, & a number of free-range chickens around. There are also 4 rather sad rock pythons in a concrete cage, who for a few thousand shillings can be draped around your neck; just hope they've had their allowance of rats for the day! B&B. **$$**

🏠 **Mabwe Roots Bungalows** [203 G3] (6 rooms) m 0777 234113; e hajimohd@ymail. com/alimohamed@ali.tf; 📘 www.mabweroots. bungalow. On the opposite side of the road from Game Fish Lodge, Mabwe Roots is owned by friendly brothers, Haji & Ali. Simple rooms have been built with care as business as grown & whilst money has not allowed for the finest fixture & fittings, there are fresh flowers in every room & the gentility of the owners goes a long way. All rooms have hot-water bathrooms & outside each is a small terrace & hammock chair. There is a pleasant bar area with cow hide & timber furniture under open-sided makuti thatch, serving food from a simple menu, & there's a rustic firepit for evening campfires with local drumming under the stars. The sea is visible, albeit though a building site at present, but at a distance, & it's worth noting that táxis or bikes are necessary to get around from this location, which is some way from the main drag & off the local minibus circuit. B&B. **$–$$**

✕ **WHERE TO EAT AND DRINK** Nearly all the hotels and guesthouses in Nungwi have attached restaurants, many of which are open to guests and non-guests alike (see *Where to stay* for more details). Along South Beach a number of casual restaurants, cafés and bars serve seafood dishes for around US$10, and snacks, pizzas and burgers for around US$6, all washed down with fresh fruit juices, milkshakes, ubiquitous Coca-Cola and African beer, whilst Z Hotel's Saruche lords over them with its fusion feasts. Between South and West beaches, a band of more structured restaurants perch on the coral cliff above the sea, all with similar menus of fresh seafood, oven-fired pizzas and local curries, and many do Happy Hours and backpacker meal-and-beer specials. North of Paradise Beach Bungalows is a clutch of funky, sand-between-your-toes bars, offering cocktails and music on the beachfront. For a more grass-roots flavour, deep in the village you are likely to find cheap local fare from around US$2–3, though venues are highly changeable.

With little building regulation apparent, beachfront bars, restaurants and guesthouses tend to close and spring up again virtually overnight as land is sold on to ever-higher bidders. For many years, simply setting up a barbeque beside a few chairs, tables or logs on the sand signalled being in business, but things are changing and more substantial restaurant structures are slowly replacing these ad hoc eateries. Here, we've listed only some of the more reliable, long-running establishments and those that are new but showing promising signs of staying the course. You're quite likely to find more newcomers on arrival, so do also ask around for current culinary hot spots. It is perhaps also best avoiding a few: **Bam Bam Bar**, a dilapidated hangout for some slightly disillusioned locals, being notable as such.

Restaurants

✗ **Saruche Restaurant** [202 A4] m 0773 535808; ⏲ dinner only daily. The formal restaurant at Z Hotel (page 201) serves an à la carte menu of African–European fusion food with a heavy emphasis on local seafood. Accompanied by an international wine list, ocean views & island antiques, it's a pleasant place to dine & one of the smartest options currently in Nungwi. Peruse the menu from the lavish daybeds & couches in the lounge, then pick a table on the deck overlooking the beach or high-tide waves. There are traditional music & entertainment nights throughout the week, featuring everything from belly dancers to troops of drummers, & after-dinner nightcaps in upstairs bar Cinnamon are very much de rigueur. $$$–$$$$

✗ **Coccobello** [202 A6] This colourful Zanzibari–Italian-owned Rasta restaurant, bar & bungalows (page 205) opened in 2014. There's a DJ every Sun playing everything from reggae to Afro-pop & country, but otherwise it's a very laidback hangout. The central bar/restaurant is under high makuti thatch adorned with psychedelic flowers & CND symbols with a semi-circular bar, dhow tables & a mosaic floor fashioned from colourful cracked tiles. Bartenders mix iced coffee (US$2.50) & cocktails (US$5) all day beneath a Bob Marley 'One Love' poster & a suspended bicycle; & there's a 'Made in Italy' menu, featuring the likes of fish panini (US$7), pesto chapatti (US$2) & piri-piri Rasta pasta (US$5). $$$

✗ **Flame Tree Restaurant** [202 B2] ☎024 224 0100; ⏲ lunch & dinner daily. Just inside the low wall of the hotel of the same name (page 206), this is a low-key gem. Offering uninterrupted sea views from its clutch of tables, you can sit back in the dappled shade of casuarinas & frangipani trees, enjoy the ocean breeze, brilliant turquoise waters & a sense of space. Chef Simai, a long-standing member of staff here, offers up crunchy salads,

fresh seafood & spicy Swahili treats, & whilst the service is a little slow, the scene is lovely & the food, when it does come, is tasty. Wi-Fi is available (vouchers on request) & there are some shaded loungers & a couple of hammocks for post-lunch chilling. By night, the restaurant twinkles under fairy lights for a little seaside romance. $$$

✗ **Gerry's Bar** [202 C2] m 0779 897707; e gerrysbarzanzibar@gmail.com; ⓕ NungwiZanzibar; ⏲ noon–06.00 daily. Immediately next door to the DoubleTree, this is a popular Nungwi hangout with an open-sided makuti thatch shade, covering its coconut bar & live music area (Tue reggae & Sun Jazz evenings). Eat & drink inside or out under shaggy palm umbrellas & always with the sand between your toes. Gerry's is a casual haunt, offering simple, well-cooked food from rock lobster to chicken schnitzel & salads (US$7.50), an array of chilled beers & cocktails (US$4–6), friendly staff, & a knowledgeable owner: Gerry is a serious game-fisherman (page 221) with some fully kitted boats & a charter yacht – ask here if you're interested in taking to the water. $$$

✗ **Infusion** [202 A4] m 0775 044719; ⏲ 09.00–late daily. Approached from South Beach, this is the first of this coast's clutch of raised seafront restaurants. The friendly staff serve a range of popular seafood dishes, including octopus, calamari, prawns & cigale (rock lobster), which is amusingly spelt 'seagull' on the menu. For something a bit different try the seafood coconut curry (US$9.50) or if you're really hungry go for the seafood platter (US$19). Lobster is reasonably priced (US$16), whilst those tired of fish can sample delights from the pizza oven (US$5–8) or a spicy satay kebab (US$10). Meals can be accompanied by a choice of fresh juices or a hot & frothy cappuccino from the restaurant's Italian espresso machine. $$$

✘ **Langi Langi Restaurant** [202 A4]
m 0773 911000; ⏱ 07.00–22.00 daily.
On a large cantilevered deck of the hotel of the same name (page 204), Langi Langi is a relaxed lunch stop by day & a Swahili restaurant by night. Serving super cappuccinos & cake at b/fast, then pizza & pasta (*US$6–8.50*), seafood grills (*US$9–15*) & fresh curries (*US$7.50–13*) for lunch & dinner. The brave can sample the Zanzibar Chili PiliPili menu – 'have fun in the sun don't get burn' warning included! It's a popular place & worth booking to guarantee a table for dinner. Service is friendly & menu variations always possible, whilst the breeze & rolling waves add to the casual vibe. Dine inside amid the monochrome photos of Stone Town & antique *objets d'art*, or out on the deck – shade or sun available. No alcohol, but beer & wine can be chilled & served if you bring your own. Couples, families & large groups are all equally well accommodated. If you like the food, ask Sele about the cookery classes here. $$$

✘ **Marina Blue** [202 A4] m 0775 044719;
⏱ 07.00–23.00 daily. Bright & breezy Marina Blue is relaxed by day but livens up during Happy Hour (⏱ *17.00–19.00*), when a selection of cocktails is offered. The expansive, mangrove-pole terrace affords diners uninterrupted views out to sea & a welcome breeze. The speciality here is grilled seafood & meats, which features in a range of salads (*US$7*), burgers (*US$9*) & sizzling platters (*US$11*). Fresh seafood is served freshly grilled or fried, & the piri piri prawns with chips are a popular choice (*US$13*). Although the staff could be friendlier, it's a welcoming enough place & there are also 2 satellite TVs in the adjoining Sunset Grill for catching up on international sports. $$$

✘ **Ombeliko del Mondo** [202 B4] m 0773 604265; ⏱ 09.00–22.00 daily. This pleasant *cucina italiana* is unusually located: tucked behind Amaan Bungalows, on the far side of the dusty access road, with precious little in the way of a nice view. Owned by Lella, a lovely Mantovan who only speaks Italian, the menu (in English & Italian) is full of traditional Italian delicacies: seafood antipasti, pastas, risottos & tempting *dolcis*. Good coffees are available. There's an open kitchen, smart lounge & a neat restaurant area, buzzing with Mediterranean chatter, all under a huge makuti roof. Starters cost around US$5.50 & main courses US$5–10, & whilst quality & reviews are

consistently good, portions are a little on the small side for some diners. $$$

✘ **New Dhow Restaurant** [202 C2] ⏱ lunch & dinner daily. This restaurant is a locally owned & run little place that's been around since the start of the millennium. Operating from a small makuti hut immediately behind the harbour, Khamis prepares tasty pilau rice & daily 'catch of the day' seafood dishes: BBQ octopus (*US$4.50*) to grilled ginger & garlic lobster (*US$16*). Round off a meal with bananas in coconut milk (*US$4.50*) & watch the dhows & fishing ladies. $$–$$$

✘ **The Nungwi Inn Restaurant** [202 A5]
☎ 024 224 0091; m 0777 418769; ⏱ from 06.00; last food orders taken 22.00. On South Beach, in front of the hotel of the same name (page 205), this restaurant receives consistently good reviews for its simple, traditional fare, which is listed in technicolour on a wall that doubles as a backboard. Guests can sink their feet in the sand, watch the beach volleyball & peruse the menu whilst seated under neat pole shading. Order a 'Nungwi Killer' cocktail (Bacardi, vodka, Cointreau, tequila, lime & coke) & little is likely to be on the agenda for the afternoon, though more popular are the open-oven pizzas (*US$5–9*), burgers (*US$6–9*) & grilled lobster (*US$13–50*), plus the regular beach BBQ. But before making your choice, look out for the amusing 'absent menu' – a list of dishes that the restaurant doesn't serve! $$–$$$

✘ **Morning Star Restaurant** [202 C3]
 A very local establishment in the heart of the village, Morning Star is signposted off the main dust road through the village between the BBS Computer Room & the dalla dalla stop. It is allegedly open daily for b/fast, lunch & dinner; however, it does seem to close regularly for 'maintenance', so best not to rely on it if you're starving. If by chance it is open, expect a set meal of Swahili seafood dishes in a basic setting & some curious villagers for company. Outside seems to be the hub of local *bao* games, so you may even be able to join the crowd for a heated match after your meal. $$

✘ **Mama Africa Restaurant** [202 B4]
⏱ 08.00–22.00 daily. Mama Africa caters very much to visitors after some genuinely local cuisine. At the end of the curio alley, furthest from the beach, local ladies can often be seen neatly chopping spinach & a handful of diners enjoying their simple Swahili dishes. B/fast, lunch & dinner

are served but special requests or groups should probably book in advance. **$–$$**

Bars

☀ ☿ **Cinnamon Cocktail Bar** [202 A4] m 0773 535808; ⏰ 07.00–late daily. This is part of the Z Hotel complex (page 201) but welcomes non-residents. With its 1st-floor location, overlooking the South Beach scene & the sea, the young & beautiful are attracted by its contemporary décor & fabulous tropical cocktails. Sipped at cushion-clad baraza benches, surrounded by ever-changing mood lights & chilled tunes, this is a great pre-dinner drinks spot & is certainly one of Nungwi's most stylish drinking dens to date. Stay for sushi & tempting tasting platters (*US$5–15*) at lunch or dinner, or just work your way through the extensive cocktail list. There is a cool vibe here & it's the only place by the beach where fashionable ladies won't feel out of place in high heels. **$$$–$$$$**

☿ **Mangi's Bar & Restaurant** [202 A4] m 0777 417042; ⏰ 08.00–22.00 daily. Relocated as part of the Z Hotel pool area expansion, long-running Mangi's is now back on the sandy beach where it first started out as Dolphin Restaurant. A shaded spot beside Nungwi Inn Hotel, it's a relaxed hangout serving fresh juices, US$4 cocktails (the 'Zanzibar Mzungu' concoction of banana, rum, milk & vodka appearing popular), & snacks like samosas, chapattis & baked potatoes on its distinctive Maasai red tartan tablecloths. For US$15pp you can join the nightly BBQ buffet on the beach & indulge in the likes of king prawns in garlic butter, octopus in coconut curry & vegetable curry – just be sure to order before 16.00. **$$$**

☿ **Cholo's Bar** [202 B3] m 0777 505434; ⏰ 10.00–late daily. For all-day drinking & wild nights, Cholo's is a perennial favourite. Tucked under palms at the back of West Beach, this eccentric establishment is well known for its 24hr music, crowd of local Rastas & backpackers & free-flowing alcohol. The bar is a piece of living art composed of 2 marooned dhows with suspended dugout canoes acting as seats & an array of motorbikes, sanitary ware & various other salvaged items used for structure, storage & décor. Beach bonfires are a periodic evening attraction along with ad hoc BBQs & dining at upturned dhow tables. Tamer than it once was since a relatively recent facelift, it's smartened up a little & added daytime appeal with a raft of 4-poster timber daybeds on the beach in front. Good spot if you like a mojito whilst sunbathing, though expect a reasonable amount of attention. Weekly beach parties & 'ladies' nights' draw crowds, & you'll likely see the expat hotel staff jostling for bar space. **$$**

Cafés

💻 **Z Café** [202 A4] m 0773 535808; ⏰ 08.00 – 18.00, daily. Above the dive centre at Z Hotel (page 201), this tiny terrace café offers homemade Italian ice cream, smoothies, iced coffees, a small selection of take-away sandwiches & pasta salads (*US$3-5*) & unusually refrigerated chocolate bars. For a quick bite or a beach picnic, it's a convenient stop along the Nungwi walkway. **$$**

💻 **Rastacafe** [202 B3] ⏰ 17.00–early morning. Behind a low timber garden fence next to Kiteboarding Zanzibar, this tiny makuti thatched bar serves fresh coffee, from spiced Zanzibari style to Italian cappuccinos. Run by a friendly Rastafarian, Girasole, it's open from early evening until the last of the beach party revellers head home in the wee hours. **$–$$**

NIGHTLIFE Three years ago, **Club Infinity** [202 B5] opened as Nungwi's first 'proper' nightclub. Located away from the beach and allegedly soundproofed, this club is not a particularly salubrious place. Advertising itself as the place 'Where Partying Never Stops' it's open most nights, and boasts free entry to ladies on Tuesday, Friday and Saturday; gentleman pay a token US$2.50–3 entry.

SHOPPING There are several small shops in Nungwi village, where you'll find an array of cheap souvenirs, including carvings, paintings and jewellery, as well as essential items. Head inland across the football pitch behind Cholo's, and you'll first come to a neat building on your right, one half of which is the well-equipped Nungwi School computer room (page 218), while the other half is

Choices, a souvenir shop that also sells swimwear. A few steps further on, there is a small parade of shops – an ever-changing array of beauticians, barbers, local cafés, and the long-standing **Nungwi Supermarket** [202 B3], a veritable Aladdin's den of imported luxuries from toothpaste and toiletries to chocolate and Pringles.

Taking the road deeper into the village, there's another internet access point, the **California Foto Store** for film processing, the New Nungwi Salon where the brave can have a bikini wax, and the local-style Jambo Mixed Shop, behind which is the Ahsanna Dispensary for villagers.

Amaan Bungalows Supermarket [202 A4] has a reasonable selection of knick-knacks and food/drink basics, whilst behind Paradise Beach Bungalows, **Mr Alibaba** [202 A3] and his sons, Abdul and Suleiman, sell everything from kangas to cold drinks, postcards and tours.

Alternatively, if you just need to grab a few essentials and don't want to stray too far from sunbathing, there are a couple of places on South Beach. **Nungwi Inn Supermarket** [202 A5], next to its namesake hotel, is very well laid out, clearly priced and stocks a good selection of snacks, drinks, toiletries and beach requisites such as sunscreen. Between the curio market and North Coast Snorkelling, up some very steep and irregular coral-rock steps, **New Worldwide Supermarket** [202 A4] sells a similar range of goods, but is not nearly as nicely laid out. There's a good selection of known-brand suncreams, a reasonable variety of alcopops and beers, some warm white wine and even some carrot cake mix. Alternatively, stay on the beach and wait for the beach traders to parade the sand with boards covered in mirrored sunglasses, beaded jewellery and cold drinks.

For artwork and souvenirs, a fairly contained **curio market** [202 A4] has steadily grown on the alley running perpendicular to South Beach, alongside Z Hotel. Known locally as the Maasai Market, on account of the traders' tribal background, you'll find some entertainingly named shacks – IKEA Zanzibar – alongside those with delusions of grandeur: 'Leonardo da Vinci' for paintings and 'Gucci' for accessories. Joking aside, this organised approach to displaying the carvings and beadwork is to be commended, though there is still some way to go to reduce the sustained mobbing of fair-skinned passers-by.

OTHER PRACTICALITIES

Internet Most of the larger or smarter hotels have internet facilities or Wi-Fi access, and a reasonable number of the smaller backpacker places will let you use an office PC to check email. Amaan Bungalows has three PCs available for general use in a small internet café off reception. Wi-Fi is becoming more widely available, though connections remain somewhat erratic and bandwidth fairly low.

If you do need a PC or internet access, we would recommend the reliable Nungwi School IT centre as a first choice, as income here is used to reinvest in the school's excellent computer initiative. Founded in 2002 by a generous tourist, Bibi Biorg, **BBs Computer Room** [202 B4] (⏰ *08.00–20.00 Mon–Fri & 08.30–19.30 on holidays & w/ends; rates are very low*) was designed to offer computer lessons to all Nungwi School's pupils as well as IT training for local adults. Four computers at the back of the class have Wi-Fi and paying customers, mostly tourists, can access these at any time during opening hours, regardless of whether classes are present. Though heavily supported by pupils and parents, and proving sustainable from its commercial activities, the centre is still heavily reliant on donations and visitors' dollars, so even if a few dollars to email home is all you can manage, the cause is a good one. If you are in a position to give more support, the headmaster can be contacted on e bbs@zanlink.com. The centre is clearly signposted beside the football field, on the right as you approach from the beach.

Post The postbox outside Mr Alibaba's offers a twice-daily mail collection for those all-important postcards home.

WHAT TO SEE AND DO Most visitors come to this area to relax on the beach, swim in the sea, and perhaps to party at night. For local attractions, the small turtle sanctuary on the beach, terrific local coral reefs and growing array of watersports are still a draw. If you want a more cultural experience, check out the village tour, head down the coast to the 16th-century Swahili ruins at Fukuchani and Mvuleni, the bustling and ramshackle market at Mkokotoni, or venture across the water to Tumbatu Island.

If you want peace, quiet and fewer people, you will probably need to visit a different corner of the island.

Watersports The sweeping cape on which Nungwi is sited is surrounded by warm, turquoise seas, making it a perfect spot to engage in countless water activities. On the west side of the peninsula, especially on South Beach, locals offer boat rides, Mnemba picnic excursions, sunset booze cruises and snorkelling trips, whilst a growing number of Europeans are setting up motorised watersports operations. Prices are all very similar; quality is highly variable. Listen to your instinct and other travellers' advice carefully when deciding who is currently offering the best trip.

Diving and snorkelling Diving is especially popular here and many of the hotels offer dives and dive courses: you can visit the local reef, or go further afield to reefs such as Leven Bank and Mnemba. Over recent years several dive operations have come, gone or changed their name or location; at the beginning of 2017, five independent dive operations were in operation in Nungwi, most long-standing, with a few resorts also offering in-house instruction. Listed in alphabetical order, the centres are very different in feel and ethos, and divers are advised to talk seriously to the individual operators about safety and experience before signing up for courses or underwater excursions. They will all also arrange snorkelling trips to local sites and Mnemba, including all the relevant equipment and a snorkel guide. For something more low-key, there are pop-up makuti bandas hiring out fins, snorkels and masks on all the beaches. The equipment will be variable in quality and will usually cost around US$5/10 per half/full day for a mask and fins. The owners may offer to take you to Mnemba, Tumbatu or Kendwa Reef for snorkelling, but do be aware of safety considerations if you opt to go to the further destinations: the more local boats will likely only have one motor and it's a long paddle back if it breaks.

8

🤿 **Divine Diving & Yoga** [202 A4] m 0777 771914/0772 299395; e info@scubazanzibar. com; www.scubazanzibar.com. Based at Amaan Bungalows, Divine Diving is a relative newcomer on the northern diving scene, offering both yoga & scuba. Breathing technique classes to improve underwater air consumption sit alongside a range of PADI specialist courses (night diving, fish ID, enriched air, deep diving, search & recovery, drift & navigation). The well-qualified, experienced expat team hail from South Africa, UK, Spain & Israel, so can teach in several languages. They regularly dive 25 local sites & encourage attention to detail: small groups, new Mares equipment, safety procedures & a link with the island's DAN hyperbaric chamber. This centre is affiliated with Zanzi Yoga (page 225). *US$65/100/190/420 (plus US$30 to Mnemba Atoll) for 1/2/4/10 dives; Discover Scuba US$105; Open Water US$500; Advanced US$395; Night Dive US$20 extra.*

✐ Diving Poseidon [202 B3] **m** 0777 720270; www.divingposeidon.com. Owned by Austrian couple Ilse & Bernhard Kotlar, this PADI dive centre is located away from the shoreline, between Baraka Beach Bungalows & Nungwi village. The small bungalow base is clearly painted with the sea god himself, & houses the dive equipment: Mares BCDs, Dacor/Cressi regulators & long/ shortie suits. They operate 1 sgl-engine wooden boat, taking 10 divers on 2-tank dives to sites around the north coast, Mnemba & Leven Bank (advanced divers only; Feb–Oct). Be aware, some dives are led by dive masters only, though there are usually 2 German instructors based here, too. *US$60/110/200/430 for 1/2/4/10 dives; Discover Scuba US$100; Open Water US$480; Advanced US$300.*

✐ East Africa Diving & Watersport Centre [202 B3] **m** 0777 416425/420588; **e** info@ sansibar-tauchen.de; www.diving-zanzibar.com. Owned & operated by an experienced, straight-talking German–South African couple, Michael & Delene Kutz, this is the oldest dive centre on the north coast. Indeed, Delene is well known among all the island's best dive centres as a walking instructor manual, & she rightly expects very high standards! On the beach in front of Jambo Brothers Guesthouse, this highly efficient PADI 5* Gold Palm Resort offers very well-priced courses to Dive Master & a host of scuba trips. Dive sites are reached by dhow, or 2 14-person RIBS, & each boat has 2 experienced captains, with power of veto over any potentially unsafe dive. Safety is taken seriously here, with all boats equipped with first aid & oxygen; dive leaders carry permanent surface marker buoys; steel tanks are continually quality tested using 2 Bauer Pure Air Stations, & the whole centre actively contributes to the DAN Decompression Chamber Support scheme (anyone completing a course here is automatically fully insured for 6 days' underwater activity). Female divers also take note that the tanks here are all squat steel tanks, making them a much more comfortable shape on your back, & significantly easier to cart down the beach to the boat. Nitrox diving was introduced in 2008. Mnemba sites are visited every couple of days; Hunga is a frequent destination; Kichafi, Mbwangawa & Haji all feature on the east coast; Tumbatu is a weekly excursion; & Big Wall at Mnemba (advanced divers only) is favoured over Leven Bank for safety &

quality of marine life. EADC also has bases within Essque Zalu, Royal Zanzibar, Z Hotel, Ras Nungwi Beach Hotel & DoubleTree by Hilton; for hotel guests confined water assessments take place in the pool at Z, Ras Nungwi or Royal Zanzibar. *US$100/190/420 (plus US$30 to Mnemba Atoll) for 2/4/10 dives; Discover Scuba US$130; Open Water US$500; Advanced US$450; Nitrox US$300.*

✐ Spanish Dancer Dive Centre [202 A5] **☎** 024 224 0091; **m** 0777 417717/430005; **e** contact@ spanishdancerdivers.com; www.divinginzanzibar. com. Taking its name from both an attractive marine creature (a nudibranch – a kind of sea slug) & one of its owners' nationalities, Spanish Dancer is based in an open rondavel on South Beach & is run by an impressive team: David & Shee, with 3 other expat dive instructors & 2 dive masters. The team regularly dives 8 sites, including 4 around Mnemba (3–5mins by speedboat), Leven Bank (divers must have a min of 20 logged dives), & for 7 months (Oct–Dec; Apr–Jul) takes advanced divers to waters just south of Pemba. Equipment & integrated BCD/15l steel tanks are in good condition, & are pre-loaded for divers onto their 2 boats (local dhow & speedboat), which are capable of carrying 12–15 divers on 2-tank trips. Mobile phone, oxygen & first-aid kits are standard on all boats, & the instructors & dive masters carry surface marker buoys. The dive centre is PADI 5* accredited & teaches in German, French, Spanish, Hebrew, English & Swahili, with confined water sessions in the lagoon off the beach or at Zanzibar Star Resort in bad weather. *US$110/205/295/445 (plus US$30 for Mnemba) for 2/4/6/10 dives; Discover Scuba US$155; Open Water US$495; Advanced US$395.*

✐ Zanzibar Watersports **☎** 024 223 3309; **m** 0773 165862; **e** info@zanzibarwatersports. com; www.zanzibarwatersports.com. With PADI 5* Gold Palm Instructor Development Centre status, offering all PADI qualifications to instructor level, Zanzibar Watersports is based within the central Paradise Beach Bungalows complex, which is open to everyone. It uses high-quality equipment with a good service & safety record, & top-notch staff. For guests coming to learn to dive, it's worth emailing in advance; there's a home-study option which allows all the Open Water course reading & paperwork to be done before you arrive. Confined-water sessions for beginners are held in the lagoon, with a strict refresher policy means that all divers who have not donned scuba gear for 6 months must do a refresher course on arrival. Between their centre in Kendwa & this satellite operation, there's a raft of permanent instructors, dive masters, reliable local boat captains & snorkel crew to keep everything shipshape on board their large dhows: 2 of these are capable of taking 10 divers on a 2-tank dive trip, whilst the other 2 sailing dhows are used for sunset cruises & snorkelling trips. Dive sites are predominantly on the west side of the island; though trips to Mnemba are also run regularly. The 12 sites they most frequently visit are painted on the centre's wall; they vary according to visibility & weather conditions. Trips to Leven Bank & Mnemba's Big Wall are strictly for advanced divers & above. Dive departure times vary & may require a short minivan transfer if the water in the lagoon is too shallow for their boat. Safety is taken seriously with life-rings, lifejackets & first-aid equipment on all boats, plus a thorough safety briefing including a lesson on using the onboard radio. There are also 1- & 2-man kayaks & wakeboarding equipment available & sunset dhow cruises for the more sedentary visitor. *US$65/115/310/460 (plus US$45 for Mnemba) for 1/2/6/10 dives excluding equipment; Refresher US$30; Open Water US$499; Advanced US$450; kayaks US$10pp/hr; waterskiing US$50/15mins.*

Sailing Aside from local sunset dhow trips, there are few opportunities to sail on board more modern vessels on this stretch of coast. For live-aboard 'learn-to-sail' options and simple cruising, *Julia* (see below), is the only real option.

Dive 'n' Sail Zanzibar m 0774 441234; e info@dive-n-sail.com/yachtjulia@hotmail. com; www.dive-n-sail.com. Dive 'n' Sail operates a lovely 50ft Admiral catamaran, *Julia*, specialising in live-aboard dive trips & fishing excursions to Pemba & Mafia. Available for charter with its own professional skipper, chef, deckhand & optional dive instructor, the boat is fully equipped for diving & deep-sea fishing. On board are 4 en-suite dbl cabins, a large galley & saloon area complete with stereo & DVD player, an outside deck & sunbathing trampoline. Complete with a Bauer 'Mariner' dive compressor for refilling tanks, it has 8 full sets of dive equipment, including 16 aluminium cylinders, BCDs, regulators, depth gauges, weight-belts & weights. With some notice, PADI Advanced Open Water & speciality courses can be taught on board. Dinner usually comprises the daily catch, so fishing is a frequent activity. Day or overnight trips to the reefs around Mnemba are possible, although the boat is more likely to be used by serious divers for week-long ventures to Pemba. *US$1,320/day private boat charter (1–5 persons) for min 4 days, excluding dives; dives US$42/dive for first 10 dives, then US$36; US$108pp Mnemba Island snorkelling day trip (min 4 persons); US$66 dive supplement; US$480 ½-day fishing.*

Fishing Nungwi's proximity to some of Africa's best deep-sea fishing grounds – Leven Bank and the deep Pemba Channel – offers serious anglers outstanding fishing opportunities (for details on the fishing seasons see the box on page 98). In addition to the weather-beaten local dhows that plough the coastal waters, four operators currently offer game fishing in fully equipped, custom-built boats.

🐟 **Fishing Zanzibar** [202 C2] e info@ fishingzanzibar.com; www.fishingzanzibar. com. Operated by Gerry Hallam (owner of Gerry's Bar), Fishing Zanzibar have 4 sport-fishing boats based in Nungwi: *Unreel, Surreel, Cobia* & *Sansuli*, as well as a 50ft sailing yacht, *Walkabout*. The sport-fishing boats are kitted out with a stand-up fishing chair, outriggers, downriggers, Shimano fishing gear (line classes 25–80lb) & a full selection of lures, & take small charter groups (max 4 anglers) to Leven Bank & the Pemba Channel. Night fishing for broadbills is an option, as are live-aboard trips. As members of the International Game Fish Association, a catch-&-release approach to billfish & sharks is encouraged, except when fish are injured or in the event of a possible record catch. *US$500–1,000 ½ day; US$1,000–2,000 full day, including lunch; live-aboard US$1,300–2,500/day for 4 persons; rates vary by boat.*

8

Game Fish Tours [203 H3] m 0772 074766; e gamefishlodge@gmail.com; www. gamefishlodgezanzibar.wordpress.com. Based out of Game Fish Lodge (page 212), this South African operation runs half-day, night fishing & 2-day Pemba tours for reef & bottom fishing. They have 2 boats: *El Shaddai* & *Karambisi*. The former is a 14ft fibreglass Super Dolphin ski boat kitted out with a fish-finder & Penn & Scarborough tackle; the latter is a Magnum 25ft game-fishing vessel offering plenty of deck space & a harness chair for fighting fish. Focusing on the serious game-fishing market, *Karambisi* has Shimano Tiagra 30WA, 50WA & 80WA rods & reels spooled with IGFA yellow 15kg, 24kg & 36kg fishing line, 8″ Scarborough reels spooled with Berkley Whiplash Pro 37.8kg Dacron line & a selection of lures, feathers & rapalas. *Karambisi* also has a toilet & sleeping facilities so is used for the multi-day Pemba trips. *US$900/ day charter (3 persons); US$1,800–2,700 for 3–5 day Zanzibar package (inc fishing & lodge accommodation; 1–3 anglers).*

Zanzibar Fishing [202 A3] m 0773 235030; e info@zanzibarwatersports.com; www. zanzibarfishing.com. One of the best game-fishing operations on Zanzibar, & certainly the longest established, Zanzibar Fishing is a division of Zanzibar Watersports (page 220). They are extremely well kitted out for both professional fishermen & have-a-go holidaymakers, with 3 sport-fishing boats, professional tackle & international safety equipment. *Baloo*, a custom built Sport Fishing 35 is used to access distant fishing grounds, *Timimi*, a custom-built Windy 24 with a fighting chair for big-game fishing, & *Suli Suli*, a 24ft T-top fibreglass boat with open decks for fly fishing, are all available for guest use. On board modern, purpose-built fittings, experienced

skippers & a raft of state-of-the-art technology are utilised. A full set of tackle is provided along with Shimano, Fenwick, Harnell or KC rods & Shimano or Penn international reels, spooled with 80lb, 50lb & 30lb mono line, although you can bring your own if preferred. Tag-&-release fishing is encouraged for all big fish unless it is the fisherman's 1st-ever catch, his biggest to date, or if it is likely to be an east African or All Africa record. ½-day (5hr) outings depart at either 06.30 or 13.30; whole days (8hrs) depart 06.30. Rates include charter of boat, skipper, bait, tackle, equipment & lunch or snacks. *US$450/600 half/full day on Suli Suli; US$600/850 half/full day on Timimi; US$750/950 half/full day on Baloo.*

Extreme Blue Water Spearfishing [202 A3] m 0787 138642/0689 138642/0777 138642/0778 138642; e info@extremebluewaterspearfishing.com; www.extremebluewaterspearfishing.com. Sharing an office with Zanzibar Watersports at Paradise Beach Bungalows, Extreme Blue is a separate company offering beginner to advanced courses in free diving & spearfishing from both Nungwi & Paje. Day & live-aboard trips are both possible with trophy fish such as wahoo, black marlin, giant trevally, barracuda, dorado, snapper, dogtooth & yellowfin tuna all being hunted. In so far as is possible with this activity, the team here appear to support 'ethical spearfishing' by varying hunting grounds, selecting fish carefully, only spearfishing whilst free diving (no underwater breathing kit allowed) & minimising waste by selling excess catch (profits to a village project fund). *US$180/280 ½-/full-day spearfishing; US$700– 1,000 ½-/full-day sport fishing. Live-aboard trips available with advance booking.*

Kiteboarding

Kiteboarding In recent years, kiteboarding has grown in popularity and Nungwi is no exception. Steady winds (approx 15–20 knots) for most of the year, level beaches, warm clear water and protected, shallow lagoons make it a great place for both beginners and more experienced kiters. The quiet, long, sandy beach on the eastern side of Nungwi cape allows for easy launching and landing, although, like all of Zanzibar's east coast, the tidal change is significant and this affects the exposed beach area. The fringe reef here creates a calm and sheltered lagoon, which is ideal for kiting, and from May to September there are great opportunities for wave-riding and surfing. There is no seaweed farming here, and consequently no danger from concealed underwater canes. It's worth checking if centres are certified by the International Kiteboarding Organisation (IKO) if you are interested in quality assurance and training courses.

Kiteboarding Zanzibar [202 B3]

e kiteboardingzanzibar@gmail.com; www.
kiteboardingzanzibar.com. Kiteboarding Zanzibar
is IKO certified, using up-to-date Cabrinha, NPX &
Dakine equipment, with qualified, experienced staff
on hand for safety & lessons. Their Nungwi base
is in a small but neat, thatched chalet alongside
Zanzibar Parasailing, whilst a kite-mobile is used
to transfer kit & kiters to selected beaches in
Nungwi & Matemwe (season dependent – Nungwi
Jun–end Sep; Matemwe end Dec–Mar), & perform
on-the-spot maintenance & repairs. Under the
management of Seif Hassan, there are usually 2–4
instructors based here, approx 15 kites, & with proof
of certification you can hire equipment here, as well
as sign up for lessons.

Motorised watersports The last few years have seen a dramatic change in the
range of aquatic activities offered on the north coast. Once strictly a swimming,
snorkelling, diving and fishing place, Nungwi now has several companies offering
increasingly thrilling, motorised watersports. From stunt wakeboarding to sedate
parasailing, and jet-ski safaris to fast-paced banana boats, the coastal waters are
significantly busier and the range of activities vastly increased.

Zanzibar Parasailing [202 A3] ⟍0779

073078; e hello@zanzibarparasailing.com; www.
zanzibarparasailing.com. Parasailing flights
arrived in Nungwi about 5 years ago and they are
a popular diversion. This Turkish-run company
uses specially adapted boats, & participants are
harnessed to a parasail & then winched into the
air from a platform at the rear of the accelerating
boat. It's unquestionably thrilling & offers
spectacular island panoramas. Solo or tandem
'flights' are possible, as is an optional dip in the
sea on your descent. The flight itself is 10mins

JET-SKIS: THINK BEFORE YOU HIRE

Jet-skiing is one of the fastest growing watersports; but its arrival on the
north coast is understandably controversial. For some it is a thrilling addition
to the aquatic activity selection, while for others it is a cause for very real
concern. If you do choose to take to the waves, make it an informed decision.

Firstly, remember that you would be unable to hire a motorbike or a
speedboat without proper training and a licence; a jet-ski is an equally
powerful machine yet neither of these is required. Very careful consideration
of your own abilities and experience is necessary before you hire. The
waters around Nungwi are full of activity: local dhows and ngalawas sailing,
women fishing, carefree holidaymakers swimming and snorkelling, and dive
operators doing scuba training. The risk of collision is potentially quite high if
you find yourself out of control, and the results horrendous to contemplate.

In addition to the safety issues, there are also areas of shallow reef and
diverse resident marine life here, so the environmental impact must be
considered. Underwater sound pollution is one of the probable reasons for
the decline in north shore dolphin sighting, there have already been cases of
damage to the reefs at low tide, and local concerns about the impact on fish
breeding habits are understandable.

If you are still keen to hire, the operators listed on pages 219–21 are reliable:
the machinery is good quality and well maintained. However, there is a danger
in this part of the world that the visible success of a company will encourage
less reputable individuals to begin hiring out secondhand, poorly maintained
jet-skis. This is likely to result in more sound and fuel pollution and a rise in
accidents, so do avoid any casual approaches, however good a deal they
appear to be.

long, though several people may be on your boat, resulting in a trip lasting up to an hour. In spite of the company's name, parasailing is only one of the thrill-seeking water activities available. Escorted Tumbatu jet-ski safaris (identical in nature to those offered by Zanzibar Watersports, page 220), stereo or mono waterskiing with lessons are available too, & wakeboarding, knee-boarding, fly-boarding & an 8-person banana boat or ringos are also on offer. On a practical note, jet-ski drivers must be over 16, though no experience is necessary; parasailing is open to anyone over 8. *Parasailing US$100/130 solo/ tandem; jet-ski safari US$220/250 1–2 riders/ bike; jet-ski rental US$60/15mins; waterskiing US$45/10mins; wakeboarding US$45/10mins;*

banana boat US$20pp/15mins; ringos US$30pp/10mins; fly-boarding US$100/20mins. 6% on debit/credit card payments.

Zanzibar Watersports See page 220 for full details. Escorted jet-ski safaris (*75mins*) head from the Paradise Beach base in Nungwi to Tumbatu, where riders can have a quick swim before pushing on to Kendwa & back around the coast to the watersports centre. Drivers must be over 16 & no experience is necessary; passengers can be as young as 8. 2011 Yamaha 110 HP 4-Stroke jet-skis can also be hired for individual use. Parasailing, kitesurfing & waterskiing can also been arranged. *Jet-ski safari US$180/200 1–2 riders/bike; jet-ski rental US$50/15mins.*

Spa and well-being

Temporary henna tattoos have long been de rigueur in Nungwi. Painted onto your skin by friendly local ladies on the beach, they seem to be a rite of passage for backpackers. As elsewhere on Zanzibar, the beach and bars are full of people with vaguely Arabic- or Celtic-style rings round their biceps. Many clearly believe they look cool; the reality seems highly variable though. Be warned that the henna can badly mark bed linen, which naturally annoys the hotel owners – many will charge for stains. For all-out African beach chic, hair-braiding services are also available by the same ladies, along with basic beach massages. For a less public massage experience, try one of the following.

Baraka White House Spa & Boutique [202 A5] In a small, immaculate room adjoining Baraka's Restaurant on West Beach, 2 very friendly therapists, Harriet & Tina, offer excellent treatments on kanga-covered massage tables. From deep muscle rubs to Indian head massage, foot treatments to facials, their super little business offers them all. They are both beauty-trained, with Harriet previously having worked in Bluebay's commended East Coast Spa, so the standard is above that available on the beach; that said, this is not in any way a 'spa'. *Body treatments US$20/hr; manicures US$10.*

Malaika Spa [202 B4] Alongside & linked with Safina Bungalows, this small, neat massage room is home to friendly Conchesta. Trained in Dar, she offers scrubs, facials, beauty treatments & spice oil massages, both aromatherapy & Ayurvedic. The room is fan cooled, & she tries hard to ensure guests relax & enjoy their treatment. *Body treatments US$30/hr; manicures US$10.*

Peponi Spa [203 H4] e info@rasnungwi.com. Set in the tropical gardens of Ras Nungwi Beach Hotel (page 211), Peponi Spa offers both guests &

non-residents 'an array of rejuvenating, pampering & holistic treatments'. It is the area's best spa by far. Run by internationally qualified therapists & using natural oils & ingredients, treatments are carried out in calm, minimalist rooms decorated with stylish monochrome photographs, billowing linen curtains & freshly picked red hibiscus flowers. With the soothing music & intoxicating aromas of a professional spa operation, this is a wonderfully relaxing place to spend a few hours, & who could resist the 90min 'Nungwi Earth Soul Signature African Celebration'? *Body treatments US$40– 115/45–75mins; manicures US$55/hr; waxing & eyebrow tinting/threading US$20–37.*

The Zalu Zanzibar Spa [203 G2] m 0778 683960; e ezz.retreat@essquehotels.com. Within the Essque Zalu Hotel (page 211), this small spa pavilion fans out into sweet-smelling treatment rooms, a Vichy shower room, a sauna/steam & gym area. Using healing EARTH products that blend the organic oils of indigenous African plants, the small team of therapists offer a range of beauty treatments, massages, body polishes & finishing touches from waxing to manicures. There are loungers amid the encircling gardens for pleasant pre- & post-treatment chilling, though the space is limited & it's not a place for all-day relaxing. *Facials US$120/90mins; body treatments US$80–280/60mins–3½hrs; manicures US$55/hr.*

Zanzi Yoga [202 B2] m 0776 310227; e info@yogazanzibar.com; www.yogazanzibar.com. Founded by South African Marisa van Vuuren, Zanzi Yoga, based at Flame Tree Cottages (page 206), offers individual yoga sessions & longer retreats year-round. Trained in India, Marisa is a registered teacher with the worldwide Yoga Alliance, & teaches relaxation, pranayama (breathing techniques), sun salutations, asanas (postures) & reiki. The teaching comes from Hatha Yoga based on the Ashtanga Primary Series

sequence, & classes are suitable for all levels with small groups ensuring a personal approach & flexibility. Yoga Retreats include morning & sunset yoga classes (08.00 & 17.15; duration 1 ½ hrs) in the cotton-covered garden pavilion or the sea-facing rooftop, followed by breathing & meditation, & short discussions on yogic techniques. This a lovely option for those seeking some body & mind well-being. Life coaching, fire poi workshops & mandala painting are also available, & more recently, Marisa has teamed up with Argentinian dancer Carlos Forte-Berg to offer tango courses (e *info@tangozanzibar.com; www.tangozanzibar.com*), either standalone or in conjunction with a yoga package.

Turtle sanctuaries

There are two neighbouring operations that allow close-up turtle viewing in Nungwi's tidal pools. Clear signposts will take you to either, but please read the descriptions of both carefully before planning a visit, as their backgrounds and motives are quite different.

Baraka's Turtle Aquarium Owned by Mr Baraka of Baraka Beach Bungalows (page 208) on West Beach, this aquarium is signposted at a bend in the road on the way to the East Beach area. It opened in direct competition with the long-established sanctuary scheme at the neighbouring Mnarani Natural Aquarium. Although it has a lovely tidal pool with a couple of large parrotfish, pretty Picasso fish, red snapper & 15 resident green turtles, all of whom appear to be healthy & well fed (for US$4.50 they practically leap out of the pool to take seaweed from your hand), this is fundamentally a business & not a conservation project. To compound this, we were saddened to be told by a very friendly, if ill-informed, manager that not only could we swim with the turtles (US$6), but that if we held onto the flippers 'like a motorbike' we could ride them, too. Clearly, this is a practice to be discouraged in every way & your support is probably better directed at the original rehabilitation & research scheme next door (see listing below).

Mnarani Natural Aquarium [203 E1] www.mnarani.com; 09.00–18.00 daily. Hawksbill turtles have traditionally been hunted around Zanzibar for their attractive shells, & green turtles for their meat. In 1993, with encouragement from Eco+Culture Tours (page 333), & tremendous assistance from a team of dedicated marine

biologists & conservationists, the local community opened the Mnarani Natural Aquarium. In the shadow of the lighthouse, at the northernmost tip of Zanzibar Island, it was created around a large, natural, tidal pool in the coral rock behind the beach. Originally set up to rehabilitate & study turtles that had been caught in fishing nets, the aquarium project expanded to ensure that local baby turtles were also protected. Turtles used to nest frequently on Nungwi Beach, although sadly, in some part due to hotel lighting, this is now a rare occurrence. If a nest is found, village volunteers now mark & monitor new nests, whilst local fishermen rescuing turtles caught in their nets receive a small fee. The resulting hatchlings are carried to small plastic basins & small concrete tanks at the aquarium where they remain for 10 months. By this time, they have grown to 25cm & their chances of survival at sea are dramatically increased. All bar 1 of these turtles are then released into the sea, along with the largest turtle from the aquarium pool. The 1 remaining baby turtle is then added to the pool, ensuring a static population of 17 turtles. Currently, this equates to 4 hawksbills (Sw: *ng'amba*), identified by the jagged edge on their shell, sharper beak & sardine diet, & 13 seaweed-loving green turtles (Sw: *kasakasa*). The aquarium manager, Mr Mataka Kasa, keeps a logbook detailing all eggs, hatchlings & releases. On 5 Jun 2005, the sanctuary released its first tagged turtle as part of a worldwide monitoring programme, & now all large turtles are released with an 'address tag' to track their movements. In spite of the aquarium being little more than a glorified rock pool, it's fascinating to see the turtles at close quarters. Further, the money raised secures the project's future & goes towards local community schemes, in a bid to demonstrate the tangible value of turtle conservation to the local population. With luck, this will lessen the trade in souvenir shell products & ensure the species' survival. When timing your visit, the water is clearest about 2hrs before high tide (Sw: *maji kujaa*). *US$5; 50% discount for children.*

Village life

Dhow-building and harbour activity
As well as being a tourist destination, Nungwi is also the centre of Zanzibar's traditional dhow-building industry. A number of hardwood trees, particularly good for boats, grow in this area (or at least did grow here, until they were chopped down to be made into boats). Generations of skilled craftsmen have worked on the beach outside the village, turning planks of wood into strong ocean-going vessels, using only the simplest of tools.

It is a fascinating place to see dhows in various stages of construction, but do show respect for the builders, who are generally indifferent towards visitors, and keep out of the way. Most do not like having their photos taken (ask before you use your camera, or join the village tour listed below for easier opportunities), although a few have realised that being photogenic has a value, and will reasonably ask for payment.

Fishing continues to employ many local men, and it's magical to watch the fishing boats bobbing in the sparkling waves of the morning, and then set out to sea in the late afternoon. There can be as many as 40 going out at once, their distinctive lateen sails silhouetted against the evening sky – it's probably been unchanged for centuries. Early in the morning, around 06.00, they return with their catch to the beach fish market. The spectacle is worth the early start, but if you don't make it, there's a smaller re-run at around 15.00 each day.

Like the east coast, Nungwi's other key marine industry centres on its seaweed. Local women tend this recently introduced crop on the flat area between the beach and the low-tide mark. The seaweed is harvested, dried in the sun and sent to Zanzibar Town for export (see box, pages 278–9, for more details).

Cultural village tour
(*US$15pp*) The base for the Nungwi Cultural Village Tours is adjacent to Mnarani Aquarium, and indeed run by the same volunteers. From the clearly marked bungalow, the 2-hour walks take in the aquarium, fish market (best visited early morning when the day's catches are landed), mosques, dhow-builders, basket-weavers and even touch on the uses of surrounding medicinal trees. A pleasant, guided trip, it offers visitors a different view of the community here, and gives photographers a great opportunity to capture the dhow-builders (always ask permission first). The money generated from these tours goes back into the community and is donated to a range of beneficiaries, from the kindergarten to the dhow-builders.

Lighthouse
[203 E1] The lighthouse at Ras Nungwi is still in operation, although it is not open to visitors. As it is a designated 'strategic point', photographing it is officially not allowed; the marines on guard may point this out. There have been a few muggings in this area, so be aware when walking on the cut-through pathways here, especially if carrying expensive cameras, and be sensible about walking here in anything other than broad daylight.

On the west coast, about 4km south of Nungwi, is the tiny, linear village and beautiful beach of Kendwa. Once offering relief from the noise and crowded development of Nungwi, its glorious, wide, sandy beach catered almost exclusively to free-spirited budget travellers and those in search of simple escapism – that is, until the arrival of La Gemma Dell'Est in late 2005. It's now somewhat less serene. A clutch of neighbouring, luxurious resorts now line its shore and the simple beach huts of old are increasingly hard to find. Unlike some areas, however, the developments here are generally well landscaped, low-level and on large plots, giving a greater sense of space and making it peaceful place to chill out. A few original beach bars remain, alongside the beachfront hotel restaurants and their banks of carefully guarded loungers, and there are three great dive schools. The beach also benefits from less extreme tidal changes than the east coast, making swimming possible all day long. Things do liven up in the evenings, with bonfires, barbeques and serious full-moon beach parties, attracting island-wide crowds, but otherwise Kendwa is still a relative haven of peace – you just have to negotiate the island's worst approach road to get here!

GETTING THERE AND AWAY From Nungwi you can simply **walk** along the beach at low tide. If you plan on doing this, it's imperative that you are aware of tide times before setting off: with steep coral cliff bordering the beach, there is nowhere to escape the incoming tide. It is also worth noting that there have been a few incidents of robbery on the 1.5km stretch of beach between Baobab Beach Bungalows and Diamonds La Gemma Dell'Est, so single travellers are not advised to take this route.

A good option is to travel by **boat** or **canoe** from Nungwi. Several places in Kendwa run a free transfer service, or it's easy to find a local boatman who will take you for a few dollars, but do check their reliability with others first.

If you're **driving**, turn off the main road about 4km south of Nungwi, and follow the very rough, badly potholed, undulating track for about another 2km. A high-clearance vehicle is essential. The public **bus** (Route 14) and **dalla dallas** (No 116) from Zanzibar Town to Nungwi will drop you off at the same junction on the tar road, leaving you to walk the final 20 minutes to the sea.

WHERE TO STAY *Map, page 228*
All of Kendwa's accommodation choices are on the coast; there are no village-stay options here. None of the hotels on this stretch have a salubrious approach, be they award-winning, members of leading hotels of the World or village guesthouses.

Exclusive

Diamonds Star of the East (11 villas)
024 224 0125; e info.sote@diamonds-resorts.com; staroftheeast.diamonds-resorts.com. A hotel within a hotel, Star of the East is the swish new sibling of La Gemma, & sits within its grounds, though masked from view & guests by a high wall & grandiose tower entrance. A member of Small Luxury Hotels of the World, the 1- & 2-bedroomed villas are seriously stylish: amazing contemporary bedrooms are flooded with natural light. There are high-end fixtures & fittings, waterfalls & fountains, walk-in wardrobes, indoor & outdoor showers, a glazed courtyard, a beautiful keyhole pool in the spacious garden, cushioned daybeds, & a lounge with all the latest mod cons. If you need anything, personal butlers carry pagers 24/7 & have 6mins to be at your beck & call! The fine-dining Ocean Blue restaurant & Tiara Lounge are in a thatched building at the centre of the complex, around which the pool snakes seductively. It's stylised & very sophisticated, but it all comes with an exceptional price tag, & however luxurious, it's hard to justify when the resort is not directly on the beach & is surrounded by an all-inclusive resort & neighbouring Hideaway of Nungwi. There are far more private places at this end of the market, not that this appears to be affecting occupancy levels. Access to all the facilities at La Gemma is included. Al.

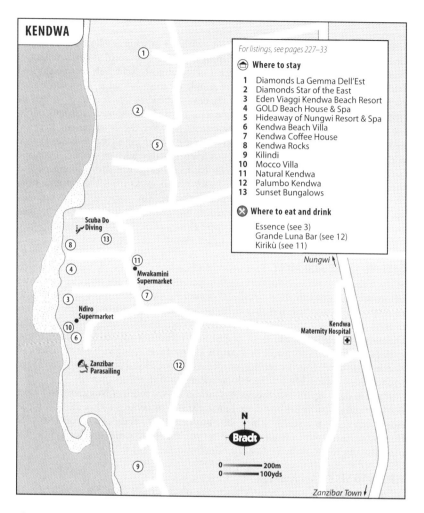

KENDWA

Scuba Do Diving

Mwakamini Supermarket

Ndiro Supermarket

Zanzibar Parasailing

Nungwi ↗

Kendwa Maternity Hospital ✚

Zanzibar Town ↓

N

Bradt

0 ▬▬▬ 200m
0 ▬▬▬ 100yds

⌂ **GOLD Beach House & Spa** (67 rooms)
m 0779 700005; e info@goldzanzibar.com;
www.goldzanzibar.com. Opened in 2013, GOLD
is a smart, stylish & (predominantly) all-inclusive
resort aimed squarely at couples in search of a
slick, contemporary beach bolthole. From the
ochre, circular reception, charming staff escort new
arrivals to the low-lying bungalows, all tucked
amid neatly manicured pathways & gardens.
Rooms here are impressive, even in the entry-level
Deluxe Garden room. Spacious, split-level rooms
are delightfully cool, with a smart cappuccino &
cream colour palette, bespoke moulded-concrete
beds swathed in gold-edged mosquito nets
& facing patio doors to take in the view; well-
appointed bathrooms & all the necessary in-room

mod cons. 3 beautiful beachfront villas are also
on offer for friends or families, but this hotel
feels very much like a couples' retreat. Meals are
served buffet style – Chinese to Swahili – in the
Kilimanjaro Restaurant (lunch US$24), or à la carte
Italian at the smaller Gold Restaurant (dinner
US$34); whilst sundowners & after-dinner drinks
are in the Omani-influenced Sultan's Bar, with its
coloured lanterns, shapely arches & cushioned
baraza benches. There is a distinctly adult air
to this resort – no children running around or
interactive guest games; instead guests spend
their time soaking up the sunshine by the large
saltwater pool or relaxing in the 6 lilac rondavels
that make up the inviting Healing Earth Spa
(⊕ 09.00–20.00, daily). Non-residents can hang

out here, too, by purchasing a US$24 'Day at Leisure' pool pass (excl Xmas & New Year). Al. ☗
🏠 **Hideaway of Nungwi Resort & Spa** (102 rooms) m 0758 818281; e info@hideawaynungwi.com; www.hideawaynungwi.com. Along a bumpy track from La Gemma Dell'Est, & past a less than pleasant smoking landfill site, Hideaway of Nungwi would do well to invest in its approach. Beyond the entrance gate, however, lush, tropical gardens of baobabs, palms, flame trees, bananas & pretty flowering shrubs run from the lantern-filled reception down to the beach. From the raised entrance, only the tops of pink castellated roofs & small white domes of the accommodation peep through the vegetation & hint at the subtle Middle-Eastern flavor of the architecture & interiors. Rooms are stylish & sophisticated: crisp linens, Arabian metalwork patterns, top-notch mod cons & idyllic terrace views, whilst the 4 beach villas offer similarly high-quality interiors with the benefit of a private pool & uninterrupted sea view. Epicurean guests are well catered for with several dining venues & cuisines of offer: The Carnivorous unsurprisingly offers 'African game from land & sea'; the indecisive can head to the colonial-inspired terrace of Aqua where buffet meals are available close to all day long; Asian food enthusiasts can enjoy stir fries & sushi amid the smiling buddas & lacquered tables of Ishi Teppanyaki; while Tue & Fri bring themed 'Gala Nights' (evening dress required), held poolside to showcase African & tropical cuisine. Activity choices are just as varied with a professional watersports centre, gym, spa & professional kids' club all onsite. It is worth noting that Hideaway is in fact in Kendwa not Nungwi, contrary to what its name suggests. HB/FB. ☗

❋ 🏠 **Kilindi** (15 rooms) m 0784 250630; e reservations@elewana.com; www.elewanacollection.com. Exclusive & upmarket without being pretentious, the complex offers pavilions spread out over 20ha & overlooking a sweep of white beach. Reminiscent of Greek Orthodox churches, the domed, 2-tier pavilions are dotted among dense, indigenous shrubbery & each is accessed through heavy wooden Zanzibari doors. Rooms are divided into 2 halves, split by a small flight of steps. On one side is the spacious circular bedroom, with a mosquito net-draped dbl bed in the centre & a wardrobe & dressing table around the edge. All are equipped with a safe & a minibar fridge.

Outside is a free-form plunge pool, & the open-sided bathroom with central rain shower, where the sea is visible from the open window. Below this is a tranquil seating area, strewn with cushions & sun loungers. It's strikingly simple with lovely Moorish detailing in the beaten metal lanterns, coloured glass & little indulgences: port decanters to tasty petit fours. With a personal butler to bring you whatever you may desire, including your meals, you may never wish to leave your pavilion. However, if you can be tempted away, head for the attractive restaurant & bar for a spiced mixed fruit juice or a deliciously chilled South African wine. This distinctly colonial chic area oozes a casual, funky vibe. The waterfall behind the bar catches the eye, while the umbrella-shaded deck is perfect for b/fast in the sunshine. Dinner, on the other hand, is served by candlelight next to the infinity pool, & is accompanied by a great selection of world music. The adjoining lounge is adorned with smart black-&-white photographs. The spa offers massages & body wraps in a laid-back atmosphere. Kilindi is also ecologically sensible, with rainwater collected & stored under each pavilion to keep it cool, whilst also providing water for the pools, showers & toilets. With its extensive grounds & stunning accommodation, this is a place for getting away from the stresses of modern life (although Wi-Fi is available). Most definitely one of Zanzibar's top spots! FB. ☗

🏠 **Diamonds La Gemma Dell'Est** (138 rooms) ☎ 024 224 0125; e info.gemma@diamonds-resorts.com; lagemmadellest.diamondsresorts.com. This large hotel is still one of Zanzibar's more stylish large resorts. Sensitive architecture & stunning landscaping create a feeling of tremendous space, while minimal tidal changes allow for all-day swimming in the sea. Rooms have been cleverly built along the natural contours of the landscape, making them appear lower-density & fairly unobtrusive, while also allowing each a sea-view veranda. Approach corridors may be dark, but inside rooms are comfortable, each having a king-sized bed or twin beds with all mod cons & an en-suite marble bathroom. Thoughtfully planted screens offer privacy on each terrace & the lawns & swathes of established exotic vegetation make a beautiful foreground to the setting sun over the Indian

Ocean. The private, raised wide beach has nice loungers & makuti umbrellas dotted around the raked sand. The enormous, floodlit pool is also set right on the beach, with a children's area, jacuzzi, waterfall & swim-up cocktail bar. There is hotel security on the beach to ensure no hassle for sunbathers yet Kendwa's clutch of beach bungalows & their associated bars & restaurants are an easy 10min walk south.

La Gemma has several bars & restaurants, from the sleek Pavilion serving tasty Mediterranean buffets to the Coral Cove alfresco pizzeria by the pool. The Sunset Lounge on the jetty (🕐 *from 17.00*) is a perfect cocktail spot before an elegant dinner of fresh seafood (lobster omelette, tuna carpaccio, seafood stew) at à la carte Sea Breeze (🕐 *closed Thu*), & dancing above the waves to the DJ from 22.00 or chilling on the turquoise cushions of Café Moresco shisha bar. With the exception of Sea Breeze & the themed Swahili Night in the faux Maasai village, all food & drink is on a totally flexible, all-inclusive basis, & the Italian influence ensures that the food is invariably very good. By day, there's a PADI diving centre operated by Scuba Do (page 233), outdoor gym, countless watersports, beach volleyball, sailing & even snorkelling over the artificial reef to keep everyone occupied; by night, the selection of optional evening entertainment kicks off with everything from quizzes to musical Swahili beach BBQs. Children are well catered for, & the staff's attitude is extremely positive towards families, making La Gemma one of Zanzibar's best choices for young families. AI. **$$$$$–☗**

Luxury

🏠 **Palumbo Kendwa** (30 rooms) m 0776 001300; e booking@palumbokendwa.com; www. palumbokendwa.com. Opposite a bright turquoise house, the striking curved coral rock structure is easy to spot from afar. Past the hibiscus bushes & through the peacock stained-glass door, this off-beat establishment boasts some beautiful, vibrant murals, rustic coral rock & shell walls & a soaring pole & makuti entrance. There's a cool arched bar-cum-lounge downstairs, a rooftop Panorama restaurant (🕐 *b/fast & dinner only*) whose steep access is not for those with vertigo. Rooms are unusually shaped but spacious, clean & with AC, fan, fridge, safe & a balcony overlooking the pool & small garden area. Palumbo is not on the beach,

but operates a shuttle minibus to ferry guests down to its seaside bar & restaurant: Grande Luna (page 232). B&B. **$$–$$$$$**

Upmarket

☀ 🏠 **Natural Kendwa** (6 rooms) m 0778 579146; e naturalkendwavilla@yahoo.it; www. naturalkendwavilla.com. Some of the loveliest accommodation in Kendwa can now be found tucked behind the seafront resorts at this gem of a hotel. Opened late 2015, it is carefully & considerately designed & constructed by its amiable Italian owner, Andrea, who put his heart & considerable experience as a film-set designer into this project. The rooms, of which 2 are suites, are gorgeous: original, contemporary & charming. Expect vibrantly coloured feature walls, indulgent silk throws & pillows, decorative arches, & plenty of practical comforts: AC, safes, built-in fridge, twin marble sinks, a separate toilet & a great shower. The interiors are both simple in style & elaborate in detail, & all are blissfully spacious. One of the suites also has a private kitchen, should you wish to order from the fishermen & make use of the private chef. Outside, manicured tropical gardens slope around the lovely free-form pool & jacuzzi that make for a beautiful setting & thoroughly enjoyable escape from the busy beach. Around the gardens, shaded seating area & on individual terraces, there is bespoke chunky reclaimed dhow furniture & cushions crying out to be sunk into with a good book. Dining is in adjoining restaurant (page 233), which is a highlight in itself; whilst beach days can be spent on the loungers at Kendwa Rocks (page 231), where Natural Kendwa guests can enjoy a free day passes. B&B. **$$$$**

Mid range

🏠 **Eden Viaggi Kendwa Beach Resort** (90 rooms) www.edenviaggi.it. Popular with Italian all-inclusive holidaymakers, rooms here run from the sandy beach, up the coral-rock cliff through sloping, tropical gardens to reception & the bumpy track behind the village. There are 4 categories, from the older rooms in small apricot, castellated buildings to a large 2-storey thatched block of holiday apts & the newly built, spacious deluxes. Those closest to the water command a worthwhile premium. All rooms are simply furnished, have mini fridges, reasonable en-suite facilities, & can accommodate 2–4 people. There is a pool, beach volleyball, soccer, tennis, boules & an extensive all-day entertainment programme. The large beach restaurant & bar (Ngarawa) serves food & drink all day under a huge makuti shade. Alternatively, the Tutti Frutti Bistro dishes up crêpes & gelato to residents only, & there is the à la carte Essence, where tagines & Arab shwarmas are popular with local expats as well as visitors. Although Kendwa Beach is beautiful, the small section immediately north of here is where the village fisherfolk pull ashore & park their dugouts & nets, & can get a little messy; though arguably this is far preferable to the nightly 'theatre' performed on the beach by Eden's Italian staff. AI. **$$$**

🏠 **Kendwa Rocks** (35 rooms) m 0774 415475; e booking@kendwarocks.com; www. kendwarocks.com. The 1st property to open on this stretch of beach, there's a wide range of accommodation offered here, which gets booked up roughly in order of luxury: the best rooms go first! The African-themed coral-stone bungalows have large Zanzibari beds & veranda, plus mains electricity & mosquito nets; most of these can be used for dbl or trpl occupancy. The all-new semi-detached Coconut Bungalows are spread out in a semicircle on a lovely stretch of sand, constructed from coral stone & boasting lots of lights, platform beds, bright blue colour accents, large showers and separate toilets. An inviting batik hammock beckons on the veranda & there's a plunge pool shared between every 2 rooms, with Kiwengwa, Pate & Madagascar enjoying access to particularly large ones. Only a few steps from the sea, their location is excellent, & without question this category is the best available. Away from the beach, towards the road, are 8 rooms in the 2-storey North & South wings; some have nice sea views from the shared balcony, as well as a terrace of simple, motel-style rooms; small, with a shared ablution block, & usually used by guests arriving without a reservation. There is also a 19-bed mixed dorm for groups of off-duty volunteers. On the beach, the Mermaid Bar is the epitome of beachside drinking dens: a hip DJ messes on decks in the corner, smiling staff stand behind a well-stocked bar festooned with laminated lists of cocktails, while sun-kissed travellers recline, chat & drink. In addition, a beach bar has opened on the foreshore, serving Italian coffees, juices & spirits, & is surrounded by chunky timber furniture (the

remnants of a cargo ship) & a bonfire area. The place is totally chilled, so don't expect anything to happen fast, just sit back & enjoy the sea views. On Sat nights (22.30 onwards) the bar hosts live music an infamous beach party (*US$7pp*), a messy affair that's often still in full swing at sunrise. Revellers come from all over the island to experience the cocktails, bonfires, dance beats & acrobatic shows. Things can get a bit rowdy, & the frequency, scale & noise from this event, & other Kendwa copycat events, are starting to change the atmosphere in the area considerably. Complaints from beach-lovers seeking a tranquil retreat are on the rise but if it's your thing, the monthly Full Moon Party is well worth checking out. For the rest of the month, The Rocks Lounge, in the middle of the 3-storey coconut clad building behind the bar, is a late-night drinking & dancing venue. By contrast, the top floor is a large open shaded terrace offering massage & mani/pedi treatments from palm-view loungers. B&B. **$$–$$$$$**

🏠 **Sunset Bungalows** (80 rooms) m 0777 413818; e info@sunsetkendwa; www. sunsetkendwa.com. An increasingly faded, upturned surfboard on the beach marks Sunset Bungalows' location. Set back from the sea, 2 widely separated rows of extremely pleasant bungalows have been built of either timber or stone, with bold fabrics, mains electricity, an electronic safe & AC in some. A terrace in front of each looks out onto sand & feathery casuarinas. Higher up, on the coral cliff above the beach, the standard rooms (no AC) are in thatched cottages dotted around a pretty garden, overflowing with hibiscus & bougainvillea. Huge 'apt' buildings at the rear offer spacious rooms with high ceilings, coconut-wood furniture, built-in cushioned baraza benches & garden-view terraces. 2 large apricot-coloured buildings, Chaza & Lulu, each have spacious rooms with sweeping views over baby palms. The surfboard out front is in fact the sign for a sizeable beachside structure, once a backpackers' drinking den known as the 'Bikini Bar', but now clearly aiming at a more affluent crowd – though Happy Hour has stuck (⏱ *15.30–18.30; 2 cocktails for US$7*). Outside, on wide wooden decking, diners indulge in Zanzibari curries with chapattis (*US$5–8*), stone-baked pizza (*US$4–5*) & surf 'n' turf grills (*US$8–10*). On the beach in front is a shaded hammock area & a bonfire pit surrounded by wooden benches, making it a popular after-

8

dinner drinks spot, while floodlit beach volleyball keeps the energetic entertained, & the relaxed laze in the local massage tent. Its quaint beach retreat vibe may have faded with development, but it remains a reliably good choice & is remarkably convenient for divers using Scuba Do (page 233). Be warned, though – the DJ at the Fri night beach party could well be spinning his discs until gone 04.00. B&B. **$$–$$$**

Budget

🏠 **Kendwa Beach Villa** (7 rooms) No contact details. Neighbouring Mocco Villa on a tiny plot, this place seems to be in a perpetual state of semi-completion & is very basic. Accessed up concrete stairs from the beach, the spartan rooms are off a dark central corridor & boast little: orange lino floors, simple beds & an adequate toilet & cold-water shower. Some rooms have a fan, though only some work, & all have dim electrical lighting. There is a thatched beach restaurant, which is a popular hangout for Italian package holidaymakers, & it's best to ask for Mohammed if you're looking for a room. B&B. **$$**

🏠 **Kendwa Coffee House** (2 rooms) m 0774 162536; e kendwacoffeehouse@gmail.com. Immediately alongside the main access road to Kendwa's beach hotels, this village guesthouse is run by friendly Aussie Nadine & her Zanzibari husband, Kombo. Opened in 2013, they currently have 2 simple guestrooms in their bungalow, each offering a clean & basic en-suite bedroom with Zanzibari beds, woven palm mats on the concrete floor & a gleaming shower room. Outside, a private veranda is allocated to each

room, overlooking the narrow strip of sandy garden & its cluster of fragrant frangipani trees. Oversized potted plants, handmade shell screens & prayer flags fluttering in the trees all hint at the gentle, homely feel of this place. Tables are neatly arranged in the sand for coffees, light lunches & evening BBQs, & there's a little shop for picking up local handicrafts or forgotten flip-flops. It's pretty dusty being next to the road, but it's relatively good value for being only a few mins' walk from the beach (albeit not on the beach), & is one of the limited budget options in Kendwa these days as the larger resorts take over. B&B. **$$**

🏠 **Mocco Beach Villa** (16 rooms) 024 550 0646; m 0777 504516; e bookings@ moccobeachvilla.co.tz; www.moccobeachvilla. co.tz. Rebuilt in 2010 following a fire, this small, single-unit villa is in fact a collection of independent rooms. Sitting on the very edge of the coral cliff at the southern end of the beach, Mocco's 4 original rooms are neat & clean with showers & 4-poster beds, although the plastic floor sheeting lets the place down a little. The rooms are all named after island towns, with 'Kidoti' enjoying the best sea view & commanding a consequential supplement. At the back, overlooking a tiny garden, a newer whitewashed block offers very simple rooms, including a family room, & some upstairs accommodation with AC. There is an affiliate restaurant on the beach where cocktails can be enjoyed to MTV tunes & traditional seafood specials are served at comfortable coir sofas. Ask for Juma at the restaurant if you're interested in staying here. B&B. **$$**

✖ WHERE TO EAT AND DRINK *Map, page 228*

Virtually all the hotels on Kendwa Beach have an affiliated beach bar and restaurant offering cold drinks, casual dining and uninterrupted sea views. The menus and quality are close to identical, relying heavily on the day's catch for fresh seafood, with a number of Swahili curry & fresh pizza options. They are all open to anyone who cares to wander by and, as with many places on Zanzibar, this includes a number of friendly (and hungry) neighbourhood cats.

✖ **Essence Restaurant** m 0779 941555. On the beach in front of Eden Viaggi (page 230), this popular hangout serves up daily specials at lunch from US$7.50, before luring beachgoers in for Happy Hour cocktails (🕐 *17.30–19.30*) or tempting romancing couples to a 'Dinner under the Stars' experience: a 4-course seafood affair with

wine & a feet-in-the-sand set up on the beach for US$25pp. **$$$–$$$$$**

✖ **Grande Luna Bar** At the southern end of the beach, under a large makuti thatch is the jolly dining outpost for Palumbo Kendwa (page 230). By day, you can sip US$5 cocktails from your sun lounger (free sunbed, if you buy a drink) whilst listing to gentle African tunes, or order an à la carte lunch for around US$12. Return on a Mon or Wed evening at 22.00 for a chilled reggae party. $$$$

✳ ✕ Kirikù   m 0778 579146; **e** naturalkendwavilla@yahoo.it; www. naturalkendwavilla.com/ristorante; ⏱ 08.00– 16.00 & 18.00–23.00 daily. This fabulous little restaurant adjoining Natural Kendwa (page 230) is a vibrant visual assault: a striking, multi-coloured

Aztec mural covering every internal wall & ceiling. Guests are seated on the floor on red-&-green cushions at coconut-wood tables or at the bijou bar. It's quirky & fun, & a happy place to hang out. Food is part Italian (a testament to the owner's nationality) & part Swahili: biryani (*US$4*), linguini with mussels (*US$10*), pizza (*US$5–6.50*) & indulgent seafood platters (*US$20*). Come for any meal of the day, & you'll likely return for another. $$–$$$

SHOPPING With the increase in accommodation and visitors, Kendwa now has two small, local-style 'supermarkets': **Ndiro Supermarket** on the very edge of the cliff at the southern end of the beach and **Mwakamini Supermarket** on the village side of Kendwa Rocks. Both sell basic supplies of tinned food, crisps, sweets and water, but little else. For **curios**, the ever-increasing span of Maasai-manned stalls on the beach bordering La Gemma offers colourful paintings, beaded jewellery and occasionally carvings, as do the makuti stalls stretching south on the sand from Grande Luna. Quality varies considerably so shop around and don't be blinded by the sun into making second-rate purchases.

WHAT TO SEE AND DO Sunbathing, beach volleyball, diving and snorkelling are the main activities in Kendwa – it's a terribly laidback beach hangout. The vast majority of the hotels and guesthouses will hire out basic snorkelling gear, organise day trips by boat to Tumbatu Island, and offer sunset dhow cruises; some will rent out kayaks, too.

Watersports For fun above and below the waterline, Kendwa has some long-established dive operators and a raft of other motorised and non-motorised activities on offer. You can pick up a mask, snorkel and fins from a basic beach hut for around US$10/day, or head to somewhere more established to guarantee kit condition or arrange more formal activities.

⚓ Zanzibar Parasailing   m 0779 073078; **e** info@zanzibarparasailing.com; www. zanzibarparasailing.com; ⏱ 08.00–18.30 daily. At the southern end of Kendwa beach, next to Ndiro Supermarket, Zanzibar Parasailing is based in a 2-tier structure under high makuti thatch. Buy a US$2 beer on the upper deck & discuss diving & jet-ski hire with the small team. They are one of Kendwa's newer operators & have another branch in Nungwi (page 223). *Snorkelling trips US$40–55 Tumbatu/Mnemba; US$60/80 for 1/2 dives.*
⚓ Scuba Do Diving   ✆ (UK) +44 (0)1326 250773; **m** 0777 417157; **e** do-scuba@scuba-do-zanzibar. com; www.scuba-zanzibar.com. For many years, Scuba Do was Kendwa's only dive operation, & it remains a superb establishment. Owned & operated by a British couple, Christian & Tammy, it is a highly professional & well-equipped dive centre, based on

the beach next to Sunset Bungalows' restaurant (& at La Gemma for resort guests). As well as a thoroughly nice guy, Christian is a PADI Master Instructor & the only Emergency First Response Instructor Trainer in Tanzania; Tammy is a PADI Master Scuba Diver Trainer & exceptional at teaching even the youngest children to snorkel & dive. She is also one of the hyperbaric chamber operators. There are up to 10 permanent dive leaders based here (season dependent), taking a max of 6 divers each to 1 of their repertoire of 20+ reef sites, chosen according to conditions & diver experience. Diving is done from 6 high-powered RIBs (rigid inflatable boats), allowing fast access to dive sites (Mnemba is reached in 30mins, as opposed to nearly 2hrs by dhow), & GPS navigation pinpoints precise dive entry points. There's plenty of good, new equipment – 'Buddy Explorer' BCDs, Sherwood regulators, masks & fins, & Reef wetsuits – & they

8

On the third Saturday of September every year since 2005, the team at Scuba Do Diving has galvanised Kendwa into a successful beach tidy. As part of International Coastal Clean-up Day, co-ordinated by conservation foundations Project AWARE and Ocean Conservancy, the aim is to collect and prevent debris littering seaside locations and aquatic environments, thus protecting their beauty and health. In Kendwa, the initiative has been greeted enthusiastically by villagers, residents, hotel staff and even thoughtful tourists, and their efforts to make a difference are clear: Kendwa does have one of the island's cleanest beaches. Ideally, the village will ultimately take ownership of this event, and to effect this Scuba Do have provided wheelbarrows to help with ongoing collection.

At the first beach clean-up, 82 people (80% being Zanzibari or Tanzanian nationals) collected 108 bags (730kg) of rubbish, but only five years later, in 2015, this had grown to over 145 volunteers and a massive 1,018kg of rubbish removed from the beach, approach roads and underwater. Sadly, the composition of the rubbish is changing too, and while village waste declines, tourist waste increases. Whilst this increase in litter, a manmade mix of drinks bottles, food wrappers, discarded building materials and plastic bags, is disturbing, this community's involvement to better the environment is positive.

Tammy and Christian at Scuba Do are totally committed to their community and work hard throughout the year to educate local schoolchildren and elders, as well as many hotels, about the effects of rubbish on the environment. In an impressively shrewd move, their latest initiative is to photograph the collected rubbish and send the images to companies whose branding is clearly visible. The aim being to request their assistance in promoting social awareness of litter related problems.

Do help their efforts by disposing of rubbish responsibly and if you're on holiday in the area in mid September, don a pair of rubber gloves and join in the clean-up campaign: snorkellers can fill crates in the shallows whilst landlubbers comb the sand. Be sure to guess the total waste weight too, and you may even win a prize at the end of the day.

---

have a code of stringent safety procedures. We were impressed that all divers are issued with surface marker buoys, whilst marine radios maintain contact between boats & base. Their on-site Bauer air compressor is regularly tested, & there's an emergency oxygen re-breather & a full medical kit. As part of this adherence to safety, Scuba Do will not take any divers underwater without proof of their qualification & insist on a US$50 PADI refresher dive with anyone who hasn't been underwater for 6 months or boasts fewer than 100 logged dives. When out of the water, the team are also involved in extensive community work, most notably their commitment to training Zanzibaris & Tanzanians to become qualified dive masters & instructors, & the

annual beach & underwater clean-up project (see box, above). *Snorkelling trips US$45–85 Tumbatu/ Mnemba; US$120/230/330/420 for 2/4/6/8 dives; Discover Scuba US$110; Open Water US$575; Advanced US$370.*

⚓ **Zanzibar Watersports** m 0773 235030; e info@zanzibarwatersports.com; www. zanzibarwatersports.com. The 3rd island base for this established watersports' company is at Kendwa Rocks (page 231). In a purpose-built, thatched bungalow, efficient staff can arrange PADI courses & an array of watersports, both motorised & not, using good-quality equipment. Full company details can be seen in their main Nungwi listing (page 223). *US$65/115/310/460 (plus US$30* *for Mnemba) for 1/2/6/10 dives (inc equipment); refresher US$30; Open Water US$499; Advanced*   *US$310; equipment hire (mask, fins, snorkel) US$15; kayaks US$10pp/hr; waterskiing US$50/15mins.*

REGIONAL EXCURSIONS

There are a handful of worthwhile detours on the road between Zanzibar Town and Nungwi. They're worth a short stop if you're driving this way, and a possible excursion from Nungwi if lying on the beach gets too much.

MKOKOTONI On the west coast of the island, about 21km south of Nungwi, Mkokotoni is a lively fishing village. Although there's no accommodation here that we could find, it's worth a short detour to soak up some rural atmosphere and vibrant village life. The bustling market, where Tumbatuans and local Zanzibaris buy and sell all manner of fresh seafood, is crowded, noisy and full of energy. Around this, an abundance of tumbledown stalls display piles of coconuts, fruits, vegetables and spices, whilst in the harbour behind age-old techniques are used to repair and build the next generation of dhows.

In 1984, a major hoard of Chinese coins was discovered on the beach north of the village, indicating that this was once a prosperous trading port between the East, Arabia and Zanzibar, long before the arrival of the Europeans. Colonial rule brought the few grand administration buildings glimpsed along the central avenue of sweet almond trees, but today village life is still centred on simple trade with neighbours.

Few tourists visit Mkokotoni, and those who do are usually part of a tour *en route* to Tumbatu Island. The village can be accessed on a fast tar road from both Mahonda to the south and Kivunge to the east. By public bus, Route 1 runs hourly from approximately 05.30 to 20.00 from Darajani Terminal in Zanzibar Town to Mkokotoni; as do frequent dalla dallas (No 101) from Creek Road.

FUKUCHANI RUINS Fukuchani Ruins are on the edge of the village of the same name, around 12km south of Nungwi. Beside a large school on the western side of the road, there's a small signpost under a baobab tree which will point you in the right direction, along a track that bisects the local football pitch. The ruins are known locally as the 'Portuguese House', but although some Portuguese settlers may have built houses on Zanzibar during this period, this structure is considered by archaeologists to be of Swahili and not foreign origin. The ruins are well maintained and the surrounding land has been mostly cleared of vegetation.

Built in the 16th century, Fukuchani is a fortified dwelling that may have belonged to a wealthy merchant or farmer. It is constructed of coral bricks, with arched doorways and rectangular niches in the walls of the main room, and surrounded by a stone wall in which small holes have been inserted. It has been suggested that these are gun slits for the purposes of defence, but a more recent theory suggests they may have been to hold projecting beams which supported a raised walkway, so that anyone inside the enclosure could see over the wall. The ruins are in good condition, compared with many others on Zanzibar of a similar age, and quite impressive. Buildings of a similar style have been found at other sites along the East African coast, though – alongside the ruins at Mvuleni – Fukuchani represents the finest domestic stone house architecture of this period.

Behind the ruin, a path leads to a small beach. Across the channel you can see Tumbatu Island, with the lighthouse at its northern tip clearly visible. At the southern end of the island are the remains of a large town, dating from around the 12th century. (For more details, see box, page 236.)

Tumbatu is one of the largest of Zanzibar's offshore islands, measuring about 8km long by 2–3km across. The people of the island, the Watumbatu, speak their own dialect of Swahili. They have a reputation for pride and aloofness, and are reputed not to welcome visitors to their island. The Watumbatu men are traditionally known as the best sailors on Zanzibar, or even on the whole east African coast.

On the southern end of Tumbatu Island are a group of Shirazi ruins, thought to date from the 12th century. An Arab geographer writing in the 13th century recorded that the Muslim people of Zanzibar Island were attacked (by whom is not clear) and retreated to Tumbatu Island where they were welcomed by the local inhabitants, who were also Muslim, and it is assumed that these people were responsible for the Shirazi ruins.

The ruins were probably abandoned in the early 16th century, but the Watumbatu still claim to be descended from Shirazi immigrants.

MVULENI RUINS Mvuleni Ruins lie just to the south of Fukuchani, on the other side of the road (east), where you'll see a small signpost. Next to a few huts and a small shop, a path leads through banana and palm plantations to reach the site. Like Fukuchani, this structure was probably once a fortified house that would have belonged to a powerful member of the community. It, too, was thought to be the work of Portuguese invaders until recent research suggested that it is more likely to be Swahili in origin. The house was once larger than the one at Fukuchani, with thicker walls, but the ruins are in poor condition, and are partly overgrown, obscuring some of the architectural features. Substantial sections of the walls remain standing, though, complete with carved door arches, conveying something of the impressive building that this once was. One of the most interesting features of this house is the large natural cavern just northeast of the house, outside the main wall. Crystal-clear, salt water flows through the cave, collecting in a pool visible beyond an entrance fringed by vegetation: this was probably a source of water when the house was occupied.

9

Northeastern Zanzibar

The northeast coast of Zanzibar boasts an almost continuous expanse of picture-perfect beach; it's arguably the island's greatest attraction for visitors. Stretching from Nungwi on the northernmost tip of the island (covered in *Chapter 8*) to the mangrove swamps of Chwaka Bay, the superb, powder white-sand beaches of the northeastern coastline are breathtaking in length and beauty. Less than 1km offshore, waves break along the fringe reef that runs the length of the island, and the warm, turquoise waters of the Indian Ocean attract divers, swimmers and fishermen. Bordering the sand, an almost unbroken strip of picturesque coconut palms provides shade for traditional fishing villages and sunbathing honeymooners, and completes many people's vision of paradise.

The beaches along Zanzibar's east coast slope very little. Consequently, when the tide is out, the water retreats a long way, making swimming from the beach difficult. It does, however, allow for fascinating exploration along the top of the exposed reef. Washed-up seaweed can also be a surprise here for uninformed visitors, (see box, page 261).

Compared with those found in Nungwi to the north, the accommodation choices in the northeast tend to have more space, both in their private grounds and between properties. However, most are still within easy walking distance along the seashore, and make useful refreshment stops on long beach walks. The central stretch of the coast around Kiwengwa is the busiest, with its cluster of large, Italian, package-holiday resorts, but there has been less tourism development to the north or south of this area, and it's still possible to find some lovely, individual places that seem to be virtually on their own.

Access from Zanzibar Town to the east coast is easy, on both private and public transport. The extension of the tar road has improved the journey and shortened transfer times, though close to the sea there is currently little more than a narrow, bumpy track connecting the villages from Pongwe to Matemwe, necessitating very slow progress and either a 4x4 vehicle or the hastening of the end for your vehicle's suspension.

MATEMWE

A long, linear village, Matemwe is the most northerly of the east coast settlements. Although less than 20km south of Nungwi, it marks the end of the coastal road heading north. It's a quintessential Swahili fishing village: little houses set among masses of elegant coconut palms with dhows and *ngalawa* (dugout canoes) bobbing in the water. The sand is so white and smooth here that the wind blows it into mounds that look like snowdrifts. In spite of some recent expansion, this remains a quieter section of coast, with some great accommodation options and the added bonus of swift access to Mnemba's reefs for divers.

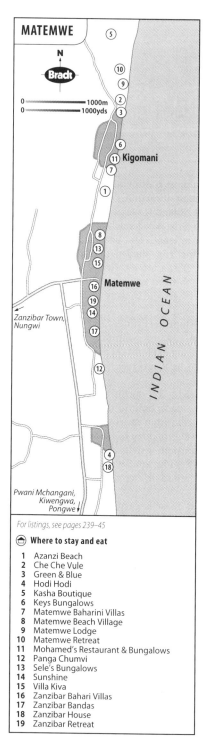

For listings, see pages 239–45

Where to stay and eat

1 Azanzi Beach
2 Che Che Vule
3 Green & Blue
4 Hodi Hodi
5 Kasha Boutique
6 Keys Bungalows
7 Matemwe Baharini Villas
8 Matemwe Beach Village
9 Matemwe Lodge
10 Matemwe Retreat
11 Mohamed's Restaurant & Bungalows
12 Panga Chumvi
13 Sele's Bungalows
14 Sunshine
15 Villa Kiva
16 Zanzibar Bahari Villas
17 Zanzibar Bandas
18 Zanzibar House
19 Zanzibar Retreat

Matemwe is very much a working beach, especially close to the village centre, and this is part of its attraction for visitors looking for just a bit more than sea and sunshine. The main employment here is fishing, and the dhows and ngalawa go out most evenings, delivering their catch onto the beach in the morning. There's also some seaweed farming here: look out for the makeshift racks of purple fronds drying in the sun. Life here is generally hard, with few opportunities and poverty evident. The local people are very conservative Muslims and whilst they don't seem to mind tourists watching the scene, this isn't a spot to be intrusive with photography.

Sadly, like many villages on the island, Matemwe has a litter problem. In spite of Matemwe Lodge arranging regular rubbish collections, plastic bags and general household garbage can be seen caught in bushes and strewn on the ground. The village roads are also in poor repair, and sadly, despite lodges offering to pay jointly for their upgrade, the village leaders have yet to approve this work, preferring instead to receive cash. To avoid corruption, this is not an option, and hence the roads have become increasingly rutted and difficult for all. On a positive note, a brilliant education NGO, Tamani Foundation (*www.tamanifoundation. org*), is working hard, often against the odds, to establish good nursery and primary education within the village, so there is some real hope for the youngest of Matemwe's residents.

GETTING THERE AND AWAY If you are **driving**, there is a direct road to Matemwe from Mkwajuni, on the island's central north–south road. Alternatively, turn east after Kinyasini to Pwani Mchangani, and head north along the new tar road.

If you're staying at one of Matemwe's smarter accommodation options, **transfers** to/from Zanzibar Town can be arranged by them. Alternatively, a private **taxi** or **minibus** can be organised by a Zanzibar Town tour company or hotel (pages 114–17).

By public transport, there's a frequent daily **dalla dalla** service (No 118) and public **bus** (Route 16) from Zanzibar Town to Matemwe village, which then continues up the coast to within about 2km of Matemwe Lodge.

WHERE TO STAY AND EAT   *Map, opposite, unless otherwise stated*
Exclusive

Kasha Boutique Hotel (11 villas) m 0778 067510; e reservation@kasha-zanzibar. com; www.kasha-zanzibar.com. Accessed down a very bumpy track north of Matemwe village, Kasha is located on the top of a coral cliff with the entrance a riot of colourful cascading bougainvillea & flame trees. The hotel sits on a sizeable plot, predominantly left as natural vegetation, with its spacious villas in 2 rows set just back from the beach, each with a substantial open-plan living room, bedroom & bathroom. In the centre of the room is a plasma TV that can be used to watch one of the limited DVDs available from reception. There's a powerful shower, twin sinks & an Arabian-style bath but no door except on the toilet, so be prepared to get familiar with your travelling companion. From the bedroom, glass doors lead out to the patio, where there's a plunge pool & a cushioned baraza for lazy afternoons. The view depends on which row the villa is in – from the front it's across the natural vegetation to the sea, but from the back row it's relatively enclosed with planting & glimpses of the villa directly in front. All rooms are equipped with safes, & European plugs, but adaptors are available. Towards the beach, there's an infinity pool with views across to Mnemba, a small pool bar & a simple spa. A coastal path & wooden stairs lead down to the sea, which at high tide covers the bottom few steps, swallowing the beach. Various signboards along this route have formal health & safety disclaimers on them – & there are additional ones in the rooms – making swimming off-putting for some, & certainly less carefree for most. Away from the beach, the high-ceilinged makuti-thatched main area contains the Nargili Bar, where guests can try the cocktail of the day (*US$9, or US$6 during Happy Hour 18.30–19.30*), the Sama Restaurant, where à la carte b/fasts & European-style dinners are served, a TV room & a small curio shop. Although well-finished & relaxed, with plenty of comforts, Kasha is a fairly pricey place, which doesn't quite live up to expectation, but this doesn't appear to discourage the young honeymooners who rave about it. FB. 👑

Matemwe Retreat   (4 rooms) e reservations@asilialodges.com; www.asiliaafrica. com; ⏱ closed Apr & May. Bordering Matemwe Lodge is its exceptional younger sibling, Matemwe Retreat. Comprising just 4 imposing, castellated villas, this is one of Zanzibar's most impressive & exclusive places to stay. Each villa has been thoughtfully & creatively designed & has strikingly unusual interiors, panoramic ocean views, a private roof terrace & highly original, locally produced furnishings. The heavy timber entrance allows access to the enormous private deck, where dbl hammocks gently sway, sofas invite siestas & reclaimed dhow timber tables are set for dinner *à deux*. The interior is decorated in coffee & muted blue tones, with a mix of Swahili style & minimalist tendencies, & thoughtful touches like luxurious linens & modern conveniences are indicative of the attention to detail & price tag. There is a king-sized bed, plenty of storage, a private bar & good use of reclaimed dhow-wood throughout. The large bathroom boasts a circular shower, separate toilet & a bath beside the sea-facing picture window for truly indulgent soaking. At the top of the internal spiral staircase, a door leads to the idyllic private roof terrace. A 2-tier area, half is devoted to sun worshippers & the other to a super-sized corner sofa under pole shading. With an easterly outlook, the terrace catches the first rays of dawn, making for wonderful photographs & all-day sunbathing. There is also an infinity plunge pool, complete with alcove waterfall, offering stupendous views. Service is top-notch with a friendly villa butler taking care of your every need. Menus are discussed daily & almost anything seasonally available is prepared on request. Food & drinks can be served anywhere: the beach, roof terrace or veranda. Retreat guests can use the small beach that the villas share, & are also free to walk the neat sandy paths to Matemwe Lodge (5mins) & have free use of all of their communal facilities. It's important for sociable guests to realise, however, that there are no public areas at Matemwe Retreat itself – no central lounge, bar or restaurant. This is really a place to get away from it all & indulge in exclusive solitude. FB. ♨

🏠 **Azanzi Beach Hotel** (35 rooms) m 0772 044171; e gr@azanzihotels.com/info@azanzihotels.com; www.azanzihotels.com. Behind the high Azanzi gates, a friendly team awaits. Snaking through the centre of the hotel are water features & a sinuous swimming pool, complete with swim-up bar, & somewhat surprisingly high makuti thatch shade. Bedrooms line the timber walkways & interior décor has strong ethnic influences: soaring high ceilings, heavy theatrical curtains, carved doorway arches & heavy wooden chests. All have minibar & tea/coffee facilities as standard, with villas offering additional outdoor showers, deluxe villas offering a small outdoor jacuzzi, & luxury suites boasting the most internal space & a small private garden or terrace. At the beachfront side of the property, there are deep-cushioned chairs in the lantern-strewn lounge & a restaurant on the breezy mezzanine level. Aquatic activities are well-catered for with an efficient ScubaFish dive centre (page 246) & some fun glass-bottomed kayaks (capacity 2 adults & 1 child). Zanzibari massage (*US$35pp*) is available or there's a TV lounge & basic games rooms. FB. **$$$$$**–♨

🏠 **Che Che Vule** (4 rooms) m 0778 919525; e reservations@moivarosouth.com; www.chechevule.com. Recently renovated, this luxury villa caters to families, small groups & even intimate wedding parties. Managed by a delightfully welcoming Italian lady, Carola, & backed by the experienced team at Moivaro, it is a cool, comfortable Swahili-style beach house, with personal, understated service. Spacious bedrooms (2 with en suites & balconies) have high makuti ceilings, concrete floors & brilliant white interiors keeping the place cool, with touches of colourful kanga fabric, chunky timber furniture & lanterns offering style & comfort. There is a large dining table seating 8, a spacious lounge & a veranda framed by delicate cotton curtains. An honesty bar operates (bottled water free of charge), otherwise a butler will try hard to meet your needs. Locally recruited staff are on duty 24hrs to provide all necessary catering, housekeeping & security services, & though day trips around the island can be arranged, the sail-cloth shaded pool, local beach

walks (bring your own reef shoes), tropical garden hammocks & leisurely BBQ lunches (veggies well catered for) are tough to leave. This is a place to laze in the sun & chill out with family & friends … take your lead from long-term resident 'Speedy' the tortoise. No credit cards. Zanzibar Town transfer US$80/up to 8 people. FB. **$$$$$**–♨

✳ 🏠 **Green & Blue** (14 rooms) m 0772 390086; e reservation@greenandblue-zanzibar.com; www.greenandblue-zanzibar.com. Standing at the opposite end of a curved beach from Matemwe Lodge, this terrific lodge lies on a pleasantly large & strikingly landscaped plot. The 2-person bungalows are all identical bar their view, whilst the larger Ocean Front Villa sleeps up to 4. Colourful interiors are meticulously designed & laid out: ochre-washed walls, a net-draped bed with indigo sheets, plus an upstairs lounge with daybed, which can double as another bedroom. On each bungalow's veranda, shaded by banana trees & palms, is a stylish plunge pool & an outdoor shell-encrusted shower. Lovely as these rooms are, the beachfront public areas are the real draw. In a large 2-storey makuti structure, the lounge, bar & restaurant, are cantilevered over the beach, offering fabulous sea views & equally appealing breezes. The excellence continues in the restaurant, where 2 celebrated Austrian chefs (both hailing from Michelin-starred establishments) have trained the staff to gourmet standards. Adjacent to this area, 2 large & inviting pools run down to the beach. Tulia Spa, in the centre of the gardens, offers various therapies in the open air as well as candlelit treatments for romancing couples, who also get private use of an additional, more sedate pool. Dive clients benefit from a water-taxi service to Dive Point in Muyuni for Mnemba dives. It's the attention to detail that really makes this place stand out, from the handmade welcome packs, to the planting on the roofs so that the rooms blend in to the surroundings. Its German–Austrian owners & managers are hospitable & ensure a great guest experience. FB; BB & HB also available. **$$$$$**–♨

🏠 **Matemwe Beach Village** (22 rooms) m 0777 417250; e matemwebeachvillage@zitec.org; www.matemwebeach.net; ⏲ Jun–Mar. In 2015, Matemwe Beach Village lost its dedicated, long-standing manager, & with her its heart and high standards. Investment & an enthusiastic manager are needed to return this simple, unassuming beach resort back to its former glory. We very much hope this will happen soon to nip disrepair in the bud. The compact Kijiji rooms (1 with AC) are next to one another in a series of rows, a mere hop, skip & a jump from the beach. The interiors are simple with blues & lilacs giving a cool, nautical air, & thoughtful touches from hats to towels are provided. With a mixture of king-sized, sgl- & twin-bed combinations, all have mains electricity, fans, mosquito nets, candles & handy torches. Outside, a selection of chairs sit on a small terrace & the sound of the sea beckons. Forming a cul-de-sac of dbl-storey rondavels with steep pitched thatch are the Shamba suites. Cross the threshold & enter the highly stylised interior of designer Ivan Sutila. Matching hats, kangas & beach bags greet every guest at the door. The spacious central lounge area has built-in seating, & the bedroom is airy with a large dbl bed & pastel lilac linen. The en-suite shower is a stand-alone circular feature, whilst the very separate toilet is dressed to look like a throne with swathes of blue & purple circus-style fabrics streaming up towards the roof. On the galleried upper level, these suites have large mattresses covered in cushions, & a suspended dbl bed. Fun as these rooms are, their real disadvantage is that they are set at the back of the complex, & even from the upper level, their views are limited. The one-off Asali Suite is most frequently used by honeymooning couples keen to take advantage of its private plunge pool & dedicated chef. The resort's raised lounge area, overlooking the beach, encourages lazy afternoons & evenings. The area is thatched but the walls are made of billowing canvas to create a cool, intimate den. The adjoining restaurant offers a daily à la carte menu at individual tables. An attractive pool area complete with pole-shaded bar & sloped loungers makes cooling low-tide dips possible, but be aware that there is little shade here. The independently owned One Ocean dive centre is housed behind the pool (page 246); upstairs in the makuti thatch a DVD & TV lounge offer sports fans & sunburnt guests a shady retreat. HB. **$$$$**–🛏

☀ 🏠 **Matemwe Lodge** (12 chalets)
e reservations@asiliaafrica.com; www.asiliaafrica.com; ⊕ closed Apr & May. Just past the northern edge of Matemwe village, occupying a windswept spot beside a sweeping sandy beach, Matemwe Lodge is a very good, smart yet informal place. Popular with well-travelled, unpretentious couples,

it's relaxed & quiet & is not really the place for families seeking action-packed adventures. Perched on the edge of a low coral cliff, lapped by the waves, each of the thatched chalets has a superb view to Mnemba Island. All rooms have been upgraded into impressively stylish, individual suites, some split-level, with private, curved verandas. Coconut-wood dbl beds are covered in bright appliqué throws; polished concrete floors are strewn with cheerful woven mats; & wooden lattice shutters conceal built-in wardrobe space. The newer suites have decadent baths, as well as a sunken, cushioned baraza that looks out through wide shutters to the sea. On the terrace, a dbl hammock & comfortable cushioned sofa make the perfect seaside retreat. Constant mains electricity, a solar-powered hot-water system, retractable mosquito nets, free-standing fan (on request), large Zanzibari safe box & a relaxing daybed are standard in all suites. Matemwe also has a self-contained beach house with 3 bedrooms, sleeping a max of 6, located just a few mins along with beach, well suited to families or groups, which comes with a private pool, & its own chef & butler. Below & behind the cottages, a stone path meanders through lush tropical gardens to the swimming pools, the main dining area & the beach, which ends where Matemwe Lodge begins, resulting in virtually no passing foot traffic & very little hassle. Some locals have set up curio stalls, but few approach guests & it's relatively low-key compared with other stretches of this coast. There is an infinity pool with a clear view across to Mnemba Island, & another pool below it, connected by a gently tumbling waterfall, offering protection when the coastal wind blows. The adjacent bar is a beautifully polished old dhow flanked by an enormous sperm whale skeleton. Tasty buffets & plated dinners are served in an open-sided dining room overlooking the beach. 2 day rooms (US$50), complete with shower area, have been added so that those leaving late in the afternoon can enjoy their final hours on the beach or sunbathing by the pool. 4 boats (1 dhow; 1 fibre; 2 ngalawa) are based at the lodge for snorkelling & sailing excursions, free escorted reef walks can be arranged at low tide (local villagers, who already work as the lodge's boatmen, are being trained to guide these), & a large wooden chess set (complete with prawns as pawns) is set up *en route* to the beach. Fishing & diving trips can also be arranged, & bikes can be rented with all proceeds going to community projects. For the more sedentary, there's the Sea & Spice Spa, poolside cookery lessons, in-room massage, a library, a stack of books & board games & free Wi-Fi throughout. With close proximity to the local community & a desire to contribute to development, the company & guests have given time & money to supply the local villagers with fresh water, build a primary school, provide 2 deep-sea mashua dhows for fishing, assist with much-needed rubbish collections & teach English. Matemwe is one of very few lodges on the island with a staff member dedicated to community relations & development. If this appeals but something more exclusive is required, neighbouring Matemwe Retreat (page 239) is the lodge's private villa alternative. FB. **$$$$$**–🛏

* 🏠 **Sunshine Marine Lodge** [map, page 198] (24 rooms) **m** 0773 236578/0778 992493; **e** info@marinelodgezanzibar.com; www. marinelodgezanzibar.com; see ad, 2nd colour section. Matemwe's northernmost property, sitting in splendid isolation, is a delightful lodge oozing understated sophistication. Gorgeous tropical gardens are tiered along the coral clifftop, dotted with 2-storey thatched buildings, each housing spacious, stylish island-style rooms. Interiors are cool, coloured concrete with large timber beds, bespoke mossie nets, beaten metal lanterns, open wardrobes & Poäng chairs to take in the lovely balcony views. Following the snaking paths towards the ocean, guests will reach the stylish restaurant-lounge, complete with the requisite dhow bar & smiling kanga-clad staff, keen to make their stay an enjoyable one. The view from the infinity pool over the reef towards Mnemba is strikingly beautiful, as are the loungers clustered under swaying palms, the picture-perfect mezzanine library vista & the shady baraza lounge, where chilled music & the sea breeze set the tone, making this the perfect place to retreat &quietly unwind. There are 3 lovely pools, including a large, purpose-built dive training pool at the great onsite scuba centre, Dive Point (*www.divepointzanzibar.com*). Here, an experienced international team offer PADI courses, friendly service, a choice of boats & the closest access to Mnemba's reefs, making this a terrific choice for those coming to Zanzibar specifically with diving in mind. The hotel's clifftop location means that there is no direct beach access; however, a 5min walk or private water taxi

away is the glorious stretch of sand at Muyuni Beach, on which the lodge has its own private feet-in-the-sand beach bar, loungers & staff. It's a cool hangout & definitely one of the island's most laidback luxurious hangouts. B&B. **$$$$$**–🛏

🏠 **Villa Kiva** (11 rooms) **m** 0772 224222; **e** villakiva@villakiva.it; www.villakiva.it. This smart, Italian-run villa, with some rooms in the villa & others in rondavels, boasts a comfortable central lounge, a bar, 2 restaurant areas & a small L-shaped pool. Even the tiny gift shop has beautifully displayed products, showing an eye for detail & high level of care. Bleached furniture, pale cushions, billowing voile curtains & a wide timber deck all give a cool, uncluttered look, & aid the relaxed vibe. It exudes a home-from-home feel & is a place to escape not to party. On the villa's 1st floor, the spacious master suite has a wrought-iron 4-poster bed, AC & fan & a small chill-out area. Decorated in white with Tanzanian trims, it's a lovely cool spot & has a spectacular balcony sea view. This room's only potential negative is drifting noise from the restaurant below. Other villa rooms can be cleverly interconnected for groups or families up to 6. The rondavels have sea or garden views & each has its own small terrace & 2 rooms high in the makuti roof with peephole windows. An infant cot & even a portable hob can be provided in the larger rooms on request. HB; FB US$20pp supplement. **$$$$**–🛏

Luxury

* 🏠 **Hodi Hodi** (7 rooms) **m** 0779 412603; **e** info@hodihodizanzibar.com; www. hodihodizanzibar.com. In her own words, Hodi Hodi owner Julia Bishop is 'a world adventurer & international corporate executive returned home to roost & now sharing her dream'. And indeed she is: Hodi Hodi is small, smart, welcoming & personal. All that knowledge & love of travel, of personal experiences deeply rooted in Africa, & especially in Zanzibar, & love of the sea & the environment are distilled in this little piece of crafted beach-chic. Julia is a delight: gentle, knowledgeable & great company; this is everything a low-key, homely beach retreat should be. For all its simplicity, every element of this place has been carefully thought-out, with love & care, style & ever an eye on the environment & community impact. On a tiny, picture-postcard little plot of coconut palms & ocean views, it consists of 3 houses: Poa, Toto & Dua – all built & run to responsible tourism standards. Dbl rooms, family suites & a self-contained 3-bedroomed villa are all available, each with lovely open rooms, coconut-wood beds, walk-in wardrobes, free-standing fans, lovely carved *jali* plasterwork (hand-carved, wet) & great showers, complete with spiced seaweed soap made in the village. Outside, neat terraces lead to the small garden & little oval pool, complete with picturesque coconut palm in its centre. There's an honesty bar, coffee & cookie station, daily cocktail hour & a blackboard announcing the day's menu of simple, freshly prepared meals, which are eaten under shade or twinkling fairly lights at thatched-shaded tables around the garden & pool. Diving can be arranged with One Ocean (page 246), & guests here often enjoy the whole-day Mnemba sandbank experience. A great spot for a quiet, chilled-out stay. B&B. **$$$$$**

Upmarket

🏠 **Sunshine Hotel** (16 rooms) 📱 0774 388662; e office@sunshinezanzibar.com; www. sunshinezanzibar.com; ⊕ Jun–Apr; see ad, 2nd colour section. On a sweeping curve of white sand, this vibrant hotel occupies a relatively small plot of land, but the immaculate gardens, stylish architectural touches & calm efficiency lend it a cool intimacy & prevent it from feeling claustrophobic. Run by the helpful & friendly team, Sunshine offers light rooms set in 2-storey chalets among banana tree-filled gardens. They share a similarly sunny colour scheme inside but vary slightly in location & facilities. The Sunshine Suites have 2 sea-view rooms on the top floor & 2 garden-view rooms on the bottom; set back from the beach are the 2 Garden Retreats; whilst 2 luxury suites are found right on the sea shore. All have dbl or twin beds draped with mosquito nets, a small cushioned seating area, a safe & 3 electric fans – 1 ceiling, 1 bed & 1 free-standing. The luxury suites also have private plunge pools & beach bandas, & either a garden or terrace, depending on which floor they are on. The furniture in these rooms is recycled from a disused Stone Town pier, while the ceiling shape channels the wind, negating the need for AC & contributing to the hotel's eco-friendly policy. Back on the beach, the main area

houses the restaurant, serving up daily specials of fresh seafood & Zanzibari curries as well as an eclectic cocktail list. Upstairs is a chilled lounge with a couple of computers, a small library & Wi-Fi. A small waterfall cascades into an infinity pool shaded by dhow sails, & the sun loungers are popular hangouts. While providing plenty of opportunities to relax, including the lovely Kianga Spa (*Swahili facial US$30; traditional massage US$60*), Sunshine also has a rack of Muddy Fox mountain bikes & can easily arrange diving/snorkeling excursions. This place has a lively buzz & should appeal to sociable young couples as much as urban escapists. HB. **$$$$**

🏠 **Zanzibar House** (7 rooms) 📱 0774 062010; e info@zanzibarhouse.it; www. zanzibarhouse.it; see ad, inside back cover. Built as a private family home to accommodate Max's 7 grown-up children & their families, this became a guesthouse somewhat by accident, when the friendly Italian owners took in some desperate guests from an over-booked neighbouring hotel & promptly received positive online reviews! Now fully established, much of the appeal here remains in the home-from-home experience. The Swahili-style building, with its wide, shady seafront terrace, whitewashed Omani arches, & coloured glass doorframes, offers reasonably spacious bedrooms (5 sea view), each with Zanzibari beds, brightly painted walls, en-suite bathrooms, a small balcony & a beach bag containing an array of practical stuff from beach towels to a fan. There's a full-sized snooker table, ping-pong, bicycles, board games & a basket of beach toys, fins, masks & reef shoes for general use, although the hammam, saun masseule & poolside loungers are pretty popular. Most guests stay HB, & food is decidedly Italian in flavour, from the homemade coconut gelato to pizza slices over cocktails & 4-course dinners that always begin with a pasta course. HB. **$$$$**

🏠 **Zanzibar Retreat** (12 rooms) 📱 0776 108379; e info@zanzibarretreat.com; www. zanzibarretreat.com. Behind a wall of cascading bougainvillea, this pleasantly peaceful hotel is popular with Nordic expats from the Tanzanian mainland & even when fully booked is exceptionally quiet by day. With 8 rooms accessed from its broad, wraparound veranda, 2 1st-floor, interconnecting rooms (1 with balcony) & 2 garden rooms, it's small & personal. The main building has decorative Moorish arches, a shady veranda & a small central courtyard from which the stairs ascend to 2 rooms. The upstairs private balcony has a wonderful view, & it is possible to see all along the coast from Mnemba Island to Kiwengwa. The bright, standard rooms are on the ground floor have polished dark timber floors, well-made louvred wardrobes, large Zanzibari beds & newly renovated bathrooms. High ceilings, fans & AC ensure they are always cool, & Wi-Fi is available. Outside is a well-tended garden with an attractive view through the beachfront mangroves to the sea & bobbing ngalawa boats, which can be enjoyed from the good restaurant, at the nice circular bar or in the lovely blue-&-white baraza lounge area. The hammock-filled raised beach & large pool are assets at low tide but for those keen to hit the ocean, activities, including diving, can be arranged at One Ocean in Matemwe Beach Village (10min walk; page 246). For something more local, talk to the fisherman-cum-gardener to arrange a reef or village walk. The lodge is consciously working to help their community by buying produce locally & ensuring responsible waste management. B&B. **$$$$**

Mid range

🏠 **Panga Chumvi** (15 rooms) **m** 0777 862899; **e** info@pangachumvi.com; www. pangachumvi.com. This small locally owned place offers surprisingly good, genuinely eco-friendly accommodation, just a stone's throw from a pretty quiet stretch of beach. The layout is somewhat unusual, with a couple of private houses lying at the centre, but the selection of room types – 3 villas, bungalows & a refurbished beach house – & tranquility make it well worth a look. The newer villas, each with 2 dbl & 2 twin rooms, all have AC, a pleasant veranda & some interconnecting rooms if required. The terraced bungalow rooms have been built with an eye on traditional Swahili cooling techniques, & maintain the same attention to detail with coconut-wood furniture, quality linen & some outdoor space. They are lovely, smart & spacious in their simplicity. The beachfront Baharini bungalow & banda offer sea-facing rooms with fan-cooling only. There is a small on-site restaurant & bar, complete with pizza oven, offering the usual Swahili fare, but otherwise it's quite a private place to be. Community support

is strong, with the owners heavily involved in Matemwe life & some interesting projects: supporting a village taxi service, fishing boat & chicken-farming projects. Equally impressive is their real commitment to environmental awareness – an aspiration that many others on the island should embrace. B&B. **$$$–$$$$**

🏠 **Zanzibar Bahari Villas** (15 rooms) **m** 0776 660104; **e** info@zanzibarbaharivillas. com; www.zanzibarbaharivillas.com. Opened in Dec 2015 on the site of the owner's house, this is a smart, friendly spot in the heart of the village with great beach access. Comprising 3 whitewashed, 2-storey buildings & a separate 3-bedroom villa, the hotel is wellconstructed (not a given in Zanzibar!), with neat, spacious, modern rooms. Bright white interiors, contemporary furniture & wide terraces feature throughout; some rooms have a claw-foot bath & a few have a lovely outdoor shower in a semi-circular coral rock nook. AC & a fridge are available in 4 rooms; some have a TV, so be specific about your requirements on booking. Some of the island's greenest grass has been laid outside & proper palm gardens run through the resort to the lovely turquoise pool above the beach. Loungers & an ocean-view restaurant are inviting & there's an array of non-motorised watersports equipment available. The spacious, nautical villa can be booked for self-catering or with a private chef. B&B. **$$$–$$$$**

🏠 **Zanzibar Bandas** (7 bandas) **m** 0773 434113; **e** milky@zanzibarbandas.com; www. zanzibarbandas.com. These simple but lovely mkeke bandas offer rustic accommodation around stylish public areas. 3 rooms are on the beachfront with stunning ocean views, whilst the others sit behind the pool & bar area. All are natural, made from woven palm leaves with solid coconut-wood doors, window frames & furniture, & palm mats adorn the floors & strings of shells screen the shower. The interiors are a little on the dark side, but outside each is a small raised deck with directors' chairs & a pretty view. The open-sided restaurant-cum-bar is stylishly simple with white chairs around a coconut-wood table & gentle Arabian background music; Swahili cuisine is served here 3 times a day. There is also a lovely rectangular pool surrounded by white sail-cloth shades, coir loungers & hammocks hung between mkadi palms. For wider-reaching views, check out the 2-storey pool banda for sundowners on high. B&B. **$$$**

Budget
⌂ **Matemwe Baharini Villas**
(12 rooms) m 0777 417768/0777 429642; e matemwebaharini@gmail.com; www.matemwebaharinivilla.com. Under the local management of softly-spoken Madia, this is a long-running mid-range option. The 3 categories of rooms are all immaculate: The 2 large bright (if slightly soulless) villas are predominantly used by families & groups, with 1 villa featuring an open-plan, self-catering kitchen & lounge area. Electricity, hot water, mosquito nets & deckchairs on the terrace are all standard. In addition, there are 10 clean rooms in traditional bungalows, one of which has an interconnecting door for family use. Set back from the beach behind a garden, they have a high Zanzibari dbl bed, a daybed & a mosquito net. The mekeke & makuti ceilings are high & unusually constructed, which combined with the gauze windows allows the cooling sea breeze to circulate. Facilities & activities are quite limited, but there is a beachfront restaurant, old volleyball net, Swahili massage, local fishing excursions on request, & Wi-Fi in the works. The raised swimming pool is the heart of the complex, surrounded by shaded loungers. For self-drivers, there is the advantage of secure parking behind the metal gate. *Villas* **$$**; *bungalows*. B&B. **$$$**

⌂ **Sele's Bungalows** (8 rooms) m 0776 931690/0777 413449; e info@selesbungalows.com; www.selesbungalows.com. A British–Zanzibari joint venture, Sele's is a hip hangout with a buzzing atmosphere, friendly staff & relaxed vibe. The funky, fruit-bedecked bar is a real draw for non-residents & guests. Food is served on the upper deck, & it's a good option for fresh seafood with a local twist: staples like spicy octopus, grilled kingfish or giant prawns in coconut curry are popular. It can get very busy at dinner time, but diners are almost never turned away. Amid dense vegetation – Sele himself planted every flower & tree over the last 12 years – the simple rooms are a mix of sizes – some at the back of the property are decidedly bijoux though perfectly nice – & have varying facilities, while the new family room can accommodate up to 8 people in 4 dbls with AC & an en suite featuring jaunty hibiscus tiling. All rooms have hot-water en suites, Zanzibari beds, Indian rugs & a free-standing fan; they are a little dark but clean & well cared for, & the owners couldn't be more hospitable. There is a safe available in the manager's office, & its use is recommended for any valuables. No credit cards. B&B. **$$–$$$**

⌂ **Keys Bungalows** (11 rooms) m 0777 411797; e allykeys786@gmail.com. Behind a collapsing mkeke-palm gate, Keys is a friendly beach bar with some surprisingly nice little rooms in gardens of casuarinas, palms & papayas. This is a good option for beach-focused backpackers seeking a chilled hangout for their ocean activities. Accommodation is in individual coral-rock cottages, the newest of which are on the beach or within a larger whitewashed building & each room is small but clean & pleasant. Behind heavy Zanzibari doors, there are nicely carved dbl beds, cheerful kanga curtains, embroidered bedding, cupboards made from cleverly adapted ngalawa boats (complete with integrated safe), & wet-room-style bathrooms. Fans, mosquito nets, cold water & a small veranda with cane & hide chairs are all standard; but only 2 rooms have hot water. The circular bar above the beach is the centre of activity here with gentle reggae music & a sociable crowd mixing under a curious array of flags from Welsh to Tanzanian. It's possible to arrange snorkelling & boat trips with the local crew (half-day Mnemba snorkelling US$25pp), but anything more will require a trip to one of the larger resorts. Meals are possible with some notice, & include some imaginative ingredients from mustard mayo to chorizo, as well as Swahili staples like octopus masala & grilled tuna (*US$7.50*). B&B. **$$**

⌂ **Mohamed's Restaurant & Bungalows**
(5 rooms) m 0777 431881. Follow the clear sign from the main road in Matemwe village & you'll find Mohamed's small, basic cottages (3 twin, 2 trpl), each with mosquito nets, fans & tiled, immaculate bathrooms with cold-water showers & flush toilets. They are basic but clean, & although the beds don't always have linen, this can usually be arranged. Simple meals can be organised with a day's notice. The beachfront location & price continue to make this a great backpacker option. B&B. **$$**

WHAT TO SEE AND DO Apart from lazing on the beach, or going for long walks along it, there are the usual diving and snorkelling possibilities which can be arranged through One Ocean's two local centres:

🤿 **One Ocean** m 0777 310003; e info@ zanzibaroneocean.com; www.zanzibaroneocean. com; ⏲ 08.00–17.00, daily. Based at Matemwe Beach Village (page 240), One Ocean's whale-tail reception desk is bound to bring a smile to even the most nervous of water babies. It's a 5* PADI dive school offering a range of certification courses, Mnemba dive trips & snorkelling excursions. The staff are happy to accept referral certificates from guests who've completed dive-course classroom work before arriving in Zanzibar, or to teach in English or French from scratch in the pool & at sea. Using RIBs *Mama Popo* & *Kelsey*, or purpose-built dhows, *MV Jessica* & *MV Anne*, daily dive trips depart from Muyuni Beach (a 35min dalla dalla ride), meaning an early-morning meet between 07.30–09.00; only twice a month do high tides allow for dhow departures from the resort's own beach. 12 divers, grouped by ability, are accompanied by 2 guides, & it is not necessary to stay at the resort to use the dive centre. There are also manned booking desks at Villa Kiva (page 242) & Waikiki Resort (page 253). *US$110/305/480 for 2/6/10 dives; equipment rental US$15/day; PADI Open Water US$500; snorkelling trips US$45.*

🤿 **ScubaFish** m 0772 730368/0779 111888; e info@scubafishzanzibar.com; www. scubafishzanzibar.com; ⏲ 08.00–17.00 daily. ScubaFish is a relative newcomer as a dive operator on Zanzibar but its staff are not. Experienced Dutch owner & dive instructor Yong Mi Janse established this after 6 years managing one of the area's other dive operations, & has since built a team of local dive masters & a South African instructor. Focusing predominantly on Mnemba atoll sites, they offer PADI courses from Discover Scuba up to Dive Master, & have a professional & friendly team at their bases at

MUYUNI BEACH

Until recently, Muyuni Beach was little more than the coastal pick-up point for guests travelling to Mnemba Island, a beautiful stretch of beach, accessed by a long, dusty, bumpy drive over the corrugated coral rock and gravel road, past a few quarries. But significant change is afoot – it is currently being developed on an unprecedented scale.

The ambitious plan of a British company, Pennyroyal (Gibraltar), **Zanzibar Amber Resort** (*www.zanzibaramberresort.com*), is a US$1 billion project comprising five five-star hotels, luxury apartments, an equestrian and polo centre, a water park, a nine-hole golf course, a marina, a private airport with a 3,000m runway, state-of-the-art medical facilities and an international school. The resort will generate its own electricity at gas and wind energy plants and initial projections show 1,500 jobs being created.

Heavy machinery is already plying the access road daily, widening it considerably, and overall project construction is slated to take between eight and 11 years. Phase One, which encompasses all the hotels, some villas, the golf course and marina, is scheduled for completion within the next three years.

With serious corporate social responsibility, the project could bring tremendous employment, education and improvement in services to the area, though traditionally large projects on Zanzibar have failed to deliver well for their local communities. The landscape is certainly set to change dramatically on this part of the island, and we must hope that the outlook of its poorest residents can be assisted as it does.

Azanzi (page 240), Sea Cliff Resort Mangapwani (page 183), Matemwe Lodge (page 241) & Zanzibar Retreat (page 243). *US$110/305/480*

for 2/6/10 dives; equipment rental US$15/day; PADI Open Water US$500; snorkelling trips US$45.

MNEMBA ISLAND

Lying approximately 2.5km off the northeast coast of Zanzibar, Mnemba Island is a picture-perfect coral atoll. Previously uninhabited, it is now privately leased by &Beyond and has become one of Africa's ultimate beach retreats.

At its centre is a tropical forest, home to nothing more dangerous than cute suni antelope, a population of cooing red-eyed doves, butterflies, an ancient well and some Ader's duiker (Africa's most endangered forest duiker). The island's circular perimeter is 1.5km of soft, brilliant white coral sand: perfect for romantic evening strolls, migrating wading birds, scuttling ghost crabs and nesting turtles. In the turquoise sea around, some of East Africa's best coral reefs hide in a relatively unspoilt aquatic wonderland. There are virtually no insects on the island, making it a very low-risk malarial area.

Officially titled Mnemba Island Marine Conservation Area (MIMCA), the island is part of a coral formation supporting a staggering variety of marine life, which was once threatened by overfishing and a general disregard for the fragility of the environment. Sustained lobbying by &Beyond and the government resulted, however, in the area being declared a Marine Conservation Area in November 2002 and its future has now been secured.

A US$3 levy is charged on all watersports, notably snorkelling and diving, within the protected zone. This revenue is paid into a community conservation fund, the primary purpose of which is to show local fishermen and their communities the very real economic value in protecting rather than exploiting these exceptional reefs. In addition to the money generated from MIMCA park levies, the lodge and Africa Foundation (&Beyond's social development partner) have invested US$180,000 in community projects on Zanzibar close to Mnemba: building eight classrooms, a windmill and ablution blocks, refurbishing the doctor's house, supporting the orphanage and assisting villagers with access to clean water.

GETTING THERE AND AWAY Mnemba Island guests are chauffeur-driven from the airport or Stone Town to Muyuni Beach, north of Matemwe, from where it's a 15–20-minute ski-boat ride to the island. It is not possible to visit the island unless you have a booking.

WHERE TO STAY AND EAT *Map, page 198*

☀ 🏠 **Mnemba Island Lodge** (12 bandas) 📞(South Africa) +27 11 809 4300; e contactus@ andbeyond.com; www.andbeyond.com; ⏰ Jun–Mar. The crème de la crème of &Beyond's impressive portfolio, Mnemba Island Lodge is the height of rustic exclusivity: a place where the term 'barefoot luxury' is reality. Overlooking the beach from the forest's edge, its secluded, split-level bandas are constructed entirely of local timber & hand-woven palm fronds, beautifully finished in a herringbone pattern. These are large & open plan & are the favoured retreats of both the rich & the famous, together with a few harmless hermit crabs. Furnished simply but tastefully, each banda has a huge bed & solid wooden furniture, softened with natural, ivory-coloured fabrics & plenty of forest-view windows. As a place to escape the trappings of the modern world, in-room facilities stretch only to electricity, a simple fan, a padlocked wooden box for valuables, a couple of cotton bathrobes & a torch. A palm-covered corridor leads to a stylish timber-&-glass bathroom. Built-in barazas on the thatched beach-facing veranda are perfect for afternoon siestas & lazy b/fasts, whilst in front, private beach *salas* (shaded, open-sided beach huts) feature traditional Zanzibari loungers for leisurely hours on the beachfront. The uncluttered indulgent luxury, peaceful isolation & stunning situation make this a blissfully romantic haven. Mnemba's cuisine is predictably excellent, with plenty of fresh seafood, fruit & vegetables, & the flexibility to cater for individual needs exceedingly well. Guests can choose what, when & where to eat, from leisurely b/fasts in bed to candlelit, lobster dinners on the beach. An engaging 'butler' is assigned to each room, & from arrival will subtly go about tailoring each guest's stay. In line with its environmentally aware beginnings, the lodge strives to be eco-friendly. Water is desalinated, the beaches are rid of any manmade debris, & organic waste is recycled & the rest shipped off the island. Solar power is used wherever possible, including to heat the water, & guests are encouraged to do their bit by the eco guide left in each room. The lodge is also involved in marine- & turtle-conservation projects: watch out for the beach signs heralding new hatchlings. Under 12s are accepted at the lodge, though only 2 are allowed on the island at any time. 1 extra bed can be put in with parents, or there are 2 bandas close to each other for convenience. Mnemba is unquestionably expensive, but its flexibility & service levels are second to none, & its idyllic location & proximity to outstanding marine experiences are very hard to match. Visa & MasterCard accepted. Al. ☕

WHAT TO SEE AND DO An American couple, Eli and Robin, run a professional **dive centre** on the island and for qualified PADI divers, up to two dives per day are included in the lodge rates. PADI courses are naturally available and one-on-one tuition may be expensive but the quality instruction and warm, shallow waters make for excellent training. Once divers are qualified, a number of superb dive sites are within 15 minutes of the lodge, from tranquil coral gardens dancing with colourful reef fish and gentle turtles to steep drop-offs: the haunt of huge, deep-water game fish. Over a delicious hot chocolate on the boat back to shore, sightings of dolphin pods are not uncommon, and even humpbacks can be spotted in season.

For the non-diver, there's snorkelling, double kayaks, windsurfing, power kiting, sailing, and fly- or deep-sea fishing. Aromatherapy, hot-stone and deep-tissue massages and reiki are all available, too.

PWANI MCHANGANI

'Pwani' means beach in Swahili and this is certainly the focus of village life. This area is particularly noted for its seaweed collection, and the dramatic low tides see women and children take to the shallow water to harvest their marine quarry, which is then usually dried on the beach. The men, like most on Zanzibar's coast, concentrate on fishing, and the village boasts one of the island's main seafood markets.

Mass-market tourism is less developed than on the coastline around Kiwengwa (9km south), and Pwani Mchangani retains a more traditional air as a result. It's a sizeable village in the seaside coconut belt, where children and poultry run riot, colourful washing is strung between thatched houses and conservative attitudes dominate.

GETTING THERE AND AWAY To travel from Zanzibar Town to Pwani Mchangani on public transport, take **dalla dalla** No 117 towards Kiwengwa or the No 118 towards Matemwe, or local **bus** Routes 15 or 16. Those with a **hire car** approaching from the north or west coast should take the right turn about 1km north of Kinyasini at Kikobweni, straight into the village. The simple coastal track has now been joined by a smart tar road, making travel along the coast infinitely faster and more comfortable.

WHERE TO STAY AND EAT *Map, page 250*

Unless stated otherwise, hotels listed below offer air conditioning and en-suite bathrooms as standard.

Exclusive

🏠 Mchanga Beach Resort (10 rooms) m 0776 590016; e info@mchangazanzibar.com; www.mchangazanzibar.com. Now managed by an Italian–Eritrean couple, this is a simple, stylish construction with high-quality interiors & a stunning location. Situated on a deep, powder-sand beach between Pwani Mchangani & Matemwe, where the sea is crushed coral & urchin free, this is a great spot for swimming, paddling & relaxing. There are steeply thatched whitewashed rooms: 6 sea-view lodge rooms, 2 garden twins & 2 family rooms, the latter with a dbl baraza seating area that neatly converts into an additional sleeping spot for children. These also have additional outdoor terracing for private relaxation. All of the rooms have new moulded-concrete beds covered in white soft cotton, fine wool blankets & turquoise-&-indigo batik throws, as well as a semicircular cushion-covered baraza alcove & a small sand-covered terrace for morning tea. There are fridges & AC in all rooms, & touches like light switches within mosquito nets, beach baskets brimming with towels, & jugs of water by the door to wash the sand from your feet show great attention to detail. Equally, a thoughtful mix of hand-crafted wooden shutters, electric ceiling fans, AC & traditional high-beamed ceilings all ensure rooms remain cool whatever the time of day. Outside, through fruit- & flower-filled gardens, towards the oceanfront palm grove, there is a lovely swimming pool, relaxed bar & an open-sided makuti restaurant. Food is a homemade seasonal mix of Italian–Swahili specials using locally produced vegetables & fresh fish where possible (dinner US$15). There are beach bandas & cheerfully covered coir loungers for sunbathing & snoozing, a simple massage room, boules & board games, & even 'Macycle' bikes to borrow. Diving can also be arranged with nearby PADI centres. All rates FB; airport transfer US$60 each way. 🏖

🏠 Melia Zanzibar (124 rooms) m 0789 743254; e melia.zanzibar@melia.com; www.meliahotels.com. In 2011, Spanish hotel group Melia, took over this former Kempinski resort. Much has remained of the original property, but some interiors have suffered under the new management & the once clean lines & contemporary style have been diluted. Set in 12ha of immaculate gardens, the spacious guest rooms & suites are housed in contemporary coral-rock buildings, each with its own private terrace or balcony. Angular in design with Moorish influences evident in the carved timber balconies, patterned shutters & cool courtyards, the architecture is some of the most modern on the island; it's strikingly different from any other large resort here. In addition to the standard rooms, there is a vast Grand Suite villa & 6 smaller villas, each with a private pool. All rooms have Zanzibari beds & heavy floral cushions & curtains, & the quality & number of in-room facilities reflect the resort's association with a serious European hotel group. Bathrooms have a contemporary free-standing bath &, in safari style, an outdoor shower in a pebbled Zen courtyard. There are 2 restaurants: a themed buffet at Spices where seating spills out onto the garden patio; & a daily set menu at Aqua, overlooking the sea. Drinks & snacks are available poolside, or there's tapas on the jetty & a book-filled Library Bar. For exercise & total relaxation, the Anantara Spa is one of the island's best well-being facilities, with private treatment rooms & professional Thai therapists, a large outdoor pool with sundeck & pool bar, a 23m lap pool & a fully equipped fitness centre. If being outside is preferable, there's basketball, tennis, a stunning swimming pool & a number of watersports on offer & diving can be easily arranged with One Ocean (page 246), who have a desk onsite. The resort is on the edge of the coral cliff so there's no real beach to speak of immediately in front of it. If it's lying on the beach you're after, then it's a golf buggy trip 1km south to Gabi Beach – the resort's satellite beach bar on Kiwengwa Beach. HB. 🏖

🏠 Diamonds Mapenzi Beach (87 rooms) m 0774 414268; e info.mapenzi@diamonds-resorts.com; mapenzibeach.diamondsresorts.com. Part of the Diamonds group, Mapenzi is a comfortable resort on a nice stretch of coast. Despite its size, it is a relatively serene place, catering to package holidaymakers from across Europe, South & East Africa. Families especially are enticed

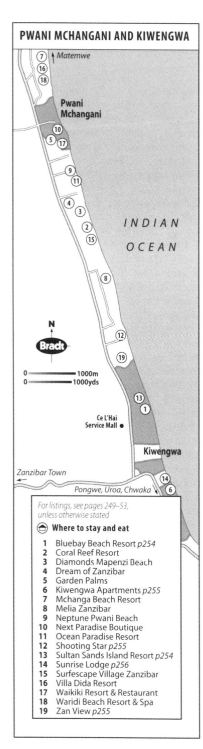

PWANI MCHANGANI AND KIWENGWA

Matemwe

Pwani Mchangani

INDIAN OCEAN

N

Bradt

0 ——— 1000m
0 ——— 1000yds

Ce L'Hai Service Mall ●

Kiwengwa

Zanzibar Town

Pongwe, Uroa, Chwaka

by the positive attitude towards children (easy availability of cots, highchairs, babysitting & even a beachfront playground). The reception area is shaded by impressive makuti thatch supported by a tremendous network of poles, & plays ethereal music to arriving guests. From here, wide corridors lead to a mezzanine-level daybed & evening shisha corner, a curio shop & stylish boutique, a business centre offering internet & the massage zone. Raised above the beach, the long swimming pool is surrounded with loungers, & affords views across the entire complex. The cottages closest to the sea fetch the premium rate but all rooms offer 24hr mains electricity, mosquito nets, electronic safe, fridge & a veranda. In true European-resort style, 'animators' encourage active participation in games & activities but at least there is a Swahili influence evident in their offerings, & their manner is not as intolerably coercive as at the all-inclusive Italian resorts. Village excursions, ngoma drumming lessons & resort botanical walks are just as likely to feature alongside ball games & boules here. There's a daily fitness programme of aqua aerobics, beach stretching & jogging, & catamarans & windsurfers can be used free of charge by all-inc guests. Football & volleyball matches benefit from properly marked pitches, diving is organised through Scuba Do & sister-property La Gemma (page 229), & there's a new purpose-built gym & fitness centre. By night, entertainment ranges from live bands to acrobatic shows & quizzes. Mapenzi is all inclusive & meal times & cuisine are set, though a seafood à la carte menu is also available. Meals are served in the spacious restaurant, under the giant fig tree at Ocean Reef Grill, or in the casual pizzeria, though Mon night sees the weekly Swahili BBQ on the beach. There are 2 bars & drinks are included in the room rates (inc those in the minibar). Late checkout rates are reasonable at US$50/4hrs, & well worth considering for those with afternoon flights. HB. **$$$$$**–👑

👑 **Next Paradise Boutique Hotel** (20 rooms) m 0773 822206; e info@next-paradise.com; www.next-paradise.com; see ad, 2nd colour section. This lovely, quiet property under Marina & Stuart's Italian–Slovenian ownership is set in an immaculate coconut grove. The resort's hub is a trio of interlinked, circular makuti structures: a large international restaurant, a small bar complete with life-sized carved Maasai & an eclectic music selection (Pink Panther to Queen during our visit), & a reception area. From here, Arusha stone paths meander around the complex to rooms housed in an assortment of multi-storey villas & 4 newer beach bungalows overlooking the pool towards the sea. All rooms & suites are different, but the interior of each is clearly the product of a high degree of thought, care & investment. Bathrooms clad in metallic mini mosaics, vibrant chiffon curtains, impressive appliqué wall hangings, & luxurious bed linen all feature, along with AC, safes, fans & Wi-Fi. Families are well catered for with large, interconnecting rooms & wide verandas to ensure everyone has plenty of space. There are 2 swimming pools, a tennis court (rackets & balls available), table tennis, & massage on demand in a voile panelled open-air spot. A good option for couples hoping to relax in tropical surroundings & with no sense of urgency. Min 3-night stay; 7 nights high season. HB. **$$$$$**–☕

Luxury

🔼 **Dream of Zanzibar** (157 rooms) m 0759 598888; e booking.dream@emerald-collection. com; www.dreamofzanzibar.com. A member of the Emerald Collection (see also Hideaway of Nungwi, page 229), this all-inclusive property is an architectural interpretation of the grand old Arab–African palaces: makuti-thatched buildings with shaded arcades, open terraces & palm-filled vistas. The detached reception is a striking introduction with a large open-sided lounge area filled with primary-coloured cylindrical lanterns suspended from the thatch. From here, accommodation heads downhill towards the beach. Bedrooms are very spacious & pleasant, with dark teak furniture, orange-&-white fabrics & a raft of mod cons. For sea views opt for the Junior Suites, or one of the 3 Royal Suites for a private plunge pool. There are an incredible 10 restaurants in the grounds, from the international, buffet-style Cape to Venice Brasserie to the beachfront Sakura Suchi Bar, & the Andiamo Pizzeria to the seafood à la carte Blue Vanilla; as well as a couple of cocktail & juice bars. With 2 pools, a well-equipped gym, a professional spa, games room & diving, activities galore are available with Team Aqua Zanzibar. There are some group activities available – tennis, football, aqua gym – although this is not a resort for coercive group activities. HB. **$$$$$**

🔼 **Neptune Pwani Beach** (154 rooms) ✆ 024 224 0396; m 0774 567893/4; e info. neptunezanzibar@neptunehotels.com; www. neptunehotels.com. With 4 established resorts

in Mombasa this was the Neptune Group's 1st departure from the Kenyan coast, a sizeable hotel extending from the beach up along the coral cliff behind. Striking dbl-storey accommodation blocks with steep makuti thatch & external timber staircases are laid out in imposing rows on the lush lawns. There is little that is soft, gentle or environmentally in keeping; rather the scale, colour & harsh geometry are quite arresting. Inside, things improve: spacious bedrooms are decorated with locally crafted furniture & there is crisp linen & wide balconies. Satellite TV, tea-/coffee-making facilities, mini fridge & electronic safe are all standard. There is an extensive network of swimming pools with a child-friendly paddling section & popular swim-up bar. A selection of non-motorised watersports is also available, & divers can make arrangements with Extreme Watersports Diving or any of the local centres. For relaxation, the autonomous Earth & Rain Spa above reception is suitably sweet smelling & is staffed by delightful Indonesian & Thai therapists. Offering flower-filled baths, scrubs & professional massage & beauty therapies, this is a good place for guests & non-residents alike to break from the sun for a few hours. AI. **$$$$$**

🔼 **Ocean Paradise Resort** (98 rooms, 8 suites) m 0777 440990/5; e info@oceanparadisezanzibar. com; www.oceanparadisezanzibar.com. This is a big hit with UK honeymooners enticed to the resort by the free bottle of bubbly, fruit basket & private lobster dinner for newlyweds. The imposing reception is a huge semicircular area, with a high, vaulted makuti roof. From here, sweeping stairs curve round what is intended to be an impressive waterfall, into manicured gardens, the beautiful central pool area, & beach-level accommodation. There are superior rooms & junior suites, all in neat, pale yellow rondavels. The circular bedrooms are stylishly understated in neutral tones & all have mains electricity, satellite TV, electronic safe & a minibar, & unlimited Wi Fi access can be purchased for US$15/week. Each room has an outside seated terrace area accessed through French doors. The junior suite rooms are exactly the same in design as the superior, but with 2 separate rooms they are twice the size. Half of these have a king-sized bed & sitting room, whilst the others have 1 king size & a twin room, which can be used by families. Transfers around the complex by golf cart can be arranged for guests with limited mobility. If splashing in the seaside pool or reclining on the beach isn't stimulating enough, there's a daily schedule of activities typically including coconut weaving, Swahili lessons & beach soccer. Alternatively, there's a One Ocean Dive Centre for scuba & snorkelling (page 246), canoeing, windsurfing, fishing, volleyball, table tennis, billiards & a small fitness centre. Beach bikes can also be rented (*US$7*). For families, there's a children's pool & 'animators' to engage children in Butlin's-style activities; cots are available & English-speaking babysitting services are provided at a standard US$5/hr. Every night musicians perform, treating guests to traditional Swahili ngoma drumming or Maasai acrobatics. Evening meals at the Jahazi Restaurant overlook the performers & are usually themed. Non-residents with a booking are also welcome to eat here. When the cabaret entertainment is over, the Jungle Disco (Fri & Sat) & terraced Bahari Bar can get lively. HB. **$$$$$**

⌂ **Villa Dida Resort** (9 rooms) e info@villadida.com; www.villadida.com. This small-scale resort under Tanzanian–Italian ownership is largely used by Italians on bush 'n' beach package trips organised by the owner's tour company. Described as a 'big Swahili villa', Dida focuses firmly on the sea view. Rooms are simple with ochre, rust & white colour schemes, polished concrete floors, coconut-wood furniture & mkeke mats. There is deliberately no AC, though dbl fans are fitted in all bedrooms for comfort. Equally, fish & vegetables for the restaurant are sourced from the local community as much as possible to keep food miles low. An inviting pool in the palms, large jacuzzi & plenty of makuti beach umbrellas make lazing in the sun appealing, & activities from local massage to jeep rental can also be arranged. Rates include flights from Italy. FB. **$$$$$**

Upmarket

⌂ **Coral Reef Resort** (28 rooms) m 0777 415549; e coralreef@zanzinet.com; www.coralreefzanzibar.com; ⊕ Jul–Apr. Coral Reef was opened by 3 Italians & virtually every guest here is a fellow compatriot, though their presence, or that of any other management, was notably absent during our last 2 visits – willfully unhelpful staff lent it an uneasy air. The sparse reception area is naturally raised above the beach & decorated with simple murals showing acrobatic Maasai. From here a long central path leads to the swimming pool, complete with its own elegant palm island & sadly a roped monkey at the shower. Signs from the main path indicate the direction of various rooms, some of which are a fair stretch from the beach. The bungalow architecture is Arabic in style: white walls with arched windows & flat roofs. There are dbl or twin standard rooms on the hillside, plus superior & seafront rooms on the beach. Each has mains electricity, mosquito nets, & hot-water shower. The standard & some superior rooms have fans only, whilst 7 of the latter enjoy AC. There is a key safe, left-luggage facility & Wi-Fi access available at the pool & bar. Buffets are served for every meal in a restaurant beside the sea; outside is a very pleasant deck with large navy parasols & a lovely view along the beach through the extensive Tingatinga painting gallery. HB. **$$$$–$$$$$**

⌂ **Garden Palms** (11 rooms) m 0713 682666; e gardenpalms@gmail.com; www.gardenpalms.pl. Immediately next door to Next Paradise, this Polish-run resort offers immaculate rooms, with refreshingly few large hotels on the doorstep. Built in a U-shaped formation around a good-sized central pool, & overlooking the beach, are the 2 neat rows of accommodation, an open-sided seafood restaurant & a dive centre. The rooms – available in a terrace or as detached bungalows – are all extremely spacious, with bright interiors, tiled floors, coconut-wood furniture & sea-view terraces. Perhaps lacking a little in soft furnishings & character, they remain pleasant, cool retreats after a day in the sun. The surrounding landscaping is rather stark sand, but it remains a quiet, efficient retreat, catering predominantly to Eastern European clients. B&B. **$$$$**

⌂ **Waridi Beach Resort & Spa** (62 rooms) m 0777 125139; e info@waridibeachresort.com; www.waridibeachresort.com. Waridi is a package-holiday resort favoured by young Italians. An assortment of room categories cater for couples & families, with satellite TV & all the usual mod cons as standard. There are 2 restaurants serving largely pasta-based dishes, a beach bar & a cushioned shisha lounge. A small fitness room, table tennis, pool, bike rental, & a 4-room spa with jacuzzi, sauna & steam room, are all on site, with entertainment staff coercing guests to participate in a range of activities from sports tournaments to cabarets. In addition, a large number of Maasai beach boys (most with adopted Italian names) congregate around the beach entrance to this property, playing football with the guests, & taking the opportunity to recommend their neighbouring souvenir stalls & 'guiding' services. HB. $$$$

Mid range

🏠 **Waikiki Resort & Restaurant** (27 rooms) m 0779 401603; e waikikibooking@hotmail. com; www.waikikiafrica.com. This delightful hotel is refreshingly small & personal, run enthusiastically by Italian–English husband & wife team, Flavio & Sarah. Life here focuses on the buzzing central restaurant, where guests quaff wine & enjoy homemade leisurely lunches, the Coco Jambo bar with intimate dhow booths & homemade gelateria, & the funky beached dhow bar Cassiopeia, with its chilled cocktail-drinking crew. There is also a beachfront 'Pizza Express' wood-fired oven serving up slices of freshly made pizza to beach lovers from Pongwe to Matemwe – delivery available (m 0775 049080)! Across the resort, the multi-lingual staff help to ensure a vibrant atmosphere prevails. In addition, every Fri from 22.00 island DJs play on the beach to a large party crowd (up to 400 revellers), there's live music on a Sat night & every Tue there's a Maasai show & market. All original bungalows are individually decorated with striking tropical murals, whilst at the back of the resort, 12 new rooms were built in 2016 around a welcome swimming pool. Of the original rooms, 'Safari' rooms are particularly spacious, & room 6 in this category has the best beachfront location. There is some basic activity equipment, free Wi-Fi, & a small massage zone. For more organized sport, diving is available through One Ocean at Matemwe Beach Village (free 10min transfer; page 246), & kitesurfing courses & equipment through onsite operators Kite Zanzibar (below). In spite of doubling in size, Waikiki remains welcoming, making it somewhere fun & offbeat on this stretch of coast. From a security perspective, this resort is one of the few covered by CCTV. B&B. *Rooms* $$$, *bungalows* $$$$

Budget

🏠 **Surfescape Village Zanzibar** (6 rooms) m 0657 420259; e hello@thesurfescape.com; www.thesurfescape.com. Billed as 'the first surf-inspired hotel', Surfescape opened in 2016 as a social hangout for aquaholics in search of a like-minded company & budget accommodation. Neighbouring Coral Reef Resort (page 252), the ocean-view rooms here are simple but clean & adequate, & share a sea-view terrace. 2–5 instructors are permanently based here offering lessons in kitesurfing, windsurfing & stand-up paddling; IKO & WDVS courses are available (*Intro kiting course from US$215; Advanced courses from US$390*). Definitely a spot best enjoyed by die-hard kiters & surfers. B&B. $$

WHAT TO SEE AND DO Any lodge or resort can arrange one or more of the ubiquitous Zanzibar Island tours (page 113). Otherwise, kiting and diving can be arranged through Kite Zanzibar, or at the One Ocean desks at Ocean Paradise and Melia.

Kite Zanzibar m 0773 114976; e info@ kitezanzibar.com; www.waikikiafrica.com/ kitesurf.html. Based at Waikiki (above) this IKO-registered kite centre offers instructor-led courses as well as hiring out North-branded equipment to experienced kiters. Beginners can join small groups (max 4 pupils/instructor), intermediates can top up their skills, & professionals can practise freestyle & wakestyle acrobatics. *Beginner lesson on sand (3hrs) US$140; intermediate lesson (6hrs) US$260; advanced lesson (9hrs) US$375.*

KIWENGWA

A small, traditional coastal village with a stunning beach, Kiwengwa is also the heart of Zanzibar's package-holiday industry. A glut of exclusively Italian all-inclusive resorts cluster along the beach immediately around the village, with several other large hotels spaced along the coast to the north. That said, with continuous in-house entertainment and exhaustive facilities, the guests at all of these resorts are rarely seen outside of their chosen hotel's perimeter walls, so the area around is generally quite quiet. The contrast between the dusty Zanzibari fishing villages and the lush, European hotel grounds is stark, and sadly the bigger developments and their visitors have often displayed a depressing lack of environmental and social consideration towards the local area and population. However, there are some who have made real efforts over many years, notably Bluebay and Shooting Star, and are good options on what is a truly beautiful beach.

GETTING THERE AND AWAY The easiest way to reach Kiwengwa from Zanzibar Town is along the good tar road, via Mahonda and Kinyasini. The small coastal road, both north and south, is narrow, sandy and badly maintained, so 4x4 vehicles are advisable if you choose to travel it. The excellent tar road north to Matemwe is parallel to this and just slightly inland of it.

You can come by **taxi**, **rented car** or **motorbike**, or arrange a **minibus** through a tour company. By public transport from Zanzibar Town, **dalla dalla** No 117 runs between 06.00 and 19.00, whilst the public **bus** on Route 15 passes through the village five times daily. The 'official' stop for both is in the village; though for a small fee the driver may well drop off at individual hotels. The major resorts and upmarket hotels all arrange transfers from the airport and Stone Town.

WHERE TO STAY AND EAT   *Map, page 250*
Exclusive

Bluebay Beach Resort (112 rooms)
m 0774 413321; e mail@bluebayzanzibar.com; www.bluebayzanzibar.com. Set on a lush, gently sloping site, spacious rooms are in thatched, 2-storey villas. Rooms in the original complex have 2 large or 1 king-sized dark wood 4-poster beds, a dressing area & private balcony or terrace; the garden & deluxe rooms also have a lounge area. Satellite TV, electronic safes, tea-/coffee-making facilities & mosquito nets are standard. Deluxe rooms enjoy a bath & a private outside shower. Honeymooners are welcomed with arches of fresh flowers adorning their doors, & families are well catered for with interconnecting rooms, a children's pool, playground, a kids' club (⏰ 08.00–15.00), the possibility of babysitting & an onsite nurse at sister property Sultan Sands (below). There are 2 rooms kitted out with a shower shelf & ramp for visitors with limited mobility. There are oodles of activities from canoeing to catamaran sailing, a One Ocean centre onsite for diving & snorkelling trips (page 256), a large freshwater swimming pool with jacuzzi & a floodlit tennis court. The professional Oasis Spa offers Vichy treatments, massage tables with a sea view, a steam room, open-air whirlpool with loungers & an adjoining fitness centre. There is free Wi-Fi throughout the communal areas. The 5 restaurants & bars cover everything from extensive dinners to beachfront seafood, coffees & cocktails,

with the majority of guests staying here on an all-inclusive basis. Bluebay is proud of being a 'Green Globe 21' organisation: a sustainable tourism certification. It recycles all room & laundry waste, purifies water to keep its gardens green, incinerates all garden & kitchen rubbish, soundproofs generators, uses energy-efficient fittings & collects rainwater from its specially designed roofs. In addition, the gardens are planted only with indigenous species. Christmas, New Year & Easter supplements apply. Airport transfer US$40pp each way. Al. **$$$$$**–

Sultan Sands Island Resort (76 rooms)
m 0774 413321; e mail@bluebayzanzibar.com; www.bluebayzanzibar.com. The newer sister property to the neighbouring Bluebay (above), this large hillside resort offers rooms in thatched rondavels dotted among planted terraces above the beach. The split-level interiors house a dbl bed, sofa-bed lounge & modern facilities including satellite TV & minibar. All rooms are sgl storey & very few have a sea view, but the gardens are well tended with snaking coral-stone paths to the beach. In the main building, arches, courtyards, fountains & colourful scattered flowers set the cool, calm tone in the reception. There is a pool, the Casablanca Lounge, the Mwambao all-day restaurant & the beachfront Asian Kivuli Bar & Restaurant. Once a place to relax with a book, the hotel has recently jumped on the animation programme bandwagon & offers a wide

range of activities from Oscar movie evenings to coconut-throwing competitions, Wed village walks, beach football, fortnightly fashion shows & w/end discos. If this still isn't enough to keep you occupied, energetic guests can venture next door to Bluebay where further facilities abound. Christmas, New Year & Easter supplements apply. Airport transfer US$35pp each way. HB. **$$$$$–**🛏

Luxury

🏠 **Shooting Star** (16 rooms) m 0777 414166; e shootingstarlodge@gmail.com; shootingstarlodge.com. Standing on a coral cliff above the stunning Kiwengwa Beach, this is a firm favourite with young, well-travelled Europeans. Built & run by the charismatic Eliamani 'Elly' Mlang'a, a charming & engaging Tanzanian, & his family, it is a delightfully social place, despite the high number of honeymooners who visit. The 3 small & simply furnished garden rooms border the lodge's central area & have a dbl/twin bed, mosquito net & en-suite bathroom. The sea-view cottages are a step up with lovely decorations & each offering mosquito nets, a large shower, a private terrace, comfortable Zanzibari beds, colourful Tingatinga pictures & dyed makuti mats. In line with the lodge's child-friendly attitude, 4 of these cottages have been designed with families in mind & include a dbl bedroom & separate twin-bedded upper room. Named after the island's trade winds – the Kusi from the south & the Kaskazi from the north – 2 separate villas offer luxurious accommodation & some real privacy. Each suite is entered through a pair of intricately carved Zanzibari doors flanked by large potted palms. Inside, both temperature & style are cool: high-quality finishes, antique furniture, AC & whirring ceiling fans. In the entrance hall, there are curved cushion-clad baraza benches, Swahili-style interior-design books piled on the coffee table & a dressed Zanzibari daybed awaiting tired travellers. With an adjoining shower, dressing room & kitchenette (complete with well-stocked fridge), this area is easily converted into an extra bedroom for families. Continuing up the curved staircase at the rear, the spacious master bedroom boasts a super-king-sized 4-poster bed, twin baraza benches & a large lockable chest for valuables. Windows have shutters to keep out the midday sun, but when opened they afford views along the coast in both directions. Up a further flight of stairs, the roof terrace is the

perfect place to enjoy a sunrise coffee, stretch out on the cushioned baraza or indulge in a moonlit bubble bath for 2, while overlooking the island vegetation & ocean beyond. There is also a private garden on the ground floor with a small plunge pool surrounded by soft sand, coir loungers & a little bar. Tasty snacks & fruit are available & meals can be served here or at the main restaurant. For all guests a stunning horseshoe infinity pool & sundeck afford superb views over the ocean, barrier reef & beach below, as well as the opportunity for a cooling dip when the tide's out. Alongside, a circular 'beach' area has been created. Dining is split among 3 adjoining areas: 2 beneath makuti thatch & 1 under date palms, but all surrounded by tropical vegetation. Meals here are simple & filling, but it's the lively bar & relaxed lounge area that is the true heart of Shooting Star. Elly's invariably on hand to offer friendly advice & help with planning, whilst card & board games are available for those content with a bottle of wine & a quiet seat. There is also a Star Bar under suitably star-shaped makuti thatch on the beach. With the waves literally crashing underneath at high tide, this is a terrifically friendly evening hangout – even before the famed lobster beach BBQ (an extra US$45pp). Diving & snorkelling trips can be organised, & fishing trips with the locals on outboard boats will give a totally different take on life on the ocean wave. For relaxation, a seaside spa room is available for massages &, appropriately, seaweed wraps. There's a phone for guest use &, with satellite connection, fast internet access. All rates FB; B&B & HB rates available; transfer from Zanzibar Town US$60. **$$$$$–**🛏

Mid range

🏠 **Kiwengwa Apartments** (12 rooms) m 0777 421824; e info@kiwengwaapartments.com; www.kiwengwaapartments.com. In neat white bungalows, complete with Omani windows, shady terraces & flowerbeds, these en-suite rooms offer hotel services with basic self-catering facilities, too. The PiliPili Restaurant offers beachfront Italian dining all day long, & there's a swimming pool & easy access to a raft of watersports activities. SC. **$$$**

🏠 **Zan View Hotel** m 0774 141803; e yourhome@zan-view.com; www.zan-view.com. Receiving consistently warm & positive reviews, this Danish–Zanzibari-owned hilltop hotel offers rooms & semicircular terraces overlooking the pool & a 2-storey, open-sided lounge/bar. Rooms – from dbl to family & honeymoon suites – are en suite & immaculate with coconut-wood beds, coir shelves & coloured mkeke mats & batik cushions. The service levels are high with Jakob & his team working hard to offer island tours, food & advice to ensure holiday enjoyment. B&B. **$$$**

🏠 **Sunrise Lodge** (4 rooms) m 0777 239296. If you can negotiate the huge craters in the road from Kiwengwa junction down towards Obama Beach BBQ, & block out the masses of roadside litter, then Sunrise is a surprisingly pleasant little lodge. Sitting right on the beach, the unassuming seafront rooms are immaculate: simple but nice. Large coconut-wood beds with neat coir-hung shelves & smart moulded-concrete bathrooms, & there's also a family room, complete with bunkbeds, available. Unsurprisingly for the area, Sunrise is run by an Italian, Silvia: a gentle, caring lady with a background in island quad-biking. The simple restaurant has a suitably fusion Italian–Swahili menu, with a selection of pasta & fresh seafood, as well as a popular tasting menu featuring lobster, squid & octopus curry & grilled fish & chips (*US$25pp*). B&B. **$$–$$$**

WHAT TO SEE AND DO   As of 2016, Kiwengwa boasts a rather lovely and practical shopping precinct. Built by an Italian firm, **Ce L'Hai Service Mall**, is opposite Veraclub Zanzibar and has a café, small supermarket, hair salon, and perhaps most importantly, an excellent medical clinic with a well-stocked, international pharmacy, and a branch of the People's Bank of Zanzibar, including an ATM – the only bank on the island outside Stone Town. It is easy to spot on the roadside with its smart, contemporary architecture, lush lawns and water features.

The major resorts and hotels can organise the normal tourist trips and watersports, as can tour operators in Zanzibar Town (pages 114–17). At Kiwengwa junction, there's something of a small beach scene with a cluster of makuti buildings offering local massage, kitesurfing & seafood meals. There is a distinctly Italian influence on account of the nearby all-inclusive mega-resorts, so expect signs, menus and pricelists to be in Italian: Bienvenuti da Massage Monica, Scuola Kitesurf & Ristorante Pesce. The notable naming exception is the Obama Beach BBQ, easily spotted under its Rasta-coloured makuti poles, where scantily clad Italians can be seen tucking into pizza slices and seafood platters with 'Maasai' warrior beach boys.

Diving

🤿 **One Ocean**   m 0774 310003; e info@ zanzibaroneocean.com; www.zanzibaroneocean. com. Well-equipped & thoroughly professional, this PADI 5* dive centre is One Ocean's area hub. Offering the usual array of courses & dive opportunities, including pool-based training & refresher courses. Diving & snorkelling trips depart at 08.00 on board *Manta*, a custom-built dive boat which concentrates on sites around Mnemba Island, & *Storey*, & both return in time for lunch. Helpful staff are always willing to answer questions & give underwater advice. PADI courses can be taught in English, Swahili, Italian & Spanish. *US$45 snorkelling; US$110/305/480 for 2/6/10 dives; equipment rental US$15/day; PADI Open Water US$500; Advanced US$470.*

PONGWE

Northwest of the Ras Uroa headland, a series of idyllic, palm-fringed, sandy coves make up Pongwe. Except for a tiny fishing village and a handful of small, individual accommodation options, there is very little else here: and that's its magic. Blissful beach relaxation, away from everything. You can wander round the few village streets to watch men stitching together fishing baskets or practise your Swahili with curious small children, but that's about it. There is a small, new office for 'Pongwe Tours' offering the usual island excursions, but otherwise visitors here have little cause to stray far from their hammocks on the beach.

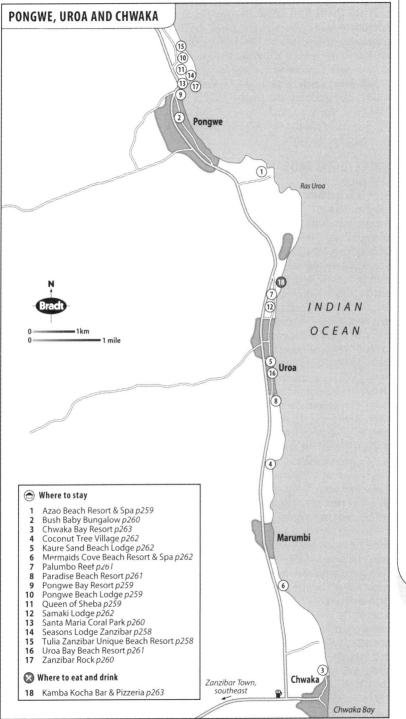

PONGWE, UROA AND CHWAKA

Pongwe

Ras Uroa

N

Bradt

0 ⸻ 1km
0 ⸻ 1 mile

INDIAN
OCEAN

Uroa

Marumbi

Chwaka

Zanzibar Town,
southeast

Chwaka Bay

⊖ **Where to stay**

1 Azao Beach Resort & Spa *p259*
2 Bush Baby Bungalow *p260*
3 Chwaka Bay Resort *p263*
4 Coconut Tree Village *p262*
5 Kaure Sand Beach Lodge *p262*
6 Mermaids Cove Beach Resort & Spa *p262*
7 Palumbo Reef *p261*
8 Paradise Beach Resort *p261*
9 Pongwe Bay Resort *p259*
10 Pongwe Beach Lodge *p259*
11 Queen of Sheba *p259*
12 Samaki Lodge *p262*
13 Santa Maria Coral Park *p260*
14 Seasons Lodge Zanzibar *p258*
15 Tulia Zanzibar Unique Beach Resort *p258*
16 Uroa Bay Beach Resort *p261*
17 Zanzibar Rock *p260*

✖ **Where to eat and drink**

18 Kamba Kocha Bar & Pizzeria *p263*

GETTING THERE AND AWAY Pongwe Beach and Nature Safari Lodge can arrange **minibus** transfers from Stone Town, or these can be organised by local tour companies (pages 114–17). By public transport, **bus** Route 6 and **dalla dalla** No 209 (only three per day) from Stone Town travel to Pongwe, with dalla dalla No 214 to Uroa often continuing to Pongwe village: ask the individual drivers.

Self-drivers will be pleased to find that the bumpy mix of sand and coral rag which once made up the coastal road is now paralleled with a smooth, fast tar road up to Kiwengwa and beyond. A **4x4** can still negotiate the original route, but patience and a good suspension are necessary for any degree of comfort and there are negligible benefits.

WHERE TO STAY AND EAT *Map, page 257*

Exclusive

* ✿ **Tulia Zanzibar Unique Beach Resort** (17 rooms) m 0773 409377; e reservation@tuliazanzibar.com; www. tuliazanzibar.com; ⊕ closed May. Created by Czech developers, Tulia opened its imposing timber gates in 2015 to reveal an unexpectedly beautiful resort. On the tumble-down site of an old budget bolthole, an oasis of calm, beauty & luxury modern design has appeared. It boasts one of the most attractive gardens on the island & every plant here is indigenous, in effect creating a resort-sized botanic garden. Off meandering tanga-stone pathways, the sgl-storey suites (3 categories) have classic interiors blending European elegance with natural materials: silk lampshades, Egyptian cotton linens, & bespoke coconut-wood furniture, all in cool ivory & aqua colours. There's an array of quality in-room amenities from a Nespresso machine & personalised minibar to satellite TV & fast Wi-Fi. All rooms have wide verandas, some with lovely sea views through the feathery casuarinas, & champagne breakfasts are readily served outside. The restaurant itself is quite lovely, too – a fitting setting for some of Zanzibar's best food. Alongside the shaded, timber restaurant, the curvaceous swimming pool hugs the bar & reaches out towards the sea, surrounded by a lawned area for sun loungers & huddles of seagrass bubble chairs, perfect for poolside lazing under smart white umbrellas. Aside from sophisticated chilling, guests (big & small) can giggle their way down the curvy water slide that snakes around a verdant, manicured mini-mountain. There's also an artificial beach within easy striking distance of the cocktail bar, & for the more active, there's a personal trainer, bicycles, kayaks, snorkelling & yoga courses in the garden. This is definitely one of the island's smartest & most sophisticated boutique hotels, with the benefit of a quiet seafront (if not beach) & top-notch staff. HB. ♔

Luxury

✿ **Seasons Lodge Zanzibar** (11 rooms) m 0776 107225; e info@seasonszanzibar.com/ seasonslodge@gmail.com; www.seasonszanzibar. com. With dreams of starting up a boutique beach hotel, Irish–Ugandan owner Michael scouted opened this peaceful hotel in 2012, built using natural materials & local craftsmen. The bright & fresh cottages & top-floor rooms (7 dbl; 2 twin) are bathed in sunlight from the numerous windows & all have fans & folding louvred doors that allow the sea breezes to enter, so no AC is necessary. Being just metres from the sea, there are 180° ocean views from all balconies & terraces. In the en-suite bathrooms sit a cast-iron claw-footed bathtub & 2 sinks, with solar-heated water on tap. The cottages are a little more private than the rooms, each with its own garden. The striking chokaa limestone design of the buildings gives a pretty mottled effect. The owners have made a conscious & commendable effort to limit their carbon footprint by growing their own herbs, spices & vegetables, & chickens, goats, ducks & turkeys are kept here by locally employed staff. They have installed solar electricity throughout & are a member of ZANREC island recycling. After a hard day's sunbathing lie back in a chair & sip a Scottish malt whisky in the ingeniously named Bar Es Salaam. The Temple Bar, a throwback to the owner's Irish roots, offers similar fare down on the sand. While the romantic cottages, privacy & sweeping vistas would suggest that honeymooners are the main target market, the owner has included a small splash pool on the side of the main pool for his young daughter, & visiting children are welcome to use it, too. If sea splashing & beach lounging isn't enough, the lodge also has brand new mountain bikes, table tennis, boules & kayaks for guest use. B&B. $$$$$

✱ ⌂ Pongwe Beach Lodge (20 rooms)
e info@pongwe.com; www.pongwe.com;
⊕ closed May; see ad, 2nd colour section. Standing within its own quiet cove, under a shady oasis of coconut palms, this is a simple little lodge in a lovely location. It is a well-managed, good-value haven for relaxing on a beautiful beach, & consistently (& justifiably) popular. There are airy, whitewashed bungalows, furnished simply with traditional Zanzibari beds & mosquito nets, woven palm mats, fans & moulded-concrete en-suite bathrooms (brackish water). 3 rooms are located in the pretty garden, while the remaining have beachfront views. Dbl & trpl rooms are available, with some rooms capable of taking 4 beds at a squeeze. Above the pool in 2 semi-detached buildings, 4 new en-suite rooms mark a distinct departure from Pongwe's original bungalow buildings, with a private sapphire mosaic swimming pool, polished tanga-stone terrace, lounge area & masses of space. From the walk-in wardrobe to the lovely black-&-white photographs & large shower room, they feel indulgent & well-designed. There are plenty of inviting hammocks & loungers, a small library, a kite for seaside entertainment, free kayak hire & an array of other individual & group beach games. The reef is only 15mins offshore & the resort has its own dhow for sailing, snorkelling trips, & game or line fishing that can all be arranged at the Captain Ali Boti beach shack. On the rock to the north of the beach, beside the border with Tulia Boutique Hotel is a lovely infinity pool. Large enough to swim lengths & with an imported beach area & decked surround, this area is a popular, if slightly exposed, spot when the tide's out. Yellow-clad pool attendants are on hand to supply drinks & fresh fruit at 16.00. Pongwe is especially proud of its food with tasty lunches from US$5 & varied set menus for dinner, including succulent spiced meats from the professional tandoori oven. Fri nights are often given over to beach BBQs with an array of seafood & Swahili favourites. There is now also a tiered baraza creating a lovely, intimate lounge area alongside the Komba Bar. Great spot for afternoon chilling or after-dinner candlelit drinks. With a little notice, children are warmly welcomed at the lodge & there are good children's discounts. HB. **$$$$–$$$$$**

Upmarket

⌂ Azao Beach Resort & Spa (43 rooms)
m 0779 567822; e info@azaoresortzanzibar.

com; www.azaoresort.com. An incongruous resort, whose entrance has all the charm of a cheap Middle Eastern office block: a wood-panelled, inordinately high, conical reception area, with high-shine floors, plastic sofas & some empty ground-floor shop units. There is no softness or obvious welcoming committee. Behind this, rooms are laid out in 'streets' like a housing community radiating from the large swimming pool. Interiors are newly furnished & clean, with an array of amenities, but remain soulless in the vein of a mid-range airport hotel. Some rooms are interconnecting via a semi-circular, primary-coloured sitting room. There is a barn-sized restaurant under a red roof, occasional volleyball net, spa, fitness suite & a distinct paucity of staff & guests. B&B. **$$$$**

⌂ Pongwe Bay Resort (20 rooms) ✆ 0777 706868; www.pongwebayresort.com. Not to be confused with long-established Pongwe Beach, this is a quiet lodge situated on the curve of the bay. Encircling the swimming pool & jacuzzi, the 2-storey whitewashed buildings offer very spacious rooms with curved sofas, silky bedspreads, sage-green moulded-concrete fittings & a good number of in-room amenities. The large, open-sided restaurant is eclectic in range – sushi platter (US$28), fresh tagliolini (US$12) & Pongwe beef filet (US$20) – though a little quiet to have real ambiance. The boutique Maji Spa offers aromatherapy & stress-relieving treatments, & there's a pool table & darts board in the grounds, whilst paddle boards, beach volleyball & a selection of Swahili games offer additional distraction. One Ocean (page 246) can collect divers for sub-aqua excursions. B&B. **$$$$**

Mid range

⌂ Queen of Sheba (10 rooms) e info@ queenofsheba-zanzibar.com; www.queenofsheba-zanzibar.com. Adapted from a private house, this has the same owners as Santa Maria Coral Park (page 260), & is well signposted off the main road. Friendly staff greet visitors in the airy central area, & the low-key, happy vibe is immediately apparent. There are few frills but for the more budget-orientated traveller this is a good option on this stretch of coast. In the original villa there are 2 dbl rooms with en-suite bathrooms; the sgl, dbl & trpl rooms in the 3 newer stone houses are clean & extremely large, with Spartan décor & bougainvillea-clad terraces. The upper rooms offer good sea views, & soon all will offer hot-water en suites. There's a pleasant stretch of beach below the vibrant orange restaurant & it's blissfully quiet thanks to little development in the immediate vicinity. For a little aquatic action, fishing & snorkelling can be arranged on the owner's boat (*US$20–30pp*), otherwise just lie back & chill by the raised pool. B&B. **$$$**

🏠 **Santa Maria Coral Park** (10 rooms)
e info@santamaria-zanzibar.com; www.
santamaria-zanzibar.com. Opened by an entrepreneurial local named Suleiman, this is a delightful hideaway. With no other developments currently along the beach here, this really is a place to get away from it all & relax. Set in a coconut grove, in the middle of a sweeping bay, there is a well-spaced collection of simple bandas & bungalows, a mix of sgl & dbl storey, with high thatch & suspended ceilings. Rooms are basic with solid wooden beds, coconut-rope & timber shelves, colourful mats on the floor & block-printed buxom mermaids adorning the walls. All rooms have hot water & there is 24hr electricity, with a backup generator. Arguably, the best rooms are the new & smarter 'Sultan & Soloman' rooms, though set back within the coconuts, the coral rock & timber building does boast superb views along the bay. Lunch & dinner are served in the bar: usually freshly cooked fish or chicken with pilau rice or 'Zanzibar Kitchen' coconut curry (*US$10*); alternatively splash out on the lobster in garlic butter (*US$20*). Dhow snorkelling trips can be arranged to the reef beyond the bay, or there's a simple thatched lounge/library area for enjoying a cooling drink & a good book, & a new swimming pool surrounded by a coral-rock wall of mosaic dolphins. The capable manager, Abubakor, will happily help organise anything; he's friendly & helpful & speaks English with ease. Airport transfer US$40. B&B. **$$$**

🏠 **Zanzibar Rock Hotel** (5 rooms)
m 0778 948704; www.zanzibarrockresort.
com. Unlike any other accommodation on the island, Zanzibar Rock is quite literally perched on a narrow coral rock outcrop in Pongwe Bay. Very simple mkeke buildings are spread around the island, some with rather lovely views of the coconut palm belt of Pongwe village. The interiors are very basic with everything made of palm: walls, floors, ceiling & even blinds. There is an en-suite shower & toilet area, screened with only a fabric curtain. At the southern end of the island, an open-sided bar-cum-restaurant serves an eclectic menu from salads & burgers to pasta & oriental prawn noodles. 2-for-1 cocktails are available at sundown & 4-course lobster dinners with wine can be arranged (*US$50pp*). In early 2016, a swimming pool was being hewn into the coral rock, which will give guests a cooling spot for a dip during low tide. For arriving & departing guests, you can walk to the island at low tide or take the small rowing boat when the tide cuts the island off. This is a very quiet & isolated spot, with low-key staff & limited options – it's idyllic or nightmarish, depending on your perspective. B&B. **$$$**

Budget

🏠 **Bush Baby Bungalow** (2 rooms) m 0776 815273; www.bushbabypongwe.jimdo.com. These basic, mkeke bandas have somewhat thrown-together interiors; the mish-mash of lino, maize sack & broken-tile mosaic flooring, patterned walls, & a dbl bed, complete with blue mosquito net (after a fashion) are almost passable. Amid the palms, there's a local-style bar, decorated with strings of shells, upcycled plastic-bottle light shades & Maasai paintings, & a wall delineating the property. B&B. **$$**

UROA

The small village of Uroa is on the coast about halfway between Pongwe and Chwaka. Neat bundles of wood are piled 'jenga-style' by the roadside, quirky pedestrian crossings have been painted on the road, and village life appears active and ordered. It's a traditional, slow-paced place, centred on fishing and seaweed collection. There have been a few low-key accommodation options here for many years, but 2008 saw the start of larger developments at either end of the village. So far these resorts have not set the trend for a flood of all-inclusive properties in the area, but with coastal land at such a premium, this may not be the case for long.

GETTING THERE AND AWAY Approaching from the south on the 9km of blissfully tarred road from Chwaka, you'll pass cultivated, plantation-style fields of casuarina pines; from Kiwengwa, 15km to the north, there is now a fast tar road too, with the old coast track the preserve of **4x4** drivers alone.

Dalla dalla No 214 plies the route from Stone Town to Uroa six times a day, between 06.00 and 18.00, whilst the public **bus** on Route 13 adds another five services from 08.00 to 16.00. If you prefer, private **minibuses** and **taxis** can also be arranged by most reliable Zanzibar Town tour operators (pages 114–17).

WHERE TO STAY *Map, page 257*
As well as those listed below, a smart new bougainvillea-clad resort, likely to be called Ocean View Resort, is currently under construction on the ocean side of the road north of Paradise Beach Resort, and may be open by the time you read this.

Upmarket

Uroa Bay Beach Resort (97 rooms) m 0778 672809; e reservation@uroabay. com; www.uroabay.com. Italian-owned but international in approach & clientele, this resort is spread over a large, lawned plot with a series of makuti-thatched accommodation blocks stretching back from the beach. Smart, well-spaced dbl, trpl & family rooms are available, with 4 being wheelchair accessible with walk-in showers & level floors. Seafront & sea view, the latter being a little further back from the sea, are otherwise identical: tiled, spacious rooms with 1 king & 1 sgl bed, cream-&-burgundy interiors, & wide terraces. Satellite TV, fridge & electric safes are standard throughout. The communal area houses the internet room, a simple boutique, Jua buffet restaurant, Rafiki bar &, behind the tropical mural, a massage room. Nearby, but apart from the accommodation, is the small Disco Mwezi for evening entertainment. There's also a floodlit tennis court, beach volleyball area, 5-a-side football pitch, a large swimming pool & a wellness centre. FB. **$$$$–$$$$$**

Palumbo Reef (102 rooms) m 0772 633063; e palumboreef@hotmail.it; www. palumboreef.com. The majority of guests here are on European package holidays, hence the pasta stations in the restaurant & Italian-speaking 'animators' encouraging guest participation in the day's activities. Accommodation is in 4-storey blocks, & all rooms have basic mod cons with Zanzibari beds. There's a pleasant swimming pool snaking down to the beach, a popular pool bar, thatched restaurant area & an adjacent TV lounge. The usual island excursions can be arranged, or there's an on-site spa. FB. **$$$$**

Paradise Beach Resort (76 rooms) 024 223 8021; e booking@hotelzanzibar.com; www.paradisebeachresort.com. Between Uroa & Chwaka rises the truly massive makuti roof of Paradise Beach Resort's reception. Beyond this, there are 56 rooms in the main resort area, 13 new suites, & a further 7 rooms at the satellite Beach House, 15mins' walk north along the beach (close to Mermaid's Cove). Each has a fridge, electronic safe, hot water & capacity for dbl or trpl occupancy. The Premium room has a lounge area & TV, whilst the Luxury rooms are identical but lack the audio-visual equipment. The 1st-floor suites are simpler but thoughtfully decorated & still very spacious. In a small coconut grove, there is a central sundeck & a popular pool. Other onsite activities are limited to the spa, a few bicycles & the pool table, although the team can arrange diving,

BEACHED SEAWEED

From December to mid February, some of the beaches on the east coast have large patches of brown seaweed washed ashore from the ocean by the wind. This can be quite a shock if you expect pristine, picture-postcard tropical beach conditions. The seaweed normally stays on the beaches until the start of the rainy season, when it is carried back out to sea.

sailing & the usual tours elsewhere on the island. The beach here is not Zanzibar's finest, with landed seaweed & little sand. There's a large buffet & à la carte restaurant under shady dhow sails, complete with open kitchen, plus a safari feet-in-the-sand beach restaurant, & a Jetty Bar on stilts over the sea, for sundowners & Sun dance classes (16.00). Most guests here are on all-inclusive holidays from Germany & the Netherlands; B&B only possible. **$$$$**

🏠 **Samaki Lodge** (35 rooms) m 0772 633063; e samaki@samakilodge.com; www. samakilodge.com. Owned by the same Mr Palumbo as its immediate neighbour (page 261), Samaki differs in both architecture & vibe. Its design is marked out by striking shell-encrusted coral walls (doing little for any environmental awareness credentials) & a fish skeleton logo ('samaki' means fish) that adorns lights, room numbering & all signage. Overlooking the pool, but set back from the beach, the L-shaped main building houses most of the accommodation & the public areas. There's an à la carte restaurant (all cuisines in spite of the 'Italian food' sign the on gate) serving b/ fast, lunch & dinner in high season (only b/fast served here in low season; all other meals at neighbouring Palumbo) & a piano tucked away for musical guests, with no organised activities, making this a much quieter establishment than Palumbo Reef, albeit still predominantly Italian. Additional rooms are located beside the beach, in a separate building. Access from these to the main area is less than salubrious, on a rough path bordered with barbed wire, but they do afford a little more intimacy & a sea view. B&B. **$$–$$$$**

Mid range

🏠 **Coconut Tree Village** (59 rooms) m 0773 201867; e info@coconuttreevillage. com/reservation@coconuttreevillage.com. Pulling up at Coconut Tree, you could be forgiven for thinking you were arriving at a low-budget, crumbling safari park. Life-size animal sculptures litter the entrance & landscaping: grimacing gorillas point at the gate, some sun-bleached giraffe greet you inside, whilst zebra & kudu hide in the vegetation around room terraces – it is undoubtedly a curious place. The terraces of standard & superior rooms are identical except in furniture choice; newer rooms are in multi-storey buildings dotted around the complex. The central area has rows of sofas, angled to the TV & its fuzzy African soap opera, & a restaurant. There's also a small gym & a pool. This resort is very quiet, so negotiating rates should be possible. B&B. **$$$**

🏠 **Kaure Sand Beach Lodge** (8 rooms) m 0774 536256; e kaure.sand@gmail.com. Taken over by a local Zanzibari team in recent years, this is set on a quiet & beautiful stretch of beach at the end of a bumpy side road (continue seaward past the Buio Bar). Rooms vary considerably by location, from 1 above the main entrance to semi-detached bungalows with sea views, but all are large (some sleep up to 4 with a dbl & wonky bunkbeds) & relatively sparsely furnished. Furniture in general is fairly low quality but it is clean & functional, & all rooms have a small terrace on the large plot. There's a large, muralled restaurant & a large weaver bird-filled tree under which to chill, but no particular activities here or in the immediate vicinity. B&B. **$$$**

🏠 **Mermaids Cove Beach Resort & Spa** (18 rooms) m 0776 434434 e info@mermaids-coveresort.com; www.mermaids-coveresort. com. Long-standing, Norwegian-run Tamarind was sold in 2016 to the owners of Stone Town's Africa House Hotel (page 129) & renamed Mermaids Cove. Renovated though not rebuilt, the rooms now have new en-suite bathrooms, AC throughout, fresh paintwork & Zanzibari beds. Along a particularly stunning stretch of coconut-lined beach, the semi-detached cottages built from coral-stone blocks & cement are each entered through traditional doors. All rooms have a dbl bed, mains electricity, 2 ceiling fans, & mosquito net. Interiors are traditionally furnished, clean & comfortable. There is a safety-deposit box at reception for valuables, a small TV room, games room, gym area & a large central pool with integrated children's pool. The restaurant (*lunch & dinner US$15pp*) offers indoor dining at individual tables, beach meals & fresh produce, with an emphasis on seafood, whilst the adjoining bar produces fabulous freshly squeezed juices & lots of cocktails. Children are generally welcome at the hotel, a cot is available & babysitting can be arranged with the staff, but, beyond playing in the pool, sea & sand, activities are limited. B&B. **$$$**

WHERE TO EAT AND DRINK *Map, page 257*

✖ Kamba Kocha Bar & Pizzeria

🕙 10.30–00.30. 'In this bar you'll never drink alone' claims the signage, & popular it is. Italian-owned & Maasai run, this timber-clad bar & restaurant is a busy seaside hangout for guests of the neighbouring resorts. Inside, the bar is decorated with graffiti: declarations of love & alcoholic words of wisdom adorn every inch of the interior. Outside on the sand, pub benches & mosaic-topped tables sit under makuti umbrellas & the clay oven serves up pizza for US$5–9, alongside a host of daily cocktails. $$

CHWAKA

Halfway down the east coast, directly due east of Zanzibar Town, Chwaka is a large fishing village overlooking a wide bay fringed with mangrove swamps. In the early 19th century, Chwaka was a major slave port, exporting human cargo across the Indian Ocean to Arabia. In more recent times, its sea breezes and lack of mosquitoes made it a popular holiday destination for British colonial administrators and affluent Zanzibari dignitaries: their grand, crumbling villas remain along the shoreline north of the village. Today, apart from some coastal researchers, there is not much in the way of facilities or activity, besides the large, lively seafood market, where for the best atmosphere, arrive in the mornings when the fishing boats dock, laden with the day's catch.

Chwaka Bay itself supports the largest swathe of mangrove forest on Zanzibar and forms a significant part of the Jozani-Chwaka Bay National Park (pages 324–9), Zanzibar's only national park. The government is currently working with international charities, like CARE International, and conservation bodies, to develop and manage the forest as a conservation area and income-generating ecotourism project. Some tours to explore the mangroves are possible, and do make an interesting diversion. There is little accommodation in Chwaka and few visitors, but it's possible to take a boat across Chwaka Bay to head further down the east coast, which may attract the adventurous.

GETTING THERE AND AWAY Chwaka can be reached by public **bus** (Routes 6 and 13), **dalla dalla** (Nos 206 and 214) or by **hired car** or **bike**. Tourist **minibuses** do not usually come here, although you could privately hire one through a tour company (pages 114–17). However you choose to travel, if you approach from the west, the smooth, tarmac road through the island's lush interior is a pleasure.

If you are heading to or from the southeast coast, and don't want to go back to Zanzibar Town in between, you can hitch a ride on an octopus-fishing **boat** (high tide only) across Chwaka Bay to Michamvi on the peninsula north of Bwejuu. Local people regularly travel this way, but only the occasional intrepid tourist is seen here. Boats from Michamvi come across to Chwaka's fish market most mornings, returning around noon. There are no set schedules, so you will need to ask around on the beach. A ride should cost little more than a few dollars.

🏠 WHERE TO STAY AND EAT *Map, page 257*

🏠 Chwaka Bay Resort (30 rooms)

m 0777 574931; e info@chwakabayresort. com; 🔧 chwakabay. North of Chwaka village on the coast road, past some near-derelict grand colonial villas, this all-inclusive Italian complex is filled with social groups of 30-somethings from Rome & Milan. The original rondavels are light & spacious, with large windows, dark furniture, AC & en-suite bathrooms. The newer villas (each with 4 independent rooms), referred to as 'deluxe' have a terracotta-tiled terrace & a view to the beach. Rooms in both categories are raised up away from the sand. The beach isn't as good as many on the east coast, but daily

Mangroves are salt-tolerant, resilient, evergreen trees, anchored by stilt-like roots in the intertidal zone (eg: *Rhizophora mucronata*) or simply growing in sandy muddy bottoms (eg: *Avicennia marina*), or even perched on fossil coral pockets with minimum soil. They are found in sheltered bays and river estuaries, where the waves have only low energy levels, and are vital components of the tropical marine environment. They ensure shoreline stability by protecting soft sediment from erosion, providing nutrients for sea organisms, and offering sanctuary to migratory birds, juvenile fish, shellfish and crustaceans.

Mangroves are nevertheless one of the most threatened habitats in the world. Environmental stress from changing tides and pollution takes its toll, but increasingly it's human interference that is the primary cause of irreparable damage. On Zanzibar, this is certainly the case: many people rely on the forests for fuel (firewood and charcoal), lime burning, boat repair and dugout manufacture, as well as material for house construction. Mangrove wood is dense and, because of its tannin content, it is termite-resistant, making it preferable for house construction. Income is also generated from trading in cut wood, poles and charcoal. The absence of alternative income-generating activities means heavy dependence on mangroves.

Ominously, as the rural population continues to grow, so does the demand for this fragile resource. It is therefore critical to fully understand and address the needs of the villagers in order to have any chance of developing successful conservation initiatives.

Chwaka Bay is fringed by Zanzibar's largest area of mangrove forest, approximately 3,000ha and accounting for 5% of the island's total forest cover. Here, fairly dense stands of diverse mangrove species, zoned by their tolerance to the conditions of the area (eg: volume of water and salt levels), are drained by a number of lovely creeks.

Over the last 70 years, assorted management plans have been drawn up with the communities bordering the forests, in a bid to control overexploitation in the area. From issuing permits to control harvesting, imposing mangrove taxes and limiting creek access, each has successively failed to halt rapid deforestation. Ever-changing forestry policy, lack of serious patrolling, a decline in the authority of village elders to command community support, insufficient alternative income sources for villagers, and minimal resources are all cited as reasons for the failure.

Conservation and development organisations continue to attempt to halt deforestation in the area, improve villager understanding of the forests' importance and lobby local and national government for support; but, without doubt, these valuable natural resources will be irretrievably ruined unless human activities are carefully controlled.

---

boat trips to the other side of the peninsula are arranged, & the kidney-shaped swimming pool is pleasant enough & alongside the open-sided buffet restaurant. B&B. **$$$–$$$$**

UFUFUMA FOREST HABITAT

The Ufufuma Forest conservation project was set up by the people of nearby Jendele village, and aims to protect the forest habitat and educate the villagers in sustainable use. The 102 local volunteers, led by the dedicated and charismatic Mr Mustafa Makame, hope to make it a place for both locals and foreigners to visit, and to preserve the traditional worship of *shetani*, or spirits, which is performed here (see box, pages 40–1). The forest area is at present only 1km², but the villagers are leaving the surrounding 4km² area uncultivated to allow the forest habitat to expand in size. Tiny paths, marked with periodic, mid-blue arrows, wind through thick vegetation, whilst underfoot a tangle of roots clings to coral rag. A visit here is not a great wildlife experience, nor is it meant to be, although you might be fortunate enough to see skittish red colobus monkeys (as we did; apparently early morning is best), island birdlife, snakes and lizards. Honey is also collected from the forest, so look out for the canopy-height hives. A few villagers act as guides, but they are not wildlife specialists and don't know a lot of the bird names. They are trying to learn, however, and are very enthusiastic about Ufufuma's cultural importance – which is the primary reason for a visit here.

There are many underground caves hidden in the dense forest undergrowth: three are shetani caves being used by the local traditional healer (aka 'witch-doctor'), which tourists may also visit. It is a source of great joy and comfort to the local Zanzibari people who come to these caves to speak with the spirits (see box, pages 40–1). When local people are sick or troubled they come to these sites with the local traditional healer and perform rituals and recitations to cure themselves. The cave entrances are adorned with tattered strips of red and white fabric and surrounded by piles of sweet offerings, often rotting, from sugar cane to Coca-Cola. Inside, the caves are dank and spooky, with the smell of smoke from recent fires and resident colonies of bats. It's a fascinating insight into a rarely seen aspect of Zanzibari culture.

Mr Mustafa and his small team believe wholeheartedly that in protecting the forest there is potential for the local communities to benefit financially from conservation tourism; they are simply unsure how to achieve their goal. Gaining support from all of the villagers is difficult – many want the timber for firewood and rocks for building, and perceive little monetary gain from conservation. But Mr Mustafa is determined, and, whilst searching for a solution, he travels to Ufufuma from Zanzibar Town every Sunday on his moped, keen to inspire and educate the villagers about protecting the forest. He even chairs the local NGO.

Six villages in the vicinity already benefit from the income of the forest. All of the money goes directly to the community leaders, who assess their village's primary needs, be it cattle medicine, wells or school materials, and channel the money as appropriate. If more people visit the forest, accepting that it's not a slick tourism enterprise, the village coffers will slowly increase, and in turn the communities will begin to see the benefits of preserving rather than plundering their surroundings. We wish the Ufufuma Forest conservation project every success.

ARRANGING YOUR VISIT To visit Ufufuma Forest, it is best to make contact in advance, to ensure that an English-speaking guide is available at the time of your visit (*Mr Mustafa Makame*; m *0777 276620/0747 491069*; e *himauje@ yahoo.com/jules8982@aol.com; ufufuma.wordpress.com*). The price of a visit is variable as a single tariff system has yet to be adopted. However, for a guided forest walk lasting a few hours, a visit to the caves, and usually a gift of fresh fruit or coconut refreshment, expect to pay US$5 per person per guide, and then volunteer to make a larger donation to the community fund. If you want to see a full shetani ceremony, consisting of about seven hours of singing, dancing and assorted rituals, this costs US$50 (for one or two people), and will have to be booked in advance and take place at a time convenient to the local 'doctor'. As the forest floor can be damp and rugged, be sure to take sturdy shoes, and, in the hot season, plenty of water to drink.

UFUFUMA'S USEFUL TREES

As in most African societies, many of the trees and plants found in Ufufuma Forest play an important role in the daily lives of the local population. Be it for medicinal or practical use, religious or cultural significance, the flora is fascinatingly versatile when viewed through the eyes of a resident guide. The trees below are a sample of what's to be seen and learnt. They are listed by their Swahili name, as the guides will not know them by anything else.

MCHOFU Across the island, the branches of this tree are commonly used as an all-purpose timber for firewood and furniture. Here, only its fruits are used as a cure for coughs, colds and flu.

MDAA (*Euclea natalensis*) Ufufuma's answer to Colgate: this is the local toothpaste. The villagers chew on a piece of the tree's root to ensure a bright, white set of teeth and healthy gums. In 1991, research into this custom by the South African Medical Research Council at the University of Stellenbosch showed that oral bacterial growth was indeed suppressed by this chewing, giving the practice some scientific validity. Sadly, it also concluded that the daily exercise is too limited to have a truly beneficial effect: this is probably backed up by the smiles around you.

MKOMWE (*Caesalpinia bonducella*) Mkomwe's Latin name derives from the Arab word *bonduc*, meaning 'hazelnut'. It's easy to see why when presented with the neat spherical seed kernels (Swahili: *komwe*) from within its fruit. These are the traditional pieces used in games of *bao*, but the dual-purpose seeds of this tree can also be boiled with water to produce a drink for sufferers of stomach ache.

MKUYU The roots of this wild fig are boiled with water to form a drink. Given to pregnant women, the concoction is believed to have an abortive quality.

MLALANGAO Hunting for birds is a patient but ingenious process. Local men must first study the avian movements in the forest, watching flight paths and routines. To catch the birds, they cut the trunk of the mlalangao tree with a *panga* (long blade machete), collect the sap (Swahili: *utomvu*), and boil it to form a type of latex. Back in the forest, the chewing-gum-textured latex is smeared onto the branches where birds have been observed resting. Then the men wait … for when the birds do land, they simply stick to the latex from where they are easily collected and taken home to make soup.

MUWAVIKALI This sweet-smelling tree is boiled with water and the resulting liquid is drunk to combat symptoms of malaria.

MKAAGA Seek out the young leaves on this little bush. They'll provide you with the freshest tea.

GETTING THERE AND AWAY To reach Ufufuma from Zanzibar Town, take the road west towards Chwaka: the forest is on the left, about 5km before Chwaka. There is currently a small, slightly rusted sign but no specific parking place, and only concealed paths lead into the forest. If you have contacted the Ufufuma volunteers in advance, then a welcoming party will likely be waiting for you. However, if your visit isn't scheduled, stop at Jendele village and ask in the market area for an official forest guide.

To reach the forest on **public transport**, talk to the dalla dalla drivers heading towards Chwaka (Nos 206 or 214), and ask to be dropped in Jendele village; be aware this is a sprawling village with little tourism connection so it may not be an easy task.

DUNGA RUINS

Equidistant from Chwaka and Zanzibar Town, in the lush centre of the island, close to the modern village of Dunga, these are the remains of the palace built for King Mohammed, the Mwinyi Mkuu (great chief) of Zanzibar. Constructed between 1846 and 1856, the palace may have been built on the site of an earlier house. Prior to this, the residence of the Mwinyi Mkuu had been at Kizimkazi or Unguja Ukuu (see pages 315 and 329 respectively).

Local legend tells that when Dunga Palace was built, slaves were buried alive in the foundations, while others were killed and their blood mixed with the mortar. It was believed that this would bring strength and good fortune to the house. There may be some truth in this story as, in the 1920s, a nearby well was found to be half full of human bones. Today, in the centre of an overgrown garden, only the main walls of the palace remain, but it is still an imposing ruin and retains something of its original grandeur.

A few old passages, pillars and staircases can also be seen. The windows are empty and their decorative frames are now in the House of Wonders in Zanzibar Town (pages 163–4), along with the Mwinyi Mkuu's sacred drums and horns. The latter were part of the royal regalia and both were kept at Dunga during King Mohammed's rule. The drums, carved from mango wood and inscribed with Arabic, were said to beat spontaneously to warn the king of impending trouble. The horns were kept in a secret hiding place, known only to the Mwinyi Mkuu. When he was near death, their location would be revealed to the heir apparent. Mohammed died in 1865 and was succeeded by his son Ahmed, but he died of smallpox in 1873, leaving no male heir. His two sisters had married into prominent families of Arab landowners, but the ruling dynasty came to an end.

A Swahili royal line is believed to have existed on Zanzibar prior to the first Shirazi immigrants arriving from Persia in the 10th century AD. Leading figures among the Shirazis are thought to have married into the family of the then Swahili ruler, as the Mwinyi Mkuu later claimed to be descended from a Shirazi prince. During the following centuries, while the island was controlled by the Portuguese, and later by the Arabs and British, a Mwinyi Mkuu continued to be regarded as the traditional leader by the people of Zanzibar.

GETTING THERE AND AWAY About 14km from Stone Town on the road to the east coast, or 30 minutes' drive inland from Chwaka, the ruins sit in the centre of the island on the southern side of the road. It is also possible to reach Dunga from the south, along the dirt track from Tunguu, on the main road to the island's southeast; a **4x4** is necessary for this route. By **dalla dalla** from Zanzibar Town, it's possible to reach the ruins on the Chwaka services, (Nos 206 and 214) or by public **bus**, (Routes 4 and 6).

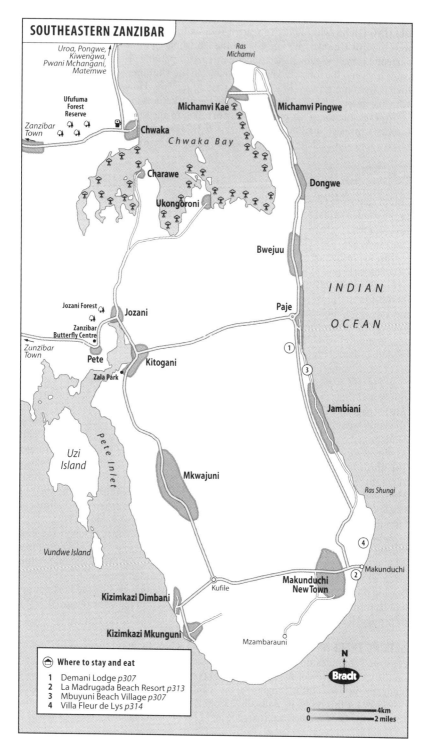

SOUTHEASTERN ZANZIBAR

Uroa, Pongwe,
Kiwengwa,
Pwani Mchangani,
Matemwe

Ras Michamvi

Michamvi Kae

Michamvi Pingwe

Ufufuma
Forest
Reserve

Zanzibar
Town

Chwaka

Chwaka Bay

Charawe

Dongwe

Ukongoroni

Bwejuu

INDIAN

Jozani Forest

Jozani

Paje

OCEAN

Zanzibar
Butterfly Centre

Zanzibar
Town

Pete

Kitogani

Zala Park

Jambiani

Uzi
Island

Mkwajuni

Ras Shungi

Vundwe Island

Kufile

Makunduchi
New Town

Makunduchi

Kizimkazi Dimbani

Kizimkazi Mkunguni

Mzambarauni

N

Where to stay and eat

1 Demani Lodge *p307*
2 La Madrugada Beach Resort *p313*
3 Mbuyuni Beach Village *p307*
4 Villa Fleur de Lys *p314*

Bradt

0 ——— 4km
0 ——— 2 miles

10

Southeastern Zanzibar

From the finger of the Michamvi Peninsula to the coastal curve at Makunduchi, the southeast of Zanzibar offers, in many ways, a continuation of the powder-white sandy beaches and traditional fishing villages found from Matemwe to Chwaka Bay. Certainly the environment here, with its large tidal range and fringe reef parallel to the beach, is almost exactly the same.

A decade or so ago, the area around the villages of Paje, Bwejuu and Jambiani used to be the busiest part of the east coast, especially for backpackers, as there was a good choice of cheap places to stay. However, things have changed in recent years and the variety of accommodation has increased considerably, whilst the arrival of tourism to the peninsula's furthest reach at Michamvi Pingwe and Michamvi Kae have opened up a whole new area. A scattering of mid-range and upmarket options have appeared, with more imagination and thought going into their design and ethos, and the success of a few large family resorts has widened the area's overall appeal.

The island's network of fast tar roads are now spreading the budget travellers between the traditionally livelier environs in northern Zanzibar, around Nungwi and Kendwa, and the burgeoning beach bars, 'flashpacker' retreats and kitesurfing centres of Paje. There remain a large number of rather uninspiring guesthouses along the southeastern coast, many almost indistinguishable from the next, but competition is forcing some improvements and among them some gems are worth seeking out.

The end result is that southeast Zanzibar now offers some of the island's quietest beach spots available to a genuine mix of budgets. The palm-fringed beaches here invariably seem wilder and more ramshackle than their counterparts on the northeast coast, and still offer fewer makuti-shaded cocktail bars and full moon parties than those of Nungwi, Kendwa and Kiwengwa. With the exception of a couple of larger all-inclusive properties, the southeast of the island is still generally an area for a lower-key, lower-impact beach retreat.

MICHAMVI PENINSULA

Along the length of the Michamvi Peninsula's 10km east coast, the sand is the fine, powder-white stuff of 'paradise' advertising, the sea is a suitably sparkling cobalt blue, and the hotels are some of the most luxurious on the island. Few local people live here, concentrating instead in Bwejuu to the south or the village of Michamvi Kae, beside Chwaka Bay. Almost all of the accommodation in this area is currently high quality, and each place is individual in its style and customers. However, the number of hotels has more than doubled in the last decade, and more are being built. For the immediate future, come for the

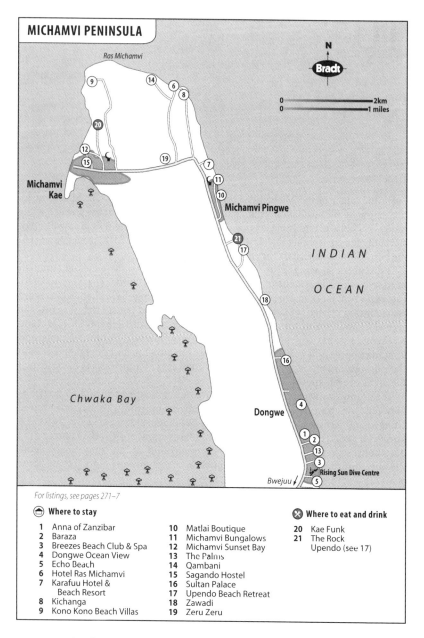

MICHAMVI PENINSULA

Ras Michamvi

N

Bradt

0   2km
0   1 miles

Michamvi
Kae

Michamvi Pingwe

I N D I A N

O C E A N

Chwaka Bay

Dongwe

Bwejuu   Rising Sun Dive Centre

For listings, see pages 271–7

Where to stay

1	Anna of Zanzibar
2	Baraza
3	Breezes Beach Club & Spa
4	Dongwe Ocean View
5	Echo Beach
6	Hotel Ras Michamvi
7	Karafuu Hotel & Beach Resort
8	Kichanga
9	Kono Kono Beach Villas
10	Matlai Boutique
11	Michamvi Bungalows
12	Michamvi Sunset Bay
13	The Palms
14	Qambani
15	Sagando Hostel
16	Sultan Palace
17	Upendo Beach Retreat
18	Zawadi
19	Zeru Zeru

Where to eat and drink

20	Kae Funk
21	The Rock
	Upendo (see 17)

pristine, palm-fringed beaches, good diving opportunities and a sense of space, and hope that development stalls.

GETTING THERE AND AWAY All of the accommodation on this stretch of coast will arrange **transfers**, though most international guests will set this up in advance with their tour operator. For those with a **hired car**, north of Bwejuu there is a single fast tar road, so getting lost is virtually impossible; a bumpy coastal track also heads north, although the arrival of the tar highway has rendered it into more of a footpath, and it is almost impassable at points. There is little in the way of public transport on the peninsula, but **dalla dalla** No 324 from Zanzibar Town will sometimes continue from Bwejuu towards Michamvi Kae village.

WHERE TO STAY Map, opposite
Exclusive

Anna of Zanzibar (5 villas) m 0773 999387; e info@annaofzanzibar.com; www. annaofzanzibar.com. Staying here feels like being welcomed into a friend's home & the spacious villas are cosy & full of charm. Split into 3 rooms – a living room, bedroom & bathroom – all are filled with homely touches like deep armchairs, dressing tables, framed black-&-white photos & an abundance of cushions. The 2 resident dogs complete the home-from-home vibe. On a practical note, all the bedrooms are fitted with minibars & a safe; for proximity to the sea, book rooms 4 & 5. The villas surround the pool, which sits behind a lovely section of powdery sand, where b/fasts & special dinners are served. On occasion, tasty 3-course meals are also eaten at the formal table in the dining room. The lounge is a popular place to kick back; there's a large satellite TV & DVD collection, plus a good range of novels left by previous guests. Free, reliable Wi-Fi is available all over the property, & laptops are available to take to rooms. For more indulgent entertainment, there's an outside bathtub & 2 massage treatment rooms (US$40/hr), or the hotel also has a telescope for stargazing. Commendably, the owners here are spearheading a campaign to provide benches for local schoolchildren who would otherwise sit on the floor, & are matching every dollar donated – so please do contribute if you stay. AI. Min stay 7 nights over Christmas & New Year. Airport transfer US$45/party each way. ♨

Baraza (30 rooms) m 0720 538148/0733 777172 e baraza@thezanzibarcollection.com; www.baraza-zanzibar.com. A member of The Zanzibar Collection group, all-inclusive Baraza aims to be more family-friendly than its sister, The Palms (page 272), & more luxurious than its eldest sibling, Breezes (page 274). With strong Omani influences in its architecture, ornate gardens, & plunge pools, its target is clearly affluent families who are not interested in the island's activity-focused mega-resorts. Whitewashed, flat-roofed villas are divided into categories based on their proximity to the sea & bedroom numbers. All have a spacious lounge, mod cons & décor of golden fabrics & glittering cushions. The imposing Presidential Villa also offers 2 massive rooms & a lap pool. Each villa has a numbered umbrella on the beach, complete with a pair of sun loungers for the sole use of the room's occupants, though the pool appears to be the focus of afternoon chilling. Diners have a choice of the equally excellent Sultan's Restaurant, serving Indian food, or the more traditional, Swahili-influenced Livingstone Terrace; afterwards, sip liqueurs in the atmospheric library. The lavish spa feels more like an Arabian palace theatre set, filled with swathes of fabric & antique-style artefacts from the Middle East & India. Scented treatment rooms & a further courtyard pool offer respite from the outside heat, while the more energetic can enjoy a fully equipped fitness centre, yoga room & tennis courts. Shoppers may be tempted by the Aladdin's Cave curio shop, which sells a range of art, swimwear, crockery & even furniture, all in a similar Arabian style to the hotel's own. The kids' club is filled with colourful toys, a small paddling pool & even miniature beds for afternoon napping. Given the success of its sister hotels & the affiliation with the respected Rising Sun Dive Centre (which also has a small base here; page 277) it's no surprise that Baraza is proving to be a slick, quality operation. AI. ♨

Echo Beach Hotel (12 rooms) m 0773 593260/0774 366794; e info@echobeachhotel. com; www.echobeachhotel.com. In 2007, British expats Sue & Andrew Page swapped life at their quaint Loire Valley B&B to create Echo Beach. This small, friendly lodge has high aspirations & is receiving some admirable reviews. 4 small detached cottages & 3 dbl-storey houses with 2 rooms in each are arranged in an arc behind the inviting kidney-shaped swimming pool, & there are 2 cottages at the rear of the property offering more privacy & a daybed in the loft. Almost every room has a sea view from its private terrace, & each is attractively screened with billowing fabric panels in a rainbow of colours, giving this lodge an original take on the

10

Zanzibari norm. Room interiors vary slightly, though all are similar in style: a 4-poster dbl bed swathed in a mosquito net, feature wallpaper, African bedside lamps, carved wardrobes, highly polished floors, good AC, ceiling fans & open bathrooms with huge walk-in showers. The large open-sided lounge/dining room is under high makuti thatch with gleaming aqua tiles on the floor; the food is consistently very good (Andrew is a chef) & the pre-dinner bar chatter makes it a cheerful hangout. It looks out towards the sea through a coconut grove, & the lovely stretch of beach is a mere stone's throw away. Echo Beach is more about relaxing than action, though there is an onsite dive operation. Children can stay at the discretion of the management, so advise at time of booking. HB 🍴

🏠 **Kono Kono Beach Villas** (27 rooms) m 0772 265431; e reservations@konokonozanzibar. com; www.konokonozanzibar.com. Kono Kono opened its doors in 2010 & promptly closed them again the following year; the same happened in 2016 after a fire. Fully operational once more, the lodge has undergone some significant refurbishment & has reopened with additional villas & a much-needed beachside restaurant & a spa. The 25 large, contemporary villas all have their own secluded gardens with plunge pools, & are well spaced over this extensive plot, but they are enclosed so don't expect sweeping sea views. There is a beachfront option, in the 2 beach pavilion rooms, right on the magnificent sandy cove, with loungers & palm umbrellas just a few steps away. The lovely infinity pool sits on top of the coral cliff, in front of the large – somewhat soulless - makuti-thatched restaurant area, complete with small bar & TV area. The open-air spa has good therapists & a treehouse feel, making this resort an overall hit for those seeking quiet relaxation over activities: the idyllic beach with a good book & a massage are the definite highlights. HB 🍴

✳ 🏠 **Matlai Boutique Hotel** (6 rooms) m 0777 300012/0772 628833; e info@hotelmatlai. com; www.hotelmatlai.com. 'Matlai' is Kiswahili for 'the gentle morning wind that blows from the ocean to the land', & this is indeed a cool spot in the centre of Michamvi Pingwe. Beautifully planted & manicured gardens of palms, tropical flowers & carefully raked sand pathways hide a dozen shady, secluded spots of loungers, hammocks & romantic dinner hideaways. Accommodation is in either 1 of 4 independent rooms within Asili House or at

Kidosho House, housing 2 separate rooms but with the feeling of an exclusive rental for 2 travelling couples. Both are very different in architectural design & style. Asili House boasts a spectacular entrance, overlooking its stylish curvaceous pool, complete with picturesque palm & swim-up stools in its centre. Rooms are named after the elements – Earth, Fire, Water & Air – with corresponding colour schemes, & created from an array of natural materials. There's a covered, open-air dining area, semi-circular barazas, a dhow bookshelf & some oversized armchairs. Kidosho is more Arab in style: a grand entrance through gorgeous flower-filled gardens, this sgl-storey house is whitewashed with curved colonnades & beds are enclosed in arched inner rooms with gold accents. There's a shared infinity pool & broad private terraces. At the northern end of the plot is a split-level beach bar & pleasant feet-in-the-sand restaurant. There's also a raised spa area, with vibrant kanga curtains, an open-fronted sea view, beanbags & a masseuse for holistic massage & body scrubs. There's a children's playground, boules area, beach volleyball, a large tortoise enclosure, open-air cinema options in the garden & a 10-min walk along the beach brings you to the dive centre, The Rock Restaurant & Upendo beach bar. In a peaceful spot, Matlai is contemporary African beach chic with delightfully attentive, friendly & accommodating staff to match. A great option for escapists. HB. 🍴

🏠 **The Palms** (6 villas) m 0777 440882; e info@palms-zanzibar.com; www.palms-zanzibar.com. Immediately adjacent to Breezes (page 274) & owned by the same family, this is significantly more exclusive & expensive. The large, luxurious villas attract young, affluent honeymooners lured by style & intimacy; however, it is immediately next door to a large family-friendly resort, & everyone shares the same beach, so romantic dinners for 2 on the sand may be subject to intrusion. Palms set out to achieve 'understated elegance', & this has broadly been achieved. The colonnaded Plantation House is the main resort building, housing its bar/lounge, dining room & mezzanine library. Here, antique cabinets, carved dark wood sofas & natural palm mats rest on highly polished floors, while heavy old-fashioned fans spin in the high makuti thatch. The billowing *organza* curtains & afternoon tea on the deck complete the colonial feel. At the ocean end of the building, tarnished mirrors &

candles fill a dining room set with sparkling crystal glasses & simple flower arrangements. Individually named after exotic spices, the villas sport shaggy thatch roofs & a large curved front terrace. Through French doors, there is a lounge with picture windows revealing the classically elegant bedroom decorated in brown, cream & apricot, with Arabian brass lanterns & wooden furniture. There's a bathroom with a bath & even a private outdoor plunge pool. The villas share a small, split-level, tiled swimming pool, & each is also allocated a private banda overlooking the beach, where intimate dinners can also be served (tide dependent). Makuti shades draped with panels of indigo fabric make these a good place to escape the heat of the day & survey the beach beyond. For most activities, head to neighbouring Breezes though Palms does have a tiny spa, The Sanctuary. AI; minimum age 16. ☕

✳ ⌂ **Qambani** (7 rooms) m 0779 754242; www.qambani.com. Qambani is edgy, chic & addictively indulgent. With only 7 rooms & a distinctly high-end home-from-home vibe, it is one of the island's finest boutique spots. The individual villas are spread along the length of this large oceanfront plot, each impeccably furnished with contemporary pieces with & a firm eye on Africa. State-of-the-art sound, light & Wi-Fi, beautiful bathrooms, lovely linens, relaxing lounges & sea-view terraces are standard – though this place is far from standard. Its expansive central area is far more luxury beach house than hotel, packed with interesting *objets d'art*, original Tanzanian pop art, stunning coffee-table books & designer furniture. From the groovy sunken bar & the lantern-filled Moroccan shisha den to the cushioned white sofas & the desk for postcards home, everything has been carefully considered. Continuing the homely vibe, meal times & menus are decided on the day to match your whim, & food can be enjoyed at the chef's table in the smart kitchen, in the formal dining room, or under the stars on the terrace; nothing is too much trouble. Venture outside along snaking stepping stone pathways & you'll find the stunning infinity pool & its funky shaded bar, or wander down the coral cliff to reach the beach: a stretch of long, linked coves, where high-tide walks are possible. Staff here are 1st class: capable, friendly & able to anticipate your every need. It's an expensive destination, but without question value for money. FB. ☕

⌂ **Sultan Palace** (22 rooms) ☎ 024 224 0173; m 0777 423792; e sultanpalacezanzibar@zanlink. com; www.sultanpalacezanzibar.com. Set high on a coral cliff, overlooking a deserted pristine beach, this elegant place has a good amount of olde-worlde charm. Rooms are widely spread & divided into Flower Rooms & Ocean, Garden & Imperial suites, with Ocean & Garden being identical apart from the view (though there is a better view of the sea from the Garden suites here than from many sea-view rooms at other nearby hotels). Colour-coordinated interiors are extremely spacious with some beautifully ornate pieces of carved Zanzibari furniture, a bed draped in a lace-trimmed mosquito net, & tasteful locally sourced antiques. Each room is named after a flowering plant, & its name is ornately painted on a ceramic tile on the door post & in reception, where a row of keys hangs below the gold flower paintings. The unusual, Arabesque main area is laid out in a circle, with striking stained-glass windows, fading old Africa maps & fascinating black-&-white photos of Zanzibar of days gone by. Up 1 floor, the restaurant has a breezy interior & a great view over the sea at b/fast time. Dinner here is a 3-course affair, & the local chefs have been trained by Italian cooks, making for some delicious fare. There's another restaurant on the beach, open for snacks & drinks, & a clifftop infinity pool for low-tide swimming. FB. ☕

⌂ **Karafuu Hotel & Beach Resort** (135 rooms) m 0777 413647/8; www. karafuuzanzibar.com. Karafuu is as friendly as you would expect from an Italian-owned resort. Carved chaise-longues, polished floors & beaded chandeliers greet arrivals, before they join the couples sipping margaritas at the poolside ZanziBar. Its rooms are all good quality & quite smart, & they're divided into 7 categories, based solely on proximity to the beach, with only the junior suite having a sea view. All have big beds with neat wrought-iron seats at the end, a daybed & minibar. Outside, a wide terrace with wooden furniture looks out onto gardens filled with beautiful white lilies & coconut palms. Children are warmly welcomed & well catered for with a children's playground & a sectioned-off baby area within the main pool. There's also a large diving & watersports base beside the pool, the Wimbi Dive Centre, & a long stretch of beach, albeit with relatively high numbers of beach boys. It's hard not to feel that a significant increase in the size of this hotel has shifted its focus from quality to quantity. FB. **$$$$**–🍽

🏠 **Kichanga** (23 rooms) m 0777 835515; e booking@kichanga.com; www.kichanga.com. This attractive cliff-top lodge sits above a lovely sandy cove at the northernmost tip of the Michamvi Peninsula. Its cottages are of stone-&-thatch or rustic timber construction & are in staggered rows to give a mix of beach-facing & garden outlooks. Interiors are a little sparse, especially in the family rooms, & slightly tired, but they do all benefit from large wooden sea-view terraces. Mosquito nets, fans & safes are standard throughout. In the main building there's an internet point, local tailor, a lounge bar & a Swahili-influenced restaurant There are organised snorkelling trips, canoe rental & kite-boarding; even beach towels are provided. The cove geography means that very few non-residents come even close to the beach, & children are pretty safe from wandering too far. The sand here migrates, & is at its best from Aug–Dec; the beach gets progressively rockier as the Kaskazi wind blows. There is a pool popular with young families, a massage banda for local treatments (*US$25/hr*), an experienced onsite yoga teacher, Ilse, & a pool bar for midday drinks & snacks. HB. **$$$$**–🍽

Luxury

🏠 **Zawadi** (10 villas) m 0720 538148; e info@ thezanzibarcollection.com; www.zawadihotel.com. Opened in 2016, Zawadi is the young, trendy sibling of Breezes, Palms & Baraza (below, pages 272 & 271), & aims to offer a more relaxed, beach-house vibe. Differing in location, Zawadi is set atop the coral cliff-face, with sophisticated villas offering fabulous ocean panoramas from their large, utterly private terraces. Interiors are calm & stylish with beaded chandeliers, marine-inspired decorations, crisp linens & indulgent bathrooms, all featuring a bath with a view. The open-sided Mali Mali lounge & dining areas have pale grey themes & an adult air: high-backed dining chairs exclusively set for couples & oversized pots sprouting lush tropical leaves (albeit plastic ones!). Alongside the pool, the 3-tier Mswakini Bar offers snacks & sundowners overlooking the bougainvillea terracing & sandy cove to the turquoise sea beyond. Neutral colours, giant wicker bell lampshades & bunches of green coconuts placed on the tables give a calm, casual simplicity. There is a much more open vista here than at the palm-fringed resorts to the north &

south, & Zawadi is definitely designed with sun worshippers in mind. Bar a few token umbrellas poolside, planting is generally low level. Below the main area, the small coral cove offers a pretty beach at low tide (there's an artificial raised beach for high-tide lounging), & thanks to an offshore channel it's possible to swim in the sea all day long (bar during spring tide when currents make this risky). Strong, experienced swimmers can paddle down to enjoy snorkelling in the Blue Lagoon, 10mins south, or the team will drop you off in a minute by boat. There are kayaks & paddleboards, & other watersports & diving can be arranged through Breezes (below), & the current manager here is an experienced diver in the area so is well placed to assist with advice or arrangements. On land, there is a 1km jogging track, & the near future should see the arrival of an onsite spa. No young children; Al. **$$$$$**

Upmarket

☀🏠 **Breezes Beach Club & Spa** (74 rooms) m 0774 440883–5; e info@breezes-zanzibar. com; www.breezes-zanzibar.com. A perennial favourite with honeymooners & families, Breezes is a large, efficient, family-run beach resort. Amid extensive gardens are rooms in whitewashed villas decorated in muted neutral colours & with all the amenities of a good hotel. Rooms are comfortably furnished with large beds, & all have safe, fridge & sofa bed, but deliberately no TVs (although the newer 2-floor villa has one). The suite & deluxe categories are closer to the sea, & are upstairs & downstairs respectively. The suite also features a walk-in dressing room, slightly larger bathroom & wraparound balcony with sun loungers. There is a large pool at the centre of the resort, surrounded by verdant lawn & a great stretch of beach. Tall palms & makuti umbrellas offer shade at both, & wooden loungers are comfortable for reading & relaxing. The excellent Rising Sun Dive Centre is based between the beach & pool (page 277) & there's a brilliant, brightly coloured watersports centre on the beachfront, where everything from reef walks to body boards & bicycles can be arranged with the enthusiastic staff. Filled with the aroma of cinnamon & cloves, the Frangipani Spa is a great retreat: the team of Thai & Balinese professional masseuses ensure you leave purified & pampered, & for indulgent couples, there's also a private spa for 2. The yoga studio (with genuine yogi), fitness centre & floodlit tennis court complete the spiritual & physical well-being offered. There's a baffling number of restaurants: the Salama Dining Room for b/fast & evening table d'hôte; Breakers on the beach for lunchtime sustenance; & the intimate Sultan's Table offering fresh seafood & Swahili cuisine in a wood-panelled tower filled with red velvet cushions & brass lanterns. For private dining *à deux*, The Tides comes complete with its own chandelier & staff. For a cocktail & bar snack, the shady Pool Bar is a fun spot, with soft sand on the floor, coir-rope sofas & smiling staff in funky indigo-blue batik shirts. By night, the sophisticated & atmospheric Baraza Bar is a cool drinking den; shrouded in silk, it offers whisky, liqueurs & cigars. HB. **$$$$–$$$$$**

🏠 **Michamvi Sunset Bay** (20 rooms) m 0777 878136; e bookings@michamvi.com; www. michamvi.com. The only east coast resort facing west across water, this underwent a complete renovation in 2011, & also turned away from large, energetic groups. At the northern end of Michamvi Kae village, overlooking the mirror-like Chwaka Bay, it's now a relaxed, family-friendly resort with a casual vibe. There's a small restaurant & a breezy bar overlooking the pretty beach. The bedrooms are in 2-storey villas set out in an arc around the mosaic pool. Entering from the back, the rooms are light & spacious with contemporary furnishings, retractable mosquito nets & original Zanzibari art (any piece can be bought with 100% of sale price going to the artist). The bathrooms have a dbl shower, with 4 rooms enjoying a bath, too. All have either a private balcony or ground-floor terrace, complete with seating. Sunset mangrove safaris (*US$50, up to 4 people*) are available & several watersports are possible from the quiet beach, whilst divers are collected by the off-site Buccaneer Diving in Paje (page 294). The team here are very adaptable & children are warmly welcomed by the hands-on management, with under 12s staying for free. Equally, there is an impressive commitment to the local community. Several sensible, well-resourced – financially & practically – projects have been tried here, sadly with mixed success, though this is not for lack of effort from the lodge. Staff do receive a share of profits though, financial assistance is available for staff to purchase low charcoal usage cooker in a bid to combat excessive wood usage, – this place firmly lives up to its 'Making a Difference' philosophy. It's

a lovely remote spot on an increasingly crowded island. HB. **$$$$–$$$$$**

☀️ 🏠 **Upendo Beach Retreat** (3 rooms) m 0777 244492; e reservations@ upendozanzibar.com; www.upendozanzibar. com. Adjacent to Upendo Bar (page 276), Upendo now boasts 3 utterly fabulous villas: Shiv, Priya & Kusum. The largest, Shiv, is the original beach house: a mint-green, makuti-thatched villa that is a dream retreat for hip, travelling friends. There are 3 spacious dbl bedrooms, all with simple built-in furnishings, stylish bathrooms, & splashes of colour from circular mkeke mats & vibrant artwork. For couples, Priya & Kusum, on the southern side of the bar, are equally cool – hugely spacious & indulgent, with roof terraces, enormous showers, top-notch mod cons & lovely treats. All villas have plunge pools, or there's a swimming pool by the lounge bar. A private chef is on hand to prepare food to order, or give you a lesson in spicy Swahili cookery, & there's a family-style timber table beside the open kitchen for social meals. An iPod docking station, raft of design & fashionista magazines, & library hint at the low level of guest activity expected here – but with a beautiful breezy deck, beach frontage & good food & drink, it's easy to see why just chilling is de rigueur. Overlooking the beach, lagoon, & the Rock Restaurant, this is a super spot for escapists. It's close to Pingwe village, but far from the large resorts & crowded budget haunts elsewhere on the island. FB. **$$$$–$$$$$**

🏠 **Dongwe Ocean View** (18 rooms) m 0777 835515; www.dongweoceanview.com. Under the same ownership as Kichanga & The Rock (pages 274 & 276), this cool, chilled, unpretentious hotel has lovely beach views, comfortable, spacious rooms & reasonable rates. Entering through the high-ceiling pillared 'Clubhouse', where kanga-covered wicker sofas, hanging bubble chairs & a TV area offer a shady retreat from the sun, you get a sense of the relaxed vibe. Accommodation is in 2 3-storey whitewashed buildings, all with a pool & sea-view terrace. Interiors are cool & clean with white linens, neat chitenge curtains & matching trimmed mossie-nets, AC, fan & en-suite shower rooms. There's a large decked restaurant overlooking the sea, a tiled swimming pool & pole-shaded loungers. It's an easy walk to neighbouring hotels & activity centres, though for a quick dip, snorkels can be rented onsite (*US$5*). B&B. **$$$$**

Hotel Ras Michamvi (15 rooms)
m 0778 067510; e info@rasmichamvi.com; www. rasmichamvi.com. Managed by the same team as Casa Del Mar (page 301), this little resort sits high up on the coral cliffs at the very tip of the peninsula. It's in a very quiet corner of the island, so unless you have your own transport or enjoy extremely long walks it's really quite remote; of course, this is also its charm for the escapist. Bordered by peach-&-pink hibiscus bushes, the paths around the complex are all on slightly raised stone pathways with neatly planted macramé hanging baskets. Rooms are surprisingly nice with tiled floors, quality Zanzibari beds & large blue bathrooms. There are some rooms classed as 'disabled-friendly' with ramp entrances & walk-in showers, though the beds remain fairly high to be practical for those who are truly wheelchair-bound. There is an impressive semicircular restaurant & bar offering beautiful reef panoramas & glimpses into the open kitchen. Outside, steep steps lead down the cliff to a large swimming pool & a small private cove, where the sand is at its deepest & best in Jun/Jul. HB. **$$$$**

Mid range

Kae Funk (6 rooms) m 0774 361768; e kaefunk@gmail.com; www.kaefunk.com. ⏲ 11.00–late daily. This beach bar (page 277) also offers rooms in woven-palm bungalows with en-suite shower rooms, simple, natural interiors & some nice touches of mosaic mirrors, metal lanterns & fresh flowers. Chilled & entertaining, it's understandably popular with backpackers & social travellers. B&B. **$$$**

Budget

Zeru Zeru (7 rooms) m 0773 235016/0772 211564; e mwerevucompany@gmail.com; www.zeruzeru.org. Behind orange metal gates alongside the main road, Zeru Zeru is home to a friendly Tanzanian–Italian couple, Monica & Alberto, their sweet young daughter & 2 giant mastiff dogs. Rooms are in emerald-&-white semi-detached bungalows & offer simple, clean, en-suite accommodation (cold water), each with a terrace 'kitchen' for self-catering (2-plate gas burner & sink). There is a restaurant on the 3rd floor of the main house, where home-cooked meals are served at kanga-clad tables & hide chairs. There are 2 bicycles available for guest use & Alberto will drive guests to Michamvi Kae or Pingwe for shopping on arrival – though don't expect much in the way of supplies as these are small village shops. There is a good swimming pool & a Tingatinga-painted broken van-cum-playhouse but not much in the way of gardens. Rates are cheap but it is worth bearing in mind that this is a good distance from the beach & public transport is limited. B&B. **$–$$**

Shoestring

Sagando Hostel (10 rooms) m 0773 193236; e sagandohostel@gmail.com; www.sagandohostel.com. In Michamvi Kae, away from the beach, Sagando comprises 7 different but equally rough 'n' ready buildings with basic rooms (sgl–quad), all of which are en suite & of a standard expected at the bottom end of the budget scale. The dugout canoe bar has a Rasta vibe & simple Swahili food & drinks are available all day. B&B.**$**

✕ WHERE TO EAT AND DRINK *Map, page 270*

✕**The Rock Restaurant** m 0777 835515; e info@therockrestaurantzanzibar.com; www. therockrestaurantzanzibar.com; ⏲ lunch daily. Probably the most remarkable location of any Zanzibar restaurant, The Rock is perched on top of a marooned, seriously undercut coral-rock outcrop, just off the shore of the Michamvi Peninsula. Accessed by wandering across the sand at low tide, or by boat or breaststroke at high tide, the local team in this dilapidated building, with its cheery yellow window frames (no glass) & sea-life murals, serve up a simple 'catch of the day' & seafood pasta dishes. It's very basic, quirky & often empty, but the views are terrific, the staff friendly & the experience unique. Call in advance or book online, especially if you're coming a distance. **$$$**

✳✕**Upendo Bar & Restaurant** m 0777 244492; e info@upendozanzibar.com; www.upendozanzibar.com; ⏲ 10.00 until last customer leaves daily. On a gorgeous sweep of beach directly opposite The Rock, this is the perfect place to while away an afternoon, where gentle female bar staff mix tantalising cocktails & exotic mocktails: try the Upendo signature drink (Sky vodka shaken with guava juice & honey, then topped with sparkling wine) or the Apple Virgin Mojito. London lounge music is piped into the shady, cushion-covered beach barazas, &

Magical place on Matemwe Beach

Sunshine Hotel, Matemwe Zanzibar

* * * * *

PONGWE BEACH HOTEL

top left You're likely to see the blue (Sykes') monkey (*Cercopithecus mitis albogularis*) on a trip to Jozani Forest (th/S) page 51

top right A creep of giant tortoises (*Geochelone gigantea*) are found on Changuu Island, descendants of four gifted from the Seychellois governor to his opposite number on Zanzibar in the 18th century (M/S) page 195

above left Between 200 and 300 types of butterfly can be spotted at the Zanzibar Butterfly Centre, including the citrus swallowtail (pictured) (AVZ) page 328

above right Coconut crabs (*Birgus latro*) are common on Chumbe Island (AVZ) page 335

below The cute Suni antelope (*Nesotragus moschatu moschatus*) can be found on Mnemba Island (CM) page 247

top left Starfish are a common sight on inter-tidal walks along the east coast of Zanzibar (A/S) pages 59–60

above A spice tour is one of the most popular activities on
& right Zanzibar, giving visitors the chance to experience familiar flavours such as nutmeg (_above_) and cloves (_right_) growing naturally (s/S) and (PS/S) pages 192–3

below Turtles have been nesting on Tanzanian beaches for millions of years; Juani Island, just off Mafia, is the best place to witness them hatching (EC/EA) page 398

left & below The large, billowing sail of the traditional dhow is a typical sight off Zanzibar, and dhow builders can be seen at work up and down the coast (AVZ) and (SM) page 45

bottom Elaborately carved doors are a sign of a home owner's wealth and status, and grace both humble village houses and historic palaces in Stone Town (BB/S) page 173

above   Maruhubi Palace was once one of the most ornate on the island; following a fire in 1899 and poor maintenance, it has fallen into a state of picturesque ruin (AVZ) pages 184–5

right   Known locally as Ngoma Kongwe, the Old Fort in Stone Town was built in 1698 by the Omanis to defend against the Portuguese (S/D) pages 164–5

below   Mtoni Palace was home to Sultan Said's wives, their children and hundreds of slaves, and is now a conservation area (AVZ) pages 185–7

*left and
below left*

Fishing is one of the main economic activities throughout these archipelagos (AT/S) and (AD/S) page 28

*below right
and bottom*

Seaweed has been farmed by coastal dwellers for centuries — it is harvested and dried before being exported (GT/S) and (AVZ) page 29

above   A dalla dalla at Jambiani post office — a popular method of transport on Zanzibar (CM) pages 111–12

below   Bullfighting is a somewhat surprising local tradition on Pemba, thought to have been introduced to the island in the 16th century by the Portuguese (DD/A) page 362

WELCOME TO

NEXT PARADISE

BOUTIQUE RESORT ZANZIBAR

Next Paradise Boutique Resort Zanzibar   info@next-paradise.com

+255 (0) 773 822206   www.next-paradise.com

• Sunshine Marine Lodge •

COMBINE THE TRANQUILITY OF A UNIQUE

Paradise Getaway

with the spectacular marine life of the Indian Ocean.

more informations
page 242

more informations page 242

Sunshine Marine Lodge   DIVEPOINT

marinelodgezanzibar.com, info@marinelodgezanzibar.com
divepointzanzibar.com, info@divepointzanzibar.com

tasty treats are cooked to order. Delights range from salt & pepper squid (*US$5*) to loaded beef tacos (*US$9*) to the 'So Loaded' seafood fiesta sharing platter (*US$100*), comprising 1kg rock lobster, slipper lobster, crab, prawns, octopus, calamari & catch of the day. If you're too comfortable (or full) to move, there are even service bells provided. Sun brunches are an island institution, but it's worth a trip any time. With it's understated beach chic: a perfect place to just lose time. Rooms are also available in the affiliated villas (page 275). **$$$**

✕ Kae Funk m 0774 361768; e kaefunk@gmail. com; www.kaefunk.com; ⏱ 11.00–late daily. A fun, laidback reggae hangout with an impressive bar – in structure & contents. Barman Simba serves up cold drinks & cocktails from the massive array of liqueurs & spirits lining the multi-tier bar backdrop. On the upper deck, guests recline on cushioned swings in the shady garden, or sit at ngalawa tables enjoying coconut spice curry. Music is played all day, & fireside beach parties are a regular occurrence. Rooms are also available (page 276). **$$–$$$**

WHAT TO SEE AND DO   With many of the hotels on this stretch offering a gamut of activities in idyllic grounds, few visitors need step outside their own resort in search of entertainment. Divers, however, may need to head to a neighbouring property to find a dive centre. Excluding the one at the Italian-speaking Club Vacanze, the dive schools on the peninsula are as follows:

⤳ Karafuu Dive Centre m 0777 413647/8; www.karafuuzanzibar.com. This dive & watersports centre sits within the grounds of the hotel of the same name (page 273). It has all the latest branded equipment, as well as welcoming divers who bring their own (10% discount if you do), & offers everything from PADI to windsurf courses, kitesurfing, canoeing & mountain biking. Dive accessories, from dive computers to underwater Seadoo scooters, can also be hired. *Diving US$50/85 sgl/dbl; US$165/230/345 for 4/6/12 dives; Open Water US$390*

⤳ Rising Sun Dive Centre m 0777 440885; e bookings@risingsun-zanzibar.com; www. risingsun-zanzibar.com. This smart, efficient company is based on the edge of the beach at Breezes (page 274), but is independently owned & operated. The scuba kit here is regularly updated & remains in excellent condition. All Rising Sun instructors & clients are also covered by DAN (Divers Alert Network) insurance, but for those travelling throughout the continent they recommend taking

out insurance online with DAN Europe (*www.daneurope.org*). The dive school is geared to take both beginners & experienced divers looking for PADI speciality courses, such as Deep Water or Photography. There are 4–5 instructors permanently based here & each take a maximum 4–5 scuba guests. Using GPS & echo-sounder technology, several brand-new sites have been discovered, & the team are always keen to show experienced divers underwater treasures rarely visited by other companies. It is also the only PADI National Geographic Dive Centre in East Africa & does genuinely have a keen eye on environmental impact & care. The centre also offers snorkelling safaris (*US$15/25 child/adult*) & sunset dhow trips to the Chwaka Bay mangrove forests. Payment in cash only. *US$80/160/450/700 for 1/2/6/10 dives; Open Water US$545 (with e-learning); Digital Photography US$240; daily equipment rental (regulator, BCD, wet suit, mask & fins) US$35; underwater digital camera rental (inc CD of images) US$40.*

BWEJUU

About 4km north of Paje, sitting just back from the beach, Bwejuu is a dense network of dusty alleys and cramped houses, interspersed with towering palm trees. Like many of Zanzibar's east coast villages, it has experienced alarming population growth in recent years, which, combined with the increase in tourism on the coast, is putting great pressure on the resources here. Given that around 80% of the children frequently fail even the basic school exam, the village's problems sadly look set to increase. That said, lodges are working hard to support education

SUSTAINABLE SEAWEED FARMING

Seaweed has been harvested by coastal dwellers for centuries. This practice led to the export of red seaweed from Zanzibar to Europe in the 1950s, and continued until the wild stocks became exhausted. However, in the late 1980s, following initial scientific experiments by the University of Dar es Salaam, several development organisations and private companies began working with Zanzibar's north and east coastal communities to develop and promote the commercial cultivation of seaweed. This later expanded to the rest of the island, neighbouring Pemba Island and more recently to the mainland coast.

Providing initial funding, seedlings and technical skills, the aim is to encourage sustainable resource management, an essential prerequisite for long-term economic growth and employment, particularly for women. It is estimated that 15,000–20,000 people (90% of whom are women) are currently engaged in seaweed farming, providing a much-needed household income for many coastal workers. The revenue from this trade is also a great foreign-exchange earner for Zanzibar's economy.

Seaweed is used commercially as a source of carrageenan, a natural gelling agent produced from it by alkaline extraction. Used in the manufacture of toothpaste, cosmetics, medicine and also as a thickening agent in many food products, particularly some which are milk-based, this is a valuable, natural product.

With real market demand, several species of seaweed are now farmed, though the most common are the reliable, profitable strains of *Kappaphyicus alvarezii (cottonii)*, *Eucheuma denticulatum (spinosum)* and *Kappaphycus striatum*. By hammering wooden stakes into the sandy intertidal zone, and stretching lines of coir rope or nylon monoline a foot above the seabed, cultivation lines are prepared and small seaweed stems are attached. Each plot can have up to 50 rows of strings 30cm apart, each line carrying ten to 15 cuttings. The seaweed grows at a rate of 7% per day, increasing to tenfold its original weight in a fortnight. This rapid growth allows farmers to harvest their crop every six weeks; a total of 697kg of dry seaweed is harvested annually per farmer, earning them an average US$50–100 per month, although some earn more with increased effort.

The seaweed is then dried in the sun for a few days, bagged, and sold to seaweed brokers who transport it to Zanzibar Town and onwards to Europe and the USA. Replanting of seedlings can be done immediately, using fragments from the old crop, ensuring sustained farming and income. According to statistics from the Department of Marine Resources Zanzibar, the current production and export volume is 12,500 tonnes per annum.

---

projects within their communities and the work of organisations such as Bwejuu Charity School, educating orphaned and vulnerable children, are important steps.

Over recent years, there has been a significant rise in small-scale, roadside shops as you enter Bwejuu, but the majority of truly local men focus on fishing, whilst the women make coir rope from coconut husks (see box, page 312) or farm seaweed. With these ancient trades remaining the major industry, Bwejuu retains a very traditional atmosphere.

North of the village, towards Michamvi, it is still a quiet area, excellent for escapism, where there are plenty of places to enjoy just the sound of the waves and the wind rustling in the trees. Like the rest of the east coast, the tide goes out for

In 2006, a group of female seaweed farmers in the northern Zanzibar village of Kidoti were trained under the Zanzibar Seaweed Cluster Initiative (ZaSCI) to further increase their income by making finished products out of seaweed. Known as Tusife Moyo ('we should not lose heart'), they are members of the Zanzibar Seaweed Cluster Initiative who are promoting innovative methods of farming seaweed, such as deep-water floating lines, promoting working together with neighbouring villages and the invention and production of value-added products. Working under the Pan-African Competitiveness Forum (PACF – Innovative Clusters Programme), the Kidoti women (aided by the Small & Medium Enterprises Competitiveness Facility and the Tanzania Commission for Science and Technology), acquired the necessary machinery to manufacture seaweed soap (they also make soaps infused with aromatic spices). Other groups under the ZaSCI that make seaweed products are located in Paje (Furahia Wanawake Group) and Bweleo (Bado Tupo Bweleo & Jitegemee Group). The first 600 bars of seaweed soap were produced in March 2008, packaged neatly in specially created seaweed boxes and distributed for sale. Spurred on by their success, members of the Zanzibar Seaweed Cluster Initiative have already embarked on creating a range of diverse products from seaweed powder, foods such as biscuits, salads and cake, to body creams and scrubs for spas, and shampoo. The women's commitment and determination are deeply impressive, and have inspired similar projects elsewhere on the island. In Paje, the smart new Seaweed Center works in conjunction with ZaSCI to help improve and maintain working conditions for the village's 450 seaweed farmers, who earn an average of US$1 per day, training them to make organic seaweed soap, providing marketing and sales channels, and ultimately increasing their earnings. It is very much hoped profitability here will allow for expansion of this and similar projects.

The personal income generated from seaweed farming and its products has helped significantly to improve many villagers' standard of living. In many parts of Africa, farming has been traditionally regarded as women's work, and this remains the case with seaweed farming on Zanzibar. Consequently, much of the money earned stays in the hands of these rural women, who would not normally have their own source of income. The advent of seaweed and the more recent development of seaweed product manufacture have resulted in many having a degree of freedom and empowerment previously impossible. Money is often used for school fees, house improvements, kitchenware or even luxuries like radios and cassette players. The villagers of Paje have collectively built two day-care centres for their children with their profits. Thus, sustained trade in these fast-growing marine algae and related products may just be a viable way out of poverty for many Zanzibari families.

miles, and as long as you're not hankering after a cool dip, there's a great feeling of space. There are still a few huts and houses dotted among the palms, but generally speaking the local population thins out and, in their place, you'll find a wide choice of places to stay from all-inclusive resorts to upmarket boutique hotels and simple bungalows. The beach to the north is beautiful, and the water deep turquoise, making this an ideal place to relax for anything from a day to a week.

Since the arrival of the tar road up the centre of the peninsula, a great deal of the tourist traffic has withdrawn from the winding village paths, making things a lot more pleasant for both the residents and drivers, neither of whom appreciated the resulting dust or track corrugations. However, there have been incidents of

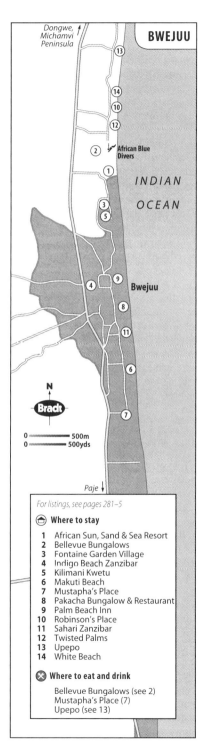

For listings, see pages 281–5

🏠 **Where to stay**

1 African Sun, Sand & Sea Resort
2 Bellevue Bungalows
3 Fontaine Garden Village
4 Indigo Beach Zanzibar
5 Kilimani Kwetu
6 Makuti Beach
7 Mustapha's Place
8 Pakacha Bungalow & Restaurant
9 Palm Beach Inn
10 Robinson's Place
11 Sahari Zanzibar
12 Twisted Palms
13 Upepo
14 White Beach

❌ **Where to eat and drink**

Bellevue Bungalows (see 2)
Mustapha's Place (7)
Upepo (see 13)

snatch-and-grab crime on the isolated tracks from beach accommodation to the bus stops on the main road, and also along some of the quieter stretches of beach. Travellers, especially women, are naturally advised to be careful and ideally to avoid unknown, remote routes. These are undoubtedly disturbing occurrences, but for now, at least, the assailants seem more interested in stealing bags than causing physical harm.

GETTING THERE AND AWAY From the roundabout at Paje, connecting the island's main east–west artery to the southeast's new tar road, **self-drivers** should turn north on the well-signposted road towards Michamvi. This fast, smooth road now runs all the way to the outskirts of Michamvi Kae. Most of the beach hotels have clear signs marking the relevant turning off the tar road, and we have marked those present in early 2017 on the area map. Tracks spring up as quickly as new hotels though, so do be aware that more of these less official routes will appear by the time you travel. If you are keen to head into the centre of the village, follow signs to Palm Beach Inn. This will take you along the old coastal road: a narrow, bumpy, dusty track that meanders between village huts and palm trees. It's not for the faint-hearted as children and chickens regularly dart across the road, and navigation through Bwejuu village's tracks is tricky and often without room for a three-point turn. If you're **on foot** or **bicycle**, hit the beach and enjoy the sea breeze as you travel.

Dalla dalla No 324 leaves Zanzibar Town for Paje three times a day, and often travels onwards to Bwejuu: check with the individual drivers as some will turn south at Paje for Jambiani. Bus Route 9 to Paje occasionally travels onwards to Bwejuu, so again check with the driver.

If you come to the Bwejuu–Paje–Jambiani area by **tourist minibus**, many drivers will be keen to take you to the hotels and lodges where they expect to be paid a good commission, often regardless of your own requests (read our comments in the box on pages 122–3). If you take a minibus from Zanzibar Town, then we strongly advise that you agree precisely where you want to go before departing, and preferably have a reservation in advance.

WHERE TO STAY *Map, opposite*

Bwejuu has something to cater to almost every taste and budget. The accommodation options below have been divided between those in the immediate vicinity of the village, and those strung out along the coast to the north of the main settlement. The pick of the bunch, offering great value for money in their class, are: Bellevue Bungalows for its laid-back vibe, food and cheery bungalows; Robinson's Place for its character and eco-credentials; and Makuti Beach Hotel for peace and escapism.

Bwejuu village
Upmarket

✳ 🏠 Indigo Beach Zanzibar
(17 rooms) m 0601 481942; e reservation@ indigobeachzanzibar.com; www. indigobeachzanzibar.com. French-owned & unsurprisingly chic, this lovely little lodge has 8 great-value guesthouse rooms & 9 private villas, all sharing the same delightfully inviting facilities. Furniture throughout is contemporary, even down to the smart skeleton loungers; details are considered & thoughtful (flower-filled footbaths at your door), & the staff are smart & joyously helpful. Pathways snake through pretty, well-tended gardens, & there's plenty of shade for midday chilling under established trees. The pleasant pool is set back from the beach & surrounded by oversized beanbags, whilst alongside the lovely tented restaurant is stylish in its simplicity: rough wood tables neatly set with simple fresh flowers in vases & turquoise condiment bottles. Villas are both sgl & dbl storey, with a distinctive ceiling-to-floor trio of windows & slick interiors. Curved baraza-bench seating, an Andalucian-influenced outdoor bathroom, complete with bougainvillea cascading down the coral-rock shower walls & dappled sunshine, high internal ceilings & contemporary furniture are standard. Yet the glass milk bottles filled with fresh flowers & carefully placed fire coral or pillar candle all add to the sense of genuine care. The charming guestrooms offer whitewashed bedrooms with Scandi-style coconut beds & vibrant batik colour accents, & there are plans to open a 3-bed beach house soon, which will make this an especially great spot for travelling friends. The owners & managers here are extremely experienced

hoteliers with an eye for quality modern design: it is a smart, stylish, low-key spot in the heart of the east coast. B&B. **$$$–$$$$$**

🏠 Makuti Beach Hotel & Club
(15 bungalows) m 0774 372947; e info@makuti-beach-hotel.com; www.makuti-beach-hotel.com. Straddling the road at Bwejuu's southern end, Makuti's simple bungalows were demolished in 2014 & replaced with a sgl- & dbl-storey block. The rooms are now spacious & neat with quality bedding, raffia rugs, good mosaic-tiled bathrooms & baraza terrace, complete with a thoughtful shower to wash the beach sand from your feet. Just metres away is the beach, speckled with shrubs, hammocks & makuti shaded loungers for chilling. Relaxation is definitely in order, as management refuse groups, ensuring peace & quiet. The simple bar & restaurant is little more than a few kanga-covered chairs & tables dotted around in the sand under a makuti roof, whilst upstairs the lounge is strewn with animal appliqué cushions, a few books & a world map. On the other side of the road, the Makuti Club is more of an acquired taste, in spite of being twice the price! Here, 2 giant family rooms with a staggering zebra theme – everything from the ceiling to the cushions & artwork is black & white 0150 are set back from a stark, Tanga-stone pool. There is no vegetation to soften the setting, making it hot & not particularly pleasant. (The lush pool at Mustapha's next door a far more appealing option!) B&B. **$$$$**

Mid range
🏠 Palm Beach Inn (21 rooms) ☎ 024 224 0221; m 0777 410070/411155; e info@palmbeachinn. com; 📘 PalmBeachInnZanzibar. In the heart of Bwejuu, sandwiched between the dusty village track & the beach, this is a real hotchpotch of a

10

place. The management makes an admirable effort to employ Bwejuu residents, particularly single mothers, & female staff have been taught to design & make woven bags to sell for extra income. Accommodation is in detached cottages & in a central building, & all rooms (from sgl to trpl) have 24hr mains electricity, universal adaptors, orange mosquito nets & a fridge. Kamilo's suite, with its sea view & tiny lounge area, is viewed as the best room, but this depends upon your taste & is not for minimalists, who may prefer the simplicity of the Abdi Karume room. Most guests stay here on a B&B basis, but other basic meals are available, served in the split-level dining room. There is a large menu but, as is often the case, it's invariably only the 'specials' menu that shows what's available that day. Order food as early as possible & accept that service is slow. There's a well-stocked bar of beer & spirits, as well as traditional dancers & stage entertainment. An inviting pool nestles among beds of cacti, frangipani & large-leafed climbers, & the grounds are also home to 3 very old tortoises & a sizeable pigeon coop. Although it's located beside the ocean, there is a fence between the lodge area & the beach. The beach immediately outside the property is strewn with sharp coral rock, & litter from the village, & staff also warn against taking valuables onto the sand due to the risk of theft. Also think twice about a night-time stroll on the beach, as high-speed motorbikes bypass the bumpy village lanes by taking to the sand. B&B. **$$$**

Budget

🛖 **Pakacha Bungalow & Restaurant** (8 rooms) m 0777 484811; e pakachabungalows@ hotmail.com; www.pakachabungalows.wordpress. com. A small village restaurant run by friendly Bwejuu resident, Ali Chamnda, the accommodation here comprises clean rooms, each with twin dbl beds & a shower (3 with hot water). Each has simple beach décor with blue-&-turquoise linen & lime-green curtains. Some rooms have AC whilst others have only a large ceiling fan, & 1 has a well-equipped kitchenette. There is a very basic 'relaxing area' upstairs with some less-than-stylish armchairs & a few concrete planters, but there is a pleasant sea view through the trees. The 'honeymoon suite' comes with a TV & DVD player (BYO movies). The adjacent Makuti restaurant serves big b/fasts of fruit & Spanish omelette, & Swahili dinners (octopus in coconut cream US$6; whole crab US$7;

grilled fish US$5). The managers here are gentle & lovely, making this a pleasant & peaceful, low-key place. Rates are highly negotiable low season. B&B. **$$–$$$**

🛖 **Mustapha's Place** (16 rooms) ☎0772 099422; www.mustaphasplace.com. Set back from the beach, across the sandy road, this long-established, totally chilled, slightly eccentric hangout has seriously upped its game in recent years. Its original name, Mustapha's Nest, bore reference to both its Rastafarian owner, Mustapha, & the site's overwhelming population of bright yellow weaver birds, which have sadly not been seen for a number of years hence the name change. Set around a neat, sandy circle (complete with bonfire, swings & miscellaneous pieces of coir rope & wood furniture) are 6 uniquely decorated bandas, 2 of which share a bathroom. An additional room is set further back beside the beehive (honey available on request), while 3 newer 2-storey rooms are spread among the trees. Inside, the white adobe walls are decorated with brightly painted patterns or pictures, & colourful kangas are used to cover the solid beds & as curtains. The floors & surfaces of the bathroom are newly tiled in sparkling white & jet black, with plants sprouting from soil-filled bottles & deliberately placed holes in the floor – a crude, back-to-nature feel in some rooms that will not suit everyone. For the best rooms, with high ceilings, mosaic-tiled bathrooms & little terraces, check out the new Bull & Hickman rooms. The eclectically decorated bar & restaurant area is as laidback as the reggae tunes it plays, & is repeatedly praised for its extensive menu & tasty food, but the *pièce de résistance* is the recent installation of a fabulously large, curvaceous swimming pool. Surrounded by tropical planting, swinging chairs suspended from the sweet almond tree & loungers, it's a lovely cool hangout, open to both lodge guests & visitors to the restaurant, & makes up for this place not being right on the beach. B&B. **$$**

North of Bwejuu village

Mid range

🛖 **African Sun, Sand & Sea Resort** (30 rooms) m 0779 666690/0763 397397; e info@africansunsand.com/gm@africansunsand. com; www.africansunsand.com. Originally White Rose Beach Resort, this little resort is now under

Tanzanian–Indian ownership & reopened in 2016 with a somewhat pedantic name. There has been some modernisation over the years, from new generators, to internal phones & new thatching, but the place remains fairly standard. Rising from the beach up the hill behind, there are garden rooms set on the slope above the coconut line, superior bungalows with slightly better views, & sea-view rooms that actually look out over the pool. The white-stone garden bungalows are all the same basic design with wide verandas, spacious bedrooms & en-suite bathrooms, whilst the pool-side rooms are in 2-storey buildings with small individual balconies or terraces. It is most definitely worth paying for the latter. The garden bungalow interiors have been styled by the owner to a very particular taste, which may well be viewed as gaudy by some visitors: frilly mosquito nets, polyester lily-covered beds & bright painted walls with fish stenciling. The swimming pool is worthy of note though, with an interesting 3-level design, including a splash pool & snack bar (🕐 10.00–17.00), & there are a few swings for children, a central TV & table tennis. The main restaurant is above the pool area & shaded by pink bougainvillea, & offers the usual array of Euro–Swahili cuisine. It's a peaceful place with pleasant staff, some tropical landscaping & a secure parking area for self-drivers, but somehow lacks energy & atmosphere. B&B. **$$$–$$$$**

✳ ⌂ **Bellevue Bungalows** (13 rooms) m 0777 209576; e bellevuezanzibar@gmail. com; www.bellevuezanzibar.com. On the top of a high rise of coral rock, this thoroughly relaxed, gentle place offers one of the best budget deals on the island. Bellevue has evolved & flourished under the leadership of a young Dutch couple, Melanie & Dim, & over the last decade, their energy, vision & hard work has paid off – as well as on Paje beachfront & various NGO projects they support. Building on the good work of recent years, they have established lush terraced gardens, transformed the restaurant into a delightfully, unassuming hotspot for fresh, tasty, healthy food, added a super swimming pool, & created rooms with vibrant co-ordinated colours & original solutions for storage & lighting. The Villa Deluxe, accommodating the honeymoon suite & 2 downstairs rooms, has been done up in the homely, relaxed vibe of the rest of the property – moulded bathrooms, colourful bedspreads & jangly

shell curtains. The whole building can be used as a family house, which shouldn't break the bank as children under 4 stay free. Alternatively, there are clean, spacious dbl rooms with fans in 3 thatched bungalows, which all have good bathrooms with mains water, matching linen, fluffy towels, fishing-basket shelves & even bedside reading lights. Each has a sunrise terrace, with clever kanga woven-coir dividers to create privacy & the raised level allows for a cooling breeze & a great outlook (the nearby residential villa is hidden by clever planting). There is now also a semi-open, 2-storey Jungle Bungalow, where the sea breeze flows freely & the same simple style & lovely African fabrics make for a further 2 inviting rooms. Outside, there are pretty hidden spots to just hang out, & most recently the completion of a terrific Tanga stone pool area, where stripy loungers & blue hammocks sit on powder sand around the turquoise water. Sitting here, under sailcloth shade, it's idyllic to gaze out to sea through the swaying palms & casuarinas. Drag yourself away though & the chefs make terrific tapas as well as a variety of fresh European & Swahili cuisine (US$5–7). Scrumptious b/fasts of spice-infused juices, fresh bread, pancakes, locally produced honey & homemade jams are a great start to the day; while crunchy rainbow salads, calamari stir-fries & chicken mango pilaf (all US$7) make excellent lunches. Splash out on the US$45 seafood platter for 2 at dinner to sample an array of locally caught fish & shellfish. With a 50m walk down to the beach & free transfers to Dim's kitesurfing school (page 295) in Paje, the focus is still on traditional seaside activities & the chance to chill under the storm lanterns with a cold beer in the evening. Bellevue is consistently brilliant & always improving to stay on top of its game, & at this price their continued success is virtually guaranteed. B&B. **$$$**

⌂ **Kilimani Kwetu Restaurant & Bungalows** (4 rooms) ☏ 024 224 0235; e info@ kilimani.de; www.kilimani.de. A partnership between 5 Germans & the villagers of Bwejuu, Kilimani Kwetu is rooted in community development. Built by local people from local materials, on a gentle hill to the north of the village overlooking the sea, this is a relaxed spot, with a positive impact on those who live in the area. Wadi & a delightfully friendly local team are happy to help any visitors. Rooms are in 2 white thatched bungalows, surrounded by palms

10

& sweet almond trees; they are basic, if a little uninspiring, with painted concrete walls, but have simple furniture, 2 deckchairs, mosquito nets with inside fan, & en-suite bathrooms with a cold-water shower. Electricity is available & there's a traditional well on site. The neat restaurant serves fresh fish & vegetarian dishes on the daily set menu, & b/fast boasts homemade tropical fruit jams & locally produced honey; culinary-inspired guests can even learn some Swahili recipes from the chef if they wish. Take any one of several zigzag paths, 50m to the sea, & there's a private beach area for guests, with makuti umbrellas, deckchairs & the Kilamani Beach Café, serving wine & beer. Development projects centred on Kilimani Kwetu have successfully financed the construction of an adult education centre & library in the past, & it remains a place for visitors keen to immerse themselves in local life. B&B. **$$$**

Robinson's Place (6 rooms) m 0777 413479; e ann@robinsonsplace.net; www. robinsonsplace.net; Jun–Mar. This is a delightfully offbeat family home set in lovely mature gardens, beside a superb beach. To Ann & Eddy, the fascinating European–Zanzibari couple who own & run the place, being here is about a particular lifestyle choice rather than business, hence you can expect a very friendly welcome, a gentle & relaxed pace, but none of the trappings of a commercial lodge. Robinson's does its best to be fairly self-sufficient – keeping chickens & geese across the road & growing tropical fruit. Simple meals are served either under the trees or on rugs & cushions on the floor in the main lounge area. There is no electricity, so wind & solar power are used to light the restaurant, portable solar lamps & petrol lamps are found in the rooms & all cooking is done in clay pots on open fires. In an effort to conserve wood, the only hot meal of the day is dinner (*US$10*). Rooms cater for a max 12 people so advance booking is invariably necessary. All rooms are very different in style & are divided amongst 2 small houses & a *Robinson Crusoe*-esque, 2-storey treehouse. All rooms, except the master & Marakesh Lodge, share immaculate, central bathroom facilities. There are 2 cold-water showers & 2 toilets, each separated by stylish cream curtains, & a large open-ended central area with mirrors & sinks. These are cleaner & more pleasant than many of the en-suite facilities offered by Zanzibar's more mid-range properties;

certainly the best 'shared facilities' that we've seen in Africa! Several dogs roam the property as effective security guards. Min 2-night stay, cash only. B&B. **$$$**

Sahari Zanzibar (12 rooms) m 0773 814929/0779 769726; e info@saharizanzibar. net; www.saharizanzibar.net. Behind Bwejuu school, the popular Sahari is a small, neat hotel in a whitewashed building overlooking a square tanga-stone pool. The suites, all of which can be converted to family rooms, have simple décor, 4-poster beds & clean en suites. The palm courtyard, shaded coir loungers by the pool & beach views all lend a relaxed air. The restaurant – with a curious Italian–Japanese fusion menu – is well regarded, serving mouth-watering platters of sushi, fresh chicken Milanese & crisp pizza. B&B. **$$$**

Twisted Palms (11 rooms) m 0753 980674; e twistedpalms@yahoo.com; www. twisted-palms-lodge.com. Under new Croatian ownership, this is a welcoming & friendly beachside retreat. Inside pink-&-peach buildings, rooms are divided between the beach & the small hill behind the property, but all contain 3 beds with delightfully eccentric lilac sheets & matching mosquito nets. Simple furnishings, cooling fans, en-suite tiled bathrooms with European flush toilets & hot-water showers are standard. 2 of the beachside rooms are quads, & 1 has a bunk bed, useful for those travelling with little ones, & in time 2 more beachfront rooms are planned. Well-tended gardens filled with shells & shaded by palms host a swinging beach sofa, great for afternoons with a good book from the book exchange. The explosion of colour continues in the restaurant (*10.00–22.00 daily*), which is the only one in Bwejuu to sit on stilts above the sea, & the menu changes depending on the daily catch. B&B. **$$$**

Upepo (4 rooms) m 0784 619579; e shareefznz71@hotmail.com; www. zanzibarhotelbeach.com. Under Canadian–Zanzibari ownership, this offers clean, spacious en-suite rooms with huge comfortable beds, pretty kanga-edged mosquito nets, hide chairs, fans & traditional ceilings. 3 rooms face the beach & 1 is set a little back with a view of the lush garden, where carved wooden zebras peer through the foliage. With just 4 rooms there'll only be a maximum of 8 guests, so you may think you'll have the place largely to yourself; don't be fooled, though, as the animated beach restaurant & bar attracts large numbers with its relaxed vibe & iced sangria (see below). B&B. **$$$**

Budget

⌂ **Fontaine Garden Village**
(12 rooms) m 0714 902618; e reception@ fontainegardenvillage.com; www. fontainegardenvillage.com. Reopened in 2014 following a fire, this Latvian-owned establishment is tucked back from the beach but well signposted from neighbouring African Sun, Sand & Sea. Accommodation is varied so it's worth looking around if you plan to stay. Rustic whitewashed rondavels with half-height walls, chipped concrete flooring, basic coir & timber furniture & kanga curtains are small & have either a shared bathroom at the edge of the plot or a pebble-tiled shower corner inside the room. In the main 'hotel' house, there are 5 dbl rooms, some en suite, & also a family room – an open area under the makuti thatch (no netting) above the villa, accommodating 4 people. Travelling parents must beware though: there is an open, ground-level well in the centre of the gardens here, & there are better family-friendly options on the island. The raked sand & palm gardens are strung with a few hammocks and the Hot Potatoe [sic] restaurant, hailed by the buffalo skull

with blazing red lightbulb eyes, serves Swahili-inspired food: squid piri-piri US$7.50, chicken salad US$5, fried beef in lemon sauce US$8.50. As a minor note, water & ice served here is boiled mains water not bottled, though the latter is available on request. B&B. **$$–$$$**

⌂ **White Beach Hotel** (6 rooms) m 0776 789181; e info@whitebeachhotelzanzibar. com; www.whitebeachhotelzanzibar.com. This Czech-owned place consists of bungalows built in a row either side of the main building. The cool interiors are a little featureless but are generally furnished with Zanzibari beds, mosquito nets, sturdy coconut-wood cupboards, fans & giant, bright bathrooms with hot-water showers. There is some variety in the rooms, so it's worth looking around to find the best available. Out in front, travel-weary guests can recover on the shaded deck filled with potted plants, or can head down to the sweeping beach which is dotted with comfortable sunloungers. Overlooking the sand, the restaurant serves up a daily menu of mainly pizza & burgers. From the loud music playing at 09.00 to the snoozing revellers on the beach-facing sofas, it would appear that the bar is the main hub of activity & it shows movies & sports on a giant screen. Free airport pickups & long-stay discounts make White Beach a pretty good deal. B&B; HB & FB available. **$$–$$$**

⊁ **WHERE TO EAT AND DRINK** *Map, page 280*
Nearly all of the hotels cater for guests and non-residents alike (see individual listings), with **Bellevue Bungalows** (page 283) deserving a special mention for their tasty offerings, and **Mustapha's Place** (page 282) for budget travellers who fancy a swim and lunch. In addition, there are a few small shops and local-style eating-houses in the village itself, and now a few European-style beach café-bars, all of which also offer accommodation.

⊁ **Upepo** m 0784 619579; e shareefznz71@ hotmail.com; www.zanzibarhotelbeach.com. You can't fail to hear the Cuban beats emanating from this chilled restaurant-cum-bar, which, with only 6 tables, offers a personal touch on local & international cuisine, influenced by the joint Tanzanian–Canadian ownership. Rum is quite clearly a best-seller, as bottles of it line the shelves

behind the bar. Thirsty beach-goers can cool off with a fruity sangria, but there's also a range of seasonal fish dishes, curries, bowls of pasta & pancakes for the hungry, though if you're after lobster they'll need prior notice to request it from the fishermen. There's a good vibe here, & you may well find that you linger longer than intended. Rooms are also available (page 284). **$$$**

WHAT TO SEE AND DO Most visitors to this area are kept occupied by resort activities and sun-worshipping. If you're staying somewhere small or simply fancy a change, you can explore the offshore reef with **snorkelling** gear hired from most of the smaller hotels, in the village (around US$5 per day for mask, snorkel and flippers), or, with better kit, from some of the larger watersports or beach activity centres. At low tide, the long **intertidal walk** to the ocean is a rewarding excursion in itself, but be sure to top up the suncream and drink lots of water on the way. It's well worth doing this trip with a good guide, decent reef shoes (the coral is sharp and water varies from ankle to thigh deep) and a walking pole: it's worth visiting Breezes (page 274) on the beach to book this trip. The reef is a 1.5km offshore and low tide makes for a really fascinating opportunity to see beneath the waves, study the starfish, little reef fish, urchins and clams, but the walk does carry some risk from slips, urchins and coral cuts, so a guide with knowledge to tell you about what you're seeing, choose your path, and also be able to call in backup in the event you do fall is invaluable.

You can also take a taxi (*US$6–8*), hire bikes (*US$10*) or scooters (*US$40*) from local villagers, with a little help from your hotel, and ride a few kilometres north up the beach to the **Blue Lagoon** at Dongwe, where the break in the reef means it's possible to swim and snorkel off the beach even at low tide (if hiring a scooter, see page 109).

Surfing

Aquaholics Zanzibar m 0776 219337/0779 721630; e aquaholics.zanzibar@gmail.com; www. aquaholics-zanzibar.com. Established in 2014, this is Zanzibar's first dedicated surf school. Operating a mobile school, this very friendly European crew collect from along the southeastern coast & take everyone from beginners upwards to the waves off Dongwe. With 3 fully licensed instructors, 30 branded boards (5ft8–8ft) & surf aid kits, this is a good little operation. Beginners can enjoy lessons in warm waters & mellow conditions, & even children are welcome to give it a try (min 15years unsupervised; younger children possible with parental supervision & ability to swim 25m). For something very different, the team have developed an underwater 'wing' that allows guests to be towed underwater while holding a purpose-

built timber wing … they say it's the closest feeling to being a mermaid you can get! *US$50/65 3½/4–5hrs inc water, snacks & gear.*

Diving

ψ **African Blue Divers** m 0777 556016/0773 095419; e info@africanbluedivers.com/ africanbluedivers@gmail.com; www. africanbluedivers.com. This small operation has a dive reception & store at the back of Evergreen Bungalows. Dutch owner, Leendert Sprey, is a PADI instructor & is generally onsite from Jul–Sep, whilst at other times there is only a Dive Master based here. PADI Open Water courses (*US$450*) are available with the team calling in freelance divers from Nungwi to assist as necessary. They run a twin-engine dhow & can also arrange local snorkelling guides.

PAJE

Once a small fishing village, straggled along the coast, Paje is centred on the junction of the tar road from Zanzibar Town with the main east coast road between Michamvi and Makunduchi. This prime location has always made it the easiest place on the east coast to reach by public transport and certainly contributed to its early success as the backpackers' choice location. After an initial peak, Paje's visitors declined as Nungwi claimed the crown for budget beach action, but the north is pulling upmarket again these days, and the backpacker pendulum is currently swinging back to the east coast. Recent years have also seen a veritable boom in Zanzibar kitesurfing, and Paje is now firmly on the map as a destination for sun-blond kiters seeking a cheap getaway in warm, tropical waters with reliable conditions. More lodges have sprung up, old ones have expanded, cafés have opened, a basic curio street now stretches back from the beach, and everywhere along this stretch, kites fill the sky. During peak season, the beach is pretty hectic with people and fluttering silk, and swimming is an absolute non-starter. The kitesurfing community – both professional centres and visitors – are generally fairly laidback and responsible, but the sheer numbers of visitors here have attracted some associated troubles: a rise in beach boys permanently lingering on the sand, some beach robbery and reports of increasing problems with drugs. By and large, the area surrounding the village remains a quiet spot for an idyllic beach break, but it's worth taking sensible precautions when wandering around. Genuine interaction with the local community is virtually non-existent here, with only the beach traders mixing with the tourists.

GETTING THERE AND AWAY To reach Paje, the main tar road from Zanzibar Town leads through Tunguu, Jozani and Kitogani before reaching the coast. From Paje, a tar road then leads north to Bwejuu and Michamvi, whilst another heads south to Jambiani and Makunduchi, in the far southeast corner of the island.

Paje can be reached by **public transport** (dalla dalla No 324 or bus Route 9), **tourist minibus** or self-drive **rental car**, **motorbike** or **bicycle**. If you want to go north beyond Bwejuu or south past Jambiani, there's no regular public transport, so you'll need to have your own wheels, be willing to hitch on a local ngalawa, or enjoy a really long, hot walk.

WHERE TO STAY *Map, page 288*

There are several places to stay in Paje, most of them closely clustered at the southern edge of the village. All the accommodation here is small scale, individual and relatively cheap; most places are owner-run. Not all hotels are on the beach though, so choose carefully if it's a sea view you're after.

Beside the main group of guesthouses is a private house, locally known as 'Paje Palace'. Ignore the aesthetic damage that this pink-and-mint monstrosity may do to your architectural sensibilities, and be grateful that it has brought floodlighting to its immediate surroundings, including the beach, as it is generally felt to have increased security here in the evenings.

Exclusive

* ⌂ **White Sand Luxury Villas** (11 rooms) m 0776 263451; e contact@whitesandvillas. com; www.whitesandvillas.com. 1km south of Paje village, White Sand is indeed luxury: uniquely designed, beautifully landscaped, impeccably furnished & has a distinct air of finesse. A French–Polish-owned resort, it offers a small collection of exclusive 2-bedroom private villas & suites within its inspiring grounds. Neutral in palette & contemporary in décor, the spacious villas boast state of the art amenities, indulgent walk-in showers, terrace hammocks, a plunge pool, private dining area & a separate lounge if you fancy chilling to a DVD of an evening. B/fast & dinner are served by candlelight on the intimate terrace off the cool central area, whilst lunch is served beachfront under pole shading on decking flush with the sand, & embraced by the surrounding low vegetated dunes. It's certainly decadent beach chic, with pale wood tables, silver wine buckets glistening with condensation, a delicious cook-to-order beach BBQ & an array of tempting salads. Guests are pleasantly eclectic, too: young & beautiful city couples clad in Valentino are just as likely to sit alongside friends taking time to relax after safari. The perfectly clear turquoise waters & entertaining & colourful kitesurfers make for an outstandingly lovely vista, & there are shaded daybeds set back along the beach for post-lunch snoozing. If something more active is needed, there's pétanque, badminton, volleyball, a gorgeous curvaceous swimming pool & an onsite professional kite centre: Zanzibar Kite Paradise (page 296). Everything here is created to a high standard with efficient staff & a commendable environmental effort to match (ask to see the onsite furniture workshop & vegetable gardens). As hip beach elegance goes, this is certainly one of Zanzibar's top spots. B&B; HB, FB & AI available. ♛

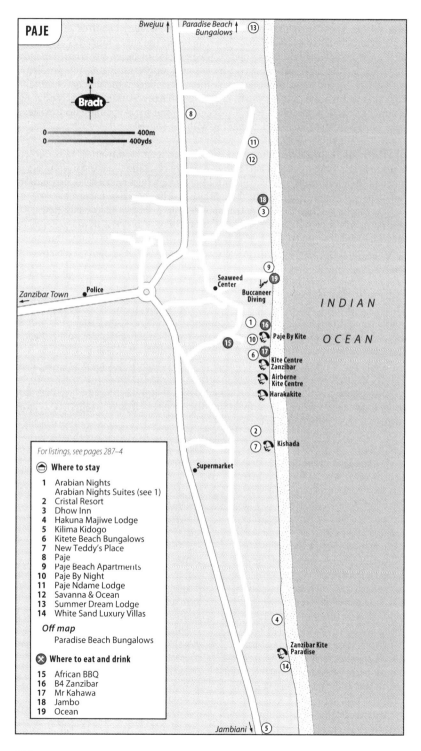

PAJE

N

Bradt

0 ———— 400m
0 ———— 400yds

Bwejuu ↑ | Paradise Beach Bungalows ↑ ⑬

⑧

⑪

⑫

⑱
③

⑨
Seaweed ⑲
Center ●
Buccaneer
Diving

Zanzibar Town ← Police ●

① ⑯
⑩ 🪁 Paje By Kite
⑮
⑥ ⑰
🪁 Kite Centre
Zanzibar
🪁 Airborne
Kite Centre
🪁 Harakakite

②
⑦ 🪁 Kishada

● Supermarket

INDIAN

OCEAN

④

🪁 Zanzibar Kite
Paradise
⑭

Jambiani ↘ ⑤

For listings, see pages 287–4

🏠 **Where to stay**

1   Arabian Nights
     Arabian Nights Suites (see 1)
2   Cristal Resort
3   Dhow Inn
4   Hakuna Majiwe Lodge
5   Kilima Kidogo
6   Kitete Beach Bungalows
7   New Teddy's Place
8   Paje
9   Paje Beach Apartments
10   Paje By Night
11   Paje Ndame Lodge
12   Savanna & Ocean
13   Summer Dream Lodge
14   White Sand Luxury Villas

Off map
     Paradise Beach Bungalows

❌ **Where to eat and drink**

15   African BBQ
16   B4 Zanzibar
17   Mr Kahawa
18   Jambo
19   Ocean

Luxury

☀ 🏠 **Dhow Inn** (28 rooms) m 0777 525828;
e info@dhowinn.com; www.dhowinn.com.
Neighbouring Paje Ndame to the south, Dhow
Inn's 3 Dutch owners are onsite & keen to
welcome guests & live up to their 'come as a
guest, leave as family' motto. The lovely, modern
rooms are built in 2 neighbouring circles, each
around a whitewashed courtyard & swimming
pool. Interiors are contemporary & thoughtfully
finished with white walls & ice-blue accents;
hot water, fans, mosquito nets & even free Wi-Fi
are standard. Set 40m back from the water's
edge, the rooms don't have a sea view but each
has a terrace, complete with directors' chairs &
a sundowner table, & their pool views & pretty
tropical flower beds make for a lovely enough
outlook. The atmospheric bar is the spot for a
cool cocktail & ocean gazing, whilst the charcoal
grill tempts with Swahili seafood & the formal
restaurant offers a chance to smarten up &
indulge. It's also worth noting that if you can't
get a room, non-guests are welcome to use the
pool as long as they buy something – perfect for
cooling dips when the tide is out & temperatures
are searing. If you fancy a further jaunt then ask
at reception for help renting bikes & cars, or check
out the proper beach volleyball court (albeit back
from the beach), onsite kitesurfing centre or
massage treatments. HB. **$$$$$**

🏠 **Hakuna Majiwe Lodge** (20 rooms)
m 0777 454505; e hakunamajiwe@gmail.com;
www.hakunamajiwe.com. About 2km south of
central Paje, & accessed from the main tar road
to Jambiani, is Hakuna Majiwe. Meaning 'a place
without stones', a reference to the wide beach &
expansive intertidal flats here, it certainly has a
lovely position & benefits from relative isolation.
The large, en-suite beach bungalows are very nice
indeed, with varnished floorboards, fluffy towels,
fans & impressive 4-poster beds. Wide individual
decks have inviting swinging beds & a cushioned
bench, whilst makuti-shaded loungers are
tucked amid the low beach vegetation to provide
some privacy. Housekeeping do a particularly
marvellous job here at making rooms look
thoroughly inviting at all times. There is a huge
open-sided makuti restaurant, where friendly
staff & African tunes make it a cheerful hangout,
a baraza lounge with dartboard, & a swimming
pool set back from the beach. HB. **$$$$$**

Upmarket

🏠 **Arabian Nights** (12 rooms) m 0777 854041;
www.zanzibararabiannights.com. Tucked down
a narrow alley to the beach beside Kitete Beach
Bungalows, this is one of Paje's more mid-range,
sedate options. Its rooms are in pink coral-rock
cottages with thatched roofs. Some surround
the large, private pool & others face directly onto
the beach. In keeping with the hotel's evocative
name, soft golds & decorative spices influence the
room décor. Very spacious bedrooms have walk-in
wardrobes & floral tiled en suites. The upstairs
Swahili & European-mix restaurant is open to
all, & along the beach, the owner's dive centre,
Buccaneer, offers good scuba opportunities. B&B.
$$$$

🏠 **Arabian Nights Suites** (18 rooms)
m 0777 844443; e info@arabiannightssuite;
www.arabiannightssuite.com. Being newer,
Arabian Nights Annex seems slightly superior to its
nearby sister property Arabian Nights. Its large, red
reception area is filled with matching red-&-gold
furnishings, giant Arabic coffee pots & deep black
sofas. The warm colour scheme continues to the
rooms, where gold curtains & lampshades, plus
generously proportioned carved coconut-wood
beds, are cosy & inviting & even the mosquito nets
are gold trimmed. Sparkling white bathrooms
with tropical-fish shower curtains diverge from the
theme a little, while modern paraphernalia such
as electric safes & flatscreen satellite TVs make life
easier. Rooms are located in various 1- & 2-storey
rondavels set around tidy gardens, where there's
also a palm-shaded pool looking out over the
waves. The garden terraced Cinnamon Restaurant is
open to guests & passers-by wishing for a taste of
its Swahili cuisine. B&B. **$$$$**

🏠 **Paje Beach Apartments** (5 apts) m 0777
098577; e contacts@pajebeachapartments.com;
www.pajeapartments.com. Perfect for divers or
those here to learn the skill, these new apts share
their site with Buccaneer Diving (page 294), &
overlook the training swimming pool. A 5min
walk north of Paje's main beach hub, they are
immaculately clean with gleaming tiled floors,
4-poster beds & limed furniture, an open-plan
kitchen & living room with thoughtful touches. The
kitchens are well kitted with a microwave, large
fridge, cooker & all the necessary accoutrements.
Rooms can also be adapted to accommodate
children on the sofa bed. There is a tiny terrace area

outside the mirrored patio doors, but with the beach & some bright, cushion-covered loungers only a few metres away, this is really not an issue. SC. **$$$$**

Mid range

🏠 **Cristal Resort** (30 rooms) m 0777 875515; e info@cristalresort.net. In 2012, the Cristal Resort absorbed the adjacent hotel, Kinazi Upepo, to create a sizeable beachfront plot just south of Paje village. Under new ownership again since 2016, it has consistently received mixed reviews, & sadly we don't sense this is likely to improve anytime soon. There are currently 3 uninspiring room types, with the safari-style eco-cabins probably the best bet. There's a good-size swimming pool & a large non-descript restaurant & an impressive dhow cocktail bar, although little in the way of guests or atmosphere. A canteen-style restaurant on the beach serves Thai food lunch & dinner (beef stir fry US$9; chicken red curry US$10; spicy soups US$7) & cocktails by night. **$$$–$$$$**

🏠 **Paje By Night** (21 rooms) m 0777 460710; e info@pajebynight.net; www.pajebynight. net. Once the only hotel with electricity on the peninsula, this is an unpretentious joint where jovial Italian owner Marco warmly welcomes 'the young & the not so young any more'. The row of hammocks & the Mondrian-inspired pool, complete with a piano-key edge & disco ball, hints at the pervading mood before you even reach the reception bar inside, for this is a slightly hippy, thoroughly original, take-it-as-it-comes place. Come here for the relaxed vibe & social atmosphere rather than for chic style, modern facilities or endless activities. Set 50m back from the beach, & without a sea view, the hub of PBN is the bar. With black-painted interiors, golden baraza benches covered in astroturf & lightbulbs sprouting from wall-mounted trumpets & saxophones, this is an edgy, off-the-wall hangout, but it's easy going & unashamedly different. There are wooden tables & faux-fur chairs, & colourful lanterns furnish the adjoining makuti TV lounge, which screens international news & sport virtually all day. The food quality is good with a definite Italian slant: fresh pasta & pizza are always available, there are regular seafood & Swahili BBQs, & even fondue nights, whilst the social cocktail bar is open 24hrs serving Italian coffees to exotic cocktails. Around the garden area are spacious standard rooms with a dbl/twin bed, & king-sized rooms. The latter refer

to the larger size of the room not the bed, for only 9 of the rooms have a king-sized bed while the other 2 are trpls. There is mains electricity available throughout the complex, & every room has hot water, tiled floors with colourful mats, cheerful batik pictures & a fan. Room 1 is a newly decorated family bungalow with 2 bedrooms, a shared bathroom & a spacious entrance hall. Each of the bedrooms has 2 sgls & 1 dbl with mosquito nets, vibrant curtains, a small desk, wardrobe & ceiling fan. There are distinctly quirky 'Concept Rooms', ranging in theme from *Alice in Wonderland* to the Captains Cabin, and in which every little detail from the shower curtains to the light switches have been sourced or upcycled to match the idea. For something more rustic African, check out the 2-storey 'Jungle Bungalows': within the downstairs coral-stone walls are twin beds & a small, hot-water bathroom; upstairs, there's an additional dbl bed & a small terrace overlooking the plot. Although a baby's cot was once borrowed from the village for a visiting child, the basic facilities & vibe here are not really conducive to holidaying with infants. Primary guest activities seem to be sleeping, sunbathing & kitesurfing at the beach, hanging out at the pool (🕐 08.00–02.00), then chilling over cocktails & fresh juices before building up to an evening party. On a practical note, there's free Wi-Fi & a safety-deposit box in the office & in the king-sized rooms. Visa, MasterCard & Amex subject to 5% surcharge. B&B. **$$$–$$$$**

🏠 **Kilima Kidogo** (12 rooms) 📞 (South Africa) +27 (84) 225 5500; m 0777 201088; e kilimakidogo.management@gmail.com; www. kilimakidogo.com. Hakuna Majiwe's southern neighbour, Kilima Kidogo is essentially a fully staffed villa, though rooms can be booked individually. Owned by South African twins, Dina & Joey, it's very much their home from home & retains that comfortable feel throughout. With en-suite bedrooms in the main villa & a small gate-side cottage in the bougainvillea-filled garden, it represents very good value for groups looking for quality accommodation & beachfront privacy. Under high makuti thatch, the central villa area has a pool table & satellite TV, a beautifully set table beside the open kitchen & a small lounge full of games, jigsaws & books; bedrooms are tastefully furnished with rustic beds, quality linen & colourful scatter cushions. There is AC, fans & an electronic safe as well as open wardrobes & shuttered windows. There is a licensed bar & small restaurant under makuti on the beach, & a flat roof overlooking the sea for sunrise sea views. Hadji is the friendly onsite tour guide who books island tours & hires out jeeps & bikes. For the less energetic, the beachfront spa offers various soothing therapies. Unfortunately, the curio shop here sells shells from the beach; please do not buy them as it will only encourage this practice further. B&B. **$$$**

🏠 **Kitete Beach Bungalows** (13 rooms) 024 224 0226; m 0778 160666; e kitetebeach@ hotmail.com; www.kitetebeach.com. Kitete has moved on from being just an old villa offering basic rooms, & has most recently added a swimming pool, albeit with minimal shade & rudimentary facilities: the pool shower is a wall-mounted hose pipe. Reception is opposite the animal murals, on the right-hand side coming from Paje by Night, & rooms are then a little further towards the beach. Housed in 2-storey, blush-pink villas, bedrooms are a little dated but offer adequate facilities: bright-green interiors, mains electricity, AC, fan, mosquito nets & a small outside terrace/balcony. Rooms are fresh & clean, with crisp linen & modern clip-on bedside lights. In the prime position beside the beach, the Kitete View Restaurant offers terrific views along the sand from its 1st-floor location, but unfortunately lacks buzz. Whilst the decent chef does serve up traditional Swahili dishes (*US$5.50–12*) alongside specials such as lobster thermidor (*US$30*), you may well be better off visiting the independent café on the ground floor, Mr Kahawa (page 293), for genuine warmth, atmosphere & tasty treats. Down on the sand, there is also a gift shop that rents out bicycles for local jaunts at US$5/day. B&B. **$$$**

🏠 **Paje Ndame Lodge** (31 rooms) m 0777 886611/0777 863421; e info@ndamezanzibar. com; www.ndamezanzibar.com. Since German manager Hans Ehrentraut took over in 2011, Paje Ndame has been catering mainly to German families & is consequently at its busiest during the European school holidays in Jul & Dec. Rooms in 2-storey villas or neat bungalows are all bright & clean with shiny pink flooring, baby-blue tiled bathrooms, & either a shared semicircular balcony with a good sea view or a garden terrace. All rooms have mains electricity, fans, mosquito nets & bedside lights. The resort sits along a lovely long stretch of soft beach on which guests laze, enjoy an African massage & watch the world go by.

There's a pleasant seafront restaurant & bar, a curio shop with a reasonable selection of colourful local paintings, a new circular beach bar for sundowners & a popular beach volleyball court. Activities are limited but the youthful crowd seems happy playing cards, snorkelling from a local ngalawa, or renting bicycles & embarking on cultural tours of Paje village (*US$10pp*). Child & student reductions available. B&B; HB & FB available. **$$$**

Budget

🏠 **Paradise Beach Bungalows** (12 rooms) m 0777 414129; e paradisebb@zanlink.com; paradisebeachbungalows.web.fc2.com. Opened some years ago by a diminutive Japanese lady, Saori Miura, who abandoned the corporate rat race to travel in East Africa, this cheap beach retreat offers basic facilities & great sushi. Through tiny doorways, there are clean & tidy rooms, of which 3 are larger, dbl-storey options. The original rooms are in semi-detached cottages with 2 ¾-size traditional Zanzibari beds with flowery sheets, mosquito nets & shuttered windows. Some of these have interconnecting doors for groups of friends or families. The bathrooms are basic concrete rooms with mostly hot-water showers, but 1 dbl & the dormitory are cold-water only. The new chalets are a better bet with a simple but spacious, ground-floor bedroom with dark wood furniture, a dbl & ¾ bed, neat coconut-wood shelves & a Zanzibari chest for storing valuables. Outside, stairs lead from the veranda to a private roof terrace with a picnic table, chairs, washing line & view into the surrounding palms & frangipani trees. There is now electricity here with low-level lights helping significantly at night, & storm lanterns still used for atmosphere; power cuts are frequent though so a good torch is essential. The central restaurant houses tables covered in pink batik tablecloths & glasses of fresh flowers, & a small multi-lingual library. The home-cooked food is all good quality, especially the Japanese options of fresh sashimi & tempura, but supplies are limited so order dinner well in advance & check Saori is around if you're coming for the sushi. B/fasts are simple affairs of fruit, fresh bread & a selection of local preserves.

It is also possible for the team here to arrange village cooking lessons for interested guests, which at US$10pp is a great way to have some

10

genuine time with the community. Next to the restaurant, a 2-storey, hexagonal lounge area offers cushioned seating, good sea views & some shade during the heat of the afternoon. In spite of its very basic amenities, Paradise's quiet location, Japanese food & inexpensive rates do mean that it can get very busy, so advance booking is advisable. It is also worth being aware that there are a number of docile-looking dogs dozing around the gardens – from experience, their bite is stronger than their bark though. B&B. **$$**

🏠 **Savanna & Ocean Hotel**   (8 rooms) m 0774 368468; e info@savanna-ocean. com; www.savanna-ocean.com. Set a row back from the beach opposite the Dhow Inn, this consists of a ring of rooms around a central circular courtyard, which is also the location of a smattering of recycled-dhow tables that make up the restaurant. Attempts have been made to spruce up the rooms & corridors with local art work, but they are still fairly simple, AC spaces with whitewashing & Zanzibari furniture. Up on the 2nd storey, the bar is raised above the courtyard, & you'll need to be early to save a seat on its kanga-covered sofas when the plasma TV is on. Out in the front of the building, a well-used snooker table is wedged into the sand, & at reception a limited but useful shop sells essentials such as suncream. Accommodation is mostly used as a base by students & Danish volunteers looking for longer stays & who don't seem to mind the lack of direct beach access. B&B. **$$**

Shoestring

🏠 **New Teddy's Place**   (9 rooms) m 0773 096306; e karibu@teddys-place.com; www. teddys-place.com. Neighbouring, & definitely not to be confused with, (old) Teddy's Place, New Teddy's is a simple, genuine backpackers' bolthole with the level of accommodation & laidback vibe that you would expect. Set out in an arc under the palms, the thatched bandas are very basic, with sand-covered floors, coir rope shelves, rustic coconut-wood beds & a free-standing fan. Ranging from sgl to trpl, with a dorm room available too, all accommodation is similar in standard & all share toilet & shower facilities. There is a very chilled bar-restaurant, serving up fresh, homemade dishes from a daily menu, cold beers & an array of cocktails. It's all very chilled out & guests consistently praise the friendly

staff. For kitesurfers, discounts are available at neighbouring Kishadi Kite Centre, or storage lockers & hanging lines can be rented for US$2/day at New Teddy's. B&B **$–$$**

🏠 **Paje Hotel**   (6 rooms) m 0773 321460; e info@pajehotel.com; www.pajehotel.com. Down a bumpy dirt track parallel to the tar road, this can be tricky to find: they advise heading for the high tin roof or calling ahead from the tar road entering Paje . . . just hope the signal is strong enough to connect. Behind the red metal gates is a 6-bedroom white villa with rooms for rent (some with shared bathroom) & a communal kitchen for self-catering. It is somewhat misleading to call it a hotel as services are extremely limited & there is no restaurant or bar; all guests here are staying on a room-only basis. There is a reasonably well kitted-out ground-floor kitchen, & a BYO bar area beside the pool, but staff involvement is nil. Rooms radiate from a narrow internal courtyard & are reasonably neat with clean bedding & fans (AC in 1 room); en suites where they exist are open plan, so be very familiar with your travelling companion if booking here. Outside, there are a few hammocks hung around the sand-covered 'garden' & a raised swimming pool surrounded by loungers. It's a fairly stark exterior with limited shade in the midday sun, but the biggest drawback is location, being both a reasonable walk from the local shops for supplies & a 10–15min walk to the beach. B&B. **$–$$**

🏠 **Summer Dream Lodge**   (8 rooms) m 0777 294809; e summerdreamzanzibar@gmail.com; www.summerdreamlodge.com. Opened in 2014, on an unremarkable plot between the main tar road & the beach, this friendly spot is popular with volunteers looking for some cheap R&R. 3 rooms are en suite, & there's a brand new, albeit very rudimentary, 8-person dormitory. The bungalows are all mkeke woven palm, with high thatched roofs, safe boxes & fans; stone en suites are large with sloping floors to channel shower run-off. The rooms are clean but quite dark, so not good for bookworms. The central bar area is the focus, with 'Tupendane Sote' ('love each other') emblazoned across the optics. It's a place for chilling, sipping some Paje Punch (rum, vodka, crème de bananes & juice) & chatting; not for partying. Enjoy the gentle reggae vibe, munch on grilled ginger lobster (US$7.50) & take your pick from the array of swinging chairs. B&B. **$–$$**

CLUBBING AFRICAN STYLE

Well signposted off the main road between Paje and Jambiani, Coco Blue (m 0777 499103; e *info@cocoblue-zanzibar.com; www.cocoblue-zanzibar.com;* ⌚ *Fri & Sat nights*) opened in 2016 and has fast become the east coast's top spot for hearing live African music and internationally acclaimed DJs. A platform for East African artists, this open-air thatched venue boasts state-of-the-art European sound and light systems, a large cocktail bar, good management and decent security. The bush location doesn't stop the beach party vibe, with sand under your feet and coconut palms around the curvaceous pool. It's worth booking a taxi to check out the local jam sessions and you may also just catch a famous DJ from New York or London hit the decks afterwards. By day, the venue also hosts art workshops and occasional markets.

WHERE TO EAT AND DRINK *Map, page 288*

All of the hotels above welcome non-guests to eat and drink, with most serving a mix of Swahili flavours and international-style dishes. On top of this, a smattering of local and European-style cafés and restaurants have appeared in recent years, all serving suitably filling and tasty treats.

B4Zanzibar m 0778 672715; e b4zanzibar@gmail.com; ⌚ 11.00–midnight daily. Under a giant tented roof, B4's deckchairs in the sand hint at the laidback vibe here. Brilliant burgers served in little brown-paper bags, milkshakes made to order & cold beers overlooking the beach at sunset are all popular. Come for chilled cinema nights, popular club nights, & a chat with Angelo & his friendly team: a runaway success since their arrival on the Paje dining scene. $$$

African BBQ m 0712 567988. Just around the corner from Paje by Night, Rastafarian-run African BBQ is not much more than 2 tables covered by makuti thatch & decorated with pictures of Bob Marley. Unsurprisingly, everything on the menu is barbequed, from fresh seafood & home-grown garden vegetables to chicken & spiced beef skewers, all served with salad & chips or rice. $$$

Ocean Restaurant At the far north of Paje village, next door to Buccaneer Diving, Ocean is accessed over an unnecessary bridge from the beach, which at high tide is partially underwater. The menu is a classic selection of Italian-style food, including pasta, steak, seafood & grilled chicken dishes washed down with a glass of wine or a cold beer. $$$

Mr Kahawa m 0776 038288; e mrkahawa@gmail.com; ⌚ 08.00–17.00 daily. Opened in 2014 by the delightful Dutch owners behind Bellevue Bungalows (page 283) & neighbouring kite centre, Mr Kahawa (meaning Mr Coffee) has brought much-needed style & quality beachfront refreshment to Paje. Offering some of the best coffee on the east coast, with a barista trained at Zanzibar Coffee House in Stone Town (page 145) & a selection of simple but delicious homemade baguettes, salads, wraps, cakes & smoothies, its neat turquoise-&-white outdoor tables, stripy hammocks & indoor communal dining table are invariable filled with a delightfully chilled & eclectic bunch. It's gentle, calm, efficient & deservedly successful. Choose from the colour-coded smoothie menu at breakfast (*US$3–5*), sample the pastry chef's delicious chocolate cake (*US$2.50*), munch on Thai beef baguettes (*US$6*) &, of course, sip coffee… all to a backdrop of sparking ocean & waves teeming with colouful kites. If you're free of an evening, there's a weekly cinema night on the beach, an event popular with expats & visitors alike, where anything form *Great Gatsby* to *Little Miss Sunshine* is enjoyed along with tasty finger food. There are also fortnightly fair-trade curio markets held here that are well worth supporting for your souvenir shopping. Plans are afoot to introduce a cocktail night in the near future, & this is a team known to deliver on their often ambitious projects, so keep an eye out for what's new here when you visit. $$–$$$

⊽ Jambo Restaurant & Bar m 0774 529960; e jambo.booking@hotmail.com; www. jambobeachbungalows.com. Fri night is a well-known local party night at Jambo's, where drinks flow, loud music plays & locals & tourists dance until late under strings of white lights. Entrance is US$4, & whilst there's a limited menu of spaghetti & burgers, most come for the intoxicating cocktails. If you don't want to travel far, there are 4 woven-palm bandas & a 6-bed dorm on the beach: all cheap (**$–$$**) & with a clean bed & shared facilities. **$$$**

WHAT TO SEE AND DO The primary activities in Paje are sunbathing on the beautiful beach and swimming in the sea. If staring out at the waves breaking along the fringe reef pricks your curiosity, there are two dive schools and a number of European-run kitesurfing operations; be aware, though, that the latter is seasonal, with the best times being December to February, or even better, from June to August. For those tired of the salt and sand, Dhow Inn's pool (page 289) is open to non-residents as long as they purchase something from the bar.

An informative diversion is the new **Seaweed Center** (m *0777 871377;* e *info@ seaweedcenter.com*). Given the visibility of seaweed farming, it's well worth checking out these lovely new 'headquarters' to better understand its very real importance to the community. Information boards are clear and guided tours are available. A few bars of organic seaweed and spice soap also make perfect, lightweight souvenirs.

There is also an old **mausoleum** nearby: a low rectangular edifice with a castellated wall, inset with antique plates and dishes. This design is thought to have originated in Persia, and may indicate that this part of the island was settled by Shirazi immigrants prior to the western side of the island, near present-day Zanzibar Town. Ask one of the local villagers to escort you for a small fee.

Diving

⤳ Buccaneer Diving m 0777 853403; e zanzibar@buccaneerdiving.com; www. buccaneerdiving.com. Based at Paje Beach Apartments (page 289), this efficient 5* PADI dive school has a purpose-built classroom, a swimming pool for course work, & a resident team of 4 experienced expat instructors & 2 dive masters, who between them speak 4 languages. Buccaneer bears the hallmarks of a reputable, safety-conscious operation with clear certification from DAN & PADI on display, a dive-briefing board

---

KITE CATASTROPHE? UPCYCLE IT!

Damaged your kite? Planning on buying a new one? Save on the return packing and donate your old kite to JENGA (m *0777 209576;* e *info@ jengazanzibar.com; jengazanzibar.com*), a brilliant Dutch-run initiative, offering Tanzanian craftsmen and women the opportunity to trade their locally handmade products. Donating your kite is just one easy way to help the community here, by providing them with a quality material for their imaginative products. The kite-upcycling scheme is run by a young, enthusiastic Tanzanian entrepreneur called Martin. Trained as a tailor, he converts old kites into vibrant bags, laptop covers and caps, and to thank you for any kite donations he'll create you a laptop or iPad case from your own kite; a lovely handmade, personalised souvenir!

You can hand in your old kite at either Kite Centre Zanzibar in Paje (page 295) or at Bellevue Bungalows in Bwejuu (page 283), or contact JENGA directly (page 151) don't forget to take your laptop measurements, too!

In the last decade, kitesurfing has literally taken off on Zanzibar, particularly in the area around Paje. A colourful and fascinating spectator sport, its rise comes as no surprise to the many operators here. Warm, calm, tropical waters, a shallow lagoon and constant steady wind (13–25 knots is ideal) for eight months of the year have all contributed to its success. There is good, flat, waist-deep water for freestylers at low tide, and choppy conditions (1–3m waves) beyond the reef at high tide that thrill the wave riders. Beginners can take courses with licensed instructors, advanced riders can bring and store their own kit or hire on the beach, and the kitesurfing community is generally professionally run on the island. Perhaps the only drawback of the popularity is that swimmers are perhaps better off away from this kiting heartland, where boards zip through the surf from dawn to dusk.

& some enticing underwater photography. Like most of the island's best centres, they encourage guests to complete the PADI e-learning scheme prior to travelling for dive courses; however, they can teach on location & have all the relevant DVDs & even tablets for poolside learning. There are now some pleasant apartments here, too, which are great for dedicated divers & those doing learn-to-dive courses. Buccaneer also have satellite bases at Uhuru Beach in Jambiani (page 305) and Arabian Nights (page 289). *Sgl/dbl dive US$77/130 inc equipment; Open Water US$490; Dive Master US$840.*

Kitesurfing

Airborne Kite Centre m 0715 548464/0776 687357; e info@airbornekitecentre.com; www.airbornekitecentre.com. Airborne's knowledgeable staff consist of 2 instructors, 2 interns, 2 helpers, & the owner who can tell you all you need to know about their IKO-accredited a courses, small group & private lessons. Kiters are never left alone in the water during a course, so instructors are confident of good progress & enjoyment. For something a little different, day trips kitesurfing at Mnemba Island, reef-kiting lessons & full-moon trips are available, as well as paddleboarding & a variety of local tours & excursions. *Kite-rental costs US$55/½-day, US$100/full day.*

Harakakite m 0777 244416; www. zanzibarkiteschool.com; ⏱ Dec–Mar & mid May–Oct. Meaning 'fast kite' in Swahili, Harakakite has been offering IKO-accredited courses for nearly a decade. All levels are catered for, &

children are accepted from the age of 3 (strength, comprehension & concentration allowing!) as long as they are accompanied by an adult, & from 9 on their own. The number of instructors here depends on the season, but there's 1 permanent instructor & founder, Mathias. After all that surfing, guests can head to the small café which offers a selection of drinks & snacks. Equipment rental is available to tour operators only. *Beginner's discovery course US$100/4hrs; complete course US$200/10hrs; max 4 per group.*

Kite Centre Zanzibar m 0776 531535/0778 385503; e info@kitecentrezanzibar.com; www. kitecentrezanzibar.com; ⏱ mid Dec–mid Mar & mid Jun–mid Oct. Owned & operated by Dim of brilliant Bellevue Bungalows in Bwejuu (page 283) & Mr Kahawa, the cool café just down the beach (page 293), this IKO-accredited activity outfit was one of original kiting operations on the island – and certainly the only dedicated centre on this stretch of coast when it opened. It continues to offer high-quality, branded kit, lessons & courses, experienced instructors & a thoroughly exhilarating seaside diversion. The courses are open to all abilities (you do need to be able to swim though), but if you are a novice to the sport, take along a T-shirt, plenty of sunscreen & a sense of humour. The centre also offers sea safaris to learn about local fishing techniques & seaweed farming, with all profits going to the village, & links with Aquaholics Zanzibar (page 286) for surfing lessons. There's a repair centre & shop for more experienced kiters, selling everything from bikins & suncream to harnesses, boards & caps. There is

10

also a raft of social gatherings for after-kiting get-togethers, so it's worth checking out the weekly timetable for dinners & add-on evening activities if you're after some fun with like-minded hydrophiles. *Beginner course (3x3hrs) US$320; board & kite rental US$45/70/290 ½-day/day/week.*

Kishada m 0776 030384; www.kitesurfzanzibar. wordpress.com. On the beach just in front of New Teddy's Place, Kishada was started by 2 local guys in 2016. From their 2-storey, makuti centre, they offer some of the cheapest deals on the coast, with additional discounts available to guests at New Teddy's. They appear to have a host of happy customers & a friendly, relaxed manner with clients.

Paje By Kite e info@pajebykite.net; www. pajebykite.net. As the name might suggest, this IKO centre is on the same plot & affiliated with the quirky Paje By Night hotel (page 290), offering kiteboarding lessons from beginner to advanced level in small groups or as private lessons, taught by 3–4 instructors. There's also wakeboarding, speedboating, sub-wings, stand-up paddleboarding in Chwaka Bay & other water & motor combinations. *Equipment rental is a steal at*

just US$16/hr for the full gear; courses US$40/hr for a group of up to 4, private lessons US$50/hr.

Zanzibar Kite Paradise m 0772 194278; www. zanzibarkiteparadise.com. Alongside White Sand (page 287) & affiliated with the lodge, this smart, efficient centre & its multi-lingual, experienced team benefit from being 1km south of Paje's main drag, where the water is quieter & has fewer boats. There are between 4 & 7 licenced instructors based here (season dependent), all are IKO & VDWS licensed, & teach in English, French & German as standard, with a wide selection of other languages on offer. The equipment is all new, & they claim to be the only school in the area with light wind boards & kites available in addition to the usual array of kites; kayak, SUP or windsurf options are also available. There is a maximum of 2 students per instructor here, although the majority of beginners opt for private lessons: expensive, but significantly increasing their chances of actually being able to ride by the end of their holiday. Check out the live webcam on their website to have a close up look at day-to-day running. *Equipment rental US$30/hr for full gear; courses US$140/3hrs for a group of up to 4, private lessons US$220/3hrs; equipment storage US$15/day.*

JAMBIANI

This sprawling, linear coastal village consisting of four amalgamated communities begins a few kilometres south of Paje, spreading for about 6km down the coast towards Ras Shungi. With around 7,000 permanent residents, of whom half are children, Jambiani still has a relatively low population density. It benefits from having two nursery schools, primary and secondary schools and a medical centre. All warmly welcome visitors to donate money to improve facilities; indeed one nursery was built entirely by money raised by the local village NGO, not by the government. There are several basic food stores, a local craft shop (selling delicious natural honey), women's pottery centre, a friendly post office and a bakery.

The village's name comes from the Arabic word *jambiya*: a dagger with a markedly curved blade. Local legend holds that early settlers found such a knife here; proof that others had been in the area before them. It emits an active community spirit; on a village tour with the local Eco+Culture team (page 333), Jambiani is probably the best place on the island to gain genuine insights into Zanzibari village life and enjoy rewarding community interaction.

The beach is wide, and is the hub of daily life: work, rest and play. For visitors it's a place to catch some sun and explore the fascinating tidal flats; for children it's a place to cool down, run and play football; for local men it's a launch for their picturesque ngalawas; and for the large number of seaweed-farming women it's a valuable natural asset. Increasingly, the sea-faring villagers are sharing the sea with kitesurfers seeking quieter waters than Paje.

Alas, for tourists, Jambiani has lost some of its energy in recent years and is increasingly run-down. It now offers a disappointing lack of variety in its choice of places to stay: depressingly deserted hotels and a lack of characterful accommodation options combine to give the place an empty feel, sending many visitors north to Paje where there's more going on.

There is clear evidence of coastal erosion too, with most hotels protected from the waves by aesthetically challenged concrete walls and rock breakwaters, creating a two-tier beach – above and below the defences. That said, the beach is kept clean

JAMBIANI MARINE AND BEACH CONSERVATION (JAMABECO)

The Jambiani Marine and Beach Conservation (JAMABECO) organisation was founded in Jambiani village in 2001, receiving official recognition in 2005. It aims to eradicate beach pollution and destruction in the area by providing villagers of all ages with environmental education and hopes, ultimately, to improve villagers' incomes by promoting sustainable, long-term use of the local marine resources.

Jambiani village life revolves around the sea – fishing, seaweed farming, coir-rope manufacture and beach tourism – so the quality of the sealife and coastal environment has the ability to impact directly upon the vast majority of villagers. Well-managed resource use and protection is important in maintaining and developing all of these industries and incomes.

The 34 JAMABECO committee members operate a year-round education programme to advocate environmental conservation; plant trees along the beaches; and regularly patrol and clean the beaches and village, removing the broken glass, bottles, batteries, iron materials and huge number of plastic bags that litter many of Zanzibar's coastal villages. Since 2003, they have also organised annual clean-up days to mark International Environment Day on 5 June. In addition, they follow Scuba Do Kendwa's excellent example (page 233) and participate in September's annual International Coastal Clean-up Day.

With support and sustained education, we must hope that their efforts pay off in Jambiani, and that the message spreads to other coastal settlements. Without question, there is already significantly less litter here than in most of Zanzibar's other villages.

Partnered with JAMABECO, Swiss-run Marine Cultures (*www.marinecultures. org*) works in a similar way, encouraging villagers to find sustainable ways to cultivate and harvest marine products. This non-profit organisation enables farmers to contact their buyers directly, allowing them to cut out the middleman and reap greater financial reward from their produce. The Marine Cultures office in Jambiani is located next to the Equinox Restaurant (page 309) and welcomes visitors who wish to find out more about their ongoing projects. They are currently investigating sponges, with the hopes of starting up sponge harvesting in the village. There's currently a test farm, and if this is successful they hope to teach locals to cultivate and sell sponges (in a similar way they do seaweed), providing them with much-needed employment.

More information is available from Abdu M Vuai or Makame Simai (e *jamabeco@yahoo.co.uk*). To visit in Jambiani, ask for directions to the JAMABECO office or head to Okala Restaurant, where owner Mohammad (*okala@marinecultures.org*) is an enthusiastic member of both organisations.

JAMBIANI

For listings, see pages 300–11

thanks to two dedicated community organisations (see box, page 297) who arrange litter collections and local environmental education, and the sand here is simply never as busy as the northern beaches of Nungwi and Kendwa.

There is a locally run tourism website (*www.visitjambiani.com*), which has some reasonable listings and an enthusiastic team hoping to build on this resource, so it's worth a look if you're travelling to the area, and a good group to contact if you want a local guide.

GETTING THERE AND AWAY The paved road has made travel to and from Jambiani a pleasure compared with the past. The road runs inland of the village with a number of well-signposted turns to various coastal lodges. The old uneven, meandering 'highway' through the village remains, though it is no longer possible to travel all the way to Paje along the coast, thanks to various boundary walls along the way.

You can reach Jambiani by **private vehicle** or **tourist minibus**. In addition, **dalla dalla** No 309 runs from Zanzibar Town about five times a day, and the public **bus** (Route 9) to Paje sometimes continues as far as Jambiani: it's important to check each individual bus's destination though. It's also worth noting that most public transport heads only as far south as Auberge Coco Beach. To get to the more southerly resorts, you will have to either make a special plan with the driver, walk, or wait for one of the few daily dalla dallas that continue on to Makunduchi.

At the southern end of Jambiani village, the dirt road heads inland past the Red Monkey Lodge to meet with the main road for the final 10km to Makunduchi. Zanzest Beach Bungalows is the only hotel along this stretch of road, and public transport is extremely limited. If you want to keep heading south to Makunduchi, you may be lucky and find a lift on one of the occasional vehicles on the main road, otherwise, if you decide to walk, it takes a very hot three to four hours.

🏠 **WHERE TO STAY** With a long stretch of small guesthouses and no resorts, nothing on this stretch of coast qualifies as truly upmarket. There are, however, a few spots

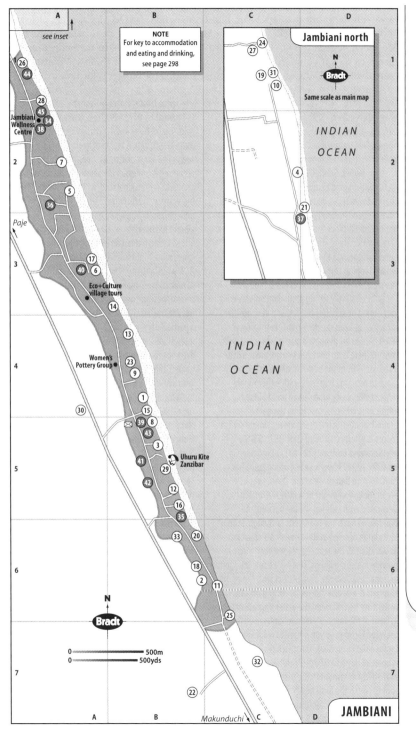

NOTE
For key to accommodation
and eating and drinking,
see page 298

Jambiani north

INDIAN OCEAN

INDIAN OCEAN

Jambiani Wellness Centre

Paje

Eco+Culture village tours

Women's Pottery Group

Uhuru Kite Zanzibar

Makunduchi

JAMBIANI

N

Bradt

0 ——— 500m
0 ——— 500yds

now with stand-out character: Nur, Blue Oyster and Casa Del Mar are very pleasant and far ahead of the pack, with Mama Mapambo following close behind. The Red Monkey Lodge at the far south of town is probably the best of the budget-choice places to stay, if you don't mind the more relatively remote location, whilst away from the beach Demani Lodge takes some beating for budget value on the island.

Upmarket

✳ ⌂ **Belvedere** [299 A2] (7 rooms) m 0774 094306; e bb@hotelbelvederezanzibar.com; www. hotelbelvederezanzibar.com. An absolute gem! Built with immense thought, care & style by its Austrian owner, Gabriel, Belvedere is refreshingly rustic whilst being beautiful, creative & full of charm. The steep-sided A-frame makuti rooms all have gorgeous views thanks to a conscious decision not to build & block the sea views. Interiors are lovely with natural chunky beds & a coral-rock open bathroom at the back. From the polished wood stepping stones to the toilet & shower sea view, every detail is full of fun & thought. For Gabriel, simply sitting around on holiday is 'not boring or negative but rather a very positive luxury'. . . & from the deck chairs in the flower-filled garden his delighted guests wholeheartedly concur. There is no pool, but you are always just a few steps from the beach, making this a lovely place to recharge batteries, with a thoroughly relaxed vibe, tasty food served amid billowing white voile curtains, cascading bougainvillea all around, unobstructed ocean views, simple stylish rooms & utterly charming staff. B&B. **$$$$**

⌂ **Seaview Lodge** [299 A1] (11 rooms) m 0777 729393; www.seaviewlodgezanzibar. com. Next to Bahari View, this clean, simple accommodation might be a little overpriced. Decorated with painted sea life outside, the bungalows have low twin beds (although 1 room has a large dbl), en-suite showers & a small fan as standard, & the team have tried very hard to provide matching linens. There are a few loungers in front of each room, a small pool with tangerine loungers & a beach shower for rinsing off salt water (but bear in mind the water immediately in front of the lodge is predominantly used for seaweed farming so you'll have to wade out quite far for a dip in the sea). The beach restaurant is open all day (🕐 07.30–22.30) with market availability determining the menu, & it's a casual spot to watch the local beach activity. Bikes can be rented for US$7/day for further village exploration. B&B; HB & FB available. **$$$$**

⌂ **Spice Island Hotel & Resort** [299 C1] (34 rooms) m 0775 020113; e reservation@ spice-island-hotel-resort.com; www.spice-island-hotel-resort.com. A breath of fresh air among what seems like a row of identikit guesthouses, this organised & professional operation is managed by energetic professional staff, with excellent facilities but without the feeling of some of the larger, more generic resorts elsewhere on the island. The 17 vibrant red bungalows, each containing 2 rooms, are all sea facing but not all with sea views, which may cause some confusion when booking. There's both AC & a fan, although the trpl-layered construction of makuti-steel-makuti keeps the temperatures cool so these are not always necessary. Each room has Zanzibari beds scattered with fresh flowers & a particularly ornate piece of furniture for added interest. All have clean en-suite bathrooms, & some even have 2 separate toilets. Within the pleasant garden, filled with over 5,000 plants & complete with a fountain, the large swimming pool is the main focus. Here, guests sunbathe & read while their children amuse themselves with pool games, stopping only for lunch in the vast restaurant where European, Zanzibari & Asian fusion food is served. Stressed parents might prefer to interrupt their poolside lounging with a massage in the Lemon Spa. For further respite, the plush leather sofas in the huge makuti lounge are a particular draw, & the sequinned cushions & saxophone music add to the relaxed feel. Spice Island's beachfront is 100m long, allowing plenty of space for the H^{2}O watersports centre (page 311), where, water babies can participate in all manner of activities, from banana boats to fishing, snorkelling to windsurfing & parasailing to aqua aerobics. Particularly unusual is supping, a form of stand-up paddle boarding. In the middle of the beach, the 100m-long jetty has a bar at the end, where an international wine list is a fitting accompaniment to sunset. If entertainment is still required, then there's always the TV, library, & the volleyball court, or the hotel rents out cars & bikes. B&B. **$$$$**

⌂ **Coral Rock Hotel** [299 C6] (18 rooms) m 0776 031955; e coraltrees@yahoo.co.uk; www.

coral-rock.com. Towards the southern end of Jambiani, this chilled-out South African–Zanzibari hotel with excellent ocean views lives up to its name, with the bungalows, pool & restaurant all perched along the coral cliffs above the beach. Smartened up over recent years, standard rooms are divided among 9 thatched bungalows, & have sunken beds, local paintings for decoration, mosquito nets & AC. Quirky carvings, Moroccan mosaic lanterns, vibrant Sasik cushions & beautiful furniture have been added for extra interest. There are lovely pole-shaded terraces in front of each with a few deckchairs, inlaid tables & sun-bleached shell strings. The glass-fronted Rocky Bar at the end of the complex offers terrific views of the craggy, notch-cut headlands to the south, & the extensive seaweed farming in front of the hotel. It's a funky hangout for sundowners with a nice vibe & free Wi-Fi. Chilling out is definitely the order of the day here, with an original triangular infinity pool & sun terraces that look out over the sand. With a private location, much-improved rooms & a cool bar, Coral Rock is establishing itself as one of the better Jambiani options at this price. B&B. **$$–$$$$**

Mid range

🏠 **Casa Del Mar** [299 B4] (14 rooms) m 0778 067510; e reservation@casa-delmar-zanzibar.com; www.casadelmar-zanzibar.com; ⏱ Jun–Mar. A long-standing, consistently reliable & friendly option in this part of Zanzibar. One of on Jambiani's more aesthetically pleasing beach lodges, consisting of rooms in 2 thatched dbl-storey houses, & a 2-room bungalow made almost entirely of organic material. It's owned & managed by a young, gentle Palestinian couple, with impressive enthusiasm, skill & environmental awareness, & a good understanding of what visitors to the island are really after. All of the unique lodge furniture & objets d'art were made onsite & every palm uprooted during its construction has been successfully replanted. Community relations are very strong, with the vast majority of the staff (14 out of 17) being Jambiani residents & the school & clinic receiving regular support. These credentials aside, the accommodation & friendly vibe are good reasons to stay, too. The ground-floor dbls with mosquito net, fan & terrace overlook the gardens, while the 1st-floor suites are dbl storey with a downstairs lounge (or children's room) & balcony, & a galleried bedroom high in the makuti thatch.

The circular restaurant is in a shady spot with colourful cushions, tropical planting & reasonable food. There's a detailed noticeboard of local activities & island excursions, & the lodge has its own boat for snorkelling trips (*US$15pp/day*) & operates its own 24hr taxi service, which is great for trying out other restaurants, checking out Coco Blue nightclub or simply visiting another part of the coast. If you do hang out at the lodge for the day though, there's a refreshing swimming pool & a lovely little massage treatment room. B&B. **$$$–$$$$**

🏠 **Mama Mapambo** [299 D2] (6 rooms) m 0773 862059; e mamamapambo@gmail. com; www.mamamapambo.com. Cheery Mama Mapambo adds a splash of much-needed colour & character to the guesthouses in this village. A wonderfully vibrant sign will direct you to this very cool, Italian-owned place immediately next to Kiddo's Café (page 310). Rooms are delightful & high quality, each painted a different shade, tastefully decorated & with Omani arches into starlit bathrooms. 4 rooms have a sea view & all have 4-poster beds draped in colour-trimmed nets as well as gauzed windows for mosquito defence. Walk-in wardrobes are a bonus, as is AC (2 rooms at the back), & bathrooms are modern. Up a spiral staircase, 2 Jungle Rooms have wooden A-frame ceilings & zebra-striped beds, & the modern bathrooms feature a shower in a circular pod in the middle of the bathroom – a striking & original design. To round it all off, the exterior of the whole lodge is painted a sunny yellow to match the owners' warm dispositions. A choice of bright & breezy seating areas both upstairs & down offers plenty of cushions & overlooks the sand, while the original furniture in the restaurant give it a funky edge. Unsurprisingly, the food has an Italian–Swahili twist with large bowls of spaghetti & curry buffets being the staples. The owners have put their hearts & souls into this project & it shows. B&B. **$$$–$$$$**

🏠 **Al Hapa Hotel** [299 B4] (7 rooms) m 0772 190901/0773 048894 e info@alhapazanzibar. com; www.alhapazanzibar.com. In association with the local villagers, this Swedish–Zanzibar-owned hotel offers a cosy & intimate stay, right on the beach, & there are plans to slowly extend, add a pool & improve the facilities in the beachfront garden. The narrow, 2-storey curved buildings are freshly whitewashed & thatched. Inside, bright yellow walls & huge flowery floor tiles clash with tangerine sheets, but rooms are clean, fresh & equipped with fans, mosquito nets & hot-water showers. It's fairly simple but added touches such as fresh flowers, scattered shells & driftwood shelves lend a dash of beach homeliness. The simple restaurant & circular beach bar is the spot for seafood dishes such as sizzling calamari fritters (*US$7*) & evening postcard writing next to an almost shrine-like wall of Bob Marley memorabilia. By day, reserve your hammock – classically tied up between curving palm trees – & lie back with one of the many well-read library books. B&B. **$$$**

🏠 **Auberge Coco Beach** [299 B5] (5 rooms) m 0777 413125/0732 940154; e info@ cocobeachzanzibar.com; www.cocobeachzanzibar. com. This long-standing small lodge offers simple & recently renovated dbl & trpl rooms. Accommodation is in little thatched bungalows, each with a simply furnished bedroom with fresh white linen, fan, en-suite bathroom & a small terrace leading to a shady garden of coconut palms & sweet almond trees. It's a quiet spot &, in the past, travellers have recommended the hedge-enclosed restaurant, which is decked out in vinyl records, shipping memorabilia & turtle-shells, but these days cuisine is much the same as the rest of the beach lodges: a selection of catch-of-the-day fish served with rice or chips & Swahili curries, though quality is still pretty good. B&B. **$$$**

🏠 **Bahari View Lodge** [299 C2] (15 rooms) m 0784 419232; e info@africanview.co.tz; www.african-view.com. The former Mount Zion Long Beach Bungalows changed hands & name in 2009, & embarked on a successful process of improvements. There's now a small pool amid the palms & a delightfully shady garden Wi-Fi zone, complete with colourful, cushioned seats. The coral-rock bungalows sit in lush tropical gardens & through the ornately carved door frames are clean, well-furnished bedrooms with lovely Zanzibari beds, pretty linens, coir easy chairs, & practicalities such as ceiling fans & mosquito nets. There are also 2 pagoda-like makuti structures on the beach, which contain simpler banda rooms. The circular sand-underfoot beach bar is a pleasant hangout for guests day & night. B&B; HB & FB available. **$$$**

🏠 **Blue Oyster Hotel** [299 A2] (14 rooms) m 0783 045796; e booking@blueoysterhotel.com; www.zanzibar.de. In lovely gardens of oleander & hibiscus, this remains one of the friendliest, most cared-for & best-value hotels in its range. The main

2-storey building has ground-floor rooms around a rear palm courtyard & a wonderfully breezy 1st-floor restaurant, from where the wide veranda overlooks the ocean. Further accommodation is available in a trio of smaller 2-storey buildings, all of which come with en-suite facilities & balconies. There is a lovely raised stretch of sand in front of the hotel laid with loungers, shaded by makuti parasols & softened with tropical planting – a perfect sunbathing spot, especially if you also opt for one of Zena's coconut-oil massages (*US$20*). With exceedingly friendly staff, clean rooms, good beds, running water & electricity, & an attractive location, this is a fine deal for the price. In the restaurant, snacks & sandwiches cost around US$5, delicious salads US$6, or pizzas & good evening meals like coconut-infused octopus with rice around US$10. Kemi Tours & Travel are based here (m *0782 214127;* e *kemitours@gmail.com; www. kemitours-zanzibar.com*); contact for advice on day trips, safaris & watersports, or simply to hire reef shoes for US$1 per day to avoid those pesky sea urchins. B&B. **$$$**

🏠 **Blue Reef Sports & Fishing Lodge** [299 B5] (8 rooms) m 0779 633234/ 0779 049419; e info@bluereeffishinglodge.com; www. bluereeffishinglodge.com. Established by Dutch brothers, Thomas & Nathan, as a family-run & family-friendly lodge on the beach, it's a chilled & friendly place. Focusing somewhat unusually on sports activities – from gymnastics & dance to beach volleyball or personal training – & fishing, they are an off-beat & likeable crew. Fisherman have endless options from casting, jigging & trawling from the fibre boat, serious big-game luxury trips (in conjunction with Ocean Blue in Paje), or even kayak fishing using specially balanced Cityindian kayaks from The Netherlands. There's a clear catch-&-release policy, bar catch-of-the-day dinners, & a raft of equipment & advice is on hand. Accommodation is in the main villa building with simple bedrooms & decent beds decked out in Dutch orange & white, & beaded curtains to en-suite shower rooms. There's an upstairs dining room with an open kitchen & a daily set menu, serving the likes of Durban chicken curry (*US$9*) & homemade apple cake with cinnamon ice cream (*US$5*). Out front, there's an enclosed beach 'garden' with a very relaxed bar area & access to the public beach. This is not a party place – music is off at 22.00 – but certainly offers good value for sports enthusiasts who don't want to spend their holiday glued to a lounger. B&B. **$$$**

🛏 **East Coast Visitors Inn** [299 B4] (63 rooms) m 0778 884647; e visitorsinn@ zitec.org/visitorsinn@hotmail.com; www.zanzibarvisitorsinn.com. Situated on the village main street, 150m south of the charred remains of the Sau Inn, this is a fairly large budget place. Reception is tucked under the 'Karibuni' arch & is a popular spot for locals to watch TV. Rooms are in white bungalows above the beach & display a selection of musty, mish-matched furniture in slightly run-down interiors with saggy ceilings & worn carpets. All of these offer AC, mini fridges, satellite TV & tiled floors, & some have a dining table, too. 2016 saw some rather dramatic expansion underway in the form of multi-storey accommodation blocks alongside the pool. The site will certainly be cramped on completion, & hopes are low for anything high-quality. Meals are available for around US$5 in the expansive & empty, fruit-painted restaurant. There is a nice stretch of beach here, a swimming pool & shade to be had under the casuarina trees. There is also a giant, blue-tinted, low-budget conference centre. Under 7s stay free. B&B. **$$$**

🛏 **Garden Restaurant & Bungalows** [299 B3] (6 rooms) m 0655 410263; e halimchozi@ hotmail.com. Now locally owned, this is a simple beach hangout for budget travellers. There are spacious if very basic rooms, with cold-water en suites, plus a small dorm, all of which are clean & well screened within the lush planting. The kitchen continues to dish up popular curries & crêpes in the restaurant, & the enthusiastic & friendly team crack jokes & enjoy the reggae tunes well into the night as much as the laidback guests. B&B. **$$$**

✳ 🛏 **Kimte Beach Inn** [299 B6] (8 rooms) m 0776 657794; e kimteguesthouse@hotmail.com; www.kimteguesthouse.com. Straddling the road, about 500m beyond Uhuru, at the quieter end of the village, this Swiss-managed lodge offers a warm welcome, stylish simplicity & a lovely garden bar on a great stretch of beach. The rooms are all within a sgl-storey house, with orange windows & a tin roof, on the right of the road as you head south of the village centre. Check in at the welcoming grey-&-white striped reception, before heading inside the main house to the cool, calm & thoroughly refurbished interior – 7

dbl rooms, 2 with a shared bathroom, & a good, spacious, comfortable dorm. Behind doors marked with a domino piece, rooms have pale stripped-wood furniture, whitewashed coral-rock walls, checkerboard floors & simple, clean bathrooms. Towels & Wi-Fi are available & management are genuinely keen to please. There is a lovely, shady palm garden & bar-restaurant on the beach across the quiet village road, where you can hang out here on hammocks, dine on Swahili dishes or sip cocktails. It's a relaxed, low-key hangout, & a great-value option in this budget. B&B. *Dorm* **$$**, *rooms* **$$$**

✳ 🛏 **Nur** [299 B4] (10 rooms) m 0777 162016; e info@nur-zanzibar.com/reservation@ nur-zanzibar.com; www.nur-zanzibar.com. Neighbouring its sister property, Casa Del Mar (page 301), Nur is gorgeous in its architectural simplicity & modern interior design. Its identical, coral rock, A-frame bungalows sit perpendicular to the sea, overlooking the slick infinity pool. Small, stylish & beautiful, they marry industrial grey moulded-concrete furniture with exposed timber beams, crisp linens, thoroughly original design features & an open-plan en-suite area. The shower head is fashioned from an intricate twisted copper pipe, whitewashed beaten metal light fittings sit either side of the bed & there's ample storage is built into the relatively bijou room. A smart grey concrete terrace with built-in baraza benches faces the turquoise pool, & give a private space – but this is a social place at heart. The open lounge-cum-restaurant area is designed to encourage guests to meet up & mingle & the utterly delightful French managers are always around to chat. Under recycled boat & bottle chandeliers, the turquoise cushioned barazas & contemporary dining tables are a great spot to enjoy tasty tapas, gazpacho, fresh fish & salads, all finished off with some delicious homemade ice cream. Take sundowners or after-dinner drinks on the Ocean View terrace upstairs or just linger in this funky hang-out. By day, there's an onsite kite centre (Zanzibar-Prokite, page 311) with a great team & a location offering easy conditions for beginners. Nur is certainly a great addition to the growing clutch of edgy, mid-range beach spots. B&B **$$$**

🛏 **Pakachi Beach Hotel** [299 C1] (9 rooms) m 0773 621086; e info@pakachi.com; www.pakachi.com. Appropriately, *pakachi* means 'border', for this pleasant little hotel is situated on the coral rock roughly halfway between the centres of Paje & Jambiani. 3 2-storey, A-frame beach bandas sit amid flower-filled gardens, each with 2 rooms designed to channel the breeze & offer a lovely view from upstairs. Inside, the rooms are simple, functional & spotlessly clean, with kanga curtains, large ceiling fans & en-suite bathroom. There is also a 2-bedroom family house available. On the other side of the bumpy road, the bar/restaurant sits overlooking the sea where the chef rustles up local & international dishes, with recommendations coming in for his pizzas. The coastline is very rocky at this point, so it's not always ideal for shore swimming, but the intertidal zone makes for fascinating beachcombing at low tide. A much-needed brackish pool & a simple Island Spice treatment room have recently been added for guest enjoyment. It's a very quiet spot currently being managed by its English owner, although this is likely to change hands at some point in the near future. B&B. **$$$**

🏠 **Stonehouse** [299 A1] (8 rooms) m 0777 414209; e karibu@stonehouse-zanzibar.com; www.stonehouse-zanzibar.com. This former family house was converted to a guesthouse nearly a decade ago & is steadily trying to improve its standards. Retaining much of its homely feel, the assortment of rooms are very simply furnished with heavy Zanzibari beds & little else. Most, but not all, of the rooms are now en suite & all rely on sea breezes for cooling. Guests are welcome to use the well-equipped kitchen, but if you don't fancy cooking, the owners can rustle up simple Swahili fare with a bit of notice, & there is a palm-woven bar area for fresh juice & local beers. It is, however, centrally located in the village with a good sea view from the 1st-floor terrace & raised beach area. B&B. **$$$**

🏠 **Villa de Coco** [?99 C1] (11 rooms) m 0776 110691; e info@villadecocoresort.com; www. villadecocoresort.com. Beside the electrical substation, about 400m off the tar road south of Paje, Villa de Coco is an Italian-run lodge with friendly managers, Marco & Marcella. The majority of the rooms are in 3 rows of coconut-wood bungalows; inside they are small but neat with attractive coconut floorboards, kanga-hung walls, clean beds, fans, open wardrobes & a small terrace. There are also 2 separate rooms in a 2-storey villa beside the raised Tanga stone swimming pool, with views over the pretty beach. There is

a makuti-thatched restaurant serving pasta, & the chill-out lounge by the beach is a great place to relax & play snooker. There has been marked investment & improvement in this little lodge over the years & it's a neat, pleasant place these days; nothing flash but quiet & homely. B&B. **$$$**

🏠 **Villaggio Seconda Stella a Destra** [299 A4] (12 rooms) m 0779 004369; e secondastella2013@libero.it; www. villaggiosecondastella.it. Taking its name from *Peter Pan's* Neverland – where responsibilities are few & you never grow up – Seconda Stella is a lovely, Italian-owned lodge with immaculate rooms, a fine kitchen & neat frangipani-filled gardens. Well-presented rooms circle the raised swimming pool & all have spotless interiors in denim blue & white, with sparkling en-suite shower rooms, pretty cushions on hide chairs, moulded-concrete beds & neat terraces. There's a friendly restaurant dishing up homemade pasta, wood-fired pizza & some Swahili classics, all washed down with glasses of Montepulciano reds (*US$19/bottle*) & Prosecco (*US$27/bottle*). The whole complex is on the 'wrong' side of the road, in that it is to the west of the tar road & as such is quite a distance from the beach, but Seconda Stella's reasonable rates reflect its location & make it pretty good value for the quality of accommodation & Italian home cooking. FB. **$$$**

✳ 🏠 **Zanzistar** [299 B6] (6 rooms) m 0774 440799; e info@zanzi-star.com; www.zanzi-star. com. Opened in 2015, this cheerfully decorated, welcoming café & guesthouse is a delightful oasis in the heart of the village, with a great vibe, happy staff & some lovely rooms. Ground-floor rooms have coconut floors, moulded-concrete beds (complete with build-in electronic safe), fans & funky details from a coat stand tree to beaten metal wall lights. There is also a neat, spacious family room with 2 bedrooms & a bathroom (7 pax). Interiors are cool, whitewashed & stylish in their simplicity, & each room has a small private garden area, surrounded by pole fencing & housing a hammock under plenty of shade. The charming central area has a small square pool, complete with in-water benches, some lovely banana trees & palms, bright pink sail-cloth shades & lovely shady coir sofas covered in vibrant cushions. There's a bar area & café (page 311) serving juices, cocktails & well-priced home-cooking. Wi-Fi is available. A great option, if you're happy staying off the beach, thanks to the efforts of Fleur & her enthusiastic team. B&B. **$$$**

Budget

⌂ **Blue Earth Bungalows** [299 A3] (8 rooms) ☎024 224 0351; m 0777 846597; e blueearthbungalows@ymail.com; blueearthbungalows.com. Approaching Blue Earth from the beach, you could be forgiven for thinking the desolate, overgrown walled plot was yet another slice of abandoned half-built wasteland. But look closer & you'll see a discrete row of thatched bungalows hidden along the far wall, each containing 2 rooms. Within, the aroma of freshly laundered linen wafts from the Zanzibari beds that sit on a cool blue-tiled floor. Furnishing is simple, with just a wardrobe, fan & a lamp, but strangely no table to put it on; flowery green curtains complete the look.
4 rooms have AC but other than that, the rest are indistinguishable. Bathrooms are again basic but have hot-water showers & are spotlessly clean. In front of the rooms stands the Dimbuni Restaurant, which is little more than a couple of tables under a makuti roof. Here, a menu of seafood, curries & sandwiches is on offer, though the probability of anything on the menu actually being available seems low. There's a lot of unused space here, & for such basic accommodation, the price should be lower. B&B. **$$–$$$**

⌂ **Changuu Beach Resort** [299 C1] (12 rooms) m 0717 109910/ 0676 22829; e changuubeach2@gmail.com Next to Villa de Coco, Changuu is the seaside retirement dream of a jovial gentleman from Lake Victoria. Sadly his infectious chuckles & warmth don't mask the scale of his towering 4-storey property right on the beach. Rooms are adequate with clean, neat bedding & large blue bathrooms, but they lack style. The top-floor 'Kilimanjaro' room, is a vast, open-plan, 8-person bedroom with Zanzibar beds, selection of miscellaneous chairs, 2 small AC units & no fan. There are an additional 4 sgl-storey thatched rooms towards the beach that are smaller in size but similar in style. There's a deep, somewhat cloudy, swimming pool & a beach with a simple, raised chill-out area. B&B. **$$–$$$**

⌂ **Art Hotel** [299 B6] (4 rooms) e kabelele@ hispeed.ch; www.arthotelzanzibar.com. This small, Swiss-owned, L-shaped B&B offers simple rooms overlooking a small lawn & pool. Each has been decorated with paintings & murals by a different Tanzanian artist, & the garden has a cluster of Hendrik Lilanga's galvanized steel sculptures. There is little atmosphere here, staff are limited & there is no security (village location with no fencing), but rooms are adequate. Across the village road, on the low cliff above the seafront, is a small concrete terrace where a few tables & benches are used for a few meals; however, it's empty & totally lacking in comfort or atmosphere. B&B. **$$–$$$**

⌂ **La Papaye Verte Bungalows** [299 B6] (5 rooms) m 0772 252670; www.zanzibar-papaye-verte.com. This French-owned & -run self-catering establishment has rooms in delightful villas set in lush, shady gardens. Under bougainvillea-clad thatch, the little bungalows offer a dbl (2 can accommodate a family with extra beds) & little kitchen with blue-&-white painted furniture, simple, homely interiors & a lovely terrace for outdoor dining or lazing in the hammock. For larger groups, there is also a 3-bedroom villa (8 pax) with its own kitchen, panoramic terrace & even an outdoor shower. If you are planning on self-catering, locally bought fruit, vegetables & eggs are available, but any meat or fish really needs to come from Stone Town, so do plan ahead. For an evening away from the stove, the family running Peace of Mind Restaurant (10min walk along road; page 310) will prepare & deliver a Swahili dinner. By day, there are pole-shaded beds beside the beach & an air of tropical calm: come here for self-sufficiency, peace & escapism, not excitement, & you'll be very happy. SC **$$–$$$**

⌂ **Uhuru Beach Resort** [299 B5] (17 rooms) m 0779 041645; e info@uhurubeach.com; www.uhurubeach.com. Along the beach, about 1km south of Jambiani centre, Uhuru started life as Shehe Bungalow's – one of the first backpacker refuges in the village. A decade later, it is being utterly transformed by its new Irish owner, Anna, with a commitment to creating a stylish budget retreat. Each of the ocean-view bungalows is right above the beach, & has a bijou patio for gazing at the sunset. Inside, bedrooms (sgl, dbl or trpl available) are slowly being renovated & simply but thoughtfully decorated with white limed timber beds, pretty mirrors, nice linen, & an obligatory mosquito net & fan. It is worth looking at a few rooms as they are slightly different inside. The main whitewashed villa offers the best ocean vista from its 1st-floor terrace restaurant & lounge.

10

Recycled dhow furniture, a few deep leather sofas, terrazzo tiling & gleaming mirrors make this a cool place to peer over the low castellations to the picture-perfect beach & sea beyond. Chef Amita serves continental b/fast to start the day & the likes of octopus curry, chicken burritos & coconut-crusted fish later in the day (*all around US$8*); Sun brunch features live music. There are also good local masseuses here, as well as yoga options & an onsite kite centre: Uhuru Kite Zanzibar (page 311). Whilst there have been some reports of issues with in-room water supplies, the current care, cost & beach location still make this a good-value option, which should only be enhanced as Anna's improvements continue. B&B. **$$–$$$**

🏠 **Dudé's Guesthouse** [299 B5] (3 rooms) m 0773 147812; e info@dudesguesthouse.com; www.dudesguesthouse.com. Immediately behind Uhuru, Dudé's (*Doo-day*) is a 2-storey whitewashed villa, kept beautifully neat & clean by its friendly namesake owner who lives upstairs. Rooms (2 en suite) are simply furnished & share a communal lounge filled with batik cushions on baraza benches, & also have access to a monochrome kitchen area for optional self-catering. There's a shady terrace & loungers under neat palm umbrellas, & the beach is 1min away through a narrow sandy path opposite the villa. B&B. **$$**

🏠 **Karibuni Beach Villa** [299 A3] (7 rooms) m 0685 408007; e pross12@t-online.de. In 2015, the old Oasis Beach Inn was taken over by a former German tour operator & her Zanzibari husband. They are in the process of upgrading this rather run-down resort, with painting, new thatch & rewiring all being undertaken. Rooms are in whitewashed bungalows literally 20m from the sandy beach, but the real luxury ends there. Behind the polished mkeke doors, interiors are pretty basic: clean but with only simple, spartan furnishings & passable hot-water en suites. There's a quiet, raised bar & restaurant area, where meals can be arranged in the sandy underfoot restaurant. Transfers can be arranged with the owner herself. B&B. **$$**

🏠 **Kobe House** [299 C1] (11 rooms) m 0772 249 000; e info@kobehouse.org; www.kobehouse.org. Behind the green turtle-stamped gate next to Villa de Coco, Kobe's rooms are spread across 2 buildings just up from the beach. Reception is something of a local hangout but the staff here are friendly, if not swift. It's hard not to feel from the incongruous layout & design of the rooms that this was originally intended as a private house, rather than a hotel. There is a basic dorm room in the makuti thatch, 1 bedroom with a dbl bed, bunkbeds & a small kitchenette, & some en-suite rooms radiating from the central white spiral staircase in the 'Big Villa'. There's a small swimming pool, rooftop relaxation spot & a buffet restaurant. B&B. **$$**

🏠 **Jambiani Guesthouse** [299 B4] (5 rooms) m 0773 147812; e anne@zanzibar-guesthouse. com; www.zanzibar-guesthouse.com. In the coconut line immediately above the beach at the southern end of the village, this is a small, thatched building, clearly signposted off the main village road, best booked by a group of friends or a family. A simple villa, nicely maintained, it has clean dbl rooms (1 en suite), 2 shared bathrooms, a small kitchen-lounge & a veranda overlooking the sandy beach & ocean. The local caretaker, Rama, lives onsite & can help with local tours, snorkelling equipment (free) &, if necessary, catering. The weekly rates are not really discounted, but you can check availability online. B&B. **$$**

🏠 **Jambiani White Sand Bungalows** [299 B5] (8 rooms) m 0777 778385; e whitesandbungalows@yahoo.com; jambianiwhitesands.com. With a lovely location right on the beach, White Sand Bungalows live up to their name. Big plans are afoot for the unremarkable rooms though, with 2017 likely to see their demolition & resurrection as a much larger resort. B&B. **$$**

🏠 **Mango Beachhouse** [299 C3] (3 rooms) m 0773 498949; e alikiddo@gmail.com; www. mango-beach house.com. At Kiddo's Café (page 310) & with the same management, this quirky guesthouse has 3 very different, self-catering rooms spread across 2 buildings, each made distinct by the owner's eye for unique decorative items & styles: 1 room has batik elephant sheets; 1 has a large orange bathroom; & 1 is adorned with shells hanging from the ceiling. All are brightened up with fresh flowers & bold paintings & share a kitchen with a hob, kettle & a zebra-print fridge. B/fast is not served here, so guests can purchase produce locally to prepare something instead. Out the front, comfortable sun loungers are spread out on the sand. For every week booked guests are offered a free night, an offer well worth taking up as this is a place to linger. It's worth noting that there are currently 11 happily adopted cats & a dog living here, too – so not a spot for anyone allergic to animals. Cash only. SC. **$$**

⌂ **Mbuyuni Beach Village** [map, page 268] (20 rooms) **m** 0773 659989; **e** mbuyunibeachvillage@yahoo.co.uk; www.mbuyuni.com. Mbuyuni is 200m north of Pakachi, accessed on a bumpy road directly from the north–south tar highway. It's not the most charming arrival, especially given the lack of reception area & staff at the back of the hotel. However, once inside, there are a selection of bandas, bungalows & newer houses, the latter somewhat strangely at the rear of the property. The 2 rows of thatched bungalows, running perpendicular to the sea, are OK with established flower beds & wide sandy paths. These rooms are simple with tiled floors, sky blue walls & matching sheets, & an enormous bathroom. All offer a fan, mosquito net & shower. The 3 houses – Furaha, Upendo & Kisima – offer giant en-suite rooms, easily sleeping 4 people, with clean concrete interiors, high ceilings & blush-coloured baraza terraces. Most recently added, the bandas are simple & functional with good storage, hammocks on terraces & an en-suite shower. The seemingly constant construction work that surrounds the site gives the place a permanently half-finished rough-&-ready feel, but it's very peaceful here & somewhat off the beaten track. There is also a relatively large pool & a seafront restaurant decorated with paintings of golden hued sunsets. The à la carte cuisine is both Swahili & international, with a range of spaghetti & fish dishes (*US$8*), & there's a lengthy cocktail menu (try a Zanzibar Pirate: local gin & Cointreau with lime, orange & passionfruit juice). B&B; HB available. **$$**

⌂ **Mfumbwi Lodge** [299 B7] (8 rooms) **m** 0784 687169; **e** info@mfumbwilodge.com; www.mfumbwilodge.com. From the tar road, take the road inland following the signpost towards Kuumbi Caves; this basic villa offering large, budget rooms is tucked into the bush on the right. Rooms are clean enough, & if you can look past the onslaught of patterns & colours in the interiors, they are quite reasonable. 4 have small, acceptable en suites, the others share bathrooms; all are cold-water only. Downstairs there is a communal lounge, with little more than an array of oversized red sofas, whilst upstairs, past the open electrical box & its spouting wires, is a wide terrace area overlooking the bar & bush beyond. Meals are currently served here, although a thatched restaurant is under construction. In the garden, there's a long dhow bar, complete with coconut-trunk bar stools & some token Bob Marley memorabilia, where service is extremely laidback. Tue nights can be pretty noisy affairs though

with a campfire BBQ & entertainment from a local Washamba band from 21.00, followed by a DJ with a penchant for very loud reggae & late nights: best to avoid if you're heading here to escape the beach buzz. There are no real activities or recreational facilities, & it's a 15–20min walk to the beach via Zanzest (below), so be sure you're happy with the location before committing to stay, & beware the dogs – they may not be as old or friendly as they appear. B&B. **$$**

⌂ **Red Monkey Lodge** [299 C6] (14 rooms) **m** 0777 713366; **e** info@redmonkeylodge.com; www.redmonkeylodge.com. About 2km from Jambiani centre, this is set on low coral cliffs & named after the Kirk's red colobus monkeys that live in the adjacent forest & pass through the grounds most days. The Austrian management ensure standards & quality: rooms are delightful, there's a nice view of the beach (which is reached by a short flight of steps), & staff are very friendly. Incredibly spacious rooms, complete with large ceiling fans, mosquito nets & high-pressure showers (some also have mini fridges), are extremely clean & represent one of the better budget deals in this part of Zanzibar. There are a few raised flower beds & palms, & up in the restaurant on the coral cliff, a skilful chef prepares fresh fish & other delightful dishes, especially at the 4-course dinners (*US$16*). There is also an onsite kite school, Kite Worldwide (**e** jambianikitecentre@gmail.com; www.kiteworldwide.com), licenced by VDWS & offering courses from beginner to advanced. Snorkelling can also be arranged using local boat captains. B&B. **$$**

⌂ **Zanzest Beach Bungalows** [299 C7] 12 rooms) **m** 0777 430992; **e** info@zanzest.co.tz; www.zanzest.co.tz. Way down the beach from Jambiani village, high up on the coral rock, this is run by the former manager of Kimte & caters for the budget travellers with 2 dorms sleeping 8 & 5, & 2 rooms with private cold-water bathrooms. Basic palm-thatched bandas have been brought a level above the norm by shell & coconut decorations, patterned lamps & psychedelic zebra-print sheets. Simple catch-of-the-day meals & pizza are available in the open-sided bar, which is laid out with benches & kanga-covered tables. It's simple, but a little different from standard Jambiani accommodation, though not helped by its location. B&B. **$$**

✳ ⌂ **Demani Lodge** [map, page 268] (20 rooms) **m** 0772 263115/0777 460079; **e** demanilodge@gmail.com; www.demanilodge.

com. Catering for those on a tight budget who still want a decent standard, delightful Demani is truly a backpackers' place, filled with chill-out music, good vibes & interesting characters. The lodge underwent a total renovation in 2014 & is in great shape, with the rooms grouped in friendly little circles around well-screened grounds. The simple but well-constructed thatched bandas have fans, mosquito nets & sturdy beds made from varnished tree trunks, or there are new coral rock dbls, & by far the island's most immaculate, sweet-smelling 7-bed dormitory. Rooms either share the smart, cold-water ablution block, or come with hot-water en suites. Hearts & stars hang from the makuti-ceilinged bar, where the lower level has swings, benches & a fire pit, & the upper chill-out zone is strung with rainbow-coloured hammocks & scattered with floor cushions. This upper area is a good spot to catch a cooling evening breeze, but you'll need to be quick to save the cocktails-at-sunset sea-facing sofa. Tasty meals made by very friendly ladies from locally sourced ingredients are all served here for rock bottom prices. Filling comfort food is always available for those on even the tightest of budgets: pumpkin soup with garlic bread (*US$3.50*); king fish fillet with wedges (*US$7*); or save up for the all-you-can-eat Swahili night on Thu (spicy rice, beef skewers, whole grilled fish & a lot more for US$10) complete with the local Wakushi Band, playing everything from jazz to reggae. It is a good walk to the beach from here, but there is now a lovely swimming pool surrounded by tropical palms & flowers that make lounging in the midday heat a great alternative. If you do fancy getting out & about, you can rents bikes for US$4/day, useful for reaching the sea which is found across the road & down a private sandy path. At such reasonable rates, this is a super budget pad, with the US$16/night dorm being probably the island's best bargain. B&B. **$–$$**

✖ **WHERE TO EAT AND DRINK** Virtually all of the places to stay listed above have affiliated restaurants, most of which serve a fairly standard range of seafood and island curries. **Casa Del Mar** (page 301), **Nur** (page 303) and the **Blue Oyster** (page 302) are all recommended for food. Good-quality meals at all of these, naturally with a seafood emphasis, cost US$5–10, and drinks, snacks and lunches are also readily available. Off the beach road, **Villaggio Seconda Stella a Destra** (page 304) is a good pit-stop for homemade Italian cooking. If your taste buds get the better of your wallet, you can often pay by credit card.

Unusually for a Zanzibari village, there are also some really very good local-style restaurants which, with a bit of notice, will prepare an excellent medley of island dishes for you to sample (talk to them in the morning if you want to eat that afternoon or evening). **Kim's** and **Okala**, listed below, warrant special mention – don't be discouraged by the ramshackle exteriors and sand floors; the food is very tasty.

If you just want supplies, there are a number of small local shops. The **Jambiani Post Office & Mini Market** on the main village road, near the Auberge Coco Beach, doesn't quite warrant its prominent signposting throughout the village, but it does supplement the usual local fare with a selection of tinned foods and a few imported goodies (sweets and crisps), and it also sells stamps.

✖ **Alibi's Well** [299 A2] m 0786 231988; www. handsacrossborderssociety.org; ◷ 11.30–17.00 daily. Part of the adjoining Jambiani Tourism Training Institute (JTTI), Alibi's Well is staffed by students who wish to gain experience in the tourism industry. Tasty fusion food such as wraps & pizzas are on the light-bites menu, as are rich coffee & tempting cakes. Colourful cocktails are shaken & stirred at the pretty pink bar, & there's a green-walled deck overlooking the sea. Dinner is served on Fri nights only & must be pre-booked, & the varied menu takes on a different theme each week – Japanese & Italian are some of the more popular choices. Many of the students here also study tour guiding – ask if you fancy a local excursion. All proceeds go to the JTTI, all tips go directly to the students, & with some of them having gone on to run lodges & hotels in Jambiani, or even set up their own business, this is a cause worthy of your support. **$$$**

✕ **Chez Hassan** [299 B5] m 0773 101603
Clearly signposted, Chez Hassan sits under high
makuti thatch & in their own words 'presents the
best food in Jambiani'. Strung with fairy lights,
& filled with primary-coloured chairs & neatly
tables set with vases of plastic flowers, Hassan
& his wife Aisha (the chef) offer a lengthy
menu with everything being cooked fresh to
order. Tandoori food is cooked traditionally on
a local charcoal BBQ (marinated chicken, beef
or octopus for US$10/2 sharing), or try some
Zanzibari favourites of special pilau rice or fish
in spiced coconut with carrot pickles & chapatti.
Unusually for a locally run place, they also serve
glasses of wine (*US$2*). If there is something
special you would like, it is a good idea to call
by earlier in the day to allow for purchase &
preparation. $$$

✕ **Equinox Restaurant** [299 A2] m 0772
608241; ⏲ lunch & dinner, daily. Owned by
a local Rastafarian, known as Captain Cook,
Equinox is tucked behind a woven makuti fence.
Chances are that Captain Cook will find you
before you find him, but if not follow the signs
from Blue Oyster & you'll locate it with ease. It's
a very basic, casual place, doubtless influenced
by Cook's own friendly, informal manner. With a
flag-flying rondavel bar & outdoor seating, it's
primarily a place to chill out & chat in the village.
There is some simple cooking equipment & if
you're keen to eat (fish in masala US$7; grilled
octopus US$6.50), Captain Cook will proudly read
you the glowing multi-national reviews in his
extensive guest book. Perseverance, a supportive
family & well-deserved success have recently
allowed Cook to build 7 guestrooms alongside
his restaurant, & at only US$20/dbl including
b/fast they may be very basic but it's a friendly
place if you're really on a shoestring. He'll equally
arrange scooter or bike rental, teach ngoma
drumming or introduce you to his delightful
family for a Swahili cookery lesson. $$$

✕ **Kim's Restaurant** [299 A2] ⏲ lunch & dinner
daily. Well signposted from Blue Oyster & owned
by a charming local entrepreneur, Kim, this simple,
shaded restaurant is the realisation of a childhood
dream. This place serves authentic Zanzibari cuisine
(best ordered in advance), all freshly prepared by
Kim & his mother. The spicy fish samosas (*US$3.50*),
fish soup (*US$2.50*) & coconut-crusted fish with
mango chutney (*US$9*) are particularly tasty.

The small palm-clad shack & sand on the floor
that make up the restaurant only add to the local
flavour, & this is one of a few reliably good village
dining options in Jambiani. $$$

✕ **Lustania Restaurant** [299 B4] m 0776
031961; e mohabduly@gmail.com; ⏲ dinner;
lunch on request. Offering the 'best dishes,
etmosphere [sic], food & very local experience',
Lustania is run by Mohhamed & his family
from a white bungalow emblazoned with their
name. Set just back from the beach, behind Blue
Reef, it specialises in seafood & Swahili classics.
Generally speaking, it's best to order dinner by
the middle of the day to allow time for shopping
& preparing their special buffet meal. At only
US$10 it includes basmati rice, green banana,
chapatti, coconut-crusted octopus, grilled fish
(spiced to your preference), omelette, creamed
spinach & potato masala. Plus, if you chat to
Mohhamed in advance, for an additional US$10
you can spend time with the family shopping,
cooking & preparing the feast, which gives great
insight in village life & makes for meaningful
interactions with the local women. $$$

✕ **Seahorse Restaurant** [299 A1] ⏲ lunch &
dinner daily. Just to the north of the Blue Oyster, this
lovely little place offers fresh home-cooked Zanzibari
cuisine in its breezy beachside restaurant. Spiced
curries & grilled lobster go for around US$7, with
light snacks about US$4, served up by friendly staff
by candlelight (if you come after sunset). The simple
makuti roof is spruced up by shell mobiles, the menu
is full of witty comments that make for amusing
reading, & traveller reports are pretty positive.
Order food in advance if you aren't prepared to wait
patiently, then sit back & enjoy. $$$

✳✕ **Seconda Stella a Destra** [299 A4]
m 0779 004369; www.villaggiosecondastella.
it. Not quite as far as Neverland, but rather on
the right of the tar road heading south of Paje,
Seconda Stella is clearly signposted with large blue
letters heralding it's genuine 'Italian Kitchen'. Stop
by at this bush oasis for some lovely homemade
crab gnocchetti (*US$10*), fettuccine alla Bolognese
(*US$9*), wood-fired pizzas (*US$8–11*) & the
occasional Swahili curry. There's karaoke on Wed
& Sat nights, a big screen for European football,
& always a relaxed, friendly vibe. Italian owners
Arnaldo & Claudia are living their dream, & if you
can cope with only Italian & Swahili being spoken,
it's worth stopping for a bite. There are also some

great-value, attractive rooms to rent around their appealing pool (page 304). $$$

✕ Step In Restaurant & Bar [299 A2] m 0773 555280; e sochs@gmx.ch; ⏰ 10.00–22.00 daily. From the beach, Step In is a fairly attractive prospect, & although the inside is an expanse of concrete, there's a large terrace & an extensive menu of octopus, coconut-crusted fish (*US$6*) & a range of tempting desserts & snacks (if they're available). Run by Sabine, a dedicated Swiss lady, all food is freshly made & the open kitchen is well stocked. Check out her homemade ice creams in Zanzibari flavours (passion fruit, coconut & sesame butter), or the Swiss speciality potato rosti. Like most little restaurants along the coast, for the best flavours & choice, it's worth ordering dinner early in the day to allow for preparation. If you are prepared to just wait though, there's an array of funky cocktails from which to choose. 2 simple, spacious bedrooms, with a shared cold-water shower, are also available for rent in the house. $$$

✕ Peace of Mind Restaurant [299 B5] ⏰ lunch noon–15.00, dinner 19.00–21.00. The well-signposted village restaurant, run by the delightful Ali Maulid & his family, is consistently highly praised for its Swahili dishes & seafood. Try the deliciously sweet steamed slipper lobster (cigale) with vegetables & rice (*US$5*), or take the chef's recommendation of the day's specials. They will also arrange Swahili tasting dinners with a day's notice. $$–$$$

✕ Pishi Restaurant [299 B5] m 0776 450127. In the centre of the village, opposite the Jaribu store, with a neat sign & bleached shell-topped fencing, the 6 tables here are surrounded by hide chairs & sit on a little terrace under a shady makuti roof. There are painted fish & shell mobiles, buoys hung for decoration & a degree of care is evident in its planting; food is predominantly Swahili (octopus masala US$7.50, peanut-crusted fish with tartare sauce US$7.50) with a few pasta dishes. $$–$$$

✕ Garden Restaurant [299 B3] m 0776 586193; ⏰ 11.30–late. Follow the yellow sign from the ruins of the Sau Inn or access this place from the beach; either way it's very clearly marked. With lovely sea views from its beachfront plot (page 303), this breezy & popular place boasts friendly staff & a mixture of both Zanzibari & European menu options, including curries & crêpes. The polished makuti bar plays reggae tracks day & night, & it's become a hangout for both locals & backpacking visitors. $$

✴✕ Kiddo's Café [299 C3] m 0773 498949; e alikiddo2hotmail.com/pl-stern@web.de; ⏰ 07.00–22.00 daily. Tucked off the main road through the village between Mama Mapambo & Bahari View Lodge, or accessed from the beach, this is an understated, calm café where gourmet fruit-juice concoctions are mixed by the dreadlocked, cool dude after whom the bar takes its name. It's a place to retreat, order a cafetière of fresh coffee or something exotic (Kiddo's Mix of pineapple, passion fruit & mango juices with coconut milk & ginger is divine) with a side of popcorn, grab a paperback from the recycled dhow bookshelf (an eclectic mix from Nick Hornby to Louis de Bernières), kick back & relax in the treehouse-like upper bar or under the sailcloth shade in the sand garden below. Wherever you choose, there's a good chance you'll be joined by one of the many resident dogs or cats, so it's probably not the best bet if you're not an animal lover. Kiddo's is particularly convenient for those staying at the affiliated Mango Beachhouse next door (page 306) & a great stop for vegetarians as the veggie owner always offers a good array of suitable dishes. There's also a lovely buffet dinner served daily (book by lunchtime) where a number of Swahili vegetarian dishes can be sampled alongside your choice of chicken or fish. Food is sourced locally in an initiative to support the community & so is highly seasonal & always fresh. $$

✕ Okala Restaurant [299 A3] m 0777 430519; e okala_6@hotmail.com; ⏰ lunch & dinner daily. In a small, unremarkable makuti building, just up from the beach (beside Oasis Beach Inn), Okala's food far exceeds any expectations arising from its architecture. Run by a small co-operative of Jambiani families, the Zanzibari fare here is really excellent by any standards, making the restaurant well worth a visit. The woven makuti walls, sand floor & crude shell mobiles may discourage some from entering, but we highly recommend that you do. With some notice, the team here can prepare a fabulous mezze of Swahili curries, grilled seafood & tasty vegetable accompaniments. Filling up on fresh coconut rice, wilted spinach with lime & rich tomato fish curry is a real Zanzibari treat. Individual dishes, such as grilled octopus or fish, are US$5–6, with special items, like the amazing (& enormous) coconut-crusted jumbo prawns costing US$10. If you like what you taste, they also offer short courses in Zanzibari cooking. The team here are closely involved with JAMABECO & Marine Cultures (see box, page

297) & several community projects, so ask them if you're interested in what's happening, or arrange to end your Eco+Culture village tour (page 333) with a deliciously satisfying lunch here. $$

✕ Palm View Restaurant [299 B5] ⊕ lunch & dinner daily. Well signposted from the beach, Palm View can be hard to spot despite the distinctive bright red-&-orange sign. In a small makuti-covered courtyard, a book-like menu of pizza, pasta, seafood & sandwiches, which also includes anomalies such as goulash for US$8, can be devoured along with an extensive list of milkshakes & juices. As with anywhere in Jambiani, it's worth ordering a few hours ahead to ensure availability. $$

✳ 📖 Zanzistar [299 B6] ⊕ 08.00–late daily. Tucked away behind the brightly painted exterior, this café is a real find in the heart of the village. Leave the dust & heat at the door, as this little oasis is a gem of colour & joy. Friendly, efficient staff, a gorgeously cheerful & colourful garden setting, & delicious drinks & meals – what more to ask? The giant blackboard mural menu tempts visitors to freshly squeezed juices for US$3 (try the 'Detox' of cucumber, ginger, spinach & lime), cold beers (*US$2.50*), cocktails (*US$5*) & a mouth-watering mix of sushi, sashimi, soup & the freshest seafood (*US$3 starter; US$10 main*). Chef Roja even came 4th in the 2016 Zanzibar Chef Competition, & it shows in both the artistic presentation & taste of his dishes. It's a lovely spot to hang out, & diners can use the Wi-Fi & small pool for a dip. Look out for the Garden BBQ nights or just check-in & stay (page 304). $$$

OTHER PRACTICALITIES If you need **money**, there's a bureau de change at the East Coast Visitors Inn (page 303). Alternatively, Auberge Coco Beach (page 302) and Casa del Mar (page 301) might be able to give you cash back from a bank card (though you'll need to have a meal at the restaurant first). The best bets for **internet** access are the hotels (mid range and above), although Wi-Fi is increasingly widespread and generally free. A good bet for a smoothie and connection is the lovely café at Zanzistar (above).

WHAT TO SEE AND DO

Watersports As with most of Zanzibar's coastal villages, the main focus of the tourist agenda is swimming and sunbathing. **Diving** and **snorkelling** can be arranged anywhere along the coast, and **kitesurfing** is experiencing a massive popularity surge.

H²O [299 C1] Based at Spice Island (page 300), H²O is an independent watersports company offering equipment rental, game-fishing & boat tours from Kizimkazi. Hire snorkelling kit for US$5, take a trip to the Blue Lagoon (*US$50pp for 4*), have a windsurfing lesson (*US$30/hr*) or go game-fishing (NB: there is no catch-&-release policy). Experienced sailors can also hire the little catamaran for US$65/hr (proof of licence essential).

Uhuru Kite Zanzibar [299 B5] m 0779 441877; e info@uhurukite-zanzibar.com; www.uhurukite-zanzibar.com. Based at Uhuru Beach Resort (page 305), this centrally located kite centre has 3 IKO-licensed instructors & 13 sets of equipment. Courses are best booked in advance, as is specialist equipment. However, there are fewer kites in the water in this area than in Paje, making it much quieter. Lessons in the waist-deep lagoon are standard whilst more experienced kiters can hit the waves beyond the reef; beware, though, seaweed farming is quite extensive in Jambiani so take heed of instructors advice on where to kite. It is also possible to store kites here (max 5 kites at a time) but this is best booked in high season. *Intro course US$125/2hrs; group course US$325/9hrs; private tuition US$75/hr.*

Zanzibar-Prokite [299 B4] m 0778 273962; e manager@zanzibar-prokite.com; www. zanzibar-prokite.com. Based at Nur (page 303), Zanzibar-Prokite is run by the delightful Anthony & Mélie. Cabrinha equipment, IKO instructors & courses, & a quieter stretch of beach than further north. *Equipment rental US$22/hr for full gear; group courses US$360/6hrs; private lessons US$360/9hrs; advanced private tuition US$75/hr.*

The fruit of the evocative coconut palm does not look as many imagine: it has a smooth, leathery, green skin. The brown nuts sold in supermarkets worldwide are simply the central element of the fruit. Between the well-known shiny shell and green exterior is a coarse fibrous husk known as coir; it is from this that rope is made.

The patient process begins when the husk is separated from the nut. The fibres are then buried in the sandy intertidal zone and covered with a cairn of coral rock. Over the coming six to ten months, microorganisms in the surrounding sand cause the husk tissues to begin biodegrading, in a process known as retting, loosening the fibre strands. The remains are then uncovered, beaten and sun-dried. When dry and clean, the long fibres are simply rubbed together to form strands which can be twined to the required thickness of rope.

According to the Royal Botanical Gardens at Kew, the total of world coir-fibre production is about 250,000 tonnes, with over 50% of the coir fibre produced annually consumed in its countries of origin. This bears out on Zanzibar where the relatively waterproof nature of the coir and its resistance to saltwater damage make it an invaluable material for boat rigging, fishing nets and seaweed-farming lines. As a tourist, you are likely to benefit from its more recent application in the manufacture of sun loungers, hammocks and the beds used by budget hotels.

Cultural tours If you want a change from the beach and water, Jambiani does have a few options. The **Eco+Culture village tour** (⌕ 024 223 3731; m 0777 410873; e info@ecoculture-zanzibar.org; www.ecoculture-zanzibar.org) is excellent and is probably the island's best insight into genuine rural life. Organised and guided by resident Kassim Mande (m 0777 469118) and his colleagues, the tours last anything from a few hours to the best part of a day (depending on your enthusiasm and heat tolerance), and take in many aspects of everyday life. Spend time helping the women make coconut paste, reciting the alphabet in unison at the efficient kindergarten and meeting the *mganga* (traditional healer). Kassim's presence, reputation within the community and ability to translate allow for genuine interaction with the Jambiani residents and a thoroughly engaging time. A percentage of your fee goes directly towards community development initiatives, such as the kindergarten and planned handicraft shop for the women's co-operative. Tours can also be arranged at their office in Stone Town, too (page 114). Do be aware, though, that of late a few villagers have apparently been operating copycat walks.

There is also a **Women's Pottery Group** [299 B4] (m 0773 239475; e babu.iddi@gmail.com), well signposted in the centre of the village, where you can either join in activities or purchase their creations. Using locally dug red clay, the crude pots and decorations are inspired by sea life, shells and village life, crafted with natural or recycled tools and fired in traditional coconut-husk fires – they make great souvenirs.

For some relaxation, **Jambiani Wellness Centre** [299 A2] (e habszanzibar@yahoo.ca; www.handsacrossborderssociety.org; ⏲ 09.00–14.00 Mon, Tue, Thu & Fri) primarily offers chiropractic treatment, homeopathic remedies and other therapies free of charge to the local community. The exact treatment on offer depends on the skills of the volunteers at the time but tourists are welcome to visit for massage, acupuncture, breema or homeopathic treatments and even Chinese medicine.

A donation of at least US$15 is asked *in lieu* of a fee. Run by Canadian–Zanzibari NGO, Hands Across Borders, the charitable work of the group now extends well beyond the clinic boundaries, with current community projects including the Jambiani Tourism Training Institute (JTTI), a vocational school that educates adults about tourism and starting up a business and also provides on-the-job training at the Alibi's Well Restaurant (page 308).

About 2 hours' walk outside Jambiani is a large underground cavern called **Kumbi**, which contains a natural spring. According to local legend, it was once lived in but today it is a traditional shrine and local people go there to pray and make offerings. You'll need a local guide to show you the way and it's an interesting trip; even if the cave doesn't leave you in awe, the walk is pleasant. Around the village, you can also see several **old tombs** decorated with plates and dishes, similar to the mausoleum at Paje.

For self-guided exploration, bicycles can be rented from a number of hotels – try Casa del Mar (page 301), which charges US$10 per day.

MAKUNDUCHI

The ill-defined settlement of Makunduchi lies at the southeastern end of Zanzibar Island, and is divided into two distinct parts. On the coast is the small fishing village of 'old' Makunduchi, with some local huts and houses, a few holiday cottages, and a small beach from where you can sometimes spot dolphins. Then, about 2km inland is 'Makunduchi New Town', complete with one main road, some dusty side streets, a bank, post and telephone office, police station, small shop and a few incongruous blocks of austere flats, built as part of a 1970s East German aid scheme.

With the exception of July's Mwaka Kogwa Festival (see box, page 314), Makunduchi receives hardly any visitors. It is significantly quieter than Bwejuu or Jambiani – not that they are particularly noisy – and its community focuses on seaweed farming and fishing, not tourism.

GETTING THERE AND AWAY From Zanzibar Town, Makunduchi can be reached by public **bus** (Route 10), **dalla dalla** (No 310), or by **rented car**, **scooter** or **bike** on good tar roads all the way. There are no tourist minibuses working regularly on this route, although you could always hire one for exclusive use through a tour company. You can also reach Makunduchi from Jambiani (page 298).

WHERE TO STAY AND EAT *Map, page 268*
Accommodation in Makunduchi consists of just three hotels, one of which (Pumzika Beach Resort) is currently closed. However, despite the isolation, visions of remote shorelines should be banished – the hotel beachfront is full of locals going about their business – and so a stay here is not the tranquil seclusion you may be envisaging.

🏠 La Madrugada Beach Resort
(37 rooms) m 0777 423331; e reservations@ lamadrugadaresort.com; www.lamadrugadaresort. com. This large established complex has slowly improved in recent years. The 2-storey, whitewashed buildings run perpendicular to the beach & surround 2 swimming pools (1 freshwater & 1 saltwater), each emblazoned with the hotel name in mosaic. There are 3 rooms per building accommodating the large suites & standard dbl rooms, each complete with a small terrace or balcony: the best ones overlooking both the sea & poolside palms. Inside, white sheets & colourful appliqué bedspreads adorn Zanzibari beds & the rooms are large & clean, with beautiful hand-painted birds of paradise & marine animals decorating the bathroom walls. There's a central restaurant & bar area, & a pleasant, very quiet

If you happen to be visiting Zanzibar during the last week of July, try to reach Makunduchi for the Mwaka Kogwa festival, when local people come from all over the island for a great get-together of singing, dancing, drumming, making new friends and meeting old ones. It's no problem for tourists to join in, and several tour companies run day trips to the village when it's on (pages 312).

Also called Mwaka Nairuz, the festival originates from Persia, marking the start of the New Year in the Shirazi calendar (for more details on the Shirazis in Zanzibar, see page 35) and involves several rituals, including a mock fight where men from different parts of the village beat each other with banana stems. It is believed that this fight gives each combatant a chance to vent his feelings, and in this way the disagreements and arguments of the past year are exorcised so that the New Year can be started peacefully. Although this is a mock fight, it can still get pretty serious. Fortunately the men are only fighting with banana stems – they used to do it with real clubs and cudgels! While the men are beating each other, the women have a far more genteel way of celebrating: dressed in their finest clothes, they parade around the village singing about love, families and village life.

The next stage of the festival is the ritual burning of a traditional hut, built especially for this purpose. A local healer goes inside before the fire is lit and runs out again when the hut is burning strongly. It is thought that the burning of the hut symbolises the passing of the old year and also ensures that, during the coming year, should any house in the village catch fire its inhabitants will escape unharmed.

After the fighting and the hut-burning, a large feast is held with all the villagers bringing food and eating together. People from other parts of Zanzibar are welcomed, as a local tradition holds that any villager without a guest must be unhappy.

After the eating, the music starts – traditional ngomas and taarab, but these days may include some more modern amplified sounds as well. The locals dance into the night, and die-hard party animals move on to the beach to continue singing and dancing until dawn.

beach, complete with the usual coir loungers under a couple of mkadi palms. Activities at the resort are limited to reading, swimming & low-tide beach walking, although trips to anywhere else on the island can be arranged. Prospective visitors should be happy with the remote location & accept that dinners out, beach bars & watersports will require you to get in a car. HB/FB/AI. $$$

⌂ **Villa Fleur de Lys** (7 rooms) m 0777 314801; e info@villafleurdelyszanzibar.com; www.villafleurdelyszanzibar.com. Billed as a boutique hotel, this striking, 3-storey blush building has more of the air of a large private villa, & indeed was originally built as the owner's

beach retreat. Its numerous large windows overlook the ocean from its cliff-top spot, there's a nice stone pool with a sea view, a ruby-red 1st-floor African fusion restaurant & large bedrooms, all with AC, en suites & a balcony, & 1 including bunkbeds for children. A lot of thought has gone into Fleur de Lys, & the owners certainly try hard to provide a good-quality place, albeit perhaps lacking in the chic implied by 'boutique hotel'. It's remote & in an extremely quiet part of the island, with private transport necessary to do anything – activities or dining – but if you're happy to just sit & read, it's not a bad spot. HB/FB. $$$

11

Southwestern Zanzibar

For most of Zanzibar's overseas visitors, the island's southwest corner holds little more than day-trip opportunities to see dolphins from Kizimkazi and troops of red colobus monkeys in Jozani Forest. Yet some of the best marine, animal and historical conservation projects on the island lie on the coast between Chukwani (10km south of Stone Town) and the ruins at Unguju Ukuu, and on the coral reefs of Chumbe Island and the Menai Bay Conservation Area. Few people stay in this area, in part because accommodation options are limited, with most opting instead for the endless beaches of the east coast or the buzz of Stone Town. Away from the main tourist attractions, the villagers in these parts rarely encounter many visitors, and their welcome is either one of genuine friendliness or great reserve. It's a refreshing contrast to the more crowded and visitor-centric feeling taking over significant parts of the island's north and east coasts.

KIZIMKAZI

The village of Kizimkazi lies at the southwestern tip of the island, about 12km west of Makunduchi. In a beautiful bay, it is one of the island's oldest settlements and the former home of the Mwinyi Mkuu (the traditional ruler of Zanzibar). It is steeped in history, though there is little evidence of this today.

Kizimkazi has a sizeable population, a school, a dispensary, a reasonable selection of places to stay, and a growing tourist industry based on dolphin watching, albeit only by day. Bottlenose and humpback dolphins are seen off the coast here and Kizimkazi has long been the major launch point for boats taking visitors out on viewing trips.

Technically, Kizimkazi consists of two villages: Kizimkazi Mkunguni and Kizimkazi Dimbani. Most boats go out to see the dolphins from the larger of the two, Kizimkazi Mkunguni, and this is generally just called Kizimkazi. As the number of tourists has grown over the last few years, so too has the number of 'guides', touts and hustlers taking to the streets – sadly some of them can be quite aggressive, rude and generally unpleasant. If you're driving, watch out for the squad that wait for custom on the roadside by the entrance to the village.

Kizimkazi Dimbani is 2km north along the coast from 'main' Kizimkazi (3km by road); it is smaller, much quieter and arguably prettier, and a few boats do depart from here as well. There are far fewer touts, probably because it's mainly groups who come here, and just a clutch of places to stay. Dimbani is also the site of East Africa's oldest mosque.

GETTING THERE AND AWAY Most people come to Kizimkazi by tourist minibus or as part of a **day tour**; the alternative is to come by **hired car**, **scooter** or **bike**.

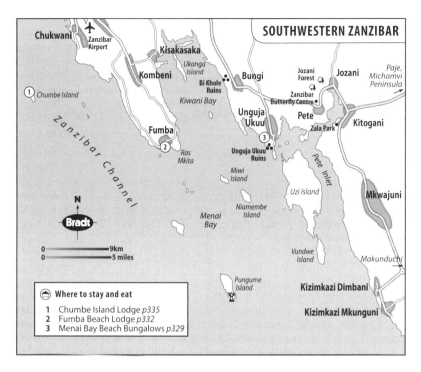

Where to stay and eat

1 Chumbe Island Lodge *p335*
2 Fumba Beach Lodge *p332*
3 Menai Bay Beach Bungalows *p329*

To reach Kizimkazi Dimbani, turn off the main road between Zanzibar Town and Makunduchi at Kufile junction, the site of a huge, half-built secondary school, and follow this road to a fork, heavily adorned with miscellaneous accommodation and tour signs. Here, right goes to Kizimkazi Dimbani and the ancient Shirazi mosque; left goes to the main part of Kizimkazi (Kizimkazi Mkunguni).

It is also possible to get here independently from Zanzibar Town on one of the five daily **dalla dallas** (No 326) or, by public **bus**. Some buses (Route 10) running between Zanzibar Town and Makunduchi stop in Kizimkazi Mkunguni, but if this cannot be arranged, get off the bus at Kufile junction for the long 4km walk along the tar road, predominantly downhill, to Kizimkazi Dimbani (3km) or Kizimkazi Mkunguni (6km).

WHERE TO STAY   *Map, page 318*
Kizimkazi Dimbani
Exclusive

✳ ⌂ **Karamba** (24 rooms) m 0773 166406; e info@karambazanzibar.com; www.karambazanzibar.com. This attractive clifftop lodge started life as a large restaurant, aimed almost exclusively at dolphin-viewing tour groups. Transformed into smart bungalows some years ago & continually improving, it remains one of this coast's most appealing places to stay. Despite the linear layout, rooms all have individual interiors & are thoughtfully decorated in nautical blues & whites with a splash of sunshine yellow in the luxury rooms. Some boast outdoor circular baths, whilst others have blissful open-air showers hewn in coral rock. Check out the whitewashed walls filled with coloured glass bottles cemented into the brickwork, whilst upstairs, a spacious terrace allows for sleeping under the stars. Most recently, a lovely Tanga-stone swimming pool has been added & its idyllic cliff-top location makes the tangerine loungers an appealing option for an afternoon chilling. Behind the pool, 4 new duplex bungalows for up to 6 people, offer dbl-storey galleried interiors, adding to Karamba's trademark smart & funky style. Beyond these, along the snaking pathway, the honeymoon villa, Nakyru, offers rustic luxury in complete privacy. Beyond the lovely airy bedroom, follow the coconut spiral stairs to the upper deck with the option to sleep out under the stars, or hang out on the ngalawa daybed; pad down your own path to the beach, take an outdoor bath or shower & enjoy the Zanzibari bush decadency in this lovely little secret hideaway. All rooms enjoy a sea view from their veranda though the harbour vista from the cushioned lounge/restaurant (page 320) is arguably the finest of them all. Once the dolphin-viewing tour groups head home in the afternoon, real peace & quiet returns, & cocktails overlooking the sunset dhow activity make for a quintessentially Zanzibari experience. If you're still in need of relaxation, yoga, reiki & Ayurvedic therapies are also available. B&B. **$$$$$–**

Upmarket

🏠 **L'Oasis Kizimkazi Zanzibar** (12 rooms) 📞 027 250 7089; e info@loasistanzania.com; www. loasiszanzibar.com. Resort-style L'Oasis is in an overall state of general disrepair – from rotting boardwalks to falling makuti thatch – & guest reviews are decidedly mixed. The rooms, built in a row either along the beachfront or behind the irregular-shaped pool, each sleep 4 with space for an extra bed in the family rooms. Colourful murals decorate the outside walls of each, whilst inside traditional Zanzibari beds have been painted white. At one end of the beach the restaurant/lounge/ bar is cantilevered over the sand, while a blue wall divides the property from the surrounding grasslands. Wi-Fi is available & there's a curio shop in the thatched reception area. B&B. **$$$$**

Kizimkazi Mkunguni

Exclusive

🏠 **Unguja Lodge** (12 rooms) 📱 0774 477477; e info@ungujalodge.com; www.ungujalodge. com. Run by a friendly, unpretentious Dutchman called Martin, Unguja is a small, quiet place with original accommodation & friendly service. Rooms (8 with sea views) are enormous & unusual, & are dotted around the dense gardens between a few large baobabs. Under vast, steep makuti roofs, the interior walls conceal a cushioned lounge, shower room, mezzanine seating area & a fully enclosed bedroom. 3 Baobab Villas have AC & a plunge pool, whilst 6 Sea-View Villas & 2 3-bed Family Villas have direct views over the coral cliff to the ocean below.

The furniture is island produced from coconut wood, & the artwork contemporary. The main restaurant & bar area is a similar mix of modern & traditional – low curved white walls, low-hanging makuti thatch & terraces of square tables with directors' chairs. Punched brass lanterns cast a patterned glow at night, wall-mounted basketry adds colour, & 3 large fans enhance the sea breeze. Well-presented, buffet meals are served 3 times a day, with social, pre-dinner drinks at the bar from around 18.30. The lovely pool is surrounded by bougainvillea, hibiscus & fan palms to one side & wide makuti umbrellas & timber loungers to the other. Alternatively, there is the beach. Diving instructor Said runs the purpose-built PADI dive centre for guests only, & snorkelling & shore diving are possible, with good sightings of lionfish & even sea horses being reported on the closest reef (70m away), though most people choose to boat dive (*Menai Bay 2-dive trip US$120pp*). Dive courses & other water-based activities – dhow cruises to sea kayaking & surfing – are all organised. There is also a village tour, escorted by 1 of the local staff (*US$5*), & the fee is donated to vital village projects such as the water pump & school furniture. If you're self-driving, be aware that there is no signposting; ask directions once you've entered the village & continue from the bumpy turning roughly opposite the nursery school, it does eventually snake round to the lodge. HB/FB; children 2–18yrs 50–75% reduction. **$$$$–**

Upmarket

🏠 **Swahili Beach Resort** (27 rooms) 📱 0777 844442; e info@swahilibeachresort.com; www. swahilibeachresort.com. At the far side of the village, this is looking very tired & run down these days. Inside the giant metal gates, guests are welcomed into a large reception area, from where views extend to the swimming pool & sea beyond. Spacious rooms are all in peach-painted coral bungalows, except the 4 'cabanas'. Each is named in Kiswahili after a marine creature & there is a fan, AC, mini fridge, TV & broad terrace as standard. The bedroom interiors are perfectly fine, if a little dated in décor, & the bathrooms spotless. There is a central, mosaic-tiled pool, with a small children's splash pool, but unfortunately the dive centre is indefinitely closed. Local tours by dhow & speedboat are possible, kayaks can be hired & the usual island excursions are offered, but onsite the atmosphere & attractions are lacking. FB/HB. **$$$$**

11

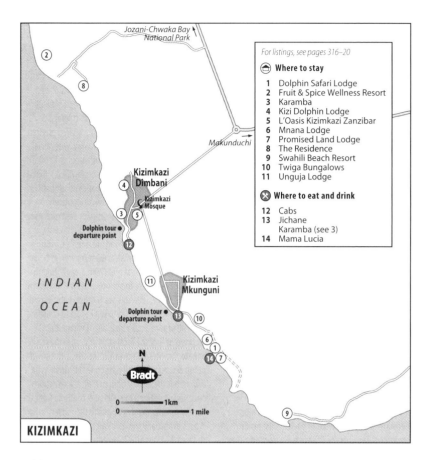

For listings, see pages 316–20

Where to stay

1 Dolphin Safari Lodge
2 Fruit & Spice Wellness Resort
3 Karamba
4 Kizi Dolphin Lodge
5 L'Oasis Kizimkazi Zanzibar
6 Mnana Lodge
7 Promised Land Lodge
8 The Residence
9 Swahili Beach Resort
10 Twiga Bungalows
11 Unguja Lodge

Where to eat and drink

12 Cabs
13 Jichane
   Karamba (see 3)
14 Mama Lucia

KIZIMKAZI

Mid range

🏠 **Dolphin Safari Lodge** (13 rooms) 📞0774 007360; e dolphinsafarilodge@gmail.com; www. dolphin-safari-lodge.com. In 2015, a charming French–Dutch couple, Astrid & Patrick, bought the old Dolphin View Lodge on impulse, & have wholeheartedly devoted their time, energy & passion to renovating & improving this place every since. By altering the lodge name, undertaking essential maintenance, beginning to beautify the rooms, empowering their staff, they have created a gentle, little place where old-fashioned hospitality aims to leave every guest with 'a banana smile'. No strangers to Africa (Patrick has lived in both West Africa & the Indian Ocean as a chef), this couple have a desire to share their dream of peace & tranquility with others. From the welcome cocktail at the low-key beach bar on arrival, to the swinging chairs overlooking the tidal flats, communal diners, Zanzibari cookery classes & 'Treasure Island' dhow

trip, this establishment offers heaps of personal service. The deluxe dbl rooms have slate grey interiors with beamed ceilings, free-standing fans & neat en suites, & it's evident from linens & decorations that care is taken in trying to make things attractive. The basic rooms are perfectly good: clean, simply furnished with fresh linen & safari-print pillows, & for something more rustic, the 3 Robinson Crusoe bandas on the very edge of the coral cliff offer a tented experience under makuti A-frame. Blessed with a terrific sea view, a solid coconut-wood deck & a separate bathroom at the rear, these are a nice safari-style option for the more adventurous. Hot water is available in all rooms in the afternoons only. An array of trips can be organised, including a very off-beat, basic camping option near Jozani, & Astrid is a professional massage therapist offering lovely cocnut-oil treatments, so if you're happy with Kizimkazi as a very quiet location, without the miles of sandy beach on the east coast, then this is a genuinely friendly, good-value option. B&B. **$$$**

Budget

⌂ **Promised Land Lodge** (13 rooms) m 0779 909168; e promisedland.znz@hotmail.com; www.promisedlandlodge-zanzibar.com. French–Zanzibari-owned & run, Promised Land has been open on & off since 2002, but does retain a certain rustic charm. Currently it's open again, offering brick-built rooms in 3 buildings as well as newer, detatched thatched bandas. Rooms are simple, with nothing more than a bed, fan & some shelves, but they are jazzed up by a colourful kanga ceiling & matching curtains, & jet-black bathrooms. The bandas have more character than the rooms & have original, open-air, shaded bathrooms, but are quite dark inside. There are relaxation opportunities aplenty, with an outdoor bed inside a thatched 'tent' & a fire pit surrounded by swing benches; Bob Marley tunes play on repeat in the sapphire-cushioned beach bar & shady seafood-focused restaurant, & guests can now enjoy the newly built swimming pool, complete with neat pole-shading over the loungers. It's very chilled out here, with friendly staff & good ocean frontage making it a very reasonable option in this price band. B&B. **$$–$$$**

⌂ **Mnana Lodge** (3 rooms) m 0776 661915. Set back from the seafront, in a very quiet spot, Mnana is the heart-&-soul venture of Italian Jenny, her Zanzibari husband & their sweet young daughter. Offering en-suite dbls in the main villa, an open dorm in the makuti thatch above the central area, & with a few more bungalows & even a pool planned for the future, plenty has happened here since its opening in mid 2015. Rooms are currently the best bet here, with small balconies overlooking the bush, colourful painted interiors with simple beds, coir shelving & shell-screened bathrooms offering hot-water showers at certain times of the day. The 'dorm' is little more than the huge upper deck of the restaurant, kitted out with a few beds, each with a wooden trunk at their foot for storage, a candle for evening light & a shared toilet/shower a short walk through the banana trees. Despite being fairly basic, guests here consistently praise the hospitality & fresh home cooking. Salads &, of course, pasta are available, or a full catch-of-the-day dinner can be prepared for US$15. Hang out in the open-sided lounge, stroke the cat,

contemplate the Lao Tzu quotes painted on the wall & feel like you're in someone's home. B&B. **$$**

⌂ **Twiga Bungalows** (4 rooms) m 0777 297683/0778 478229; e twigabeachbungalows@gmail.com; www.twigabeachbungalow.com. Opened in 2013, Twiga's simple rooms are in 2 neat, thatched buildings with a 1-up-1-down configuration & small flowerbeds to the front. The Zanzibari–Canadian owners are only occasionally about, but someone is usually around the pole-shaded Hakuna Matata bar to help, just don't expect speed. Rooms are basic with a dbl bed & cold-water en suite (unless the sun happens to have warmed up the tank of water). The sandy central chill-out area has rainbow hammocks, an upper cushioned deck, & a menu (order in advance) offering the usual fare of octopus & rice, fresh fish or simple vegetarian dishes for lunch & dinner. The beach is a good 5min walk, & the views are pretty limited, but this place is cheap if you don't need to be close to activities or restaurants & very quiet. B&B. **$$**

North of Kizimkazi

Exclusive

⌂ **The Residence** (66 rooms) ✆ 024 555 5000; e info-zanzibar@theresidence.com; www.theresidence.com. Just 3km north of Kizmikazi Dimbani stands one of the most talked about hotels on the island, a place where movie stars & supermodels wouldn't seem out of place. Set on a delightfully calm stretch of powdery beach, with gently lapping waves washing up intricate pink-&-lilac shells, The Residence offers plush villas, each with its own generously sized swimming pool & personal butler. They are divided into 6 categories, with varying views, sizes & number of bedrooms, but all are extremely well appointed with satellite TV, DVD player, Wi-Fi, minibar, safe, bathrobes, slippers ... the list goes on. Indoor & outdoor showers plus a bathtub are found in the contemporary curvaceous, glass bathroom. Each guest is provided with a bicycle to explore the complex, but you can also give reception a call for a lift in a golf buggy. It's worth bearing in mind that the oceanfront villas have little privacy from passing beach-goers (& each other), & the patio doors leading onto the pools are clear glass, so close the curtains for modesty. The main complex is spread over a number of buildings, including 2 restaurants: the Dining Room, with Arabic & African influences; & the

11

Pavilion, with Middle Eastern & Mediterranean dishes. These are complemented by 2 bars, the modern Dining Room Bar & the more traditional Library Bar. The adjacent swimming pool is raised above the deck, & with glass sides observers are able to clearly see under the water – an unusual & intriguing design. The spa complex has yoga classes as well as therapies, & is the first hotel spa to offer ohashiatsu, an energy-based massage therapy. For further beautifying, there's a 'hair spa' & hairdressing pavilion. To burn off the rich food, hit the gym, head for the tennis courts or out on a nature walk or take part in the watersports. The Residence is not a small & intimate lodge, but nor does it pretend to be. As with its international counterparts, this is a vast complex, with bowing staff pandering to every whim. On arrival, there's even someone to unpack for you, plus a tempting selection of welcome chocolates. With all this, plus scheduled evening entertainment, there's plenty to keep you amused, & for anything else your butler will be on hand to assist at any time. Despite all the luxury, it's hard not to feel that it's all a bit sterile – you could be anywhere in the world. FB. 🍽

🏠 Fruit & Spice Wellness Resort
(32 rooms) m 0776 676867/0779 210953; e info@resort-zanzibar.com; www.resort-zanzibar.com. With a striking position overlooking Kizimkazi Bay from Mchangamle, this lovely resort offers raw natural beauty & one of the island's wildest & quietest spots. Stetched along 300m of coral cliff, rooms enjoy far-reaching ocean views, expansive tropical gardens & bush, & complete peace. Built using only natural, local materials & with great craftsmanship, the bungalows & villas are sympathetically constructed & stylishly fitted out. Lovely moulded-concerete beds & en-suite bathrooms, thoughtful amenities from beach towels to fluffy gowns, co-ordinating linens & plenty of space are all standard. For something more sizeable, the 2 villas – Honeymoon & Luxury – boast small private pools & living rooms in addition to their swish bedrooms. Linked by stone paths & boardwalks over the coral rag, rooms all lead to the large central pool area, with its beach-sand surround & clusters of loungers. There are 2 restaurants: buffet-style dining at Frangipani, complete with high-backed chairs at the formal tables & dozens of mini, candle-lit Omani arches; & the seafront Maoni where à la carte, starlit dinners can be pre-ordered at lunch. There's also a pool snack bar & a long jetty for sundowner cocktails. There's a popular Jungle Spa tucked away in the bush, an air-conditioned gym, a small library & a 2km strip of beach adjacent to the resort, perfect for walks, sandcastles & stepping into the Indian Ocean. Overall, a thoroughly relaxing spot on this rugged stretch of coast. B&B. $$$$$–🍽

✕ WHERE TO EAT AND DRINK *Map, page 318*

In the main part of Kizimkazi, near where the boats are launched, is the **Jichane Restaurant**, mostly serving lunches for the tour groups from Zanzibar Town.

In Kizimkazi Dimbani, there are two places – both geared mainly to feeding large groups. Friendly, reliable **Karamba** (page 316) serves noodles, tapas, pasta and traditional Swahili seafood dishes from US$3–6. **Cabs Restaurant** (m *0777 415554*), on the opposite side of the harbour mouth, has meals like chicken and chips or grilled seafood for around US$5. For good coffee and simple homemade pasta with a sea view, Italian-run **Mama Lucia Restaurant & Café** (m *0689 218217*) is worth a pit-stop.

WHAT TO SEE AND DO

Kizimkazi Mosque Hidden behind its new plain walls and protective corrugated-iron roof, the mosque at Kizimkazi Dimbani is believed to be the oldest Islamic building on the East African coast. The floriate Kufic inscription to the left of the *mihrab* (the interior niche indicating the direction of Mecca) dates the original mosque construction to AD1107 and identifies it as the work of Persian settlers, working under the orders of Sheikh Said bin Abi Amran Mfaume al Hassan bin Muhammad. The silver pillars on either side of the niche are decorated with pounded mullet shells from the island of Mafia, and the two decorative clocks, which show Swahili time (6 hours different from European time), were presented by local dignitaries. However, though the fine-quality coral detailing and columns date from this time, most of the building actually dates from an 18th-century reconstruction, attested to by a further inscription, to the right of the mihrab. The more recent additions of electrical sockets and flex have not been installed with a comparable degree of style or decoration.

Outside the mosque are some old tombs, a few decorated with pillars, one covered by a small makuti roof, and all with prayer flags. The raised aqueduct that once carried water from the well to the basin where hands and feet were washed is no longer used: running water is piped straight into a more recently built ablution area at the back of the mosque.

Archaeological evidence suggests that when the mosque was built Kizimkazi was a large walled city. Tradition holds that it was founded and ruled by a king, Kizi, and that the architect of the mosque itself was called Kazi. Legend has it that when the city was once attacked by invaders, Kizi prayed for divine intervention and the enemies were driven away by a swarm of bees. Later the enemies returned, but this time Kizi evaded them by disappearing into a cave on the shore. The cave entrance closed behind him and the enemies were thwarted once again.

Today, very little of the old city remains, but non-Muslims, both men and women, are welcome to visit the mosque and its surrounding tombs. It's normally locked, and you'll probably have to find the caretaker with the key (he lives nearby, but is usually under the trees near the beach a few hundred metres further down the road). Show respect by removing your shoes and covering bare arms and legs (this part of the island is very traditional so, out of politeness, your arms and legs should be covered anyway – see page 102). On leaving you'll be shown the collection box and be able to make a donation.

Dolphin tours Most visitors to Kizimkazi come on all-inclusive 'dolphin tours' that include road transport, the boat, snorkelling gear and lunch. If you don't take an all-in tour, or want to spend the night at Kizimkazi, you can make your own way here, then hire a boat on the spot or arrange to join a group.

Generally, dolphin-viewing trips last for about 2–3 hours – usually enough time to locate the dolphins – although some captains trim the time down to about 90 minutes. Sometimes tourists become bored if they don't get quick and easy sightings, and decide to go back even sooner.

Dolphin tours are often promoted in a misleading light. It is important to realise that sightings cannot be guaranteed, and swimming with the dolphins is a rare occurrence. This is not a Florida-style dolphinarium; these are wild animals and their whereabouts cannot be predicted. It is they who choose to interact with people, not the other way around.

Observing dolphins in their natural environment, as with any other animals, requires time and patience. Shouting and excessive movement will not encourage them to approach your boat. Be satisfied with passive observation – do not force the boat driver to chase the dolphins, cross their path, or approach too close, especially when they are resting. If you decide to swim, slip quietly into the water and avoid splashing. Never jump in. Stay close to the boat and let the dolphins come to you instead of you trying to catch up with them. You could try attempting to excite their curiosity by diving frequently and swimming below the surface, maintaining your arms alongside your body to imitate their own streamlined shape.

In reality, unless you charter your own boat and go out early in the morning, so as not to be disturbed, you're unlikely to be able to put any of these theories into practice.

THE KIZIMKAZI DOLPHINS

The shallow coastal waters around Kizimkazi have been favoured by dolphins for many years (quite possibly for millennia) because the area offers a reliable food supply and is a good place to nurse calves or simply to rest and socialise. Two species of dolphin are resident all year round: the Indo-Pacific bottlenose dolphin (*Tursiops aduncus*) and the Indo-Pacific humpback dolphin (*Sousa chinensis*). The bottlenose dolphin is more sociable, and more readily observed, whereas the humpback dolphin is a shyer creature.

Studies conducted have revealed that there are about 150 bottlenose and 60 humpback dolphins inhabiting the area. A catalogue of all the individual dolphins has been compiled based on the shape, nicks and marks of their dorsal fins and most of the animals have been given names. (Look closely if you see the dolphins and you'll notice that they all look different.)

Tourists first started coming to see dolphins at Kizimkazi in the early 1990s. The continued presence of these popular creatures has attracted growing numbers of visitors, such that tourism has now created new job opportunities for the local villagers. Contrary to the practices of other fishing communities in the Indian Ocean, the fishermen of Kizimkazi are very protective of the dolphins and no longer hunt them, seeing instead the economic rewards from conservation. In 1997, villagers from Kizimkazi also helped to arrest dynamite fishermen from Dar es Salaam, knowing their methods destroyed the coral reefs and important habitats for the dolphins. Today, other fishing methods, such as drift nets, pose the greatest threat to the dolphins as they are liable to get tangled up in the nets and drown.

Over the years there have been a number of studies carried out at Kizimkazi, to monitor the interaction between dolphins and tourists. It's widely believed that the overall effect is detrimental. In 2005, all the stakeholders involved in dolphin tourism formed the Kizimkazi Dolphin Tourism Operators Association (KIDOTOA), to create a management plan and run training courses to teach boat operators how to conduct their tourism activities in a responsible, sustainable way. The creation of KIDOTOA was very promising for the conservation and management of both the dolphins and the tourism and remains an important organisation. It has not solved the problems, and sadly, more than a decade on, many boat operators continue to compete for the best views of the dolphins. It remains up to *everyone*, operators and visitors, to ensure best practice. As a tourist, you should read the dolphin tourism guidelines (see box, page 323) and ask the boat operators to follow them strictly. This should minimise the impact on the dolphins and ensure that they remain in the area for many years to come.

This section is based on information from the Marine Mammal Education & Research group at the Institute of Marine Sciences, Zanzibar, and Dr Per Berggren, Department of Zoology, Stockholm University, Sweden.

On some days it's not unusual to see 20 or more boats, carrying at least ten people each, all chasing the dolphins and desperate for a sighting. When the dolphins are seen, big groups of people jumping in do little to entice them any closer. One visitor commented: 'it's billed as "swimming with dolphins" but it's actually "jumping into the water a long way from the dolphins"'; another called it a 'shambolic turkey-hunt'.

DOLPHIN-WATCHING GUIDELINES

Kizimkazi is one of very few places where wild dolphins can be admired in their natural habitat. The following guidelines minimise the disturbance to the dolphins while allowing tourists to make the most of the experience. By following these, and encouraging your boat driver to do likewise, it is possible that tourists may continue to enjoy dolphin-watching for the foreseeable future.

GUIDELINES FOR BOATS
- Drive the boat slowly with a steady speed; do not rev the engine and avoid going in and out of gear
- Approach the dolphin group from the side or from behind; never head-on
- Do not chase the dolphins; let them come to the boat
- Always make sure the dolphins have a clear escape route
- Never be more than two boats on one group of dolphins
- Never approach a mother and calf
- Never stay longer than 30 minutes with the same group of dolphins
- Dolphins slapping their tails at the surface, making coughing sounds, leaping or turning away from the boat, indicate that they are disturbed: leave them alone and look for other animals

GUIDELINES FOR SWIMMERS
- Enter the water as quietly as possible; do not jump or dive in
- Stay close to the boat and hold on to the rail or to lines alongside
- Do not swim after or chase the dolphins; let them come to you

It's little wonder that the dolphins are beginning to head for somewhere more peaceful. In recent years, the number of sightings has definitely gone down. They used to be almost guaranteed, but it's not unusual now for groups to return without having seen a single dolphin. Sadly, as the disturbances from too many boats and people increasingly outweigh the benefits of food and shelter, this trend is likely to continue, with fewer and fewer dolphins appearing in Kizimkazi's waters in the future.

When to visit The best time of year to see the dolphins is between October and February. From June to September, the southerly winds can make the seas rough, while during the rainy season (March to May) conditions in the boat can be unpleasant. Regardless, out at sea you're likely to get wet anyway. You should also protect yourself against the sun.

Organised tours Most people who visit Kizimkazi come on a fully organised tour. These are easily arranged before you arrive, in Zanzibar Town, or by one of the hotels elsewhere on Zanzibar. Costs for these tours vary between US$35 and US$100 per person from Zanzibar Town, including transport to/from Kizimkazi, the boat, all snorkelling gear and lunch.

These prices vary considerably depending on the season, the quality of the vehicle, the standard of driver and guide, the number of passengers, and whether you want a private tour or are happy to share with others. Obviously they also depend upon where you are coming from: if you're taking a day trip from Zanzibar Town, then it's going to be cheaper than driving here from Nungwi.

Private boat charter Excursions can be arranged with local fishermen through any of the guesthouses and restaurants in Kizimkazi Mkunguni and Kizimkazi Dimbani. (The latter is more group orientated; it might be harder finding spare seats here unless you can muster a group together.) Traditional wooden fishing boats are most commonly used, although several fishermen have upgraded to modern fibreglass boats. Chartering a boat costs about US$40 and if you're in a small group, you can of course share these costs, although you'll probably find that for groups of five or six the price for a boat may go up to about US$50. You can also hire snorkels, masks and flippers (around US$5–10pp) from the souvenir stalls beside Jichane Restaurant. This is essential if you want to get in the water and observe the dolphins below the surface – which is highly recommended. As competition between the boatmen is stiff, some include free snorkel gear in the price of the boat, so it's always worth asking.

Cabs Restaurant in Kizimkazi Dimbani (page 320), has a fleet of boats for dolphin-viewing. It caters mainly for large groups from the all-inclusive east coast resorts, but it's reckoned by local operators to be one of the safest and best-organised outfits based here, so it may be a good bet if you don't arrive with a trip pre-booked.

JOZANI-CHWAKA BAY NATIONAL PARK AND AROUND

Roughly halfway between Zanzibar Town and the broad beaches of the southeast coast is a lush area of protected forest reserve, the Jozani-Chwaka Bay National Park, and small, rural villages lining the road. It's a gentle part of the island, with little development and some of Zanzibar's best opportunities for viewing land animals. The communities here are increasingly involved in a number of conservation projects and even though the forest is an ever-popular, sometimes busy, destination for visitors, the neat boardwalks, diversity of dense vegetation and terrestrial mammals make for a great escape from the sunloungers and souvenir stalls of the rest of the island. For smaller-scale insect and reptile encounters, the new Butterfly Centre and Zala Park (page 328) are worthy add-ons to a trip in the area.

JOZANI-CHWAKA BAY NATIONAL PARK (⏲ 07.30–17.00 daily; admission US$10)
This national park incorporates the largest area of mature indigenous forest remaining on Zanzibar, although today it is only a tiny remnant of the forest that once covered much of the island. It stands on the isthmus of low-lying land which links the northern and southern parts of the island, to the south of Chwaka Bay. The area is prone to flooding in the rainy season, giving rise to its unique 'swamp-forest' environment, and the large moisture-loving trees, stands of palm and fern, and high water table and humid air give the forest a cool, 'tropical' feel.

Historically, local people have cut trees and harvested other forest products for many centuries, but commercial use started in the 1930s when the forest was bought by an Arab landowner and a sawmill was built here. In the late 1940s, the forest came under the control of the colonial government and some replanting took place. Jozani has been protected since 1952 and, as the forest areas in other parts of the island have been cleared, much of the island's wildlife has congregated here. The forest was declared a nature reserve in the 1960s, but despite this the trees and animals were inadequately protected. Local people cut wood for building and fuel, and some animals were hunted for food or because they could damage crops in nearby fields.

Nevertheless, Jozani Forest retains much of its original natural character and now forms the core of the island's first national park, Jozani-Chwaka Bay National Park. Developed from a partnership between the Zanzibar government's Commission for Natural Resources and the charity CARE International, with funding from various sources including the government of Austria, the Ford Foundation and the Global Environment Facility, the park now has clear targets to protect natural resources and improve conditions for local people and wildlife in the area.

When to visit Keen naturalists who want to watch wildlife undisturbed, or those who just like a bit of peace and quiet, should try to visit the reserve either very early in the morning or in the early afternoon, as most groups come at about 09.00–10.00 on their way to the coast, or 15.00–16.00 on their way back. The monkeys and birds seem subdued in the midday heat, so from about 14.00–15.00 seems to be the best time for watching their behaviour. You can visit at most times of the year, but in the rainy season the water table rises considerably and the forest paths can be under more than 1m of water.

Getting there and away The entrance to Jozani Forest is on the main road between Zanzibar Town and the southern part of the east coast, north of the village of Pete. The reserve is clearly signposted, and the entrance fee includes the services of a guide and the mangrove boardwalk (see below).

Many **tour companies** include Jozani on their east coast tours or dolphin tours, but you can easily get here by frequent public **bus** (Routes 9 and 10), **dalla dalla** (Nos 309, 310, 324 or 326), **hired bike** or **car**. Alternatively, take a tourist **minibus** heading for the east coast, and alight here. This road is well used by tourist minibuses and other traffic throughout the day, so after your visit to the forest you could flag down a vehicle and continue to the coast or return to Zanzibar Town, though it's best to be waiting roadside by 17.00, when the frequency of buses decreases.

Getting around the forest A network of **nature trails** has been established. The main one takes about an hour to follow at a leisurely pace, with numbered points

RULES FOR RESPONSIBLE MONKEY-WATCHING

Jozani Forest asks all visitors to observe the following rules. They apply to watching primates anywhere in Zanzibar, or elsewhere in Africa:

- You must be accompanied by an official guide.
- Do not get nearer than 3m to a monkey, and preferably remain at a distance of 5m. This is for your own safety – the monkeys are wild animals and can bite or pass diseases to you.
- Do not invite any interaction with the monkeys or try to feed them. If they come close, avoid eye contact and move away. Do not make noises to attract their attention.
- You are one of the major threats to the monkeys, as primates are susceptible to human diseases. Do not visit the monkeys if you are suffering from any illness, particularly a cold or flu.
- Observe the speed limits if driving through Jozani, and ask your driver to slow down if you're in a minibus. Even though speed-humps have been introduced, monkeys are regularly killed by cars.

11

of interest which relate to a well-written information sheet which you can buy for a nominal cost at the reception desk. There are also several shorter loops. Some other information leaflets and species lists are also available, and there are a few very good display boards and other exhibits.

As you walk around the nature trails, it's possible to see lots of birds and probably a few colobus and Sykes' monkeys, but these animals are shy, and will leap through the trees as soon as they hear people approaching. On the south side of the main road live two groups of monkeys who are more used to humans and with a guide you can come and watch these at close quarters. This is ideal animal viewing – the monkeys are aware of your presence but not disturbed. They are not tame, and don't come close, but just get on with their usual feeding, playing, grooming or resting. As the colobus monkeys look so cute, some visitors have been tempted to try to stroke them or give sweets to them. This is bad for the monkeys, but can be bad for tourists too – several people have been given a nasty nip or scratch (see box, page 327). Look, but don't touch.

South of the forest, a long thin creek juts in from the sea, and is lined with mangrove trees. A fascinating **boardwalk** has been constructed, the only one of its type in East Africa, so you can easily and harmlessly go deep into the mangrove to experience this unique ecosystem. This is also a community project, and revenue from visitors coming to the boardwalk helps fund local development projects.

Flora Several distinct habitats exist within Jozani's borders – evergreen bushland to the west; dense groundwater forest of laurel wood (*Calophyllum inophyllum*), screw palm (*Pandanus rabaiensis*) and untidy oil palms (*Elaeis guineensis*) in its heart; thickets of flowering *Macphersonia gracilis*, cloves (*Eugenia*), and cabbage trees (*Cussonia zimmermannii*) to the north; and mangrove forest forming the eastern border along Chwaka Bay, dominated by the common red mangrove (*Rhizophora mucronata*), yellow mangrove (*Ceriops tagal*) and grey mangrove (*Avicennia marina*).

Other trees in the reserve include moisture-loving palms (five species, of which three are true palms), figs (two species) and red mahogany, plus some introduced species such as Sydney blue gum. Red mahogany (*Khaya nyasica*) was formerly regarded as an introduced exotic, but the weight of evidence is that it is native or anciently naturalised; this tree is found on other Indian Ocean islands and, like the mangrove, its seeds can float and survive in seawater. Although the size of the trees in Jozani is impressive, few trees become truly huge as the soil is too shallow to allow deep roots to penetrate, and they get blown over by strong monsoon winds. With several diverse habitat types, each brings its associated and equally varied wildlife to the reserve.

Fauna Several rare and endemic animal species occur in Jozani, making it a major attraction for wildlife fans. Even if you've got only a passing interest, a visit can be fascinating. The main reason most visitors come here is to see some of the resident red colobus monkeys (see box, page 327); their local name is *kima punga* meaning 'poison monkey' and they are unique to the Zanzibar archipelago. Many wildlife fans rate the red colobus of Jozani as one of the best monkey-viewing experiences in Africa. Nowhere else can you get so close to a monkey in the wild that is not aggressive or likely to bite, and is also attractive, endearing and very rare.

Brochures produced in the mid 1990s said there were 1,500 individual colobus monkeys in Zanzibar, but this was an estimate, and more accurate surveys in 1997 put the figure at around 2,700. More recent researchers estimate between 1,600 to

Kirk's red colobus (*Procolobus kirkii*) are named after Sir John Kirk, the 19th-century British consul general in Zanzibar, who first identified these attractive island primates. They are endemic to the archipelago and one of Africa's rarest monkeys. Easily identified by their reddish coat, pale underside, small dark faces framed with tufts of long white hairs, and distinctive pink lips and nose, the monkeys are a wildlife highlight for many visitors to Zanzibar.

Kirk's red colobus live in gregarious troops of five to 50 individuals, headed by a dominant male and comprising his harem of loyal females and several young (single births occur year-round). They spend most of the day hanging out in the forest canopy, sunbathing, grooming and occasionally breaking away in small numbers to forage for tasty leaves, flowers and fruit. Their arboreal hideouts can make them hard to spot, but a roadside band at the entrance to Jozani-Chwaka Bay National Park allow for close observation and photography.

Timber felling, population expansion and a rise in agriculture have resulted in the rapid destruction of the tropical evergreen forests in which the Kirk's red colobus live, thus dramatically reducing population numbers. Researchers estimate that less than 2,000 of these monkeys currently exist, a fact verified by their classification as 'endangered' on the IUCN Red List (2016) and their inclusion in Appendix I of CITES.

Human behaviour has undoubtedly caused the decline in Kirk's red colobus population numbers, yet now tourism may help to save them. With national park status now protecting their habitat in Jozani Forest, and visitor numbers increasing, the local communities are beginning to benefit from the tangible economic rewards that come from preserving these striking monkeys. If this continues, the future survival of the species should be secured.

3,000 individuals remain, with over half being found on the islands, such as Uzi, which are outside current protection zones, whilst the IUCN (International Union for Conservation of Nature) has the number at under 2,000. Whatever the precise figure, the red colobus population of Jozani is certainly growing, which is partly a result of conservation efforts. Sadly, recent research shows that this is most likely caused by monkeys fleeing ongoing destruction of the small patches of forest elsewhere on the island into the safety of the Jozani area, rather than their numbers increasing as the result of breeding. Researchers generally agree that Zanzibar's total population of red colobus is probably stable, but emphasise that habitat destruction is still a major threat.

Other residents of Jozani include a population of blue or Sykes' monkey (*Cercopithecus mitis albogularis*), which you are also quite likely to see. The forest is also home to Ader's duiker (*Cephalophus adersi*), a species of small antelope found only on Zanzibar and some parts of the Kenyan coast, and suni (*Nesotragus moschatu moschatus*), another antelope which is even smaller than the duiker, but both of these are extremely shy and unlikely to be seen. The Ader's duiker is virtually extinct in Kenya now and is one of the two rarest antelopes in the world. Its only chance of survival is on Unguja. Its population is between 400 and 1,000 and efforts have been under way over recent years to ensure its survival, including protecting Jozani, working with local communities to establish sanctuaries and the proposed translocation of some individuals to Chumbe Island.

There are even reports of leopards (*Pathera pardus adersi*) in Jozani. If present they would be a local subspecies, smaller than the mainland version, although

Southwestern Zanzibar   JOZANI-CHWAKA BAY NATIONAL PARK AND AROUND

11

the veracity of these claims is highly questionable. (For more details of wildlife in Jozani, see pages 48–68.)

Birds Jozani has a fairly good bird population, with over 40 species recorded, although many of the forest birds are shy and therefore hard to spot. Species occurring here include Kenya crested guineafowl (*Guttera pucherani*), emerald-spotted wood dove (*Turtur chalcospilos*), little greenbul (*Andropadus virens*), sombre greenbul (*Andropadus importunus*), cardinal woodpecker (*Dendropicos fuscescens*), red-capped robin-chat (*Cossypha natalensis*), dark-backed weaver (*Ploceus bicolour*), golden weaver (*Ploceus xanthops*), olive sunbird (*Nectarinia olivacea*) and crowned hornbill (*Tockus alboterminatus*). An interesting endemic is the Fischer's turaco (*Turaco fischeri*), which is slightly larger than those on the mainland, with blue-purple on the wings instead of green. In the mangroves you'll see various kingfishers, including the localised mangrove kingfisher (*Halcyon senegaloides*), sunbirds and coucals.

If you're especially keen on birds, it is well worth engaging the services of a bird guide. Jozani has two bird specialists on the staff: Ali Addurahim is an ecologist and chief bird guide; Ali Khamis Mohammed was trained by the other Ali, and also knows his stuff. They have a bird checklist and a copy of the big fat *Zimmerman Birds of Kenya and Northern Tanzania* book, which includes most species that occur on Zanzibar.

AROUND JOZANI-CHWAKA BAY NATIONAL PARK
Zanzibar Butterfly Centre (ZBC) (m *0774 224472*; e *mail@zanzibarbutterflies. com*; *www.zanzibarbutterflies.com*; ⊕ *09.00–17.00 daily; admission US$6/3 adult/ child*) Situated in Pete, this aims to show visitors the forest's fluttering friends close up whilst also generating income for local villagers and preserving the forest.

Villagers around Jozani-Chwaka Bay National Park are being encouraged to protect the surrounding vegetation in an unusual initiative which has them trained to sustainably farm native butterflies. Participants (currently 35 farmers) are taught to identify butterfly species, gently capture female butterflies, net small areas for breeding, harvest eggs, plant appropriate caterpillar fodder and ultimately collect the resulting pupae for breeding the next generation and sale back to the centre. The pupae are then sold on to overseas zoos and live exhibits or displayed for visitors in the large, netted tropical garden. Here, 200–300 colourful butterflies can be seen in the enclosure, making for a fascinating diversion and one of Africa's largest butterfly exhibits. There are good guides and clear informative signs to explain the project and butterfly lifecycle, and experienced photographers can also get some wonderful shots.

The income generated from visitors to ZBC is channelled back into further funding local conservation and poverty-alleviation projects, whilst the message is made clear to the communities that protecting the natural habitat of these insects provides much-needed income. The centre is a fun, worthwhile 30-minute stop, and its location just outside Jozani Reserve, makes it a convenient addition to a forest trip. For a little more insight into the farming of the butterflies, and for a chance to meet some of the families benefitting form the project, it is also possible to go on a tour through the village for an extra US$9/6 adult/child. It's a lovely, low-key way to spend a little time with rural Zanzibaris, and an opportunity that's close to impossible nearer the coast.

Zanzibar Land Animals Park (m *0777 850816*; e *mohdayoub2@hotmail.com*; ⊕ *10.00–17.00 daily; admission US$8 free adults/children*) The Zanzibar Land Animals

Park (ZALA for short) is in the village of Muungoni, just south of Kitogani, where the main road from Zanzibar Town divides into roads towards Paje and Makunduchi.

At first glance it's just a zoo, with various pens and compounds to hold the animals (mostly reptiles). However, this community-based project, run by the tireless and enthusiastic Mohammed Ayoub, has a more important purpose. It's primarily an education centre where groups of Zanzibari schoolchildren come to learn about their island's natural heritage.

For tourists this is one of the few places on Zanzibar where you can observe snakes and lizards at close quarters; the chameleons are particularly endearing. Also look out for the geometric tortoises which are not native, but were brought to the park by customs officials who confiscated them at the airport from a smuggler of exotic pets. There are a few other species on display, most notably the small group of tree hyrax who spend time in their pen and time in the nearby forest. These part-time zoo animals come back mostly at feeding time, then seem quite content to rest or play in their pen before returning to the trees at nightfall.

Zala Park is only about 3km down the road from Jozani Forest Reserve, and can be combined with a visit there. If you have an overwhelming interest in wildlife, conservation or education, it is sometimes possible to stay in the small one-roomed guesthouse, though this is often used by visiting volunteers. Mohammed offers a nature trail in the nearby forest and mangrove stands, and can organise guided walks if you are interested in seeing more of this area; ideally, this should be arranged in advance. Supporting this project with a brief stop on your journey is well worth it, especially if you have children: not only for your own understanding and experience, but also to support a thoroughly worthwhile, long-running community project.

UNGUJA UKUU AND BI KHOLE RUINS

For keen fans of history and archaeology, there are two places of interest in the southwest of the island. Both are just off the main road between Zanzibar Town and Jozani-Chwaka Bay National Park, Paje and Kizimkazi, so make convenient stop-offs *en route* there or to the southwest coasts.

There is now also an excellent full-day dhow trip in the Menai Bay Conservation Area that launches from Unguja Ukuu, run by ethical local operator Eco+Culture (page 114).

WHERE TO STAY AND EAT *Map, page 316*

Menai Bay Beach Bungalows (10 rooms)
m 0743 605860/0779 614430; info@menaibay. com; www.menaibay.com. Set beneath the palms along an impossibly beautiful crescent beach at Unguja Ukuu, these bungalows closed in 2008, but have since quietly re-opened. 5 neat, thatched, semi-detatched cottages &

the simple open-sided Ubuyu restaurant, offer total escapism. Whitewashed interiors, simple furnishings with mossie nets & ceiling fans open onto little verandas overlooking the gardens. Come here to do nothing but read a book & gaze out to sea from the low coral-rag cliff. B&B. **$$**

WHAT TO SEE AND DO

Unguja Ukuu This is the site of the oldest known settlement on Zanzibar, dating from the end of the 8th century AD. It was believed to have been founded by early Shirazi immigrants from Persia, but recent archaeological evidence from here and other sites on the east coast of Africa suggests that it was Swahili in origin. Research at Unguja Ukuu is still taking place and more evidence may yet come to light.

Unguja is the local name for Zanzibar Island today, and Ukuu means 'great'. It is believed that the settlement may have been quite large, but was probably abandoned in the 10th century when the local Muslim population came under attack. An Arab geographer, writing in the 13th century, recorded that the people of 'Lenguja' had taken refuge from their enemies on the island of Tumbatu, off the northwest shore of Zanzibar Island (see box, page 236).

Despite this site's fascinating history, today there is very little remaining that would be of any interest to anyone except the keenest archaeologist – just some shallow earth pits and the remnants of a few crumbling walls.

Getting there and away To reach this site, you need to pass through the modern village of Unguja Ukuu, reached by turning south off the main road between Zanzibar Town and the southern part of the east coast, at a junction about halfway between the villages of Tunguu and Pete. South of the village, a small track branches off the dirt road that leads to Uzi Island (reached by tidal causeway); follow this to reach the remains of old Unguja Ukuu. If you don't have a **car**, **dalla dalla** No 308 takes passengers to Unguja Ukuu from Zanzibar Town as does the public **bus** on Route 8.

Bi Khole Ruins Situated about 20km to the southeast of Zanzibar Town, the Bi Khole Ruins are the remains of a large house dating from the 19th century. Khole was a daughter of Sultan Said ('Bi' is a title meaning 'lady') who came to Zanzibar in the 1840s, after Said moved his court and capital from Oman. With her sister, Salme, she helped their brother, Barghash, escape after his plans to seize the throne from Majid were discovered (see box, pages 14–15).

Khole had this house built for her to use as a private residence away from the town; she is recorded as being a keen hunter and a lover of beautiful things. The house had a Persian bathhouse where she could relax after travelling or hunting, and was surrounded by a garden decorated with flowering trees and fountains. The house was used until the 1920s but is now ruined, with only the main walls standing, and these are often overgrown.

The main front door has collapsed into a pile of rubble but this is still the way into the ruin. Directly in front of the door is a wide pillar, designed so that any visitor coming to the door would not be able to see into the inner courtyard, in case Khole or other ladies of the court were unveiled. In this room are alcoves and niches with arabesque arches, although the windows are rectangular. With some imagination, it's possible to see what an impressive house this once was.

Getting there and away The Bi Khole Ruins lie a few kilometres to the west of the main road from Zanzibar Town to the southern part of the east coast, about 6km south of the village of Tunguu. The road passes down a splendid boulevard of gnarled old mango trees, supposed to have been planted for Khole (though they may date from before this period): about halfway along is the track to the ruins. If you're travelling on public transport, take any of the **buses** (Routes 9 or 10) or **dalla dallas** (Nos 309, 310, 324 or 326) heading to the southeast and ask the driver to tell you when to alight.

FUMBA AND MENAI BAY

At the far end of the island's southwestern peninsula, on an increasingly rutted coral road 15km from Zanzibar Town, is the peaceful village of Fumba. It's a quiet, scenic place and very few tourists ever come here, which gives it a good deal of its charm. There is only one upmarket lodge offering accommodation, but day trips to the marine conservation area of Menai Bay are run by two reputable operators (page 333), so even if you can't stay it's still possible to get a taste of this area. From the beach south of the village, local fishermen take their ngalawa outriggers and

INTEGRATED SEAWEED AND SHELLFISH FARMING

Tremendous effort is being made by the government, research institutions and NGOs to increase the returns from seaweed production (see box, pages 278–9). At the beginning of 2006, a pilot scheme began to integrate seaweed and shellfish farming. Funded and supported by the Institute of Marine Sciences in Zanzibar, Woods Hole Oceanographic Institute in Massachusetts and the McKnight Foundation, the scheme aims to maximise workers' time by engaging them in the farming of both seaweed and shellfish, particularly oysters. Some 200 women from Fumba, Bweleo, Nyamanzi and Unguja Ukuu are now involved in the project and it's hoped that the benefits of a dual income will considerably improve their independence and standard of living.

To initiate this work, the Institute of Marine Science worked with the Western Indian Ocean Marine Sciences Association (WIOMSA), the Coastal Resource Center (CRC) at the University of Rhode Island and USAID on a programme called Sustainable Coastal Communities and Ecosystems (SUCCESS). All of these operators aim to promote the inclusion of shellfish on tourist hotel menus so as to increase its overall consumption. It is hoped that this raised demand for shellfish will drive market prices up, and ultimately improve the incomes of the shellfish collectors and farmers.

The SUCCESS programme has successfully developed a floating line system for seaweed farming and adapted it to shellfish and mabe pearl farming. (A mabe pearl is a hemispherical pearl which has grown against the inside of an oyster's shell, rather than in its tissues.) The pearl farming, which started in 2006, had the first crop of 28 mabe pearls in November 2007. The mabe pearls were subsequently sold, with 19 of these being bought by a US company for US$2,000. The company donated three resulting necklaces back for the project's first Zanzibar pearl auction in February 2008. These pieces, together with the remaining raw mabe pearls earned the group of seven (three men and four women) a further US$1,000 at auction, and clearly shows the tremendous success for the aptly named project. There are currently an estimated 400 oysters implanted for mabe pearls at different stages of development and this is set to be a potentially significant marine crop.

The group have also been trained on other aspects of entrepreneurship including pearl and shell polishing, making ornaments, packaging and marketing, as well as running co-operatives. Three of these people, all women, have become so successful that they are earning approximately US$170 per month out of the part-time activity. This is significant: a low-ranking government officer will earn US$70 per month, and 50% of the island population is still on the US$1 per day poverty line. The group, together with the seaweed soap manufacturers of Kidoti (see box, pages 278–9), have been successfully selling their merchandise to tourists and residents and we very much hope that the opportunity and their entrepreneurial skills can be passed on to other coastal communities within the archipelago.

Southwestern Zanzibar   FUMBA AND MENAI BAY

11

dhows to the islands and fishing grounds beyond, and here too is the departure point for one of the boat trips. It's truly stunning in the surrounding waters but if you also want to get a deeper insight into the community, ask around for a local villager called Issa Kibwana, who conducts small tours of the nearby fruit and spice plantations, or arrange a meeting with him through Sama Tours (page 115).

As an interesting aside, there is currently a German-engineered prefab 'new town' under construction on the western side of Fumba peninsula. Billed as affordable, quality housing, it's a Western-style development with parks, practical facilities from medical centres to cafés and nurseries, and a range of apartments and houses. Still far from affordable for the majority of Zanzibaris, it is likely to be highly desirable to the upwardly mobile and some expats.

GETTING THERE AND AWAY To get here, take the road from Zanzibar Town towards the airport, then fork left (east) down a main road just after a petrol station. This will lead you northeast, before turning east and heading south, along the airport runway's eastern boundary fence. Leaving the airport behind you, you'll continue southeast along a bumpy, but picturesque, tree-lined road.

After around 5km there is a right turn from the main road, signposted to the Menai Bay Conservation Area. You can continue straight on or turn right to get to Fumba, as these roads join up at the rocky, southern end of the peninsula. Alternatively, if you don't have your own transport, take one of the four daily local **buses** (Route 7) from Zanzibar Town.

WHERE TO STAY AND EAT *Map, page 316*

Fumba Beach Lodge (26 rooms) m 0777 876298; e info@fumbabeachlodge.co.tz; www. fumbabeachlodge.com. Built on 16ha of private land, including 3 separate sandy coves, Fumba Beach Lodge is just 30mins from the airport, & is currently the only upmarket lodge in the WWF's Menai Bay Conservation Area. Designed & built by Edwin van Zwam, a Dutchman with a solid African background, Fumba was created in line with contemporary safari camps, & the result is a fabulously original place, with clean lines & bold colour. There are well-spaced, deluxe rooms with canopied dbl beds, mains electricity, en-suite showers, fans & a sea view; 3 can become family rooms using inter-connecting doors. There are also special suites with huge dbl beds, sunshine-yellow details, beautifully carved wooden wardrobes with safes & tremendous views. There's a stylish outside shower & a dbl bath with a view. Large, shuttered terrace doors open onto a private deck & the beach beyond, or there's a delightful rooftop terrace with views out to Kwale Island. 2 of these suites are built on the edge of a low coral cliff, around a baobab tree, into which an additional large outdoor bath has been set. Beside the large, infinity pool is a comfortable, colourfully cushioned lounge & an open-fronted restaurant specialising in seafood, though candlelit meals are often enjoyed on the beach. Nearby, the outside bar, Dhow FumBar, is a stunning spot for sundowners or pre-dinner aperitifs. The tropical Baobab Spa has been expanded, though still incorprates its original open-air treehouse. With high makuti for shade, & curved internal walls for privacy, it's a pleasant enough afternoon experience. This is an African spa with local therapists – don't come expecting sophisticated Thai masseuses, though neither will you be charged premium prices. Yoga classes can also be arranged. For more active excursions, there's a well-equipped onsite dive centre & some wonderful day trips around Menai's idyllic islands. The lodge is involved in local community projects including school & water initiatives, & is a member of the Fumba Peninsula Environmental Conservation Organisation. HB/FB. **$$$$$–**

WHAT TO SEE AND DO The Menai Bay Conservation Area has a number of picturesque, uninhabited islands and sandbanks to explore as well as some fascinating marine life. It's well worth taking one of the full-day **sailing** and **snorkelling** excursions here, either through Fumba Beach Lodge, if you're a guest, or with Safari Blue departing from the Fumba Peninsula or Eco+Culture departing from Unguja Ukuu.

Some shade is available on these boats and beaches, but remember to apply sunscreen and preferably wear a T-shirt for protection when snorkelling. Towels and waterproof shoes are also recommended as you'll most likely have to wade out to the boat across coral rock.

Eco+Culture \024 223 3731; m 0777 410873/0755 873066; e ecoculturetours@gmail. com; www.ecoculture-zanzibar.org. This socially & environmentally aware tour operator (page 114) runs a fabulous full-day Menai Bay excursion: the Unguja Ukuu Boat Trip. On a traditional dhow, small groups are taken past rich mangrove forests to the pristine beaches of Miwi, Nianembe or Kwale islands & accessible sandbanks. Snorkelling kit is provided & the shallow reefs around the bay & islands provide excellent opportunities to spot brightly coloured fish & corals. After a good amount of time in the water, a delicious BBQ lunch is prepared on the beach, which invariably features a selection of freshly caught fish, Swahili side dishes & tropical fruits. On all trips, there is an English-speaking guide alongside the 2 crew & local chef, all of whom are happy to answer questions & talk about the surroundings & traditions of the area. Life jackets, a small first-aid kit & outboard motor are also kept on board for emergencies. Eco+Culture have a firm policy of limiting numbers on their trips with the express aim of protecting the environment & making the trip more enjoyable for their guests. A max of 8 people per dhow & only 12 guests (in 2 boats) are ever taken out at the same time. This is a real pleasure & one of the main differentiators of this trip over its competitor. The trip leaves Stone Town at 08.00, returning at 17.00; US$65pp for 4 people, US$55pp for groups of over 5.

✴ **Safari Blue** m 0777 423162; e adventure@ zanlink.com; www.safariblue.net; ⏰ (tours) Sat–Thu. Trips are made on traditional sailing dhows, 10–13m in length (capacity 16 pax), which have been kitted out with Yamaha

outboard engines, life jackets, sunshades, boarding ladders, first-aid kits, fire blankets & waterproof bags for cameras & valuables. Public liability & marine insurance complete the adherence to safety.

The trip pauses at a few of the bay's islands & sandbanks for exploration, a tasty lunch & relaxation, in between guided snorkelling forays & hopeful spotting for humpback & bottlenose dolphins. The 1st stop of the day is usually Kwale sandbank for gentle snorkelling. If conditions allow, a 2nd snorkelling session takes place at West Kwale. Sailing on further, BBQ seafood lunches await on Kwale Island, where tamarind trees offer shade (vegetarian/non-fish options must be ordered in advance). It's worth noting that there's also a toilet block on the island. There's a visit to a mangrove lagoon, where swimming is possible during high tide, a walk across the island, & a chance to try your hand at sailing a ngalawa, before the dhow's lanteen sail is hoisted & the boat heads back to Fumba. Fumba Beach is remote with no formal changing facilities, so it's best to wear swimwear under your clothes & bring beach shoes & a towel.

Recommended by so many travellers over the years, Safari Blue is a victim of its own success with higher numbers of guests & boats now heading out into the bay; however, it is still a delightful trip. Leaves from close to Fumba Beach at 09.30, returning about 17.00; US$60 adult, US$30 child aged 6–14 years, children under 6 years free; transfers from Stone Town to Fumba cost an additional US$60/vehicle.

CHUMBE ISLAND

Chumbe lies about 10km south of Zanzibar Town, and is one of the largest of the offshore islands in this area. The surrounding coral reef is in good condition, bar some bleaching from the El Niño effect,

For information on visiting the ruins of Chukwani, go to www. bradtguides.com/chukwani.

11

because until recently the island was inside a military area and public access was not allowed. Consequently, it has not been damaged by high volumes of tourists, transfer boats or the destructive fishing techniques employed by local fishermen. The reef on the western side of Chumbe Island was officially gazetted a Marine National Park (the first in Tanzania) in 1994, and the island has since been declared a forest reserve. Together, the island and reef are known as Chumbe Island Nature Reserve or Chumbe Island Coral Park (CHICOP; *www.chumbeisland.com*).

CHICOP's own information states: 'Chumbe Island is a rare example of a still pristine coral island ecosystem in an otherwise heavily over-fished and over-exploited area. It includes a reef sanctuary and a forest and bird sanctuary of exceptional biodiversity'. This has been verified by various global conservation and scientific bodies, including IUCN, WWF and UNESCO. A specialist from the Australian Institute of Marine Sciences called Chumbe 'one of the most spectacular coral gardens to be found anywhere in the world'.

Over 400 species of fish have been identified in the marine park and other marine wildlife frequently seen includes turtles, dolphins, and–seasonally–even the great humpback whale. On the island, 60 species of bird have been recorded, including breeding pairs of the rare roseate tern (*Sterna dougallii*). The island is also home to various lizards and a population of rare giant coconut crabs (see box, page 335). Six Ader's duiker (*Cephalophus adersi*), an endangered small antelope whose range is restricted to a handful of coastal forests in and around Zanzibar, were reintroduced to Chumbe Island in 1999 and 2000, and the small population is reproducing and appears to be thriving in the dry and rough coral-rag forest on the island.

Buildings of historical and cultural interest on Chumbe include a **lighthouse** built by the British in 1904 and still clearly visible from ships approaching Zanzibar from Dar es Salaam. The lighthouse is still functioning but is now also used as an observation tower with a spectacular view of the island and the marine park. There is also an old **mosque** built in an Indian style unique to Tanzania that is still frequently used by the local Muslim staff. A cottage originally built for the lighthouse keepers has been converted into a **visitor information centre**, including an education room for local schoolchildren who are brought here by the Chumbe management and other conservation organisations to learn about local environmental issues.

Tourism is being developed on Chumbe in a very sensitive manner. Former fishermen have been employed as park rangers on the island. They have been trained by CHICOP and now take visitors on **guided walks** along trails in the dense forest and along the intertidal flat around the island at low tide. The most popular excursion on the island is the **guided snorkelling tour** to the protected reef, where the tourists learn more about the delicate coral reef ecosystem. Profits from tourists visiting the island are channelled back into local education and conservation projects.

Chumbe Island's unique situation has been recognised by an almost unparalleled string of awards for its responsible approach to tourism, and its ecologically sensitive approach to the environment. Meanwhile Chumbe seems effortlessly to combine a tourist attraction with a centre for ongoing education projects for the local people. It is an exceptional place.

GETTING THERE AND AWAY For tourists, **day trips** to the island are available when the island isn't full – these cost US$90 per person including all transfers, snorkelling

Common on Chumbe Island, yet endangered elsewhere in the South Pacific and Indian Ocean, the rare and remarkable 'coconut crab' (*Birgus latro*) is the world's largest land invertebrate.

A member of the Coenobitidae family, it is one of only a few hermit crabs that is wholly adapted to spending most of its life away from the sea. In some areas coconut crabs are known to move several kilometres inland; however, they do begin life in the sea, with the female depositing hatched eggs in the water as planktonic larvae (*zoea*). Over a matter of a few weeks, the larvae develop claws to become *megalopa*, and sink to the seabed as tiny crabs, in search of a protective shell. They retain these shells when they reach land, discarding them only when their carapace is fully hardened. Unlike other hermit crabs, these creatures develop a dual-purpose shell over their abdomen, similar in appearance to a lobster. This guards against water loss and saves on 'house-hunting'. And without the need to fit inside abandoned shells, the coconut crab is free to grow indefinitely, accounting for its serious size (adults have been recorded with a 1m leg span).

Nocturnal by nature, the crabs scavenge and feed on decaying vegetation, fruit, small animals and, naturally, coconuts. Although adept at climbing palms to reach the coconuts, these crabs do not actually have any special adaptations for scaling tree trunks. The crab will use its powerful claws to heave itself up to the coconut, snip it off the palm using its sharp pincers, descend the tree backwards (facing up), gather its prize and feast. With its razor-sharp claws, the crab attacks the coconut, ripping away the husk, cracking its shiny nut and devouring the flesh inside.

The coconut crab is listed on the IUCN endangered species list, with no record of the number in existence. Habitat destruction, human hunting and introduced predators continue to threaten their global survival. Happily, Chumbe Island reports a healthy population and is working to gain international support for the protection of this amazing species. Guided by one of the island's staff, you are likely to be able to watch them forage by night (especially in the salubrious surroundings of the camp's compost heap) – but keep still and quiet; the crabs have poor eyesight and so detect predators and threats by vibrations.

equipment, guides and lunch – but visitors are encouraged to spend at least one night here and two or three would be perfect.

🏠 WHERE TO STAY AND EAT *Map, page 316*

✳ 🏠 **Chumbe Island Lodge** (7 rooms)
m 0777 413232/0672 413582/0777 413582;
e book@chumbeisland.com/ask@chumbeisland.com; www.chumbeisland.com; ⌚ mid Jun–mid Apr. This superb, trailblazing lodge is an example of truly eco-friendly accommodation. Its bungalows are simple but clean, comfortable, ingeniously designed & genuinely ecologically sensitive. Each 2-storey dbl bungalow is made from predominantly local materials using traditional construction techniques, & employing cutting-edge eco-architectural systems. Downstairs there's an open-fronted lounge terrace, complete with sea-view hammock & animal mosaics. Upstairs, the bedroom comprises a comfortable mattress on the floor, mosquito net, & a stunning view of the ocean or stars through the triangular front wall. The bungalows are completely self-sufficient with solar panels to provide electricity, funnel-shaped roofs to catch, filter & store rainwater (there is

no good groundwater on the island), & 'compost toilets' to avoid septic tanks & the pollutants they often produce. Used water from the showers goes onto flower beds where specially chosen plants absorb nutrients before the water drains into the ground. This accommodation is unique in Zanzibar, & very unusual in the whole of Africa. The central area is a huge, star-shaped makuti structure – perfect for catching the sea breeze in the heat of the day. Simple, fresh meals are served on the terrace (at the sounding of a large gong), & there's a lovely upper deck of hammocks & chairs where the reference library & education centre can also be found. Activities are all escorted & focus on learning about the surrounding environment & ecology. They include snorkelling (scuba diving is prohibited) on the nearby reefs, forest walks & walks across the intertidal zone, with its plethora of rock pools. The coconut crab is a nocturnal creature & seldom seen in daylight, but if you ask the staff to take you into the woodland at dusk or after dark, you are virtually guaranteed to see several! The lodge is a private company with not-for-profit aims, & ploughs its proceeds back into great community education & conservation initiatives, making it not only a stunning holiday spot, but a worthy cause. Al reduced rates Oct–Nov & Mar–mid Apr. 👑

12

Pemba

Pemba Island lies about 80km to the northeast of Zanzibar Island, and about the same distance from the Tanzanian mainland, directly east of the port of Tanga. Smaller than Zanzibar, at just 67km long, it covers an area of 985km² and has a more undulating landscape, even though its highest point is only about 95m above sea level. But one of the first things that most strikes the visitor is how green it is. More densely vegetated than Zanzibar (with both natural forest and plantation), Pemba has always been seen as a more fertile place. The early Arab sailors called it El Huthera, meaning 'The Green'. Today, as always, far more cloves are grown here than on Zanzibar.

With 406,848 inhabitants recorded in the 2012 census, Pemba is – like Zanzibar– one of the most densely populated areas of Tanzania, although this is no urban jungle. Most of the population live in traditional square houses, with a wooden frame, mud walls and thatched roofs (occasionally upgraded to corrugated iron). The largest town is Chake Chake, the island's capital and administrative centre, about halfway down the western side of the island. Other main towns are Wete, in the north, and Mkoani, the main port, in the south.

As in the Zanzibar archipelago as a whole, people are predominantly Muslim. Right across the island, women wear the veil, most in bright colours but some in sombre black, while schoolgirls look immaculate in the uniform dark skirts and cream veils. Typically it's a subsistence economy, with cloves the only real revenue earner, and few jobs available, so the nascent tourist industry brings much-needed employment. Pembans are naturally hospitable, but while English is spoken in the larger hotels, and by most of those who regularly come into contact with tourists, few villagers speak anything other than Swahili, so it's advisable, and polite, to learn at least a few words of the language.

The low number of tourists to the island can make the independent traveller stand out, and visitors to Chake Chake, Mkoani or Wete will find they are likely to be the only foreigner in town, and a cause of much interest to the locals. Inland villages are visited even less; those passing through will be greeted with a mixture of broad grins and suspicious stares, while excited children squeal 'Mzungu!' (white person). There is some concern as to the effect that increased tourism will have on Pemba. As infrastructure, roads and telecoms gradually improve, it is inevitable that confidence to invest in the island will eventually increase, prices will rise and the island will change. Hopefully, this transition will be carefully and positively managed.

HIGHLIGHTS

For today's visitor, Pemba's greatest attractions include long, empty beaches, some excellent diving and snorkelling–particularly around Misali Island–and

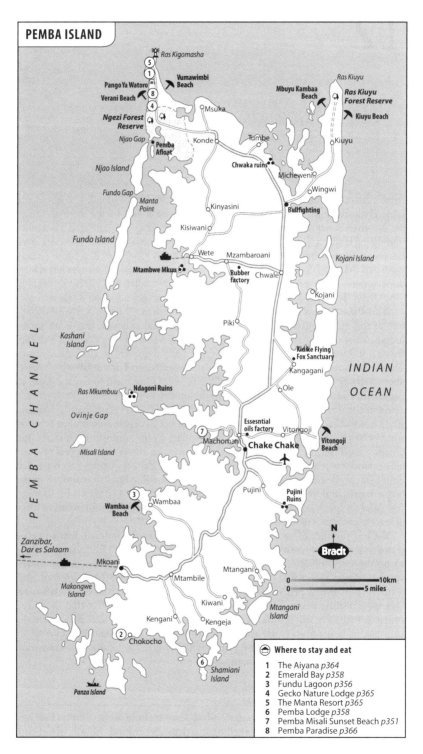

PEMBA ISLAND

Ras Kigomasha

5

1
Pango Ya Watoro
8
Verani Beach
4
Vumawimbi
Beach

Ngezi Forest
Reserve

Msuka

Mbuyu Kambaa
Beach

Ras Kiuyu

Ras Kiuyu
Forest Reserve

Kiuyu Beach

Njao Gap

Pemba
Afloat

Konde

Tumbe

Kiuyu

Njao Island

Chwaka ruins

Micheweni

Fundo Gap

Manta
Point

Wingwi

Kinyasini

Bullfighting

Kisiwani

Fundo Island

Wete
Mzambaroani

Kojani Island

Mtambwe Mkuu

Rubber
factory
Chwale

Kashani
Island

Piki

Kojani

Kidike Flying
Fox Sanctuary

Kangagani

INDIAN

OCEAN

Ras Mkumbuu
Ndagoni Ruins

Ole

Ovinje Gap

Esesntial
oils factory
Vitongoji

Misali Island

7
Machomani
Chake Chake

Vitongoji
Beach

Pujini
Pujini
Ruins

3
Wambaa
Wambaa
Beach

Zanzibar,
Dar es Salaam

Mkoani

N

Bradt

Makongwe
Island

Mtangani

0   10km
0   5 miles

Mtambile

Kiwani

Mtangani
Island

Kengani
Kengeja

2
Chokocho

Shamiani
Island

6

Panza Island

Where to stay and eat

1   The Aiyana *p364*
2   Emerald Bay *p358*
3   Fundu Lagoon *p356*
4   Gecko Nature Lodge *p365*
5   The Manta Resort *p365*
6   Pemba Lodge *p358*
7   Pemba Misali Sunset Beach *p351*
8   Pemba Paradise *p366*

P E M B A   C H A N N E L

the unspoilt forest reserve at Ngezi. There are several small historical sites which, although not 'must sees', certainly repay a visit if you use just a little imagination. Perhaps more important, though, with under 10,000 visitors per year, and little in the way of tourist facilities, Pemba is still a place where travel for its own sake (by car, bus, bike or on foot) remains a prime reason for visiting.

NATURAL HISTORY AND ENVIRONMENT

Verdant and very fertile, Pemba was once densely forested, although all that remains now is Ngezi Forest, on the northwestern tip of the island. Nevertheless, numerous spice and fruit trees dominate the rest of the landscape. **Cloves** represent the biggest cash crop, with Pemba responsible for the vast majority of cloves exported from Zanzibar, and sales monopolised by the government (see box, pages 50–1). For several months each year, cloves are left to dry in the sun on mats by the side of the road.

Consumption of almost all other **fruit** and **spices**, however, is restricted to domestic use. Mango, banana, avocado, coconut, citrus fruits, pineapple and papaya grow almost side by side with less familiar fruits such as breadfruit, custardfruit, plantain, tamarind, bungo and jackfruit (a huge and hard sponge-looking thing that yields an improbably sweet flesh). Spices such as ginger, vanilla, cinnamon and pepper also grow in abundance.

Of the three **primates** that inhabit the island, the most visible is the Pemba vervet monkey (*tumbili au kima*; *Cercopithecus aethiops nesiotes*), while the small-eared galago or bushbaby (*komba*; *Otolemur garnettii garnettii*) is more likely to be heard

WITCHCRAFT ON PEMBA

For the people of East Africa, the island of Pemba is particularly known as a centre for traditional medicine and witchcraft. The British writer Evelyn Waugh, in his classic travel book *Remote People* (1931), described Pemba as a centre of 'black art' learning, and went on to record how:

> novices would come from as far as the great lakes [of central Africa] to graduate there. Even from Haiti, it is said, witchdoctors will come to probe the deepest mysteries of voodoo. Nowadays everything is kept hidden from the Europeans, and even those who have spent most of their lives in the country have only now and then discovered hints of the wide, infinitely ramified cult which still flourishes below the surface.

Sixty years later, little had changed. A 1995 travel story in a British newspaper reported that the village of Vitongoji, in the centre of the island, was 'the capital of Pemban sorcery ... a place of dark secrets. Some years ago a witchdoctor was arrested for eating children in the course of his duties.' This report may have been tongue-in-cheek, but it's an inescapable fact that local people seeking cures for spiritual or physical afflictions still come to the local doctors of Pemba from Zanzibar Island, mainland Tanzania, Kenya, and even as far as Uganda and Congo.

As a visitor to Pemba from the West, you shouldn't expect to be taken to see any cures or ceremonies. This type of thing is strictly for the locals. Even the most innocent of questions about witchcraft from tourists will be met with nothing more than embarrassed smiles or polite denials. (For more details on traditional religion and witchcraft, see box, pages 40–1.)

12

than seen, its human-sounding cry disturbing many an otherwise peaceful night. A small population of Kirk's red colobus is also present in Ngezi Forest.

Relatively easy to spot is the **Pemba flying fox** (*popo wa Pemba; Pteropus voeltzkowi*), a large fruit bat which is the only fully endemic mammal on Pemba, and is classified as a globally endangered species. Its name comes from its orange fur and dog-like snout and ears. This animal seeks out the high canopies of undisturbed forest with a ready supply of fruit and tree blossoms. Pemba flying foxes roost throughout Pemba, particularly along the west coast and on islands off it, but are readily seen at Ngezi Forest where the forest rangers monitor their whereabouts, and at Kidike. They feed on soft fruits and weigh up to 1.5kg. Local people consider their flesh a delicacy; it tastes like oily chicken.

The **Zanzibar tree hyrax** (*pelele; Dendrohyrax validus neumannii*) is present not only at Ngezi but also on Njao and Fundo islands, whereas the rare and threatened **Pemba blue duiker** (*paa wa Pemba; Cephalophus monticola pembae*) and **marsh mongoose** (*chonjwe; Atilax paludinosus rubescens*) are found only in Ngezi Forest.

Bird species on the island include three endemics: the russet or Pemba scops owl, which is fairly common in the clove plantations and at Ngezi; the Pemba white-eye and the Pemba violet-breasted sunbird. A number of sub-endemic species include the Pemba green pigeon, the African paradise flycatcher and the Pemba African goshawk. Without doubt, the best place to see birds on Pemba is in Ngezi Forest.

GETTING THERE AND AWAY

BY AIR
Domestic services Daily services run between Dar es Salaam and Pemba, although all flights go via Zanzibar, and some may involve a change of plane. The duration of the flight is just over an hour. The modern terminal, located 7km southeast of Chake Chake, has few facilities – just a small shop selling drinks and snacks and a couple of toilets. At the time of research, the following flights and times were correct. The schedules for these flights change frequently, so do contact the airline as your trip draws closer.

To/from the mainland
✈ **Auric Air** www.auricair.com. 3 daily flights from Dar to Pemba via Zanzibar, departing 07.45, 13.30 & 15.30 (*1hr5mins; US$140 one-way*). There are also 2 daily flights from Tanga, departing 09.40 & 15.25 (*20mins; US$100 one-way*).
✈ **Coastal Aviation** www.coastal.co.tz. 2 daily flights from Dar to Pemba via Zanzibar (*65mins; US$140 one-way excl tax*). Flights depart Dar at 07.30 & 14.00, with the later flight waiting for earlier connections from Selous & Ruaha. Return flights leave Pemba at 08.45 & 15.15.

✈ **ZanAir** www.zanair.com. 2 daily flights between Dar & Pemba via Zanzibar (*1hr 15mins; US$300 return inc tax*); 08.45 & 14.00 from Dar, returning 10.15 & 14.15.

To/from Zanzibar
✈ **Auric Air** www.auricair.com. 3 daily flights to Pemba, departing 08.20, 14.05 & 16.05 (*30mins; US$140 one-way*).
✈ **Tropical Air** www.tropicalair.co.tz. 1 daily flight from Zanzibar to Pemba (*30mins; US$90 one-way excl tax*). Departs Zanzibar at 14.00; returns from Pemba at 15.00. These can be used to connect with flights to/from Tanga & Dar.

Private plane charter If you can get a group together and charter a whole plane, it can sometimes be cheaper per person than buying a ticket on a regular flight. From mainland Tanzania and Kenya, travel agents in Dar, Nairobi or Mombasa will be able to help you – they will probably phone the airport or one of the local charter companies to see if anything is going your way. To book scheduled or charter flights to the mainland from Pemba, contact ZanAir's agent opposite Barclays Bank in Chake Chake, or Pemba Aviation & Airport Services (the coastal agent) on the other side of the road. Alternatively you can phone the airport control tower (✆ *024 245 2238*) and enquire yourself. This is a fairly standard procedure – the charter companies often tell the tower if they're looking for passengers to fill spare seats.

For planes from Zanzibar Island, contact one of the local air-charter companies in Zanzibar Town. In high season there are flights at least every other day, so it's worth contacting the companies direct, or getting a travel agency to do it for you, to see if there's anything going (for contact details, see page 340).

Departure tax On leaving Pemba, don't forget that there is a US$6 departure tax (made up of US$5 'safety' tax, and a further US$1 airport tax), and be prepared to hand this over in cash.

BY SEA

By ferry Nearly all passenger ships, and some cargo ships, coming into Pemba arrive at the southern town of Mkoani, while it's mostly cargo ships and dhows that go to/from Wete (in the north). Very few ships or dhows, other than local fishing boats, go to/from Chake Chake. (In fact the old harbour of Chake Chake is silted up and only canoes can get here; the town's port is now at Wesha, about 10km west along the coast.)

It is possible to buy tickets online directly from Azam or for all ferries from Stone Town tour operators (pages 114–17); to buy tickets on Pemba, contact the relevant local agent in Chake Chake, Mkoani or Wete (see pages 349, 355 and 360). Do not buy tickets from touts, and be aware that these ferry schedules are notoriously subject to change, so do double-check with Azam close to your time of travel. If your time is tight, seriously consider flying.

Azam Marine & Coastal Fast Ferries
✆022 212 3324; e info@azammarine.com; www. azammarine.com. The best of the commercial passenger boats to Pemba from Zanzibar. It's a twice-weekly service (*Wed & Sat; US$35/45 economy/1st class one-way*), departing at 07.00 & arriving around 10.00. There is no direct service from Dar, but it is possible to leave form Dar at 18.00 the previous evening & travel via Zanzibar to Pemba, albeit a lengthy trip.

MV *Mapinduzi II* m 0777 438739; e znz@shipco.go.tz; www.shipco.website/shipco. go.tz/index.php. Zanzibar Shipping Corporation (ZSC), the state-owned line, runs the new MV *Mapinduzi II* ('Revolution'). This Korean-built cargo-passenger ship is generally used by local people because it is cheap (*Mon & Fri; US$25/35 economy/1st class one-way*), but some travellers on a tight budget also travel this way. Although slow, the cabins are quite airy & comfortable.

By dhow Most of Pemba's dhow traffic goes to/from Tanga on the mainland, and only occasionally do dhows go between Zanzibar Town and Pemba. Of those that do, most land at Mkoani. Although it is illegal in Tanzania for tourists to travel by dhow (and in Mombasa, police at the port are unwilling to let tourists board), and generally extremely unsafe (see box, page 81), some intrepid travellers still report finding captains willing to take them on board. If you're determined to consider this, see page 80.

Immigration formalities Whichever type of boat you use to reach Pemba from the mainland (Kenya or Tanzania), you need to show your passport to the immigration officials at the port. This is a very relaxed and low-key affair. So low key in fact that sometimes the office is empty, and you have to go to the police station in town to present your credentials, or get redirected to wherever the immigration staff might be.

TOURIST INFORMATION

Tour operators are the most reliable source of tourist information, although they will of course expect any bookings to be done through them. The Zanzibar Tourist Corporation (ZTC) has an office in Chake Chake, where staff may be able to assist, but their main purpose is to regulate the tour operators on the island rather than provide visitor guidance.

GETTING AROUND

Pemba's road system was given a boost in 2005 with the completion of the tarred road across the island from Mkoani to Konde, paid for by the World Bank. North of Konde, and elsewhere, however, most of the roads are pretty poor, with access to some of the outlying villages requiring 4x4 vehicles, particularly in the rainy season. From Chake Chake to Wete, a bumpy alternative to the main road is the 'old' – and, more direct – road via Mzambaroani, which goes through some beautiful scenery. This has now been tarred in places, but the road conditions are not great and time-wise, the new road is considerably quicker, despite the apparent diversion.

Options for getting around on Pemba are limited, although public transport allows independent travellers to see at least some parts of the island. To get further afield independently you'll have to hire a bike, motorbike, car or boat. For many travellers, though, the easiest way to set up an excursion or a tour of the island is to contact a driver, either direct (below) or through your hotel or guesthouse. Alternatively, there are a number of companies in Chake Chake and Wete that can organise this for you (pages 349 and 360).

TAXIS AND CAR HIRE It is rare for tourists to hire cars in Pemba, and it's not the easiest thing to organise, but with some effort it can be done through the tour companies in Chake Chake. Organising this in advance with erratic communications is challenging, and do bear in mind that conditions in Pemba for the self-driver are not great: few signposts, overconfident local drivers, sandy or rocky roads, and livestock in the street and remote hotel locations. For those heading north, the drive from Wete to the Ngezi Peninsula is particularly tough, and not at all easy to navigate.

Alternatively, it's pretty straightforward to rent a car with a driver for around US$60 a day, including petrol, depending on the distance you want to travel. Most of the hotels can organise this for you, as can tour companies. Try contacting one of the individuals listed below (giving plenty of notice), both of whom offer tours to various places of interest around the island. They are reliable, interesting guides, and both speak excellent English.

🚗 **Said Mohammed** m 0777 430201. Based in Chake Chake & known to everyone as Saidi. Offers city tours, spice tours, transport to the north & east (inc 4x4 by arrangement), & visits to all Pemba's places of interest.

🚗 **Suleiman Seif** m 0777 431793. The driver for Fundu Lagoon hotel also offers a range of tours. He is a mine of information & is particularly knowledgeable about the island's spice & fruit trees.

In Chake Chake, taxis (or at least men with cars) wait for business outside Barclays Bank, near the clock tower; in Mkoani and Wete they can be found near the market. Rates vary according to the vehicle: pickups, saloon cars, minibuses, Land Rovers and small Suzuki 'jeeps' are often available. Rates are also negotiable and should be discussed fully (and agreed) in advance. To give you an idea, a trip from Chake Chake to Wete or Mkoani costs about US$40 return. If you're planning a tour, a newish vehicle covering a round trip from Chake to Wete, Ngezi Forest and the Manta Resort and back would cost about US$150 per vehicle. All rates include petrol. Whatever you hire, part payment in advance is usually required, and the first stop is likely to be the petrol station.

Although in theory it's possible to self-drive, in practice this is less easy to set up. Some of the tour companies, such as Coral Tours or Msewe Travel in Chake Chake, may be able to help, with costs starting at US$60 per day. Do check the insurance details, and see pages 107–9 for further information.

MOTORBIKE AND BICYCLE HIRE Bikes can be hired from any of the tour operators in Wete or Chake Chake, while elsewhere it's perfectly possible to hire both motorbikes and pedal bikes on more of an ad hoc basis. The system seems to involve simply finding somebody who is not using their bike and doesn't mind making some extra shillings lending it out to tourists. Rates start at about US$10 per day for a bicycle, and US$30 for a motorbike. Alternatively, you can sometimes arrange to hire a bike or motorbike through your hotel. Tell the staff what you want to do, and they may well know someone who can help you out – prices will be the same as mentioned above. Sharook Guesthouse in Wete (page 360) rents out bikes for around US$10 a day.

Be warned that motorbikes or scooters – locally known as *piki piki* – can be extremely dangerous, both on pot-holed side roads and on the main north–south road, where erratic driving, sharp bends and numerous chickens or goats are just some of the hazards. If you're determined to go down this route, remember that you probably won't be insured. Check that your vehicle is in reasonable condition, particularly the tyres and the rims, and don't even consider it if you've no previous motorbike experience.

BUS, MINIBUS AND DALLA DALLA Pemba's main form of transport is dalla dallas (pages 111–12), which replaced the quaint old buses (actually converted trucks with wooden benches and canopies on the back) that used to serve the island, as well as the occasional minibus. Routes and numbers are listed below. On the main routes, of which the number 606 seems to have the most frequent service, there are several buses each day (at least one an hour after 06.00 until midnight), but on the minor routes buses might operate only a few times – or just once – per day, and that'll be in the morning. Services to/from Mkoani are tied in closely with ship arrival and departure times. In fact, it seems that Pemba Island's entire public transport system revolves around ship timetables. Other buses connect Chake Chake and, to a lesser extent, Wete with outlying villages. There will be a station manager at the bus depot in each town so check with him for details.

The fare on the longer routes (eg: Chake Chake to Mkoani) is about US$1.50. For shorter trips it's half that. The most useful routes for visitors are as follows, though it's worth noting that dalla dallas will stop to collect or drop off passengers at any point along their route.

Route

601   Wete to Konde
602   Chake Chake to Konde
603   Chake Chake to Mkoani
606   Chake Chake to Wete
305   Chake Chake to Wesha (Chake's port)
316   Chake Chake to Vitongoji (5km east of Chake Chake)
319   Chake Chake to Pujini
330   Chake Chake to Wambaa
10   Wete to Wingwi/Micheweni

BOAT HIRE Aside from booking through one of the hotels, there's no organised means of getting from Pemba across to the individual islands, although it's worth asking any of the tour operators in case they can help. Alternatively, some of the local fishermen are prepared to carry passengers for a fee, which is fine for short distances, but do remember that the longer crossings – especially to Misali Island – could take a considerable period of time, and be pretty uncomfortable, especially in rough seas.

ACCOMMODATION

Pemba has a very small number of places to stay compared with Zanzibar Island but there is increasing variety, from rock-bottom hotels and a smattering of guesthouses, to an ecolodge and a couple of more exclusive hideaways. While rumours of further options have been mooted for some time, Pemba Lodge and Emerald Bay (both page 358) is the only new accommodation to have appeared in recent years. Low visitor numbers to Pemba, especially independent travellers, have had a negative impact on budget accommodation options, as lack of income and investment has forced many to close. While nobody wants Pemba to turn into the cramped sprawl seen along some of Zanzibar's beaches, with so few facilities and lack of a reliable public transport network it is difficult for the independent traveller to visit, so most come on pre-paid trips to the larger lodges, and bypass the smaller, simpler hotels completely.

As on Zanzibar, all accommodation on Pemba must officially be paid for with hard currency; US dollars in cash are preferred, and, unless otherwise stated, anything else (eg: pounds sterling, euros) may not be accepted. If you have only Tanzanian shillings, these are usually accepted at the current rate of exchange. Breakfast is normally included in the room price; other meals are payable in Tanzanian shillings. As on Zanzibar Island, during quiet times many of the lodges and guesthouses on Pemba lower their rates, and even if reductions aren't advertised, it's worth asking. At the cheaper places, rates are often negotiable at any time of year.

EATING AND DRINKING

All the hotels on Pemba serve food, although at the cheaper places it has to be ordered, even by residents – sometimes quite a long time in advance. The island's main towns have simple restaurants where you can get local dishes, featuring varying combinations of chicken, fish and chips, or Indian-influenced dishes such as pilau and biryani.

Roadside stalls proliferate during market hours, most selling variations on meat kebabs (*mishkaki*) and omelettes. For a cheap meal, try *chipsi mai yai* – an omelette filled with chips, sometimes served with shredded cabbage, for around US$1. On the drinks front, it's easy enough to get branded fizzy drinks; and look out for the local pineapple drink, brand-named Zed, a strong alcoholic tipple with a dangerously low price. If you fancy a snack (or a simple souvenir), seek out the tamarind sweetmeat sold in small, hand-woven palm-leaf baskets. Called *haluwa*, it's made from oil and sugar, costs just a few shillings, and is so sweet that one packet will happily serve a whole group. Open it with caution, though – haluwa is very sticky. The best on the island is said to come from Wete.

For lunches or picnics, you can buy fruit at the markets and roadside stalls in Chake Chake, Mkoani, Wete or Konde. You can also buy bread, either from the occasional stall, or from men on bikes with baskets of fresh loaves on the back. Shops in the towns sell a reasonable range of food in tins and packets, imported from the mainland or elsewhere in the Indian Ocean, but in the smaller villages this kind of stuff is more difficult to find.

OTHER PRACTICALITIES

BANKS AND BUREAUX DE CHANGE Banking is limited to Chake Chake, which has branches of the People's Bank of Zanzibar and Barclays Bank; the latter even has an ATM (⊕ *08.30–16.00 Mon–Fri, 09.00–13.00 Sat*). The banks will change money, but expect a wait of 30 minutes or so, and be advised that US dollars are best. Financially, you may do slightly better at a bureau de change, a couple of which can be found in Chake Chake but they may not have shillings available and rates still won't be favourable. There's one in the ZTC building, and there are various less reliable local exchanges dotted among the shops. An alternative is to ask at a local shop or seek advice from staff at your hotel who may be able to direct you to a local trader who could change cash dollars, though naturally rates may well be higher than at the banks. If you're travelling to Pemba from Dar es Salaam or Zanzibar, you'd be well advised to change money at one of the bureaux de change at the airport or in town beforehand. Travellers' cheques are unlikely to be accepted anywhere.

COMMUNICATIONS Although there are **communications centres** in each of the main towns, the introduction of yellow public phone booths has made these somewhat redundant for the visitor. Phones take TTCL phonecards, which cost US$10 and are available from the Tanzanian Telecommunications office and numerous other outlets – just look for the TTCL sign outside. International calls cost US$1.50 a minute. For a fee, Coral Tours also have a landline that tourists can use (page 349). For more general information on telephone services into and out of Zanzibar, see page 102.

There are **post offices** in Chake, Wete and Mkoani and Konde (⊕ *usually 08.00–13.00 & 14.00–16.30 Mon–Thu, 08.00–noon & 14.00–17.00 Fri, 09.00–noon Sat*), but **internet** services are confined to the internet bureaux in Chake Chake (page 353). For Wi-Fi access, you'll be restricted to the more exclusive resorts, and even then connection speeds may be variable.

ELECTRICITY Since joining the mainland Tanzania grid in 2011, the electricity situation on Pemba has improved and power cuts have become far less frequent than they used to be. However, the power is still only on for eight to 14 hours a day, after which it switches to a less-consistent battery store. Backup generators are still necessary, though this is a drastic improvement on recent years.

HOSPITALS AND PHARMACIES The island's main **hospital** in Mkoani is a modern place, built with overseas aid. Although staffed by dedicated Chinese, Cuban and Tanzanian doctors, the hospital suffers from shortages of drugs and other essential supplies. There's a smaller hospital in Chake Chake, which has Western doctors and the island's only obstetrics unit, while X-ray facilities are based at the hospital in Wete, near the ferry port.

There are several **pharmacies**, including near the hospital in Chake Chake (close to the museum), where reportedly most things are available – if you know what you're looking for, that is.

ACTIVITIES

DIVING Recreational diving off Pemba is, for the most part, confined to the Pemba Channel on the more sheltered west of the island. Misali Island in particular provides a wonderful array of corals and fish life. Unlike the reefs around Zanzibar Island, many of the reefs off Pemba fall away into steep walls, offering opportunities for some exciting drift dives and the chance to see creatures such as the spotted eagle ray, with its 3m wingspan. Despite Pemba's undoubted reputation for the big pelagics, such as barracuda, trevally, giant groupers and the endangered Napoleon wrasse, sightings of shark are extremely rare on the west of the island, and even to the south. If it's sharks that you're after, you need to deep dive in the east, where the steep walls and fast currents attract hammerheads.

Most operators use either speedboats or motorised dhows to get to the dive sites. While the former are undoubtedly faster, there's a lot to be said for the leisurely pace of a dhow, giving the opportunity to take in the beauty of the islands or to watch large teams of fishermen working with their nets from narrow wooden boats. On the way to the dive sites, particularly in the morning and further north, you may be joined by schools of common or spinner dolphins, just tagging along for the ride, and occasionally humpback whale sightings have been reported.

Diving on Pemba, as on Zanzibar Island, is good all year round, with visibility ranging from 10m to 30m or even more. Between December and March, the water is warm – around 30°C, but even quite early in the season the water temperature is a reasonable 25°C or so, and most operators have good wetsuits if you didn't bring anything suitable (for more details, see box, page 98). Visibility, current and thus the choice of dive sites are strongly affected by the state of the tide: not just the level, but also whether it is spring or neap. Be guided by your dive instructor on this – it's important: there are a number of dives that should not be attempted by beginners, especially in the southeast of the island. On almost all boats, entry is a backward roll into the water.

Dive sites Although much of the reef around Pemba was adversely affected by the El Niño of 1998 (page 387) and the situation hasn't been improved by dynamite fishing (which sadly continues, despite being illegal), pristine, virgin reef can still be found, and groups do tend to be small, so divers, especially at advanced levels, are spoilt for choice. Dive sites on Pemba tend to have been given different names by the individual dive outfits, so the following is an overview of what to expect.

Particularly popular is the protected area to the west of **Misali Island** (pages 356–8), with its calm waters and spectacular coral gardens, where most (but not all) of the dives are suitable for novice or relatively inexperienced divers. Improbably giant clams hug the reef, as do numerous smaller creatures, such as exquisitely coloured nudibranchs: keep an eye out especially for the 30cm Spanish dancer, only visible at night. At one dive site to the northwest of the island, currents can be strong, making it more suited to advanced divers with considerable experience. The rewards can be great, however, with eagle rays and some big pelagics. Dives around the southwestern tip of Pemba are for the most part in the vicinity of **Panza Island**, and are also normally recommended for advanced divers, as the currents can be strong. Sites here are relatively spread out, with 'blue dives' offering good opportunities to see pelagics. There's also the wreck of a 1950s freighter in 12m of water.

North of Misali, some excellent sites around **Ovinje Gap**, **Fundo Gap** and **Njao Gap** with their steep walls are usually better explored by more advanced divers with plenty of experience, able to cope with strong and sometimes unpredictable currents. Diving through the 'gaps' between the islands can be seriously exciting, earning plenty of comparison with fairground rides and express trains. Even the more leisurely drift dives may not be suitable for a just-certified novice, so be clear of your limitations and do be sure to tell your dive leader if you have any doubts. **Manta Point**, just off Fundo Gap, is a great circular dive, affording regular ray sightings, as its name would suggest, although the number of mantas has significantly dwindled with overfishing. Also present are huge mushroom and cabbage corals; even if you don't get to see the manta rays, there are plenty of ocean-going fish in the vicinity, and all sorts of nudibranchs. Out of the currents, gentler dives offer plenty to see, while sheltered lagoons to the east of the islands are good locations to learn to dive and hone your skills. North of Njao Gap, however, the quality of the reef is poor, and dive operators rarely visit the area.

Dive companies There are currently three dive operators in Pemba, each linked to one of the island's resorts and with its own style. Be sure to check out what is available and choose the right operator for you. Equipment is available to hire from all companies, with standards generally pretty high. All offer PADI-certified courses, including the popular Discover Scuba and Open Water; night dives can usually be organised with advance notice. For those interested in underwater photography, cameras can be rented from Fundu Lagoon (*US$30/1 dive; US$50 including image CD*) or from Swahili Divers, who run photography courses.

On a practical note, some of the operators do not carry water on their boats, so check this before you leave and take your own if necessary, particularly in hot weather. For other practical advice, see pages 95–9.

For comparison purposes, prices below have been given for a single- or two-tank dive, and the PADI Open Water course. Inevitably, though, options vary considerably, and many other courses are offered, so do check these out.

⇘ **360 Dive Pemba** m 0776 718852; e diving@ themantaresort.com; www.themantaresort. com. On the northwestern tip of the island, this efficient 5* PADI dive school is run by the Manta Resort (page 365) & has good access to most of Pemba's west coast dive sites. A split-level training pool & professional instructors are always on hand, & divers from novice (advance e-learning recommended) to professional are well catered for. As many guests here come with their own equipment, the regulators, BCDs, marine conservation fees, boat trips & wetsuits are charged separately, with packages offering better value. *Equipment rental US$29; Dive US$52/104 sgl/dbl; Open Water US$540.*

⇘ **Dive 710** m 0774 438668; e reservations@ fundulagoon.com; www.fundulagoon.com. Dive 710, the professional yet friendly dive centre at Fundu Lagoon (page 356), is a PADI 5* Gold Palm operation used exclusively by the resort's guests. Its location, just 20mins or so by speedboat from the dive sites of Misali Island, makes it possible to leave at a civilised hour for the morning dive & be back in time for lunch. A more leisurely day allows for 2 dives, with a picnic lunch on the island. *Dive at Misali US$85 (further afield* additional US$20/dive, min 4); Open Water US$675; Marine Park fee US$10/day.

〰️ **Swahili Divers** m 0773 176737/8; e resort@kayakpemba.com; www.swahilidivers.com. The longest-established dive operator on Pemba is a relaxed & friendly outfit. In 2007, the company, which was the 1st on the island to attain both PADI 5* status & BSAC Resort Dive Centre, moved from Chake Chake to its new base at Gecko Nature Lodge (page 365) in the northwest, near Ngezi Forest & in 2017 it changed ownership. The crew take divers all over the central & northern dive sites of the island in fast RIBs, with the nearest dive sites just a 4-min journey. There are 2-tank dives every morning (departing 09.00; returning 13.30), with afternoon dives at 14.30, each taking a max 5 divers. Snorkelling is also on offer, as are sunset cruises. There's a purpose-built training pool for novice divers & some of Pemba's most knowledgeable instructors are on hand. US$170/450/650 2/6/10 dives; equipment US$30pp/day; Refresher US$55; Discover Scuba US$205; Open Water US$550, or US$650 for individual tuition.

Live-aboards There used to be a number of live-aboards operating around Pemba, with many originating in Kenya. Recently these have all but ceased to operate, with only one left. **Pemba Island Sailing** (m 0768 123464; e sailing@ecotz.com; www.sailing.ecotz.com) operates a fully crewed, 19m live-aboard catamaran called *Kaskazi*. Accommodating up to eight or, more comfortably, six guests, the boat sails from September to November and March to May, when the weather and sea are calmest. Charters are available from as few as three days, with bespoke itineraries usually including snorkelling, diving (request in advance to ensure a qualified dive master is present) and swimming, with wakeboarding and waterskiing from the motorised dinghy or mangrove kayaking also available. Guests are collected from Pemba Airport before being transferred to the port at Wesha, near Chake Chake, where dinghy transfers take seafarers to board *Kaskazi*. The boat moves daily, mainly among quiet lagoons surrounding the island, with the multi-national crew working hard to ensure a relaxed and enjoyable trip.

SNORKELLING While there is no shortage of places to swim and snorkel off Pemba, most are viable only at high water. One of the best places for snorkelling lies in front of the visitor centre on Misali Island, where – in just a few feet of water, and regardless of the tide – countless fish and other underwater life can be seen in almost perfect visibility. As you drift through the water, keep an eye out for unicornfish, sea goldies, cleaner wrasse, deep red and blue parrotfish, and the startling Moorish idol. Giant clams grip the reef, and sea cucumbers edge along the sandy bottom; you may even spot a grouper. Other possibilities include areas around the sandbanks that dry out at low tide along the west coast. Snorkelling trips can be organised through all the hotels and lodges; expect to pay US$20–40, depending on the distance to the site.

FISHING The waters of the Pemba Channel are well known for their abundance of fish, including blue marlin, sailfish, barracuda, trevally, mahi mahi, rainbow runner and kingfish. The lodges listed below are well geared up to offer safe, responsible fishing excursions. Alternatively, you could try asking around in the harbours at Wete, Wesha or Mkoani; there are few fishermen nowadays who are prepared to take visitors on board. The boats are small, however, and safety records are none too great, so it is probably advisable to stick to one of the established operators.

🛥️ **Fundu Lagoon** Page 356. Offers 4–5hr trips for their own guests on 2 boats captained by Rusty Rauscher, the only International Game Fish Association-accredited captain in Tanzania.

Taking 2 guests only, *Vumba* offers scenic ½- & full-day trips (*US$500/800*), including food & drink, & Fundu's chef can cook up any fish caught for dinner. Long fishing trips lasting up to 4 days can be arranged in advance, on board luxurious *Combava*. Taking up to 6 anglers, she comes on request for marlin-hunting trips to the north of the island (*US$1,500 boat relocation to Pemba plus US$1,200/day*).

🎣**Gecko Nature Lodge** Page 365. Offers fishing from a 7m Yamaha vessel, kitted out with electronics & echo sounder, & sometimes ranging

as far as 8km offshore. This is suitable for 2 serious fishermen, or 3 if they know each other, & needs to be booked in advance (*US$250pp/day, plus fuel & lures; equipment hire US$50pp/day*). Trolling, fly fishing, spinning gear & vertical jigging rods are all available for rent.

🎣**The Manta Resort** Page 365. Offers low-key fishing trips (*US$75/hr*) & locally guided handline trips on board its dhow (*US$30*). Deep-sea fishing trips can be arranged for serious anglers (*US$770/1050 ½/full day*), or on an hourly rate (*US$295/1st hr*) if you want give it a go.

KAYAKING All the larger tourist lodges and hotels have kayaks, with short guided trips offered by **Fundu Lagoon** for their guests. The **Manta Resort** offers kayak safaris (*US$30pp*), while at **Swahili Divers** (page 348), marine anthropologist Cisca Jah runs kayak tours under the name Kasa Kayaking. A half-day guided mangrove tour with snacks and support boat costs US$70.

CHAKE CHAKE

Chake Chake is the largest town on Pemba, just over halfway down the western side of the island. The island's capital and administrative centre, it forms the hub of the bus and dalla dalla network. Although Chake Chake has been settled for as long as Zanzibar Town, it has never achieved the same degree of importance, and thus has little in the way of grand palaces or the winding narrow streets of Stone Town, although part of the Omani Fort, near the hospital, is open to the public as a very informative museum.

When the first edition of this guide was researched in the early 1990s, Chake Chake – and Pemba itself – was a sleepy backwater. Today, it's a bustling community with more than a hint of modernity: there are a couple of phone shops, and many of the tin-roofed houses have sprouted satellite dishes. In other ways, though, it's still very quiet and traditional, with ox-carts trundling up the high street (although there are even more scooters). The market, around the bus station, is lively, and the old port, down the hill from the town centre, is also worth a walk. Down the back streets, particularly on the road opposite the market, are countless shops selling everything from foodstuffs and car parts to plastic mops and all types of clothing. In tiny booths, tailors will knock you up a suit or skirt on an ancient treadle sewing machine. The whole place is more peaceful than Zanzibar Town, with a laidback atmosphere, and tourists get no hassle at all, just friendly hellos or shy waves from children, so it's great just to stroll around.

TRAVEL AND TOUR COMPANIES The tourist who arrives in Chake Chake in the hope of organising something on the fly could well be disappointed, since the town is less geared to visitors than in the past.

Azam Marine Next to the market, this is the main agent for ferries to Zanzibar (page 341).
Coastal Travels 📞024 245 2162; 📱 0777 418343; ⏰ 07.30–17.00. This helpful bureau, almost next to Barclays, is set up to handle

bookings of Coastal Aviation flights between Pemba & Zanzibar, Tanga & Dar.
Coral Tours 📞024 245 2045; 📱 0777 437397; ✉ coralnasa@yahoo.com; ⏰ 08.00–16.00 daily. Enthusiastic & incredibly helpful Pemban manager

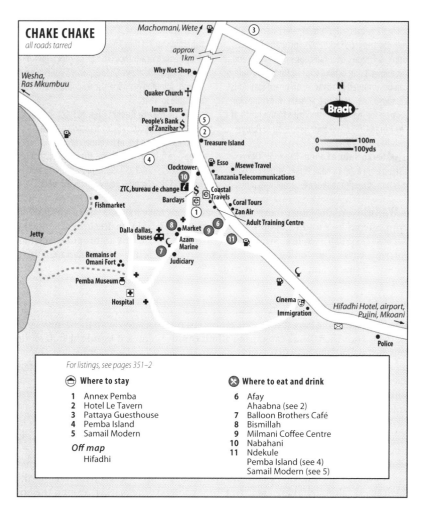

CHAKE CHAKE
all roads tarred

Machomani, Wete

approx 1km

Why Not Shop

Wesha, Ras Mkumbuu

Quaker Church

Imara Tours
People's Bank of Zanzibar

Treasure Island

N

Bradt

0 — 100m
0 — 100yds

Clocktower
Esso · Msewe Travel
Tanzania Telecommunications
ZTC, bureau de change
Coastal Travels
Barclays
Coral Tours
Fishmarket
Zan Air
Adult Training Centre
Dalla dallas, buses
Market
Azam Marine
Jetty
Remains of Omani Fort
Judiciary
Pemba Museum
Hospital
Cinema
Immigration
Hifadhi Hotel, airport, Pujini, Mkoani
Police

For listings, see pages 351–2

⬠ **Where to stay**
1 Annex Pemba
2 Hotel Le Tavern
3 Pattaya Guesthouse
4 Pemba Island
5 Samail Modern
Off map
    Hifadhi

✖ **Where to eat and drink**
6   Afay
    Ahaabna (see 2)
7   Balloon Brothers Café
8   Bismillah
9   Milmani Coffee Centre
10 Nabahani
11 Ndekule
    Pemba Island (see 4)
    Samail Modern (see 5)

Nassor has been running Coral Tours since 2000 & has built up extensive local knowledge of everything from dalla dalla routes to up-to-date road conditions. He's happy to give out tourist information & book all manner of accommodation, tours & tickets, plus car, motorbike & bicycle hire. A whole day trip to the north of the island including Kidike, Ngezi Forest & Vumawimbi Beach, plus lunch & an English-speaking guide costs US$55pp, but is cheaper if you can get a group together. He also books ferry & flight tickets. The shop can be found on the ground floor of the ZTC building opposite the adult training centre.
Imara Tours & Travel ✆024 245 2648; m 0777 842084; e info@imaratours.com; f Imaratours; ◷ 08.00–15.30 Mon–Fri, 08.00–14.00 Sat,

09.00–13.00 Sun. Located on Chachani St, next door to the People's Bank of Zanzibar, Imara offers a range of tours & water-based activities on Pemba as well as ferry & flight bookings, car hire & bike hire (*US$20/day*). They try hard to be environmentally aware & community focused.
Msewe Travel ✆024 245 2774; e msewetours@ gmail.com; f MseweTravelLtd. Managed by the very friendly & enthusiastic Kassim, Msewe is down a tiny side street just across the road from Barclays Bank. The office provides lots of information on excursions, flights, ferries, diving, bullfighting & transfers can be found, as well as safari options on the mainland, which are arranged through their Arusha office. They have a further base in Pemba Airport. Full-day tours of Pemba cost around US$90 for 2 people.

ZanAir ✆024 245 4990; m 0775 044101. The booking office for ZanAir flights is just down the hill from Barclays Bank, diagonally across from Coastal Travels.

🏠 **WHERE TO STAY** *Map, opposite, unless otherwise stated*

Chake Chake's renowned Old Mission Lodge, for years the home of Swahili Divers and a first-rate hangout for laidback scuba enthusiasts, closed its doors when owners Raf and Cisca Jah moved their operation north to Gecko Nature Lodge (page 365). This left something of an accommodation vacuum for a while, though fortunately there are now a few central alternatives, of which the Samail or Hifadhi are probably your best bet. One by one, the small collection of clean and basic guesthouses just north of town have closed down, leaving just one, plus a newer resort further along the coast in Wesha.

In town
Mid range

🏠 **Annex Pemba Hotel** (15 rooms) ✆024 245 2216; m 0777 428303/90041; e pembaislandhotel@yahoo.com. The sister hotel to Pemba Island, this is another strict Muslim establishment with no alcohol allowed & a marriage certificate compulsory for couples. Rooms are spread over 3 floors leading off a central communal area with a sofa & a TV, which also doubles as reception. Shiny yellow-&-orange tiled floors & white walls enclose simple fan-cooled rooms with mosquito nets & shaky old TVs. The bathroom is so small that the toilet is underneath the shower head. Guests are welcome to use the rooftop restaurant at the Pemba Hotel. **$$$**

🏠 **Pemba Island Hotel** (16 rooms) ✆024 245 2215; e pembaislandhotel@yahoo.com. This clean hotel is a welcoming & pleasant place to stay in the centre of town. Painted white with bright pink decorative tiles, it's easy to spot just down the hill from the People's Bank of Zanzibar. En-suite rooms have dbl beds (even the 'singles') with AC/fans, mossie nets, TV & fridge; splashes of colour come from pink curtains, red plastic chairs & green bathrooms. In keeping with the hotel's strict Muslim ethos, no alcohol is permitted on the premises, & a marriage certificate is required for a couple to share a room. Rooftop restaurant. **$$$**

🏠 **Hifadhi Hotel & Conference Centre** (14 rooms) m 0654 473772; e reservation@hifadhihotel.com; 📷 HifadhiHotel. In pale blue & white, with banks of mirrored windows, this has the look of a hospital yet offers 'comfortable modern chick accommodation'. 15mins from the airport, it's certainly one of Chake Chake's better options, if not exactly glamorous. Clean rooms all have Zanzibari beds with heavy bedspreads & en-suite bathrooms,

& it does benefit from a swimming pool. With self-proclaimed '5* luxury at 3* prices without cutting corners', it's worth a try if you have to stay in town, just accept that you may be the only one staying who's not attending a conference: there are 3 conference rooms here. **$$–$$$**

Budget

🏠 **Hotel Le Tavern** (8 rooms); ✆024 245 2660. On the main street, opposite the People's Bank of Zanzibar, Le Tavern is above a small row of shops – look for the blue-&-white-striped awning. If you're asking for directions here, forget French; it's pronounced 'lay' Tavern. Clean, en-suite rooms with sgl beds have nets, fans & crackling TVs (local channels only), but are in desperate need of a fresh coat of paint. Meals to order for around US$5. **$$**

🏠 **Samail Modern Hotel & Restaurant** (16 rooms) m 0776 627619/0718 010960; e samailmodernhotel@yahoo.com. Opened in 2012, Samail is next door to Le Tavern in a freshly painted 3-storey building. The bright restaurant serves a selection of spiced chicken & fish dishes with rice or biriyani (*US$3.50*) on glass-topped tables. Cakes, bread & fresh fruit juices make for quick snacks & there's even an ice-cream machine. Upstairs, spacious rooms are cooled by both AC & fans, & all have TVs; bathrooms are fine & functional. **$$**

Out of town
Upmarket

🏠 **Pemba Misali Sunset Beach** [map, page 338] (20 villas) ✆024 223 3882; m 0775 044717; e pembabeach@oceangrouphotel.com 📷 misalisunset. North of Chake Chake, near the village of Wesha, Pemba Misali Sunset Beach's row of pea-green villas occupies a pretty waterfront spot, with sea views for all, albeit mangrove not powder-sand beaches. The interior is neutral with, wooden king or twin beds & a shiny white bathroom. AC, ceiling fans & mosquito nets are standard, as are shuttered, handcrafted louvre doors. There's plenty of privacy & space, & outside is a small terrace. Cantilevered over the sea, the restaurant offers sunset views while serving up a buffet mix of Swahili & European meals along with the fisherman's daily catch, although sadly reviews of food quality & service have not been great of late. Diving is arranged through the onsite dive centre & all sorts of local trips can be organised. Camping facilities are also available. B&B. **$$$$**

Shoestring

☝ **Pattaya Guesthouse** (6 rooms) m 0773 172445. This simple local guesthouse is fine if you want a feel of Pemban suburban living. Rooms, 1 of which is en suite, have nets & ceiling fans, & are named after local football teams. To get here, head north out of town, then take the first major right turn you come to – look out for the big white wall with railings on the top. Pattaya Lodge is signposted on your left, about 20m from the junction. Simple suppers of chicken & rice cost US$4 & must be ordered in advance. B&B. **$–$$**

✖ WHERE TO EAT AND DRINK *Map, page 350*

All the hotels and guesthouses listed above will serve meals to non-residents, although normally food has to be ordered several hours in advance. Elsewhere, most of the town's street restaurants open from approximately 07.00 until 15.00, when the market closes.

There's no shortage of street stalls around the market or on the main road near Le Tavern selling simple hot food during these hours, with chipsi mai yai at US$1, beans and rice for around US$1.30, or chicken and rice at US$3. In the same area around the road junction, more small stalls open up in the evening, selling food such as fried fish and chapattis.

✖ **Pemba Island Hotel** ⏰ 07.00–10.00 & 19.00–22.00. A large TV dominates this hotel's pleasant rooftop restaurant, which boasts views across the town to the trees beyond. For evening meals, you'll need to order ahead. Food available includes vegetable dishes (rice US$2) & chicken curry at US$6. Soft drinks only. **$$–$$$**

✖ **Ahaabna** On the top floor of Le Tavern (page 351), this dinner-only restaurant serves a simple rice dish – pilau or biryani – with accompanying chicken or fish. **$$**

✖ **Bismillah** This is one of the better small places around the market, & is good for a no-frills lunch. **$$**

✖ **Samail Modern Hotel & Restaurant** m 0776 627619. Samail's modern ground-floor restaurant cunningly displays its cakes & ice cream in the window to tempt in passers-by. For something more substantial, hot meals such as spiced chicken & fish dishes are served with rice or biriyani (*US$3.50*). No alcohol. **$$**

✖ **Afay Restaurant** Popular with local people, central Afay is often open till around 22.00, with the terrace closing at 19.00, depending on trade & whether there's any food left. It serves good tea & offers pleasant service. **$**

✖ **Balloon Brothers Café** Market St. Close to the market, this is a reliable spot for street food, with a good range of snacks on offer: samosas, cake, popcorn, *ubuyu* (sugar-coated baobab fruit) & *chiahoro* (like Bombay mix), as well as more substantial dishes, notably the *mishkaki* (marinated meat skewers) or *chipsi kasava* (fried cassava chips) which are so good they inspire long queues during the lunch hour. To one side of the stand, a small seating area is available for diners. **$**

✖ **Nabahani Restaurant** Misufuni St. m 0777 460414. A friendly local choice next to Barclays Bank, Nabahani serves chicken & dumplings, curry & rice, soup, biriyani & omelettes for around US$2. It even does take-away. **$**

✖ **Ndekule Restaurant** Set among the shops in the town centre, this is a good, local-style place, clean & tidy with wipe-clean plastic tables. There's usually only a few choices, such as chicken & chips or fish & rice (or vice versa) for about US$1. If you stroll in at lunchtime you should find something ready, while for those in a hurry there's a small take-away stand outside. **$**

☕ **Milmani Coffee Centre** Down a narrow side street between Afay & Ndekule, Milmani serves freshly brewed spiced coffees for just TSh100. **$**

SHOPPING Chake Chake's **market** is in the centre of town, around the bus station. In the narrow streets leading away from the market, small shops sell an almost infinite variety of goods. If you're craving *mzungu* food, look no further than the **Why Not** shop at the northern end of town, where the likes of chocolate, cereal, biscuits, cheese triangles and even Pringles may be in stock. The more basic shop on Wete Street, **Chake-Chake Needs,** sells a similar if smaller selection.

OTHER PRACTICALITIES
Post and internet The post office is on the way into town from Mkoani, on the left-hand side. For internet users, Chake Chake's **Adult Training Centre** (⏰ 07.30–22.00; TSh1,000/hr), opposite Coral Tours, has five computers and is the most reliable internet café in town. Alternatively, **Tawasul Internet** is found opposite the NMB bank, and there are a couple of computers at **Naeem Telecommunication** next to Chake Chake Library, both costing TSh1,000 per hour.

WHAT TO SEE AND DO Chake Chake itself has a dusty charm that repays a walk through its small market, and around its narrow streets and alleys crowded with shops selling a wide range of goods. Definitely worth a visit is the informative **Pemba Museum** (⏰ 08.30–16.30 Mon–Fri, 09.00–16.00 Sat/Sun; admission US$3). Located in part of the town's 18th-century Arab fort, it retains the original wooden door, but other features were lost during restoration, and the cannons at the entrance came from Wete. Diverting exhibits are clearly laid out on five broad themes, covering every aspect of Pemba's history, economy and culture. Of particular interest are the display on the ruins of Pemba, and the room on the island's maritime history and boatbuilding, complete with a model of a *mtepe* – a boat made of coconut rope, with sticks for nails and a sail of palm leaves, that was in use until the 1930s; the original is in the House of Wonders in Zanzibar Town (pages 163–5). In addition to exhibitions on politics, fishing and farming, and a jailhouse (the fort was at one time Pemba's prison), there is also a considerable amount of space devoted to Swahili society. Several rooms are set out like the interior of a Swahili house, complete with relevant furniture and implements for cooking, while related displays focus on individual aspects of Swahili culture, from initiation and burial rituals to the use of herbal plants and traditional musical instruments. In the final archives room, researchers will delight in papers that have been painstakingly boxed and labelled.

AROUND CHAKE CHAKE While most places in Pemba are within easy reach of Chake Chake, there are a few places of interest that are particularly well placed for those staying in the town.

Essential oils factory (*admission US$2*) At this factory, oils are extracted from a variety of plants – cloves, of course, but others include citronella and eucalyptus. Interestingly, spent cloves are used to power the burners – a guide can tell you about the production process. To get there, head north out of Chake Chake to the village of Machomani, then turn right towards Vitongoji; it's a 10–15-minute drive from the town centre, or you could take dalla dalla No 316. You could combine this with a trip to the attractive, baobab-fringed beaches of Makoba, Vitongoji or Liko La Ngezi, the closest being Makoba at 2km from town. The waters are rocky here, so time is best spent walking, relaxing and taking pictures.

Kidike Flying Fox Sanctuary (m *0777 472941;* ☺ *09.00–18.00 daily; admission US$5/1 adult/child*) Home to more than half of Pemba's flying foxes, Kidike is a shared initiative between villagers and the government. Located about 7km north of Chake Chake, it is clearly signposted from the main road. Several tour operators run trips here, and individual drivers charge around US$25 from Chake Chake, including entrance. Alternatively, you can take a dalla dalla from Chake Chake, and then walk the 45 minutes or so along the 3.5km track to the reserve. At the reserve, a local guide will show you the pathways through the forest to see the flying foxes roosting in the treetops, feeding and, of course, flying overhead with their distinctive silhouette. There are close to 4,000 undisturbed animals here, making it an impressive sight for wildlife enthusiasts and photographers.

Pujini Ruins The remains of a fortified palace built around the 15th century by Swahili people, these lie about 10km to the southeast of Chake Chake, near the village of Pujini. Locally the place is called Mkame Ndume, meaning 'milker of men', derived from the name of a reputedly despotic king who ordered the palace walls be built by local inhabitants who were forced to carry large stones while shuffling on their buttocks.

Today, the ruins of the palace cover an area of about 1.5ha, and the remains of the defensive ramparts and surrounding ditches can still be seen, although much of the area is overgrown. The ditch was once connected to the sea by a 1km-long channel. Inside the walls, a team of archaeologists working here since the mid 1990s have found remnants of three large buildings, and an underground shrine with plaster bas-reliefs on the walls, and several other features. It is also possible to see some wide stairways that presumably allowed access to the defensive ramparts, the remains of a walkway that joined the town to the shore, and the site of the well. Legend tells of a wall that was built across the well so that the ruler's two wives, who lived in separate parts of the palace, would never meet if they came to get water at the same time.

The ramparts are the most interesting feature of the Pujini Ruins, in that they can be seen and appreciated by any visitor, and also because there is nothing else like them at any other Swahili site along the east African coast. They were built when the Swahili civilisation was at its zenith, and when the presence of Portuguese ships in the area posed a very real threat. It seems, however, that the walls may not have been strong enough to withstand the invaders: some Portuguese records dating from the 1520s mention the sacking of a fortified 'treasury' on the east coast of Pemba.

Archaeological evidence suggests that, although the palace may have fallen on hard times after this invasion, it remained occupied (or was possibly re-occupied) and was only finally abandoned in the 19th century. Remains of other buildings, including a mosque, have been found in the area around the palace, suggesting that it did not stand alone, and that a town or larger settlement also existed here – possibly for many centuries.

Getting there and away You can **walk** the 8km or so from Chake Chake to the Pujini Ruins and back in a day, or take **bus** Route 319 as far as Pujini village, but it is easier to travel by **hired bike** or **car**. To get there, leave Chake Chake on the road south, and turn left onto a dirt road just after the tar road turns off to the airport. Follow the dirt road to a fork near a small dispensary, where you go left. At the next junction, go right to reach a flat grassy area which is usually wet. The ruins are amongst the trees and bushes on the far side of the grassy area. If you get lost, ask for directions to Mkame Ndume.

Ras Mkumbuu Ruins The headland of Ras Mkumbuu is at the end of a long peninsula about 14km to the west of Chake Chake. The relatively well-preserved ruins are at the tip of the peninsula and also seem to be called Ndagoni (although Mkumbuu and Ndagoni may have been different places). This is the site of a Swahili settlement, thought to have been one of the largest towns on the coast (and in East Africa) during the 11th century. It is also considered to be the site of the earlier port of Qanbalu, where Omani sailors traded in slaves and timber.

Today, the remains of a large 13th-century mosque can still be seen, although they are becoming very overgrown, and there are also several 14th-century pillar tombs, graves with a tall 'chimney' at one end, used to mark the burial place of prominent Muslims. Pillar tombs are found in other parts of East Africa and are held to be one of the most distinctive forms of monument built by the Swahili people. The tombs here are in poor condition, although an inscription on one states that they were restored in 1916.

Getting there The easiest and most enjoyable way to reach the ruins is by **hired boat** from Wesha or on an **organised tour** – which may also visit Misali Island (pages 356–8) on the same day. Near the ruins is a small fishing village, and to reach the mosque and tombs you walk through maize fields and a plantation of tall palms with smooth white trunks. A road from Chake Chake leads westwards along the peninsula towards Ras Mkumbuu, but it becomes impassable and turns into a track for the final 5km, which is negotiable only on foot or by bike.

SOUTH OF CHAKE CHAKE

The main road from Chake Chake south to Mkoani follows a winding route through hilly terrain covered by an abundance of fruit trees, interspersed by villages at every turn. Bananas grow freely, with jackfruit, passion fruit, breadfruit, mango and papaya all very much in evidence. In season, cloves lie drying on mats by the side of the road, their scent pervading the air. Look out in particular for the trees to the east of the road that are home to the Pemba flying fox.

MKOANI Mkoani is the smallest of Pemba's three main towns, but the passenger-boat services linking it to Zanzibar Town and the mainland make the port the busiest and most important on the island. Any time a boat is docking or leaving there's a buzz in the air, and perhaps the opportunity to watch boats being loaded with cloves for Zanzibar, but for the rest of the time Mkoani is very quiet and sleepy. Although a few businesses are located near the port, and the market is just along the coast, the main town of Mkoani is up the hill towards Chake Chake. A footpath leads up some steps from opposite the port towards the town, cutting out the bends. The deserted port area is unlit at night and it's not advisable to walk there unaccompanied.

Where to stay and eat For some visitors, Mkoani remains the main gateway to Pemba, and a couple of local guesthouses cater for this, but the closure of some in recent years reflects the increasing reliance by visitors on air travel. Places to eat are equally very limited. There's a small restaurant close to the hospital, at the eastern end of town, but that's pretty much it. A couple of stalls sell fruit, sweets and biscuits for the passing boat-passenger trade.

Zanzibar Ocean Panorama (4 rooms)
\024 245 6166; m 0773 545418; e booking@
oceanpanorama-zanzibar.com; www.
oceanpanorama-zanzibar.com. This hotel's
name was obviously inspired by the excellent
sea view from its advantageous location high
up on a hill. Don't let the ramshackle exterior of
the bungalows put you off; inside, the rooms are
better than expected, with stone floors, Zanzibari
beds, a desk & chair, fan & AC, a fridge, & en-suite
showers. Outside, each has a tidy terrace with a
hammock facing the sea. There is also a cheap &
cheerful dorm room. B/fast is served in the shaded
restaurant at neatly laid plastic tables (other meals
with advanced notice; dinner US$15). **$–$$**

Other practicalities

Almost next to the quay, Mkoani's port office (⏲ *08.00–15.30 daily*) sells tickets for the ferries to Zanzibar Island (page 341). Aside from the hospital, towards the eastern end of town, Mkoani has very little to offer the visitor. A couple of communications centres lie on the road near the port, and in the centre of Mkoani is the post office and a small shop selling groceries, towards the north of town.

WAMBAA The small village of Wambaa is to the north of Mkoani. Nearby is the long and idyllic Wambaa Beach, facing southwest overlooking Mkoani Bay and out towards the Pemba Channel. At its northern end lies Pemba's most exclusive hotel, Fundu Lagoon.

Where to stay and eat   *Map, page 338*

✳ ⌂ **Fundu Lagoon** (18 rooms) +44 (0)870
240 6008 (UK); m 0774 438668; e reservations@
fundulagoon.com; www.fundulagoon.com; ⏲ mid
Jun–mid Apr. Just 15mins by boat from Mkoani,
it's not difficult to see why honeymooners & retired
couples flock to this secluded lodge. Combining the
flexibility of a hotel with the individuality of a smaller
lodge, it's a relaxed hideaway on the beach with
attentive service & a lively atmosphere. Linked to the
central area by sandy walkways, tented rooms nestle
among the trees to form the core of each carefully
designed, thatched bungalow. Interiors are simple:
natural wicker & wood furniture, white bedding & a
small en-suite bathroom with a range of handmade
aromatherapy toiletries, created for the hotel. Each
bungalow has its own veranda: either a few steps
from the beach or facing out to sea from the hillside.
The suites also offer a private plunge pool, whilst
the superior suites have a 2-storey lounge area. The
restaurant serves 3-course meals – fish dishes are a
speciality – & tables overlook the beach; light bites
& cocktails are served in the breezy jetty bar. There
are also regular BBQ & Swahili nights, complete with
traditional & very enthusiastic singing & dancing.
When it comes to activities, snorkelling, kayaking
& fishing are on offer, & there's a fully equipped
dive centre (page 347). Rather less strenuous are
the sunset dhow cruises, boat trips to Misali Island
& poolside loungers with panoramic ocean views.
There's also a popular treatment room with a wide
range of massages & beauty treatments (*US$20–
175*), a games room with satellite TV & central Wi-Fi
zone. Excursions to the village of Wambaa can be
arranged, as can hair braiding, & in the evenings
a local lady is on hand to give free henna tattoos.
It's quite isolated here but that's part of the appeal.
It's also fairly relaxed, & bare feet are actively
encouraged. It's worth noting that researchers for this
book & holidaymakers have consistently disagreed
over the quality of the finishing & food. FB. ☕

MISALI ISLAND Misali (also spelt Mesali) Island lies to the west of Chake Chake town, an easy boat ride from Chake Chake or Mkoani. Surrounded by a coral reef, it's a popular destination for tourists, with some idyllic beaches, trails through virgin forests, good swimming, and even better snorkelling, with clear shallow water, and a good display of corals. It's also a favourite spot for divers. Misali is the only island around Pemba to be accessible in all tides, although low tide is necessary for visiting the caves. No overnight stays are allowed, except for researchers, who need special authorisation to do so.

The island is covered in forest, with a mix of evergreen and deciduous species, and most notably many large baobabs. Vervet monkeys cavort among the branches, peering down at visitors. Birds to be spotted here include red-eyed dove, mangrove kingfisher, paradise flycatcher, Pemba white-eye and Pemba sunbird. Fischer's turaco has also been recorded. An increasing number of green sea turtles are successfully nesting on the beach on the western side of the island, with hawksbill turtles also present.

Locally, Misali has 'holy island' status. When the Prophet Hadhara found himself without a prayer mat, it is said that he made use instead of the teardrop-shaped island which faces Mecca; the word *msala* means 'prayer mat'. The strong Islamic environmental stewardship ethic is being used to support management and environmental education, and the island was a 'sacred gift for a living planet' from the Islamic faith as part of a millennium celebration organised by WWF in 2000.

The notorious pirate Captain Kidd is reputed to have had a hideout on the island in the 17th century, and even to have buried treasure here. Today, the island and the surrounding reef are incorporated in the government-owned Misali Island Marine Conservation Area, under the auspices of the Misali Island Management Committee. Formed as a partnership between the Zanzibar government, the local fishermen's association and the Pemba Ecological Conservation Authority (PECA), with support from CARE International, the committee is dominated by fishermen, while the rangers, who can also offer guided island tours, are employed by PECA. It's not entirely satisfactory, with considerable concerns locally about infringements of the no-take zone to the west of the island, and armed soldiers have recently been introduced to support the rangers. In its previous incarnation as MICA (Misali Island Conservation Association), PECA's authority covered a smaller area. With the change to MICA, a larger area is still covered by the same number of rangers, whose workload has now escalated while their motivation has decreased.

Almost two-thirds of the revenue from visitors goes towards managing the island, with the rest earmarked for community development. Conservation measures involve the input of local fishermen, who can continue working here in a managed environment. As just one example of how the scheme is working, local fishermen are prevented from camping on the beach itself (they camp among the trees), so as not to disturb turtles nesting. Additionally, the nests are monitored and protected, along with the rest of the island, by the rangers.

Just 1.4km long, and covering a total area of 90ha, the island consists of 15,000-year-old uplifted coral, with a surrounding coral reef to a maximum depth of 64m. Mangroves fringe much of the island, making a fascinating place for snorkelling during spring high tides. A series of walking trails has been established through the forest, where there are three caves that are considered sacred. In time of need, local people would come to one of the caves with a witchdoctor to pray for help, making payment in the form of a chicken, a goat or even a cow. It takes about 2½ hours to walk round the island (at low tide only), taking in an intertidal trail to the west of the island. At the landing point for visitors, there is a shaded information centre, with benches for picnics, rudimentary toilets and displays on what to see with a good map showing the various trails. On the beach in front, a few sunbeds and umbrellas have been set out, but banish all thoughts of commercialism – it remains a tranquil spot visited by just a few people at any one time.

Getting there and away Misali Island can be reached by **hired boat** from Chake Chake or Mkoani (page 344). There are also **organised excursions** run by various local tour operators, as well as by individual hotels for their guests. In addition, a few of the dive centres based in the northern part of Zanzibar Island run trips here. Occasionally, the island is also visited by groups from passing cruise ships and live-aboards.

Some unlicensed **fishing boats** run to the island, but few have life jackets or backup engines. One that does is the *Victoria*, owned by Captain Hamoud, who can be found at Chake Chake's port area of Wesha.

CHOKOCHO Through forested hills southwest of the main tar road, Chokocho is a remote valley village, beside a natural harbour, and the stepping-off point for Emerald Bay.

Where to stay and eat *Map, page 338*

Emerald Bay (7 rooms) m 0789 759698/0777 979667; e info@emeraldbay.co.tz; www.emeraldbay.co.tz. This friendly, low-key resort lies in an undeveloped part of the island. The 3-storey central area, complete with its castellated roof terrace, is traditionally built with white Omani arches & red concrete floors, with spacious, dbl-storey makuti-roof rooms either side. Inside, they are plainly decorated with chunky wood furniture, & are equipped with fan, en-suite bathroom & small veranda. There is a new mosaic swimming pool, along with a few simple makuti umbrellas & coir loungers in front of the main hotel area for much-needed cooling off. Sea swimming is not possible directly in front of the hotel, which is predominantly mangrove, but complimentary trips are offered daily to nearby picture-perfect sandbanks. Be warned, there is a lack of shade on these trips so hats, T-shirts & plenty of suncream are strongly advised. Meals here receive regular praise, & the terrace dining area offers lovely bay views. Otherwise, this is a quiet, remote spot & not a place for jam-packed days of activities or long beach walks. HB/FB. **$$$**

SHAMIANI ISLAND Surrounded by mangroves, Shamiani Island, also called Kiweni Island, is a remote and beautiful spot east of Mkoani, just 100m or so off the far southeastern tip of Pemba Island. Shamiani was originally settled by Persian immigrants in the 17th century, who built the island's first mosque, the ruins of which can still be visited. Shamiani's population of around 150 families rely on fishing and farming for their livelihood and live in just one small village with a school, a doctor and a mosque. Until recently there were no visitors, as the island was accessible only to the very determined. Now, the development of a new, eco-friendly lodge brings a smattering of tourists, providing income and employment to the island, as well as endless fascination to the local children, still not used to the unfamiliar ways of the *mzungu*. The tourist industry on the island is still in the fledgling stages, and there's no electricity, cars or bikes on the island, just boats.

Getting there and away Travel to Shamiani involves taking some form of transport from Chake Chake to the village of Kengeja, reached by branching off the main Mkoani to Chake Chake road at Mtambile. Then from either Mpene or Kiwimbini harbours, both located on small inlets south of Kengeja, locals wade across but visitors sail across to Dongoni, Shamiani's access point. Guests heading to Pemba Lodge will have the entire transfer from Chake Chake organised by the lodge.

Where to stay and eat *Map, page 338*

Pemba Lodge (5 bungalows) ☏ 024 224 0494/024 224 0496; m 0777 415551/0655 417070; e info@pembalodge.com; www. pembalodge.com; ☉ May–Mar. Pemba Lodge is the vision of enthusiastic Pemban Nassor Ali, owner of the popular Mnarani Beach Cottages on

Zanzibar (page 212), who tries hard to be 'eco'. Built on remote Shamiani Island, just off the southern coast, it attracts those seeking both privacy & R&R, & has been designed to create minimum environmental impact. Inspiration has been taken from Chumbe Island's excellent example of how an eco lodge can work & some of the staff have trained there, as well as at Mnarani. The 4 dbl & 1 family timber-frame bungalows are constructed from natural materials, with makuti thatch, woven palm walls & locally crafted coconut wood & recycled dhow furniture. Features include not just solar-powered lighting (which can make the room seem a little dark), hot water, & composting toilets, but also a building design that harnesses the breeze from the Pemba Channel, obviating the need for energy-guzzling AC. No plastic bottles are used & rainwater is collected in a 10,000-litre reservoir. Access to the lodge is an adventure in itself: arrive by traditional (though motorised) boat through the mangroves, passing sailing villagers & children heading for school, schoolbooks held above their heads as they wade across at low tide. Boats dock at Dongoni in a low or neap tide & it's

a hot & hard 20min walk over unforgiving coral rock to the lodge, with luggage carried by porter or ox-cart. For all other tides the boats can land right on the beach. Dinner is 'catch of the day' cooked over a gas flame; filtered drinking water is free in the bar, there's an honesty bar & all non-alcoholic drinks are included in the rates. There's no pool, but the beach is simply stunning, with white sand & turquoise sea; it's also blissfully deserted. When the tide's in, kayaking trips can be undertaken in the mangroves. There's also a 30ft catamaran with 2 cabins, based between here & Mnarani in Nungwi. For something more cultural, try a Pemban cooking class or a trip to the local village. The lodge is heavily involved with the conservation of green turtles – they pay compensation to the fishermen for any caught up in fishing nets that are brought in. These turtles are put in a tidal lake to breed & groups are released every 6 months, an event that guests are welcome to get involved in. There is very slow dial-up internet here but do not rely on it; instead come for ecological sensibility & peace & quiet on a deserted beach. FB. ♛

WETE

The second-largest town on Pemba, Wete is at the head of a large inlet on the west coast, in the northern part of the island. Spread out down a long central street, it's quieter than Chake Chake, with more ox-carts and fewer mopeds. For most travellers Wete is a good base for exploring northern Pemba: from here Tumbe, the Chwaka Ruins, Konde and Ngezi Forest can all be easily reached. The people are exceptionally friendly and willing to assist, although as most just pass through on their way to the northern resorts, you'll more than likely be the only foreigner in town.

Wete has a large harbour, mainly used by cargo ships and dhows. It can sometimes be busy here, with vessels from Tanga offloading cement or timber, and loading up with cloves, coconuts or other Pemban commodities. Local ferries also sail across the inlet to Mtambwe Island, where you can get to the ruins of Mtambwe Mkuu, and to Fundo Island.

GETTING THERE AND AROUND North of Chake Chake, the dense vegetation of the south gives way to open pasture and scrubland. The main road bypasses Wete entirely as it hugs the eastern side of the island, but it is still the quickest route between the two towns. The turn-off to Wete is about 20km from Chake Chake at the village of Chwale. From here it's a reasonable, intermittently tarred road to Mzambaroani, past the rubber plantation where what look like old flannels are hung out on racks to dry in the sun, before winding the last few kilometres to Wete.

If you want to reach the places of interest around Wete independently, Royal Tours can help with **car hire** and the Sharook brothers (page 360) can hire out **bikes** for US$30 per day.

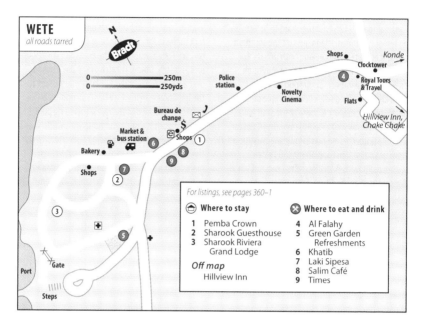

WETE
all roads tarred

0 ——— 250m
0 ——— 250yds

Shops
Konde
Clocktower
Royal Tours & Travel
④
Police station
Flats
Novelty Cinema
Hillview Inn, Chake Chake
Bureau de change
Market & bus station
Shops ①
⑥
Bakery
⑧
⑨
Shops
⑦
②
③
⑤
Gate
Port
Steps

For listings, see pages 360–1

🏠 **Where to stay**
1 Pemba Crown
2 Sharook Guesthouse
3 Sharook Riviera
    Grand Lodge
Off map
    Hillview Inn

⊗ **Where to eat and drink**
4 Al Falahy
5 Green Garden
    Refreshments
6 Khatib
7 Laki Sipesa
8 Salim Café
9 Times

Travel and tour companies Various shacks and shops along the main street advertise that they sell ferry tickets, but the only tour operator is **Royal Tours & Travel** (m *0778 143426/0777 429244*; e *royaltours@live.com*). Up in the north of town, this helpful office handles everything from tour guiding services, flights, hotels, Pemba tours, diving and snorkelling and it sells tickets for the fast ferries. Good English is spoken, as long as the manager is in.

For additional services, the **Sharook Guesthouse** (below) offers a good range of tours: a boat ride to Mtambwe Mkuu Ruins costs US$5 per person; a minibus to Ngezi Forest costs US$35. Highly recommended all-day trips to Fundo Island cost US$30 for the whole motorboat (seating up to ten) or slightly less for a dhow; or you can go to Misali Island for US$55.

🏠 **WHERE TO STAY** *Map, above*

🏠 **Pemba Crown Hotel** (12 rooms) 🤙024 245 4191; m 0777 493667/0773 336867; e pembacrown@gmail.com/sales@pembacrown. com; www.pembacrown.com. Right in the centre of Wete, Pemba Crown is a striking, white, 3-storey hotel above a row of shops on the main street, & remains Wete's best accommodation option. Rooms are comfortable, bathrooms clean & functional, & the staff smiley & helpful, albeit with limited foreign-language skills. Spotless bedrooms come with AC, fans & TVs, while colour is added by pretty linen. Soaps are even provided– a rarity in Wete's basic guesthouses. All rooms have a large balcony overlooking a busy (& sometimes noisy) street, & it's interesting to see people going about their everyday business. B/fast is generally the only meal

served; however, with a day's notice, a Swahili dinner of curry & rice can be arranged. B&B. **$$**

🏠 **Sharook Guesthouse** (4 rooms) 🤙024 245 4386; e sharookguest@yahoo.com; www. pembaliving.com/sharook_guesthouse.html. Owned & run by brothers Sharook & Ismail, this long-standing guesthouse is in the lower part of town, on a quiet side street near the market & bus station. It's a small, family-run place with a peaceful & friendly atmosphere. With its own generator, it offers constant running water & functioning TV. Dinner (*US$10*), with local dishes, must be ordered well in advance, & is served in front of the TV in the dining room. Bike hire (*US$10/day*) can be arranged, as can a range of tours around the island. B&B. **$$**

🛏 **Sharook Riviera Grand Lodge** (8 rooms)
📞 024 245 4076; e sharookguest@yahoo.com;
www. pembaliving.com/annex_to_sharook.
html. Located in a sleepy, residential area
overlooking the harbour, this rather impressive-
sounding annex to Sharook Guesthouse is not
nearly as magnificent as the name suggests.
The building itself is more recently constructed
though, & inside sgl & dbl rooms plus a dorm are
filled with Zanzibari beds covered in colourful
bedspreads, & have a fan, AC & an en-suite
bathroom with hot water. The communal space
is made up of the b/fast room & a lounge with a
computer & TV. Meals can be ordered in advance
& are freshly prepared; juices, water & soft drinks
are served but no alcohol. There have long been
plans for a rooftop restaurant, but for now they
remain just that. B&B. **$$**

🛏 **Hillview Inn** (10 rooms) m 0777
863310/428365; e omarjumakhatib@yahoo.co.uk.
When approaching Wete from Chake Chake, you'll
spot the large signpost to Hillview just before
reaching the town itself. In a rather unsavoury
residential area, the basic rooms contain little
more than a bed, fan, mosquito net & crinkled
lino flooring. 5 rooms have a bathroom, while the
others share, although strangely the rooms all cost
the same (*US$12*). Decoration comes in the form
of mismatched curtains & rather scary paintings of
dogs. 1 room has a balcony with a disappointing
view of a hill, hence the hotel's name. The whole
place could do with a good scrub & a fresh coat
of paint, but the linen is freshly laundered & the
manager a jovial, helpful sort. The room price
includes a 'continental' b/fast but other meals must
be ordered in advance for around US$6. B&B. **$**

✕ **WHERE TO EAT AND DRINK** *Map, opposite*
All the hotels and guesthouses serve food with advance notice, and Wete also has
a choice of local eating-houses, most open until the last buses have left at 16.00.
Several are located to the west of town, close to the port and bus station. There's
also a good bakery next to the market. In the north of town near the clock tower,
a number of small local cafés vie with street stalls selling the usual range of fare,
including – we've heard – very good octopus and chapattis, with sugar-cane juice
to drink at less than a dollar.

✕ **Times Restaurant** Next door to Salim, Times
is worth a visit for the AC alone, but it also serves up
good pizza, curries, grilled meats (*US$4*), fishcakes
(*US$1.50*) & sandwiches (*US$2*), all served on neatly
laid tables & accompanied by English-language
newspapers. Probably, Wete's best dining option. **$$**
✕ **Salim Café** ⊕ 07.00–22.00 daily. Further
up the main street, away from the port, this large
place is popular with locals, who recommend the
biryani & pilau at US$1 each – don't be put off by
the loud TV. **$–$$**
✕ **Al Falahy Hotel** Up towards the clock tower
in the north of town, this place (which is not a

hotel despite the name) serves tasty snacks &
fried bread. **$**
✕ **Green Garden Refreshments** This pleasant
open-air café sells omelette & chips or beans &
rice for around US$1, with more expensive meals,
based on beef & chicken, also available. It's open
all day, but not always at weekends. **$**
✕ **Khatib Restaurant** Next door to Lake Sipesa,
this dishes up omelettes & bread & has a fridge full
of cold sodas outside. **$**
✕ **Laki Sipesa** Opposite the market & bus station,
Laki Sipesa (which means '100,000 has no value')
serves pilau rice & meat, plus bread, chapattis & tea **$**

OTHER PRACTICALITIES The **post office** (⊕ *08.00–13.00 & 14.00–16.00 Mon–Thu,
08.00–noon & 14.00–17.00 Fri*) is on the right of the main street about halfway
towards the port. Wete's only **internet café** is found in the small row of shops
opposite the Pemba Crown Hotel, where there's also a **bureau de change**, although
shortages of Tanzanian shillings are common and the rates aren't great.

WHAT TO SEE AND DO The ruins of **Mtambwe Mkuu** are on the small island of
Mtambwe, which is joined to the mainland at low tide, directly south of Wete. For
over 1,000 years, it was one of the most prosperous ports of East Africa. The

'Mtambwe hoard', a collection of coins found near the beach in 1984, included gold coins dating from 11th-century Egypt, and one of very few examples of pre-colonial minted silver currency anywhere in East Africa. Despite its rich past, there's little to see at Mtambwe Mkuu these days, although a trip there from Wete is a very pleasant way to spend the day.

To reach them you go by small **dhow** or **canoe** from Wete harbour to Mtambwe village, then **walk** south, west and north around a creek and through mangrove swamps to reach the ruins. Apparently, when the water is high, you can get cut off at the ruins, or be forced to wade back to Mtambwe village through the mangroves, so careful checking of the tides is recommended. Sharook Guesthouse or Royal Tours (page 360) in Wete can arrange tours or give you advice.

NORTH OF WETE Although there are more direct routes from Wete to the north of the island, it is quicker to head east to Chwale, then take the main tarred road north. This also has the advantage of passing close to many of Pemba's places of interest, so makes for an interesting journey in its own right.

From Chwale, the landscape is mainly farmland, dotted with coconut palms as it heads up the east coast. Just before the turn-off to Micheweni, in an area generally known as Wingwi, is a rather unprepossessing stretch of green which, come the end of the year and at times of government celebration, plays host to the island's bullfights (see box, below).

Kiuyu Peninsula To the east of the main north–south road, a narrow isthmus separates the rest of Pemba from the Kiuyu Peninsula. A rough road, north of the 'bullring', leads to the village of **Micheweni** (about 5km), which has a school, a hospital and a few shops, but no place to stay. (Confusingly, Micheweni is also sometimes called Wingwi, the name not only of the area but also of another village a few kilometres to the south.) The road deteriorates from here passing through

---

BULLFIGHTING ON PEMBA

Somewhat surprisingly, the island of Pemba is a place where you might see Iberian-style bullfighting. The origins of this sport are uncertain although it is thought to have been introduced by the Portuguese during the 16th century. Bullfights take place close to Wingwi, in the northeast of the island, during holiday times, mostly between August and November after the harvest and before the short rains, but also between December and February after the short rains. Local matadors put on a brave display, posing in front of the bull, goading him into a charge and then standing aside at the last moment, much to the appreciation of watching villagers. At the end of the fight, the bull is not killed but praised by the fighter, and sometimes decorated with flowers and leaves, then paraded around the village.

If you happen to be in Pemba when a bullfight is planned, it's worth going to see, but, although sometimes it can be a lively and fascinating spectacle, a few visitors have reported that in reality some bullfights can be fairly uneventful, and seem to involve a group of local wide boys annoying an apathetic cow by beating her with sticks, while the local girls shriek loudly.

Exactly when a bullfight is about to take place is hard to find out. Ask at your hotel or a reliable tour company, such as Msewe Travel in Chake Chake (page 350) for more details.

the village of **Kiuyu**, and becoming a deep-red dirt track, reminiscent of mainland Africa, before it reaches **Ras Kiuyu Forest Reserve**, almost at the tip of the peninsula. It's a remote and somewhat inaccessible place, smaller than the forest at Ngezi and with a less impressive range of vegetation and wildlife. Nevertheless, it has been highly recommended as a day trip from Wete or even Chake Chake, as much for the interesting journey through the fields and villages as for the forest itself. The unspoilt **Kiuyu Beach**, to the east of the forest, is an added attraction.

To get here by public transport, you can catch an early **dalla dalla** from Wete to Micheweni. From here, it's a 5km walk to the village of Kiuyu and another 5km into the forest itself. About 3km beyond Kiuyu village, a narrow track branches right (east) to Kiuyu Beach. Nearby, another track branches left to a small beach on the west of the peninsula called Mbuyu Kambaa. The only alternative is to hire a driver with a **4x4**, since the road beyond Micheweni is unsuitable for other vehicles.

Chwaka ruins Continuing north from the bullring, near the coast, are the ruins of the town of Chwaka. Dating from as early as the 9th century, the town was active as a port in the 15th century, probably linked to a network of villages trading with the east African coast and beyond. The ruins are sometimes referred to as Harouni, a reflection of the town's association with a local king called Harouni, who was the son of Mkama Ndume, builder of Pujini (pages 354–5).

The most easily recognised buildings are two small mosques, standing well apart. The larger and better-preserved Friday mosque is also the site of the king's tomb. Local legend has it that the two mosques were built because the king's two wives were constantly at loggerheads, and that the town was eventually destroyed by the second wife's family.

There are also remains of houses and tombs. Nearby stood another group of tombs and an 18th-century fort built by the Mazrui group of Omanis, and on the other side of the road are some more remains called Old Tumbe. As with most of Pemba's ruins, don't go expecting a major archaeological find, but it's an interesting place and offers free rein to the imagination.

Chwaka is signposted to the east of the main road between Wete and Tumbe, just north of where it crosses a swampy area on an embankment with metal crash barriers on either side. The 10-minute **walk** takes you through cassava fields and past lofty palms, with a splendid view over the bay towards Micheweni as you approach the ruins themselves.

Tumbe This village, not far from the Chwaka Ruins, has the largest fish market on Pemba. Particularly busy in the mornings, it attracts people from all over the island to buy fish, which they carry away in plaited baskets strapped to the back of bicycles. It's an interesting place for visitors to watch the boats come in with fish of all sizes.

Tumbe lies off the main tar road about 5km east of Konde, and can be reached by **bus** or **bike** from Wete, or with a **hired car**. A **dalla dalla** stops at the junction, from where it's a pleasant walk through the long, narrow village to the coast; by **car**, it's about a 10-minute drive from the main road.

Konde Near the end of the tarred road, the small town of Konde is also the end of the road for the dalla dalla network, and the last place to stock up for a picnic before venturing further north to Ngezi Forest and Vumawimbi Beach. Men on bicycles weave up and down the dusty main street, with palm-leaf baskets strapped to the back laden with produce. During market hours, until 14.00, fruit stalls line the road, and there's a bakery selling fresh bread. There's also a restaurant where dishes such as pilau and *chipsi mai yai* (chip omelette) can be bought for around US$1.50. Konde is well known for making excellent breads.

NGEZI PENINSULA

The Ngezi Peninsula is the northernmost point on Pemba, jutting out from the northwestern corner of the island. Beyond Konde, a significant area is taken up by **Ngezi Forest**, the last remains of a huge tract of indigenous forest which used to cover much of Pemba.

Curving round the eastern side of the peninsula is **Vumawimbi Beach**, one of the most beautiful on Pemba, with miles of dazzling white sand flanked by pristine forest. Here and there fishermen sit and mend their nets, watching over their ngalawas as they wait for the tide, and occasionally an ox-cart rolls along the sand. Rumours have abounded for years about the construction of a hotel, but for now the beach remains remote and unspoilt. You can walk to the beach across the fields from Ngezi Forest or the Manta Resort, or go with a driver.

The west of the peninsula is flanked by the long expanse of **Verani Beach** with, at its northern end, a place called **Pango Ya Watoro** ('the cave of the fugitives'). At low tide, sandbanks dry out offshore, and boat trips from the nearby Manta Resort take visitors out with a picnic to swim and snorkel. It's possible to walk along the beach to the **lighthouse** near Ras Kigomasha, but only at low tide, so do check carefully before setting out; there's an alternative route through the fields if the water is up. Built by the British in the 1800s, the lighthouse offers some outstanding views out to sea and across the lush green landscape of northern Pemba. It costs US$4 per person to climb the 95 narrow steps to the top – just ask at the house nearby for the lighthouse keeper.

GETTING THERE AND AWAY You can get from Wete as far as Konde by **dalla dalla**, but from there you'll have to **walk** the 5km along the road, bordered by farmland, to the Ngezi Forest entrance gate. If you make an early start this walk is a nice part of the day out. Alternatively, and especially if you want to go on to one of the beaches, you'll need to hire a **car** from Wete or Chake, for which you can expect to pay US$50–70 for the day, or travel as part of an **organised tour** (pages 360 and 349 respectively). Beyond the entrance gate to Ngezi Forest the road is rough, and to get to the beach is sandy too, so unless it's dry a high-clearance **4x4** is recommended.

WHERE TO STAY AND EAT *Map, page 338*
It's possible to visit the forest and beaches around Ngezi for the day, and stay overnight in Wete or Chake Chake. Alternatively, there's one basic guesthouse and a couple of more upmarket places to stay nearby.

Exclusive
The Aiyana (30 villas) m 0777 006341/0772 833263; e reservations@theaiyana. com; theaiyana.com. A recent addition to the Pemba boutique hotel scene, the all-inclusive Aiyana is a collection of 30 luxury, thatched villas in lush gardens. Located on a picture-perfect crescent at the north of the island, each traditionally influenced, whitewashed villa boasts a gorgeous view across the powder sand to the turquoise ocean waters, with private outdoor space & stylish interiors to match. The design is contemporary: clean lines, coordinated accessories, design-conscious fittings, & plenty of mod cons including: satellite TV, Wi-Fi & iPod docking station. The enormous bathroom has his & hers sinks, a free-standing bath & an outdoor shower with Gilchrist & Soames amenities. The

surrounding courtyards & gardens are filled with palms, tinkling fountains, bougainvillea-covered pergolas & fragrant frangipani & lily beds; the seafront is idyllic. So given the setting & views, simply chilling comes highly recommended here. For the more active, diving & snorkelling are good, the usual range of island excursions are on offer & there's a beautiful spa. Meals are served either in the colonnaded restaurant or around the resort & beach, with a variety of cuisine on offer. There's a resident sommelier for wine lovers, an emphasis on locally sourced ingredients & home cooking, & a cushioned shisha lounge is available after dusk. AL. 🐚

🔺 **The Manta Resort** (17 rooms) m 0776 718852; e sales@themantaresort.com; www. themantaresort.com; 🕐 Jun–Apr. Overlooking the northern end of Verani Beach, in a truly stunning location, the Manta Resort is a smart beach resort catering to divers through its own PADI dive centre, 360 Dive Pemba (page 347), & landlubbers alike. The seafront villas have terrific panoramic views across the Pemba Channel, & with AC, a large dbl bed, small lounge area & en-suite bathroom, these are the resort's premium rooms. The superior garden rooms set behind the villas are more enclosed, with views across the gardens; however the option of interconnecting doors makes them good for families. As with the premium rooms they are cooled by AC, but the more standard garden rooms have only a standing fan. Manta's most unique room, however, is somewhat spectacular: a mind-blowing underwater room, inspired by a piece of installation art on a Swedish lake. Floating in the Indian Ocean in front of the hotel, this timber cube, boasts a dbl room 3m below the surface of the sea, with windows onto a floodlit watery world: essentially you sleep inside an aquarium! Above water, there's an open-fronted lounge area & a rooftop sunbathing (or star-gazing) deck. It's pretty incredible... albeit you need sea legs & a cool US$1,500/night to check in. Back at the main resort, a central area serves as dining room, bar, lounge & lobby, with a large, ocean-view terrace with steps leading down to the beach & a 2-tiered beach bar, though be careful of sea urchins. For entertainment & relaxation, there is a lovely swimming pool, a cocktail bar serving up Pemban special cocktails (try the Voodoo Juice) & a little library with books to while away sunbathing hours. There's deliberately no TV or phones at the resort, although communal dining is sometimes arranged to encourage a social vibe. Diving aside, guests benefit from a wide range of birdlife & some interesting walks to the lighthouse, Vumawimbi Beach, Ngezi Forest (5km) & village tours. There's also free kayaking, boat & fishing trips (*US$770/1,050 ½-full-day game fishing*), hand-line fishing with a local fisherman (*US$30*), & massages in the Kipepeo Spa, where 1 treatment per day is included in the FB rates. Internet is available, & there's Wi-Fi & a computer in the lounge. No children under 7. FB; airport transfer US$45pp, under 125 free. 🐚

Upmarket

🔺 **Gecko Nature Lodge** (22 rooms) m 0773 176737/0778 661489; e swahilidivers@ outlook.com; 📘 swahili.divers. Formerly Kervan Saray Beach, Gecko Nature Lodge came under new ownership in early 2017, & though it has undergone some renovations since, it remains a simple & unpretentious affair. Located close to the small village of Makangale, its thatched cottages are just above a sand-&-rock beach that is excellent for swimming at high tide. Bungalows contain cool & spacious rooms, with a dbl bed raised up on a plinth, complete with colourful bedding & mosquito nets, an en-suite bathroom & a solar-heated outdoor shower (warm water on sunny days only!). There is generator power 18.00–06.00 for light, but laptops & cameras can be charged in the office at other times. The rooms are lovely, with fresh flowers, slatted windows & oodles of colour. The lodge boasts a PADI 5* Resort Dive Centre with a team who are experienced in the surrounding reefs & sometimes challenging waters (page 348). Snorkellers, sunbathers & cruisers are more than welcome to hop on board, too. Birdwatching tours can be arranged to see Pemba's 4 endemic species, & trips are free for guests who pre-book as birders, but park fees are extra (see below). Kayaking (*US$70pp/½-day*), fishing, yoga, paddleboarding, local hikes & trips to the Ngezi Forest are also on offer. Aside from making sure everyone has a good time, the lodge is trying hard to maintain a low carbon footprint & to work with the local community. From backpackers to chilled families & hardcore divers, this is a super spot for a low-key beach break. FB. **$$$$–$$$$$**

12

Mid range

⚓ **Pemba Paradise** (16 rooms) m 0777 848783; e pembaparadise@gmail.com; www. pembaparadise.com. Just outside the Ngezi Forest & within walking distance of Vumawimbi Beach, Pemba Paradise opened in Makangale village in 2017. Owned by Kamis Mussa, a local gentleman firmly established in the tourist scene with his tour operation, Zanzibarfree Nakupenda Island Safaris, it is a welcome addition to the island's mid-range offering. Rooms are clean & simply furnished, all enjoying a veranda & en-suite bathroom, with 8 suites boasting sea views & daybeds, which can be easily used to accommodate children. A swimming pool is under construction at the time of writing, diving is available with neighbouring Swahili Divers (page 348), & excursions are available island-wide. B&B. **$$$**

NGEZI FOREST RESERVE (⏱ *07.30–15.30 daily; admission short tour US$5pp, longer tour or birdwatching US$10; transit fee US$2; night walks by prior arrangement*) This reserve is virtually all that remains of a vast area of indigenous forest that used to cover much of the island. One of the highlights of Pemba, especially if you have an interest in wildlife, is that it offers the opportunity to discover Pemba as it once was. It's advisable not to arrive too early because mosquitoes remain active in the morning.

A 2km **nature trail** takes in sections of moist forest, and several large ponds. A **guided walk** with the rangers takes about an hour, and is a must if you want to have a brief insight into the forest's different habitats and to spot some of the animals and birds that live among the trees. Tips are negotiable, but it's reasonable to give around US$5 for a small group. Birdwatching trips can be organised, too, as can walks in the late evening, or at night, when you have a much better chance of seeing the Pemba flying fox and the russet scops owl. To set up a trip of this ilk, contact the rangers' office in advance, during opening hours.

History Historically, the forest was used by local people, as it provided timber, fuelwood, edible plants, medicinal plants, and material for baskets and ropes, but at the same time areas of forest were being cleared for small-scale agriculture, and since the early 19th century for large plantations – especially for cloves. Although the first forest inventory was carried out in the 1920s, it wasn't until 30 years later that the reserve was established. Even then, a commercial sawmill owned by one Vi Arnjosh continued to extract timber until the mid 1960s, when the government officially took control. The crude hut in which he lived and the rusting remnants of his sawmill can be seen on the nature trail.

Through the 1970s and 1980s Ngezi was virtually ignored by the government, while encroachment and overuse by local people endangered the forest and its wildlife. Then, in 1995, funds were received from the Forest and Park Service of Finland, and a management plan was drawn up to preserve the remaining forest by strengthening conservation efforts and improving management. In this way, people from the ten villages within the reserve could still utilise the forest, but at a sustainable rate, and wildlife could also benefit. It is hoped that the forest can be developed to attract tourists as a way of raising revenue – which would in turn ensure its future protection.

Ecology The reserve covers just 1,476ha but the variety of soil types has resulted in a wide range of vegetation. Dominant are 943ha of tropical moist forest, which once covered most of the island. Found mainly in the central and eastern parts of the reserve (the part most easily reached by visitors) it has some trees reaching over 40m in height – most notably the *Odyendea zimmermanii*, known locally as *mbanko*. Also to be found is the endemic Pemba palm (*mpapindi*; *Dypsis pembanus*), an ornamental tree whose red seeds are attractive to birds.

Other vegetation types include swamp forest, coastal thicket, heathland, pockets of mangroves and palms, and raffia stands. The mix is unique in East Africa, with several species more usually found in lowland mountain regions, as well as those more often found in coastal areas, plus eastern Indian and Malagasy species, and even a southeast Asian wild banana. There are also several introduced tree species.

The forest is home to several animal species, most notably the Pemba flying fox. Other animals found in Ngezi include the Pemba vervet monkey, the greater bushbaby, Zanzibar tree hyrax (*pelele; Dendrohyrax validus neumannii*), blue duiker (*paa wa pemba*) and marsh mongoose (*chonjwe; Atilax paludinosus*). A band of wild European pigs, descended from domestic animals introduced by the Portuguese centuries ago, also lives in the forest. As most people on Pemba are Muslim and abstain from pork, these animals are not hunted.

For birdwatchers, Ngezi Forest is undoubtedly the best place on Pemba, with all the endemics and sub-endemics present here. Visitors could also see palm-nut vultures, crowned hornbills, red-billed hornbills and kingfishers, as well as turacos and starlings. For more details, see page 59.

12

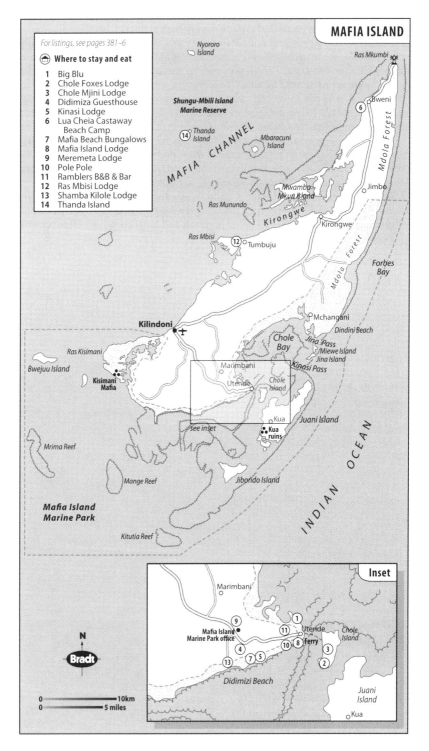

MAFIA ISLAND

For listings, see pages 381–6

Where to stay and eat

1 Big Blu
2 Chole Foxes Lodge
3 Chole Mjini Lodge
4 Didimiza Guesthouse
5 Kinasi Lodge
6 Lua Cheia Castaway
   Beach Camp
7 Mafia Beach Bungalows
8 Mafia Island Lodge
9 Meremeta Lodge
10 Pole Pole
11 Ramblers B&B & Bar
12 Ras Mbisi Lodge
13 Shamba Kilole Lodge
14 Thanda Island

Nyororo Island

Ras Mkumbi

Shungu-Mbili Island Marine Reserve

Bweni

Mdola Forest

Thanda Island

MAFIA CHANNEL

Mbaracuni Island

Mwamba-Mkua Island

Jimbo

Kirongwe

Kirongwe

Ras Munundo

Mdola forest

Forbes Bay

Ras Mbisi

Tumbuju

Kilindoni

Mchangani

Dindini Beach

Ras Kisimani

Chole Bay

Jina Pass

Miewe Island

Jina Island

Kinasi Pass

Bwejuu Island

Kisimani Mafia

Marimbani

Utende

Chole Island

Kua

Juani Island

see inset

Kua ruins

INDIAN OCEAN

Mrima Reef

Mange Reef

Jibondo Island

Mafia Island Marine Park

Kitutia Reef

N

Bradt

0 ————— 10km
0 ————— 5 miles

Inset

Marimbanj

Mafia Island Marine Park office

Utende

Chole Island

Ferry

Didimizi Beach

Juani Island

Kua

13

Mafia Archipelago

While Zanzibar is entrenched as probably the most popular ocean resort in East Africa, the small archipelago around Mafia Island, 160km to its south, remains virtually unknown. Poor communications with the mainland and a rather unfortunate name have not served Mafia well, but a growing trickle of visitors over recent years, currently around 4,500 annually have been unanimous in singing the island's praises. A few interesting Swahili ruins notwithstanding, Mafia lacks an equivalent to Zanzibar's atmospheric Stone Town, so cannot be recommended as an alternative destination for those whose primary interest in Tanzania's islands is cultural or historical.

By contrast, the combination of a clutch of small, high-quality lodges, offshore diving and snorkelling that ranks with the very best in the Indian Ocean, and a conspicuous absence of hassle and crime, make it the ideal destination for those seeking an exclusive but low-key Indian Ocean retreat. Paradoxically, perhaps, Mafia also has considerable potential for budget travellers seeking a truly off-the-beaten-track and adventurous experience, and if boats connecting Mafia to the mainland become more reliable, their numbers are sure to increase.

The Mafia Archipelago, which lies approximately 20km east of the Rufiji River Delta in central Tanzania, probably became isolated from the mainland some 20,000 years ago. The archipelago consists of about 15 sandstone and coral-rag islands and numerous smaller atolls and sandbars, none of which reaches an elevation above 80m, and all but two of which are little more than 1km^2 in extent. The central island, known today as Mafia (though it seems that this name applied to the archipelago rather than any specific island prior to the 20th century), is by far the largest, approximately 50km long by 15km across. The second-largest island is Juani, about 8km long and up to 4km wide, which lies to the southeast of the main island and was the centre of local political activity in medieval times. Sandwiched between these two larger islands, the tiny Chole Island superseded Juani as the local centre of trade in the Omani era.

The archipelago's population of 46,850 (2012 census) lives in rustic fishing communities and farming villages dotted all over the archipelago, although many of the islands are theoretically uninhabited. The largest town and port on Mafia Island is Kilindoni in the southeast, the site of the airstrip, and the main landing point for dhows from the mainland. A couple of hotels can be found along the beach from Kilindoni, as well as a few local guesthouses in the town itself, but the centre of upmarket tourist development is Chole Bay on the southeastern side of the island. Here a number of tourist lodges, ranging in standard, line the coast around Utende, roughly 10km from Kilindoni by road. Further accommodation options are found on Chole Island within the bay, up in the north of the island near Ras Mbisi and Bweni, and more recently on the islands of small Fanjove and Thanda.

VEGETATION Natural vegetation on Mafia ranges from tidal mangrove thickets (eight species of mangrove grow here), marshland, heath and scrubby coastal moorlands to palm-wooded grassland and lowland rainforest, although the evergreen forest was cleared for coconut plantations in the 1980s. Baobabs are prominent along with the native *Albizia*. A patch of coastal high forest, the Chunguruma Forest towards Ras Mbisi, is a dense tree canopy interlaced with lianas and having an abundant floor covering of ferns.

WILDLIFE
Mammals A large, reed-lined lake in central Mafia, probably a relic lagoon dating from when the island was joined to the mainland, harbours about 20 hippos that were washed out to sea during flooding in the Rufiji River system. Unpopular with locals, they eat from the rice farms at night and can cause considerable damage, but are hard to see. Other island fauna includes a colony of flying foxes (the lesser Cormorant fruit bat), while bush pigs are found in Mdola Forest and Juani Island. The pigs eat the cassava from farms on Juani, so are a menace to farmers, who try to trap the pigs where possible.

Mdola Forest stretches along the east coast of Mafia Island for about 30km, from Bweni to Chole Bay, and has a high level of diversity, as well as a number of endemic species, such as the blue duiker, a subspecies endemic to Pemba and Mafia. Other fauna includes at least one bushbaby species, the genet, and the black-and-rufous elephant shrew. Monkeys (Sykes' and vervet) and squirrels were introduced for the pot by the Portuguese.

Reptiles and insects The leaf-litter toad has been recorded in Mdola Forest, and may be endemic to Mafia; the writhing gecko is found both in Mdola Forest and on the Tanzanian mainland. The monitor lizard is known locally as *kenge*. Butterflies (there are five endemics) are best seen in the wet season, particularly around Ras Mbizi and mangroves, which flower during the rains.

Birds More than 120 species of bird have been recorded on Mafia, including five different types of sunbird. The island is of particular interest for its concentrations of resident and migrant shorebirds, which have breeding grounds in northern Europe but come to Mafia from October to March for the nearby mangrove estuaries, where they feed on the mudflats. Waders include ringed plover, crab plover, grey plover, Mongolian plover, great sandplover, curlew, whimbrel and turnstone, and the island is also a nesting area for fish eagles and open-billed storks.

MARINE LIFE Of far greater ecological importance than Mafia's terrestrial habitats is the immensely rich marine environment, which provides some of the finest snorkelling and diving sites in the Indian Ocean. It may be surprising that the biodiversity of the Rufiji–Mafia complex has global significance, and of 21 sites in East Africa it has been described as having 'one of the world's most interesting and diverse ecosystems'. The coral-reef habitats around Mafia have a diversity of species rivalled only by rainforests, with at least 380 species of fish and 48 of coral. The beds of seagrass (12 species of which are found here, the only flowering plants to have colonised the sea) and the deep open waters support some of the planet's most endangered marine life.

Four species of turtle live in Mafia's waters, and two of these use Mafia as a nesting ground. The hawksbill (*Cretmochelys imbricata*) lays eggs between December and January; the green turtle (*Chelonia mydas*), between April and June. The east African coast is one of the last strongholds for the critically endangered dugong (*Dugong dugon*), and during the 1960s and 1970s these gentle sea cows were regularly caught in the shark nets of Mafia's fishermen. Despite two separate sightings in 1999, there are fears that the dugong may now be extinct here.

The lowland coastal forest of the eastern seaboard has been 'recognised as a critical site for biodiversity', and the intertidal flats are important for octopus, while in the open sea marine mammals like the humpback whale give birth and nurse their young. Sadly the demand for shark-fin soup in the Far East is one contributor to diminished populations of shark along the coastline. The large pelagics such as marlin, billfish and tuna also inhabit the deeper sea.

Oceanographers often talk of the Rufiji River Delta–Mafia–Kilwa area being one extended ecosystem. It's particularly exciting that a coelacanth was caught here in 2003. Archaeologists have found fossils of this very rare, bony fish which dates back to the era of the dinosaurs, and today's specimens are almost identical.

From October to April, whale sharks (*Rhincodon typus*) are seen in the area. Peaceful creatures, sometimes in excess of 20m in length, they are the world's largest fish, and survive on a diet of plankton. Kitu Kiblu, in Kilindoni, is the headquarters for the Mafia Island Whaleshark Conservation Project and during the season offers regular dhow excursions for research scientists and guests to visit these gentle giants, which are spotted mainly on the western side of the island off the shore of Kilindoni. There are a few other operators in recent years who have begun offering trips, most with reasonable responsibility; however, it is very important to familiarise yourself with the whale shark code of conduct (see box, page 393) for your own safety and the animals' protection. It is our view that Kitu Kiblu (see box, page 372) are still the gold standard for care, quality and responsibility when it comes to these magical marine encounters.

CLIMATE

The Mafia Archipelago experiences a tropical climate tempered by ocean breezes. Rainfall averaging 2,000mm a year occurs mainly between April and May, although November can also be wet. February and March are hot and humid, while a strong southerly wind, the *kusi*, blows during July. The best holiday period is from June until mid October, when the islands enjoy blue skies with temperatures kept pleasant by light coastal breezes. The water temperature varies from 24°C to 31°C while the air temperature rarely exceeds 33°C or drops below 20°C.

HISTORY

Little is known about the early history of the Mafia Archipelago, but presumably it has been settled for millennia, and it may well have participated in the ancient coastal trade with Arabia. The eminent archaeologist Neville Chittick regarded Mafia as a strong candidate for the 'low and wooded' island of Menouthesias, described in the 1st-century *Periplus of the Erythraean Sea* as being two days' sail or 300 *stadia* (roughly 50km) from the river port of Rhapta (which, according to this theory, was situated in the Rufiji Delta; and if recent discoveries prove positive,

13

Kitu Kiblu ('a little blue thing') was established to offer responsible marine encounters with whale sharks for visitors and also to support the work of the Mafia Island Whale Shark Conservation Society (WHASCOS), which aims to raise awareness about whale sharks and their conservation. It is a highly principled organisation, with a clear understanding of how solid, long-term conservation must be approached. Staff work hard to demonstrate the whale sharks' worth to the authorities who are able to protect them and they believe fervently in the whale sharks' right to live free and undisturbed. They understand sharks' importance within the ecosystem, and support scientific research to better understand whale-shark behaviour and how to interact with them without harming or harassing them.

Half-day encounter trips offer visitors utterly incredible experiences with the whale sharks, and always in a safe and respectful way. On board traditional dhows, guests not only have the chance to spot and swim with these amazing animals, but also to be guided by knowledgeable people, able to translate the whale-sharks' behaviour and explain their biology. Resident marine biologists involved in current research may also be on board, giving opportunities to gain real insight into these fish and the area's conservation projects. It is as eye opening as it is magical.

For budding marine conservationists, there is also a well-organised internship programme, offering hands-on experience of scientific research and working at sea. From spot pattern data collection and 3D photometry to rural development projects, up to eight interns at a time can join the team on two-to 12-week placements from October to February, working and staying at the Kitu Kiblu Magemani beach camp. Interns even learn to sail and scuba dive while they are there.

If you are in Mafia during whale-shark season, you can book Kitu Kiblu trips directly (m *0784 520799/0787 712427;* e *4whalesharks@gmail.com; www.kitukiblu.co.tz*) or through your tour operator, dive operator or hotel.

is actually off Ras Mbisi – see page 385). Although the anonymous writer of the *Periplus* also mentions the sewn boats and hollowed-out tree canoes that are still used widely on Mafia today (as they are elsewhere on the coast), several other aspects of the description count against Mafia. Two days rather exaggerates the sailing distance from the island to the Rufiji Delta; furthermore, either the *Periplus* was mistaken in its assertion that there are 'no wild beasts except crocodiles' on Menouthesias, or the crocs have subsequently vanished and the island's few hippos are a later arrival.

The earliest known settlement on the archipelago, Kisimani Mafia, was situated at Ras Kisimani in the far southwest of the main island. Archaeological evidence suggests that this town, which covered about 1ha, was founded in the 11th century, possibly by a favoured son of the Sultan of Kilwa. Several coins minted at Kilwa have been unearthed at the site, as have coins from China, Mongolia, India and Arabia, all minted prior to 1340. A second important town, Kua, was thought to have been founded in the 13th century, again as a dependency of Kilwa, and it must surely have usurped Kisimani as the islands' political and economic hub soon after that. In its prime, Kua was probably the second-largest city along what is now the southern coast of Tanzania, boasting seven mosques as well as a double-storey palace and numerous stone homesteads spread over an area of more than 12ha.

Following the Portuguese occupation of the coast, Kua was chosen as the site of a Portuguese trade agency in 1515, when a fortified blockhouse was built at the town. The name Mafia (more accurately Morfiyeh) was well established by this time, and the islands are marked as such on the earliest Portuguese naval charts. Several explanations have been put forward for the origin of this name (see box, below). Because the archipelago lies 20km offshore, Mafia attracted a large influx of refugees from the mainland during the cannibalistic Zimba raids that dealt the final deathblow to so many coastal settlements during the late 16th century.

Control of Mafia changed hands frequently in the 17th century as Portugal's fortunes declined. An Omani naval raid in 1670 effectively terminated the Portuguese presence on the Mafia islands, and by 1598 the entire east African coast north of modern-day Mozambique was under Omani control. Little is known about events on the islands over the next two centuries. In about 1829, however, the archipelago was attacked by the cannibalistic Sakalafa of Madagascar, who succeeded in wreaking havoc at Kua, one of the few coastal towns left untouched by their Zimba forebears 250 years earlier. Kisimani, though also attacked by the Malagasy, stumbled on into the 1870s, when a devastating cyclone dealt it a final death blow, while Kua was abandoned to go to ruin.

One reason why Kua was not resettled after 1820 is that a new seat of the Sultanate of Zanzibar had been founded on the north end of Chole Island barely ten years earlier. Known as Chole Mjini (Chole Town), this settlement was also attacked by the Sakalafa, but it was soon rebuilt to emerge as the most important town on the islands. Chole became the established home of a number of wealthy Omani traders and slave owners, while the main island of Mafia, known at the time as Chole Shamba (Chole Farm), was occupied by newly established coconut plantations and the slaves who worked on them. Although Chole was not as directly involved in the slave trade as Pangani, Bagamoyo or Kilwa Kivinje, it was an important stopover for slave ships heading between Kilwa and Zanzibar, and the ruined mansions that survive today indicate that it was a very wealthy settlement indeed.

Mafia was part of the Zanzibar Sultanate throughout the Omani era, and it should have remained a part of Zanzibar in the colonial era, according to a treaty that placed it under British protectorateship along with Zanzibar and Pemba islands. However, in the complex Anglo-German treaty of 1890, Mafia was ceded to Germany in exchange for a part of what is now Malawi, and it has been administered as part of mainland Tanzania ever since. In 1892, Germany

WHAT'S IN A NAME?

There are a number of suggestions for the source of the archipelago's name, but it isn't derived from the Sicilian crime syndicate. It may have origins in the Arabic word *morfiyeh* meaning 'group', describing the archipelago of Mafia, or be named after the Ma'afir, an Arab tribe from Merku (Mocha) in present-day Yemen. An unlikely suggestion is that the name derives from the Arabic *mafi* meaning 'waste' or 'rubbish', or perhaps from the Kiswahili *mahali pa afya* meaning 'a healthy place to live'. The authors would be grateful for any further suggestions!

13

sent a local administrator to Chole, who constructed the two-storey Customs House that can still be seen on the beach today.

In 1913, Germany relocated its administration from Chole to the deeper harbour at Kilindoni on the main island. Two years later, Mafia was the first part of German East Africa to be captured by British forces. The island was subsequently used as the base for a series of aerial assaults on the German cruiser *Königsberg* which, having evaded capture in the Rufiji Delta, was finally sunk on 11 August 1915. A six-cent German Tanganyika Territory stamp overprinted 'Mafia' by the British and listed at £9,000 in the Stanley Gibbons catalogue makes philatelists one of the few groups of people aware of the existence of the islands.

ECONOMY

Coconuts were the main source of income for the islands until the 1970s, when the price of coconut products dropped, and the fishing industry grew in importance, thanks in part to the efficient production of ice on the island. Cultivated since the 19th century, coconuts remain a secure income source and, although the trees are still climbed by hand, some 30 tonnes are exported to Dar daily in dhows from all over the islands. There are three main harvesting periods in the year (after the rains, in October/November and in February/March) after which the nuts leave in sacks for processing elsewhere. Coconut products have a number of local uses: leaves are used for roofing; coconut coir makes doormats and ropes; ribs are used to make fishing traps and brooms; and the wood can also be used to make furniture.

Other produce grown on Mafia is used for subsistence farming, particularly the primary crop, cassava. Rice, sweet potato, maize, pumpkin, okra, banana, pineapple, passion fruit, lime, mango, oranges and tomato are also seen growing on the islands, some of which are exported to Dar. Cashew nuts are either sold locally or exported. At subsistence level, raffia fibre, medicinal plants and game (monkey, bush pig and duiker) play a little role. Mangrove trees provide many raw materials; their wood is used for building poles, and boatbuilding and repair. Dead mangrove branches are used for firewood; leaves, bark and fruit are all used for medicines and colour dyes. **Firewood** is collected to burn coral rag for lime, and also for charcoal, which is sold to locals, hotels, and the market at Kilindoni, as well as exported. The charcoal industry is now a disturbingly big business. The attempt at a ban on charcoal production on Zanzibar sadly created an instant market for Mafia, where hardwoods are now being removed at an alarming rate to fuel the trade to the Gulf States and, more locally, Forodhani's night market in Stone Town. This deforestation comes with a raft of aesthetic and environmental impacts for the island, notably significant erosion along the formerly wooded valleys, which act as important water channels during the rains.

The **sea** is vital to the livelihood of many of Mafia's inhabitants. Seaweed farming exists on a small-scale basis on Jibondo, with some questioning the sensibilities of introducing vigorous species from the Philippines within the marine park. It is grown on lines attached to wooden stakes across the seabed of shallow lagoons, and is dried on palm leaves, before being exported for processing into food additives. Traditionally the intertidal area has been the women's domain, where they fish for shellfish at spring tide. In the 1990s, however, men began collecting octopus on the intertidal flats as well, as fish catches were declining yet prices increasing. Today, 60% of octopus is caught by men, through free-diving or harpoon-fishing at low tide in Jibondo reef's rocky crevasses. Sea cucumbers are harvested mainly off Kilindoni's sandy seabed for export to Zanzibar or Dar, then out to the Far East, although thanks to over-fishing, this practice is happening less. Fish is also exported. Chole and Jibondo were well known for their boatbuilding in the past, but having declined somewhat as secondhand fibre-glass boats were brought in, this traditional skill is in decline, although you can still see people working in the shipyards. The majority of the work is now repairing smaller dhows rather than building large cargo-carrying boats. Put simply, the depletion of hardwood forest reserves has resulted in the cost of timber doubling every three years, so maintaining existing boats rather than building them anew is increasingly necessary.

RELIGION AND CULTURE

The majority of the islanders are Muslim, but there are also many Christians, and both religions are sometimes mixed with local beliefs which are older in origin. While traditionally reserved, the islanders are tolerant of visitors provided they dress discreetly and behave in a manner in keeping with local customs. Mafia women wear the colourful patterned kanga of the Swahili coast (see box, page 89), and on weekends and religious holidays men exchange Western dress for the long, white *kanzu*. Older folk who remember the British era can speak some English, as can staff working at the tourist lodges, but it can help to know a little Swahili when talking to other islanders.

Mafia is a conservative society, and the passing visitor is unlikely to be asked for handouts. Children who beg from tourists are quickly reprimanded by their elders. Please make sure that you, and your travelling companions, keep it this way. (For further information, see page 102.)

GETTING THERE AND AWAY

BY AIR The most efficient way of getting to Mafia is by light aircraft (Cessna Caravan or AIRVAN). The flight path to Mafia is within sight of the Rufiji River Delta, at 40km² the largest delta in East Africa with the region's greatest concentration of mangroves. The views are impressive; the dhows look tiny as they go about their fishing unfeasibly far from shore. At the time of writing, and after much stalling, the new 1.9km runway is finally under construction in Kilindoni, so a bumpy arrival on Mafia's uneven gravel airstrip should soon be a thing of the past.

In addition to using one of the airlines below, you can also **charter planes** to Mafia from a range of companies in Dar es Salaam and Zanzibar, with the cost of a small aircraft from Coastal or Tropical costing around US$900. Note that an airport **departure tax** of US$5 per person, which includes a US$1 'safety fee', is payable in cash on leaving Mafia, although flights with Coastal normally include this in the ticket price.

Airlines

✈ **Coastal Aviation** www.coastal.co.tz. 2 daily flights from Dar (*30mins; US$125 one-way*) leaving at 10.45 & 15.00. Return flights from Mafia depart at 12.45 & 16.00. Connecting flights to Zanzibar, Pemba & the Tanzanian safari circuit are available at Dar. Also 1 daily flight from Kilwa to Mafia (*25mins; US$190 one-way*), departing 12.10 & returning 11.25.

✈ **Safari Airlink** www.flysal.com. 2 daily flights from Dar to Mafia via Zanzibar & other destinations along the coast. Check website for schedule & prices.

✈ **Tropical Air** www.tropicalair.co.tz. 1 daily flight from Dar to Mafia (*30mins; US$120 one-way*), leaving Dar at 09.00 & returning from Mafia at 10.00.

Mafia airport Mafia's small airport (⏰ *around 08.00–18.30, unless there's an early morning flight*) is situated on the edge of the main town of Kilindoni, a 15km drive from Utende, where most of the tourist lodges are located. It's Mafia's centre of communication for visitors, and even if tourists arrive on Mafia by boat they tend to be directed the 1km from the harbour to the airport. Currently, the airport has a simple waiting room with huge leather sofas and basic toilets, while outside a reasonable curio shop sells kangas, kikois and imported wooden carvings for those last-minute souvenirs. Plans for a new terminal and decent runway have been 'ongoing' for many years now. There's no longer a currency exchange at the airport, but there is a branch of the National Microfinance Bank in Kilindoni, albeit the ATM only accepts cards from account holders. Lodges will take credit cards, but it's still wise to bring an amount of cash with you from the mainland.

Visitors with a hotel reservation will be met at the airport for their transfer. If you don't have a reservation, most of the lodges have representatives who speak English, and can radio the lodges to organise accommodation subject to availability. They can also help individual travellers to find a Land Rover taxi, costing a fixed price of Tsh40,000 (*US$18*) to Utende one-way; note that you'll cross the border into the marine park *en route,* so have the fee (*US$20pp/day*) for the requisite number of days ready in US dollars cash, and remember to keep your receipt as proof of payment when you leave the island. Taking a tuk tuk will be cheaper but it takes longer.

BY BOAT The options for budget travellers who wish to visit Mafia are limited to boats that connect Kilindoni to the mainland. Many of these dhows are uncomfortable and crowded and the trip can take anything from 10 to 24 hours; the safety record is none too inspiring either (see box, page 81). Equally, if it's too windy, none will sail. If you want to take a boat, make sure you check that they're properly licensed to carry passengers or vehicles, and at the very least have marine radios and lifejackets on board.

For the incorrigible, a tide table is incorporated in the free booklet, the *Dar Guide*, available from bars and hotels in Dar es Salaam. This is invaluable when trying to organise a boat trip to Mafia, as the boats have to arrive at high tide, and often leave on a high tide, too. In Kilindoni though, a jetty is under (painfully slow) construction, and has been in use for some time in spite only being half-built. Should it ever finish, it would mean that boats no longer have to restrict their arrival to high tide. This should lead to a much more regular service in the future.

The closest mainland port to Mafia is Kisiju, 30km from Dar, and 45km southeast of Mkuranga on the Kilwa road. From the Kariakoo bus depot in Dar, take a bus to Kisiju and then a dhow to Mafia. Make sure you arrive in Kisiju before 14.30, when the last dhow leaves for Mafia. Another possibility from Dar es Salaam is via Kimbiji, easily reached by catching the motor ferry from the city centre to Kigomboni (boats leave every 10 minutes or so and take 5 minutes) then dalla dalla direct to Kimbiji (about an hour). There are also dhows connecting Mafia to Kilwa Kivinje. Finally, a rather sporadic service

Over the past 2,000 years, turtle-shell, mangrove poles and seashells have been part of East Africa's trade to Arabia. By the 1960s, however, it had become clear that natural resources were not coping with human progress. In Tanzania, dried and salted fish, exported to the mainland, contributes more to the national protein consumption than meat and poultry combined. Dynamite fishing became very popular on Tanzania's coast, despite the destruction that it causes to fish populations and to coral. Small-mesh, beach-seine nets were catching all sizes of fish, again damaging populations. In some areas the only source of building materials has been coral, used as bricks and in the production of lime: this was the second-largest industry on Mafia at one time. Mangrove wood is very hard, insect-resistant, and makes excellent building material, so vast areas were cleared to provide timber, fuelwood, farmland and salt pans for salt production.

In the 1970s, four islands were declared marine reserves to slow the damage, but in the absence of facilities to police the park, fishermen ignored the rules and continued as usual. By 1995, it was clear that conservation had become an urgent priority, so the following year a partnership of investors, communities and the government set up the Board of Trustees of Marine Parks and Reserves of Tanzania, and on 6 September 1996, an area of Mafia extending across 822km² was gazetted as Tanzania's first marine park, to protect the ecosystems as well as the future livelihood of coastal people. The park embraces most of the southern and eastern shore of Mafia, including Chole Bay and associated reefs, a number of isolated atolls to the south of the main island, and the reefs enclosing Juani, Jibondo and Bwejuu islands.

The marine park now owns seven boats and has one full-time park warden plus many rangers. The park authorities are aiming to co-operate and collaborate with local residents, using community-based projects to dispel conflict between groups. If the islands are to be protected, the success of the marine park is imperative. Mangroves trap river sediments that would be otherwise washed out to sea and, along with coral reefs, protect the shoreline from the erosion of rising sea levels. The natural forest shields the island's crops from storm damage from the ocean, and a healthy ecosystem helps in the recovery from natural disasters such as cyclones, hurricanes and floods. Significantly, wetlands have also been shown to provide clean water, perhaps the most significant issue in terms of sustainable development of the islands.

For further details, contact the warden in charge, Mr George Msumi, Mafia Island Marine Park (✆ 023 240 2690; e mafiaisland@marineparks.go.tz).

runs from Niamisati in the Rufiji Delta once a day, leaving around midday and arriving in Kilindoni six hours later, before departing for the return journey at around 08.00. To reach Niamisati it's a 3–4-hr drive from Dar, or 2 hours' taxi ride from Mbalala. There is also a 04.00 departure from Kilindoni to Kisiju, though this is fundamentally a coconut-export vessel that happens to allow passengers on board.

The island infrastructure is generally basic. Hardly any villages are connected to mains water or electricity and there is only one tarred road from Kilindoni to Utende. Throughout the rest of the island the best you'll find is a bouncy sandy track. Vehicles are few, mainly Land Rover pick-ups and 4x4s belonging to the hotels and other organisations. Most local people use bicycles and motorbikes to get around, although the former are quite hard work on the sandy roads. **Bicycles** can be rented by arrangement with the New Lizu Hotel in Kilindoni (page 381), or from any of the lodges, whilst **motorbikes** are available for hire from Whale Shark Lodge (page 381).

A not-very-reliable **minibus** runs every 3 hours or so between Kilindoni and Utende charging less than US$1 one-way. It seats a minimum of 12 and has no fixed timetable – it departs when it's full. **Dalla dallas** shuttle between Kilindoni and Utende, picking people up along the way. They're not the most comfortable means of getting around, but are a good way of meeting local people and really getting to understand life on Mafia. Alternatively, a **motorbike taxi** can be picked up in Kilindoni – but safety should be seriously considered first. **Hitchhiking** is an accepted means of getting about, but it usually entails a long wait. Islanders also use *jahazis*, widely referred to in English as dhows, to commute between Kilindoni and outlying villages on Mafia, and for inter-island travel.

Free **maps** of Mafia can be obtained from the friendly Mafia Island Marine Park office, an obligatory stop to pay fees *en route* from the airport to all Utende lodges.

WHERE TO STAY AND EAT   *Map, page 368, unless otherwise stated*

Mafia isn't really the place for easy backpacking, but budget travellers who do come here may stop in Kilindoni itself. Meanwhile, the majority of Mafia's tourists head straight through town and over to one of the more upmarket small lodges in Utende or on Chole Island. There were lovely lodges in Bweni and Ras Mbisi for a period, encouraging tourists to venture a little further into the island, but sadly these are both closed at the time of going to press. With luck they will reopen by the time of your visit and both locations are well worth considering as part of a twin-centre Mafian adventure (see box, below). If budgets are higher, the private islands of Fanjove and ultra-luxurious Thanda offer tremendous experiences. For **camping**, there is a fully kitted-out campsite at Big Blu in Utende (page 383) and, if you have your own tent, Meremeta (page 383) offers camping for US$10 per person including breakfast. It is possible

---

BEACH AND BAY – MAFIA'S PERFECT COMBINATION

Mafia's attraction has long been its quiet charm and the easy access to the marine park centred on Chole Bay. Yet for some visitors, these perks have had to be weighed against the lack of endless beaches found on its busier northern rival, Zanzibar. What many don't realise, however, is that Mafia does have miles of powder-sand beach…just not on Chole Bay, where many visitors stay. It's well worth considering an organised trip to some of the picture-perfect ocean sandbanks, heading to the 7km beach at Ras Mbisi or Bweni, or indulging in beach life on Thanda or Fanjove islands. All of these can be easily combined with snorkelling or diving trips from Utende's lodges, making a beach and bay experience the very best of both worlds.

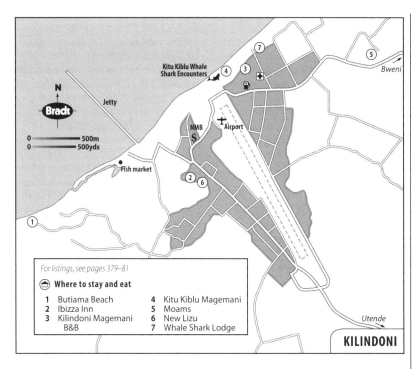

For listings, see pages 379–81

that camping may also return at Whale Shark Lodge. Otherwise, check with the marine park authorities before camping independently, as it's not legal to camp in Tanzania unless you're in a specified area – don't take any chances.

KILINDONI *Map, above*

The guesthouses here are all pretty basic, with little to draw travellers to most of them. They are still generally better in value and appeal than their price-matched Zanzibari counterparts, but a far better bet is to head to the more upmarket Butiama Beach or the simple treehouses at Kitu Kiblu Magemani.

Upmarket

❋ ⌂ **Butiama Beach** (15 rooms) m 0787 474084; e maura@coraldivers.co.za; www. butiamabeach.com. On the edge of the Mafia Island Marine Park & just a 10min walk south along the beach from Kilindoni, or a bumpy 10min drive through the village outskirts, Butiama Beach is charming, cool & calm: an immediately likeable lodge with winding sand pathways, well-tended lawns, lovely public areas, a super beach & brilliant bungalows. Rooms, in trademark aquamarine blue buildings, are both creatively stylish & practical. Spacious, both inside & out, the well-designed detached rooms offer comfort & style, with tremendous care & creativity taken in their thoughtful, colour co-ordinated décor & amenities.

Terraces are broad, with welcoming hammocks, tables for al fresco dining, batik shadecloths for privacy & totally tropical outlooks, with palms, flowers &, for many, the glittering sea. Aside from the majority dbl & twin rooms, there is a spacious trpl & 2 conjoined rooms perfect for travelling friends or families, who will appreciate the relaxed, laidback vibe of the place, not to mention the giant, cuddly whale shark hanging up in the bar. The heart of the lodge is the seafront circular bar area, surrounded by colourful cushion-clad baraza booths, just crying out for afternoon chilling or pre-dinner cocktails. There's a well-stocked bookshelf, a snooker table & a beautiful palm-shaded swimming pool, complete with loungers, pole shading & cracking sea views: simply marvellous at sunset. If you can drag yourself away, guests can borrow kayaks from the beachfront to explore the neighbouring mangrove creeks or experience village life with a walk to market (staff guides available on request) or the morning fish auction on the adjacent beach. Snorkellers & divers must head to the other side of the island around Chole Bay, a 20–30min drive, where they can visit Big Blu (page 383), also owned by Butiama, but guests here do benefit from a better beach than many around Chole Bay. All in all, it's outstanding value for money. B&B/HB. **$$$$$–⚲**

☀ 🏠 **Kitu Kiblu Magemani** (5 rooms)
m 0748 520799/0787 712427; e 2chole@gmail.com; www.cholemjini.com; ⏱ Jul–Mar. This is Chole Mjini for backpackers! Built by the formidable husband & wife team behind Chole's ingenious treetop lodge (page 384), this delightful tented camp is found on the forested slopes behind Kilindoni Beach. Initially a base camp for whale-shark researchers & those on internships with the Kitu Kiblu conservation project (see box, page 372), Magemani now happily accepts travellers, too. Each of the 5 spacious safari tents is raised on stilts, with wraparound decks, & cool shaggy makuti-thatched roofs. Inside, there's a simple timber bed, electricity point & free-standing fan; immaculate composting toilets & showers are currently in a shared ablution block, though en suites are planned. The treehouses & stilted tents are not only tremendous fun, but they allow for better air flow & views without cutting down any trees, demonstrating the extreme conservation aims of the owners. For socialising & chilling, there's a beachfront area & simple restaurant, an evening fire pit (ukuleles may even be on hand) & a stunning sandy beach with a brilliant view of the dhows heading to the nearby harbour & sunsets on the watery horizon. Long term, the Magemani team is hoping to expand to 20 tents, whilst carefully retaining its seclusion & forest, & also to add a dive centre, pool, & a treehouse bar/restaurant in the most strikingly beautiful giant sweet almond tree beside the beach. A great-value spot if you can get space. B&B; HB available. **$$$$**

Mid range

🏠 **Kilindoni Magemani B&B** (10 rooms)
m 0675 168893/0624 722538; e ali.hatibu@gmail.com/maura@coraldivers.co.za. Opened at the end of 2015, Kilindoni Magemani (not to be confused with Magemani Camp at Kitu Kiblu,

above) is a neat, efficient place, with charming staff, but somehow no soul. Rooms are in sgl-storey-red-roofed cottages at the back of a flat lawned area. Interiors are neat, cool & clean, with AC & satellite TV, a desk & marble bathrooms; outside, they have small terraces with neat flower beds. The white-marble restaurant is in the main house with an open-kitchen; food is prepared fresh to order, so is best ordered at least 1hr in advance. For US$12 you can enjoy a 3-course meal, or for US$7–8 you can settle for some calamari or chicken & rice. There are plans to expand this resort to 40 rooms & add a raised swimming pool & restaurant, so its atmosphere & facilities may change dramatically. There is no beach access here & taxis will be necessary to get around. B&B. **$$$**

🏠 **Moams** (16 rooms) m 0659 666222;
e moamshotel@gmail.com; www.moamshotel.com. Rising incongruously from the backstreets of Kilindoni, Moams's gleaming apricot-coloured buildings are the brainchild of 5 local government officials & businessmen keen to establish a hotel (Moams is, in fact, an acronym for their names). Opened in 2016, rooms are in 4 identical 2-storey buildings, complete with mirrored windows, small balconies & a central staircase. Inside, grey tiled floors, white wrought-iron beds & an eclectic mix of other furniture fill the rooms, & there's a bijou en suite where the shower tray backs right up to the toilet! Outside, there's a sizeable black-&-white-striped car park & a shaded area under blue tarpaulin where heavy iron bar stools surround high glass-topped tables. The large restaurant has ceiling-to-floor arched windows overlooking the complex & red tartan tables set for 2, but a distinct lack of any atmosphere. The pièce de résistance, however, is the (allegedly soundproofed) 'nightclub' above. Follow the royal blue staircase, complete with a few token purple strip lights, to find this drinking den. There's a large semicircular granite bar selling Dodoma's finest Tanzanian wine & local firewater, a serious lighting rig, DJ box, smoking balcony, & a few strategically placed sofas around the edge of the room. Wed is African night here & Fri/Sat are club nights … though it's hard to see any night being terribly appealing. The hotel is clean, adequate & better built & kitted out than most local establishments, but it's missing warmth & character, & as such is more likely to appeal to the local business travel market. B&B. **$$$**

Budget

🏠 **Ibizza Inn** (12 rooms) 📱 0783 133988/0658 273733; 📧 ibizzainn@hotmail.com. Around the back of the main street, this tangerine-coloured establishment, with neat, well-tended gardens, is the most comfortable of the central Kilindoni guesthouses & by far the cleanest. The sofas might be straight out of the 1970s, but rooms are bright, cheery & a good size, with wrought-iron beds, a small wall-mounted TV, large bathrooms & efficient AC in some. The entrance hall doubles as a cosy lounge & TV room, & feels homely & welcoming, whilst the outside bar/restaurant enjoys lovely views over the banana- & coconut-filled valley below. Here, groovy African tunes, free Wi-Fi & delightful staff make it a pleasant & relaxed spot to enjoy a Swahili meal or watch the football projected on the wall. Used mainly by Dar professionals working at the hospital, it's primarily a local guesthouse, but it's well maintained, efficient & good value. B&B. **$$**

🏠 **Whale Shark Lodge** (6 bandas) 📞023 201 0201; 📱 0755 696067; 📧 carpho2003@yahoo. co.uk. Outside central Kilindoni, a good 15min walk from the airport past the main hospital, this camp (formerly Mafia Pwani Camp) is one of the only basic lodges to offer great service & a relaxing atmosphere. The camp is in a beautiful, peaceful area overlooking the sea, excellent for spotting rufous elephant shrew & vervet monkey, & has considerable potential. Individual tangerine-hued bandas (5 en suite; 1 with outside bathroom) are sizeable & clean, with bright interiors, red concrete floors, nets on windows, sturdy coconut-wood beds made up with colourful batik sheets, fans & 24hr electricity. Despite the good standard of building, facilities are very basic & there's no hot water, although buckets of boiled water are available on request, & the lodge tries hard to make the best of what they have. Between the rooms & the beach below, the covered cliff-top lounge & bar is encircled by comfy wooden chairs. Here, filling seafood dishes (*US$6*) are offered as well as a selection of sandwiches, & a wine list. If you follow the steep pathway down to the beach, you'll come to the campsite (*US$7*). Whale Shark rents out motorbikes on request & once allowed self-sufficient camping, which may return in the future. **$$**

Shoestring

🏠 **New Lizu Hotel** (5 rooms) 📞023 201 0180; 📧 lizuhotel@yahoo.co.uk. Used almost exclusively by local traders, this is a 1min walk from the market & 10mins from the dhow landing jetty. With 24hr electricity, mosquito nets & fans, it is fairly clean but extremely basic. Rooms are en suite but with limited cold water (hot water can be boiled on request), & toilets are flushed with a bucket. The hotel does offer a laundry service, a stationery shop (effectively acting as reception), a phone, Wi-Fi, & an internet café (*US$1/30mins*). A simple bar/restaurant sells sodas, & rice & seafood meals, but no alcohol. B&B. **$**

UTENDE The number of accommodation options around Utende has increased in recent years, but thankfully remains at a low level and retains its escapist charm. There's a reasonable amount of choice, even for those on a tighter budget, although the more upmarket places remain the most popular.

Exclusive

☀️ 🏠 **Pole Pole** (7 bungalows) 📧 book@ polepole.com; www.polepole.com; 🕐 Jun–Mar. Italian-managed Pole Pole, meaning 'slowly, slowly' in Swahili, is a superb destination for relaxation & is consistently a pleasure to visit. Designed to be fairly luxurious whilst retaining a rustic charm, it's smart without a hint of pretence. Set in a garden of coconut palms, & connected by pathways of the softest sand, it has a small beach, perhaps 100m wide, with mangroves on either side. The bungalows, built almost entirely from organic materials, have en-suite bathrooms with a shower, twin sinks & an eco-friendly flush toilet – waste water is collected into a phytopurification bamboo pool where it is filtered for use on the garden. Bedrooms have a polished wooden floor, simple furniture, ceiling fan & 24hr electricity plus a back-up generator; dbl or twin beds are surrounded by a walk-in mosquito net. Large dbl-doors lead onto a very wide, shaded veranda overlooking the sea below, complete with relaxing Zanzibari daybeds & well-cushioned chairs. In keeping with its chill-out vibe, Pole Pole operates a strict mobile-phone policy with guests requested to keep phones on silent mode & only make calls from within their rooms, & Wi-Fi is only available in the office. Italian-influenced 4-course dinners are served in the airy restaurant; Swahili dinners are offered once a week or on request. Service is attentive, gentle & helpful,

& there are also 2 good masseuses on hand for decadent relaxation. Pole Pole has a lovely sail-shaded swimming pool, & snorkelling, diving, game fishing & island excursions are offered. 1 dhow trip – usually including some snorkelling & perhaps a BBQ picnic lunch – is normally offered every day on a complimentary basis. Between Oct & Mar the lodge operates trips to see (& on occasion swim with) the migratory whale sharks. If you're looking for somewhere small, comfortable & fairly remote with great diving & snorkelling, low-key excursions & a totally chilled atmosphere, then Pole Pole offers very good value indeed. FB inc 1 daily activity; min age 10. ♨

Luxury

🏠 **Kinasi Lodge** (14 bungalows) m 0787 424588; e holiday@kinasilodge.com; www. kinasilodge.com; ⏲ Jun–end Mar. On grassy banks above a lovely, coconut-clad sandy beach sits this Indian Ocean hideaway, named after the indigo pass through the outer reef that leads into Chole Bay. Kinasi has large, landscaped lawns studded with coconut palms, which slope steeply down to a small sandy beach & the ocean. There's a swimming-pool area, complete with poolside bar & grill, & dotted around are solid, self-contained bungalows with makuti roofs & stone verandas furnished with armchairs & hammocks. Inside, Zanzibar-style queen-sized beds are enveloped in vast mosquito nets. The lodge's multi-level, open-sided bar & lounge area contains a top-notch reference library, book-swap service & comfortable long couches & armchairs plus a TV & free Wi-Fi. The adjacent dining area serves an eclectic fusion menu & themed dinners ranging from a seafood fondue to poolside Swahili nights. A separate grill & pizza kitchen has also been installed for more casual dining, & meals can be taken in a group or individually. There's a well-stocked walk-in wine cellar & cocktail bar for pre-dinner wine tastings & canapés. Kinasi has its own fully equipped watersports & PADI dive centre beside the beach, & the resident instructor can arrange dives in & around Chole Bay, as well as snorkelling trips, windsurfing, kayaking & game fishing. An 'activity manager' in the lodge organises various excursions (at additional cost), which include the usual range of dhow trips, village visits, & 4x4 excursions across the island, plus the option of borrowing mountain bikes to explore local villages. The lodge has also

constructed a 2hr nature trail for birdwatching along the coastal flats & through patches of coastal scrub. To complement these activities, the Isis Spa has 3 treatment rooms, including the romantic Pharaoh bath, & a charming, professional Thai therapist. HB/FB. ♨

🏠 **Shamba Kilole Lodge** (6 rooms) m 0786 110671; e info@shambakilolelodge.com; www. shambakilolelodge.com; ⏲ mid Jun–mid Apr. Quiet & peaceful, Shamba Kilole's 3 chalets & 3 suites each have a different theme & colour scheme. They're all thoughtfully decorated with ochre exteriors, traditional ceilings, reclaimed dhow furniture, mosquito nets & an individual theme. Each has a couch that doubles as a 3rd bed, as well as a fan, 24hr electricity & a semi-open bathroom. A cosy 2-storey lounge is filled with wooden & coir-rope chairs, shelves stuffed with books, & cats who steal the comfiest spots. There is beach access, but it's more of a 'bush beach', with the sea itself only occasionally visible through the band of mangroves, baobabs & palms. Sea swimming is difficult, but for those who do fancy a splash, walking for just a few mins brings you to a small bay where water access is easier. Diving is the main focus here, & there's a classroom & a lovely pool for novice/refresher dives (page 388). Alongside it, emerald lawns are perfect for candlelit Italian dinners or wine tastings from the well-stocked cellar. The lodge tries its best to be eco-friendly, with all wood taken from authorised cultivators, rainwater collection & no septic tank. It's a delightful place to stay, popular with honeymooners, thanks to its design aesthetics & charming Italian owners. HB/FB. $$$$$–♨

Upmarket

🏠 **Mafia Island Lodge** (40 rooms) m 0763 527619; e info@mafialodge.com; www.mafialodge.com; ⏲ Jun–Apr. This simple government-built lodge is situated on one of the island's few open palm-lined beaches, directly opposite the ruins of Chole Mjini on Chole. Under new Italian management since 2016, Iris & her builder-cum-chef husband, Giuliano, have brought genuine warmth & a great deal of East African experience to the lodge, which, given some investment, could really improve things here. The lodge itself consists of reasonable recently renovated rooms, with standard & superior options available for couples, friends & families. There are plans to upgrade the bathrooms, & perhaps enlarge some rooms, but for now, they have dark wood furniture, built-in storage, terracotta-tiled floors & sea-facing French windows. There's 24hr hot water, & despite the uninspiring interiors, it's a reliable, functional place offering easy access to Mafia's superb diving without breaking the bank. The main bar/restaurant is a large & fairly pleasant spot, with an airy terrace & an Italian–African fusion menu. Myriad games are available & there is a small shop selling a few essentials. There's also an internet access point (*US$10/hr*), a pool table & equipment for beach volleyball. Diving is arranged through the PADI-affiliated Mafia Island Diving (page 388), whose instructors speak English, French & Italian. Mafia's only real tour company, Mafia Island Tours, is based here & is an obvious choice for booking excursions: a short hop to Chole Island for a village tour (*US$15pp inc village fee*); & ½-day trip to the Kua Ruins & Channel (*US$30pp*); picnic/snorkelling trip to Marimbani or Kitutia (*US$50pp*) & a full-day island excursion to Ras Mkumbi or Bwejuu Island (*US$75pp*). B&B; HB & FB available. **$$$$$**

Mid range

⌂ **Big Blu** (3 rooms) m 0787 474108/0654 089659; e info@bigblumafia.com; www. bigblumafia.com. What started off as a dive centre in 2005 now has 5 rooms & a circle of bell tents, too. Although the diving emphasis remains, guests do not have to be divers to stay. The 3 palm-woven beach bungalows house pretty bedrooms, decorated with pastel kikois & blue mosquito nets, plus a hot-water shower. There are also 2 new stone bungalows offering similar accommodation with AC. Across the beautiful gardens, the well-kept bell tents represent truly amazing value on this side of the island. In a lovely cool area behind the main lodge, the semicircular collection of little tents sit under permanent protective shade, & each has 2 wooden beds, clean linen, a lock box for storage, simple *mkeke* mats & 24hr electricity (plug point & light). A shared ablution block provides campers with clean showers & toilets. Meals, including a 3-course b/fast, are offered in a chilled-out restaurant right on the beach, & there's a lovely ocean-facing lounge area: white, curved seating booths, blue-hued cushions, sand underfoot & a good collection of nature reference books. As well as diving (page 387), Big Blu also offers

seasonal whale shark-watching trips from sister property Butiama Beach (page 379), snorkelling, cycling, dhow sandbank trips & windsurfing. Considerable discounts are available for room & dive combinations. B&B/HB. **$$$–$$$$$**

⌂ **Mafia Beach Bungalows** (11 rooms) m 0755 828825; www.mafiabeachbungalows. com. High up on a steep hill, with only a glimpse of sea through the trees, this low-budget backpacker place is falling slowly into disrepair. There are 5 lacquered, woven mkeke huts, each identical & all named after nearby islands. There's just about enough floor space for a bed, but not enough to walk around it, although there is a fan & mosquito net. Basic bathrooms have no hot water & are just about functional; red concrete terraces are crumbling from the edges in. In addition, there's a half-built 3-storey block just above the beach, which, if ever completed, will offer an additional 6 rooms & a roof-top restaurant, but for now it is just unsightly concrete-block walls. Meals are served in the makuti-thatched bar on the mangrove beach, accessed down a precariously steep path. It's compact with just 2 tables & is fair to say that the menu will be extremely limited. B&B. **$$$**

⌂ **Meremeta Lodge** (8 rooms) m 0787 345460; e meremetalodge@hotmail.com; www. meremetalodge.com. It's impossible to miss this place, with its kerb-side location on the tar road just outside Utende, & frivolous dolphin cut-outs along its external wall. Quirky Meremeta receives consistently favourable reviews for its friendly atmosphere & relaxed vibe. Chintz dominates, & everything here is decorated: fish & whale sharks are painted on the pink walls & giant shells & driftwood adorn the gardens, but it all adds to the curious charm. Rooms are a vision in pink, filled with carvings, ornaments & a fan. Outside a small veranda covered in cushions is filled with ornamental trees, silk flowers & swathes of fabric draped from the ceiling. One room is actually a tent with solid walls around it & makuti thatch above it, to give a 'camping' feel. There's an open-sided dining room, where heavy tables for 2 on sandy floors are the setting for simple but fresh 2-course lunches (*US$10*) & 3-course dinners (*US$15*), although meals can always be served alfresco on request. Outside, chickens roam among the pineapple & passion-fruit trees, & the active can rent quad bikes (*US$75/hr*) & motorbikes (*US$50/ hr*) or use the mountain bikes free of charge.

13

There's also a new swimming pool for 2017. The level of service here is stellar: the charming & formidable owner will bend over backwards to ensure his guests have the best possible stay. It's not on the beach, but the passion & enthusiasm of the management go a long way to making up for that, especially at this price. There are currently plans to build a 16-room sister ocean-front hotel, just north of Didimiza. It's a lovely coconut-filled plot, with views across to Jibondo Island. Meremeta is a man who tends to embrace his projects with gusto, so this may be worth checking out. The service, if nothing else, is bound to be good. B&B. **$$–$$$**

Budget

🏠 **Didimiza Guesthouse** (4 rooms) m 0787 071543; e alawia75@yahoo.com; www. didimizamafia.blogspot.co.uk. Coming from Kilindoni, turn right just before the marine park offices, & head through the rice fields towards the rickety bridge that signals Didimiza's entrance. A simple, locally owned guesthouse, it offers 3 dbl & 1 family room in baby-blue thatched buildings, all connected by flower-lined, raked sandy paths. Solid wooden beds, brilliant white sheets & towel-filled shelves furnish the rooms, while smiling whale sharks offer light relief on the walls & yellow bathrooms are tidy & clean, with a wide shady veranda. There is a solar-powered fan & light, too. 3 meals a day (*US$7/15 lunch/dinner*) are served around 1 communal table in the semi-complete restaurant area with plans, when the money's available, to have a lounge area as well. It's cool & breezy, & there are loungers scattered around the garden for relaxation, but no easy beach access. B&B. **$$**

🏠 **Ramblers B&B & Bar** (3 rooms) m 0786 524207; www.mafiabeachbungalows.com. Right in the middle of Utende village, behind high gates, Ramblers serves as overflow accommodation for its sister property Mafia Beach Bungalows (page 383), an activity base for Nungwi Diving Mafia Island Dive Centre (hence the number of boats sitting in the car park), & a bar area. Rooms are very basic & there are better options nearer the beach. B&B. **$$**

CHOLE ISLAND The two lodges on Chole are polar opposites: one an originally designed, ecologically friendly retreat; the other a bottom-of-the-scale backpacker hangout. Regardless of your accommodation choice, all visitors to the island must pay a US$10 per person village levy.

✳ 🏠 **Chole Mjini Lodge** (6 treehouses, 1 chalet & dhow) m 0784 520799; e 2chole@ gmail.com; www.cholemjini.com; ⊕ Jun–Mar. This fabulous lodge, situated in the north of Chole Island, boasts large, treehouse bedrooms perched high in the baobabs, situated amongst the crumbling 19th-century ruins of Chole Mjini. This place is emphatically not catering for people seeking Sheraton-style luxury or a conventional beach retreat – there is no electricity for starters (lighting is by paraffin lamps at night, so bring a good torch!) & the waterfront in front of the lodge is overgrown with mangroves. Nevertheless, this must rank as one of the most original & aesthetically pleasing lodges on the East African coast. It's also an atmospheric base for exploring Chole Island & the surrounding waters. Lunch is usually served at group tables in a family atmosphere, with fresh seafood & vegetable dishes in a mixture of African & European styles, usually with tasty sauces. B/ fast & dinner are served at individual tables dotted around the garden, jetty or ruins. 6 of the bedrooms stand high on stilted platforms; 3 are in or beside their own huge baobab tree. Each is made almost entirely of wood, thatch & local materials by the people of Chole – & the sheer quality of the carpentry says much for the islanders' reputation for building fine dhows. All rooms are slightly different, but climb the stairs & inside you'll generally find a large dbl bed surrounded by a walk-in mosquito net, an open wardrobe & dressing area, & a large, padlocked wooden box for your valuables. Most also have an upper floor, with relaxing daybeds or hammocks. Each of these treehouse rooms has private ablutions – but all are separate & down on the ground. The sit-down toilet is a long-drop, using ash to keep it dry & composting; they rank as one of the cleanest long-drops in Africa. Hidden from view behind a circular bamboo enclosure, the ingenious, open-air showers are good & hot. Another popular contraption is the pulley system used to deliver morning coffees to guests; children will love playing with it! Chole Mjini has just 1 more conventional chalet, which is on the ground level, next to the lodge's main lounge/dining area. Its walls are open to the breeze, & it has a huge bed, a conventional flush toilet (the only one on the island) & a large sunken bath. It's not quite as romantic as the treehouses, but might be just the place if stairs to the toilet don't appeal. Finally, a recent addition to the lodge's range of accommodation is a converted 40ft wooden dhow with 6 berths, allowing guests to spend a night or 2 on the water or fly-camping on a secluded beach. In keeping with the eco-friendly ethos, a community fee is included in the rates. There's no dive centre here, but scuba activities can be arranged through Big Blu or Mafia Island Diving just across the water (pages 387–8). There is no pool either, nor any beach to lie on, but there are organised walks, snorkel trips & excursions to nearby sandbars (usually 1–2 complimentary

trips organised daily). Visitors need to accept the lodge for what it is & then a really enjoyable stay is almost guaranteed. FB inc 1 daily activity; Mafia Airport transfers US$40/vehicle. 🐚

🏠 **Chole Foxes Lodge** (3 rooms) 📞023 201 0209; m 0787 877393; e cholefoxeslodge@ yahoo.com; 📘 CholeFoxesLodge. Named after Chole's population of flying foxes, Chole Foxes has recently been taken over by a retired Tanzanian doctor, Dr Mudy, & his wife. Together they are working steadily to improve this simple spot, whilst injecting some charm & genuine hospitality into the place. The neat bungalow bedrooms have simple but clean bathroom facilities & solar power. Along a sandy path, a couple of wooden dining tables overlook the sea, where homemade meals, predominantly seafood (excl b/fast), are lovingly served & well-regarded by guests. There are a few coir-rope loungers dotted about the garden & tours can be arranged on Mafia (tide dependent). **$$**

BWENI At Mafia's northern reaches, Bweni boasts a truly beautiful beach, and can be visited as part of a whole-island day trip. Its only lodge, the high-end Lua Cheia, is closed at the time of writing pending a major renovation. When reopened, it's certainly worth considering in combination with the one of the lodges around Chole Bay: the perfect beach and bay combination (see box, page 378).

🏠 **Lua Cheia Castaway Beach Camp** (8 rooms) m 0777 424588; e stay@mafiaisland. com; www.luacheiabeach.com; 🕐 Jun–end Mar. In the far north of Mafia, at Angel's Beach near Bweni, stands Lua Cheia. On a boomerang-shaped 2km stretch of white sand scattered with shells, its appeal is in its isolation – guests can truly escape modern life & there's a max of 16 guests so it's never crowded. The owners (those of Kinasi Lodge, see page 382) have tried to leave the area as natural as possible; there's no electricity, & solar power is used for the water, lights & fans, which are assisted by sea breezes. Mothballed for 4 years, Lua Cheia is scheduled to reopen for rustic beach chic in the near future, & very possibly by the time you are travelling. New

tented rooms, all under thatch for shade, will have verandas overlooking the beach from where there are lovely views of the surrounding bays. The style here has always been simple but comfortable: nightly driftwood fires are used for tasty cooking & there's a limited but good bar selection. Staff are friendly, so apart from appreciating the remote, desert-island feel, you can explore by dhow or kayak, swim or snorkel (even at low tide), visit the nearby lighthouse, or trek through the forest to the deserted beach on the opposite side of the island. Catch-&-release game-fishing trips are offered & there's a lovely island picnic trip to idyllic Barakuni, 5 miles offshore. Rates don't include the bumpy 55km transfer from Mafia airport. (US$120/vehicle, 1-way). FB. **$$$$**

RAS MBISI This is a 45-minute drive from the airport, largely on a bumpy, sandy track, but the scenery *en route* is lovely and the journey's end simply gorgeous. The powder-soft white sand and miles of deserted beach make this a truly fantastic location. Over the last decade simple Ras Mbisi Lodge had single-handedly opened this area up to those who wish to linger longer than just a day; sadly, however, it was struck by a devastating fire at the end of 2016, leaving an accommodation gap in this beautiful area. If you do venture here though, watch the daily catch arrive

13

on the beach as nets are hauled in from the shallow reef in front of the village. The teamwork and effort is immense: get involved with the tug-of-war effort if you're game, it'll provide entertainment for the villagers and makes for a good ice-breaker with the local community (see box, page 392).

THANDA ISLAND Roughly halfway between Mafia and the Rufiji Delta entrance on the Tanzanian coast, Thanda Island sits in the recently declared Shungi Mbili Island Marine Reserve. A picture-perfect tropical island, it's just over 1km in circumference, ringed with super-soft sand and protected by underwater reefs. There is only one place to stay on this piece of paradise: the ultra-luxurious private villa of the same name.

✳ 🏠 **Thanda Island** (5 rooms) ⚓ (South Africa) +27 35 772 6076; e info@thanda.com.za; www. thandaisland.com. Thanda is truly spectacular. Approached by sea or air, it is the quintessential Indian Ocean island idyll: a tiny patch of low, lush green vegetation, encircled by powder-white sand, lapped with intense turquoise waters. Yet it is exceptional, too, for there is no rustic *Robinson Crusoe* hut, no string hammock strung between a few palms, no remote fishing community. The only bottle on the shore here is likely to be chilled champagne, served in crystal & with style, for this is private-island luxury at its best. Reminiscent of the Kennedys' Cape Cod home, Thanda is a private villa of a kind previously unseen in these parts: American beach house glamour meets natural Scandi design in a truly exotic location. Marketed for exclusive use only, this is very much a luxury home, where charming, efficient staff encourage shoes-off relaxation. There are silky-smooth floating wooden floors throughout, high ceilings, beautiful colours & textures in the soft furnishings, an integrated Bose sound system & far-reaching ocean views at every turn. The gorgeous bedrooms all open onto the wraparound deck, & each has an outdoor designer bath & shower, the odd playful fabric & oodles of style. Everywhere is about decadent relaxation: places to sit in every corner – colourful ashanti beanbags, rattan cocoon chairs, cushioned loungers. The central lounge, in the cooling shades of Delft pottery, has lovely deep armchairs, a banqueting table under clusters of twine lamps, well-stocked wine fridges, a cigar humidor & some truly unbelievable indulgences: a giant marine aquarium, a white Steinway grand piano & some fascinating tribal artefacts, original art & seashells all of which merit closer inspection. The whole room opens onto the cool veranda, overlooking the beach, sea & phenomenal glass-sided swimming pool. If you crave a touch more 'Africa', cross the island to Turtle Beach & 'sleep out' in one of the rustic open-fronted 'bandas', albeit with beautiful Zanzibari beds & the same impeccable service. Activity options are endless; there's jet skis, kayaks, lasers, wakeboards, bodyboards, baskets of snorkels, fins & masks, deep-sea fishing, picnics to remote sandbanks, & even a tennis court in the making. That said, the pool is so magical that leaving it can be hard. Aimed squarely at multi-generation family groups, adults & children area equally well catered for with bunk beds, toys & games all readily available. Although off-grid, Thanda is 100% self-sufficient in energy & clean water, with an impressive solar farm, immaculate desalination plant & successful rainwater harvesting scheme all playing their part. Remarkably, there is also Wi-Fi & mobile phone reception. If the incredible island, accommodation & service weren't enough to tempt you here, then the exquisite food, courtesy of talented young chef, Melissa MacDonald, is reason enough to travel. From mackerel tartar with orange zest & basil, to intensely fruity watermelon sorbet; roast kingclip with caramelised carrots in ginger to lobster thermidor; decadent Crêpes Suzette to simple pizza from the wood-fired oven . . . the food is utterly scrumptious, original & prepared fresh from the finest seasonal ingredients. At US$10,000 a night for 10 guests, it's eye-wateringly expensive; but given its exclusive location, superlative staff & all-inclusive nature, is it value for money? Well, yes AI. 👑

DIVING *With Jean de Villiers*

Many people visit Mafia purely for its diving, which is often considered the best anywhere in East Africa. It's easy to dive two sites outside the bay on a single outing;

the trip out and back can also be great for fishing, sunbathing, sailing and dolphin spotting. The marine park off Chole Bay is home to 48 species of coral, including giant table corals, delicate sea fans, whip corals and huge stands of blue- and pink-tipped staghorn coral.

As well as the spectacular variety of reef fish there are turtles and large predatory fish such as grouper, Napoleon wrasse and barracuda. Stingray, manta rays (rare) and several species of shark are encountered in Kinasi Pass. November to January is best for the more common black-tip and white-tip reef sharks. The corals of Chole Bay, in the heart of the marine park, have recovered dramatically from damage caused by El Niño (of 1997–98) and the destructive fishing practices used before the establishment of the park, and the number of fish is now increasing again. The number of manta rays has sadly decreased significantly in recent years.

Almost all Mafia's best diving is in depths of less than 26m. Between June and September you can dive only within the lagoon-like Chole Bay, albeit in almost any weather. For the more challenging dives outside the bay, you have to wait until the calmer conditions from mid September to November. Outside the bay the average size of the fish is bigger, and you've a good chance of seeing a 2–3m grouper; these are friendly and let you come quite close. Inside the bay, visibility from June to September tends to be 10–15m, whereas from October to February it can be 25m, and high tide gives better visibility than low tide. Mafia is good for beginner divers, as it's very safe inside the bay. However, diving outside the bay on an outgoing tide can be extremely dangerous, with strong currents that can sweep you out to sea: if you miss your rendezvous with a boat, the next stop is Mogadishu. Make sure you check the tides before you set out.

When diving in the open ocean, divers are advised always to carry two means of signalling: one audible (a whistle or air horn) and one visible (an inflatable surface marker, a flare, strobe light or mirror). In addition, always wear a full wetsuit as protection against exposure, and drink water before commencing a dive. Don't take any risks or push the safety boundary while diving here; it's a long way to the nearest decompression chamber in Zanzibar. Note that you can't buy diving insurance in Tanzania – you must have this before you travel; it can be arranged online.

All of the lodges on Mafia offer diving excursions as well as full PADI courses, and those listed below offer specialist diving courses with every conceivable type of dive site – reefs and bommies, channels, walls, caves, drift, ocean and night dives. All these are accessible in a day, while diving safaris catering for 12 people can be arranged to destinations further afield such as Ras Mkumbi, Forbes Bay southeast of Mafia, and the spectacular reef complex around the Songo Songo Islands, which lie about 80km south of Mafia and about 50km north of Kilwa, and so an overnight trip is needed.

DIVE OPERATORS There are a number of dive operations in Mafia – all listed below. It's worth organising any specialist or 'learn to dive' courses in advance to guarantee space and talk through the options. The majority of operators are very good, and if you are planning on learning to dive on Mafia, it's well worth completing the e-learning scheme before you travel. It allows you to undertake the 'classroom' work online in advance, and so avoid spending your holiday reading up on the facts and physics! Do also remember to check if you need medical clearance to undertake any planned courses, so that this can be arranged in good time.

⚓ Big Blu Mafia Island Dive Centre
m 0787 474108; e diving@bigblumafia.com;

www.bigblumafia.com. This dedicated dive centre is the heart of the Big Blu complex (page 383),

13

operating within the lodge on the fringe of Utende Beach. With 3 instructors, 5 dive masters, 5 traditional dhows & a fibre-glass boat, this is one of the island's largest scuba operations. Teaching PADI courses from Discover Scuba introductory dives to Rescue Diver specialisms, & even Dive Master training through internships, it's a comprehensive outfit. There's a new classroom for courses, quality, up-to-date equipment & both groups or individuals can be catered for. *Diving US$45/80/215 sgl/dbl/6 dives; Open Water US$495; Advanced US$375; Rescue Diver US$375; equipment rental US$25/day.*

Blue World Diving m 0777 424588382; e kinasi@mafiaisland.com; www.kinasilodge.com. Based at Kinasi Lodge (page 382), this is a small PADI 5*centre, with a smart base, professional staff & good equipment. The team of 2 instructors & a dive master offer snorkelling trips, PADI novice & refresher courses, plus professional-standard qualifications like Dive Master certification. Night diving is occasionally possible but requires a minimum of 4 divers, & other specialisms such as Medic First Aid can be arranged. There are 3 dhows & a 26-inch twin-engine, fibre-glass boat (with a convenient water-level side door) based here, making both diving & fishing possible. *Diving US$45/90/240 sgl/dbl/6 dives; Open Water US$470; Advanced US$360; Medic First Aid US$180; equipment rental US$25/day.*

Mafia Island Diving m 0688 218569; e welcome@mafiadiving.com; www.mafiadiving. com. Operating at the heart of Utende Beach since 2005, this is one of the longest-standing dive operations on the island. A professional PADI 5* resort, expertly run by David von Helldorff, the centre offers high-quality snorkelling, diving & sailing experiences in the marine park & beyond. They have 6 instructors, 3 dive masters & a fleet of 6 boats, making it possible to arrange activities with ease. Their sandbank picnic day trips & sundowner cruises are particularly superb: friendly staff, dhows equipped with cushions, even a daybed on beautiful *Mawimbi*, stunning scenery all make for a decadent & totally tropical experience. Children & adults of all experience levels are well catered for with scuba courses, from novice to advanced & speciality, always available. From deep diver to underwater photography, night diver to peak performance buoyancy, or coral, sea turtle, seahorse or shark awareness specialisms, there are knowledgeable, multi-lingual staff on hand to teach in & out of the water. Also on land, you can embark on a series of community-focused trips around the island with the 4 dedicated excursion guides: head up to Bweni, the lily-filled hippo pools, to see the whale sharks or over to nearby islands. *Diving US$45/105/300 sgl/dbl/6 dives; Open Water US$580; Advanced US$350; Underwater Photographer US$260; equipment rental inc in all rates.*

Nungwi Diving Mafia Island Dive Centre m 0786 524207/0683 893318; e info@mafiabeachbungalows.com/ryanbritzz@ gmail.com; ✦ mafiaislanddivecentre. Based out of Ramblers B&B in Utende (page 384), Nungwi Diving appears to be something of an all-round island tour operator & informal dive centre. Offering trips around the island, seasonal whale-watching & deep-sea fishing trips as well as snorkelling & diving. The owner is not always around but there is currently 1 British dive instructor & 1 local dive master based here, along with a disproportionately large number of boats: 3 dhows & 3 speedboats for trips to Mange Reef.

Shamba Kilole Dive Centre m 0786 903752; e info@shambakilolelodge.com; www. shambakilolelodge.com. Operating from a lovely purpose-built dive centre, clearly visible beside the main tar road at Utende, Shamba Kilole is a very friendly, professional PADI centre with good classroom facilities, a large swimming pool for novice teaching & well-maintained equipment. Run by Marco, behind the lodge of the same name, courses are available from the introductory Discover Scuba course right through to the more serious Rescue Diver certifications & entry-level professional qualifications. The instructors here are warm & dedicated with a keen eye on minimising environmental impact. *Diving US$50/90/255 sgl/ dbl/6 dives; Open Water US$495; Advanced US$400; Speciality courses US$200–300; equipment rental US$20/day.*

DIVING AND SNORKELLING SITES IN MAFIA MARINE PARK In general terms, there is greater variety and volume of fish inside Chole Bay than out; however, it is equally the case that clarity and chance of spotting white tip sharks is often better outside the bay, although this is really reserved for advanced divers investigating the two massive walls and coral gardens. Without question, there are accessible and enjoyable sites for all levels around the island, from those just learning to experienced professionals.

There are at least half a dozen marine park dive sites in addition to those listed below and numerous snorkelling sites, too. Wherever possible, names given are those used by local fishermen.

The first three sites are relatively close together and can be reached on a stronger drift dive starting near the Pinnacle in Kinasi Pass. These sites sometimes suffer from being in the mouth of a bay in that the visibility can be poor for a few days after stormy periods at sea and when tidal currents are very strong at full moon or new moon.

Within Chole Bay

Kinasi Pass: South Wall (aka Kinasi Express) *Dive depth: max 27m. Recommended for experienced divers.* Justifiably Mafia's most famous dive site, this has it all: overhangs with caverns, big critters and corals. At times huge volumes of water flow through the pass, creating an exhilarating drift dive, or dive at slack water to enjoy the 26m wall and its resident potato cod and giant grouper. Schools of snappers and sweetlips are often here, as are their predators: barracuda, giant trevally, jacks, cobia, wahoo and kingfish. Rays and morays are common, with eagle rays and occasional stingrays visitors (late December to March is best). Finish the dive in a splendid coral garden, and maybe catch up with a Napoleon wrasse or a feeding turtle.

Kinasi Pass: Pinnacle *Dive depth: max 29m. Recommended for experienced divers or beginners under professional supervision.* In the entrance of the bay, 50m north of Kinasi Wall, this pinnacle rises sharply to within 8m of the surface, usually surrounded by a school or two of sweetlips or trevally and their attendant predators. When the visibility is good, this is the most likely place within the bay to meet a bull shark (or zambezi), although this is a less than an annual occurance. We also occasionally come across a 3m guitar fish (a shark that is half ray, with a flat, triangular head) and a huge mottled green-black giant grouper accompanied by a bevy of attendant yellow-and-black-striped pilotfish. It's an excellent site at slack water.

Utumbi (or Kinasi Wall) *Dive depth: 5–25m. Recommended for all certified divers. Outstanding snorkelling site nearby, mainly at low tide.* If you don't tackle the pass right off then this is the must-do dive in Mafia. About 300m before the pass, inside the bay, is a truly gorgeous reef: the ease of access and safe, sheltered location and the obliging currents all add up to a world-class dive. The corals rapidly change from soft corals (gorgonians and whip corals at the pass end), to more and more hard corals, until finally you find yourself in shallow gardens of tabular and staghorn acropora. The fish fauna is mostly typical reef inhabitants, with a huge variety of multi-coloured wrasses, parrotfish, damsels, surgeons, triggerfish and anthiases. Big wahoo and barracuda cruise off reef, and 2–3ft greasy cod and malabar grouper are abundant.

Milimani *Dive depth: max 20m. Recommended for all skill levels; often used for courses & Discover Scuba experiences.* Meaning 'mountain tops' in Swahili, this is an excellent site and the most-requested repeat dive in the park. This is a long reef characterised by spectacular coral turrets rising above corals to form mini mountains and alleys. A gentle entrance in just 6m of water over pure white sand makes this the easiest dive in the park, and the diversity of the coral is phenomenal: the topology of the reef is stunning and it just goes on and on. As you explore the twisting, turning reef interspersed with mounds of coral teeming with fish, you may become so absorbed that you suddenly find you're 20m deep with a towering reef above. A small gap in the reef is an excellent place to view planktivores, usually swarms of counter-shaded fusiliers and schools of unicorns, but occasionally a cruising stingray, accompanied by a flotilla of remoras and pilotfish. There are also a lot of layfish, nudibranchs and moray eels. You can end the dive by climbing over the reef crest to look for turtles or to join the millions of kasmira and blackspot snappers in the very shallow water among the magnificent fire corals.

Beyond Chole Bay

Dindini or Shangani Wall *Dive depth: max 24m. Recommended for experienced divers only.* Dindini is only accessible seasonally (Oct–Mar): it's directly in front of surf-pounded cliffs and about 1½ hours by boat. There are a lot of fish: big fish, small fish, sharks, rays and also turtles. In periods of good visibility, usually November–March, this is one of the better places in Mafia to see sharks, along with Mkadini (usually reef sharks). It's also good for large groupers and, very occasionally, big-game fish like tuna, sailfish and marlin. The wall has many caverns and U-shaped tunnels, and some deep, unexplored caves where there is the occasional appearance of large creatures. The dive ends on the top of the wall, with really spectacular powder blue, purple and pink alcyonaria soft corals teeming with fish, especially red-toothed triggerfish, and a variety of sturgeons.

Mlila or Jina Wall *Dive depth: max 24m. Recommended for experienced divers.* Seasickness can be a problem due to sea surges. Just over 1km away, or an hour by boat, the wall has formed a slight fold close to the cliffs. It starts out quite mediocre but rapidly changes as you get where fishing boats seldom penetrate. In the pocket there are more grouper than you'll probably ever see. There are also lots of other fish around and this is likely to be your best chance of seeing big Napoleons or getting close to a feeding turtle. At the base of the wall is a lot of coral, with many holes to investigate; look out for lobster and small stingrays, snappers, moray eels as well as giant and ribbon-tailed rays.

Miewe Shoulder – the 'Washing Machine' *Dive depth: max 25m. In slack water possible for all levels, in deep water just outside the bay during spring tides, 2hrs before high tide, this is almost white-water diving & only for experienced and advanced divers who can control their buoyancy instinctively and know how to surf currents without fear of injury.* Outside the bay, this is a sloping fringing reef north of the pass, with a fabulous diversity of fish, corals and topology. The reef is teeming with fish but you can't stop because the relentless current drags you over the top. The trick is to then drop down into one of the many deeper pools that lie just behind the jagged reef crest for a 'rinse and spin' cycle and watch the fish rush in and out. When you have been thoroughly wrung out you leave this lunar landscape of craters and spires and head south, across the current as much as possible, and will soon drift along the drop-off through Kinasi Pass for a very satisfying and relaxed end to an awesome experience.

Mkadini *Dive depth: max 25m. Recommended for all skill levels.* Off Miewe Island, there is a short vertical step in shallow water (12–14m max), this flattens out into a deeper shallow-sloping reef. There are many alcyonaria soft corals and diverse hard corals, lots of turtles (green and hawksbill), diverse groupers (back-saddled, lyretail, greasy cod, potato cod), schools of batfish, guitarfish and a chance to see white-tip reef sharks and dolphins.

Juani Reef *Dive depth: max 30m. Recommended for experienced divers.* A sloping fringing reef south of the pass extends for 12km. This is a good place to see turtles (green and hawksbill) and guitar fish, as well as stunning purple alcyonaria soft corals.

Mange Reef *Dive depth: max 24m. Recommended for all skill levels.* South–southeast of Chole Island (12 nautical miles), this is another beautiful coral-encrusted sandbar, once feared by local fishermen because of the many sharks. There is a good variety of reef fish and this is easily combined with Kitutia (page 397) for an excellent day trip with a sandbank picnic. Unfortunately, Mange did suffer bleaching the effects of El Niño and has succumbed to some poaching.

Chole Wall *Dive depth: max 16m. Recommended for all certified divers; good training site.* A reef inside the bay, with a gentle slope. About 1km in length with lots of coral and reef fishes. A grand skin-diving site when the weather is calm.

Musambiji *Dive depth: max 16m. Recommended for Open Water or equivalent; good training site.* This is a submerged island inside the bay, with terrific topography: diverse walls and sloping fringing coral reefs akin to underwater paddy fields.

AROUND MAFIA ISLAND

Although Mafia is predominantly visited for its waters, many choose to explore the islands beyond the marine park. It's easiest to arrange this through one of the lodges. For a good English-speaking guide, ask for either Moussa from Big Blu (page 383) or Halfani at Mafia Island Diving (page 388), who was sponsored through school by Pole Pole, where he also once worked. Having extensively researched these islands, Halfani is now also a knowledgeable snorkel guide. To go it alone, you could either hire a bike or negotiate a price with the 4x4 drivers parked in Kilindoni to take you on an excursion.

KILINDONI All arrivals on Mafia pass through Kilindoni, the main town as well as the island's airport and sea port, but few visitors venture into Kilindoni for any length of time. New by East African standards, the town was established by the Germans in 1913 on discovering that Chole Island lacked a deep-water anchorage. While it has none of the Arab architecture of Stone Town on Zanzibar, its coral and lime-mortar shop-houses with quaint signs and rusting corrugated-iron roofs exude an ambience of old Indian Ocean days.

At first, Kilindoni appears to have all the accoutrements of a small town: a district hospital, school (complete with science laboratories), police station, bank, petrol station, post office, airport, mosque and churches. Then suddenly the sandy road opens into a square full of clothes for sale, music and activity, as well as a cluster of tuk tuks awaiting business.

Peaceful rather than bustling, the **market** is the centre of local life. Tomatoes, chillies, potatoes, onions, limes, coconuts, dried prawns, bananas, cassava and whatever the trader can get his hands on are arranged in little piles. A large amount of food here is from Dar, grown elsewhere on the Tanzanian mainland. Spices are from Zanzibar, naturally, all wrapped up in little plastic packets.

13

If you decide to stay in Kilindoni, it's worth waking up early to experience the fishermen returning to shore with their overnight catch, and the ensuing spectacle of the fish auction and beachfront cooking. The dhows usually return around 06.30, hitting the beach just south of the jetty. Hauls of fish and octopus are brought ashore and sold in a noisy marketplace, before groups of local women set up all along the beach, laying out carpets of *dagaa*, a small pelagic fish, before scooping them into buckets by hand and cooking them in troughs of bubbling seawater over smoking logs on the sand. It's quite a remarkable scene, and you can always offer to help with the cooking. If you can stomach the gut-wrenching smell and handfuls of slimy fish, you will bring tremendous amusement to these hard-working local women and gain some insight into everyday island life. It's a great opportunity for some genuine community interaction.

Baobab seeds for kids to chew are sold in piles and the fish stalls are pungently gathered together a little further off. Other stalls sell pottery, kangas and secondhand clothes, and if you're brave enough to buy a homemade snorkelling/diving mask, ingeniously made of pieces of metal stapled to thick black rubber, it'll set you back US$2.50. In stark contrast to the ramshackle surroundings, there's a few video rental stores and a surprising number of mobile-phone shops, with some unexpectedly up-to-date models available; it seems everyone in town owns one, and Wi-Fi is generally available at even the local guesthouses.

A number of small **local shops** are of interest to the visitor, and most are found on the square or just off it down one of the five road branches. Here various stalls, shacks and shops sell a surprising variety of goods for such a small place. A couple of local tailors tout for business while a tiny shack sells various snacks and sundries. On the square itself the **KMB MIN mini-market** sells cold Cokes and Fantas for US$0.50, as well as items such as chocolate, toilet paper and toothpaste, although note that suncream is a rare commodity – the locals don't use it so it's next to impossible to find. If you're desperate, lighter-skinned lodge staff might be able to lend you some, but it's far better to come well prepared. The **Kisoma Store** next to New Lizu sells basic stationery and offers internet access from four computers.

There are more stores on the road descending to the dhow landing. The **Market General Supply Store** and the **Peace and Love** sell soft drinks, and off the main square, Utende Road has a rather vulgar monument presented by the fish factory. On the left is a grey weather-beaten **mosque** and further along the Roman Catholic **church**, one of at least six churches.

The **landing** in Kilindoni usually has 15–20 *jahazis* moored on the beach. Whether unloading fish or mending their nets, the fishermen object strongly to being photographed, as do the people frying cassava chips and cooking octopus on small stoves under the trees.

✗ Where to eat and drink

A basic African establishment, the tiny **Royal Pub Mafia**, with a woven palm door, may be rather surprised by visitors, but sells local beers: Kilimanjaro, Tusker, Serengeti, Bin Bingwa for US$1, and Konyagi (a local firewater with rather descriptive flames on the bottle) for US$2.50. It also sells food: chips are US$0.50, egg and chips US$1, and a beef kebab US$1.50. Another basic, open-sided restaurant is found opposite New Lizu – look for

From October to March, Mafia's visitors are blessed with wonderful whale shark-watching opportunities. Visitors during this period are more than 90% likely to see these marvellous marine creatures and have the chance to swim with them – it is really magical. To minimise the disturbance to the whale sharks, ensure their time around Mafia continues well into the future, and to keep both whale sharks and watchers safe, relaxed and happy, it is imperative that both boat operators and swimmers adhere to strict guidelines when approaching, watching and interacting with these huge creatures. The negative effect of not doing so is significant. The whale sharks risk intense, unpleasant harassment, disrupted feeding and even being hit by speeding boats. The code of conduct aims to control and mitigate the impact of human presence and to ensure high-quality experiences.

Please take the time to read these guidelines, and choose carefully an operator who is familiar with, cares about and guarantees to abide by them. Insisting upon this will help to promote truly responsible whale-shark encounters.

GUIDELINES FOR BOATS
- All boats must observe a 50m 'Contact Zone' radius around whale sharks.
- Only one boat at a time may operate in the Contact Zone, and not for longer than 90 minutes, or closer than 10m.
- If a second boat arrives in the Contact Zone, it must stand at least 50m away. Any further boats must wait at least 100m away from the whale shark.
- Boat operators in the Contact Zone should approach from ahead of the shark's direction of travel when dropping swimmers into the water.
- The speed limit for boats in and near a Contact Zone is 2 knots and speeds greater than 5 knots are discouraged because of the high risk of collisions with whale sharks.

GUIDELINES FOR SWIMMERS
Swimmers in the Contact Zone **must not**:
- Exceed more than ten people in the water with one animal at any one time.
- Approach closer than 1.5m from the head or body and 3m from the tail fin.
- Attempt to touch or ride on the whale shark.
- Restrict the normal movement or behaviour of the whale shark.
- Use flash photography.
- Use any underwater motorised devices.

the plastic chairs and tables behind a large gate where chips, omelettes and rice dishes are on offer. The best food will be found at the restaurants in lodges, like Butiama Beach (page 379), and better guesthouses, such as Ibizza (page 381).

Other practicalities   The **National Microfinance Bank** (⏰ *08.30–15.00 Mon–Fri, 08.30–12.30 Sat*), is located on airport road but note that its ATM can only be used by account holders. The **post office** (⏰ *08.00–13.00 & 14.00–16.30 Mon–Fri*) is just

Mafia Archipelago   AROUND MAFIA ISLAND

13

past the bank, but be aware that your letter may take months to leave Mafia. A better option may be to ask your lodge to post your letters in Dar es Salaam.

NORTH OF KILINDONI One of the few places that travellers visit on Mafia is the lighthouse at Ras Mkumbi, via the charming village of Bweni. This is approximately 47km north of Kilindoni, and the drive there, over bouncy sand roads that follow or run parallel to the west coast of Mafia, takes about 2 hours direct, or all day if you want to include swimming and a picnic. Note, though, that while there are some stunning white-sand beaches along this coast, with excellent swimming opportunities, the sea on this side of the island is largely devoid of the underwater attractions around Chole Bay to the east. The excursion is best organised through one of the lodges; you'll find an English-speaking guide is invaluable. Alternatively, a full-day excursion to Ras Mkumbi with Mafia Island Tours costs US$75 per person. Bring everything you are likely to need from your hotel, not forgetting clothes to cover knees and shoulders, suncream, and insect repellent in case you return after dark.

Driving across Mafia is a good way of seeing the island, and finding out about everyday life. As you drive through the villages, you'll see crops of mangoes, pineapples, bananas, cassava and cashew nuts, as well as sweet potatoes, which grow after the rainy season. About 8km from Kilindoni is a picturesque swamp covered in mauve lotus. Small tilapia and catfish dart among the reeds. Further on, the old agricultural village of **Kirongwe**, with a tradition of making clay pots, counts a score of houses, a handful of shops and a market selling the usual dried octopus, bananas and coconuts. Beyond here the countryside is intensively cultivated with beans, pigeon pea and cassava, and – rather less attractive – numerous indications of slash-and-burn agriculture. Sykes's and vervet monkeys raiding the crops flee at the sound of any vehicle.

The north of Mafia is markedly different from the wetter southern part of the island, which is dominated by vast coconut plantations. After **Jimbo**, where you may see local blacksmiths working by the side of the road, the landscape suddenly becomes more undulating open grassland with outcrops of mia'a or palm, and baobabs similar to those on the mainland coastal plain. Birdlife is plentiful with bee-eaters and lilac-breasted rollers flashing amongst the trees and large flocks of guineafowl scuttling off the road. While only about 30m above sea level, it is noticeably cooler here than on the coast.

Bweni village, built behind 2km of beach, was an obvious spot for tourism development, and realised its potential briefly in 2010 with the opening of lovely Lua Cheia Castaway Beach Camp (page 385) – which then closed and is currently being refurbished for reopening. The village's traditional Swahili-style houses of coral and lime plaster are dotted among slender coconut palms, and electricity lines have recently been run as far as the village, and may hopefully soon be turned on. You need to stop to collect the lighthouse key from a keeper in the village if you plan to visit, and will be soon surrounded by excited and curious children, delighted at the chance to shout '*Mzungu!*' at the unexpected visitor. Their behaviour is polite, however, and their fascination mixed with a fear of the unknown, although this is slowly changing. Bweni women are experts at weaving striped prayer mats from the palms on the plateau, and you only need to show interest for items to be shyly produced. The larger mats are 2.5m by 1.5m, and cost around US$4; smaller oval mats go for US$3.

The **lighthouse** at **Ras Mkumbi** is a 3km drive on a good stretch of road from Bweni. Built on coral rag on the northern tip of Mafia, it is worth climbing the 15m up to the top of the red-and-white structure for a spectacular view of the Mafia Channel lying between the archipelago and the mainland. The stretch of deep-blue water is reputed to offer some of the best big-game fishing in East Africa. This working lighthouse also has concrete outbuildings, now owned by Pole Pole (page 381), who organise trips to the area. One of the buildings has basic rooms with beds and mosquito nets, but no running water. At present it is used for overnight fishing trips but is being developed into a small guesthouse.

The grassy area in front of the lighthouse leads towards a rocky beach which offers half an hour or so of exploration at low tide. Black kites swoop low over the cliffs, while further out fishermen search for octopus in their race against the tide. It's possible to rent a bike from the village, or to go on a forest walk to see birds and monkeys. Snorkelling, fishing and diving trips can also be organised in this area.

KISIMANI MAFIA Kisimani (Kiswahili for 'the place of the well') lies on Ras Kisimani, at the south end of the island 30 minutes' drive from Kilindoni, or a 2-hour boat trip. The town was an important centre during the Shirazi domination of Kilwa between the 12th and 14th centuries (page 372). The hands of the sultan's chief mason were cut off after he built the palace, so that he could never repeat the task. The story goes on to claim that this was why a few months later Kisimani was inundated by the sea. There is little left of the submerged medieval settlement, but you can see the well for which it is named on the beach. Wandering about, you might find a few coins and pottery shards.

The shady coconut palms are a nice spot for a picnic, and there's a lovely beach with good birding and snorkelling, but bring everything you want to eat or drink.

UTENDE The majority of Mafia's tourist lodges lie along the beach below this small village, at the end of the 15km road west from Kilindoni. Many of Utende's inhabitants are Makonde people from the mainland, who keep their fishing boats in Chole Bay. One or two shophouses sell strings of dried octopus and fish. Like everywhere else on Mafia, the village is quite safe to explore, being only 10 minutes' walk from any of the hotels. The beach in front of Utende (close to Mafia Island Lodge) is where local dhows leave for Chole Island.

Schools here are developing with aid from the lodges. A new primary school was built on the site of the old school, offering Standards 1–6, and nursery education for 31 pupils. Since 2000, this has been financed by Pole Pole who sponsor some of the pupils. The government was then helped to build another school building for seven to 14 year olds. Visitors are welcome to visit the projects of the non-profit community development organisation Karibuni Onlus (*www.misaada.it*), which aims to improve education and health care in Utende village and all over Mafia. They have sponsored students and contributed towards the building and upkeep of a school and a well in Utende, but they also provide volunteer doctors, distribute mosquito nets all over the island and are renovating a school in nearby Kiegeani. Mafia Island Tours (m *0688 218569;* e *welcome@mafiadiving.com; www.mafiadiving.com*) offers a trip to see the well and the school, plus learn about Karibuni Onlus's work for just US$5 per person, all of which goes directly to the organisation.

Utende also has a couple of small shops, and you'll notice a number of buildings made with cement blocks and corrugated iron. Although not picturesque, cement blocks are relatively cheap and an easy material for building, while corrugated-iron roofs last longer than a palm-leaf roof, which has to be replaced every three years or so.

For a fascinating insight into local life, visit the morning fish auction on the beach and see the night's catch sold and prepared. It is on a smaller scale to the fish preparation in Kilindoni (see box, page 392), but still an eye-opening snapshot of Swahili island ways.

13

OTHER EXCURSIONS Most other villages on Mafia are inaccessible by road and, like the offshore islands, may be visited only by boat. Given advance warning, the lodges can usually arrange trips to visit them.

However, the most popular excursions are probably those to isolated sandbars. You'll sail to these from your lodge, and then the boat crew will set up some shade on the beach, and cook lunch over a barbeque. Meanwhile, you can relax, sunbathe, swim and snorkel with nothing around you except miles and miles of deep-blue ocean. Trips like these are included by some of the lodges, while others will charge you extra, depending on the destination (US$40–75 per person per trip is typical).

Destinations for excursions include Chole, Juani and Jibondo islands, described in the following pages, and several smaller spots including the following.

Mchangani This village is the end of an interesting excursion winding for nearly 3km up a creek on the north side of Chole Bay. Sykes' monkeys can be seen in the mangrove forests and fish eagles are commonly observed. The village lies on the east bank of the creek; it takes about an hour to reach by vehicle, or 90 minutes if you'd rather walk over sand and rock. Depart only on a high tide.

Dindini Beach Likewise accessible only at high tide. It faces the ocean from Mafia Island just north of Chole Bay, and from December to February can see big waves. Behind the beach is a large, sea-fed rock pool, which contains a variety of marine life. There are also low sand dunes and interesting vegetation on the coral rag.

Didimizi Beach This is the lovely beach seen from Chole Bay, around 4km from the main tourist lodges, or a 45-minute walk. You could arrange for a vehicle going to Kilindoni to drop you at the turn-off and walk back, not forgetting to take refreshments and a hat. Alternatively, a short trip by dhow brings you straight to the beach dotted with little pyramids of sand caused by the white ghost crabs that scuttle around – they'll be all you share the sandbar with.

Bwejuu Island Off Ras Kisimani to the west of Mafia, Bwejuu has its own small village and makes a good day trip. Located between the Rufiji River Delta and Mafia's main island, it offers good snorkelling at Mange Reef, as well as diving and fishing. You can also camp on Bwejuu Island for a few nights. Further afield, the Rufiji River is close enough for trips which can go all the way to the Selous Game Reserve (page 404).

Ras Mbisi Only 90 minutes by road from Kilindoni, Ras Mbisi has an ideal beach for picnics, swimming and snorkelling. Ras Mbisi Lodge, right on the beach, was razed to the ground by a devastating fire in 2016. Its resurrection is still very uncertain, but should accommodation spring up here, it's a great spot for beach escapists, and just after dawn the villagers put on a tremendous display of teamwork, hauling in their nets on the beach.

Mbaracuni Island Lying 12km northwest of Mafia, this island can be visited by arrangement. Uninhabited, quiet and said to be very beautiful, it is used by fishing dhows. This is a good place to see black kites and occasionally two or three fish eagles.

Miewe Another small, uninhabited island used by fishermen to clean and dry fish, it can be visited for picnics, as can the sandbank of **Marimbani**. If you're interested in sailing a little further, and for a good chance of seeing dolphins, you can take a day excursion to the island of **Kitutia**. After a couple of hours under sail, you'll be rewarded by some stunning snorkelling on a reef which surrounds a pure-white sandbank. This is all covered by the sea at high tide, so the trip needs to be timed carefully.

ISLANDS AROUND MAFIA

CHOLE ISLAND Chole is the lush, tropical island lying to the west of the Kinasi Pass. With the adjacent islands of Juani and Jibondo, it forms a barrier between Mafia and the open ocean. The shallow reef in front is rich in soft corals, sea anemones and sponges, and, sloping to 15m, it is a good spot to practise drift diving. The bay itself is ideal for sailing, windsurfing and kitesurfing. The town of Chole Mjini was the main urban centre on the archipelago for much of the 19th century, the home of wealthy merchants whose plantations lay on the main island of Mafia. Ruins dating from this era include a reasonably preserved **German Customs House** on the waterfront, and several more **ruined mansions** dating to the Omani era. A path behind the new market leading to the village brings you to a **prison**, whose broken cells are invaded by tangled tree roots. Farther along and also in ruins is a **Hindu temple**.

Hanging upside down in a nearby baobab is a colony of **fruit bats** of the same family as the Comoros Islands' lesser flying fox (*Pteropus seychellenis comorensis*), found in the Comoros, the Seychelles and Mafia, but nowhere on mainland Africa. Each evening the bats fly across Chole Bay to feed on the cashew nut and mango trees of Mafia, as well as marula fruit, figs and mangrove flowers. Like the Comoros bats they dip over the surface of the water – an action which scientists believe may be an attempt to rid themselves of parasites. A more enchanting local explanation claims 'they are washing before evening prayers'. Bats are nocturnal, so it's imperative for the continuation of the Chole colony that visitors allow them to sleep in the day, ensuring that neither they nor their guide throw stones at them, or shake their tree, just to wake them up and take photos of the bats in flight. Remember that it is a bat sanctuary.

Chole's human population was estimated at 5,000 during the early years of German rule, but today it is no more than 1,000. The islanders cultivate smallholdings of cassava, beans, mangoes, paw-paw, citrus (including very sweet oranges) and passion fruit. Encouraged by the lodges, these smallholdings have flourished and produce is now exported to Mafia, with the oranges also making their way to the mainland. Most of the menfolk fish, while many of the women are engaged in catching octopus beyond the mangroves at low tide. Winding past traditional houses, the path brings you to a beach where fishermen can be seen mending nets, or making sails and coconut-coir ropes. Chole was once a centre of boatbuilding, and boats are still repaired and occasionally built on the island. The boatyard is indicated on the circular walk available from Chole Mjini, about half an hour from the lodge.

The Norwegian Women's Front and Chole Mjini Lodge have been instrumental in much of Chole's development. They have funded the building of a hospital and a free clinic for the under fives, a kindergarten, a market, and the Society for Women's Development (which runs savings and loan schemes). They have also helped to set up a school, so that children no longer have to walk across to Juani Island at low tide, and a learning centre to help educate adults.

For places to stay, see page 384. Note that Chole Mjini Lodge does not cater to passing custom or serve meals to non-residents.

13

Getting there and away The lodges at Utende (pages 381–4) operate **boat trips** to Chole, or you can visit it independently from Mafia, or on a '**bat and village tour**' with Mafia Island Tours (*US$10*). A dhow dubbed the '**Chole taxi**' leaves the beach in front of Mafia Island Lodge every 30 minutes or so throughout the day – last sailing at 16.00 – a crossing of 10–15 minutes depending on the wind and tide, for a cost of US$0.60 one-way for visitors. It is also possible to charter a local boat across for a fee of about US$10.

On arrival you will need to hand over a village levy of US$10 per person – which goes straight to the village – payable at the Red Herring Café where the boat docks. You can also charge camera batteries here because there's no other electricity on the island. If you plan to stay more than a few hours on the island it is advisable to bring a picnic and refreshments from your hotel, and note that you'll have to wade a short distance from the boat. Make sure that you're wearing shoes, as there are stingrays in this area.

There is no motorised transport on Chole Island, and the locals all use **bikes**.

JUANI ISLAND The boat trip from Mafia to Juani, site of the ruined city of Kua, takes about 10 minutes longer than the one to Chole, but the island can be approached only at high tide. The landing, in a small bay sheltered by dense mangroves, is covered in thousands of opened oyster-shells, so remember to wear good shoes, as you'll have to wade to shore. Seafood is the staple diet on Juani, but, unlike Chole, Juani has no well water, and locals practise rain-dependent cultivation.

Beneath three big baobabs near the landing, your shoes crunch on the rocky paths of a buried civilisation. Bits of blue-and-white Shirazi pottery suggesting trade links with China are embedded in the dirt. In the past, people from the mainland came to Juani to bathe in a seawater cave reputed to have curative properties for rheumatism. It is a long, difficult walk across to the ocean side, where there are three protected turtle-nesting beaches (see box, page 399). The Kua Channel slices a tiny chunk off Juani as it opens into Chole Bay. It makes a superb picnic excursion with birdwatching and swimming. A friendly grouper lives in one of the rock pools at the southern end.

The ruined city of **Kua** (page 373), spread across 6ha on the west coast of Juani, was the Shirazi capital of Mafia. It was one of the few east African ports to be continuously inhabited from medieval times into the early 19th century, when it was sacked by raiders from Madagascar. A trail hacked out of the undergrowth leads up to a large building shedding masonry: the former palace, still revered locally as a 'spirit place' where offerings such as bits of glass are left. The ruins here have been defeated by the powerful strangler figs that dominate a number of the walls, and the tomb of the sultan himself has been destroyed by a tree growing in its centre. The path passes other ruined edifices, including two 14th-century mosques and a series of tombs.

The buildings are made from coral rock and lime cement, which does not survive well in this sea air. Looking at cracks in the walls you wonder how long they will remain standing, with the occasional monkey as the only inhabitant. If you see the caretaker, he expects and deserves a small gratuity; ask him to show you the foundations of the house referred to in the box on page 400.

You depart on a beautiful sail home between the islands, watched by the scores of ibis on the mangroves. There is a guide and map of the ruins, as well as the report on its archaeology, in the library at Kinasi Lodge (page 382).

JIBONDO ISLAND Jibondo is a long, low-lying island another 20-minute sail from Juani. This traditional village community is rather different from the rest

TURTLE-HATCHING ECOTOURISM

Turtles have been nesting on Tanzanian beaches for millions of years, and thanks to a successful NGO called Sea Sense (*www.seasense.org*), visitors to Mafia can now witness this spine-tingling spectacle. Established in 2001, they work in partnership with the local community to promote the importance and protection of marine turtles and their habitats. Over the last 15 years, the initiative has been so successful that it has significantly increased the number and survival rate of turtle eggs, and in doing so, it has made sea-turtle ecotourism viable.

Managed by conservation officers and local 'Turtle Tour Guides', the ecotourism venture offers visitors a truly remarkable experience and also generates a sustainable source of revenue for the community. Aside from local staff employment and donations, the community also receives half of all ecotourism revenue to fund their own development projects, making them both aware and proud of the benefits that come from protecting their marine environment.

Between June and September, the baby turtles hatch in their hundreds on the eastern beaches of Juani Island and make their long sandy journey to the lapping waves of the Indian Ocean. It's a magical sight! Leaving by dhow from Utende, excited turtle enthusiasts arrive on Juani's western coast, before walking across the island's densely forested interior (*45mins*) and past the village, to reach the hatching beaches. Here, the Turtle Tour Guide will point out the subterranean nests, and thanks to impeccable monitoring, the near-exact time of hatching. Furiously flapping their fins, the tiny turtles appear through the parting grains of sand, allowing for close-up heart-melting viewing of their first steps into the sun. It's terribly exciting and very moving to watch them head down the beach and onwards with their life's journey, and well worth supporting if you're here.

You can book the Sea Sense turtle hatching trip though any hotel or dive centre on Mafia (*US$40 plus US$10 Sea Sense charity fee*).

of Mafia, and the atmosphere is somehow more charged than in other villages. Coming ashore, a big **jahazi dhow** is one of the first things you see. Built 15 years ago, it has never been launched and is subsequently something of a museum piece, but the old men sitting under the quinine tree nearby have already learned its value to tourism, wanting to charge US$1 for a photo.

Behind the boat is a rather plain white **mosque**, built in 1979. Some of its furniture was taken from the queen's palace in the ruins at Kua, and it's worth wandering around the back to see the carved wooden door from Kua (by contrast, the window frames were made of wood from India). This is all set off by the pungent smell from the row of long-drop loos that literally drop into the sea. Jibondo does not have a fresh water supply, so the islanders depend on frequent deliveries from Mafia's main island.

Jibondo people are well known as shipbuilders and, as on Chole, use only traditional tools. Even the nails are handmade and the holes are plugged with local kapok and shark fat. Local women play a prominent role in trading as well as fishing. They also sail boats, which is unusual in African society, and are more affable and confident than women elsewhere. Jibondo people also collect and dry seaweed to export.

13

The political relationship between Kisimani and Kua is unclear, but an intriguing if unverifiable oral tradition recounted by T M Revington in an essay in *Tanganyika Notes & Records* suggests that it was not always amicable:

> The people of Ras Kisimani constructed a ship, and when it was finished and still on the stocks, they made a feast to which they invited the people of Kua. From amongst the guests they took by force several children, laid them on the sand, and launched the ship over their bodies. When the Kua people heard what had been done at Ras Kisimani, they were infuriated and thought out a scheme of revenge. Seven or eight years later, when they thought that the incident had been forgotten, an invitation was sent to the inhabitants of Ras Kisimani to attend a wedding at Kua. When the guests arrived in the evening they were ushered to a room that had been especially prepared beneath a house; the hosts one by one left their guests on the excuse of inquiring into the food, until only an old man remained to entertain them. This he did so well that the doors were bricked up without the guests perceiving it. The bodies are there to this day. So, too, is the sealed-off basement in which the bodies lie, according to the site's caretaker, who claims that it is situated below the ruins in front of his hut.

Another unusual aspect of Jibondo is that cultivation is carried out at one end of the island while the people live in an urban community at the other. The village, which consists of traditional Swahili-style houses with makuti roofs, is laid out in a grid pattern. As on Chole and Juani, there is no transport other than boats which shelter on the western side of the narrow neck of the island.

The island has one school, easily identified by the football field in front. If the tide is good for fishing, the children – encouraged by their parents – go straight out on the water, ignoring lessons. In a year, only one child is likely to leave the island and go to secondary school on Mafia. There are, however, three *madrasas* on the island, where there is a strong Muslim faith. There are no other social services, and only a basic shop. On the other side of the island is **Flamingo Beach**, which makes an interesting 2-hour trek. The village trail and sailing dhow with Mafia Island Tours costs US$30.

FANJOVE ISLAND Part of the Songo Songo Archipelago, Fanjove is situated 16km from Tanzania's east coast and 48km south of Mafia Island, and is dominated by a 17m-high lighthouse that was built in 1894 by Germans occupying Tanzania before World War I. Following the war, the island became uninhabited and, aside from a few fishermen, very few people have set foot on Fanjove, until an environmentally friendly lodge was built there in 2013.

Fanjove Island is teeming with wildlife: its white sandy beaches are a nesting site for green turtles, the young hatching between April and July; as well as a variety of crabs including the endangered coconut crab. Fanjove's tropical vegetation is home to many native birds, including herons, weavers and egrets; there are also a multitude of migrant species visiting its shores between November and March. Over 10km of coral reefs sit offshore, which is home to a wide variety of marine life including butterflyfish, grouper, triggerfish and parrotfish species. Pods of spinner and bottle-nosed dolphins are frequently seen; as are migrating humpback whales from June to October.

Getting there and away Coastal Aviation (*www.coastal.co.tz*) flies twice daily to Songo Songo from Dar es Salaam via Mafia (*1hr; US$220*). Boat transfers from Songo Songo to Fanjove are done by local dhow, rather than speedboats, to reduce fuel consumption and this takes around 40 minutes.

Where to stay and eat

Fanjove Private Island Lodge (6 bandas)
022 260 1747; e info@ed.co.tz; www.ed.co. tz. Fanjove is a low-impact lodge that offers intrepid travellers a unique island experience. Designed to be in keeping with its surroundings, the 2-storey A-frame bandas were constructed to look like a dhow sail, with the peak of the roof facing seaward, receding into the vegetation behind. The structure is made from wood beams, covered by a vast makuti-thatched roof. The thatch windows & doors can be raised & lowered independently, much like a sail would be, with a rope-pulley system. Clever positioning means that even with the doors wide open, all you see is the vegetation, sand & sea beyond. Each banda is simply but stylishly furnished & contains a 4-poster bed, swathed in a mosquito net, solar-powered reading lights, shelves & hangers crafted from driftwood, & there is also a lockable trunk. Up wooden steps is a mezzanine level with a day bed & views out to the Indian Ocean. The large en-suite bathroom is at the back of each banda on the ground floor, with a single basin & mirror & a big rain shower with running hot-&-cold water. The flush toilet is tucked around the corner out of sight. For most, simply sunbathing & swimming in the crystal-clear waters will be more than enough to fill time. However, guests are also free to explore the island on foot or by kayak; snorkelling, diving, dhow sailing, sand bank excursions, birdwatching, fishing & dolphin excursions are also offered. When you've worked up an appetite, meals, served both inside & out, are delicious with especially tempting seafood prepared with both Swahili & Mediterranean influences. Tempting à la carte b/fasts offer everything from eggs to pancakes & free-flowing fresh juices; light lunches of salads & delicate dishes of stuffed octopus & bruschetta are all that's needed; followed by creative 3-course dinners, including a terrific curry night. FB. ♛

13

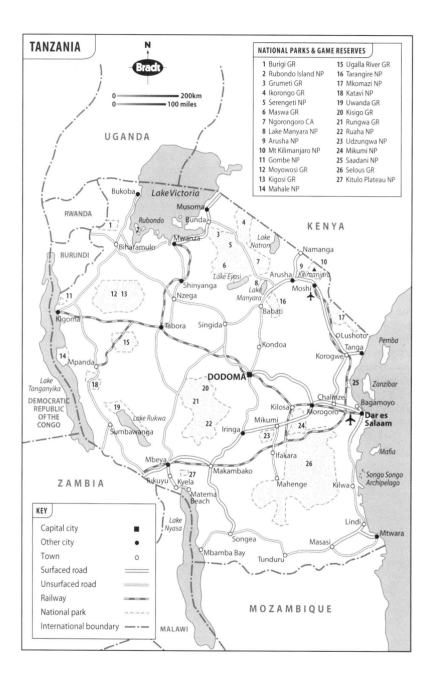

TANZANIA

N

Bradt

0 ——— 200km
0 ——— 100 miles

NATIONAL PARKS & GAME RESERVES

1	Burigi GR	15	Ugalla River GR
2	Rubondo Island NP	16	Tarangire NP
3	Grumeti GR	17	Mkomazi GR
4	Ikorongo GR	18	Katavi NP
5	Serengeti NP	19	Uwanda GR
6	Maswa GR	20	Kisigo GR
7	Ngorongoro CA	21	Rungwa GR
8	Lake Manyara NP	22	Ruaha NP
9	Arusha NP	23	Udzungwa NP
10	Mt Kilimanjaro NP	24	Mikumi NP
11	Gombe NP	25	Saadani NP
12	Moyowosi GR	26	Selous GR
13	Kigosi GR	27	Kitulo Plateau NP
14	Mahale NP		

UGANDA

RWANDA

BURUNDI

Bukoba

Lake Victoria

Musoma

Rubondo

Bunda

KENYA

Biharamulo

Mwanza

Lake Natron

Namanga

Shinyanga

Lake Eyasi

Arusha

Kilimanjaro

Nzega

Lake Manyara

Moshi

Kigoma

Tabora

Singida

Babati

Lushoto

Pemba

DEMOCRATIC
REPUBLIC
OF THE
CONGO

Lake Tanganyika

Mpanda

Kondoa

Tanga

Korogwe

DODOMA

Zanzibar

Chalinze

Bagamoyo

Sumbawanga

Lake Rukwa

Iringa

Kilosa

Morogoro

Mikumi

Dar es Salaam

ZAMBIA

Mbeya

Ifakara

Mafia

Tukuyu

Kyela

Makambako

Mahenge

Kilwa

Songo Songo Archipelago

Matema
Beach

Lake Nyasa

Lindi

KEY

Capital city ■
Other city ●
Town ○
Surfaced road
Unsurfaced road
Railway
National park
International boundary

MALAWI

Songea

Mbamba Bay

Tunduru

Masasi

Mtwara

MOZAMBIQUE

14

Southern Tanzania Safaris

with Philip Briggs

In recent years, there has been increasing interest in southern Tanzania's Ruaha National Park and Selous Game Reserve. For decades these areas have been overshadowed by their more famous northern counterparts (Lake Manyara, Ngorongoro Crater and the Serengeti), but today the secret is out, and southern Tanzania is a favourite amongst safari aficionados as well as first-time visitors who are put off by the crowds which so often mar the northern parks.

Zanzibar is barely 200km from the Selous, the largest of all Tanzania's (and indeed Africa's) game reserves, making it easily accessible by air. Ruaha is further – about 400km – from Zanzibar, and having been extended to cover an area of 22,200km² in 2008, is now Tanzania's largest national park.

Gradually a 'southern circuit' has developed, with many individuals and small groups flying to the Selous (and sometimes also Ruaha) before finishing their trip with time on the islands. Daily flights make this a very straightforward option. If you want to combine the parks of southern Tanzania with a trip to the islands as part of your travels, then this chapter aims to help you plan your trip, and enjoy it to the full.

OVERVIEW OF YOUR TRIP

It's often difficult for first-time visitors to decide which reserves to visit – so an overview here might help.

If you're planning on a beach-and-safari trip then first be mindful that safari time will usually cost much more than beach time; it's often double the nightly cost. For example, an uncomplicated safari lodge will easily cost US$350 per person per night, whilst you'll have to try hard to find a mid-range beach lodge at more than US$180 each per night. The reason for this is partly that most safari lodges include a full day of activities and all your meals, whereas a beach lodge often provides only a room and breakfast; and partly because the logistics at most safari lodges are that much more expensive.

With this in mind, consider how long you want to spend on each part of your trip. A 50/50 split (a week on safari and a week by the beach) is typical for a two-week trip, but this depends on your priorities and budget.

If you decide on five nights or less on safari, then our advice is that you should probably stick to the Selous – and spend all your time there. If you decide on eight nights or more on safari, then you should consider combining time in the Selous with time in Ruaha – as then the extra cost of flying between the parks is worth it for the change in scenery and environment. If you decide on six or seven nights on safari, then it's less clear if Ruaha is worth the extra travelling or not; you need to consider your own personal requirements.

SELOUS GAME RESERVE

Extending over 47,500km², the Selous (pronounced 'Seloo') is Africa's single largest game reserve, three times larger than the Serengeti, more than twice the size of South Africa's Kruger National Park, and roughly 50% bigger than either Belgium or Swaziland. It is, furthermore, the core sanctuary within the greater Selous-Niassa ecosystem, which extends over 155,000km² of practically uninhabited wilderness in southern Tanzania and northern Mozambique – the largest chunk of comparably untrammelled bush left in Africa.

The claim that the Selous lies at the core of the greatest surviving African wilderness is supported by the prodigiously large mammal populations protected within the reserve and the greater ecosystem. The buffalo population of 120,000–150,000, is probably the largest anywhere in Africa, while estimated tallies of 40,000 hippo and 4,000 lion must also be there or thereabouts. It is also the most important remaining stronghold for the endangered African wild dog, which is seen with some regularity in the developed northern part of the reserve. Other significant populations protected within the reserve include an estimated 100,000 wildebeest, 35,000 zebras and 25,000 impalas. It is also one of the most important sanctuaries in Africa for the endangered black rhinoceros, plus sable and puku antelope. Until as recently as 2010, the greater Selous ecosystem supported around 70,000 elephants, representing some 10% of the continental total. Tragically, however, a renewed outbreak of commercial poaching has reduced the elephant population to an estimated 15,000 in mid 2016, with some conservationists predicting they will be hunted out entirely by 2022.

BACKGROUND INFORMATION That the Selous ranks as one of East Africa's most alluring and satisfying safari destinations is not in dispute. However, given that much of the publicity surrounding the Selous bangs on about its vast area, prospective visitors should be aware that the extent of the reserve is in practice something of a red herring. The Selous is divided into two disproportionate parts by the Rufiji, Tanzania's largest river, which together with the great Ruaha, a major tributary, runs through the reserve from west to east. About 90% of the Selous lies to the south of the river and has been divided into a number of privately leased hunting concessions, all of which are off-limits to casual tourism. A proportion of the northern sector has also been set aside for hunting concessions. The remainder – no more than 5% of the reserve's total area – forms what, to all intents and purposes, is the Selous Photographic Reserve. The lodges (and most activities for visitors) are actually concentrated within an area of about 1,000km² immediately north of the Rufiji.

Fortunately, this photographic part of the Selous is wonderfully atmospheric, a dense tract of wild miombo woodland abutting the meandering Rufiji River, and an associated labyrinth of five pretty lakes connected to each other and the river by numerous narrow streams. Arriving by light aircraft, as most visitors do, it is exhilarating to sweep above the palm-fringed channels teeming with hippo and waterfowl, the swampy islets where immense herds of elephant and giraffe graze alongside each other, and exposed sandbanks where antelope drink and all manner of shorebirds scurry about.

No less exciting are the boat excursions along the Rufiji, which generally culminate with a brilliant red sun setting behind the tall borassus palms and baobabs that line the wide sandy watercourse. Gulp-inducing dentist's-eye views of the Selous's trademark gigantic crocs can pretty much be guaranteed from the boat, as can conferences of grunting, harrumphing hippo – and you'd be unlucky not to be entertained by herds of elephant, buffalo or giraffe shuffling down to drink.

The most memorable aspect of the boat trips, however, is the profuse birdlife. Characteristic waterbirds along this stretch of the Rufiji include yellow-billed stork, white-crowned and spur-winged plovers, various small waders, pied and malachite kingfishers, and African skimmer. Pairs of fish eagle and palmnut vulture perch high on the borassus palms, seasonal breeding colonies of carmine and white-throated bee-eater swirl around the mud cliffs that hem in some stretches of the river, and pairs of trumpeter hornbill and purple-crested turaco flap between the riparian trees. Worth looking out for among a catalogue of egrets and herons is the Malagasy squacco heron, a regular winter visitor, while the elusive Pel's fishing owl often emerges at dusk to hawk above the water.

Game drives along the network of rough roads to the north of the Rufiji are reliably rewarding, especially towards the end of the dry season, when large mammals concentrate around the five lakes. More frequently seen ungulates include impala, common waterbuck, bushbuck, white-bearded wildebeest, eland, greater kudu, buffalo and common zebra.

The northern sector of the park has been dubbed 'Giraffic Park', with some justification, as herds exceeding 50 individuals come down to drink in the heat of the afternoon. Giraffes seem exceedingly common here, which is odd as they are entirely absent south of the Rufiji. The river also forms a natural barrier between the ranges of the distinctive white-bearded and Niassa races of wildebeest. The endangered African wild dog is commonly observed, as is the spotted hyena, while leopards are common but elusive, and cheetahs exceedingly rare.

Much in evidence are Selous's lions, with two or three different prides' territories converging on each of the five large lakes. The lions typically have darker coats and less hirsute manes than their counterparts elsewhere in East Africa. During the dry season, the lions of Selous evidently rely on an unusual opportunistic diurnal hunting strategy, rarely straying far from the lakes, where they rest up in the shade to wait for whatever ungulate happens to venture within pouncing distance on its way to drink.

The Selous receives few visitors when compared with Tanzania's more famous northern parks – about 1% of tourist arrivals to Tanzania. Particularly if you are based at one of the western lodges – Beho Beho, Sand Rivers and Amara – it is still possible to undertake a game drive in the Selous without coming across another vehicle.

Whereas the national parks of northern Tanzania are dominated by large impersonal hotels that evidently aim to shut out the bush the moment you enter them, the Selous boasts a select handful of low-key, eco-friendly, thatch-and-canvas lodges whose combined bed capacity amounts to a few hundred visitors. Furthermore, because the Selous is a game reserve and not subject to the regulations that govern Tanzania's national parks, visitors are offered a more primal and integrated bush experience than the usual repetitive regime of one game drive after another. In addition to boat trips, all lodges offer guided game walks for those aged 12 and over (16 at Lake Manze and Impala), which come with a real likelihood of encountering elephant or buffalo – even lion – on foot. Better still are the overnight fly-camping excursions offered by some of the camps, which entail sleeping beneath a glorified mosquito net in the middle of the bush.

Note that the roads within the Selous become impassable after heavy rain. Hence camps here close towards the end of the wet season, in April, and reopen in July.

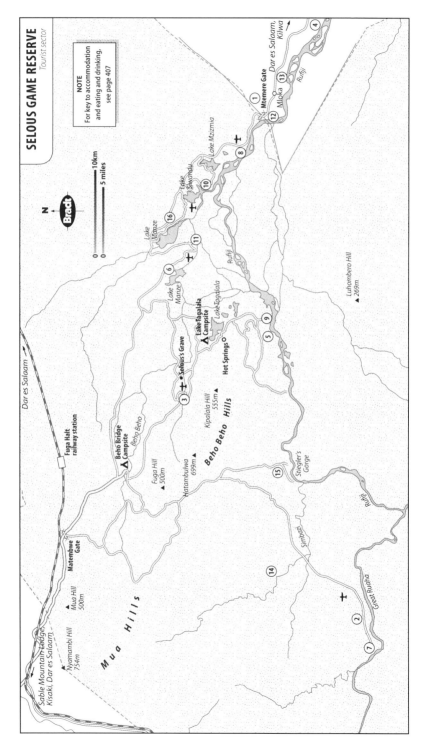

SELOUS GAME RESERVE
Tourist sector

NOTE
For key to accommodation
and eating and drinking,
see page 407

SELOUS GAME RESERVE *Tourist sector*
For listings, see pages 408–12

🛏 Where to stay and eat

1 Africa Safari Camp
2 Azura Selous
3 Beho Beho
4 Great Water Lodge
5 Kiba Point
6 Lake Manze Tented Camp
7 The Retreat Selous
8 Rufiji River Camp
9 Sand Rivers

10 Selous Impala Camp
11 Selous Mbuyu Safari Camp
12 Selous River Camp
13 Selous Riverside Camp
14 Selous Serena Camp
15 Serena Mivumo River Lodge
16 Siwandu Camp

Off map
   Sable Mountain Lodge

FEES AND FURTHER INFORMATION An entrance fee of US$75 per person per day is charged (US$50 for park fees and a US$25 conservation charge), subject to 18% VAT. On most organised trips this will be included in the overall price, but it's worth checking this when booking. Most lodges aimed at the fly-in market include reserve fees in their rates, but some of the cheaper camps, especially those outside the park, may not. There has been talk of these fees increasing in the near future so do check before you travel. Note, too, that if you are paying fees yourself at the gate, you will need a valid Visa or MasterCard, as cash is no longer accepted, irrespective of the currency tendered.

Two useful booklets are *Selous Game Reserve: A Guide to the Northern Sector* by Rolf D Baldus and the glossier *Selous: Africa's Largest & Wildest Game Reserve* by Rolf D Baldus and L Siege. Most lodges stock both and they are similar textually. For details on the man behind the park's name, read *The Life of Frederick Courtney Selous* by J G Millais, published by Gallery Publications and available in Zanzibar.

GETTING THERE AND AWAY Many tour operators, both overseas and in Tanzania, offer a variety of trips to the Selous. These usually include flights to/from the reserve, accommodation and activities. Most use frequent daily **flights** between Dar es Salaam and Selous operated by Coastal Airlines, Safari AirLink and ZanAir. These generally connect very easily to/from Zanzibar. The early-morning Coastal flight continues to Ruaha daily. Once inside the parks, these flights will all stop at any of the camp airstrips by prior arrangement, although it is not possible to fly between camps in the Selous – for this, a road transfer must be arranged in advance.

If you are travelling in mainland Tanzania it's perfectly possible to reach the Selous by **road**, although that's generally more costly than flying. For full details of these options, Bradt's *Tanzania Safari Guide* guide by Philip Briggs and Chris McIntyre is highly recommended (page 427).

ACCOMMODATION PRICE CODES

Prices in Tanzanian reserves are slightly higher than those in Zanzibar, so price codes are as follows:

$	< US$15
$$	US$15–40
$$$	US$40–75
$$$$	US$75–200
$$$$$	US$200–500
$$$$$$	US$500–1,000
$$$$$$$	US$1,000+

Over the last few years, accommodation options in Selous have increased significantly, although the sheer size of the park still ensures privacy in the majority of areas. All of the camps listed below are within the park boundaries and levels of service and experience are almost invariably high. A growing number of camps are found along the sandy road leading to the Mtemere Gate, while Sable Mountain Lodge is located 1km outside the Matembwe Gate. For further details of these see Bradt's *Tanzania* guide by Philip Briggs.

Inside Mtemere Gate
Exclusive

⌂ **Azura Selous** (12 suites) m 0784 747265; e reservations@azura-retreats.com; www.azura-retreats.com. Formally Amara Selous, Azura took over in 2014 & have been working hard to improve standards. The lodge is one of the most westerly in the park & is in a pretty location overlooking the Great Ruaha River. Marketed as a 'boutique camp', its designer's influence is apparent throughout, with stylish leather furniture & beaded chandeliers in the cosy lounge, plus interesting objets d'art & wooden carvings scattered throughout the property. The tiered main area looks out over the river & the tempting pool. The half-tented, half stone-built suites offer plenty of light & space, AC (although with gauze windows its efficiency is somewhat dubious), & a private deck & plunge pool overlooking the river. The stylish rooms are bright & colourful offering a modern take on a traditional safari tent. The en-suite bathrooms are decked out in high-quality fittings & tiles, & have both an indoor & outdoor hot shower. Twiga house was completed in 2016 & provides more spacious accommodation with an outside lounge & even a bubble bath. Activities focus on game drives plus romantic sundowners & bush dinners under the stars. Azura Selous aims to offer boating safaris; however, these are very dependent on water levels & can never be guaranteed. The standard of guiding at Azura is excellent, with many of the guides holding international guiding qualifications. While tired parents relax with an in-suite massage, children will be educated & entertained on the popular 'Amaradillos' programme, a series of informative games & activities designed to teach children about the local flora & fauna. All participants are given a colourful workbook that keen children will love to fill in & keep. The service at Azura is slick & the camp well run, & although there's a fair amount of game around, it's a little sparser than the more easterly lodges. But for a relaxing & indulgent safari it's a great choice that would especially appeal to honeymooners. *US$1,575/2,100 sgl/dbl FB inc drinks & all activities & park fees.* **$$$$$$$**

⌂ **Beho Beho** (9 bandas) ☎ 022 260 0352–4, (UK) +44 (0)1932 260618; e reservations@behobeho.com; www.behobeho.com. Beho Beho's site, in the west of the northern Selous, was used for a safari camp as early as 1972, one of the first such sites in the Selous. Its location is unusual in the Selous: high on a hill, dotted with baobabs on the slopes of the Beho Beho (meaning 'breezy') Hills. You'll find few other visitors in this district, but those who come are rewarded with the best lodge in the park. Accommodation is in large, attractively decorated en-suite bandas built of local stone & sheltered by high, thatched roofs. All are uniquely decorated, & each has a lovely open-fronted lounge area with panoramic views, large bathrooms with great outdoor showers, & bedrooms complete with canopied king-sized beds. In 2012, Bailey's Banda was completed, a private house named after the camp's owner. With 2 bedrooms, a lounge & a dining room with its own chef, this is the option to choose if you want complete privacy. Romantics can opt to stay in a super-luxurious treehouse in the branches of an ancient leadwood tree. Central areas are decadent: the elegant dining area serves beautifully presented food & guests generally eat together, hosted by the managers & 1 or 2 guides. There are comfy sofas to relax in around the bar area & a full-sized slate-bedded billiards table. Between the lodge's central areas & the upper bandas, the small swimming pool & its sundeck command a spectacular view. Beho Beho is the only Selous lodge away from the river; however, the permanent pool in the valley below supports a resident pod of noisy hippos & attracts elephants & other mammals & birdlife. Beyond the luxury and style, it's the quality & enthusiasm of Beho Beho's guiding team that has earned it its well-deserved reputation.

They take turns to accompany you on 4x4 game drives, excellent bush walks and boat trips on Lake Tagalala, and they deliver a consistently rewarding and impressively well-informed experience. It's not unknown for morning activities to last for 5 or 6hrs if you are enthusiastic & energetic. Beho Beho is certainly expensive, but it is the best camp in the Selous & arguably one of the best in Tanzania. The camp prefers guests to book through an operator & you are likely to get a better rate by doing so. Min age 12; no discount. *US$1140/2280 sgl/dbl, FB inc drinks, all activities & park fees; Treehouse US$350pp extra; Bailey's Banda US$1000 extra on top of normal room rates based on min 4 guests.* $$$$$$$

☀ 🏠 **Sand Rivers** (8 rooms in main camp, & 4 at Kiba Point) m 0787 595908; e info@nomad-tanzania.com; www.nomad-tanzania.com. Set above a wide, sandy bend in the Rufiji River, this has long been regarded as a 1st-class camp. Run by Nomad Tanzania, it's situated in an isolated area of the Selous, the wild southwest of the photographic section of the reserve – a district that is only infrequently visited by vehicles from the other lodges. The comfortable and welcoming central area consists of a large, open-fronted, thatched boma dotted with sofas & cushions. Watching the river life of the great curving Rufiji below adds greatly to the special feel of the place. There is also a stylish curved swimming pool under a large baobab tree. Meals are very good & eaten either together around a large table, or separately if you prefer. The lodge's stone-&-thatch cottages are large & elegant with secluded balconies. There are 5 standard rooms & 3 suites (each with a small plunge pool & separate lounge area), all open fronted & perched high above the river with wonderful views. For small groups seeking exclusive use, Sand Rivers has a satellite camp – **Kiba Point** – 1km downstream – with just 4 cottages. The style is similar to Sand Rivers, with the benefit of individual plunge pools, a private chef & guide. Activities focus on 4x4 game drives, boat trips along the river & up through the impressive Stiegler's Gorge, & walking safaris. The standard of guiding here is exceptionally high & the camp is very proud of its Tanzanian guides, some of whom have been there for many years. Sand Rivers also runs very popular fly-camping trips, on which a small group of guests sleep out on a dry riverbed or lake shore with their guide – usually having had a meal under the stars,

complete with table linen, crystal glasses & some fine food. *US$1,024–1,454/1,558–2,218 sgl/dbl FB inc drinks, all activities & park fees; suites US$125pp extra.* $$$$$$$

🏠 **Selous Impala Camp** (8 units) m 0753 115908; e reservations@adventurecampstz.com; www.selousimpalacamp.com. This unpretentious but attractive camp boasts a magnificent location on a wooded stretch of the Rufiji River, co-owned with Lake Manze Camp in the Selous, & Kwihala & Mdonya Old River camps in Ruaha National Park. The camp has one of the most scenic locations in the park & its thatched lounge & raised, communal deck look out over the river to the hills beyond – although your gaze is usually drawn back to the Rufiji River by the birds & other wildlife. Activities are fairly flexible, including game drives & boat trips, & the camp has a lovely swimming pool, which allows you to look out over the river while you're in the pool. Impala is a relatively small camp, with just 8 tents, built on wooden platforms with private balconies. These are very comfortably furnished, in a bright, warm style. There is a family option here, with 2 full-sized tents sharing a common platform allowing parents to have their own space but keep tabs on their children. The unfenced camp uses Maasai guards to escort guests to their rooms at night. This camp may not be quite so self-consciously stylish as some of its pricier peers elsewhere in the Selous, but it gets all the important stuff right: great food, a flexible attitude to activities & timings, & above all a team of drivers, boat captains & guides as knowledgeable & skilled as any we've encountered in Tanzania. *US$677.50–818.50/1,178–1,430 sgl/dbl FB inc activities & park fees.* $$$$$$$

🏠 **Siwandu Camp** (13 tented rooms) ☎ 022 212 8485; e reservations@selous.com; www.selous.com. Formerly Selous Safari Camp, this plush tented lodge is set back slightly from the shores of Lake Siwandu. Approaching the lake, all you see of the camp over the treetops are the tall apexes of the main central areas, built on piles. The camp consists of a 'south camp' (7 rooms) & a 'north camp' (6 rooms), both with raised, spacious, very stylish octagonal en-suite tents set well apart from each other & with fans, huge, open-air showers & private decks. Guests usually stay in south camp unless it is full. North camp can also be used by larger groups or big families. The main lounge & dining area is a fabulous treehouse, built several metres off the ground in the south camp area, lit at night by dozens of lamps & serving some of the best food in the Selous. There's a good-sized

14

swimming pool, set further back among the trees. North camp has its own very attractive dining area on decking near a second pool. Game drives, boat trips & guided walks are all on offer. A pontoon boat (larger than the usual Selous camp vessels) allows for relaxing lake trips with sundowners & canapés, or even full meals. Siwandu Camp is a very high-quality, professional operation that pays great attention to detail. Guiding here is variable, but the best guides are extremely good. *US$822.50–1,405/1,209–2,028 sgl/dbl FB inc activities & park fees.* $$$$$$$

🏠 **The Retreat Selous** (12 rooms) 📞(UK) +44 (0)208 785 6145; m 0783 213951; e welcome@retreat-africa.com; www.retreat-africa. com. In a remote section of the park, The Retreat is architecturally striking & impressive. Its ochre walls, Omani arches, stunning pool deck & impressive array of African objets d'art are testament to its Swiss owners' attention to detail & high standards. Reminiscent of a fort, the imposing main building is entered through a 200-year-old carved wooden door from Rajasthan. Accommodation is divided between the main clay 'fort', hillside tents & riverfront suites (complete with waterside plunge pools & viewing decks), including a honeymoon hideaway boasting a private chef, guide, butler & pool. 2 tents at Hippo Point share a pool bar & dining area. The tents, raised on teak decks, are spacious & well furnished & all have inviting outdoor baths to complement the en-suite facilities. In the public areas, there are lovely shaded lounge areas & there's also has a well-equipped professionally run outdoor spa on the riverbank offering traditional & holistic therapies. Food is served in the main restaurant overlooking the infinity pool & river or, for romantics, atop one of the 2 towers for panoramic views. Cocktail & sundowner spots are equally varied, with bars both riverside & raised on the hillside. If you can drag yourself away from the obvious comfort of the lodge, activities include game drives, river cruises (when the water is high enough), guided walks & line fishing. Open 4x4 vehicles & aluminium boats are used for these, with Tanzanian guides (who have received mixed reports) escorting all trips. Fly-camping needs to be pre-booked & costs an additional US$325pp. As there is more emphasis on sitting back & relaxing than game viewing, the Retreat appeals to honeymooners & those looking to get away from it all. *From US$775pp FB inc non-premium drinks & 1 activity/day. The 2 units at Hippo Point, sleeping up to 6 people, can be taken at a flat rate of US$5,000 per night.* $$$$$$$

Upmarket

☀ 🏠 **Lake Manze Tented Camp** (12 units) m 0787 817591; e reservations@ adventurecampstz.com; www.adventurecampstz. com. Part of the highly regarded Adventure Camps circuit, this is an excellent choice for a good-value safari in the Selous. Distinct from many of the other camps in the Selous, Lake Manze is about enjoying bush simplicity & being in the wilderness: the dining area has a natural sandy floor; atmospheric paraffin lanterns are used; bathrooms are partly open-air; & dinner is often eaten under the stars by the campfire. Dining here is usually communal, with meals hosted by the managers. Dotted under borassus & doum palms, the guest tents are spacious & have traditional insect mesh windows to allow for long views & a cooling breeze. Tent furnishings are simple but reasonably high quality, with wood or wrought-iron beds & chairs. There is an en-suite bathroom complete with a hot shower & flush toilet. Perhaps the greatest asset is the slightly raised elevation of the shady stone veranda, which affords good views across the lake, the floodplain & passing wildlife. There is a good standard of guiding & the activities are varied, with 4x4 safari drives, boat safaris & morning walks all available. *US$538.50– 643.50/1,017–1,087 sgl/dbl FB & activities inc park fees; US$393.50–503.50/627–827 sgl/dbl FB for drive-in clients (no activities) inc park fees.* $$$$$$

🏠 **Rufiji River Camp** (14 units) 📞022 286 2357 or (UK) +44 1452 862288; m 0754 237422; e info@tanzaniasafaris.info; www.rufijirivercamp. com. One of the first lodges established in the Selous, the ever-popular & reasonably priced Rufiji River Camp is situated at the eastern extremity of the tourist sector, in a lush stretch of woodland populated by monkeys & numerous birds, & overlooking a magnificent stretch of the Rufiji River alive with hippos, crocs & waterbirds, & regularly visited by elephants. The widely spaced accommodation is in spacious en-suite standing tents, each with 2 netted dbl beds, shaded by a thatch roof & set on a wide wooden platform with a balcony offering superb river views. The 3 suites also have private plunge pools. The central area is a massive dbl-storey wood-& thatch construction with a bar, dining room, plentiful seating & swimming pool. It offers an excellent range of boat & foot activities, as well as half-day game drives encompassing the 3 nearby lakes, full-day excursions further afield &

overnight fly-camping. The guides are generally experienced Tanzanians, most of whom have been guiding here for many years & many of whom worked as game scouts before joining the lodge. *US$503.50–598.50/867–997 sgl/dbl FB inc activities & park fees.* $$$$$$

🏠 **Selous Serena Camp** (12 tents) ✆022 211 8113/4; e darreservations@serena.co.tz; www. serenahotels.com. Formerly known as Selous Wildlife Camp, this Serena offering lies on the Simbazi River, a tributary of the Rufiji. Each of the individual tents, sheltered under grass thatch, is identical, with soft carpeted floors, comfy sofas & sparkling chandeliers & individual bathroom. Interiors are rather dramatically decorated with high-quality dark wood furnishings, & dressing gowns & slippers are provided. Central to the lodge is a natural waterhole, overlooked by the dining area & lounge. There's also a viewing deck & an infinity swimming pool. Guests can take part in nature walks, river cruises & game drives, which often last a full day in order to reach the well-dispersed game. *US$622/856 sgl/dbl FB inc local drinks, activities & laundry; children over 7 welcome.* $$$$$$

🏠 **Serena Mivumo River Lodge** (12 rooms) ✆027 254 5555; e reservations@serena.co.tz; www.serenahotels.com. Situated on the banks of the Rufiji close to the eastern entrance to Stiegler's Gorge, this spacious lodge has an unbeatable location in terms of scenery & boat trips into the gorge. The modern suites are perhaps the most comfortable accommodation on offer in Selous, coming with a wooden floor, leather furnishings, king-sized bed, large bathroom with indoor tub & outdoor shower, as well as AC, which might offend the purists, but can feel very welcome in this muggy climate. There is also a large deck with a spectacular infinity swimming pool looking over the river. The one big drawback about this lodge is that the surrounding miombo woodland supports low game densities & plenty of tsetse flies, which makes for unrewarding game drives unless you opt for the long full-day drive to the lakes. *US$652/1,028 sgl/dbl FB inc local drinks, activities & laundry; children over 7 welcome.* $$$$$$$

Moderate

🏠 **Sable Mountain Lodge** (12 rooms) m 0713 323318; e info@tentwithaview.com; www. selouslodge.com. This sensibly priced lodge lies in a patch of small hills 1km outside the western park boundary near Matembwe Gate. It consists of 4 cottages & 5 tented bandas, a private villa & separate rooftop suite, all with en-suite hot shower & toilet & 24hr electricity, set spaciously across the hillside. A treehouse on one of the slopes, offering a grandstand view over a waterhole regularly visited by buffalo & elephant, now includes a suite for overnight stays. The surrounding woodland is very thick, & guided walks offer the opportunity to see forest-associated species such as blue monkey, black-&-white colobus & the amazing chequered elephant shrew, as well as a host of forest birds including the exquisite Livingstone's turaco, a variety of hornbills & the vociferous forest weaver. Between Dec & May, sable antelopes move into the area. Game drives concentrate on the plains north of the main cluster of lodges, which can be very worthwhile seasonally, with very few other vehicles around. Fly-camping is also available, as are boat safaris on Lake Tagalala. *Stone cottages cost US$250/390 sgl/dbl FB, US$490/630 sgl/dbl inc activities, with no seasonal variation. Other units are slightly pricier.* $$$$$

🏠 **Selous Maji Moto Camp** (up to 4 units) m 0786 019965; e enquiries@authentictanzania. com; www.authentictanzaniasafaris.com. A welcome throwback to the old-school safari, this private mobile camp is set up by request (min 2 nights) at a variable location on the banks of one of the 5 lakes, which means that elephant, hippo & other wildlife passes through on a regular basis. Activity-wise, the focus is on game drives, but guided walks & river trips are also offered, & since it is reserved for private parties, individual guests can decide their day-to-day schedule in conjunction with an experienced guide. The emphasis is on providing guests with a down-to-earth & immersive bush experience rather than slick designer safari chic. The tents are comfortable enough, but rather cramped, & they come with narrow twin camp beds, bucket shower & portable loo, so are not suited to those seeking a high level of comfort. *Rates depend on group size & duration of stay, ranging from US$620pp/night for 2 people staying 2 nights to US$250pp/night for 6+ people staying 5+ nights. Meals, drinks & activities are included, but park fees are extra.* $$$$$$

🏠 **Selous Mbuyu Safari Camp** (16 units) m 0689 133010; e sales@selousmbuyusafaricamp. com; www.selousmbuyusafaricamp.com. Well positioned for game drives along the productive eastern lakes circuit, this camp also offers perhaps the best in-house game viewing of any camp in the Selous. It is set on a rise overlooking a river channel frequented by hippo, elephant, giraffe & various antelope, while the central baobab after which it is named is visited by bushbabies & genets after dark. There's also an attractively sited swimming pool & a lovely bar/dining area running down to the river. Sadly, the functional tiled standing tents have a rather fuddy-duddy feel that don't quite match the setting, & the camp as a whole looks a little frayed at the edges. Despite these shortcomings, it is very reasonably priced, at least by Selous's wallet-draining standards, & you can't argue with the location or quality of game viewing, especially if you score one of the riverfront units farthest from the main reception area. *US$402/650 sgl/dbl FB inc game drives but not boat trips.* $$$$$$

CAMPS OUTSIDE MTEMERE GATE

A string of riverside camps set outside Mtemere Gate are less convenient than their counterparts within the reserve, but they also tend to be a lot cheaper. Although there are around a dozen camps set outside the gate, most are semi-functional and/or poorly tended. The quartet listed below stand out as the least ephemeral and best-run options.

Moderate

⌂ **Selous Riverside Camp** (14 rooms)
📞022 213 6770; e info@selousriversidecamp. com; www.selousriversidecamp.com. Set on the lushly wooded south bank of the Rufiji about 5km east of the reserve boundary as the crow flies, this well-managed camp is the smartest option outside Mtemere Gate. A large thatched dining & bar area leads to a small swimming pool overlooking the river, while accommodation is in large stilted tented units with king-sized beds, walk-in nets, bright furniture, 24hr electricity & private balcony with river view. Some rooms also have a private plunge pool. Very good value. *From US$190pp FB or US$275pp inc activities.* $$$$

Budget & camping

☀ ⌂ **Selous River Camp** (12 units) m 0784 237525; e reservations@selousrivercamp.com; www.selousrivercamp.com. Owned & managed by a hands-on British–Tanzanian couple, this well-priced camp (not to be confused with its pricier near namesake listed above) also has an idyllic location immediately outside the reserve boundaries close to Mtemere Gate. Accommodation is in simple standing tents using common showers, or en-suite mud huts, all with bedding provided & meals included. Independent travellers coming from Dar es Salaam by bus can be met at nearby Mloka by prior arrangement. Guided walks, boat trips & game drives into the park can be included in game activity packages of 2–5 nights' duration; see the website for full details. *US$100/155 sgl/dbl in standing tent, US$230/300 sgl/dbl mud hut, all rates FB.* $$$$

⌂ **Africa Safari Camp** (21 units) m 0777 699000; e info@africa-safari.com; www.africa-safari.com. Practically bordering the reserve, this popular & well-run new camp lacks for river frontage but has a genuine bush location overlooking a newly created waterhole designed to attract elephant & other passing wildlife. Accommodation is in spacious & attractively rustic bandas & smarter bungalows, all with fitted nets, fan, organic décor & en-suite hot showers. The grounds are studded with baobabs & include a swimming pool, curio shop & attractive thatched dining area & bar. Game drives cost US$85pp & boat trips outside the park US$35pp. *US$100/140 sgl/dbl banda or US$200 dbl banda. All rates inc b/fast but exclude lunch (US$15) & dinner (US$20).* $$$$

⌂ **Great Water Lodge** (4 rooms) m 0684 651337; e info@selouslodge.co.tz; www. selouslodge.co.tz. The most remote of the Mtemere lodges, situated about 10km downriver of the reserve boundary, this intimate & unpretentious lodge is set in a patch of riverine woodland on a low cliff above a stretch of Rufiji frequented by crocodiles & occasional hippos. Although it is too far from the reserve for large wildlife to pass through, colobus monkeys are resident in the vicinity, bushbabies make their presence felt as they cry through the night, & birdlife is abundant. Despite their rustic rough-&-ready appearance, the stilted chalets are well screened & have good natural ventilation, while simple home-style cooking is served in a restaurant with sand underfoot & thatch overhead. Activities include game drives (*US$220 per vehicle/day*), boat trips outside the park (*US$40pp*) & bush walks (*US$15pp*). *Fair value at US$140/230 sgl/dbl FB.* $$$$

With the addition of the Usangu Game Reserve in 2008, Ruaha doubled in size to become Tanzania's largest national park. It extends over 20,200km² of wooded hills and open plains to the west of Iringa, and lies at the core of a greater ecosystem that is 2½ times larger, embracing six other protected areas including the contiguous Rungwa and Kizigo game reserves. Ruaha is widely regarded by Tanzania's safari cognoscenti to be the country's best-kept game-viewing secret, and it has unquestionably retained a compelling wilderness character that is increasingly savoury when compared with the package safaris and 100-room game lodges common in the parks of northern Tanzania. Let's hope it stays this way.

BACKGROUND INFORMATION The dominant geographical feature of the park is the Great Ruaha River, which follows the southeast boundary for 160km, and is known to the local Hehe people as the Lyambangori (Ruaha being a corruption of the Hehe word *luhava*, which simply means 'river'). Only the small part of the park around the river is developed for tourism, with around a dozen small lodges currently operating. Its limited 400km road circuit sees relatively few visitors and has a reassuringly untrammelled mood.

Ruaha has a hot and rather dry climate, with an average annual rainfall of around 500mm falling almost exclusively between October and May, and peaking in February and March. Daytime temperatures in excess of 40°C are regularly recorded, particularly during October and November before the rains break, but a very low humidity level makes this less noticeable than might be expected, and it cools down reliably at night. The best game viewing is generally from May to November, but the bush is greener and prettier from January to June, and birding peaks during the European winter months of December to April. The vegetation of Ruaha is transitional to southern miombo and eastern savanna biomes, and a wide variety of habitats are protected within the park, including riparian forest along the watercourses, swamps, grassland and acacia woodland. The dominant vegetation type is brachystegia woodland, and several areas of the park support an impressive number of large baobab trees.

The floral variety of Ruaha is mirrored by the variety of wildlife likely to be seen over the course of a few days on safari. The most common ungulates, not unusually, are the widespread impala, waterbuck, bushbuck, buffalo, zebra and giraffe, all of which are likely to be encountered several times on any given game drive. The park lies at the most southerly extent of the range of several east African ungulate species, including lesser kudu and Grant's gazelle. Yet it also harbours a number of antelope that are rare or absent in northern Tanzania, most visibly the splendid greater kudu – some of the most handsomely horned males you'll come across anywhere in Africa – but also the more elusive roan and sable antelope. The elephant population is the largest of any Tanzanian national park, despite heavy losses due to poaching in the 1980s, with some 12,000 elephants migrating through the greater Ruaha ecosystem. The most impressive pair of tusks weighed in the 20th century – combined weight 201kg – were from an individual shot in Ruaha in the 1970s, but the poaching of the recent past means you're unlikely to see anything comparable these days.

Ruaha is an excellent park for predators. Lions are not only numerous and very habituated to vehicles, but the prides tend to be unusually large, often numbering more than 20 individuals. The park also boasts a justified reputation for good leopard sightings, and, while it's not as reliable as the Seronera Valley in the Serengeti, leopard are usually seen every few days and they are less skittish than in many game reserves. Cheetah, resident on the open plains, are quite often encountered in the Lundu area – known locally as the mini Serengeti – northeast of the Mwagusi River. More than 100 African wild dogs are thought to be resident in the greater Ruaha ecosystem. Wild dogs are known to have very wide ranges, and their movements are often difficult to predict, but one pack of about 40 individuals regularly moves into the Mwagusi area, generally hanging around for a few days before wandering elsewhere for a couple of weeks. Visiting in July gives a higher chance of seeing a wild dog, as they are normally denning, and are thus easier to locate than at other times of year. However, in recent years their behaviour has been more varied, and so this seasonal activity is not as reliable as it once was. Black-backed jackal and spotted hyena are both very common and easily seen, and the rarer striped hyena, though seldom observed, is found here at the southern limit of its range.

With 573 species recorded, Ruaha also offers some excellent birding, once again with an interesting mix of southern and northern species. Of particular note are substantial and visible populations of black-collared lovebird and ashy starlings, Tanzanian endemics associated with the Maasai Steppes, found here at the southern extreme of their distribution. By contrast, this is perhaps the only savanna reserve in East Africa where the crested barbet – a colourful yellow-and-black bird whose loud sustained trilling is a characteristic sound of the southern African bush – replaces the red-and-yellow barbet. Two other noteworthy species, both recently described based on observations within the national park, are the Ruaha hornbill, a locally abundant Tanzanian endemic formerly regarded to be a race of the more widespread red-billed hornbill, and the Ruaha chat, a variant in Arnot's chat associated with western Tanzania and eastern Rwanda. Raptors are well represented, with bateleur and fish eagle probably the most visible large birds of prey, and the localised Eleanora's falcon quite common in December and January. The watercourses support the usual waterbirds.

Ruaha is best visited between July and November, when animals concentrate around the river. Internal roads may be impassable during the rainy season (December to May), when many of the camps are closed.

FEES AND FURTHER INFORMATION There is a conservation fee of US$30 per person per night (US$10 for children aged 6–16) plus 18% VAT. On most organised tours this will be included in the quote, but it's worth checking when booking. If you need to pay the fee yourself, be warned that cash is not accepted, you need to have a Visa or MasterCard, or a loaded Tanapa smartcard.

Sue Stolberger's *Ruaha National Park: An Intimate View* (Jacana Media, 2012, available at the entrance gate for US$45) is an exemplary field guide to the park's plants and smaller wildlife – erudite, informative, and littered with fascinating fact boxes. Another excellent publication, essential for birders, is Robert Glen's comprehensive *Annotated Checklist of the Birds of Ruaha National Park* (self-published, 2011), which is also sold at the gate for US$10. Another useful resource is the website www.ruahanationalpark.weebly.com.

RUAHA NATIONAL PARK
For listings, see pages 416–19

Where to stay and eat
1 Chabo Africa
2 Ikuka Safari Camp
3 Jongomero Tented Camp
4 Kigelia Camp
5 Kwihala
6 Mdonya Old River Camp
7 Msembe Headquarters
8 Mwagusi Safari Camp
9 Ruaha Hilltop Lodge
10 Ruaha Kilimatonge Camp
11 Ruaha River Lodge
12 Tandala Tented Camp
13 Tungamalenga Camp

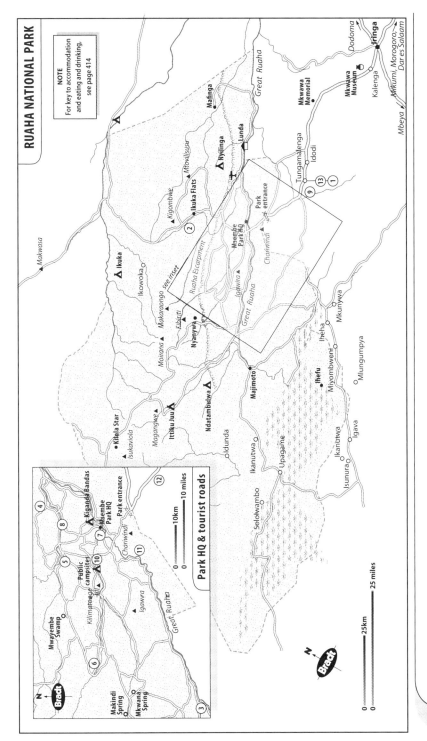

RUAHA NATIONAL PARK

NOTE
For key to accommodation
and eating and drinking,
see page 414

Park HQ & tourist roads

14

GETTING THERE AND AWAY The most straightforward way to reach Ruaha from Zanzibar is by **air**. Coastal Aviation (*www.coastal.co.tz*) flies daily via Dar es Salaam, which also serves Selous. As with the Selous, if you are travelling in mainland Tanzania you can reach Ruaha by air from Dar es Salaam, without going to Zanzibar. Safari Air Link (*www.flysal.com*) offers a daily shared air charter service from Dar es Salaam to Ruaha via Mikumi and Selous. It's also possible to get there by **road**, although this is usually at least a two-day trip; for more details see Bradt's *Tanzania Safari Guide* by Philip Briggs and Chris McIntyre (page 427).

WHERE TO STAY AND EAT *Map, page 415*
Inside the national park
Exclusive

☀ ⌂ **Ikuka Safari Camp** (6 tents)
m 0763 598027; **e** info@ikukasafaricamp.com; www.ikukasafaricamp.com. Set on a tall ridge offering views across the rolling foothills of the escarpment to the Mwagusi River about 5km to the south, Ruaha's newest & most spectacular camp is owned & managed by a family with years of experience in East Africa's guiding & lodge industry. Accommodation is in fabulous open-sided, thatch-roofed constructions set on a stilted platform positioned to catch the welcome breeze & to make the most of the wonderful view. Each unit comprises a spacious bedroom with king-sized bed & completely openable canvas walls on 3 sides, a large modern bathroom, a comfortable & brightly coloured sitting area, & a wide wooden balcony. The architecture throughout is organic but stylish, while the extensive use of the lovely white quartzite rocks that dominate the area gives it an individualistic feel. The food is excellent & is normally eaten communally with the hospitable owner-managers, but individual parties can eat alone if they prefer. Guided game drives to the nearby Mwagusi/Ruaha confluence area are included, & it has 1 of only 2 swimming pools in the park. The introductory rates listed below represent the best value in Ruaha at the time of writing, but expect increases once the camp is more established. *US$550–650/900–1,100 sgl/dbl FB inc drinks & activities.* **$$$$$$**

⌂ **Jongomero Tented Camp** (8 tents)
☏ 022 212 8485; **m** 0784 953551; **e** reservations@ selous.com; www.selous.com; ⏰ closed Apr–May. Sister camp of Siwandu in the Selous (page 409), this is one of the most luxurious lodges in Ruaha & one of only 2 with a swimming pool. Stylish & excellently run, Jongomero consists of spacious tented rooms with private balconies carved into the dense riverine woodland bordering the

eponymous seasonal river. It's about 2km upstream of its confluence with the Great Ruaha River, where a semi-permanent pool hosts a resident pod of around 50 hippos. Situated 60km southwest of the entrance gate, Jongomero has a very isolated feel, & the little-used road running back towards the entrance gate often yields good elephant & buffalo sightings. The area to the south of camp sees few other vehicles, & functions much as a private game reserve, but with slightly lower game densities & thick vegetation, it takes a little more effort to see the game here than in other areas of the park. However, this is more than made up for by the top-notch guiding &, in the dry season, fascinating walking safaris led by the camp's manager & head guide. The birdlife within camp can be excellent, with Livingstone's turaco topping the gaudiness stakes, while the localised Böhm's spinetail can be distinguished from the other swifts & swallows that soar above the camp by its distinctive, bat-like voice. For something a bit different, try fly-camping to complement the existing game drives. The catering is to an exceptionally high standard, but, unlike several other lodges in this price range elsewhere in Tanzania, drinks are not automatically included, although they can be added for a supplement of US$40pp/night. *US$695– 1,278/998–1,820 sgl/dbl, FB & inc 2 activities/day, laundry & park fees but not drinks; walking safaris US$40pp extra park fee.* **$$$$$$**

⌂ **Kichaka Expeditions** (3 tents) **m** 0763 782982; **e** info@kichakaexpeditions.com; www. kichakaexpeditions.com. This private mobile camp opened in 2013, far from any other camps, in the northeast of Ruaha. The focus here is on exploring new areas of the park while getting close to big game, often on foot. The camp is owned, run & excellently managed by Andrew 'Moli' Molinaro & his partner Noelle Herzog. Noelle is a great chef & hostess & Moli a superb walking guide, who, along with another experienced guide, leads the safari walks & game drives, which are considered to be some of the best in Tanzania. The camp is booked exclusively for a minimum of 2 people & a maximum of 6. This, coupled with the fact Kichaka is owner-run, creates a very intimate experience. It is also possible to book on to a group trip of up to 6 people that makes staying here slightly more affordable. The camp itself comprises of simple, yet very comfortable, cream canvas tents, each with a covered veranda at the front & a slightly separate bathroom at the side, complete with a basin, bucket shower & short-drop toilet. Each tent has a huge dbl bed, writing desk & plenty of hanging space. The camp moves periodically, depending on which areas Moli & Noelle decide to explore next, & Kichaka also has 3 smaller tents that allow for ad-hoc fly-camping. *Rates depend on group size & season, ranging from US$1,043–1,728 dbl to US$652–779pp for 6 people, inc activities, drinks, laundry & park fees; all rates FB.* **$$$$$$**

🏠 **Kigelia Camp** (6 tents) ↘(South Africa) +255 787 595 908; e info@nomad-tanzania. com; www.nomad-tanzania.com. Named after the sausage trees (*Kigelia africana*) that line the seasonal Ifuguru River on whose bank it stands, this rustic yet elegant semi-permanent camp offers accommodation in secluded standing tents with king-sized beds, hot outdoor showers & private balconies. The open-sided lounge is filled with solid wooden furniture, made from reclaimed dhow wood, & the shelves & tables scattered with coffee-table books. It's a popular spot for afternoon tea & biscuits. In the evening, a roaring campfire is set up overlooking the riverbed, where guests gather for pre-dinner stargazing. Tasty 3-course meals are usually served outside, depending on the weather. Although great walking safaris are also offered, the main activity here is game drives with knowledgeable & informative guides. The extremely comfortable vehicles are equipped with soft, armchair-like seats; hot-water bottles & blankets are provided for the colder mornings. Kigelia is one of the few camps in Ruaha where guests can also do night drives (US$59pp supplement). *US$995–1,260/1,500–1,830 sgl/dbl FB inc laundry, drinks & park fees.* **$$$$$$**

🏠 **Kwihala** (6 tents) m 0736 500515; e reservations@asiliaafrica.com; www.asiliaafrica. com. Kwihala opened in 2006, & is comparable to Kigelia in many ways. It has a similar layout & actually used the same tent designer, although

they have adopted a slightly different style. The en-suite canvas tents are spacious & tastefully decorated with glass beads, & the camp's signature blue baobab design adds a touch of interest. The lounge & dining room are adjoined & set back from the tents, while a short walk away is the camp fire, where safari-goers gather in the evening to discuss the day's sightings. Dining locations vary, but a popular choice is a tasty bush dinner served under the stars by lantern light. The camp cleverly mixes style, luxury & comfort while managing to retain a feeling of wilderness. As well as the usual game drives, safari walks & night drives are also offered here, & unlike most camps these are included in the cost. Kwihala's popularity has increased steadily over recent years, due to its great value, good management & excellent standard of guiding. With plenty of game in the surrounding area – leopards are often sighted here – it's a justifiably popular choice. Following its success, Kwihala has plans to open a luxury camp nearby, called Jabali Ridge, in the next couple of years. *US$680–1,131/1,360–1,670 sgl/dbl inc activities, drinks, laundry & park fees; all rates FB.* **$$$$$$**

✳ 🏠 **Mwagusi Safari Camp** (10 tents) ↘(UK) +44 (0)1822 615721; m 0752 5170940; e safaris@wingsoverthewild.co.uk; www. mwagusicamp.com. This small & exclusive tented camp, situated on the north bank of the seasonal Mwagusi River, is one of the most alluring lodges anywhere in East Africa. Immensely comfortable, yet with a real bush atmosphere, accommodation is strung through the woodland fringing the river & consists of spacious walk-in tents, enclosed in shelters of wood, thatch & reed, each of which has a large shower & toilet area, & a private balcony with inviting armchairs & hammocks. Because the lodge is owner-managed, the service is top-notch, & includes some great touches – most memorably, starlit bush dinners around the campfire in a clearing above the camp or in the riverbed. Game viewing is superb, with elephant & greater kudu regularly putting in an appearance, & plenty of birds hopping through the trees. Although wild dog habits have become more changeable in recent years, leopard are regularly sighted in the area, several lion prides are resident, & the nearby game-viewing circuits are far enough from the larger Ruaha River Lodge & park HQ to give you the feeling you have the whole park to yourself. Game walks with an armed ranger are also offered, with

14

a good chance of encountering elephant & other large animals on foot; it is best to book these in advance & they cost around US$50pp. For early risers, Mwagusi also runs free, early-morning bird walks around the camp – a lovely way to start the day. *US$690/1,251 FB sgl/dbl inc all activities & park fees; drinks are extra.* **$$$$$$$**

Upmarket

⌂ **Mdonya Old River Camp** (12 tents) ☏ 022 260 1747; e info@ed.co.tz; www.mdonya. com. Like its sister camp, Lake Manze Camp in the Selous, this was set up with help from the airline Coastal Aviation. It stands on the wooded banks of the 'old' Mdonya River, which has not flowed in earnest since a newer path was carved by the river a couple of decades back. Comfortable, rather than luxurious, the en-suite tents all have a private veranda, while the culinary emphasis is on tasty home-style cooking eaten beneath the stars. The camp makes no apologies for being fairly simple: it aims for an elemental experience of Africa, & not for the comforts & fripperies that so many camps seem to have been striving for in recent years. There's no electricity, although the open-air bathroom does have a hot-water shower & a flushing toilet. A few sofas dot the lounge area, while the bar is really just a tree with bottles stored in the nooks & crannies. Isolated though it may be, the camp offers good access to the superb Mwagusi Sand River game-viewing circuit. The old riverbed is an important wildlife passage, & plenty of animals pass through camp daily, most abundantly elephant, warthog & giraffe, but also the occasional lion, while the helpful staff will gladly show you nocturnal visitors such as honey badger, genet & bushpig. The birding is also superb, with the likes of purple-crested turaco, bearded woodpecker, crested barbet, black-necked weaver, orange-breasted bush-shrike & green-winged pytilia among the colourful & conspicuous residents. *US$295–350/430–540 sgl/dbl for drive-in clients (exc activities & park fees), US$495–550/830–940 sgl/dbl for fly-in, inc activities, laundry & park fees; all rates FB.* **$$$$$$**

⌂ **Ruaha Kilimatonge Camp** (up to 4 units) m 0786 019965; e info@authentictanzania. com; www.authentictanzaniasafaris.com. This private mobile camp is set up by request for a minimum of 2 nights at a superb location on the bank of the seasonal Mdonya River as it flows

past Kilimatonge Hill, a massive granite dome that towers overhead. It lies in superb big cat country, with lions often passing within a few metres of the tents at night & a near guarantee of leopard sightings on the surrounding rocks. Because the camp is always reserved for private parties, guests can decide their daily schedule in conjunction with a guide. Emphatically aimed towards those seeking an intimate in-your-face bush experience as opposed to stylish safari chic, the camp comprises as many standing tents as are required to house the party, & are just about tall enough to stand up in, but rather cramped, with narrow twin camp beds, bucket shower & portable loo. Game drives & optional walks are led by very experienced guides with exceptional tracking skills. *Rates depend on group size & duration of stay, ranging from US$615pp/night for 2 people staying 2 nights to US$240pp/night for 6+ people staying 5+ nights. Meals, drinks & activities inc, but park fees are extra.* **$$$$$$**

⌂ **Ruaha River Lodge** (24 rooms) ☏ (UK) +44 (0) 1452 862288; m 0754 237422; e info@ tanzaniasafaris.info; www.tanzaniasafaris.info. This scenic & comfortable camp is the oldest in Ruaha, situated on a rocky hillside above a set of rapids on the Ruaha River some 15km from the entrance gate. Game viewing is excellent, with rock hyrax scuttling around everywhere, hippo resident in the river, elephant passing through regularly, & many other animals coming down to drink. Accommodation is in unpretentious stone chalets & each unit has a dbl & a sgl bed & a comfortable lounge area. The chalets are very spread out with 12 rooms along the river & 14 rooms further up the hill. One of the dining areas is raised up with great views over the river; the other is nearer the water's edge, giving a closer view of drinking animals. Fly-camping & walking safaris can be arranged. *US$437–487/714–814 FB sgl/ dbl inc most activities, laundry & park fees; drinks & walking safaris are extra.* **$$$$$$**

Budget & camping

⌂ **Msembe Headquarters** (16 rooms) This national park camp near the HQ lies close to the river & some extensive open plains teeming with game. The accommodation isn't up to much – prefabricated en-suite dbl & family bandas that look like they must get seriously hot in the middle of the day – but it's the cheapest on offer within the park. There's a shower with hot water & the newer bandas have more space & indoor bathrooms. Bedding, firewood & water are provided, & drinks & very basic provisions can be bought at the nearby staff bar, but it's best to bring all food with you. Payment can only be made at the park entrance or headquarters using Visa or MasterCard (or the special cards issued by Tanapa) – cash is not accepted. *Old banda US$20pp, new banda US$50pp, camping US$30pp.* **$$–$$$**

Outside the national park The camps listed below lie alongside the Iringa Road between the main national park entrance and the village of Tungamalenga, which lies 18km to the east and is accessible on a daily bus service from Iringa. They are all a lot cheaper than their counterparts within Ruaha, and arrange day safaris into the park.

Moderate

🏠 **Tandala Tented Camp** (11 units) m 0755 680220/0757 183420; e info@tandalacamp.com; www.tandalacamp.com. Situated 6km outside the entrance gate along the Tungamalenga road, this attractive bush camp overlooks a seasonal river in a private conservancy buffering the national park, & makes for a good compromise between the costlier accommodation within the park & more basic options further east. The comfortable en-suite tents stand on stilted wooden bases, while facilities include an attractive makuti restaurant & bar area alongside a small swimming pool. The greater kudu for which the camp is named is quite common in the surrounding woodland, while a waterhole attracts a steady stream of wildlife in the dry season, including elephant on most days. Because it lies outside the national park, activities such as night drives, guided game walks & fly-camping are offered on the property. Game drives into the park are offered as an extra. *US$250/450 sgl/dbl FB.* **$$$$$**

Budget

🏠 **Ruaha Hilltop Lodge** (18 rooms) m 0784 726709; e info@ruahahilltoplodge.com; www. ruahahilltoplodge.com. Situated on a steep hillside 16km from the park entrance gate & 2km from Tungamalenga, this well-organised lodge is comfortably the pick of a few budget options in the vicinity. Small but clean en-suite thatched bandas come with fitted nets, bright ethnic fabrics, hot water, solar power & a private balcony. There's a stunning view from the restaurant/bar area, & the management can arrange transfers from Iringa

(*US$200 return for up to 6 people*), free transfers from Tungamalenga to coincide with the bus, game drives into the park, & guided walks into the surrounding hills. Good value. *US$95pp FB.* **$$$$**

🏠 **Tungamalenga Camp** (16 rooms) 📞 026 278 2196; m 0768 093853; e tungacamp@yahoo. com; www.ruahatungacamp.com. This well-run camp & curio shop is situated on the western edge of tiny Tungamalenga village about 18km from the park entrance gate. Neither the setting nor the small en-suite bandas, each with 2 beds & netting, compare to the far nicer Ruaha Hilltop Lodge, but it is considerable cheaper, though it would seem somewhat overpriced were it not for its proximity to the park. Camping, with access to a clean shower & toilet & a self-catering area, is permitted, too. There is a good restaurant & staff can organise game drives into the park. *US$65 FB, camping US$10pp.* **$$$**

Shoestring

🏠 **Chabo Africa** (7 rooms) m 0784 893717/0715 893717; e info@chaboafricasafari. com; www.chaboafricasafari.com. This unpretentious small lodge operated by Iringa's Chabo Safaris stands in Tungamalenga village (right next to Tungamalenga Camp) & offers accommodation in no-frills en-suite rooms with cold water & net. The management can arrange transfers from Iringa (*US$150 one-way*) & game drives into the park. It wouldn't be anything special in any other context, but it does stand out as far & away the cheapest place to stay in the vicinity of Ruaha. *US$10 dbl bed only.* **$**

Appendix 1

LANGUAGE *with thanks to Said el-Gheithy*

PRONUNCIATION Pronunciation of Swahili is generally straightforward: every syllable is sounded and there are no 'silent endings'. In longer words the stress is on the penultimate syllable. The most confusing feature for learners is that many words have a prefix and suffix which change according to subject and tense. However, when speaking, beginners can ignore these additions, and still be understood.

Of course, the best way to learn is to listen to the people around you. For more detailed information, use a phrasebook (page 427), or visit the Institute of Kiswahili and Foreign Languages (page 158).

USEFUL SWAHILI WORDS AND PHRASES The following basics are necessarily very simplified, and may not be grammatically correct, but by using them you will be understood in most situations. Many Zanzibaris will be delighted to hear a visitor using a few Swahili words – even if they are mispronounced or put in the wrong order!

Introductions and greetings Introductions and salutations are very important in Swahili culture, particularly when speaking to adults or people older than yourself, even if the age difference is slight. (Children are not usually greeted by adults outside their family.)

The most common forms of address are the traditional Muslim greetings (in Arabic), regardless of the religion of the people being greeted, each with its own response:

Salama aleikum	Peace be with you
Aleikum salam	And peace be with you (response)

You can also use the following greetings when addressing older people:

Sblakheri	Good morning
Msalkheri	Good afternoon/evening
Shkamoo	(a general greeting which can be used at any time of day)
Marahaba	(response to '*shkamoo*')
Habari zako or *hujambo?*	How are you?
Al humdul allah	Everything is well (response: literally 'Thanks be to Allah')

For people of the same age, and especially for friends, you can use *Habari*, which means 'Hello' (also meaning 'How are you?', literally 'what news?'). The reply might be *Al humdul allah*, or the more casual *Nzuri* ('good'), *Nzuri sana* ('very good') or *Safi* ('fine').

In areas where Swahili is not spoken as a first language the reply is often *Mzuri*, with an 'M', rather than 'Nzuri'. *Habari* can also be used for 'Excuse me' (when attracting somebody's attention), but it is still considered impolite to simply say '*Habari*' ('hello') to someone older than you.

Mambo is an even more casual way of greeting friends, meaning 'how's it going?' The response is *Poa* (something along the lines of 'neat', 'cool' or 'dandy').

Although *Jambo* also means 'Hello', Zanzibaris never use this word speaking to each other, and it tends only to be used by Zanzibaris talking to tourists. (In the same way, the oft-quoted '*Hakuna matata*' – 'no problem' – is mock-Swahili-for-tourists imported from Kenya, and not used by Zanzibaris. If you want to express this idea, a more correct alternative would be '*Hamna neno*' or '*Haidhuru*'.)

Children in Zanzibar greet adults with *Chechei*, usually followed by the title of the adult. The response is the same.

Even when speaking in English a Swahili acquaintance will ask 'How are you?', 'How are things today?', 'How is your husband/wife/friend?' You should do the same. Launching straight into any subject without the opening questions is rude. Traditional Zanzibaris expect women to be less forward than men, although in areas used to tourists this does not apply.

Hodi means 'Hello, anyone at home, can I come in?' used when knocking on somebody's door. *Karibu* is the response, meaning 'welcome' (literally 'come near').

You may hear the word *mzungu* ('white person') directed to you, particularly by children, but it is not disrespectful.

The basics

Goodbye	*Kwaheri*
Welcome	*Karibu*
Please	*Tafadali*
Thank you (very much)	*Asante (sana)*
Yes	*Ndiyo*
No	*Hapana*

Conversation starters and enders

What is your name?	*Jina lako nani?*
My name is Susie	*Jina langu Susie*
Where are you from?	*Unatoka wapi?*
I am from …	*Mimi ninatoka …*
	(the *mimi* is often dropped)
Where do you live?	*Unakaa wapi?*
Where are you staying? (ie: locally)	*Umefikia wapi?*
I am sorry, I don't understand	*Samahani sifahamu*
I don't speak Swahili	*Sijui Kiswahili*
I speak a very little Swahili	*Nazungumza Kiswahili kidogo tu*

Other useful words and phrases

OK (agreement)	*sawa*	there is	*ipo*is
sorry (condolences)	*pole* (not used for apologies)	there…?	*iko* …?
		there isn't…	*hakuna* …
where?	*wapi?*	how much?	*bei gani?*
what	*nini*		(literally 'what price?')
here	*hapa*	how many shillings?	*shillingi ngapi?*
there	*hapo*		

I want to go to Bububu		Nataka kwenda Bububu	
Where is the bus for Makunduchi?		Liko wapi basi la Makunduchi?	
Where is the ruin?		Liko wapi gofu?	
I am ill		Mimi mgonjwa	
Where is the hospital?		Iko wapi hospitali?	
Where is the doctor?		Yuko wapi daktari?	
I am lost		Nimepotea	

left	kushoto	tomorrow	kesho
right	kulia	yesterday	jana
straight on	moja kwa moja	bank	benki
near	karibu	shop	duka
far	mbali	market	soko
today	leo	café, eating-house	hoteli ya chakula

Food and drink

beef	nyama ya ngombe	water	maji
chicken	kuku	tea	chai
eggs	yai	coffee	kahawa
fish	samaki	milk	maziwa
potato	viazi	sugar	sukari
rice	mchele		

The word *soda* means any fizzy drink in a bottle. In the smarter hotels in Zanzibar Town, if you want soda water try asking for a club soda.

Numbers

1	moja	21	ishirini na moja
2	mbili	30	thelathini
3	tatu	40	arobaini
4	nne	50	hamsini
5	tano	60	sitini
6	sita	70	sabini
7	saba	80	themanini
8	nane	90	tisini
9	tisa	100	mia
10	kumi	101	mia na moja
11	kumi na moja	102	mia na mbili
12	kumi na mbili	200	mia mbili
20	ishirini	300	mia tatu

Time Swahili time starts at 00.00, the hour of sunrise, which is at 06.00 in Western time.

What time is it?	Saa ngapi?	08.00	saa mbili
07.00	saa moja (literally one o'clock)	noon	saa sita
		13.00	saa saba

When finding out about bus or boat departures, check if the time you've been told is Swahili time or Western time. This can be complicated further by some buses leaving outlying villages very early in the morning.

Appendix 2

FURTHER INFORMATION

BOOKS
History and background
General histories of Africa The following books are general histories of Africa or the East African region, which include sections on Zanzibar. Some are old and now long out of print, but make interesting reading if you can find them – try a specialist historical bookshop. Pakenham's classic history of Africa from the 1870s onwards is particularly compulsive, and often reprinted in paperback. Taylor's book about the European settlers who 'stayed on' in East Africa after the countries gained independence, looks at the colonial past in the present context, and neatly combines history with contemporary travel writing.

Coupland, R *The Exploitation of East Africa 1856–1890: The Slave Trade and the Scramble* Faber, London, 1939
Davidson, B *The Story of Africa* Littlehampton Book Services Ltd, London, 1984
Freeman-Grenville, G S P *The East African Coast: Select Documents* Oxford University Press, 2nd edn, 1975
A History of East Africa Oxford University Press, London, 1963
Pakenham, T *The Scramble for Africa* Weidenfeld & Nicolson, London, 1991
Prestage, E *Portuguese Pioneers* A & C Black, London, 1933
Taylor S *Livingstone's Tribe* HarperCollins, London, 1999

Early histories of Zanzibar The next six books cover Zanzibar specifically, but they are old guidebooks and histories from British colonial days. Most are out of print, though a local Zanzibar publisher, Gallery Publications, has reprinted some of the titles.

Brode, H *Tippu Tip: His Career in Zanzibar and Central Africa* Gallery Publications, Zanzibar, 2002. This is a reprint of the original 1903 study of the career of Tippu Tip, Zanzibar's most famous (or infamous) trader. A fascinating and highly readable account of life on Zanzibar and the east African mainland over a century ago.
Gray, J *History of Zanzibar from the Middle Ages to 1856* Oxford University Press, London, 1962
Ingrams, W H *Zanzibar: Its History and People* Witherby, London, 1931
Lyne, R N *Zanzibar in Contemporary Times* Darf, London, 1905. Reprinted 1987
Ommanney, F D *Isle of Cloves* Longman, London, 1957
Pearce, Major F B *Zanzibar: The Island Metropolis of Eastern Africa* Fisher Unwin, London, 1920

General histories of Zanzibar and the Indian Ocean

Hall, R *Empires of the Monsoon* HarperCollins, London, 1999. A fascinating history of the lands around the Indian Ocean, including good sections on Zanzibar.

Hamilton, G, *In the Wake of da Gama* Abacus, London, 1951

Hamilton, G, *Princes of Zinj* Hutchinson, London, 1957. Comprehensive and accessible historical accounts, with an emphasis on readability, sometimes at the expense of accuracy.

Modern histories of Zanzibar

Nurse, D and Spear, T *The Swahili: Reconstructing the History and Language of an African Society* The Ethnohistory Series, University of Pennsylvania Press, Philadelphia, 1985. This is an excellent, short, readable book which argues convincingly that the Swahili culture is more of an African (and less an Arab) phenomenon than previously thought. Highly recommended.

Horton, M C 'The Swahili Corridor'. This article was published in *Scientific American* 255(9) 86–93 (1987). Horton has been one of the most influential archaeologists to work on the east African coast, and has done excavations and surveys on Pemba and Unguja (Zanzibar Island). This is an excellent short piece that touches on some of the Mediterranean connections with East Africa.

Mapuri, O *The 1964 Revolution* (published 1996). This short, locally published book is a concise history of Zanzibari politics, covering the period from 1964 up to the 1995 elections.

These three books are modern, post-revolution, textbook-style histories:

Martin, E B *Zanzibar: Tradition and Revolution* Hamish Hamilton, London, 1978

Sheriff, A *Slaves, Spices and Ivory in Zanzibar* James Currey, London, 1987

Sheriff, A, and Ferguson E D *Zanzibar under Colonial Rule* James Currey, London, 1991

Zanzibar and Oman

Four modern and very detailed books, with specific reference to the Oman–Zanzibar link:

Al-Maamiry, A H *Oman and East Africa* Lancers Books, New Delhi, 1979

Al-Maamiry, A H *Omani Sultans in Zanzibar* Lancers Books, New Delhi, 1988

Bennett, N R *A History of the Arab State of Zanzibar* Methuen, London, 1978

Bhacker, M R *Trade and Empire in Muscat and Zanzibar* Routledge, London, 1992

Railways and ships

Hill, M H *The Permanent Way* East African Literature Bureau, Nairobi, 1949 and Miller, C *The Lunatic Express* Macmillan, Ballantine Books, Random House, 1971. These two books are histories of the east African railways, both with good sections on Zanzibar.

Patience K *Zanzibar and the Bububu Railway* (published by the author, 1995). A fascinating little booklet about the only railway on Zanzibar, which existed at the beginning of the 20th century.

Patience K *Zanzibar and the Loss of HMS Pegasus* (published by the author, 1995) and Patience K, *Zanzibar and the Shortest War in History* (published by the author, 1994). Two excellent booklets written and published by Zanzibar historian Kevin Patience. Well researched, they describe in full events which might otherwise be confined to the footnotes of history. The gunship *Pegasus* was sunk during World War I and this book also contains background information on British naval ships in East Africa, while *Shortest War* describes the 1896 bombardment of the sultan's palace, with several fascinating archive photos.

Patience, K *Königsberg: A German East African Raider* (published by the author, 1997). The *Königsberg* was the German gunboat which sunk the British *Pegasus*, fully described in an earlier book by the same author. This painstakingly researched book covers historical events before and after the *Pegasus* incident, including the *Königsberg*'s final sinking by another British ship in the Rufiji Delta, southwest of Zanzibar. The chapter describing the present-day position of the *Königsberg*'s relics scattered all over East Africa is particularly interesting.

Architecture and history

Mwalim, M A *Doors of Zanzibar* Gallery Publications, Zanzibar, 2002. Using hundreds of photographs by Uwe Rau, this fascinating book catalogues the unique doors which have become an icon of Zanzibar Stone Town, and covers the various Indian, Arabic and Swahili influences.

Pitcher, G and Jafferji, J *Zanzibar Style* Gallery Publications, Zanzibar, 2001. This celebration of Zanzibari architecture is listed under *Large-format photo books* below.

Siravo, F, and Bianca, S *A Plan for the Historic Stone Town* Gallery Publications in association with the Aga Khan Trust for Culture, Zanzibar, 1997. A large and detailed discussion document, full of fascinating photos, plans and drawings, which analyses the current situation then proposes a major and systematic plan for the repair, preservation and conservation of the many old buildings in Stone Town. This is a vital reference for anyone interested in the history and architecture of Zanzibar.

Sheriff, A *Zanzibar Stone Town: An Architectural Exploration* Gallery Publications, Zanzibar, 1998. With skilful photographs by Javed Jafferji and illuminating text by a leading Zanzibar historian, this handy little pocket-sized book is an ideal guide and companion for your strolls around the narrow streets of Stone Town. Highly recommended.

Sheriff, A *The History and Conservation of Zanzibar Stone Town* James Currey, Ohio, 1995. This book is part of Currey's Eastern African Studies series, and although quite academic in tone, it has a lot of useful information for anyone keen on the history of Zanzibari architecture.

Princess Salme

Ruete, E (born Salme binte Said Al-Busaidi), *Memoirs of an Arabian Princess from Zanzibar* Gallery Publications, Zanzibar, 1998. This book is a translation of *Memoiren einer Arabischen Prinzessin*, which was first published in 1888. It was also reprinted by Markus Wiener Publishing (New York, 1989), but the latest translation is now easily available in Zanzibar bookshops. It is a very readable first-hand account by a unique figure in the history of Zanzibar, providing a good overview of the period and several fascinating personal insights. Highly recommended.

Ruete, E (born Salme binte Said Al-Busaidi), *An Arabian Princess Between Two Worlds: Memoirs, Letters, Sequels to the Memoirs*, ed E Van Donzel, E J Brill Publishing, Leiden, Netherlands, 1993. Volume 3 in a series on Arab History and Culture. This is a very detailed and comprehensive account of Salme's life in Zanzibar, Germany and Syria. Includes a biography of her son, Said-Rudolph Ruete. Expensive and hard to obtain.

Travel and exploration

Batchelor, J and J *In Stanley's Footsteps* Blandford Press, London, 1990, and Wilson, C, and Irwin, A, *In Quest of Livingstone* House of Lochar, Scotland, 1999. Two books in which British couples follow the routes of the great explorers in Africa. Livingstone started many of his travels in Zanzibar. The Batchelors mount a full expedition, while

Colum Wilson and Aisling Irwin trace Livingstone's final journey through Tanzania and Zambia at a more grass-roots level.

Burton, Richard Francis *Zanzibar: City, Island and Coast* London, 1872. Many early European explorers in Africa mentioned Zanzibar in their journals, but Burton, perhaps the most 'colourful' of them all, is the only one to write a specific book on Zanzibar. Although published first over a century ago, reprints are sometimes available.

Hugon, A *The Exploration of Africa* New Horizons, Thames & Hudson, London, 1999. This is a fascinating and beautifully illustrated little book, with good coverage on the journeys of Livingstone, Stanley and others in East Africa.

Moorehead, A *The White Nile* Hamish Hamilton, London, 1960. A classic book on the history of European exploration in the east African region. Often reprinted. Readable and recommended.

Mountfield, D *A History of African Exploration* Domus Books/Hamlyn, London, 1976 and Richards, C, and Place, J *East African Explorers* Oxford University Press, London, 1960. Two books on exploration in Africa, although both out of print and hard to find, including some mentions of Zanzibar where many journeys began and ended.

Royal Geographical Society (ed John Keay), *History of World Exploration* Paul Hamlyn, Reed International, London, 1991. Includes sections on the exploration of East Africa.

Teal, J *Livingstone* Putnam, New York, 1973. A fine biography of the great explorer.

Waugh, E *Remote People* Duckworth, 1931, republished 1985 by Penguin Books, UK, as part of their 20th Century Classics series. Waugh travelled to many parts of Africa, including Zanzibar, as a newspaper correspondent, and his dry observations are as engaging today as they were when first written.

Large-format photo books

Jafferji, J, and Rees Jones B *Images of Zanzibar* HSP Publications, London, 1996. Much of East Africa has been covered by publishers of lavishly illustrated 'coffee-table' books, but until recently Zanzibar seems to have escaped their notice. Local photographer Javed Jafferji has made up for this with a portfolio of his finest work, showing rich colours and an eye for detail perfectly capturing the spirit of the islands.

Jafferji, J, Jafferji, Z and Waterman, P *A Taste of Zanzibar: Chakula Kizuri* Gallery Publications, Zanzibar, 2001. Not hungry? You will be if you read this bountiful cookbook which celebrates (and helps you create) Zanzibar's delicious cuisine, enhanced with 250 mouthwatering colour photos.

Pitcher, G and Jafferji, J *Zanzibar Style* Gallery Publications, Zanzibar, 2001. This sumptuous and stimulating book combines evocative photos by Javed Jafferji and text by Gemma Pitcher to explore the themes that have inspired Zanzibar's unique architecture and interior design – from Europe, Oman and India, as well as of course the natural forms of Africa – and also covers related aspects such as crafts, textiles and furniture. Listed by *The Times* as one of the 'Top 20 travel books for Christmas' 2001.

Sheriff, A *Historical Zanzibar: Romance of the Ages* HSP Publications, London, 1996. Accomplished photographer Javed Jafferji compiled this fascinating collection of archive photos from the late 19th and early 20th centuries – the text and captions were provided by Abdul Sheriff, Professor of History at the University of Dar es Salaam and Principal Curator of the Zanzibar Museums.

Fiction and autobiography

Bateman, G *Zanzibar Tales* Gallery Publications, Zanzibar, 2002. Another reprint from the industrious Gallery house; a collection of amusing (and sometimes confusing)

Zanzibari folktales originally recorded and translated into English by George Bateman almost a century ago, and enhanced by lively illustrations by Walter Bobbett.

Haji, M M *Sowing The Wind* Gallery Publications, Zanzibar, 2002. This autobiographical novel explores life and politics on the islands of Zanzibar during the turbulent years which led to independence in 1963, and the revolution which followed.

Kaye, M M *Death in Zanzibar* Penguin, London, 1984 – first published as *The House of Shadows*, Longman 1959 and Kaye, M M, *Trade Wind* Longman, 1963, Penguin, 1982. Two historical romantic novels set in Zanzibar. *Death in Zanzibar* is also published with two other M M Kaye *Death in…* stories in a larger book called the *House of Shade*.

Field guides
Mammals and birds

Kingdon, J *The Kingdon Fieldguide to African Mammals* Academic Press, USA and UK, 1997. For animals on Zanzibar, a field guide to the more common species of East Africa is of limited use. However, Kingdon's book is by far the best, as it covers every species in Africa in detail, including those on Zanzibar, with excellent illustrations and background notes.

van Perlo, B *Illustrated Checklist of the Birds of Eastern Africa* HarperCollins, London, 1996 and Williams, J, and Arlott, N *A Field Guide to the Birds of East Africa* Collins, London. For birds, the field guide you choose is determined by your level of interest. Of the books listed above, the van Perlo *Illustrated Checklist* is complete, with illustrations of every bird occurring in Africa, including those on Zanzibar, while the classic Williams and Arlott also has fairly good coverage. The large and comprehensive *Birds of Kenya & Northern Tanzania* by Zimmerman is used by keen birders, and it includes most species which occur on Zanzibar, but it's quite heavy to carry around.

Marine wildlife

Richmond, M (ed), *A Guide to the Seashores of Eastern Africa and the Western Indian Ocean Islands* Sida/SAREC, 1997. This excellent book contains around 450 pages, including over 150 of colour illustrations. More than 1,600 species of marine plants and animals are illustrated, plus notes on geology, climate, ecology and human activities. This is an essential tool for scientists, and a useful handbook for all visitors to the region. Proceeds from the sales of this book are put towards marine education purposes in the region, administered by the SEA Trust. Although hard to find overseas (only specialist stores stock it), this book is readily available in Zanzibar from all good bookshops.

Forstle, A, and Vierkotter, R *Marine Green Book* Green Ocean, Zanzibar, 1997. This handy little pocket encyclopaedia covers everything you need to know about marine life (from algae to zooxanthellae) and marine activities (from anchor damage to the Zanzibar Sea Turtle Project) in and around the Zanzibar archipelago. It also covers snorkelling, diving, coral reefs, fish and marine habitats. It is available in Zanzibar bookshops at a very reasonable price, and all proceeds go to fund environmental education projects.

Manuals, guidebooks and phrasebooks

Bogaert, P *The Krazy Kanga Book* Gallery Publications, Zanzibar, 2002. An offbeat 'adult' study of the kanga or 'wrap', the ubiquitous and vital garment for the women of East Africa.

Briggs, P, and McIntyre, C *Tanzania Safari Guide* Bradt Travel Guides, 8th edn 2017. The most comprehensive guide to Tanzania, ideal both for those heading off the beaten track and travellers visiting the country's major attractions.

Dawood, R *How to Stay Healthy Abroad* Oxford University Press, Oxford, 2012

Benjamin, M *Swahili Phrasebook* Lonely Planet, London, 2014

Hatt, J *The Tropical Traveller* Pan, London, 1993

Koornhof, A *Dive Sites of Kenya & Tanzania, including Zanzibar, Pemba & Mafia* New Holland, London, 1997

Wilson-Howarth, J, and Ellis, Dr M *Your Child Abroad: A Travel Health Guide* Bradt Travel Guides, 2nd edn 2014

WEBSITES You can get further information on Zanzibar from the following websites. Most have links to other useful relevant sites.

Africa Confidential (*www.africa-confidential.com*) gives the inside story on political events across Africa, including Tanzania and Zanzibar.

Africa Travel Association (*www.africa-ata.org*) has close links with the US-based *Africa Travel* magazine and is an interesting source of information on the whole continent.

African Travel and Tourism Association (*www.atta.co.uk*) represents many tour operators covering Africa, and is an excellent directory of useful contacts.

The Hunger Site (*www.thehungersite.com*) is not directly related to Zanzibar, but if you visit this site (no more than once per day) and click on a 'donate' button, the site's sponsors will give two *free* cups of food to a developing country.

Swahili Coast (*www.swahilicoast.com*) excellent online version of the free Tanzanian magazine by the same name. Topical articles on island life with a strong bend to tourist interests.

Zanzibar.Net (*www.zanzibar.net*) has sections on history, diving, touring, beaches, history, travel tips and so on. It also has a good selection of links to other sites which cover Zanzibar.

Sites for general news and information

www.allafrica.com Huge pan-African news site with vast amounts of topical content.

www.tanserve.com Interesting and slightly offbeat Dar-based portal with a mix of news and information.

www-sul.stanford.edu/depts/ssrg/africa/tanzan.html Extensive listing of links for Tanzania and Zanzibar.

www.zanzibar.go.tz Official site of the government of Zanzibar.

www.africa.upenn.edu/Country_Specific/Tanzania.html University of Pennsylvania African studies course – linking to useful Tanzania-specific sites.

www.zanzibar-travel-guide.com Online site where you'll find much of the text of this guide, plus many additional useful links.

Index

Entries in **bold** indicate main entries; entries in *italics* indicate maps.

INDEX OF ADVERTISERS